Gendering Globalization, Globalizing Gender

Postcolonial Perspectives

Edited by Gül Çalışkan

OXFORD

UNIVERSITY PRESS

OXFORD
UNIVERSITY PRESS

Oxford University Press is a department of the University of Oxford.
It furthers the University's objective of excellence in research, scholarship,
and education by publishing worldwide. Oxford is a registered trade mark of
Oxford University Press in the UK and in certain other countries.

Published in Canada by
Oxford University Press
8 Sampson Mews, Suite 204,
Don Mills, Ontario M3C 0H5 Canada

www.oupcanada.com

Library and Archives Canada Cataloguing in Publication
Title: Gendering globalization, globalizing gender : post-colonial perspectives / edited by Gül
Çalişkan.
Names: Çalişkan, Gül, editor.
Description: Includes bibliographical references and index.
Identifiers: Canadiana (print) 20190192291 | Canadiana (ebook) 20190192321 | ISBN 9780199030729
(softcover) | ISBN 9780199030736 (EPUB)
Subjects: LCSH: Sex role. | LCSH: Globalization. | LCSH: Women—Social conditions. | LCSH: Feminism.
Classification: LCC HQ1075 .G475 2020 | DDC 305.3—dc23

Cover image: © Lonspera/Shutterstock.com
Cover design: Sherill Chapman
Interior design: Sherill Chapman

Oxford University Press is committed to our environment.
This book is printed on Forest Stewardship Council® certified paper
and comes from responsible sources.

Printed and bound in the United States of America

1 2 3 4 — 23 22 21 20

Contents

Tables and Figures

Figures

Tables

Contributors

Anna M. Agathangelou
Department of Political Science, York University

Sara Ahmed
Independent Scholar

Melissa Baldwin
Aging Activisms collective, Trent University

Gül Çalışkan
Associate Professor, Department of Sociology,
St Thomas University

May Chazan
Associate Professor and Canada Research Chair in
Gender and Feminist Studies, Trent University

Ruth A. Clowater
DMin, President, SIGA Ministry Partners, Inc.

Tia Dafnos
Associate Professor, Sociology, University of New
Brunswick

Tracy Glynn
PhD Candidate, Interdisciplinary Studies,
University of New Brunswick

Aleyda Marisol Cervantes Gutierrez
Alumna Western Washington University; Outreach
Services, Highline College

Jasmin Hristov
Assistant Professor, Sociology, University of British
Columbia–Okanagan

Ana Isla
Indigenous Peruvian feminist; Professor Emerita,
Brock University, Department of Sociology, Centre
for Women and Gender Studies

El Jones
poet and activist; 15th Nancy's Chair, Department
of Women's Studies, Mount St Vincent University

Gary Kinsman
Longtime queer liberation and anti-capitalist
activist; Professor Emeritus, Sociology, Laurentian
University

Vanessa Lynn Lovelace
Assistant Professor, Crime & Justice Studies,
University of Massachusetts Dartmouth

Robyn Maynard
Black feminist writer and activist; Vanier scholar
and PhD student, Women and Gender Studies
Institute, University of Toronto

Deborah McGregor
Anishinaabe from Whitefish River First Nation,
Birch Island, Ontario; Associate Professor, Canada
Research Chair in Indigenous Environmental
Justice, Osgoode Law School, York University

Ghaida Moussa
PhD, Social and Political Thought, York University

Tahlia Natachu
Member of the Zuni Pueblo in New Mexico;
Alumna, Western Washington University

Colleen O'Manique
Professor, Department of International
Development Studies, Department of Gender and
Women's Studies, Trent University

Kayla Preston
MA Candidate, Dalhousie University

Clelia O. Rodríguez
University of Toronto

Belina Letesus Seare
ለተሱስቲ ንርኹረስ ቼራ
ሃንሱቲ ንርቼረስ ቼራ
Western Washington University

Fariba Solati
Assistant Professor, Department of Economics, St Thomas University

Tamara Lea Spira
Associate Professor, Western Washington University

Denise Spitzer
Professor, School of Public Health, University of Alberta; Adjunct Professor, Institute of Feminist and Gender Studies, University of Ottawa

Laura Stokes
Associate Professor, History, Stanford University

Lina Sunseri
The Oneida Nation of the Thames, Turtle Clan; Associate Professor, Department of Sociology, School of Behavioural and Social Sciences, Brescia University College

May Telmissany
Associate Professor, Communication and Film Studies, University of Ottawa

Heather M. Turcotte
Associate Professor, Crime & Justice Studies; Co-director, Urban Studies, University of Massachusetts Dartmouth

Verónica Nelly Vélez
Associate Professor, Western Washington University

Amar Wahab
Associate Professor, School of Gender, Sexuality and Women's Studies, York University.

Rinaldo Walcott
Professor, Women and Gender Studies Institute, University of Toronto

Mollie Jean West
Western Washington University

Acknowledgements

This project started with the belief and inspiration of my parents, Şemsi Çalışkan and Muharrem Çalışkan, who instilled in me a sense of social justice long before I could articulate what that meant. More recently, it has been Lyle Davidson and Ayla Davidson's unwavering love and encouragement that have made me enjoy academia so much. It has been the same for this project. These four have remained my unconditional sanctuary, to whom I return whenever I need to recharge, even though at times I may appear to take them for granted.

Even though she is not named as co-editor of the volume, Kayla Preston has been an integral part of the idea, the proposal, and the project management. The Canada Summer Jobs Program (2017 and 2018) and the JOBS Program (2016–17 and 2017–18) each provided two grants, enabling me to hire Kayla as a research assistant. During this process, someone who was once my undergraduate student has grown into a valued writing partner.

I would also like to acknowledge the students who took my Globalization and Gender course at St. Thomas University between 2015 and 2017. I asked them what they would like to read in a textbook for this course. They enthusiastically offered me feedback, which helped set the course for this book.

I also want to express my deep gratitude to all the collaborators whose work is included in this edited volume. Some were friends, some mentors; others revealed themselves during the process. All inspired me with their commitment to a postcolonial vision. I am grateful that they allowed me to include their work in this volume. Nevertheless, all errors remain mine.

Connecting with Debbie van den Hoonaard and Will van den Hoonaard has been a special gift. They have been my guides ever since I arrived in Fredericton. Our weekly coffee meetings have been occasions for mentorship, friendship, and kindness. Their presence in my life has kept my soul nourished and given me confidence. They have been my sounding boards during the different stages of this project, offering thoughtful answers to my many questions concerning "what" and "how."

My dear friend, Janine Muller, cheered me on through throughout the process. Our phone conversations over tea or lunch have inspired me more than she can ever know.

Brian Griffith and Douglas Vipond both offered copyediting at different stages and for several segments, always with care, generosity, and passion.

Amy Gordon, Associate Editor with Oxford University Press, has been the single most important anchor behind this project. Amy kept the venture going even during the times I felt uncertain. She answered all my questions with utmost patience and kindness. She was always there to be my guide, reference person, and much more.

During our earliest conversations, when it was still just a proposal, Ian Nussbaum, Senior Acquisitions Editor with OUP, had a profound impact on the project. He encouraged me to consider it as an original edited volume rather than a collection of already published pieces, as he recognized the significance of the emerging contemporary interest in globalization and gender from a postcolonial point of view.

Thanks also to Dorothy Turnbull, Copyeditor, Patricia Berube, project manager, and Michelle Welsh, Senior Production Coordinator with OUP, for their assistance and attention to detail.

Lastly, I wish to thank the following peer reviewers for providing generous and constructive feedback: Umme Al-wazedi of Augustana College, Anita Anantharam of the University of Florida, Emerald L. Christopher-Byrd of the University of Delaware, Lori Leonard of Cornell University, Marieme Lo of the University of Toronto, Grace Adeniyi Ogunyankin of Carleton University, Laura Parisi of the University of Victoria, Mythili Rajiva of the University of Ottawa, Kimberly A. Williams of Mount Royal University, together with a number of others who chose to remain anonymous.

As you can see, I had a whole community of supporters helping to make this project a reality. Editing a volume of this scope, as a solo editor, is not an easy job. However, because of the unstinting support of this community, the process was both pleasant and smooth.

I dedicate this book to marginalized communities in all corners of the world, and Black, Indigenous and other People of Colour (BIPOC), whose lives have been impacted by colonialism, imperialism, and globalization. Also, to the many writers and activists around the world whose social justice work has paved the way, and whose demand for human dignity and call for unity have inspired every line of this book.

—Gül Çalışkan

Introduction

Gül Çalışkan and Kayla Preston

Background: Locating in Contemporary

The scholars of postcolonial, Indigenous, anti-racism, and queer studies have long been engaged in revealing how the forces of globalization are intimately connected to colonialism and how those forces have their most dramatic impacts on marginalized people across the world. These scholars have been calling for action to dismantle those forces and offering intersectional analyses that place gender at the centre of their work. Many current events illustrate how the processes of globalization disproportionately affect women and gender minorities in areas such as mining, health, militarism, and migration. The importance of these issues is further demonstrated in the activist responses to them.

Perspective and Thesis

Taking a transnational/postcolonial feminist perspective, *Gendering Globalization, Globalizing Gender: Postcolonial Perspectives* includes contemporary studies that examine how definitions of gender and sexuality are established, negotiated, and positioned in the context of globalization and transnational flows. In its engagement with a gendered analysis of globalization, this collection engages questions of feminist epistemology and research while exploring how the processes of economic, cultural, and political globalization are embedded in gendered representations, discourses, and policies. It offers a lens for decolonial global studies.

This book provides a compilation of important feminist and postcolonial contributions that is bound to draw the attention of anyone interested in the field of globalization and gender studies. Addressing issues regarding the gendered processes of globalization requires an understanding of how gender intersects with race, class, and sexuality. It requires an examination of how the structures of nationalism, colonialism, and transnational capitalism affect these identity constructs and the social, material, and political differences they impose.

This collection of studies, as it locates decoloniality to the center as its method, poses a number of questions for its audience. How are the various processes that are associated with globalization, such as trade, production, and migration, gendered in their effects? What are the effects of globalization on gender relations and on different groups of women, and gender minorities? What are the roles played by various groups of women in constructing globalization in terms of social, economic, and political life and in terms of personal and social identity?

A key question raised in this book is how global transformations affect gendered global subjects and influence worldwide understandings of masculinity and femininity. The chapters provide a critical examination of the following topics:

- the framing of global issues through analysis of the colonist subject rather than by analyzing the colonized subject
- the varied impacts of militarization, war, and violence on women
- the consequences of global crises involving health, climate change, and national governance

- the narratives of identity and belonging in the context of globalization
- the implications of modernity for global studies
- critical interventions and methodological issues for future scholarship
- activism and resistance movements through a postcolonial feminist lens

The Pedagogy

The chapters present contemporary case studies and assessments by the leading authors in the field in a framework suitable for an undergraduate class or seminar. The volume as a whole aims to provide students with a variety of perspectives for understanding the relations between globalization and gender and to further their critical understanding of societal complexity in any given context, from local to global or from individual to group. It is important that students understand human experience in a multi-dimensional way, which extends beyond any particular culture, race, class, gender, ethnicity, religion, sexual orientation, or (dis)ability. We aim to go well beyond basic examinations of what is different about "other" cultures and experiences. We aim to help students realize how they themselves are defined and ranked by prevailing conventions and to give them tools to combat, undermine, and dismantle these conventions.

By applying theoretical analysis to examples of the interconnections between these topics, this edited collection helps readers to make connections between their everyday lives and the global processes at work around them. Through critical inquiry into a variety of topics, theoretical frameworks, ethnographic case studies, and analyses of activist movements, the students will:

- reconceptualize the relationships between women and the state, between gender and globalization, and between feminist theory and practice;

- engage with questions of postcolonial, Indigenous, and anti-racist feminist epistemologies and research methods from an intersectional perspective;
- investigate the opportunities and challenges that are inherent in postcolonial and transnational feminist scholarship and activism.

More specifically, we believe this volume will help students to build several important and meaningful skills. They will:

- gain insight into various approaches to the gendered analysis of globalization and the politics of gender in a globalizing world;
- understand how structures of power shape people's lives differently in the globalizing world;
- identify the institutions and power relationships that create and sustain global inequalities;
- perceive why postcolonial and transnational feminists study globalization and why feminists argue that globalization is a gendered process;
- grasp the implications of the term "globalization" and identify the key terms and institutions associated with it, such as global labour flows, migration, militarization, neoliberalism, and the construction of the gendered global subject.

Distinctive Features and Chapter Structure

This collection presents a postcolonial theoretical analysis of topics such as modernity, race, politics, masculinity, insecurity, identity and belonging, migration, economic activities, queer intersections, and global movements. In addition, the collection provides case studies that capture the practical, experiential implications of theoretical analysis on these topics. The various chapters give students a glimpse into current developments in the field, offering up-to-date research that relates to real-life situations. Each chapter incorporates a gendered analysis, an intersectional emphasis, and a feminist postcolonial perspective.

The book also takes an interdisciplinary approach, with perspectives from sociology, anthropology, geography, political science, cultural studies, environmental studies, economics, history, literature, and theology. Each chapter includes pedagogical tools that enable students to engage critically with the material. These tools include:

- lists of learning objectives
- "Tying It Together" boxes at the end of each chapter to bring the entire reading back to the context of the book as a whole
- brief "Call to Action" boxes that advise students on what they can do to help deal with the inequalities or the global problems discussed in the chapters
- discussion questions
- annotated lists of further readings and video suggestions

Additionally, a glossary of key terms at the end of the book provides important support for students who may be having their first exposure to these concepts within the context of the chapter discussions.

Overview

The volume has 23 chapters organized into six parts.

Part I: Global Studies, Feminism, and Gender Analysis

The chapters in Part I set the tone for the volume by examining globalization through a gendered analysis lens and by providing a conceptual framing of modernity. Anna Agathangelou looks at global studies as a project of modernity whose roots are embedded in slavery and colonialism. Lina Sunseri locates globalization at the intersections of colonialism, Indigeneity, gender, and nationalism. She reminds us that **survivance** of Indigenous peoples is omnipresent. Gül Çalışkan and Kayla Preston's interviews with Gary Kinsman, Ghaida Moussa, and Amar Wahab explore decolonial interventions to queer necropolitics and homonationalisms. Rinaldo Walcott urges us to reveal, examine, and challenge the commitment to the idea that white people must be eased into dismantling the structures of whiteness. He presents this kind of commitment as a problem to be overcome.

Part II: Gender, Christianity, and Modernity

Laura Stokes and Ruth Clowater explore the intersections of gender, Christianity, and modernity. Stokes offers a transhistorical perspective on "witch hunts," connecting this early modern mode of persecution to the methods of demonizing others in a postcolonial world. Clowater takes a critical theology perspective, engaging in an exploration of the historical role of Christianity in colonialism and its continuing influence on racism, gender bias, and Othering.

Part III: Gender and Development

Deborah McGregor, Fariba Solati, and Denise Spitzer invite us to an intersectional exploration of economic processes through a critical postcolonial analysis of development studies. Deborah McGregor gives an overview of Indigenous feminist perspectives on environmental justice. Fariba Solati's survey chapter provides a critical overview of development studies from a postcolonial feminist perspective. Denise Spitzer explores the challenges facing migrant domestic workers in two parallel registers, both in terms of their precarity and their resistance.

Part IV: Gendering Politics: Militarism, Violence, and Security

The chapters in Part IV highlight the differing effects of war, violence, and the politics of security on women and men, within specific states and on the global stage. A particular focus is placed on violence against women in times of postcolonial conflict. These chapters cover the issues surrounding hegemonic masculinity and patriarchy as they intersect with colonization. Jasmin Hristov gives an overview of militarization and repression in Latin America as these developments relate to globalization. She then explores the capital–state nexus and its war on women. Vanessa L. Lovelace and Heather M. Turcotte examine the ways in which surveillance is weaponized to immobilize resistance. Tia Dafnos provides an overview of how the interests of pacification, accumulation, and colonialism intersect in the state-backed drive for security. Colleen O'Manique explores another form of security as she explores the discourses on global health security and the ways these discourses can erase and silence, or marginalize, gender minorities and women.

Part V: Bodies of Activism

The chapters in Part V consider the various forms of global solidarity movements that are emerging around the world. These movements include Black Lives Matter and Idle No More as well as a mobilization of age groups—such as elders or young adults—and local communities, transnational advocacy networks, and international "occupy" movements. These chapters seek to capture the voices of protesters or leaders of global movements that are rising in the context of transnational or global feminism and analyze how globalization affects the ways women see and advocate for human rights.

Robyn Maynard critically reflects on race, resistance, and global movements for Black liberation, as informed by the rise of the Black Lives Matter movement. Tracy Glynn's work focuses on decolonial feminist activism in response to global mining operations. Ana Isla examines the impact of forced sterilization in Peru, which has been done in the name of sustainable development, and the resistance to this policy by Indigenous women. May Chazan and Melissa Baldwin provide a case study that explores the concept of mobilizing age as a mobilization of elders in intersectional climate justice alliances. Finally, the joint authors, Aleyda Marisol Cervantes Gutierrez, Tahlia Natachu, Belina Letesus Seare, Tamara Lea Spira, Mollie Jean West, and Verónica Nelly Vélez explore the pasts, presents, and futures of Black, Indigenous, and queer of colour feminisms.

Part VI: Narrative as Activism

The final part of the volume is a collection of narratives presented as radical demands for decolonization. May Telmissany explores the transnational work of women filmmakers in the Arab diaspora. El Jones contributes two poems: "Migrant Slavery" and "Ralph Goodale on Abdoul." Clelia O. Rodríguez's narrative "Untitled" offers a methodology for decolonization. Sara Ahmed's "A Killjoy Manifesto" is, as the title suggests, a manifesto for changing what gives us joy. These narratives provide examples of how decolonial feminist work can be done through global studies.

REFERENCES

Al Jazeera. (2018). UN calls on US to stop separating migrant children from parents. 5 June. Retrieved from https://www.aljazeera.com/news/2018/06/calls-stop-separating-migrant-children-parents-180605101014315.html.

Bhalla, Nita. (2018). War leaves one in four girls in South Sudan suicidal: Report. *Reuters*, 29 May. Retrieved from https://www.reuters.com/article/us-southsudan-women-war/war-leaves-one-in-four-girls-in-south-sudan-suicidal-report-idUSKCN1IU2H3.

Goldberg, Mark Leon. (2018). How colonialism explains female HIV rates in Africa. UN Dispatch, 15 May. Retrieved from https://www.undispatch.com/how-colonialism-explains-female-hiv-rates-in-africa.

Human Rights Watch. (2018). Diamond trade still fuels human suffering. 10 May. Retrieved from https://www.hrw.org/news/2018/05/10/diamond-trade-still-fuels-human-suffering.

Tsai, Alex. (2018). Black Lives Matter co-founder, Women's March co-chair probe activism. *The Stanford Daily*, 22 May. Retrieved from https://www.stanforddaily.com/2018/05/22/black-lives-matter-co-founder-womens-march-co-chair-talk-activism-reform.

PART I

Global Studies, Feminism, and Gender Analysis

Global studies, in its broadest sense, is the study of political, economic, social, and cultural relationships across the world. It is an examination of events, activities, ideas, processes, and flows that go beyond the boundaries of any nation-state and have globe-wide effects (Juergensmeyer & Anheier, 2012). Although this field has expanded exponentially since the early 1990s, global studies originated in the founding period of social science. It is intimately connected to modernity, although gender analysis emerged more recently, along with studies regarding the impact of modernity on marginalized, racialized, and colonized subjects.

The interdisciplinary readings featured in Part I of this collection help us to understand the complex relationships between modernity, colonialism, and globalization. These chapters invite readers to think about what it means to conduct a gendered analysis of globalization from a postcolonial perspective and to consider how gender intersects with race and class in the field of global studies. The Part I chapters offer conceptual and methodological tools for examining these interactions. They interpret globalization through a gendered analysis that considers feminism and the postcolonial politics of queer identities. These chapters offer a critical insight into how gender functions in the globalization process: specifically,

how gender serves to further neo-imperial goals and establish heteronormativity.

In "De-enslave This! 'Whose Global Studies Is It Anyway?'" Anna Agathangelou offers a critical perspective on global studies as a field dominated by monocultures and monolithic systems of knowledge and power. She offers an alternative vocabulary for reconceptualizing global studies and viewing globalization from the vantage point of enslavement and colonization. Readers will survey the formative experiences, insights, and social activism of Ida B. Wells and W.E.B. Du Bois and explore their impact across the world. We are invited to examine Black and postcolonial thought on the questions of enslavement, colonization, settler colonialism, and the rise of racial capitalism. Agathangelou offers a historical context on the structural role that lynching and colonization have played in the formation of globalized systems. The chapter applies Black, transnational feminist, and global anti-racist frameworks and analysis. Readers will learn about the key texts and movements that have shaped the ways we imagine and interact with the contemporary global world.

Lina Sunseri's "Intersections of Colonialism, Indigeneity, Gender, and Nationalism" explores the ways in which modern nation-building and settler colonialism reinforce each other in settler states like Canada, the US, Australia, and New Zealand. Sunseri shows that although settler-colonized states create meta-narratives regarding their march of progress and civilization, for the Indigenous peoples these nation-building projects have brought centuries of land dispossession, cultural genocide, socio-economic and political marginalization, substandard housing, high rates of suicide, transformed gender relations, and gendered violence. Although the chapter focuses on the Canadian context, it makes relevant comparisons to other settler-colonial societies. Sunseri invites us to consider the steps needed for moving toward a decolonized relationship between Indigenous peoples and settler colonialists.

In "Decolonial Interventions to Queer Necropolitics and Homonationalisms," Çalışkan and Preston conduct a lively conversation with Gary Kinsman, Ghaida Moussa, and Amar Wahab as they apply a critical lens to the issues of queerness in the nation-state. This conversation, with its engaging framework for understanding queer necropolitics and homonationalisms, explores the intersections of race, class, gender, and sexuality. Each interviewee examines how nation-states use queer bodies to justify their expansions of power and control. They interpret the policing of queer bodies and the ways that proponents of national security use the queer body to justify racialization and xenophobia. The chapter provides an overall examination of how queer bodies actively mediate and resist the nationhood projects of national security as queer people stand up to racialization and oppression. The interviewees provide a critical analysis of masculinity as it is negotiated and shaped by migration, violence, and gender norms in a globalizing world. Their discussions present a postcolonial perspective on globalization and gender through the lens of queer theory.

"White Lies: Race, Power, and the Future" by Rinaldo Walcott is a crucial reading on the ways that whiteness has been embedded in the institutions of settler societies such as Canada. Walcott's chapter centres on a critical exploration of whiteness and its role in the systematic marginalization of Black, Indigenous, and other people of colour. The chapter sheds light on the discourses that keep white supremacy intact in Canada and helps the reader to expose the "unconscious biases" involved in creating and maintaining white supremacy. Walcott examines the role of language in keeping racism alive while allowing "whiteness" to be seen as raceless. Two other key concepts that Walcott explores are "white rage," as constructed in the white body, and the "pure decolonial project."

REFERENCE

Juergensmeyer, M., & Anheier, H.K. (2012). *Encyclopedia of global studies.* Thousand Oaks, CA: Sage Publications.

CHAPTER 1

◇

De-enslave This! "Whose Global Studies Is It Anyway?"

Anna M. Agathangelou

Learning Objectives

In this chapter, you will:

- develop a critical vocabulary for conceptualizing global studies and globalization from the vantage point of enslavement and colonization;
- familiarize yourself with the experiences, activism, and expressive practices of Ida B. Wells and W.E.B. Du Bois in the US and in the world;
- consider Black and postcolonial thought on the questions of enslavement, colonization, settler colonialism, and their entanglement with racial capitalism;
- understand the structural role of lynching and colonization in the formation of globalization;
- examine Black, transnational feminist, and global anti-racist frameworks, key texts, and figures that have influenced and continue to shape the way we imagine and remember the configuration of the contemporary global world otherwise.

Introduction

In this chapter, I argue the "global" is an experimental and ongoing instituted perspective based on global racism. The work on globalization and **global studies** is dominated by thought and conceptual systems that focus on the emergence and sustaining of power structures. These systems emphasize narratives of origin, the reproduction of capital and settler colonial relations, and the desire of the "White Man" to dominate the world (Deleuze & Guattari, 1968; de Sousa Santos, 1995; Shiva, 1993). Even radical works that descriptively expand the geopolitical scale of globalization depend on an epistemological frame that centralizes and understands capital, modernity, and the nation-state as a given category. That is, we often presuppose that "the nation" and its ways of seeking its own global position in a globalized structure need to be excavated and categorized rather than explained or questioned. Some of these presuppositions are also shaped by a "**Eurocentric**" way of thinking and organizing the world.

Agathangelou and Ling's Worldist Theory

Agathangelou and Ling's *Transforming world politics* (2009) draws on **postcolonial feminist political thought** and is an attempt to account for colonialism in the making of world politics and the discipline of international relations. They connect the empire's dependence on hierarchical segregation with the hyper-rational and hypermasculine state that arose in response. It denigrated anything evoking of the feminine, including a sense of welfare and compassion for all, natives and aliens alike.

Colonizers and colonized alike came to accept and legitimize these hypermasculine values and placed them at the centre of how to order societies and conduct politics, local, international, and global. Colonizers did so to maintain their status "on top" while the colonized appropriated the same hypermasculine discourse to assert that they, too, were masculine (i.e., had power in the world). The division of the world post–World War II presumes a developmentalist ideology that comes with the nation-state, with the Global North offering the aspirational vision of how to order and sequence the Rest of the World. However, this political imagination is limiting and subordinates the rest of the world in a distant past or distant geopolitics as if its inhabitants are not active participants in the making of the world.

The authors challenge this Eurocentric colonial and imperial vision of world politics and global studies. They offer an analytical and descriptive framework called worldism that takes seriously the relational materialism in world politics and provides a different outlook on power relations, including the transformation of empire. Worldism presents the international system as composed of multiple worlds rather than just states. These worlds are made up of different languages, stories, myths, and collective memories. World politics is presented as a site in which these characteristics of the multiple worlds interact, while also including trade, development, conflict, and war.

By looking at multiple worlds and asking critical questions, worldist theory proposes that we can better understand violence and therefore have a better understanding of how to transform it. The authors invite the imagination of a worldist dialogical world politics that can conceptualize multiple worlds, promote coexistence, and produce a truly global world.

What Is the Global?

In *The birth of the modern world,* Bayly provides a history of the global nature of the modern world. Bayly argues that modernity—i.e., the rise of the nation-state—was a process that began at the end of the 18th century and has continued up to the present day. Its rise depends on the "centralization" of power. Bayly insists that "all historians are world historians now" and we do not need to reinvent world history but to decentre it (2004, p. 469).

Even if we take the nation-state as the central unit of analysis for the global, Bayly evades the question that he is setting out to understand: what is the historical role played by the formation of the nation-state in the formation of modernity? If we take the nation-state as the process through which "capital" makes itself local to "legitimate its own existence," as Walker tells us (2016, p. 69), then the nation-state plays a significant role in making possible this localization. However, what Bayly does not tell us is that core to modernity is a presumption about the "backwardness" of other geographies and other subjects. This backwardness seems to be a fixed and non-changing reality taken for granted in the ordering of difference (men vs women, whites vs Blacks, whites vs Indigenous, developed vs underdeveloped). If this presumption is missed, then we miss that capital depends on an apparatus of raciality, the hierarchical ordering of peoples and sequences of events on a global scale (Walker, 2016). As Walker states: "The forms of exclusion and inclusion that have historically structured the modern world, have been formed on the basis of this judgment of backwardness (p. 69). Walker underscores that structures of commodification and classification—i.e., this assumption of "backwardness"—required colonialism, the nation-state, and capitalism to function at the same time that they were required for these systems to develop.

Africana and postcolonial studies have systematically queried these epistemological and methodological assumptions of difference, arguing that the modern world depends on racialized, gendered, class, ability, and sexuality as positionalities of power to decipher how to position subjects and geographies in a global racial matrix. This global racial matrix inscribes the colonial and **enslavement** in the national itself (Du Bois, 1915; Spivak, 1999). Da Silva takes it further by saying the global order depends on a raciality matrix. She connects raciality to the state's ability to accumulate global capital through racial subjugation, specifically through "exclusion and obliteration" (da Silva, 2016, pp. 186–7). Da Silva argues that inclusion and exclusion become pivotal in the production of the global racial matrix and world politics. This raciality division and hierarchization of bodies and geographies further divide the world into those who deserve to be integrated and those who deserve to be obliterated.

Along with these authors, I argue that readers of the global ought to grapple with the centrality of colonialism, empires, and raciality and their entanglement with the development and history of the West and of the Rest. Bayly critiques this literature as **subaltern** speech, as in speech from those who are socially, politically, geographically, racially, and fiscally excluded from structures of power. The nature of subaltern speech challenges the instituted perspective of the global as a discipline whose focus is on bringing the world into view (Krishnan, 2007, p. 4). For Bayly, subaltern speech moves away from what he calls the global perspective (i.e., a univocal and unilinear approach to understanding events in world politics) and the global as an empirical process. Bayly orients us to a dominant condition of knowledge production in which the consolidation of Eurocentrism is primary.

Hobson's *The Eurocentric conception of world politics* (2012) could challenge Bayly. Hobson's immense undertaking shows how several theories have been configured by a complex notion of Eurocentrism, ranging from explicit to subliminal. For Hobson, however, there is a way out of this Eurocentrism. To think beyond the West and challenge the Eurocentric bias of history, we need to reframe historical-sociological notions into epistemological ones to nuance our understanding of global or world history (Hobson, 2012, p. 25). His contribution is his emphasis on Eastern agency. In effect, what Kenneth Pomeranz calls the "Great Divergence" (2000) between Europe and the Rest has been retroactively placed epistemologically and materially into what is known as global history.

This point is significant. Could this kind of projection retrospectively tell us how capital relations create the possibility of the global? If capital depends on this retroactive reframing of history, what do postcolonial theory's analytics of the West and the Rest suggest about Europe's **adaptiveness**—that is, in the context of global studies, the capacity of Europe to self-start the "global" and change and transform the world?

Hobson's articulation makes an important move strategically but reinserts Europe at the centre. If we remain focused on Europe's capacity to self-start the world (i.e., capitalize it), we are enslaved to the usual questions: How did capitalism originate in Europe? How do Europe and capital think about their own operation as "global"? This focus always orients the reader to begin and end with Europe and the history of capitalism. It reinserts European imperialism without ever orienting us to whether other sites, economic forms, and subjects were pivotal in the co-industrialization of the world.

Global history remains captive to Europe's fictional narratives, to its Eurocentrism, of birth and origin: namely, that the modern world, and global capitalism, owe their existence to Europe. When our examination of the history of the global cannot move us beyond what is already understood and predefined as the history of global capital, a question remains: what is the purpose of these productions of knowledge and ideas?

To deal with this basic question, I draw on two theorists of Black thought, Ida B. Wells and W.E.B. Du Bois. Both centralize the enslaved and the colonial (i.e., what the postcolonial theorists call the subaltern) of global capitalism. They challenge dominant assumptions of the production of the conditions of backwardness of the enslaved and Black subject. Their work problematizes the understanding of European adaptiveness (i.e., Europe vs Rest) as the essential element in the history of capitalism.

The Race Question and Configuration of the "Global"

Many theorists argue that white Americans used **lynchings** to racially control and terrorize Black Americans "into submission, and into an inferior racial caste position" (Lartey & Morris, 2018). These terrorist acts were common from 1877 until the 1950s. More recently, they have transmuted:

Victims would be seized and subjected to every imaginable manner of physical torment, with the torture usually ending with being hung from a tree and set on fire. More often than not, victims would be dismembered and mob members would take pieces of their flesh and bone as souvenirs (Lartey & Morris, 2018).

Lynching as a method of sorting US society was also fundamental in the making of the global white supremacy and white empire. One of the major reasons for this brutal approach was capitalism, whose basic premise is surplus value and profit. Plantation owners did not want their enslaved to escape or become free. The loss of plantation workers meant the loss of wealth and loss of possibilities for its making. To suppress revolts or protests, white Americans used violence.

What is the relationship of enslavement and lynching to the global? Wells and Du Bois explicitly say this question cannot be answered without linking it to global capitalism. Wells's thorough analysis of lynching at the end of the 19th century and the start of the 20th century goes a long way toward answering this question. She argues that lynching, capitalism, and the global are interlinked. Lynching divides the world into people who can be enslaved and people who rule the enslaved, based on race. Lynching is not just a political and a moral question but also an economic and existential one. Enslavement and lynching were/are strategies to ensure and protect white (European) life and its economic power by creating and sustaining in place a captive and pliable Black labour force. Lynching is thus a foundational condition of white supremacy and global capitalism.

The lynch-law—that is, the practice of administering the penalty of death without due process—reached a peak in 1892 when 241 Black people were lynched (Wells-Barnett, 1900). Each execution was intended to strike fear into the nation's Black communities. Lynching Black people made their bodies into examples of those who broke written or unwritten laws of social custom. Lynch mobs also staged mock trials with testimony from witnesses, and state authorities attended them. Thus, lynch-law was used to maintain the global hierarchy of Black and white people. It oriented both state and local authorities to protect "whites," even when they committed terror systematically against Black people. Mobs were never prosecuted but were supported by the state and local authorities.

Lynch-law also provided an opportunity for white women to actively participate in the configuration of the white supremacy structures. As Jones-Rogers argues, white women determined who they wanted to be beyond their gender through a set of feminist practices that were violent: "Slavery was their freedom. They were able to exercise control and autonomy by owning enslaved people" (Jones-Rogers, 2019).

The most significant way white women exercised control and autonomy was by systematically accusing Blacks of rape. In October 1886 in De Soto Parish, Louisiana, a white woman accused Reeves Smith, a Black man, of attempting to rape her. A mob comprised of "the best people in the parish" broke into the city's local jail and lynched him. The *Democrat,* a Democratic newspaper, wrote:

While we deplore the necessity for mob law, we must commend it in this instance, for if the accused had been convicted of an "attempt at rape," the penalty would only have been two years in the Penitentiary, which is worse than farce. . . . [T]he action of the mob is approved by the best people in the parish, who realized that they had to do something to protect their families, as three men had been arrested within one month charged with attempting to outrage white ladies. . . . As we have said before,

"the will of the people is the law of the land," and all such monsters should be disposed of in a summary manner (*Democrat*, cited in Tolnay & Beck, 1995, pp. 87–8).

Lynching was not a form of exceptional violence but a fundamental material apparatus in the configuration and maintenance of white supremacy and global capital. Its basic work was terrorizing and killing Black people and their communities all in the name of morality and protection of white femininity (i.e., "attempting to outrage white ladies").

Lynch-law put a certain kind of sexual desire and terror at its centre; thus, thinking about lynching without sex or understanding lynching without the ways dominant powers used it to create sexual empire is not possible. Sexual assault, specifically the rape of white women, was the excuse for and the justification of this violence toward and fear of Black men (Gray, 2015).

This white anxiety bonded to rape was entangled with the principles of white supremacy. Its focus was to protect the "nationalized" and "gendered" subject at the expense of Black people, who were imagined as genderless, asexual, and above all "bestial" (Gray, 2015) and exterior to global imperial structures.

Wells's work on US racial history highlights more than just notions of European adaptiveness. It speaks to the ways Europe's role in the US and its adaptiveness are entangled with the "negro question" as inflected with sexual empire. Like Wells, I question this notion of Europe as the sole originating source of globalization. For one thing, as Ascione (2016) rightly critiques, Hobson's move from the how to the why Europe adapts does not permit the equivalency of the agency of the East or the African (aka) enslaved subject. Moreover, this conceptual move does not allow us to understand the retrospective moves of capital to integrate some and exclude others, always positing enslavement and Blackness as its ultimate limit.

In deploying the enslaved body as the end, capital and white supremacy reassemble themselves, making sure their power is reproduced, expanded, and secured in place.

One way of reading Wells is that she is writing about women's work. But more than that, I read Wells as arguing that lynching is the most fundamental technology (or means) in the making/unmaking of global sexual imperial history and capitalism. In this way, she challenges easy and problematic white southern narratives (e.g., Mississippi's Governor James K. Vardaman and novelist Thomas Dixon), whose primary explanation of lynching was that Black men raped white women.

The deranged "new" economies required the production of the Black male as assaultive and the Black female flesh (Spillers, 2003) as a unit of unending property. Thus, the Black male and female slave flesh served as limit zones within settler colonial and capital imaginaries. Though largely omitted from the analytic frames of lynching, as well as settler colonialism, Black women's flesh is materially and symbolically pivotal in the contestation of lynching and the narratives of rape of white women. Black women's flesh as **commodity** and property sutures slavery with Blackness.

Spillers argues that "flesh" can never enter subjecthood. Black flesh is always relegated to zero social conceptualization (Spillers, 1987).

Wells worked with this insight long before Spillers wrote and made these innovative distinctions between flesh and body. Wells's insights come directly from the making of the US settler colonial sexual nation through lynching. She describes how the rape of Black women by white men is not met with anywhere near the same degree of horror (Wells-Barnett, 1892, p. 3). Wells shows how Black women are at the forefront of the creation and foundational principles of America and its empire. Yet Black women are raped without any outrage, juridical intervention, or opportunity to defend themselves and are turned into the defendants of the nation-state. Her intervention raises questions about the role of the state and its protection of peoples:

> Our country's national crime is lynching. It is not the creature of an hour, the sudden outburst of uncontrolled fury, or the unspeakable brutality of an insane mob. It represents the cool, calculating deliberation of intelligent people who openly avow that there is an "unwritten law" that justifies them in putting human beings to death without complaint under oath, without trial by jury, without opportunity to make defense, and without right of appeal (Wells-Barnett, 1900).

In The crusade for justice, Wells elaborates on a lynching that struck home to her. In 1889, Thomas Moss, a friend of Wells, founded a cooperative enterprise, the People's Grocery. The business boomed. As a result, it became a target of William Barrett, a white grocer whose store had served the community before the Black-owned grocery store arrived. Barrett felt threatened because the People's Grocery brought money into the hands of African Americans, engendered a sense of pride, and made possible Black people's integration into the market economy. On 9 March 1892, a white mob lynched Moss and two of his workers, Calvin McDowell and Will Stewart. They explained away the lynching by arguing that Moss was plotting a war against whites. The "skillful executioners" threw the corpses into the Chesapeake and Ohio rail yard a mile outside of Memphis, Tennessee, and left them to rot.

Wells began to investigate the lynching, publishing her findings in the *Memphis Free Speech* newspaper. She challenged the common linking of lynching to rape by pointing out that lynching cannot be understood in terms of sex and outside capitalism. In this case, the lynch mob functioned to destroy the white grocer's business rival (Wells-Barnett, 1970, p. 51). This lynching took place to protect white economic power and subvert Black capitalist development:

> Like many another person who had read of lynching in the South, I had accepted the idea meant to be conveyed—that although lynching was irregular and contrary to law and order, unreasoning anger over the terrible crime of rape led to the lynching; that perhaps the brute deserved death anyhow and the mob was justified in taking his life. . . . This is what opened my eyes to what lynching really was. An excuse to get rid of Negroes who were acquiring wealth and property and thus keep the race terrorized and "keep the nigger down" (Wells-Barnett, 1970, pp. 64–5).

Wells further complicates the dominant narrative of rape by explaining that the Memphis lynching was a technology of state economic repression (Ming Francis, 2017). In so doing, she also highlights how the ongoing enslavement of Black flesh was at the forefront of the power of both the state and capital and their dynamics.

In the same article, Wells calls on African-American residents to take their labour and capital and go elsewhere. This call had a serious effect on Memphis's economy. Within six weeks, many African Americans left. Faced with a loss of revenue, the local white-owned railway company came into her office at the *Free Speech* and requested Wells to ask Black people to come back:

> When I asked why they came to us the reply was that colored people had been their best patrons, but there have been a marked falling off of their patronage. There were no Jim Crow streetcars in Memphis then, I asked what was the cause. They said they didn't know. They had heard Negroes were afraid of electricity. . . . I said that I couldn't believe it, because "electricity has been the motive power here for over six months and you are just

now noticing the slump. How long since you have observed the change?" "About six weeks," one said, "you see it is a matter of dollars and cents with us. If we don't look after the loss and remedy the cause the company will get somebody else who will." "So your own job depends on Negro patronage?" . . . "Why, it was just six weeks ago that the lynching took place," [Wells said]. "But the streetcar company had nothing to do with the lynching," said one of the men. "It is owned by northern capitalists." . . . "And run by southern lynchers," I retorted. "We have learned that every white man of any standing in town knew of the plan and consented to the lynching of our boys" (Wells-Barnett, 1970, p. 54).

Her response brilliantly explains that lynching is the raw violence of expropriation of resources and life, as well as the deployment of apparatuses meant to generate Black people as dehumanized flesh. Lynching eliminates all blocks to capital's possible erection and reproduction. It establishes the conditions for capital's smooth motion, while relegating Black people to capture, expropriation, and obliteration outside its coordinates. As Wells articulates it, post-Reconstruction whites were concerned that the industrial revolution in the North would leave them behind or move their companies elsewhere. They proceeded to lynch Black people as if they were the ones responsible for the structural shifts and transitions of dominant power and capital relations and its dire effects. In this way, white supremacy is consistently consolidated without ever allowing for its premises and the coordinates of imperial capital to be challenged. Blacks become the scapegoat. The scapegoat is the sacrificable body that the state and capital either murder or expel, thus deflecting a violence that could otherwise be turned upon the structure itself. This displaced violence, lynching, protects all whites and the whole structure from acknowledging that its making and unmaking depends on its own generated violence. Its social fabric cannot be maintained without it.

Wells moved to New York and continued her writing and reporting. Her radical inquiry systematically challenges the fantasies of sexual violence of Black men against white women. What is at stake, she says, is not rape but sustaining in place white supremacy (Ming Francis, 2017) and the reconfigurations of the global capitalist system. Racial violence is a technology used to keep Blacks enslaved, in both the South and the North, and thwart their economic and ontological power; using rape as an excuse is simply an "empty state justification" (Ming Francis, 2017).

The constant shifts and changes to the global colour line come from white men, Wells argues. Their conquest and rape of Black women teach Black people that the colour line and law are permeable. And explicitly taking up the idea of nation and regional "autonomy" for the white South, Wells argues compellingly that the "negro problem" is not well handled within regional boundaries; instead, extra-regional (i.e., federal and international) action against lynching is required. In moving lynching to the extra-regional scale, she challenges easy readings of thinking about the negro problem as one of the South, of power between Blacks and whites, and of sexual desire.

Lynching is a global material relation of raw violence. It is a technology of dominant power and capital that materializes, zones, orders, and institutionalizes enslavement repetitively, legitimating it by the eugenic logic of science and its promotion of the need to master the flesh, the enslaved, if civilization (aka white supremacy) is to make it. The global juridical architectures tethered it to necessity, producing racial subaltern subjects to whom modern universal principles such as protection from force, as well as liberty and equality, do not apply. These subjects are governed by "necessity—that is, by violence" (da Silva, 2016, p. 187). Although we may read the law and the state through a liberal lens, these two modern juridical entities have a contradictory relationship.

Several authors (e.g., Agamben, 2000) argue that through lynch-law, the state suspends normative legal procedures, articulating a form of legal abandonment. However, Africana studies theorists (Gray, 2015) problematize such easy readings. Agamben's reading centralizes Europe. If we read Wells's work carefully, we see that at the forefront of any liberal/constitutional project is a distinction that guides the relationship of states with other nation-states and the social contract and direct terror committed with impunity on Black bodies.

Wells's intervention in the violent lynching of Sam Hose, who killed his white employer, points to this. She wrote a short pamphlet, situating Hose's murder within a "reign of outlawry" that swept Georgia over six weeks in March and April 1899 (Wells-Barnett, 1899). In it, she brilliantly explains the lynching of Hose by pointing to the role of the Constitution. This form of terror was not "the work of the lowest and lawless class." Instead, the Constitution, she argues, distinguishes between those upon whose bodies terror can happen with impunity and those with rights of liberty and equality who are legitimately protected even when they actively participate in mob-lawless-violence:

> The real purpose of these savage demonstrations is to teach the Negro that in the South he has no rights that the law will enforce. Samuel Hose was burned to teach the Negroes that no matter what a white man does to them, they must not resist. Hose, a servant, had killed Cranford, his employer. An example must be made. Ordinary punishment was deemed inadequate. This Negro must be burned alive. To make the burning a certainty the charge of outrage [i.e., rape] was invented and added to the charge of murder. The daily press offered reward for the capture of Hose and then openly incited the people to burn him as soon as caught. The mob carried out the plan in every savage detail (Wells-Barnett, 1899, p. 9).

This form of terror and violence with impunity, Wells tells us, shows the negro is not considered a human but a savage. Ironically, the savage is the white man. The terror of lynching is central to the un/making of the global and the ordering of sexual empire and is co-constitutive with the making of the US global empire. Put otherwise, lynching as a material practice made possible the boundaries between the interior and the exterior of capital, or what Frank Wilderson (2011) calls the savage/native/citizen/worker.

Wells also notes that violence committed on Black women does not register in the statistics of the state. Lynching is seen and understood as an act perpetrated against Black men suspected of raping or attempting to rape white women, a clearly problematic assumption because, of those lynched between 1882 and 1946, only 25 per cent were so accused. Further, many were women. Between 1884 and 1903, about 40 Black women were lynched, charged with such crimes as murder, "well poisoning," "race prejudice," arson, and theft (Cutler, 1969, p. 172). Finally, during Reconstruction those raped were Black, not white, women (Lerner, 1972). The making and unmaking of the sexual empire both as a structure of enslavement and settler colonialism thus depended extensively on the terror on Black women's bodies, with lynching a material apparatus to separate the interior and exterior of imperialism and capital.

The sexual nature of lynching was not a characterizing element until after the Civil War. Until then, lynching occurred mostly as a tactic against abolition activities, and white males were the primary targets. Moreover, before emancipation Black life was too valuable as labour to be wasted. After emancipation, Black life was posited as a source of non-value to ex-masters and as a threat to the order of white supremacy and capital, especially the economic opportunities of the largely unskilled white population. However, what is at stake in these narratives is something deeper and not the opportunities or the slaves' value. What is

at stake is the realization that capital cannot create life. Capital depends on capturing and folding into its structure any "energy" that is released in the system (i.e., the slaves were now "free" and up for grabs) for its own reproduction. The enslaved and the lynched are reminders that capital cannot create life unless it uses raw violence (that is, it steals the energy available) to self-start and reproduce itself anew. However, to secure in place the fantasy that it creates life (Walker, 2016), capital uses white supremacy and lynching as its technologies of subjection and obliteration.

How do we make sense of slavery and **colonization** when thinking and writing on the emergence and configuration of a global history and postcolonial theory? How do we read authors like Wells, whose life spans a terror period in American and world history? The word "transition" to explain the movement from one state to another, from the plantation to Reconstruction, normalizes spectacular violence. Lynching was central in the making of US civic and civil life, and the US "transition" into a global empire ultimately became mob business as usual. Thus, "transition" is a problematic euphemism for the egregious acts methodically organized, enacted, and circulated to govern and exterminate Black desire and Blacks in the name of (unacknowledged) economic development.

In her work, Wells grapples with "transition," calling out against lynching and relating the re-ordering of US society to an industrialized global force and its configurations. For Wells, the violent, systematic murder of African Americans is a way to reorder social relationships by drawing extensively from the familiar material zonings of enslavement. The goal, she says, is to thwart African Americans' efforts to be politically and economically successful (Wells-Barnett, 1892, p. 64). Put otherwise, the consolidation of the North as the site that would lead the US into a global empire depended on the ongoing theft and obliteration of the energy—that is, the lynching—of those who were now "free" to move.

White American attempts to consolidate power over Black Americans in the post-emancipation era occurred simultaneously with US expansion of its dominion over non-white people in the western United States and overseas. The late 19th century, especially the 1890s, saw the closing of the frontier and the expansion of American **hegemony** to transpacific and transatlantic locales, as well as the rise of popular belief in the inevitability of Anglo-American rule over lesser races, aided by the emergence of evolutionary social sciences validating the supremacy of the Anglo-Saxon race (Bradley, 2009, pp. 27–33). Lynching inflicted on Blacks at home was a harbinger of the acts of violence used to subdue and "civilize" those in Cuba, the Philippines, and the Hawaiian Islands at the turn of the century (Kramer, 2006). European immigrants, believed by many white Americans to be from lesser racial stock, also became the victims of hysterical lynch mobs (Kendell, 1891). In the context of perceived challenges to the racial status quo, the lynching of African Americans reflected white American understandings of the "integration" of geopolitical power. The racial violence and economic and political exploitation drew connections between the experience of Black Americans and colonized peoples throughout the world, anticipating theories of Black America as an internal colony (Gutiérrez, 2004; Kaplan, 2005).

The Global Problem of the "Colour Line" and the Un/making of the Global

In "The problem of the color line," W.E.B. Du Bois says a colour line runs through not only the segregated American South but also the territories occupied by European powers in Africa, South America, and Asia (2007, p. 8). The history of racial violence in the form of lynching—and by extension, responses to it and efforts to end

it—lends itself to a broader global analysis. This systematic raw terror against African Americans fits into a worldwide resurgence of white supremacy and imperialism, forcefully and violently committed on those constituted as Black and brown peoples.

W.E.B. Du Bois was a Black Atlantic anti-colonialist. He, along with several others, including Nnamdi Azikiwe (Nigeria), George Padmore (Trinidad), Kwame Nkrumah (Ghana), Eric Williams (Trinidad), Michael Manley (Jamaica), and Julius Nyerere (Tanzania) drew on approaches and strategies used in Asia, such as those of the Indian National Congress. The Black Atlantic anti-colonialists focused on slavery, colonization, and race. They saw enslavement and colonialism as entangled with white supremacy and imperialism. They challenged the emerging global racial domination and hierarchy by struggling to overcome foreign rule and gain self-determination. The stakes involved in the struggles to constitute a post-imperial world order organized on the principles of national autonomy and equality were high.

Du Bois argues that the unequal incorporation of non-European communities in international society amounts to the consolidation of white supremacy on a global scale. One of his best-known comments, "the problem of the twentieth century is the problem of the color line" (Du Bois, 2007), points to the international order as an extension of the Jim Crow system whereby the "white world" is superior and its role central in the zoning, ordering, and organization of capital. Although European states were competitive and in conflict with each other, they collaborated in their exploitation of non-European societies and obliteration of Blacks and other subaltern subjects. According to Du Bois, "the theory of [imperialism] is this: It is the duty of white Europe to divide up the darker world and administer it for Europe's good" (1915, p. 707). This collective right over the dark world, Du Bois argues, entailed an international order that organized people in a global racial capitalist hierarchy. In his essay *Black Reconstruction in America*, he shows how the hierarchization of races and racialized nations is historically entangled with capital: "The abolition of American slavery . . . started the transportation of capital from white to Black countries where slavery prevailed . . . and precipitated the modern economic degradation of the white farmer, while it put into the hands of the owners of the machine such a monopoly of raw material that their dominion of white labor was more and more complete" (Du Bois, 1979, p. 48, cited in Johnson, 2018). For him, the ending of slavery in the US did not end enslavement but made possible the "generalization on a global scale of the racial and imperial vision of the 'empire of cotton'" (ibid.).

The expropriation of land, labour, and raw materials in the Americas, Asia, and Africa contributed to the economic and political development of Europe and the underdevelopment of the rest of the world. According to Du Bois, this pattern of increasing inequality reached its zenith in the late 19th and early 20th centuries. At the moment of democratization and economic redistribution within European states, those elsewhere became subject to a new form of slavery that denied subject peoples voice and legal protections (1915, p. 36). Reiterating an anti-imperial critique, Du Bois argues that the economic and political developments in Europe cannot be disentangled from the rest of the world. Hierarchy was thus both the cause and effect of European imperial expansion. It generated unprecedented political and economic inequality between political communities.

When faced with the problem of international hierarchy, nationalists did not simply seek to reproduce the nation-state and gain inclusion in international society. Instead, they reinvented self-determination as a project of securing autonomy and equality within a reconstituted international society. In this effort, anti-colonial nationalists went beyond the achievement of national

independence and imagined the formation of a post-imperial order in which the principles of autonomy and equality would govern interstate relations.

The end of World War II reopened the question of a new international order. US President Truman opened the United Nations Organization Conference in San Francisco in 1945 by noting the importance of international institutions. For him, such institutions would guarantee peace and justice through collaboration among states. He rejected the Axis slogan "Might makes right." He echoed Woodrow Wilson by calling for a new world order in which justice could be backed by the power of an international organization (Truman, 1945). In an editorial in the *West African Pilot* published the same day, Nigerian nationalist Nnamdi Azikiwe questioned Truman's vision because it would not be extended to colonized peoples. Azikiwe argued that the rise of international organizations would only extend imperialism: "There is no new deal for the Black man at San Francisco. We are worried about San Francisco because colonialism and economic enslavement of the Negro are to be maintained" (Azikiwe, 1945, cited in Sherwood, 1996).[1]

Although some participated in the San Francisco conference hoping the platform might be a site for the end of colonialism and racial discrimination (Sherwood, 2003), many Black Atlantic anti-colonialists noted its problems and limitations. The UN, for them, extended existing hierarchical structures. Although the charter's preamble affirmed a commitment to equal rights, this entailed neither an end to colonial rule nor equal membership in the UN. Colonies and trusteeships would have no representation. Resolutions were non-binding, and the scope of the General Assembly and its action in economic affairs were limited (Kennedy, 2007, pp. 58–9).

Jan Smuts representing South Africa, drafted the preamble (Mazower, 2009, pp. 45–74). Du Bois noted the irony; Smuts envisioned extending apartheid from South Africa to Kenya but was now appealing for a preamble that affirmed human rights (Du Bois, 2007, p. 154). Du Bois comments, "We have conquered Germany . . . but not their ideas. We still believe in white supremacy, keeping Negroes in their place and lying about democracy when we mean imperial control of 750 million of human beings in colonies" (Du Bois, quoted in Mazower, 2009, p. 63).[2] He observes: "There will be at least 750 million colored and Black folk inhabiting colonies owned by white nations, who will have no rights that the white people of the world are bound to respect" (Du Bois, 2007, pp. 248–9).

In this latter statement, Du Bois draws on Chief Justice Roger B. Taney's majority opinion in the 1857 *Dred Scott v Sandford* decision of the US Supreme Court. The Scott decision concluded that Blacks "had no rights which the white man was bound to respect; and that the Negro might justly and lawfully be reduced to slavery for his benefit" (Taney, 1857). A watershed decision, the Dred Scott ruling permanently barred freed and enslaved Blacks from citizenship and extended slavery to the western territories while securing the rights of slave owners (Taney, 1857). Drawing on the decision, Du Bois linked the conditions of enslavement and colonization. Both the enslaved and the colonial subject were positioned in a global racial hierarchy that constituted them as racially different and inferior, thus allowing legal exclusion, political domination, and economic exploitation.

The application of enslavement to colonial rule led to renewed interest in transatlantic slavery and its aftermath among Black Atlantic intellectuals. Du Bois's 1935 *Black Reconstruction in America* was a central text in the project of challenging white supremacy. In it, he problematizes and challenges more centrally the discipline of history and the ways it understood and explicated the role of Blacks in Reconstruction. Writing against the dominant trends of American historiography that presented emancipation and Reconstruction

as failures, Du Bois seeks to establish the transatlantic slave trade and New World slavery as constitutive events in world history and the Reconstruction of the US. He constructs Blacks as central political agents, arguing that the end of slavery emerged from self-emancipation in the form of a general strike and insisting Reconstruction was a modem experiment in democratic self-government (Du Bois, 1992)

In *Africa: Its place in modern history* (1930) and *The world and Africa* (1947), Du Bois extends his reflections to consider the global history of enslavement. Enslavement and colonialism, he argues, were the primary mechanisms through which capitalism enabled Africa's integration into the modern world. Although Africa was integrated into the global economy as a source of cheap labour and raw materials, the continent was relegated as outside world history and civilization and without any agency in the creation, production, and configuration of the global (Du Bois, 2007) and global studies. Mirroring his argument in *Black Reconstruction*, Du Bois highlights African contributions to world history to counter this long history of domination and to correct historiography constructing Africa as a place without history. Du Bois reconstructs the problematic white supremacy's historiography and provides evidence of Africa's political and social contribution:

> It all became a characteristic drama of capitalist exploitation, where the right hand knew nothing of what the left hand did, yet rhymed its grip with uncanny timeliness; where the investor neither knew, nor inquired, nor greatly cared about the sources of his profits; where the enslaved or dead or half-paid worker never saw nor dreamed of the value of his work (now owned by others); where neither the society darling nor the great artist saw the blood on the piano keys; where the clubman, boasting of

great game hunting, heard above the click of his smooth, lovely, resilient billiard balls no echo of the wild shrieks of pain from kindly, half-human beasts as fifty to seventy-five thousand each year were slaughtered in cold, cruel, lingering horror of living death; sending their teeth to adorn civilization on the bowed heads and chained feet of thirty thousand black slaves, leaving behind more than a hundred thousand corpses in broken, flaming homes (Du Bois, 2007, p. 46).

As Johnson explains, Du Bois points to both "the intimate, violent proximities and the material and cognitive distances of region, race, and scale (global and imperial, intimate and proximate)." Johnson adds:

Du Bois's account is particularly interested in the material culture of racial capital, of how the suffering of dead elephants and enslaved Africans was reassembled elsewhere as sensory pleasures for the parlors and pool halls of imperial London. It is an environmental history of the resource-extracting, race-differentiating, world-wasting race to the end of time. Uncannily, the most ambitious and perceptive examples of the "new history of capitalism" turn out to have been written over seventy years ago (Johnson, 2018).

This emerging critique of enslavement, political domination in the colony, and their entanglement with **racial capitalism** countered the account of empire as a sacred trust serving the interests of the ruled. Anti-colonialists argued that imperialism was not undertaken for the sake of native subjects but for European powers and their economic interests. By the early 20th century, two such critics, J.A. Hobson and V.I. Lenin, had articulated an economic critique of late imperialism. According to Hobson, late 19th-century imperialism emerged from the need for new sites of investment for surplus capital (Hobson, 2012). However, for Black Atlantic anti-colonialists, the economic logic of imperialism had characterized Europe's relations with the non-European world since the 15th century. Lenin and Hobson emphasized the novelty of finance capital and its role in European expansion and competition, but anti-colonial nationalists spoke of the connections and displacements by locating enslavement, colonization (i.e., the theft of land and invasion of territories), and labour at the centre of imperial economics. According to Du Bois: "Today instead of removing laborers from Africa to distant slavery, industry built on a new slavery approaches Africa to deprive the natives of their land, to force them to toil, and to reap all the profit for the white world" (Du Bois, 1999, p. 33). Like transatlantic slavery, the new imperialism was premised on the extraction of African labour, the theft of land, and the destruction of the environment to serve metropolitan ends.

Linking slavery in the Americas with the expansion of empire in Africa, Du Bois rejects an account of late imperialism that understood it as a humanitarian or local project. Article 6 of the General Act signed during the 1885 Berlin Conference on West Africa declared European colonial powers would "care for the conditions of [the native's] moral and material well-being and help in suppressing slavery, and especially the slave trade" (General Act, 1905). Du Bois and other anti-colonialists challenge this notion of care, pointing to a restructured and emerging global project guided by finance capital. The European rule transmuted the conditions of enslavement and thefts of land and also generated new forms of coercive terror mechanisms and labour for its reconstructions. As in the Americas, where abolition was followed by coercive strategies that returned free Black labourers to the plantations of the West Indies and the US South, emancipation in the new colonies of Africa was accompanied by efforts to enlist African labourers in the production of cash crops, mining, and the development of infrastructure projects (Holt, 1992).

Expulsion from land and taxation were the primary means by which colonial subjects in Africa were forced into production for export (Padmore, 1936, p. 3). Similarly, the displacement of colonial subjects from lands used for subsistence farming meant they had to take employment in European-owned mines and plantations and were taxed on their earnings. Together, landlessness and taxation subjected the colonized to European employers (Padmore, 1936, pp. 53–4). In Africa, an independent and autonomous peasantry became dependent on wage labour. These workers' rights, however, were not protected as was expected in Europe. Trade unions were often illegal, and where they were allowed, workers remained unorganized. This was not modem free labour with legal and political protection but a transmutation of enslavement. Du Bois argues that under imperial rule, "there will be no voice of law or custom to protect labor, no trade unions, no eight-hour laws, no factory legislation—nothing of that great body of legislation built up in modern days to protect mankind from sinking to the level of beasts of burden" (Du Bois, 1999, p. 36). While emancipation in the Americas was thought to have ended "the slave status of the African," imperial expansion in Africa "forced the Natives into wage-slavery" (Padmore, 1936, p. 386).

Through the question of Black life and Black labour, anti-colonialists tied transatlantic slavery and imperialism together. Moreover, in linking the exploitation of labour to questions of exclusion and domination, they broadened the definition of enslavement. In key documents, including the League of Nations' 1926 Convention on Slavery, slavery was reduced to the problem of property in which one person assumes "all of the powers attaching to the right of ownership" over another (League of Nations, 1926). From the anti-colonial position, however, a person could be reduced to the status of a slave without becoming property and subjected to dehumanization and violation (Nkrumah, 1963, p. 33). In short, colonized subjects were denied the rights and protections of personhood and citizenship. They were also subjected to terror and other forms of raw violence.

The Jim Crow colour line was a global phenomenon that zoned, ordered, and organized the world. The "whites" were positioned as superior, the non-white peoples as incapable of full membership in international society, and the Blacks as non-subjects. This constitution of white supremacy on an international scale was a collaborative project of the European states in that they collectively exercised a right of ownership and expropriation over the rest of the world (Du Bois, 1915, p. 707). This asymmetrical international hierarchy also tended to exacerbate conflicts between imperial powers as they competed over the domination of peoples and colonial spaces. As each imperial power sought to extend its reach within the emerging international space, enslavement and colonial violence moved beyond the colony to destabilize interstate relations. Such conflicts as the Boer War, the battle at Fashoda between England and France, and the Tripoli battle between Italy and the Ottoman Empire lit "the desperate flames of war," exacerbating tensions between European powers and setting the foundations for world war (Du Bois, 1915).

In a 1944 article, Du Bois notes: "Not only does Western Europe believe that most of the rest of the world is biologically different but it believes that in this difference lies congenital inferiority; that Black and brown and yellow people are not simply untrained in certain ways of doing and methods of civilization; that they are naturally inferior and inefficient; that they are a danger to civilization as civilization is understood in Europe" (p. 451). Domination in the colony could not be separated from a broader structure of racial hierarchy in the international order whereby a global colour line enabled the organizing, ordering, and zoning of the world or from the ongoing enslavement of Africans and subordination of colonial and quasi-sovereign territories.

Toward a Truly Global Studies

My engagement with Wells and Du Bois highlights that the configuration of the world depends on a global racial hierarchy whose premise is to sort out peoples based on terror, lynching, and raw violence. This global racial hierarchy becomes co-constituted with racial capitalism and is marked by the global colour line. It sorts out those who belong to empire, those who are to be subjected, and those who are fundamentally relegated again and again as external to capital because of their supposed incompleteness as subjects, labourers, or territories. Understood as a racial hierarchy by critics of imperialism, this supposed incompleteness has generated unprecedented political and economic inequality based on shifting notions of capital and capital's use of the state apparatus to reassemble its power by linking together and redeploying capture practices such as relegation of the other outside itself and history, dislocations, expansion, contraction, crisis.

Wells and Du Bois use the history of enslavement and colonization as the fundamental vantage point from which to rethink our notion of the global and justice. I draw on their work to show how global studies cannot be thought of and materially understood as truly global; that is, it cannot participate in the invention of a world whose basic material reality is justice if it begins with the dominant and critical epistemologies of the making of Europe, empire, and capitalism. Both authors expose the dominant logics and material relations that guide the co-production of white supremacy and global capitalism. A belief that the white subject is superior over the Black is an epistemological and material strategy. It evades what capital's and empire's ends are as well as their dependence for their making on Black life and its labour. Black life is the foundation of the conditions of their making and also expansion.

In challenging dominant disciplines that narrate the sexual empire via problematic rape myths and history and ethnographies, both Wells and Du Bois point to the ways narrations and histories bond the enslaved with capital and the state. The narration and historical articulation of a global that begins and ends with European empires and the imperial-nation-state without accounting for the ways the global colour line and capitalism have jump-started and ordered the world asymmetrically and antagonistically is part and parcel of white supremacy. The global colour line fundamentally depends on memory, imagination, and the material practice of enslavement and colonization. Without these three, it cannot configure its global and dominant power.

These authors systematically point to how enslavement and colonialism have immured native, colonized, and Black life and the writing of history. The dominant narrative codes, genres, and genealogies of enslavement, lynching, colonialism, and imperialism have blocked the potential of the subjected and also seem to have blocked what we understand as global studies. As disciplines such as history, anthropology, sociology, and even politics of anti-imperialism epistemologically leverage the global line and raciality apparatus to do their projects (Johnson, 2018), our work requires a literacy that moves us beyond the familiar frameworks of globalization. Our work on global studies demands that white supremacy and capital as well as its hypermasculine approaches and values have to be questioned. Questioning, thus, what it means to be subject, a world, a system without attending to their making and their contingent ideologies evades the violence of allowing them to become the norm, to become what the whole world aspires to.

In a larger sense, Wells and Du Bois articulate frameworks and impulses that allow us to challenge our notion of globalization and global studies by pointing to how important it is to zoom in on the methods and dominant epistemologies that orient us and pedagogically train us to think, understand, and relate to the world. Through a close reading of these authors' work, we come to realize that how and why we know the global and how and why we study it depends much on terrorizing and exterminating the source of its reproduction and expansion: enslaved life. Globalization and global studies are caught up in a discursive machinery of power and political economy that distorts the knowledge that the global colour line of the hierarchy of racial capitalism and its contingent hierarchy of violence (i.e., force, terror, and lynching) are its basic foundational premises. They trouble the dominant and liberal move to propagate a form of global studies that obliterates systematically the life and struggles of the enslaved and the subaltern by producing certain genres and codes to exclude them, foreclosing the possibility of imagining a world otherwise (or worldism; see box) (Agathangelou & Ling, 2009).

Reading Ida B. Wells and how lynching and rape ideological justifications are central in the making of white supremacy and capital allows us to rethink and re-understand global studies. Her work points to the making of the global by providing for us a much longer trajectory than the moment of finance capital. She begins with the plantation and the lynching of "free" Blacks to undermine their access to capital. She points to the making of the global through the use of sex and rape as justifications.

Du Bois clarifies the role global studies can play in the making of the world anew. He tells us that we cannot think of global studies without thinking how the global colour line is entangled with capitalism:

Black labor became the foundation stone not only of the Southern social structure, but of Northern manufacture and commerce, of the English factory system, of European commerce, of buying and selling on a world-wide scale; new cities were built on the results of black labor, and a new labor problem, involving all white labor, arose in both Europe and America (Du Bois, 1935, p. 5).

He names the violence that makes possible the material reality of the global and racial capitalist order and "names the history of American slavery 'The Black Worker'—a subject, at once, of capital and of white supremacy" (Johnson, 2018). He challenges dominant critical thinkers like Adam Smith or Karl Marx, who "viewed slavery as a residual form in the world of emergent capitalism"; instead, "Du Bois treats the plantations of Mississippi, the counting houses of Manhattan, and the mills of Manchester as differentiated but concomitant components of a single system" (Johnson, 2018).

Ultimately, Wells and Du Bois challenge us to understand that the production of the global is itself bonded to enslavement and lynching. It is not possible, thus, to take this global for granted without understanding its emergence, its transitions, its assemblages, and making and unmakings. An analysis that grapples with enslavement and lynching can allow us to grapple with the material orderings of the world and the dominant apparatuses of knowledge systems that guide such relations to think the global world and its making otherwise. They point to us an orientation and articulate an impulse of how to think and imagine a global studies which is not white-washed and does not depend on the fictions of the "wages of whiteness" or its promises. Such a truly global understanding can rupture regimes of value and valuation and controlled cultivation of monocultures—plant, animal, and human.

Call to Action

Choose either carceral capitalism, international sex-trafficking, or transnational "sponsorship" arrangements that bind migrant workers to their employers: i.e., one of many global issues that call out for interdisciplinary and global investigations of how historical and present-day forms of slavery have shaped—and continue to shape—capitalism. Explore your chosen issue in your community and how it affects different lives based on the global colour line. Then research which organizations, if any, in your community address these issues, and choose a way to be involved (such as collecting stories, writing campaign leaflets, writing to political leaders, or even organizing a group to mobilize action in your own community).

Tying It Together

Recent historical and Black thought investigations speak of the centrality of racialized chattel slavery to the origins of capitalism—along with activists' efforts to expose the ongoing practice of New World slavery—and how they inspire a broad reconsideration of the connections between capitalism, the global colour line (see Du Bois in the chapter), and coerced labour across time and around the world. These investigations challenge theories of capitalism that see slavery as something distinct because under slavery, workers do not labour for a wage. In *The Red Record* (1895), Ida B. Wells collected and published the newspaper accounts of hundreds of lynchings of African Americans across the southern states for 1892, 1893, and 1894. Wells expands on the raw statistics with accounts of specific incidents in which legal due process was denied, families and individuals were targeted arbitrarily, and innocent people were killed to prevent them from gaining access to

the produced and structured claims on economic value. The historical and empirical investigation of W.E.B. Du Bois reveals that plantation and factory co-evolved; both are entangled with global racial capitalism. They are two artifacts of two discrete economic systems. Property and property rights, as Du Bois says in *Black reconstruction in America* (1992), are the foundation of global racial capitalism. Historically, and as Wells and Du Bois have shown, socially recognized rights and entitlements—in the form of raciality, specifically, whiteness—have produced and structured claims of economic value, preventing some from gaining access to it through lynching and other forms of genocide.

It is impossible for us to speak of globalization without attending to the transmutation of enslavement and colonization in the emerging structures (i.e., the configurations of capital, states, and subjects) and institutions (such as the World Bank, the United Nations, the International Monetary Fund) of globalization.

DISCUSSION QUESTIONS

1. What are the central aspects of **Black feminist** and postcolonial critique of global studies as expressed by Ida B. Wells and W.E.B. Du Bois?

2. What kinds of problems do these two authors highlight? Do Black feminist and postcolonial thought offer any new insights into how to understand global studies today?

3. In this chapter, the author argues that global studies ought to be de-enslaved for a truly global studies. What are some elements of **de-enslavement** and with what implications on rape and savage myths?

4. How does an analysis of enslavement and colonization allow us to make sense of the creation and ongoing existence of global hierarchies? Why should we care about the global colour line?

5. What lessons can we draw from Ida B. Wells and W.E.B. Du Bois about the importance of positionality and location in the act of theorizing?

SUGGESTIONS FOR FURTHER READING

Robinson, Cedric J. (2000). Introduction, and Racial capitalism. In *Black Marxism: The making of the Black radical tradition* (pp. 1–28). Chapel Hill, NC: University of North Carolina Press. This book discusses the inability of Marxist theory to fully understand Black people's history of resistance and the evolution of a modern world system of "racial capitalism" dependent on slavery, violence, imperialism, and genocide in the West.

Smith, Andrea. (2012). Indigeneity, settler colonialism, and white supremacy. In Daniel HoSang, Oneka LaBennett, & Laura Pulido (Eds.), *Racial formation in the twenty-first century* (pp. 66–90). University of California Press. This chapter focuses on the interrelationships of indigeneity, settler colonialism, and white supremacy within the concept of the racial state and highlights new intellectual and political projects that address these intersecting logics.

Chakravartty, Paula, & da Silva, Denise Ferreira. (2012). Accumulation, dispossession, and debt: The racial logic of global capitalism—An introduction. *American Quarterly, 64*(3), 361–85. This article discusses the targeting of economically dispossessed communities and race-based blame cast during the bailout of the largest investment banks in the United States by beginning with the notion of the house as an "unsettling hybrid structure" with economic, juridical, and ethical elements.

MULTIMEDIA SUGGESTIONS

Glen Coulthard. Global Red power: Fourth world resurgent, Glen Coulthard's Antipode lecture

https://jeremyjschmidt.com/tag/glen-coulthard
This presentation, by Yellowknives Dene member and University of British Columbia professor Glen Coulthard, focuses on Global Red power and the movement of ideas between Indigenous and Third World intellectuals and political anti-colonial leaders. His intervention articulates a new fourth world resurgent project challenging global racial capitalism and white supremacy.

Audra Simpson. Indigenous women and intellectual traditions in anthropology

https://www.youtube.com/watch?v=PBvJLKEWeq0
This presentation, by anthropologist Audra Simpson, points to the ways dominant research frameworks evade the transnational materialities among Indigenous peoples.

NAACP: A century in the fight for freedom
https://www.loc.gov/exhibits/naacp/prelude.html
This online source traces the major contributions of African Americans in the production of global ideas and visions about the world. Several of these featured authors and political activists changed the way we think and practise global studies.

Library and Archives Canada
https://www.bac-lac.gc.ca/eng/pages/home.aspx
This is the official page of Library and Archives Canada. It contains records related to Indigenous heritage and immigration processes helpful to exploring the configuration of global Canada.

REFERENCES

Agamben, Giorgio. (2000). *Means without end.* (Vincezo Binetti and Cesare Casarino, trans.) Minneapolis, MN: University of Minnesota Press.

Agathangelou, Anna M., & Ling, L.H.M. (2009). *Transforming world politics: From empire to multiple worlds.* New York, NY: Routledge.

Ascione, Gennaro. (2016). *Science and the decolonization of social theory: Unthinking modernity.* London, UK: Palgrave/Macmillan.

Azikiwe, Nnamdi. (1934). *Liberia in world politics.* London, UK: Arthur H. Stockwell.

Bayly, Christopher Alan. (2004). *The birth of the modern world, 1780–1914.* London, UK: Wiley.

Bradley, James. (2009). *Imperial cruise: A secret history of empire and war.* New York, NY: Back Bay Books.

Cutler, James Elbert. (1969). *Lynch law: An investigation into the history of lynching in the United States,* Montclair, NJ: Patterson Smith.

da Silva, Denise Ferreira. (2016). The racial limits of social justice: The ruse of equality of opportunity and the global affirmative action mandate. *Critical Ethnic Studies, 2*(2), 184–209.

de Sousa Santos, Boaventura. (1995). *Toward a new common sense.* London, UK: Routledge.

Deleuze, Gilles, & Guattari, Felix. (1968). *Différence et répétition.* Paris, France: PUF; *Difference and repetition.* (1994). trans. Paul Patton. New York, NY: Columbia University Press.

Du Bois, Edward Burghardt. (1915). The African roots of war. *Atlantic Monthly, 115* (May), 707–14.

Du Bois, W.E.B. (1930). *Africa: Its place in modern history.* W.E.B. Du Bois Papers (MS 312). Special Collections and University Archives, University of Massachusetts Amherst Libraries. http://credo.library.umass.edu/view/full/mums312-b218-i033.

Du Bois, W.E.B. (1935). Course schedule of W.E.B. Du Bois, 1935. W.E.B. Du Bois Papers (MS 312). Special Collections and University Archives, University of Massachusetts Amherst Libraries. http://credo.library.umass.edu/view/full/mums312-b073-i155.

Du Bois, William Edward Burghardt. (1944). Prospect of a world without race conflict. *American Journal of Sociology, 49*(5), 450–6.

Du Bois, W.E.B. (1947). *The world and Africa: An inquiry into the part which Africa has played in world history.* New York, NY, Viking Press.

Du Bois, William Edward Burghardt. (1992). *Black Reconstruction in America, 1860–1880.* New York, NY: Free Press.

Du Bois, William Edward Burghardt. (1999). The hands of Ethiopia. In *Darkwater: Voices within the veil* (pp. 32–43). Mineola, NY: Dover Publications.

Du Bois, William Edward Burghardt. (2007). *Africa, its geography, people, and products* and *Africa–Its place in modern history: The Oxford W.E.B. Du Bois.* Henry Louis Gates (Ed.). New York, NY: Oxford University Press.

El-Ayouty, Yassin. (1971). *The United Nations and decolonization: The role of Afro-Asia.* The Hague, Netherlands: Martinus Nijhoff.

General Act of the Berlin Conference. (1905). *The American Journal of International Law Supplement: Official Documents 3,* May, 7–25.

General Assembly. (1960). Resolution 1514 (XV). Declaration on the Granting of Independence to Colonial Countries and Peoples, A /R E S/1514/X V. 14 December. https://www.un.org/en/decolonization/declaration.shtml.

Getachew, Adom. (2015). *The rise and fall of self-determination: Towards a history of anti-colonial world-making.* Dissertation, Yale University.

Getachew, Adom. (2019). *Worldmaking after empire: The rise and fall of self-determination,* Princeton, NJ, and Oxford, UK: Princeton University Press.

Gray, Erin. (2015). Necrography at the lynching block. *GLQ, 21*(1), 13–15.

Gutiérrez, Ramón Arturo. (2004). Internal colonialism: An American theory of race. *Du Bois Review: Social Science Research on Race, 1*(2), 281–95.

Hobson, John Montagu. (2012). *The Eurocentric conception of world politics: Western international theory, 1760–2010.* Cambridge, UK: Cambridge University Press.

Hobson, John Montagu. (2004). *The Eastern Origins of Western Civilization.* (Cambridge UK: Cambridge University Press).

Holt, Thomas C. (1992). *The problem of freedom: race, labor, and politics in Jamaica and Britain, 1832–1938.* Baltimore, MD: Johns Hopkins University Press.

Johnson, Walter. (2018). To remake the world: Slavery, racial capitalism, and justice. *Boston Review,* 20 February. Accessed 10 December 2018. http://bostonreview.net/forum/walter-johnson-to-remake-the-world.

Jones-Rogers, Stephanie. (2019). *They were her property: White women as slave owners in the American South.* New Haven, CT: Yale University Press.

Kaplan, Amy. (2005). *The anarchy of empire in the making of U.S. culture.* Cambridge, MA: Harvard University Press.

Kendell, S. John. (1891). The mafia and what led to the lynching. *Harper's Weekly, 35*(1778), 602–12.

Kennedy, Paul Michael. (2007). The conundrum of the Security Council. In Paul Michael Kennedy (Ed.), *The parliament of man: The past, present, and future of the United Nations* (pp. 51–76). New York, NY: Vintage Books.

Kramer, Paul Alexander. (2006). *The blood of government: Race, empire, the United States and the Philippines.* Chapel Hill, NC: University of North Carolina Press.

Krishnan, Sanjay. (2007). *Reading the global: Troubling perspectives on Britain's empire in Asia.* New York, NY: Columbia University Press.

Lartey, Jamiles, and Morris, Sam. (2018). Pain and terror: America's history of racism. How white Americans used lynchings to terrorize and control Black people. *The Guardian,* 1 May. Accessed 10 December 2018. https://www.theguardian.com/us-news/2018/apr/26/lynchings-memorial-us-south-montgomery-alabama.

League of Nations. (1926). Slavery Convention. OHCHR. 25 September. Accessed 9 May 2019. https://www.ohchr.org/EN/ProfessionalInterest/Pages/SlaveryConvention.aspx.

Lerner, Gerda. (1972). *Black women in white America: A documentary history*. New York, NY: Pantheon Books.

Mazower, Mark. (2009). Jan Smuts and imperial internationalism. In Mark Mazower (Ed.), *No enchanted palace: The end of empire and ideological origins of the United Nations* (pp. 28–65). Princeton, NJ: Princeton University Press.

Ming Francis, Megan. (2017). Ida B. Wells and the economics of racial violence. *Items: Insights from Social Sciences*, 24 January 2017. Accessed 8 May 2019. https://items.ssrc.org/ida-b-wells-and-the-economics-of-racial-violence.

Nkrumah, Kwame. (1963). *Africa must unite*. New York, NY: International Publishers.

Padmore, George. (1936). *How Britain rules Africa*. London, UK: Wishart Books.

Pomeranz, Kenneth. (2000). *The great divergence China, Europe, and the making of the modern world economy*. Princeton, NY: Princeton University Press.

Sherwood, Marika. (1996). "There is no new deal for the Blackman in San Francisco": African attempts to influence the founding conference of the United Nations, April–July 1945. *The International Journal of African Historical Studies*, 29(1), 71–94.

Sherwood, Marika. (2003). Pan-African history. London, UK: Routledge.

Shiva, Vandana. (1993). *Monocultures of the mind: Perspectives on biodiversity and biotechnology*. London, UK: Palgrave.

Spillers, Hortense. (1987). Mama's baby, Papa's maybe: An American grammar book. *Diacritics, 17*(Summer), 65–81

Spillers, Hortense J. (2003). *Black, white, and in color: Essays on American literature and culture*. Chicago, IL: University of Chicago Press.

Spivak, Gayatri. (1999). *A critique of postcolonial reason: Toward a history of the vanishing present*. Cambridge, MA: Harvard University Press.

Taney, Roger B. (1857). Opinion of the court. In *Scott v. Sandford*. 60. U.S. 393. 6 March. http://www.corneU.edu/supct/html/histotics/USSCCR00600393ZO.html.

Tolnay, Stewart Emory, & Beck, E.M. (1995). *A festival of violence*. Champaign, IL: Illinois University Press.

Truman, Harry S. (1945). Address to the United Nations Conference in San Francisco. Delivered 25 April. Accessed 1 December 2018. https://www.trumanlibrary.gov/library/public-papers/10/address-united-nations-conference-san-francisco.

Walker, Gavin. (2016). *The sublime perversion of capital Marxist theory and the politics of history in modern Japan*. Durham, NC: Duke University Press.

Wells-Barnett, Ida. (1892). *Southern horrors: Lynch law in all its phases*. New York, NY: New York Age Print.

Wells-Barnett, Ida. (1895). The Red Record: Tabulated statistics and alleged causes of lynching in the United States. 8 February 2005 [1895]. Accessed 3 January 2010, www.gutenberg.org/files/14977/14977-h/14977-h.htm.

Wells-Barnett, Ida. (1899). *Lynch Law in Georgia*. Chicago: Chicago Colored Citizens, archive.org.

Wells-Barnett, Ida. (1900). "Lynch Law in America" *Digital History* http://www.digitalhistory.uh.edu/active_learning/explorations/lynching/wells4.cfm

Wells-Barnett, Ida. (1970). *Crusade for justice: The Autobiography of Ida B. Wells*. (Alfreda M. Duster, Ed.). Chicago, IL: University. of Chicago Press.

Wells-Barnett, Ida. (1990). Lynch law in America. Speech, Chicago, IL. Digital History. http://www.digitalhistory.uh.edu/disp_textbook.cfm?smtID=3&psid=1113.

Wells-Barnett, Ida B. (1997). *Southern horrors and other writings: The anti-lynching campaign of Ida B. Wells, 1892–1900*. (Jacqueline Jones Royster, Ed.). Boston, MA: Bedford/St Martin's.

Wells-Barnett, Ida. (1999). Lynch law in Georgia. 20 June. https://iowaculture.gov/history/education/educator-resources/primary-source-sets/reconstruction-and-its-impact/lynch-law.

Wilderson, III, Frank B. (2011). *Red, white & black: Cinema and the structure of U.S. antagonisms*. Durham, NC: Duke University Press.

NOTES

1. Nnamdi Azikiwe was a leading figure in the Nigerian nationalist movement. He became governor-general in 1960 when Nigeria became independent and president in 1963. During the 1930s, he founded and edited the *West African Pilot* (Getachew, 2015).

2. Despite Du Bois's fears, in 1960 16 African states gained independence, and the General Assembly passed Resolution 1514, conceiving self-determination as a right of all peoples: "The subjection of peoples to alien subjugation, domination and exploitation constitutes a denial of fundamental human rights" (General Assembly, 1960). To ensure equal application, the General Assembly created a Special Committee on Decolonization to oversee it. The committee had oversight over trusteeships and colonies, welcomed petitions and requests for investigation from colonized peoples, sent missions to investigate colonial rule, and made recommendations for specific territories (El-Ayouty, 1971, p. 217, cited in Getachew, 2015, p. 104). In only 15 years, self-determination was transformed from a secondary principle to a human right. The UN shifted from being an international body that largely maintained imperial structures to a central site for constructing a post-imperial world order (ibid.). See Getachew, 2015, 2019, and other chapters in this volume, e.g., Chapters 8, 9, and 12, for ways in which neoliberal policies and, in particular, debt programs allowed for the maintenance of global inequalities and postcolonial imperialism.

CHAPTER 2

◇

Intersections of Colonialism, Indigeneity, Gender, and Nationalism

Lina Sunseri

Learning Objectives

In this chapter, you will:

- examine the links between colonialism, Indigeneity, gender, and nationalism that have existed in settler colonies like Canada, the US, New Zealand, and Australia;
- learn of the effects of settler colonialism on the ability of Indigenous peoples to exercise their self-determination;
- learn of the impacts of settler colonialism on the gender relations of Indigenous communities;
- consider some of the necessary steps needed to move toward a decolonized relationship between Indigenous peoples and settler colonialists.

Introduction

This chapter aims to illustrate that nation-building projects that marked modernity across the globe resulted in settler colonialism in places like Canada, the US, Australia, and New Zealand. Beginning in Europe in the 19th century, modernity and industrialization were accompanied by the formation of unified nations and the development of statehoods (Sunseri, 2011). But constructions of nation and national identity have existed outside of European modern statehoods and predated settler colonialism (ibid.). For the purpose of this chapter, Indigenous nation means a collectivity with a shared language, culture, territory, and specific principles of kinship relations and

political organizations (ibid., pp. 36–43). Differently from modern nation-states, Indigenous nations were not characterized by private ownership of lands or capital or by a centralized political institution like the state.

In contrast to settler colonial historical narratives, the global proliferation of modern nation-states outside of Europe did not always lead to progress or civilization. As the underlying intent of this volume is to gender global social, economic, and political phenomena, this chapter demonstrates that globally, for Indigenous peoples in settler colonial nation-states, modernity led to centuries of land dispossession, cultural genocide, poor socio-economic and political conditions, sub-standard housing, high rates of suicide, transformation of gender relations, and gendered violence.

The chapter begins with an introduction to the earlier phases of settler colonialism, with a focus on the Canadian experience. This section shows that following a brief period of cooperation between European settlers and Indigenous nations, centuries of colonial relations were established, which led to dispossession of lands, white supremacy, and colonial policies such as the Indian Act and residential schools. Next, the chapter examines the gendered implications of settler colonialism by demonstrating how colonial laws and policies transformed what once were gendered egalitarian Indigenous nations into (hetero)sexist and patriarchal systems. Through this transformation, Indigenous women's lives and roles became devalued, and eventually they became at risk for disproportionate cases of violence at the hands of both individuals and states. The gendered aspect of settler colonialism is covered in detail in the following section, which provides concrete examples such as the Missing and Murdered Indigenous Women and Girls (MMIWG) and forced sterilization practices. It will become evident to readers that global settler colonialism has devastated the lives of Indigenous peoples worldwide, and the last section of the chapter covers the healing journey we are all travelling as we recover from such traumatic experiences, repair the harms inflicted upon Indigenous nations, and all work together to (re)establish healthy and just relations.

Canada 150 Celebration: Exactly What Are We Celebrating?

2017 marked the 150th anniversary of the Canadian Confederation. Both during the preparations for this social phenomenon and throughout 2017, Canadians were invited to join in the celebration of the "founding" of the nation and in the

process to promote the vision of a multicultural, diverse, just society to the rest of the world. However, many Indigenous peoples (see below for further discussion) did not jump onto the celebratory bandwagon, and some publicly criticized the Canadian governments for spending so much money on the commemorative events. Undoubtedly, for many settler Canadians the country has been a welcoming place that they are proud to call home, and for some it is a refuge from previous conflict zones. Hence for them, 2017 could be a year to celebrate. However, the reality for Indigenous peoples has been very different.

As Rachael Yacaaʔał George states, for "Indigenous peoples, this year marks 150-plus years of resistance against an ongoing colonial assault. It is a reminder of our strength, our resilience, and the vitality of our nations. It is a moment to recognize our resistance and resurgence, as well as the work that still needs to be done" (2017, p. 49). So perhaps there was room for some celebration for Indigenous peoples, but it was not directed toward the Canadian state but toward themselves for having survived centuries of **settler colonialism**. Some of the work that still needs to be done involves raising global awareness of the entire history of Canada and, in so doing, rewriting the official narrative of Canadian nation-building. For example, we all need to acknowledge that "Indigenous peoples' labour and lands have shaped the political economy of Canada from the time of the fur trade to bankrolling industrialization with their lands and resources, and today, from confronting neo-liberal policy in the form of continental restructuring and intensified resource grabs" (Pasternak, 2014, p. 40). What Indigenous peoples are asking of non-Indigenous individuals residing within and outside of Canada is that while waving the maple leaf flag they reflect more deeply about the heavy price Indigenous nations have been paying through centuries of settler colonialism.

The (Re)making of Settler Colonial States

By settler colonialism, we mean "a particular form of European colonialism . . . [one wherein], unlike colonialists in South Asia and most of Africa, settlers in Canada and the U.S [and Australia and New Zealand] did not go back to live in their colonial metropoles" (Mackey, 2016, p. 4). Upon settling in these already-occupied Indigenous lands, colonialists set up new ways of governance by slowly dispossessing Indigenous peoples of their lands and forcing upon them economic and socio-political domination (Mackey, 2016; see also Cannon & Sunseri, 2017). Although this particular form of colonialism began globally centuries ago, as Battell Lowman and Barker argue, "colonialism continues: Indigenous nations are still losing their land base, facing infringement from resources extraction and mining companies, property developers, and the pressures of urbanization" (2015, p. 3). Meanwhile, colonialism continues outside of Canadian borders as the push for oil and other resource extraction is also happening in the US (as the Dakota Access Pipeline protests that began in 2016 highlighted). The Canada 150 celebrations symbolized to Indigenous people a continual denial of the ongoing colonialism that still shapes their lives and is embodied in legislation such as the **Indian Act**, the **gendered colonial violence** facing Indigenous women and Two-Spirited individuals, and the multiple legacies of residential schools. During their criticisms of and protests against the commemorative events, Indigenous peoples reminded all that everyone is implicated in the current settler and non-settler relationship in places like Canada, the US, Australia, and New Zealand. A strong symbolic act of resistance of the Canada 150 anniversary was a four-day ceremony that took place on Canada's Parliament Hill, accompanied by the erection of a teepee just days before

1 July, also known as Canada Day. The participants chose that particular location to stress that Canada's federal government sits on the unceded lands of the Algonquin people. In the US, recurrent protests have taken place against the celebration of Columbus Day (Fortin, 2017). Protesters have drawn attention to the fact that Columbus's exploration opened the door to the colonization of the American continent, bringing along many diseases and destruction to the Indigenous populations. In response to the anti-Columbus protests, cities like Salt Lake City and Los Angeles now recognize the second Monday in October as Indigenous Peoples' Day (ibid.).

The word "settler" points to the relationship many have to the land in which they live, to each other, including Indigenous communities, and to various institutions and laws. Not surprisingly, the word might result in "uncomfortable realisations, difficult subjects, and potential complicity in systems of dispossession and violence" (Battell Lowman & Barker, 2015, p. 2). The discomfort might result from the realization that the land their house sits on, whether purchased in good faith or inherited from their ancestors, had been originally taken from Indigenous peoples through colonial means. Or some might begin to critically examine how a social system in which they are employed or from which they have benefitted, such the educational system, was built on years if not centuries of miseducation about the history of the relationship between Indigenous nations and Canadian society.

Not all of those living in settler colonies have equal positions or interest in maintaining the current hierarchical colonial systems. For example, many immigrants who arrived in Canada, as in other global settler colonial states, were "imported as labour by the settler nation. These immigrants later become encompassed (although they are still racialized) in the ideologies of settler nations during the 20th century re-inventions of national identities through ideologies of multiculturalism (Canada and Australia) and the 'melting pot' (United States)" (Mackey, 2016, p. 4). While it is true that "nonindigenous settlers [might] participate in white supremacy through their disavowal of Native American sovereignty in the many manifestations and their hesitancy to critique the historical and continued formation of the United States and Canada" (Teves, Smith, & Raheja, 2015, p. 276), we must critically examine the term "settler" to avoid homogenizing a variety of groups that settled (and not always permanently) on Indigenous lands, since the conditions under which they left their original home and how they experience their new "home" might greatly differ. Hence, we must not equate "distinct types of migration such as enslavement, trafficking, and the displacement of refugees with the institution of settler colonialism" (ibid.). As Vowel states, "non-European migrants do not have the power to bring with them their laws and customs, which they then apply to the rest of the peoples living in Canada—no matter what some alarmists like to claim. The dominant sociopolitical structures remain European in origin, and, as Indigenous peoples are well aware, they are not so easy to change" (2016, p. 17).

Individuals forced to migrate for a multitude of reasons to settler colonies have often been historically marginalized, stigmatized, and discriminated against. As a consequence, they hold a different relationship with the state and other settlers that are in a position of **privilege**, and ultimately they form a complicated relationship with Indigenous peoples. Possibilities for coalition between these groups can exist and have existed, as we witnessed during the Idle No More movement in 2012, which included both Indigenous people and non-Indigenous allies and brought attention to "settler colonial, legislative, and treaty violations in the Canadian and international context. . . . [And on] 13 April 2016, Black Lives Matter joined in solidarity with Indigenous activists to occupy the federal offices

of the Department of Indigenous and Northern Affairs of Canada in Toronto, Canada . . . to draw attention to the living conditions of leading Indigenous youth to take their lives" (Cannon & Sunseri, 2017, pp. 248–9). In 2016 in the northern US, when the Standing Rock Sioux tribe protested the proposed construction of the Dakota Access Pipeline project because of the threat to its water and lands, non-Indigenous allies, including people of colour across the globe through social media exposure and even Hollywood celebrities like Susan Sarandon, Mark Ruffalo, and Shailene Woodley joined the protest. More recently, recognizing that migration is not the issue but settler colonialism is, many Indigenous individuals and groups have critiqued the anti-immigration rhetoric and policies implemented in the US that have resulted in the detention of asylum-seekers from Latin American countries. Facebook pages like Indigenous Life Movement have been filled with many posts supporting these families who are escaping violence and poverty. Through signs and hashtags like #NoOneIsIllegalOnStolenLand, they point out the hypocrisy of such anti-immigration sentiments, since nation-states on the North American continent were built by settler colonialism and, poignantly, the reality is that most of these families seeking refuge are indeed of Indigenous descent themselves.

Earlier Phases and Ideologies of Settler Colonialism

Settler colonialism took slightly different forms and phases across the globe, although ultimately Indigenous peoples shared a similar fate, meaning death, physical and cultural genocide, assaults on their economic and social systems, violation of their human rights, and ongoing **historic trauma** affecting communities (Palmater, 2015; Sunseri, 2011; Wesley-Esquimaux, 2009).

In Canada, the early years of contact between Indigenous peoples and Europeans were marked

Idle No More Flash Mob Round Dance event in London, Ontario, in December 2012

by merely economic relations and semi-equal cooperation because the labour of and social relationships with Indigenous societies were needed for successful trade (Stevenson, 1999). During this period, an original treaty was made between the Dutch and the Haudenosaunee League (also known as the Iroquois Confederacy), the Two-Row Wampum, which later was also exchanged with other Europeans. The Wampum belt is made of two rows of purple shells in a bed of white ones. The two purple rows represent the Indigenous nations with their own laws and cultures and the European nations, each to travel parallel in the sea without imposing on the other, sharing the land and forming a relationship of respect and friendship (Sunseri, 2011). The intent of this treaty was indeed that the two parties would respect

each other's autonomy and sovereignty and coexist in a peaceful and just manner.

However, once trading declined and Europeans began to settle in North America permanently and envisioned a "New World," treaties like these and the overall relationship between Indigenous peoples and settlers changed drastically, and what followed were centuries of settler colonialism. Similarly to places like the US (see Dunbar-Ortiz, 2014), New Zealand (see Mikaere, 2011; Walker, 1990), and Australia (see Moreton-Robinson, 2015; Wolfe, 1999), in Canada this particular form of colonialism involved restructuring of original economies, extraction of natural resources, (re)development of lands, and imposition of European religions, moral values, and legal systems. What resulted was the creation of dependent and marginalized Indigenous communities worldwide. Lands originally occupied by Indigenous nations were transformed to facilitate the expansion of capitalism on non-European lands. Hence, we need to "focus on how the theft of Indigenous peoples' lands and other racialized forms of violence are linked to imperialism and were vital to the foundation of the Canadian [and other similar] nation state" (Sunseri, 2011, p. 82; see also Dunbar-Ortiz, 2014). Of course, the experiences of colonized peoples have not been identical, although they are fundamentally similar. For instance, as Altamirano-Jiménez points out, "settlers and extractive colonialism pursued different strategies, modes of governance, and operation . . . in Mexico, extractive colonialism implied that Indigenous peoples were recognized as *subjugated peoples* who had to render tribute and pay taxes to the colonial authority" (2013, p. 8). What also accompanied settler colonialism wherever it went was an ideology of racial superiority that served as a justification for domination.

This history of settler colonialism contained an ideology of superiority that in places like the US has meant "white supremacy, the widespread practice of African slavery, and a policy of genocide and land theft" (Dunbar-Ortiz, 2014, p. 2). The US national narrative ignores this ugly reality while perpetuating its Columbus Discovery myth, which tells its believers that Europeans have a right of title to the lands that they so "discovered" (ibid.). Similarly in Canada, the conceptualization of Canada as a *terra nullius* enabled the settler colonial process whereby property became equated with whiteness (Cannon & Sunseri, 2017, p. xiv). This process was facilitated by constructing European settlers as a racially superior, civilized Self and Indigenous peoples as the uncivilized Other, thereafter allowing Europeans their missionary quest to civilize (and Christianize) the peoples and "develop" (read imperialize for future capitalist adventures) their territories (ibid.). Settler colonialism began during the modern era,

influenced by the philosophy of the Enlightenment and its belief in rationalism. Because this belief system was intended to replace tradition and emotional subjectivity with objective rationality, "mysticism, miracles, spirituality and anything similar were frowned upon . . . the traditional knowledge of North American Indians were simply pushed aside—because that traditional knowledge included notions of spirituality" (Little Bear, 2017, p. 40). All these civilizing projects used colonial legislation and other social practices; in Canada, two major instruments of colonial domination have been the Indian Act and the **Indian residential schools**.

Colonialist Instruments of Assimilation

The transformation from independent, striving Indigenous nations to colonized peoples in Canada began with the establishment of pieces of lands "reserved" for "Indians" through legislations such as the 1857 Act for the Gradual Civilization of the Indian Tribe and the 1859 Civilization and Enfranchisement Act. These acts allowed for increasing dispossession of Indigenous traditional territories, settlement of Indigenous nations into small areas, and the eventual control of Indigenous peoples by colonial administrators of the Canadian state, which heightened with the passing of the 1876 Indian Act (Sunseri, 2011).

The Indian Act "provided for the appropriation of Indigenous territories and the accumulation of capital . . . imposed an elected band council system of governance upon Indigenous nations . . . [which] represented an imposition to already established traditional governance" (Cannon & Sunseri, 2017, pp. xiv–xv). A major colonial instrument of the act was the institutionalization of the legal category of Indianness through imposition of an Indian status category constructed by the state. Indeed, the Indian Act represents "the very first instance of racialized thinking and institutionalized racism in Canada" (ibid., xv). While before colonialism each Indigenous nation had its own specific criteria of national belonging and identity (for example, Oneida and other nations of the Haudenosaunee followed a matrilineal line of descent to one of the three clans, and anyone could be adopted into a clan as long as the clan mother welcomed them), eventually the Indian Act imposed its own construction of Indian, which was patriarchal as well as racist. Only those registered as Indians in the Indian registry can live on reserves and have a fiduciary relationship with the Canadian state. Such definitions are not traditionally Indigenous but creations of the colonial state, which linked legal Indigenous identity with notions of blood quantum and a lifestyle associated with reserve residency (Sunseri, 2011). Although a series of amendments to the act have occurred through the decades, it is still in existence and a reminder, therefore, to Indigenous peoples that we still live in a colonized world (hence, the impossibility of celebrating Canada 150 for most of us, Indigenous and non-Indigenous).

Such colonial policies involving Indigenous identity are not foreign to Indigenous peoples outside of Canada. In Hawaii currently, there are "popular notions of cultural authenticity and biological differences through the use of blood quantum, notions that have been reinforced by the law" (Kauanui, 2008, p. 2). This policy, similar to Canada's Indian Act, is closely linked to racist and sexist assumptions and practices. "Racialization is the process by which racial meaning is ascribed—in this case to Kanaka Maoli through ideologies of blood quantum" that gives preference to patrilineal constructions of Indigeneity (ibid., p. 3). It replaces Indigenous Hawaiian criteria of national belonging that were more fluid, inclusive, and less patriarchal with colonial ones that eventually "undercut indigenous Hawaiian epistemologies that define identity on the basis of one's kinship and genealogy . . . with destructive political consequences for indigenous peoples" (ibid., p. 3). The consequences include lingering divisions within Indigenous communities about

who is "an authentic Indian" and internalization of patriarchal practices of belonging. Reducing the legal eligibility of status Indians ultimately serves the purpose of genocide, since "histories of genocide are made possible through rigid assertions of difference between 'real Indians' and Others" (Cannon & Sunseri, 2017, p. 19). Moreover, the consequences have had a gendered impact because Indigenous women right from the early colonial policies have been specifically and more negatively targeted, as will be examined in a later section of the chapter. And even as recently as 2017, Indigenous people, and women in particular, are still experiencing legislative concepts of Indianness in Canada (see box, p. 33).

Another major mechanism of colonialist assimilation to mainstream Canadian society was the establishment of the residential schooling system mandated by the state and run by Christian churches until the early 1990s (Sunseri, 2011). The explicit goal of these schools was to "get rid of the Indian problem" by separating children from their families' and community's influence and educating and socializing them into European so-called civilized ways. In the schools, students received a very low quality of education needed to succeed in the society, were forbidden to speak their Indigenous language and engage in any other cultural practices, and were often subjected to many kinds of abuse (Truth and Reconciliation Commission, 2015). In 2008, the Canadian federal government formed the Truth and Reconciliation Commission (TRC), giving it the task of collecting stories from the survivors of the schools about their past experiences so that a road toward truth and reconciliation could begin. In 2015, the TRC released its final report highlighting the impacts the residential schooling system had on the survivors, their families, and Indigenous communities. It reported that many had been abused, died from malnutrition or diseases, and were forced to assimilate to Canadian norms and values (ibid.).

The lingering impact of the experience has been a breakdown of familial relations and what Wesley-Esquimaux (2009) calls a historic trauma, meaning a transmission of years of trauma from one generation to subsequent ones. "The combined effects of unexpressed historic trauma and the resulting emotional, psychological, and physical abuses have led to collective symptoms of repressed emotions, numbness, and the expected social and emotional depression that comes with unresolved issues and the loss of inherent identity" (2009, p. 20). In moving toward repairing the negative impacts of the residential schools, the final report of the TRC outlined 94 Calls to Action, urging all levels of government, social institutions, and ordinary community members to take the necessary steps to raise awareness of the historic trauma. Ranging from areas like education to legislation, the TRC pointed to the need to invest in all levels of education of Indigenous children and youth, to reform the child welfare system, to educate the Canadian public on Indigenous history and issues, to develop culturally relevant social programs, and to form a sincere nation-to-nation relationship between Indigenous peoples and Canadians.

While centuries of settler colonialism has produced devastating, lasting damage to Indigenous peoples globally and its symptoms are evident in the high rates of poverty, poor health, and high suicide rates, especially among the youth, Indigenous women have also felt the sexist and patriarchal dimensions of racist colonialism. One of the colonialists' initial and ongoing targets has been the transformation of Indigenous gendered norms and relations. It is to this dimension that the chapter now turns.

Gender and Colonialism at a Crossroad

It is important to note that, just as is the case with colonial experiences globally, gender identities and relations have never been identical across all Indigenous peoples worldwide, either pre- or after contact with settler colonials. Hence, "[w]hile we can never claim to adequately represent the extremely nuanced diversity of Indigenous maternal [and other] experience, Indigenous peoples do share some values, epistemologies, and world-views, including a belief in the centrality of strong powerful women" (Lavell-Harvard & Anderson, 2014, p. 2). This section of the chapter gives a brief overview of some similar gender experiences shared by Indigenous peoples, beginning with what they were prior to settler colonialism and then examining how the latter transformed Indigenous gender relations.

Indigenous Gender Relations Prior to Settler Colonialism

In North America, Indigenous gender relations were quite egalitarian, and women were valued for their roles as life-givers, carriers of culture, and participants in the economy and other activities in their nations (Anderson & Lawrence, 2003; Cannon & Sunseri, 2017; Lavell-Harvard & Anderson, 2014; Sunseri, 2011; Valaskakis, Stout, & Guimond, 2009). "Referencing the teachings of the Dakota nation, Anderson has explained that according to our traditions Indigenous women not only literally 'birth the people' they are also given a 'lifetime responsibility to nurture the people'" (Lavell-Harvard & Anderson, 2014, p. 3). Haudenosaunee societies have also been reported as having a gendered power balance whereby all sexes worked together and shared responsibilities in all spheres of their nations, with no sex seen as superior to the others (Sunseri, 2011). Women held important leadership roles: they sat in separate women's councils in the confederacy, Clan Mothers appointed—and could remove—hereditary male chiefs, they held jurisdiction over adoption rules and declaration of wars, and they held the land communally by following their matrilineal and matrilocal rules (ibid.). Moreover,

Indigenous nations of North America treated gender roles as complementary but not dichotomous (Tsosie, 2010, p. 32). "For example, in the Southwest [of the US], men and women have complementary roles in planting, growing, harvesting, and preparing corn . . . it would be inappropriate to say that one gender has primary responsibility for growing corn. It is an obligation of both genders, but it manifests in distinct duties and responsibilities" (ibid.). Indeed, for the well-being of their nation, Indigenous gender identities were fluid, and all individuals were self-determined in their own sexuality (Sunseri, 2011).

Outside of North America, we can see similar patterns. For example, Kanaka Hawaiians "had a range of models of gender and sexual diversity. . . . Both men and women were autonomous in all conjugal relations . . . bisexuality was normative and . . . polygamy and polyandry also were not uncommon. . . . High-ranking Hawaiian women and men held governing positions as paramount chiefs and lesser chiefs before the formation of the monarchy in the early nineteenth century" (Kauanui, 2017, p. 49). Sami women, together with men, lived off traditional economies and "made use of own expertise within the Sami landscape" (Eikjok, 2007, p. 108). Women had responsibility for agriculture, were producers of food and clothing, and held ownership over the reindeer industry (ibid.).

However, settler colonialism had a major negative impact on gender relations in Indigenous territories globally. Eventually, the imposition of patriarchal notions of gender and sexist discriminatory laws devalued Indigenous women, and gender equity diminished. In its place we begin to see gender inequality and an attack on Indigenous women's lives, with its legacies still felt in today's world.

Gendered Impacts of Settler Colonialism

Indigenous feminist scholars (Green, 2007; 2017; Suzack, Huhndorf, Perreault, & Barman, 2010) have recently increased awareness of the interconnections between colonialism and gender discrimination and inequality that have affected Indigenous peoples. Their analyses have highlighted how "colonialism affects both Indigenous men and women, but not identically" (Green, 2017, p. 5). The ongoing consequences of setter colonialism for Indigenous women have included: racist and sexist laws that have robbed them of rights to their territories and entitlements to legal Indian status in Canada; inability to practise Indigenous self-determination in children and family relations; poor economic and social conditions; decrease in their leadership roles; and high risk to many forms of violence. As the following section shows, "there is no doubt that colonialism was shaped by patriarchy and racism and that Indigenous peoples were subjected to the consequent normative assumptions and structural processes" (ibid.).

Not surprisingly, settler colonial institutions such as schools and churches played a pivotal role in "producing and reproducing ideologies about what it means to be a man or a woman or a family" (St Denis, 2017, p. 51), and such meanings exclude Indigenous notions and practices. While prior to settler colonialism, most Indigenous societies valued women, their conditions were drastically altered (Sunseri, 2011). The changes occurred shortly after early contact with Europeans, who judged the Indigenous women they encountered against their own preconceived "cult of true womanhood" (ibid., p. 89). Their ideal saw women confined within restrictive domestic spheres, subordinate to their patriarchs, and forced to accept double standards of sexuality. "This Victorian ideal of womanhood was seen as proof of civilization, whereby European women had been liberated of their burden of hard public labour and could now reserve their labour for a docile, feminine role" (ibid.; see also Olsen Harper, 2009; Stevenson, 1999; Wesley-Esquimaux, 2009).

Since Indigenous societies were structured upon gender egalitarianism and women, especially in matrilineal/matrilocal nations, were autonomous leaders, they were seen as a threat to the patriarchal order of the colonizing structures (Lavell-Harvard & Anderson, 2014). Consequently, colonizers set out to "denigrate, disempower, and dehumanize [them], thereby serving a racist and sexist colonial agenda" (ibid., p. 4). A locus of such disempowerment lay in Indigenous familial and communal relations, and laws such as the Indian Act and residential schools indeed targeted these Indigenous traditional practices.

The Indian Act, although its most oppressive sections have been removed, has been the main instrument of colonialism in Canada because its main goal from its inception has been to assimilate all Indians into mainstream Canadian society, thus getting "rid of the Indian problem." A major way it has attempted to accomplish this is by establishing "a narrow definition of 'Indian' . . . the fewer Indians that Canada recognizes, the less land must be allocated as reserves, the more people who are excluded from bands, the more quickly the government-recognized Indian population shrinks. The faster bands shrink and ultimately disappear, the more quickly the land may be taken by Canada" (Eberts, 2017, p. 79).

The definition of Indian has historically been a patrilineal one: "an Indian was any male person of Indian blood, or any child of such a person, or any woman married to such a male person. In 1951 . . . it terminated the Indian status of Indian women who married non-Indian men and prevented these women from passing Indian status to their children" (Sunseri, 2011, p. 90). Patriarchal definitions of Indigeneity were also imposed in other settler colonies like Hawaii (Kauanui, 2008). Such sexist laws removed Indigenous women of their ability to equally pass on their legal Indigenous status to their offspring and to fully participate in the daily social and political activities in their communities. This was quite a change from the autonomy and leadership roles they had held in their nations, especially for Indigenous women of traditionally matrilineal societies like the

Haudenosaunee. Indeed, as Eberts argues, "this places Indian women at a great legal disadvantage" (2017, p. 79).

In 1985, after Indigenous women fought the Canadian state both nationally and internationally through recourse to the United Nations, Canada passed Bill C-31, through which "women who had lost status when they married non-Indians were eligible to apply to acquire status under section 6(1) (c)" (ibid.). However, Bill C-31 ended the one-parent rule for determining status, requiring in its place that now "those with section 6(2) status would have to parent with a registered Indian in order to be able to confer status on their children. . . . And that is a new host of inequality among Indians brought about by the vexed provisions of the Indian Act" (ibid., p. 87). More recently, the *McIvor v. Canada* legal judgment "restores federal recognition to the grandchildren of Indian women who were involuntarily enfranchised (i.e. legally assimilated) because of sexism and Indianness" (Cannon & Sunseri, 2017, p. 62). However, the Canadian courts did not recognize the racialization embedded in its ongoing definition of Indian status; hence they have not addressed the racialized injustice that they have continued to apply to Indigenous peoples (ibid.). As well, not all of the sexist implications have been removed from the Indian Act (see box, p. 33). Aside from the issues arising from the status criteria, the Indian Act imposed new forms of governance in the established reserves, modelled after the European electoral system, and until the mid-1960s, women could not participate in the elections or hold office, nor could they own property. This should lead us to question exactly what kind of progress, what kind of liberation, did modern civilization projects like settler colonial nation-statehoods bring to Indigenous women!

Transformations in gender relations were also made possible through the residential schools in Canada and in similar educational systems in other settler colonial places like New Zealand

Ongoing Sexist Discrimination in the Indian Act

In November 2017, the Canadian Senate passed an amendment to Bill S-3 to address a Quebec Court judge's ruling that had asked the federal government to make changes to the Indian Act to restore status to all women and their descendants who had lost it after marrying someone not registered as Indian. However, as Dr Lynn Gehl and other activists have argued, this new bill falls short of eliminating all the existing sexist discrimination. The bill restores status to those who "married-out" post-1951, but those of pre-1951 will have to wait. As it stands, the federal government is promising that it will consult with First Nations groups to address the remaining gap and will report on that process to the Parliament within three months, a year, and then three years after the passing of the bill. But as critics have pointed out, there is nothing forcing the government to actually eliminate all the sexist discrimination. As Pam Palmater, an Indigenous scholar, has pointed out, "a promise for future equality doesn't reach the Charter guarantee of equality" (*Winnipeg Free Press*, 2017).

(Lavell-Harvard & Anderson, 2014) and Hawaii (Kauanui, 2017). In these schools, Indigenous girls and boys learned new gender norms that reinforced patriarchal and heteronormative ideals. As well, they were taught to view their Indigenous sexuality as sinful and Indigenous parenting practices as uncivilized and inferior to those of European families. Together with residential schools, the child welfare system in Canada also attacked traditional family structures by removing children from what they viewed "dysfunctional" homes. Most often, children were apprehended by the state either because their families broke away from Euro-Canadian nuclear family, middle-class values or because families could not properly meet their needs because of social inequities resulting from centuries of settler colonialism (Cannon & Sunseri, 2017). "Breakdowns of traditional Aboriginal kinship and family structures are attributed to these experiences and they impact parenting across generations, disrupting traditional systems of social support" (Baskin & McPherson, 2014, p. 113). What were once sovereign families structured around gender equity were broken spiritually, psychologically, and emotionally. Sexism and patriarchy slowly penetrated

Indigenous communities, and the lingering traumatic effects are still evident today, as the Truth and Reconciliation Commission of Canada reported (TRC, 2015). Current social ills affecting Indigenous women must be examined through a critical analysis of the damage settler colonialism continues to cause, and one evidence is the tragic loss of Indigenous women's lives through gendered violence.

Gendered Colonial Violence against Indigenous Women

To better grasp the height of the issue of violence against Indigenous women, we can begin with the reported numbers across different regions of the world: in Canada, an RCMP report documented more than 1000 missing or murdered Indigenous women and girls (MMIWG) in Canada between 1980 and 2012 (Lavell-Harvard & Brant, 2016). In the US, "one in three Native American women have been raped or experienced attempted rape, and the rate of sexual assault on Native American women is more than twice the national average" (Dunbar-Ortiz, 2014, p. 214). In Guatemala,

Mayan Ixil women were often raped during the civil war as part of the systematic and intentional plan to destroy the social fabric and thereby ensure the destruction of the Ixil population" (Jayakumar, 2014, p. 132). While the violence experienced by Indigenous women is similar in some ways to that of other women because of their shared gender variable, it is quite different, since it has been shaped by its link to colonial violence.

To begin with, as Amnesty International reported in 2010, Indigenous women of Canada are at least 3.5 times more likely to experience violence than non-Indigenous women. Moreover, their homicides are disproportionally unresolved or not taken seriously by police and other justice systems (Cannon & Sunseri, 2017, p. 79). Indigenous scholars and activists have repeatedly argued that violence against Indigenous women is connected to colonial policies, laws, attitudes, and stereotypes of Indigenous peoples in general but particularly affect women. This colonial history has placed Indigenous women's lives at very high risk of many forms of violence, including sexual exploitation, assault, and murder (Bourgeois, 2017; Cannon & Sunseri, 2017; Eberts, 2017; Olsen Harper, 2009).

Indigenous women's lives remain at risk today. For example, a study conducted in the US revealed that "from the early mid 1960s up to 1976, between 3,400 and 70,000 Native women were coercively, forcibly, or unwittingly sterilized permanently by tubal ligation or hysterectomy" (Ralstin-Lewis, 2005, p. 71). These state-sponsored procedures led to a decrease in the birthrate of Indigenous women so must be considered a program to reduce the Indigenous population, a genocidal practice. Indigenous women in the US who were coerced and/or forced into these medical procedures were often very poor and dependent on the state and health care professionals, therefore vulnerable. Moreover, they most likely lacked the medical and legal knowledge needed to make an informed decision about

their reproductive rights. Lastly, "because all titles to land in the United States must, at some point, follow a path from the original inhabitants of the country to the United States government, the property can only be owned after the aboriginal title can be extinguished" (ibid, p. 83). Reducing the Indigenous population through forced sterilization cleared the path to such extinguishment of Indigenous lands and natural resources, therefore indicating the genocidal implication of such medical procedures.

The violation of Indigenous women's reproductive rights has also occurred in Latin American countries like Peru, where more than 200,000 women were sterilized between 1996 and 2000 (Cavallo, 2016). Health care providers in Canada have also performed such unjust procedures, as reported by Dr Boyer and Dr Bartlett in 2017 (Hamilton & Quenneville, 2017). Using anecdotal evidence, the report stated that "women felt pressured and harassed to sign consent forms while under the trying conditions of labour" (ibid.). The report made recommendations to prevent future violations, and these included: creating an advisory council that would include Indigenous elders and community members, hiring Indigenous workers, and setting up a support group. Additionally, a United Nations committee has recently recommended that Canada criminalize any further involuntary sterilizations of Indigenous women, a move applauded by the Assembly of First Nations of Canada (Smoke, 2018).

Even the singular variable of Indigeneity has put Indigenous women at risk of violence, since racist and sexist portrayals of Indigenous women as promiscuous, easy, wild, associated with the label of "squaw," which emanated from early accounts by European traders and missionaries, still affect the minds of many in Canada. In turn, these stereotypes influence their behaviour against Indigenous women, at times leading to violence (Cannon & Sunseri, 2017, p. 79). As well, the Canadian state itself has been complicit in this violence (Bourgeois, 2017; Eberts, 2017). As Bourgeois argues, "the political consolidation of the Canadian State in 1867 marks the starting point of an aggressive multipronged colonial war waged by the Canadian State against Indigenous women and girls" (2017, p. 261). For example, colonial rules of status registration in the Indian Act discriminated against Indigenous women and their children, often pushing them outside of their communities and into urban settings. Once in the cities, racism and poor socio-economic conditions have made them vulnerable to sexual exploitation and violence (ibid.).

This vulnerability has been compounded by the multi-generational impacts of residential schools and the child welfare systems (ibid.). We must identify "the violence and intergenerational trauma caused by the Indian residential school system as an underlying factor of the violence against MMIWG" (ibid, p. 263). As a matter of fact, many of the missing and murdered Indigenous women and girls in Canada have had a history either with the residential school system or the child welfare agencies (ibid.). Hence, the state has been partly guilty in the ongoing violence inflicted upon Indigenous peoples, and women in particular. Its justice apparatus has also been complicit in this because it has failed to adequately protect Indigenous women and girls. When Amnesty International reported the alarming cases of missing and murdered Indigenous women and girls in Canada, it pointed out how the police and the courts had not taken the issue seriously. With the support of the media, often more attention was given to "the high risk lifestyle" of the victims rather than to the crime itself (Olsen Harper, 2009; Bourgeois, 2017; Cannon & Sunseri, 2017). "Canada (in)justice system has long used prostitution as justification for minimizing the violence perpetrated against Indigenous women and girls and for exonerating perpetrators" (Bourgeois, 2017, p. 265).

It was not until 2015 that the Canadian federal government, after decades of outcry and activism by Indigenous groups and allies, initiated the Missing and Murdered Indigenous Women and Girls Inquiry to examine both the roots and consequences of violence against Indigenous women and girls and the steps needed to stop it. The inquiry needs to critically look at the role of the colonial state, the influence of racist and sexist attitudes and policies on violent behaviours, and the complicit roles of the media and the justice system in order to fully comprehend the causes of the violence. In addition, it needs to be transparent, be trauma- and culturally competent, be accessible to Indigenous communities, and have good long-term support systems for both the survivors and their families, as well as the staff of the inquiry, and as much as possible it should be staffed by Indigenous women and men. Ultimately, the results of the inquiry should constitute initial steps toward healing and recovery and actions toward a more equitable relationship between Indigenous peoples and settler nation-states and their residents.[1]

Moving toward a Decolonized Future

"Currently, First Nations women (and men) are on what has been termed in the United States and Canada 'a healing journey,' which can also be described as the process of discovering and escaping the temporality of traumatic life experiences and creating a new social reality of unfavorable circumstances" (Wesley-Esquimaux, 2009, p. 25). Indigenous women have always resisted settler colonialism, and the fact that many of our Indigenous knowledges, languages, and cultures have survived is testament to their resilience.

This chapter has examined the links between settler colonialism, Indigeneity, gender, and nationalism in settler colonies like Canada, the US, Australia, and New Zealand. It has shown how global settler colonialism has resulted in genocide,

Call to Action

Every year on Valentine's Day, 14 February, memorials to commemorate and draw awareness to the issue of Missing and Murdered Indigenous Women and Girls are held across Canada. Locate an Indigenous organization in your area that participates in this activity, volunteer to assist in the preparation for the event, and take part in the vigil.

dispossession of lands, attacks on Indigenous cultures, and the imposition of sexist and patriarchal laws and practices. These social phenomena have ruptured healthy Indigenous nations and caused Indigenous women's lives to deteriorate. We have just begun to uncover the truth about the history of settler colonialism through reports like the Truth and Reconciliation Commission of Canada and are now in the process of addressing such historical trauma.

At the core of this healing journey is targeting colonial policies and laws as the main guilty parties of Indigenous women's current oppressive conditions; therefore, the main focus has been a restoration of precolonial ways of being and governing and a demand for a true nation-to-nation relationship with settlers (Cannon & Sunseri, 2017). Since global settler colonial experiences for Indigenous women also meant the intersection of patriarchy and sexism with colonialism, it is crucial that a critique of modern global colonialism and decolonization contain a gender analysis (Sunseri, 2011). We need to realize that although precolonial Indigenous societies were gender egalitarian, Western patriarchy has transformed gender relations and that "if not all Aboriginal peoples, both men and women, who are living in Western societies are inundated from birth until death with Western patriarchy and Western forms of misogyny" (St Denis, 2017, p. 54). An empowering decolonizing movement would need to be less essentialist and divisive, incorporate different experiences of contemporary Indigeneity, and meet Indigenous women's needs so they can reclaim their traditional powerful spaces in their Indigenous nations.

Tying It Together

This chapter, taking a postcolonial Indigenist approach, has shown how global modern nation-states projects are intimately tied to settler colonialism. In places like Canada, the US, Australia, and New Zealand, settler colonialism led to dispossession of Indigenous territories and transformation of their social, economic, and political systems, including gender relations. We saw how the latter moved from gender egalitarianism to gender inequity.

DISCUSSION QUESTIONS

1. In what ways have the experiences of Indigenous peoples been similarly affected by settler colonialism? What have been some of the specific elements of it for Indigenous peoples of Canada?

2. Discuss how Indigenous gender relations were transformed from the precolonial era to the postcolonial one. How did the interconnection between patriarchy, racism, and colonialism play out in this transformation?

3. What is the Indian Act? How did it, and other colonial policies, play a central role in the marginalization and oppression of Indigenous women in Canada?

4. Explain what is meant by gendered colonial violence. How is violence against Indigenous women similar to, but also different from, that against non-Indigenous women?

5. How did the Indian Act redefine Indigenous legal status in Canada? What have been some of the sexist consequences of such redefinitions? How do recent amendments to the Indian Act still fail to remove all gender discrimination?

SUGGESTIONS FOR FURTHER READING

Altamirano-Jiménez, Isabel. (2013). *Indigenous encounters with neoliberalism: Place, women, and the environment in Canada and Mexico*. Vancouver, BC: University of British Columbia Press. This book compares Canada and Mexico in terms of Indigenous struggles against colonialism and neoliberalism by looking at the interconnections between gender, place, and colonialism.

Cannon, Martin J., & Sunseri, Lina (Eds.). (2017). *Racism, colonialism, and Indigeneity in Canada: A reader*, 2nd ed. Don Mills, ON: Oxford University Press. This book is a collection of readings examining issues of racism, colonialism, Indigeneity, gender, and resistance in Canada. Indigenous scholars wrote all the readings.

Green, Joyce (Ed.). (2017). *Making space for Indigenous feminism*, 2nd ed. Halifax, NS, and Winnipeg, MB: Fernwood Publishing. This book contains contributions by Indigenous writers in the fields of gender and feminist studies. It covers themes of racism, patriarchy, colonialism, gendered violence, activism, and resistance.

MULTIMEDIA SUGGESTIONS

https://native-land.ca
An online resource with information about Indigenous lands and languages.

Native Women's Association of Canada
http://www.nwac-hq.org
This is the official website of the Native Women's Association of Canada, and it provides useful information and resources about/for Indigenous women.

Trick or Treaty (2014; 85 minutes)
https://www.cbc.ca/player/play/2669994872
This documentary, directed by Alanis Obomsawin, follows Indigenous leaders in communities affected by Treaty 9 (the James Bay Treaty). These leaders seek dialogue with the Canadian government in order to urge action for their people.

Missing: The Documentary (2014; 55 minutes)
https://www.youtube.com/watch?
    v=wSS6mRaMSHA
This documentary, directed by "Yonge Jibwe," brings attention to missing and murdered Indigenous women in Canada through interviews with family members and friends of the victims.

We Were Children (2012; 88 minutes)
This docudrama tells the stories of Lynn Hart and Glen Anaquod, survivors of the Canadian Indian residential school system. The film underlines the experiences of First Nations children taken from their homes and put in the care of schools run by people who tried to strip them of their cultural identities.

REFERENCES

Altamirano-Jiménez, Isabel. (2013). *Indigenous encounters with neoliberalism: Place, women, and the environment in Canada and Mexico.* Vancouver, BC: University of British Columbia Press.

Anderson, Kim, & Lawrence, Bonita (Eds). (2003). *Strong women stories: Native vision and community survival.* Toronto, ON: Sumach Press.

Baskin, Cyndy, & McPherson, Bela. (2014). Towards the wellbeing of Aboriginal mothers and their families: You can't mandate time. In D. Memee Lavell-Harvard & Kim Anderson (Eds.), *Mothers of the nations: Indigenous mothering as global resistance, reclaiming and recovery* (pp. 109–30). Bradford, ON: Demeter Press.

Battell Lowman, Emma, & Barker, Adam J. (2015). *Settler identity and colonialism in 21st century Canada.* Halifax, NS, and Winnipeg, MB: Fernwood Publishing.

Bourgeois, Robyn. (2017). Perpetual state of violence: An Indigenous feminist antioppression inquiry into missing and murdered Indigenous women and girls. In Joyce Green (Ed.), *Making space for Indigenous feminism* (2nd edn, pp. 253–73). Halifax, NS, and Winnipeg, MB: Fernwood Publishing.

Cannon, Martin J., & Sunseri, Lina (Eds) (2017). *Racism, colonialism, and Indigeneity in Canada: A reader.* Don Mills, ON: Oxford University Press.

Cavallo, Shena. (2016). Peru fails to deliver for Indigenous women. Available at https://opendemocracy.net/democraciaabierta/shena-cavallo/peru-fails-to-deliver.

Dunbar-Ortiz, Roxanne. (2014). *An Indigenous peoples' history of the United States.* Boston, MA: Beacon Press.

Eberts, Mary. (2017). Being an Indigenous woman is a "high-risk lifestyle." In Joyce Green (Ed.), *Making space for Indigenous feminism* (2nd edn, pp. 69–102). Halifax, NS, and Winnipeg, MB: Fernwood Publishing.

Eikjok, Jorunn. (2007). Gender, essentialism and feminism in Samiland. In Joyce Green (Ed.), *Making space for Indigenous feminism* (pp. 108–23). Black Point, NS: Fernwood Publishing.

Fortin, Jacey. (2017). Columbus Day has drawn protests almost from Day 1. Available at https://www.nytimes.com/2017/10/09/us/columbus-day-protest.html.

George, Rachael Yacaaʔał. (2017). Inclusion is just the Canadian word for assimilation: Self-determination and the reconciliation paradigm in Canada. In Kiera L. Ladner & Myra J. Tait (Eds.), *Surviving Canada: Indigenous peoples celebrate 150 years of betrayal* (pp. 49–62). Winnipeg, MB: ARP Books.

Green, Joyce (Ed.). (2007). *Making space for Indigenous feminism.* Black Point, NS: Fernwood Publishing.

Green, Joyce (Ed.). (2017). *Making space for Indigenous feminism* (2nd edn). Halifax, NS, and Winnipeg, MB: Fernwood Publishing.

Hamilton, Charles, and Quenneville, Guy. (2017). Report on coerced sterilization of Indigenous women spurs apology, but path forward unclear. Available at https://www.cbc.ca/news/canada/saskatoon/report-indigenous-women-coerced-tubal-ligations-1.4224286.

Jayakumar, Kirthi. (2014). The impact of sexual violence on Indigenous motherhood in Guatemala. In D. Memee Lavell-Harvard & Kim Anderson (Eds), *Mothers of the nations: Indigenous mothering as global resistance, reclaiming and recovery* (pp. 131–46). Bradford, ON: Demeter Press.

Kauanui, Kēhaulani J. (2008). *Hawaiian blood: Colonialism and the politics of sovereignty and Indigeneity.* Durham, NC, and London, UK: Duke University Press.

Kauanui, Kēhaulani J. (2017). Indigenous Hawaiian sexuality and the politics of nationalist decolonization, In Joanne Barker (Ed.), *Critically sovereign: Indigenous gender, sexuality and feminist studies* (pp. 45–68). Durham, NC, and London, UK: Duke University Press.

Lavell-Harvard, Memee, D., & Anderson, Kim (Eds.). (2014). *Mothers of the nations: Indigenous mothering as global resistance, reclaiming and recovery.* Bradford, ON: Demeter Press.

Lavell-Harvard, Memee, D., & Brant, Jennifer (Eds.). (2016). *Forever loved: Exposing the hidden crisis of missing and murdered Indigenous women and girls in Canada.* Bradford, ON: Demeter Press.

Little Bear, Leroy. (2017). Canada is a pretend nation: REDx Talks—What I know about Canada, In Kiera L. Ladner & Myra J. Tait (Eds.), *Surviving Canada: Indigenous peoples celebrate 150 years of betrayal* (pp. 36–42). Winnipeg, MB: ARP Books.

Mackey, Eva. (2016). *Unsettled expectations: Uncertainty, land and settler decolonization.* Halifax, NS, and Winnipeg, MB: Fernwood Publishing.

Mikaere, Ani. (2011). *Colonial myths—Māori realities: He rukuruku whakaaro.* Wellington, Aotearoa/New Zealand: Huia Publisher.

Moreton-Robinson, Aileen. (2015). *The white possessive: Property, power, and Indigenous sovereignty.* Minneapolis, MN: University of Minnesota Press.

Olsen Harper, Anita. (2009). Sisters in spirit. In Gail Guthrie Valaskakis, Madeleine Dion Stout, & Eric Guimond (Eds.), *Restoring the balance: First Nations women, community, and culture* (pp. 175–200). Winnipeg, MB: University of Manitoba Press.

Palmater, Pamela. (2015). *Indigenous nationhood: Empowering grassroots citizens.* Halifax, NS, and Winnipeg, MB: Fernwood Publishing.

Pasternak, Shiri. (2014). Occupy(ed) Canada: The political economy of Indigenous dispossession. In The Kinonda-niimi Collective (Eds), *The winter we danced: Voices from the past, the future, and the Idle No More Movement* (pp. 40–4). Winnipeg, MB: ARP Books.

Ralstin-Lewis, Marie. (2005). The continuing struggle against Indigenous women's reproductive rights. *Wicazo Sa Review*, 20(1), 71–95.

Smoke, Penny. (2018). UN committee recommends Canada criminalize involuntary sterilization. Available at https://www.cbc.ca/news/un-committee-involuntary-sterilization-1.4936879.

St Denis, Verna. (2017). Feminism is for everybody: Aboriginal women, feminism and diversity. In Joyce Green (Ed.), *Making space for Indigenous feminism* (2nd edn, pp. 42–62). Halifax, NS, and Winnipeg, MB: Fernwood Publishing.

Stevenson, Winona. (1999). Colonialism and First Nations women in Canada. In Enakshi Dua & Angela Robertson (Eds.), *Scratching the surface: Canadian anti-racist feminist thought* (pp. 49–80). Toronto, ON: Women's Press.

Sunseri, Lina. (2011). *Being again of one mind: Oneida women and the struggle for decolonization.* Vancouver, BC: University of British Columbia Press.

Suzack, Cheryl, Huhndorf, Shari M., Perreault, Jeanne, & Barman, Jean (Eds). (2010). *Indigenous women and feminism: Politics, activism, culture.* Vancouver, BC: University of British Columbia Press.

Teves, Stephanie Nohelani, Smith, Andrea, & Raheja, Michelle H. (2015). *Native studies keywords.* Tucson, AZ: University of Arizona Press.

Truth and Reconciliation Commission of Canada. (2015). *Honouring the truth, reconciling for the future: Summary of the final report of the Truth and Reconciliation Commission of Canada.* Ottawa, ON: Government of Canada.

Tsosie, Rebecca. (2010). Native women and leadership: An ethics of culture and relationship. In Cheryl Suzack, Shari M. Huhndorf, Jeanne Perreault, & Jean Barman (Eds), *Indigenous women and feminism: Politics, activism, culture* (pp. 29–42). Vancouver, BC: University of British Columbia Press.

Valaskakis, Gail Guthrie, Stout, Madeleine Dion, & Guimond, Eric (Eds). (2009). *Restoring the balance: First Nations women, community, and culture.* Winnipeg, MB: University of Manitoba Press.

Vowel, Chelsea. (2016). *Indigenous writes: A guide to First Nations, Métis & Inuit issues in Canada.* Winnipeg, MB: HighWater Press.

Walker, Ranginui. (1990). *Ka whawhai tonu matou: Struggle without end.* Auckland, Aotearoa/New Zealand: Penguin.

Wesley-Esquimaux, Cynthia C. (2009). Trauma to resilience: Notes on decolonization. In Gail Guthrie Valaskakis, Madeleine Dion Stout, & Eric Guimond (Eds), *Restoring the balance: First Nations women, community, and culture* (pp. 13–34). Winnipeg, MB: University of Manitoba Press.

Winnipeg Free Press. (2017). Accessed at https://www.winnipegfreepress.com/local/contentious-bill-on-indian-status-backed-by-senate-heads-to-house-456559293.html.

Wolfe, Patrick. (1999). *Settler colonialism and the transformation of anthropology.* London, UK: Cassell.

NOTE

1. On 3 June 2019, after this chapter was written, the final report of the Missing and Murdered Indigenous Women and Girls Inquiry was released. The report included 231 Calls for Justice and characterized the violence against Indigenous women and girls as "genocide." The report can be found at www.mmiwg-ffada.ca/final-report.

CHAPTER 3

◇

Decolonial Interventions to Queer Necropolitics and Homonationalisms

Gül Çalışkan and Kayla Preston, with Gary Kinsman,
Ghaida Moussa, and Amar Wahab [1]

Learning Objectives

In this chapter, you will:

- analyze how we view queerness within the nation-state;
- engage with the notions of race, class, gender, and sexuality in order to understand how state relations use these notions about queer bodies to justify expansion of power and control;
- apply a framework for engaging with and defining what scholars mean by queer necropolitics and homonationalisms;
- consider the intersections between policing queer bodies and the ways that proponents of national security use the queer body to justify racialization and xenophobia;
- examine how queer people actively mediate and resist the nationhood projects of national security as they stand up to racialization and oppression.

Introduction

This chapter is crafted around interviews with Gary Kinsman, Ghaida Moussa, and Amar Wahab in which these researchers, teachers, and activists discuss the effects and forms of colonialism that intersect with issues of racialization, violence, and queer identities. The interviews also explore the politics of governance, surveillance, and criminalization of racialized queer identities. As Haritaworn, Kuntsman, and Posocco argue,

"In queer theorizing, debates over the place of rights discourses in regimes of border fortification, militarization and incarceration have arrived belatedly, to collide with a context of LGBTQ+ politics and sexuality studies which, especially in Europe, lack any serious engagement with racism, coloniality, positionality, and intersectionality" (2014, p. 1). "Necropolitics" was a term coined by Achille Mbembe to describe power dynamics in which some people (those with more social and political power) create and maintain political or social structures that condemn others (those with less social and political power) to precarious positions that could result in loss of life. In other words, through extreme inequality, certain people live as the "walking dead" (for example, under slavery). Puar (2007, p. 36) articulates a "**queer necropolitics**" to make sense of the expansion of liberal gay politics and to analyze the combination of post-9/11 queer outrage regarding gay bashing with simultaneous queer complicity toward the US "war on terror" (Haritaworn, Kuntsman, & Posocco, 2014, p. 2).

Homonationalism refers to patriotic claims by members of the LGBTQ+ community that migrant (racialized) people are homophobic, that Western society is not, and that therefore their opposition to homophobia justifies racist and xenophobic policies, especially against Muslims. Puar's queer necropolitics explores these new tensions and fissures between people who have attained LGBTQ+ rights (who are mostly persons who enjoy class and race privileges in the Global North) and those who seek to protect the social and physical lives of "queerly racialized populations" (Puar, 2007, p. xxvi).

Who Are the Activist Researchers Interviewed?

Gary Kinsman is a long-time queer liberation, anti-oppression, and anti-capitalist activist in solidarity with Indigenous struggles. Most recently, he has been involved in the AIDS Activist History Project, the No Pride in Policing Coalition, and the Anti-69 Network against the mythologies of the 1969 criminal code reform. He is the author of *The Regulation of Desire*, co-author of *The Canadian War on Queers*, and author of many book chapters on sexual and gender politics.

Ghaida Moussa is a PhD candidate at York University in social and political thought. Her dissertation explores racial, gendered, and neoliberal

regimes of knowledge in relation to chronic medically unidentified illness. Her master's thesis from the University of Ottawa focused on (neo)colonial oppression and Palestinian queer resistance. She is co-editor of three anthologies: *Min Fami: Arab feminist reflections on identity, space, and resistance*; *Queering urban justice: Queer of colour formations in Toronto*; and *Marvellous grounds: Queer of colour histories of Toronto*.

Amar Wahab is associate professor in gender and sexuality, York University. His research interests include: race and sexual citizenship in liberal/multicultural and postcolonial nation-states; critiques of queer liberalism; and race, sexuality, and the politics of representation. His work in queer and critical sexuality studies has been published in the *Journal of Lesbian and Gay Studies*, the *Journal of Postcolonial Studies*, and the *Journal of Homosexuality*. He is the author of *Disciplining coolies: An archival footprint of Trinidad 1846* (2019, Peter Lang Publishers) and *Colonial inventions: Landscape, power and representation in nineteenth-century Trinidad* (2010, Cambridge Scholars Publishing) and co-author of *Envisioning LGBT human rights: (Neo)colonialism, neoliberalism and activism* (2018, Institute for Commonwealth Studies, University of London).

Situating Scholarship

How do you situate yourself in relation to notions of homonormativity, homonationalism, **racialization**, **colonialism**, and **imperialism**? How do you think your work relates to this book project in general and with this chapter in particular?

Gary Kinsman

Homonormativity, popularized by Lisa Duggan, is about how some layers of white, middle-class queer people, cis gay men in particular, come to identify with **neoliberal** capitalist relations. Jasbir Puar has extended and pushed this notion much further, developing homonationalism, in the context of the so-called war on terror, to conceptualize how some white, middle-class queer people, especially in the West, come to identify with their nation-states as being more "advanced" and "civilized" in relationship to the "backward" countries in the Global South, identified with homophobia and heterosexism.

Both homonormativity and homonationalism are suggestive terms pointing in important directions. However, sometimes they get used in ways where they're not grounded in historical and social relations. Part of my project is, in the "Canadian" context, on the northern part of Turtle Island, to try to concretize them, to root them in the historical, social processes through which they come into being.

These terms are interrelated with racialization, colonialism, and imperialism. You can't engage with what's going on in the world right now without engaging with questions of racialization, and the very foundation of state formation in what is now called Canada is in colonial practices and practices of extermination and marginalization directed against Indigenous people.

In this context, it's important to clarify that there are different forms of homonationalism. In the Canadian context, we face at least settler colonial forms of homonationalism, and built on that and in relationship to it, we have orientalist forms of homonationalism, which Jasbir Puar, in her earlier work, focuses on.

I am using "Canada" (in scare quotes), since it always needs to be troubled because of the history of colonization of Indigenous people. Colonialism operates in the Canadian context and within Canadian state formation in relationship to Indigenous people and with the legacies and afterlives of slavery and racialization that come after that. But colonialism also operates externally to Canadian state borders in its relation to people in the Global South.

Imperialism is still important as a term describing what goes on at the global level. Michael Hardt and Antonio Negri's (2000) notion of empire is also useful in that it's not so much that you have all these competing imperial powers now, but you often have the development of more global capitalist forms of regulation and extraction of resources and exploitation. There are also some ways that anti-imperialism can be used to deflect attention away from capitalist social relations, as the Zapatistas have reminded us.

Ghaida Moussa

In my master's thesis, I focused on the ways that the occupation of Palestine is justified and strengthened through the Israeli state's **pinkwashing** of **settler colonialism**, war, and apartheid. I also evaluated the role of Western LGBTQ+ solidarity movements in reproducing colonial dynamics that support homonationalism, occupation, and queer necropolitics. Since then, I have taken up that subject again in a chapter I co-authored with Nayrouz Abu Hatoum in the *Queering urban justice* collection I co-edited with Jin Haritaworn and Syrus Marcus Ware. This chapter builds on my master's work by looking at how solidarity with Palestine has been a way for Western LGBTQ+ groups to claim radical politics, all the while supporting settler colonialism right here in the West.

Queering urban justice is one of the collections to emerge from my work with the Marvellous Grounds collective (the other being *Marvellous grounds: Queer of colour histories of Toronto*), a Toronto-based queer and trans Black, Indigenous, and people of colour (QTBIPOC) mapping and counter-archiving project that challenges the whitening of queer and trans histories and argues that this story relies on the violent erasure and displacement of QTBIPOC.

Finally, my PhD work is on the racial, neoliberal, and gendered regimes of knowledge that affect how we understand medically unidentified chronic illness. I look at how scientific justifications are mobilized to determine which populations are deserving based on notions of sanity, ability, and productivity, which are highly reliant on the racial, gendered, and economic structures of a time and place.

Amar Wahab

Since 2013, I've investigated the intersections of race and sexuality through the concept of homonationalism (Puar, 2007)—an extension of Lisa Duggan's homonormativity. I have focused on this intersection in Canada and outside of Canada through a transnational perspective.

My work in Canada has focused critically on the gay community within Toronto, especially looking at communities at the edges of the LGBTQ+ margins, to think about how *some* others are positioned differently from *other* others, especially in terms of race. For instance, I investigated the neoliberal rebranding of the Toronto Fetish Fair as being much more inclusive, attracting normative heterosexual society. Rebranding—as a respectabilizing strategy—erased many of the sex-positive aspects and mobilized Islamophobia within the fetish/queer communities whereby Muslim subjects, especially Muslim women, are represented as terrorizing queerness. Gendered Islamophobia thus allows those in the fetish community—for example, the stigmatized BDSM community—to call themselves into nationhood and citizenship.

Focusing on the transnational linkages between race and sexuality, I explore places like Jamaica, Uganda, and St Lucia, which have been projected in the Canadian mainstream media as exceptionally homophobic. Canada also projects itself as exceptional in terms of being queer-tolerant (i.e., pinkwashing). I focused on the activism of queer diasporic Jamaicans and Ugandans in Toronto to examine two questions: How these activists navigate and mediate that intersection between race and sexuality; and how, regardless of the kinds of complexities they raise about their activism, the Canadian state, together with the mainstream LGBTQ+ community, reauthorizes its dominant constructions about the exceptional homophobia of these *other* places.

New Techniques of Governance: The Language of Rights and Protection

What new techniques of governance can be used in a context of power that increasingly speaks the language of women's rights, gay and transgender rights, and protection of diversity?

Ghaida Moussa

Women's rights, gay and transgender rights, and the language of diversity exist to fortify the distinction between deserving and undeserving subjects. State institutions are the gatekeepers of this process, since they create the knowledge needed to produce this distinction in the first place and then uphold it and enforce the interventions necessary to preserve it. This distinction is made along the lines of social hierarchies of race, class, gender, and ability, all integral to the decisions of inviting populations into neoliberal citizenship. Thus, our inclusion is reliant on our conformity to and reproduction of the same systems that are responsible for our oppression.

In the health sector, we see a rise in research on discrimination against queer and trans patients, for example—an embrace of diversity. Yet, at the same time, the conservative push for privatization and the discourse of individual responsibility is getting stronger. These two factors make it impossible for marginalized people to properly access care. The rights discourse often leaves out the structural factors. Incorporation through rights allocation does nothing to fundamentally change the structures weighing on our survival. Often, we are used as pawns to confirm the progressive politics of nation-states that need excuses to trigger wars and invasions in the name of sexual liberation. Thus, it comes at a serious cost, too, on a global level.

In *Marvellous grounds* (2018), Kusha Dadui's chapter gives a good example of this when discussing the Canadian benevolence toward gay refugees that helps to uphold the image of Canada as a sanctuary while differentiating it discursively from the homophobic Middle East. The targeting of Iranian gay refugees by the Canadian state as symbols of Canadian benevolence happens as the Middle East is discursively reinforced as a homophobic region, and this justifies it having to be managed by force and keeps obscuring Canada's own oppression of local QTBIPOC, Black communities, and Indigenous communities.

Amar Wahab

This relates to neoliberalism and how states are developing their biopolitical and necropolitical projects by refining their capacity to control populations through a rhetoric of tolerance and inclusion. We need to think of the conditions of agency, which seems only possible within a rights-based framework. Is the choiced self-integration of queers conditioned by a rights-based discourse, as something they cannot refuse?

States have also self-integrated into the margins as a benevolent regulator of the other and at times take on a certain minority status. This is exemplified in the Toronto Pride debates (2017), especially through Black Lives Matter's critiques of police inclusion in the Pride parade and the policing of Black communities (queer as well as non-queer and non-trans communities). Interestingly, it was not just the police but the state that produced itself as victimized by Black Lives Matter politics. This is an interesting dynamic, since any critiques of the state are constructed as terrorizing (i.e., victims of intolerance).

The turn to inclusion is also about the regulation of the included and their recruitment into citizenship. We see increasing members of the LGBTQ+ community becoming very strong supporters and agents in the war on terror. This not only recruits citizens—as well as those who are willing to stay silent and not critique the state—but also increases the legitimacy and capacity of the state to define which populations are impossible. Through its contract with new citizen categories, the state is able to legitimize the disposability of some populations.

Also, under neoliberalism, citizenship privileges the rights of the individual. It makes critical collective resistance unintelligible and unviable. Neoliberal formations—such as homonationalism—tend to be very simplistic and based on single-issue politics, which erases intersectional and complex critiques (e.g., Indigenous critiques of settler homonationalism and colonialism) and which works against solidarity across political sites and movements.

Added to this is the question of what we mean when we speak of something called "sexuality." In Canada, we talk about sexuality as if it is something that is already given, that we all have, and that therefore we must all assume. The discursive horizon, then, can only be about sexual normativity and sexual non-normativity. We also need to question: what is sexuality? How has it emerged especially under neoliberalism as a domain of intelligibility and control? Why does colonialism matter to sexuality in one politic and not matter in another? How does access to food banks matter to sexuality in one politic but have no resonance in another? It is this contrapuntal critique that is being suppressed under neoliberalism.

Gary Kinsman

It is important to understand how certain forms of neoliberal governance have moved to the fore but also have a longer history. We can go back to the establishment of multiculturalism in Canadian state practices in the early 1970s to see some of its roots. The practice of multiculturalism was about recognizing—but only on cultural grounds—that there was ethnic and racial diversity within the Canadian social formation. It recognized that different ethnic groups should have their own cultural festivals and cultural differences. Multiculturalism was also a strategy, as many feminists of colour have pointed out, that ignored the pervasive forms of social and class inequality that exist between different groups in Canadian society. It noted cultural features of racial and ethnic differences, but it didn't root these in institutional and capitalist class relations. Multiculturalism is one example of something that becomes more generalized in neoliberal forms of governance, and what you see now with the emergence of neoliberal capitalism is the ways in which certain forms of equality for some people are pushed forward. So there's now a language that we supposedly accept women's rights and gay rights, but what is meant by that is very limited individual formal rights that largely benefit white middle-class people, and what it means is that the vast majority of women and queer people continue to be oppressed. This is not about more substantive collective forms of rights and equality. Instead, this has to do with class and racialized notions of class in particular. An example I often use is that most of us have the same formal rights to go to the most expensive hotel in whatever city we're living in. But in practice, in concrete terms, many of us can't. There might be barriers in terms of access related to questions of ability, racialized practices that prevent people from going to it, and there is going to be the question of money, of people simply not being able to afford to go to these places. So here we begin to see the limitations of notions of formal rights, and we need to talk a lot more about substantive, collective rights and equality. That also leads into the whole language of diversity and inclusion. For me, it's important that we always ask critical questions of these terms. As Himani Bannerji (1995) points

out, whose diversity are we talking about, and on whose terms are people being included? These words can sound nice, but they become hegemonic vehicles for neoliberal governance through including only certain groups and excluding others.

There's all sorts of other languages of neoliberal governance, including the languages of participation and consultation whereby people participate in formulating policies that will come to regulate and oppress themselves, and languages of consultation that are set out on the terms of ruling institutions. There's languages of apologies and the social form of apologies, which means that once the apology is given, we can forget about what has happened historically. So these terms can work to suck us in, but we need to think about them much more critically, always asking how they relate to these new forms of neoliberal governance.

Challenges Rising from Queer Necropolitics and Homonationalisms

What challenges rise from queer necropolitics and homonationalisms, and how are these issues best addressed?

Ghaida Moussa

A big challenge is the discursive sleight of hand of claiming progress for all at the same time that there is increasing state intervention and policing of marginalized people. It creates lateral violence between community members; it invisibilizes what is truly going on (because now we have rights!). It hurts resistance and solidarity, too, by manipulating people into believing that their country is as progressive as they really want it to be and by providing class mobility to some. Black Lives Matter (BLM) has been integral in reminding us that, beyond solidarity, what we really need is a critical and deep understanding of what we all lose in a **patriarchal**, **anti-Black**, **white supremacist**, homonationalist police state.

Another challenge is the actual death, disability, and debility of innumerable marginalized people and how this disproportionality affects trans people—especially Black trans women—Indigenous women, and Black communities. The blanketing of their deaths by illusionary progress discourses diminishes the gravity of the situation and preserves it. Finally, rights can be taken away depending on the government in power, so we need to tear down structures and strengthen our communities.

Amar Wahab

Homonationalism and multiculturalism are about bordering and silencing others under the illusion of freedom and rights. How do we think about racism, misogyny, homophobia, and transphobia under these neoliberal formations anchored in a rhetoric of inclusion and tolerance? Have these oppressions disappeared, or have they become much more insidious with the neoliberal turn to legal rights and inclusion? How do we make them visible beyond what seems obvious?

Necropolitics and homonationalism (as biopolitical) are attached to state hegemony based on an unquestioned presumption that the nation-state matters centrally to organizing and defining the social. We therefore need to unsettle the taken-for-grantedness of the nation-state as the arbiter of social justice. That's a huge challenge, which is being voiced, especially from critiques of settler colonial homonationalism. For example, Andrea Smith talks about the ways in which queer studies imagines the idea of "no future" and celebrates the idea of "no future" precisely because the nation is premised on a future. However, according to Smith, this is a white settler queer-normative politics, which stands in tension with Native and Indigenous politics, precisely because Indigenous communities have already been rendered as having "no future." So within queer politics there are interesting tensions about whose politics counts.

In addition, if we are to think ourselves out of homonationalism, we need to think contrapuntally about social justice. What is oppression? How do we recognize oppression? How do we re-organize social justice, especially when justice is predominately framed through the legal domain? How do we make sense of "homosexuality" and "homophobia" across different contexts (as raised by scholars such as David Murray and Ashley Currier)? Even thinking about what, in the Global North, is defined as "hateful," since the state reserves the power or the right to authorize what counts as hate—within both the Global North and the Global South.

Gary Kinsman

It's important to remember that at the core of homonationalism is a racialized class politics. In this sense, it's important to see how racialization and class operate together in providing a social basis for homonationalism. The social basis for homonationalism is those policies that the Canadian state has come to adopt but also in particular the emergence of neoliberal queers or groups of largely middle-class white gay men who are integrated into the relations of neoliberal capitalism. That's the social basis that wants to be fully integrated into Canadian state formation and wants to be fully accepted into the white middle class. After these formal barriers are broken down, the acceptance of some elite white queer people in the middle class is all these people want to achieve. You have white, middle-class queer people engaged in a racialized class politics against the majority of other queer and trans people but doing it under the guise of the politics of the "community." Using that type of rubric, there has been a one-sided class struggle that has never been named as such, and we have to start to organize the other side of that racialized class struggle against neoliberal queers and homonationalist politics. It is important to think of the ways in which that has to take place in the so-called Canadian context, including queer support for Indigenous people and for actual nation-to-nation relations, opposition to anti-Black racism, and support for organizations like Black Lives Matter. But we also need to engage in it at the more global level. This is one of the more interesting features of the group Queers Against Israeli Apartheid (QuAIA) and the controversy generated around it. In Toronto Pride, there was an attempt to continue to raise progressive queer positions on global politics and support for the Palestinian people, which is one of the reasons why it generated such hostility, not only from state forces but also within certain layers of queer communities who are invested in Pride being an occasion for homonationalist performances that support the policies of Canadian state formation. QuAIA was an obstacle to that. So we also need to find ways we can oppose homonationalism on a global scale, to develop an internationalist queer and trans politics that does not participate in the construction of "Canada" as a more "advanced" or "civilized" country, that does not participate in suggesting to people engaged in different sexual and diverse gender practices in the Global South that their future is to look more like us, that we are more "advanced" and a more "adult" form of what they will become.

National Security, the Queer Canadian Body, and the Persistence of Homophobia

How has national security been enacted on the queer Canadian body? How has homophobia persisted even after the legalization of same-sex marriage?

Gary Kinsman

I will take this up in two stages. First, I am going to take up what is national security more generally. National security in the Canadian context

is a national security based initially on the colonization of Indigenous people. Later on, there is the development of a very racialized Canadian state in terms of people of colour and immigration policies. When we look at national security, we always need to ask whose national security are we talking about—what nation and whose security? Those questions are important because we need to move beyond the taken-for-grantedness of national security. We have to challenge the hegemonic character of national security to raise critical questions about it. National security always and everywhere includes only some people in the nation and excludes others. In the Canadian war on queers, queer people were identified as national security risks and were expelled from the fabric of the nation, but the other side of that was the construction of heterosexuality as the "national," "normal," "safe," "secure" sexuality. National security is not simply about expelling certain groups from the nation; it's also about constructing other groups at the centre of the nation and has a more "productive" dynamic.

Now, in the context of the "war on terror" in the Canadian and other contexts, this has been about expelling people identified as being Arab or Muslim from the fabric of the nation. Denying them rights, constructing them as enemies, while constructing whiteness and Christianity as being at the centre. National security is always an ideological practice and is something we should never support. It is always based on the oppression and exclusion of some groups of people. John Holloway (2005) talks about how it is "we"—that is, people in struggle—who are the crisis of capitalist social relations. But it's also important to understand that "we" are also the crisis of national security. National security practices are directed against oppressed people and the movements that have developed out of our communities to fight for liberation and freedom.

Going back to the Canadian war on queers, what happened to queer bodies with these national security campaigns? What happened in the late 1950s in the context of the Cold War, and the Cold War was not simply about the Soviet Union but was a national security campaign against communists, leftists, union activists, women activists, immigrants, anti-colonial and national liberation movements, and people defying gender norms, and it was extended to include queer people. Queer people were identified as being a risk to national security because we supposedly suffered from a "character weakness," which meant that we were susceptible to blackmail by "evil Soviet agents." But the people Patrizia Gentile and I interviewed for our book *The Canadian war on queers* said that the only people who ever tried to blackmail them were the RCMP or Canadian national security agents. They tried to blackmail people into giving the names of other lesbians and gay men so they could be purged by the national security regime. So there were measures that were undertaken against queer people from the late 1950s to the early 1990s, and in some ways these practices still continue. It is still possible for someone to be denied a national security clearance if they or their partner have something to hide: for instance, if someone is not out. But what happened, starting in the late 1950s with purges of anyone identified as homosexual from the public service, was combined in the military with earlier disciplinary proceedings against "sex deviants" so that thousands of people were purged from their jobs. There was even an attempt in the 1960s to develop a scientific detection technology, which the RCMP labelled the "fruit machine." Thousands of people were affected. People were interrogated, people were followed, and people outside the public service were interrogated to get them to identify their friends. The RCMP would also use local police, "morality squads," to try to round people up. They would threaten legal charges against people for homosexual activity, which was technically all-criminal at the time. So these campaigns continued in the public service,

beginning to die down in the 1980s. They continued quite vociferously in the Canadian military until 1992 with the Michelle Douglas case when the military said it could not continue to fight it on constitutional grounds because the Charter would not allow it. After 1992, major informal practices of discrimination continued in the Canadian military, and they continue to this day in terms of sexist, racist, and heterosexist practices as well.

Ghaida Moussa

It is imperative to notice how this happens once again along the lines of race, gender, ability, and class. As an example, one of the recurring themes of the chapters featured in *Queering urban justice* is how what is seen as progress relies on the displacement and erasure of marginalized people. For example, the gentrification of the Toronto Gay Village was made possible through the ousting of sex workers, homeless folks, drug users, Indigenous people, disabled people, and QTBIPOC. The increased policing of these areas and the combined efforts of police and social services to help other institutions in orchestrating a housing crisis, a loss of community, a threat to street jobs and gathering places is a very clear example of how that can play out (see Ramirez's chapter in the collection, for example).

Amar Wahab

National security is about the securitization of respectable heterosexuality and heteronormativity and now, even more so, respectable homonormativity—discursively and institutionally. With the previous Conservative (Harper) government and to some extent with the Liberal Trudeau government, we see a revamping of a family values agenda within different arms of the state, which promote certain privileged forms of respectable heterosexual, gay, or queer kinship. This helps to cover up Canada's homophobic past. Trudeau's apology pushes us to simultaneously remember and forget this past.

We also see the closing down of venues for sex and sexuality in public and shifts away from sex positivity to a respectable queerness. The bathhouses in Toronto are on the decline, and one has even been revamped for heterosexuals. This pushes us to rethink Gayle Rubin's understanding of the binary (in "Thinking Sex") of "The Charmed Circle" of heterosexuality as opposed to what she called the "The Outer Limits," which points to constructions of "bad" sexuality. The binary is now not just between heterosexual sexuality and non-heterosexual sexuality, but even within the domain of non-heterosexuality there is a distinction between good gays versus bad queers. Connected to the discourse of national security, we have to think about which queer Canadian body is secured or deemed worthy of securitization and which bodies, subjects, and populations are constructed as not deserving security because they are projected as not-really-queer.

As per the persistence of homophobia, there is the Toronto example of Project Marie (2016)—a police crackdown on public cruising at Marie Curtis Park. In 1981, there were the bathhouse raids by police ("Operation Soap"). In 2000, we had the Pussy Palace raids in Toronto. It is ironic, given the gains in legal rights for the LGBTQ+ community throughout the 1990s, that we still see police violence against the queer community. And we also need to understand that the gains during this period went predominately to white, gay, cis-male, middle-class, respectable members of the queer community. For example, why could the lesbian, non-binary, and non-normative women who went to the Pussy Palace in 2000 not depend on some of the protections of the state? Despite the rhetoric of Canada as a gay-tolerant nation, Project Marie represents a form of state-sanctioned violence against those who threaten the state's prescriptions for respectable sexual citizenship.

National Security Policies: Queer and Not Only Queer but Also Racialized

How do national security policies differentiate between those who are queer and those who are not only queer but also racialized?

Amar Wahab

National security in Canada is centrally pivoted on race, especially the defence of whiteness. Whiteness is the very root of Canada's settler colonial foundations, and as such we are expected never to question this whiteness. Whiteness is also the queer norm, as many queer of colour scholars have argued (e.g., Puar). The racialized queer other is seen as tentatively queer and never fully entitled to claim this category of selfhood, precisely because queerness is now a recognized category of selfhood and racialized others have historically been denied access to selfhood. They can only demonstrate a desire for it—a desire that is constantly denied by the homonational state. This is because a defence of queerness is simultaneously a defence of whiteness.

I also want to highlight the homonationalist focus on gay/lesbian liberation through a discourse of rights. This has occasioned the racialization of both homophobia and heterosexuality (as "culturally" saturated). For example, within Canada we see diasporic communities of colour and immigrant communities being marked under the banner of culture. So multiculturalism becomes very important to contextualizing this entire discussion. It is through the lens of "culture," which is an essentializing discourse, that immigrant others are constructed as naturally queerphobic. That is happening within Canada as a way of regulating internal others, but it is also happening outside of Canada in relation to countries in the Global South (especially where Canada has invested its peacekeeping and military missions). It is premised on projecting other places as culturally homophobic and ultra-heteropatriarchal. Most of these nation-states are racialized, so it becomes a vehicle for disconnecting homophobia and patriarchal oppression from whiteness. This is what I see as national security—i.e., a reinvention of whiteness through its disconnection from these forms of hatred, which are supposedly now attributes of nation-states in the Global South. It provides an occasion for policing racialized others as naturally capable of hate and incapable of tolerance. This helps to produce Canada as post-homophobic and post-race. Moreover, it suggests that anti-racism (under multiculturalism) is a finished project, spoiled by intolerant, hateful, and ungrateful racialized others and queers within the nation. These discursive moves have folded the discourse in a very different direction whereby whiteness is now the potential victim of racialized homophobia.

It is important to think intersectionally about racialized queer others who are rendered non-normative or not-quite-citizen but are seen to compete with dominant or white queers because this is precisely how liberalism sets up the treatment of difference. Again, there are questions here in terms of how liberalism—as a national doctrine that is important for national security—must be defended, whereas racialized queer others are seen as contesting white queerness. This is related to the conditions of citizenship, which prioritize single-issue politics over intersectional politics (and the common denominator across all single-issue politics in Canada is whiteness—which must be defended at all costs). One recent example is the failure of the Toronto police to prioritize an investigation into the disappearance and murder of several gay/queer men of colour, some of whom went missing almost a decade ago. It was only when a gay white man disappeared that the investigation of a serial murderer made progress. While we may hold the Toronto police

and arms of the state responsible (for not seriously and consistently pursuing an investigation), we also need to call mainstream queer communities to account for their lack of consistent pressure on state institutions to investigate the missing queer men.

Gary Kinsman

I'll talk first about the earlier years and then move into the more contemporary period. Indigenous people who organized and resisted were always considered a national security risk; that was the first national security threat; that was the first risk identified in the history of the Canadian national security regime. This included the bodies of Indigenous people who defied European gender and sexual practices. In the 1960s and early 1970s, Black activists, including in Montreal and in Halifax, were identified as being major national security risks. But at that point in time, there wasn't particularly a connection made between queer bodies and these racialized bodies, though that begins to change. So what we begin to see, especially in the military, is that with the racist practices that exist in the military, including in the Somalia operation in the 1990s, you see the bringing together in the right-wing white supremacist components of the military of incredible forms of racism, sexism, and opposition to queer people. And you also begin to see more forms of surveillance that uncover bodies that are Black *and* queer. You have combinations of forms of regulation of those bodies that are not simply about them being queer bodies but also about them being Black or racialized queer bodies. You begin to see those practices taking place, and you also see that intensified in the "war on terror" later on in terms of how some white middle-class queer people were being accepted into the fabric of the nation and into national security. We find that queer people who are also Arab and Muslim continue to be expelled from the fabric of the nation;

their bodies continue to be suspect. Racialization becomes a major way in which the national security regime differentiates between different bodies. The ones that have been allowed into the fabric of the nation after the 1992 military decisions have largely been white middle-class cis queer people, but only some of them. If they're considered unrespectable, if they engage in sexual practices that are seen as suspect, they can still be expelled from the fabric of the nation, but the effort is now much more focused on queer and trans people who are racialized and who are not seen as fitting into that white, middle-class stratum.

Ghaida Moussa

Those most affected by local and national "security" policies are the groups I have been talking about throughout this interview, and what is targeted—such as homelessness or drug use, for example—is most often the result of socioeconomic and political structures in the first place. Also, another point to make is that while, nationally, our lives are policed, managed, pathologized, and criminalized, our bodies are also used to justify wars and interventions abroad (see References and Suggestions for Further Reading).

Queerness and National Security Policies or Practices

How has queerness been used to justify biased national security policies for protection of the nation from the Other? How do those who identify as queer or LGBTQ+ play a role in this Othering? If you can talk not only about the Canadian context but also about any other context that you are familiar with, that would be great.

How do national security practices currently differentiate between white queers and those who are both queer and racialized?

Ghaida Moussa

First, let's acknowledge that this practice of using sexuality and gender to justify conquest, colonization, invasions, and imperialism has a long history. What we see now with the language of rights is a reversal of that history. Originally, people's sexualities that were deemed to be "deviant" were used as a reason for conquest. Now, touting gay rights is seen as a form of progress so that war is waged against "regressive" or "homophobic" countries (meanwhile, much of the homophobia seen in countries across the world today is a direct result of colonialism).

In the Palestinian context, queer and trans people are used to justify occupation and apartheid by the Israeli state through blackmailing, pinkwashing, and huge promotional campaigns meant to portray Israel as a progressive, gay-friendly state.

This is a concerted effort by Israel to reach the outside world through tourism ad campaigns that have been massive in terms of gay tourism. Gay-friendly becomes synonymous with progressive. This equation happens by also producing Palestinians and Arabs as regressive, and if they are regressive, if we follow this logic, then Palestinians need military intervention. It is in this way that it can be a tactic to justify occupation and apartheid. Many scholars and groups such as Aswat and Alqaws in Palestine have been calling out this tactic and resisting it in numerous ways. One of the tactics they've used, for example, is the creation of pinkwashing websites. They scout the Internet to find evidence of pinkwashing, and they've had very good success at propagating this information and reaching queers to get them to not be complicit in these Israeli tactics.

But this also happens locally. Refer back to my mention of Kusha Dadui's discussion of the use of Iranian refugees to confirm Canada's progressive benevolence. Also, during World Pride in Toronto a few years ago, Toronto was portrayed as a gay and diverse haven through the tokenization of QTBIPOC. On the Marvellous Grounds blog, you can read some accounts of that—by Unapologetic Burlesque, for instance. Nadijah Robinson's account of her Mourning Dress project in the Marvellous Grounds book collection (2018) is another excellent reflection on Black interventions into celebratory homonationalism.

Amar Wahab

This is a question about homonationalism and how it operates and the basic premise of integration of dominant queers, especially predominantly white, cis, gay men. It relies on a permutation of the blueprint of heterosexuality and heteronormativity, which also reinforces the fiction of identity as the basis of governance. Those who might not label themselves queer but label themselves as categories that are not recognized by the state are very difficult for the state to control, and as a result they are marked as disposable. Some aspects of the queer community are recognized by the state—for example, the category "gay." They become participants in the project; they become very complicit in that project of disposing of the racialized queer community that either does not choose to name themselves in ways that are recognized by the state or has complexities so incomprehensible that they're rendered, in some way, invisible according to those categories. This reminds me of Sara Ahmed's work about how *some others* other *other others.*

On another note, it is also interesting that we see the inaugural Pride March in Steinbach, Manitoba, in 2016 following the Pulse nightclub shooting in Orlando during which many queers of colour were the targets of shooter Omar Mateen. This points us to the intersection of race and sexuality, Islamophobia and homophobia. This is the moment in which, for example, within the Toronto queer community, we also see the emergence of a rampant Islamophobia within the community, especially against queer Muslim activists by members of the mainstream queer community.

Also, in Steinbach, Manitoba, this is the moment in which we see the rise of the first Pride parade in what was considered a bible-belt town. Again, this was an interesting movement taking place in a space that is not urban, that is imagined by the urban as not-gay-friendly. Curiously, we are witnessing an incipient rural homonationalism through which rural queers are being called into the state's Islamophobic relations of ruling.

Gary Kinsman

It's still possible for white queer people to experience discrimination—for instance, people can still be denied national security clearances, which are necessary to have higher levels of employment in the public service, if they were identified as having something to hide. Some white queer people continue to experience police repression. But what we see is that more white queer people, particularly more white cis middle-class gay men, have been accepted into the fabric of the nation and into national security but that other queer people haven't been. So queer people who are also Indigenous or Two-Spirit, people of colour, or racialized people can still be identified as being threats to national security. Not necessarily on the grounds that they're queer but that they live their lives in relationship with being Indigenous or being people of colour and racialized. It's also important to note that queer people involved in other than queer movements—and there's lots of us, for instance, in the global justice movement, in anti-poverty organizing, or among climate justice activists, especially those people that have been organizing against the tar sands and the pipelines—are still identified as being risks to national security. It's important to note that surveillance has shifted away from white middle-class people to focus on other queer people and also on other people who are Indigenous, who are people of colour, or who are political activists in a more contested fashion. That's where the major national security policing now takes place.

White Middle-Class Queers as Accomplices with Oppression?

How do some white middle-class queers play a part in otherization of Indigenous people and people of colour?

Gary Kinsman

This is crucial to examine, and we can look at a number of different sites where it takes place. First, the acceptance of the Charter of Rights by the mainstream movement as the framework through which LGBTQ+ people are to supposedly achieve our rights also aligned them with the existing social form of Canadian state relations in ways that are counter-posed to Indigenous struggles that support nation-to-nation relations and put in question Canadian state formation. This identification with Canadian state relations set the mainstream LGBTQ+ movement against Indigenous struggles and generated a widespread settler homonationalism.

Second, we can look at this in relation to Pride Toronto. A major controversy that occurred in Toronto Pride after its corporatization and after it changed its character was over the participation of Queers Against Israeli Apartheid (QuAIA). I was involved in the original organizing group for Toronto Pride in 1981 after the bath raids, and we saw it as a very political event as well as being a moment of celebration. But once Pride becomes a festival, a celebration just to party and loses its radical political roots, problems take place. You see people opposing the participation of QuAIA, which was a queer group that was formed explicitly to oppose the apartheid—the separation and the subordination policies—of the Israeli state. At that time, people were trying to kick QuAIA out of

Toronto Pride, both people within Toronto Pride and municipal and political authorities. Now QuAIA fought back and stayed in Pride but also expended an incredible amount of time just trying to defend itself, so it didn't have enough time to build up more support in the Toronto queer and trans communities for the Boycott, Divestment and Sanctions (BDS) campaign against Israeli state policies. So that's one instance where you see many white middle-class queers coming out to oppose the struggles of Palestinian people and people who want to build Palestinian solidarity.

You also see this in the response to the Black Lives Matter Toronto protest at Pride in 2016 when they had the wonderful sit-in that stopped Pride, which I was able to participate in as their ally. They raised significant community demands that had already been put forward previously by Indigenous and racialized people within Pride, as well as the demand for the police to no longer have any institutionalized presence in Pride as long as they were going to continue to be involved in racist practices toward Black people, other people of colour, and Indigenous people. That generated a major racist response from many white middle-class queers, mostly men—who denounced Black Lives Matter. The racism that was going down for a period of time was quite intense and horrific. They saw Back Lives Matter as a group that was outside their "community" even though it was a largely queer- and trans-led group. You certainly see in both those instances practices of otherization of people supporting Palestine but also of people supporting Black Lives Matter and fighting against anti-Black racism.

Queer Resistance to Security Measures

In what ways have some queer and transgender people resisted homophobic and racist national security measures?

Ghaida Moussa

Grassroots activism and activist scholarship have been key. Interesting alliances have also been formed across borders, which helps to recognize that these problems are happening globally and are part of a larger project. Issue-based alliances have had great success at bringing together people from various communities.

Some interesting resistance strategies also used a platform afforded to them by homonationalist endeavours to loudly reject it. A good example of this was Unapologetic Burlesque's intervention into the tokenization of QTBIPOC at World Pride Toronto (the script of their speech is available on the Marvellous Grounds blog—see box below). They took the stage at Toronto Pride, but they used that time to read an open letter criticizing the homonationalism, tokenization, and displacement that was orchestrated for the event.

Amar Wahab

Naming homonationalism is important to unsettling it. This is why Puar's and Duggan's works were so popular because it allowed us to name and therefore get a handle on something that was taking place that we were part of, that we were witnessing, but we could not fully make sense of. Not that the term "homonationalism" allows us to make full sense, but it is important to do that naming. Public protest is also important to queer resistance. Protests by Queers Against Israeli Apartheid and Black Lives Matter offer critiques of "the good" gays—i.e., the "respectable" LGBTQ+ movement—but they also critique the militant whiteness of the Canadian state. These kinds of public protests are not only about sexuality but a contest to define and struggle over what counts as queerness. These contestations also insist that a queer agenda must include a rebellion against all kinds of neoliberal normativity, which must include state-sanctioned and state-created normativity as well.

Gary Kinsman

It's important to point out that the mainstream movement hasn't particularly played any role in this aside from being a major obstacle or problem. So we're looking at groups like QuAIA or Black Lives Matter Toronto and other BLM groups, which had many queer and trans people involved, groups like No One Is Illegal, which include many queer and trans activists who've been challenging these heterosexist and racist national security practices, and also Idle No More. It's these groups, which are often queer- and trans-identified but also able to connect queer oppression with other forms of oppression in our society, that have been in a position to be able to challenge the current heterosexist and racist national security practices. Here it's important to talk about the moment of the state apology in 2017 to people who were purged from the public service and military. This apology was demanded from below through years of LGBTQ+ resistance, but the way it was delivered to people was as though it was a gift from above, infused with ideologies of Canadian "inclusion," "diversity" but also patriotism and loyalty to "Canada."

Emerging Forms of Art and Speech as Resistance

What can emerging forms of art and speech teach us about feminist and queer ways of resisting homonationalism and queer necropolitics?

Ghaida Moussa

Artistic resistance is a cornerstone and a huge part of both community-building and queer resistance, particularly in QTBIPOC communities. Disabled artists, too, like Mangos with Chili, are creating powerful responses to the privileging of certain bodies in our society. That is a big part of the struggle, questioning which bodies are automatically celebrated and which are dismissed as disposable, not valuable, to be managed, to be killed, etc. QTBIPOC are also resisting by turning toward their home communities, heritage, and ancestry to fortify connection, learn their histories, and find models of how to live, connect, and relate differently.

Amar Wahab

The language of "emerging" as a potential of unsettling art and speech is important because it suggests that there are still spaces in which certain forms of resistance remain "impossiblized"—i.e., constructed as always already futile. Even though homonationalism, as such, has only recently been named, it has been called out by activists and scholars prior to being coined by Puar (e.g., Cathy Cohen's work). I think that scholars have something to contribute to that naming and its legibility in the social sphere. So I see the scholar as activist in the sense that when we are putting heart, soul, energy, and hope into critical engagement, that is also a form of activism.

The other aspect of these forms of creative production and creative speech is that they're opportunities for making the personal political because these are some of the few spaces left in which to collectivize and come together in ways that could be disruptive. Artistic creation, therefore, can be a vehicle for re-politicizing what counts as public and for prying open counter-public spheres. One example is the work of Gein Wong—an Indigenous, queer activist, artist, performer in Toronto, who brings together queer Indigenous critiques of settler homonationalism in their work. Another is the Rhubarb Festival at Buddies in Bad Times (Toronto) where different queer artists and especially queer artists of colour come together to feature some of their work, much of which is disruptive of heteronormativity and homonormativity as well as critical of whiteness within the queer community. Another example is the publication *Queer and trans artists of color: Stories of some of our lives*, done by Nia King et al. on queer and trans artists of colour.

Questions to Reflect On

Next, I would like to ask you if there are any particular questions we didn't ask that you want to reflect on.

Amar Wahab

What is beyond this neoliberal moment of homonationalism, and how might a rethinking of intersectionality matter to such an intellectual project? This is key to understanding what social justice would look like and would perhaps entail critical analytical vigilance about the intersections of race, sexuality, and queerness.

Also, how are those in the (postcolonial) Global South responding to the critique of homonationalism? I haven't seen much research on this. I've been working on a chapter on LGBTQ+ voices in the small island state of St Lucia. One of the things that strike me is that we need to think about a new language to talk about the production of vulnerability in the Global South as expanding the political itinerary of queerness as a concept. One of the questions I ask is: how might we complicate the figure of "the homophobe" when this very projected figure has also been rendered vulnerable under (neo)colonialism? How might we create a different language for understanding the connections between different registers of vulnerability?

Gary Kinsman

You said you wanted to talk a little bit about teaching practices as well. Given I've been retired since 2014, that is more distant to me, but I did want to say two things. First, in terms of pedagogical

Marvellous Grounds, by Ghaida Moussa

Marvellous Grounds is a collective Toronto-based QTBIPOC mapping and counter-archiving project. It currently features an online blog with multiple issues (marvellousgrounds.com) and two book collections: *Marvellous grounds: Queer of colour histories of Toronto* (Haritaworn, Moussa, & Ware, 2018a) and *Queering urban justice: Queer of colour formations in Toronto* (Haritaworn, Moussa, & Ware, 2018b). Featured in these texts is the work, art, and words of QTBIPOC elders and younger activists, scholars, and artists, making them an intergenerational conversation on QTBIPOC histories and spaces that troubles the dominant story of white gay heroism in queer history and sheds light on processes of displacement and erasure at the heart of this dominant narrative. Thus, these collections offer important interventions on many of the themes of this chapter, including homonationalism, queer history, neoliberalism, and urban justice.

practices in the classroom, it's important for us to realize that classrooms are also sites of struggle and sites of contestation. It is important for us as radical professors, or instructors, to try to create safety for oppressed people but to simultaneously try to make these challenging places for people in positions where they might participate in oppression and exploitation. That means that you can't simply construct a classroom as being a safe place. I understand the notion of where a safe place comes from, but my pedagogy is also about confrontation, about transformation, and sometimes that requires challenging people who are in positions of relative social privilege in our classrooms. That's something I've tried to work on in my teaching, largely around sexuality and gender although sometimes around racialization as well. Students would tell me there was no racism in the community they grew up in, implying that if there were only white people, there is no racism. But I had remembered that they had told me that there was a First Nations reserve six miles away from where they grew up. So this is untenable; racism was everywhere in their lives. In the social construction of whiteness, there is racism. We need to realize that sometimes challenging confrontational forms of pedagogy can be

useful in classrooms. At the same time that we recognize that as professors, we are also imposing labour on students. Sometimes I was rewarding good labour for them, but also it was labour they were engaging in. It was unpaid labour that they had to pay to be able to do in terms of their fees, right? This entails understanding the class relationships that exists in the university context. The other thing was I always tried to get students engaged in social movement initiatives. That is, to get involved in some progressive social change movement, to help build it, to learn from it, and to then present on it or write about it in the classroom context to bring the social movements and social struggles into the classroom in more reflexive ways.

There is this interesting line from bell hooks for those of us who beat our heads because we don't like the way things are going in our classrooms, and the line is: "you can't have a revolutionary feminist classroom without revolutionary feminist students in it." That's also important for us to hold on to, that we can start this transformation, but unless there's students there to take it up and push it further, then it's always going to be limited just on the basis of what universities are.

Tying It Together: Message to the Undergraduate Students

What is the most important message that this chapter should give to the undergraduate students who are studying this text and this chapter?

Ghaida Moussa

Develop your critical mind, and always ask: who and what is benefitting from discourses of progress and homonationalism? Whose back was this "progress" built on? Trace those lineages, follow

---

Call to Action

Add your stories to the Marvellous Grounds blog, or create your own mapping project. Reflect on how the issues of homonationalism appear in your community and in your life, and share these stories with each other. We often feel more called to action when things feel connected to our lives.

Create timelines. Take one gentrified neighbourhood, and draw its changes across time. Who lives there now, who lived there then, and what processes contributed to those changes (e.g., colonialism, rent hikes, increased policing)?

Watch a YouTube video from Israel's ad campaign promoting gay friendliness, and have a discussion around what themes that you just read about come up. Apply what you learn to real life. For example, if you have queer friends going to Israel on vacation, you have a perfect opportunity to discuss these issues. Most people don't know about them; they only hear the mainstream message, and this doesn't just happen in Israel. You know these stories now, and the best way to honour them is to let them move you and influence how you live your life.

Write letters to elected representatives, whether you agree with the political system or not. That can have a huge effect that's often underestimated and possibly underused because it's not seen as radical. But especially in local contexts (e.g., increased policing in your neighbourhood), it can have a very big impact.

Write to prisoners. Most people end up in prison because of the way that the legal system is set up, and initiating that kind of contact and providing someone with comfort and interest in their life can be very impactful for them. There are also some initiatives for trans and queer people in prisons in particular.

Develop Pink Watching kits on campus by identifying the different forms of violence on campus but especially in relation to the policing of queers of colour. You might work with organizations on campus to develop a Pink Watching kit. Alternately, link students in classrooms with artists and queers of colour artists to generate art-based manifestos and foster mentorships with some of these artists.

Do not be limited by the traditional forms of activism. Those often celebrated are often ableist. How can we develop ways of doing activism that are not limited to traditional forms of activism? Think about what skills you have and how they can contribute. Some people are great at creating websites, some people are great at art, and some are lawyers or have special knowledge. Some people can offer listening support; we need everyone!

the story, and ask: who is missing from this story and why? Trace to wherever it leads you, and then work your way forward: what were the impacts? What impacts are still playing out today? When wealth and progress and abundance happen, where does poverty move and grow? How are you (we) benefitting from these systems and discourses? And, most important, how can you (we) leverage our positions and access to stay accountable to and responsible for our communities?

Amar Wahab

I see homonationalism as a discourse of national security; it is about re-bordering whiteness through the domain of "the sexual." While its main target is the domain of "sexuality," (e.g., demarcating "the good gays" from "the bad queers"), the different facets of this domain are deeply enmeshed in a larger apparatus dedicated to the reproduction of whiteness. I say that because I want students to read homonationalism and whiteness as inseparable.

Gary Kinsman

If we can give people some critical perspectives on the emergence of gay normality, the neoliberal queer, racialized class politics within queer communities, if we can get people grappling with that and understanding it and perhaps offering some suggestions about how to move into action, that would be great.

DISCUSSION QUESTIONS

1. What are some examples of queer necropolitics or homonationalism in your community?
2. How does the nation-state view queerness?
3. How does the Canadian state use the language of rights in controlling queer bodies and to further justify its expansion of power and control?
4. How does the policing of queer bodies intersect with national security discourses? How does the state use the queer body to justify racialization and xenophobia?
5. What are some examples of the ways in which queer activists mediate and resist nationhood projects of promoting national defence through increased racialization and oppression?

SUGGESTIONS FOR FURTHER READING

Gentile, P., Kinsman, G., & Rankin, P. (Eds). (2017). *We still demand! Redefining resistance in sex and gender struggles.* Vancouver, BC: University of British Columbia Press. This book explores the history of sex and gender activism in Canada from the 1970s to the present day, highlighting queer, trans, sex-worker, and feminist struggles.

Haritaworn, J. (2015). *Queer lovers and hateful others: Regenerating violent times and places.* London, UK: Pluto Press. This book posits the idea that queer people have become subjects of societal approval and acceptance only by being cast in the shadow of the "homophobic migrant," who in turn is disapproved of by society.

Haritaworn, J., Kuntsman, A., & Posocco, S. (Eds). (2014). *Queer necropolitics.* New York, NY: Routledge. In this book, queerness in the face of death is explored across various geopolitical contexts.

Haritaworn, J., Moussa, G., & Ware, S. (Eds). (2018). *Queering urban justice: Queer of colour formations in Toronto.* Toronto, ON: University of Toronto Press. This contributed volume explores the intersections of social, racial, urban, and disability justice in regards to queer, trans, Black, Indigenous, and people of colour (QTBIPOC).

Haritaworn, Jin, Moussa, Ghaida, & Ware, Syrus Marcus. (Eds). (2018). *Marvellous grounds: Queer of colour histories of Toronto*. Toronto, ON: Between the Lines. This collection begins to document the history of queers of colour in Toronto through its collection of art and writing by people in the queer, trans, Black, Indigenous, and people of colour (QTBIPOC) communities.

King, Nia, et al. (2014). *Queer and trans artists of color: Stories of some of our lives*. This book is a collection of conversations by queer and trans artists of colour about their personal and professional lives.

Murray, David A.B. (2015). *Real queer? Sexual orientation and gender identity refugees in the Canadian refugee apparatus*. London, UK: Rowman & Littlefield International. This book is an ethnographic study of the LGBTQ+ asylum process in Canada.

Schotten, C. (2016). Homonationalism: From critique to diagnosis, or, we are all homonational now. *International Feminist Journal of Politics, 18*(3), 351–70. doi: 10.1080/14616742.2015.1103061. This article analyzes what has happened to the concept of homonationalism over time in terms of how the concept has lost its radical disruptive potential and instead has become both more descriptive and less analytical.

Upadhyay, Nishant. Pinkwatching Israel, whitewashing Canada: Queer (settler) politics and Indigenous colonization in Canada. https://www.academia.edu/12132163/Pinkwatching_Israel_Whitewashing_Canada_Queer_Settler_Politics_and_Indigenous_Colonization_in_Canada. This paper discusses Israel's use of gay rights discourses as a distraction from the occupation of Palestine ("pinkwashing") and how settler colonialism in Canada is normalized by Canada's reputation as a progressive, queer-friendly state.

MULTIMEDIA SUGGESTIONS

alQaws
http://www.alqaws.org
This is the website for alQaws for Sexual and Gender Diversity in Palestinian Society, a civil organization promoting the building of LGBTQ communities and new ideas about the role of gender and sexual diversity in Palestinian society.

Art by Syrus Marcus Ware
https://syrusmarcusware.com
This website showcases the art of Syrus Marcus Ware, a queer artist and activist.

Aswat
twitter.com/aswatgroup
This is the Twitter account of a group of Palestinian gay women who regularly make posts supporting lesbian, intersex, queer, transsexual, transgender, questioning, and bisexual women.

Black Lives Matter Toronto
https://blacklivesmatter.ca
This is the main webpage for the Black Lives Matter Toronto movement. Black Lives Matter is an international movement against violence and systematic racism toward Black people.

feral feminisms, special issue
https://feralfeminisms.com/complicities-connections-struggles
This is a discussion about the connection between settler colonialism and feminism for people of colour.

Julien Salgado—"I am undocuqueer."
https://juliosalgadoart.com/post/15803758188/i-am-undocuqueer-is-an-art-project-in
This art project in conjunction with the Undocumented Queer Youth Collective and the Queer Undocumented Immigrant Project by Julio Salgado aims to give undocumented queers a greater presence in the discussion of migrant rights.

Marvellous Grounds
http://marvellousgrounds.com
Interactive mapping to generate stories about Toronto and processes of displacement; click and read stories that have been generated from a lot of people in Toronto about specific locations where things have happened, where things have shifted in Toronto.

Mangos with Chili

https://mangoswithchili.wordpress.com

This is the website of Mangos with Chili, a California-based arts group that promotes queer and trans artists of colour.

Queer (Self) Portraits: Syrus Marcus Ware

https://www.youtube.com/watch?v=MMsr6ukWKBA

This short interview with visual artist and community activist Syrus Marcus Ware describes how his activism is linked to his artistic practice.

REFERENCES

Bannerji, H. (1995). *Thinking through: Essays on feminism, Marxism and anti-racism.* Toronto, ON: Women's Press.

Dadui, K. (2018). Queer and trans migration and canadian border imperialism. In J. Haritaworn, G. Moussa, & S. Ware (Eds), *Marvellous grounds: Queer of colour histories of Toronto* (pp. 107–17). Toronto, ON: Between the Lines.

Hardt, M., & Negri, A. (2000). *Empire.* Cambridge, MA: Harvard University Press.

Haritaworn, J. (2014). Introduction. In A. Kuntsman & S. Posocco (Eds), *Queer necropolitics* (pp. 1–27). Abingdon, UK: Routledge, Taylor & Francis Group (a GlassHouse Book).

Haritaworn, J. (2015). Queer lovers and hateful others: Regenerating violent times and places. *Decolonial Studies, Postcolonial Horizons.* London, UK: Pluto Press.

Haritaworn, J., Kuntsman, A., & Posocco, S. (Eds.) (2014). *Queer necropolitics.* New York, NY: Routledge.

Haritaworn, J., Moussa, G., & Ware, S. (Eds). (2018a). *Marvellous grounds: Queer of colour histories of Toronto.* Toronto, ON: Between the Lines.

Haritaworn, J., Moussa, G., & Ware, S. (Eds). (2018b). *Queering urban justice: Queer of colour formations in Toronto.* Toronto, ON: University of Toronto Press.

Holloway, J. (2005). *How to change the world without taking power.* London, UK: Pluto Press.

King, N., et al. (2014). *Queer and trans artists of color: Stories of some of our lives.* CreateSpace Independent Publishing Platform.

Kinsman, G. (1996). *The regulation of desire: Homo and hetero sexualities.* Montreal, QC: Black Rose.

Kinsman, G. (2018). Policing borders and sexual/gender identities: Queer refugees in the years of Canadian neoliberalism and homonationalism. In Nancy Nicol, Adrian Jjuuko, Richard Lusimbo, Nick J. Mulé, Susan Ursel, Amar Wahab, & Phyllis Waugh (Eds.), *Envisioning global LGBTQ+ human rights: (Neo)colonialism, neoliberalism, resistance and hope* (pp. 97–129). London, UK: Human Rights Consortium, School of Advanced Studies, University of London.

Kinsman, G. (2019). Forgetting national security in "Canada": Towards pedagogies of resistance. In Aziz Choudry (Ed.), *Activists and the surveillance state: Learning from repression* (pp. 129–52). Toronto, ON: Pluto Press, Between the Lines.

Kinsman, G., & Gentile, P. (2010). *The Canadian war on queers: National security as sexual regulation.* Sexuality Studies Series. Vancouver, BC: University of British Columbia Press.

Moussa, G. (2011). *Narrative (sub)versions: How queer Palestinian womyn "queer" Palestinian Identity.* Master's thesis, University of Ottawa.

Moussa, G. (2013a). Breathing borders. In Ghadeer Malek & Ghaida Moussa (Eds), *Min fami: Arab feminist reflections on identity, space & resistance.* Toronto, ON: Inanna Publications and Education.

Moussa, G. (2013b). My colonized tongue. In Ghadeer Malek & Ghaida Moussa (Eds), *Min fami: Arab feminist reflections on identity, space & resistance.* Toronto, ON: Inanna Publications and Education.

Puar, J.K. (2007). Terrorist assemblages: Homonationalism in queer times. Durham, NC: Duke University Press.

Ramirez, A. (2018). In J. Haritaworn, G. Moussa, & S. Ware (Eds), *Marvellous grounds: Queer of colour histories of Toronto.* Toronto, ON: Between the Lines.

Robinson, N. (2018). In J. Haritaworn, G. Moussa, & S. Ware (Eds), *Marvellous grounds: Queer of colour histories of Toronto.* Toronto, ON: Between the Lines.

Wahab, A. (2015). Unveiling fetishnationalism: Bidding for citizenship in queer times. In Suzanne Lenon & OmiSoore Dryden (Eds), *Disturbing queer inclusion: Canadian homonationalisms and the politics of belonging* (pp. 35–48). Vancouver, BC: University of British Columbia Press.

NOTE

1. The interviewers were Çalışkan and Preston, with interviewees Kinsman, Moussa, and Wahab (names in alphabetical order). This chapter is a product of equal collaboration of the authors. Çalışkan and Preston conducted the interviews separately with each scholar and then merged their responses under relevant questions. Each contributor revised their parts once the transcripts (or interviews) were collated within the chapter and prepared the pedagogy.

CHAPTER 4

◇

White Lies: Race, Power, and the Future

Rinaldo Walcott[1,2]

Learning Objectives

In this chapter, you will:

- consider how whiteness has been embedded into the very intuitions of settler societies such as Canada;
- define whiteness and how whiteness has been used to marginalize Black and Indigenous people and people of colour;
- consider the different lies perpetuated in Canada that have kept white superiority intact;
- learn how unconscious bias has directed blame away from individuals while also not acknowledging the structures that have created white superiority;
- understand how language has been used to keep racism alive and to keep whiteness seen as raceless;
- consider white rage and how it is constructed in the white body;
- examine what a "pure decolonial project" would look like.

Introduction

We're living at the juncture of a significant historical moment. From the white supremacists in the US White House; to the assertion that colonialism was good for the colonized, to neo-Nazis marching in the streets of Europe, the US, and Canada, to legislative wins of extreme right parties across Europe, whiteness as a structure of authority, power, and violence has reasserted itself in our present time. The measure of this moment depends on where we will turn. Will we turn toward truth and ethics, or will we turn toward a retrenchment of our horrible past? Should we turn toward truth and ethics, it would mean that we are seriously ready to tackle the conditions and the terms under which we might come to live differently together, in the present and the future. However, to achieve such a desire and to make it an actuality, we will have to come to terms with the lies that at present structure our current social relations and sociology.

The lies I refer to are a set of ideas that are propagated concerning the "evolved" nature of our society in which contemporary individual and personal life is cut off from the dreadful collective past that produced it in the first instance. We must, therefore, not reference that past as still animating our collective present. Some scholars have called this "white innocence," but I prefer to call it lies. Lies for me mean that the force of these ideas is such that one cannot escape them. One must go through them to potentially arrive at a different place. But I also call them lies because even our more important ideas for producing a different kind of world become compromised in the context of the routinized and enforced idea that the terrible past is "behind us" now. In essence, we must lie to our collective selves to even get the conversation going. But more specifically, white people must collectively lie to themselves that the current organization of human life is arranged to give us all access to what I will short-handedly call the "good life."

The **whiteness** that I refer to here is multiple. First, it is the people that we have come to call "white people," and it clearly relies on phenotype, but more important, whiteness is also a structure. And by this I mean: a set of logics, ideas, and practices that work to reproduce white people as superior to others and, therefore, as benefitting from a society built to confer and confirm that superiority. Second, by whiteness I mean to signal "*a structure of feeling*" in which those marked as white share in and benefit from the conditions that produce advantages for white people. Additionally, those not marked as white are positioned as aspirants to it. These aspirants I call, following Frank B. Wilderson (2003), "junior partners" in white supremacy and white superiority. The important thing to note is that whiteness as a structure keeps in place a post-Columbus global **compact** in which "not-white" people are generally and ideologically positioned as "less than" in a crude and right order of beings.

The Crisis and Its Manifestation

The institutional organization and arrangements of contemporary human life are currently in crisis everywhere. And here in Canada, the crisis manifests itself in a number of different ways. Chief among those ways is who belongs, who counts as Canadian, and how might the network of institutions (both public and private) that organize our collective lives and govern and administer our social relations come to represent our collective interest in ways that all of our lives might be fulfilled.

Canada: The Multicultural Lie

Since Canada is a settler colonial state and outcome of the post-Columbus world, Canada fundamentally understands itself as a white nation-state derived of the Europeanness that is also understood to be white. The ideas that hold such a claim together are replicated, reinforced, and perpetually propagated by the governing, administering, and ruling institutions of the state. These institutions enforce a monocultural political and cultural order that is Eurocentric in both nature and practice. In the execution and maintenance of this **Eurocentrism**, we are asked to accept the lie that European Enlightenment and post-Enlightenment understandings, interpretations, and impositions of a particular way of experiencing the world (and living in it) is the only way to do so.

Canada as a nation-state is foundationally built on that logic. However, that logic has continually come under duress. It has been consistently contested. Resistance by Indigenous people, Black people, other "not-white" people, and some white ethnic minorities has often forced Canada to revise its Eurocentrism. But the nation-state has never fully abandoned it. It is the revisions, often felt to be progressive as ushering in change, that become the platform for other kinds of lies that keep the Eurocentric white supremacy firmly in place in Canada.

So the first lie is the multicultural lie. The most significant post–World War II lie is the multicultural compact. This is a significant lie because it asks us to collectively confirm a set of ideas that refuse to be translated into everyday life for many, even though we repeatedly insist that these ideas represent what Canada is and how we actually live. From the inception of multiculturalism as policy, not-white Canadians have criticized its inadequacies and its performance as policy that might stem racism and other forms of discriminatory practices. Indeed, in the now more than 40 years of official multicultural policy, not-white Canadians, and Black Canadians specifically, have lived under conditions of racism that have been relatively unchanged since post–World War II—and might be said to have intensified from the 1990s to the present. Nonetheless, Canada is understood as having produced a multicultural society, one that is settled around living with racial and cultural difference that is supposed to be enviable around the world.

However, the lives of Black and Indigenous peoples are the counter to the national lie that multiculturalism is a successful policy for organizing Canadian life. One might argue that multiculturalism works to confirm the white founding mythology of Canada but does not undo that founding's execution of its white supremacist logics. Nonetheless, multiculturalism as both a policy and an idea remains standard to Canada as a way to think about the scene of the nation-state. While I call multiculturalism a lie because it continually keeps in place the idea that Canada is a white nation, with all the other "not-white" others constituting its coloured adjunct citizenry, to accept that multiculturalism is a policy of citizenry organization and administration is to accept the lie that whiteness in Canada has de-centred itself. We know collectively that the latter is not the case. The lie of multiculturalism, then, functions to produce a compact whereby certain kinds of diversity can be celebrated as standing in for collective representation. To accede to those kinds of representational practices is to agree or at least become complicit with the lie.

"Ashamed to Be a Canadian": Strategies of Whiteness

Just recently when an article about the 2018 White Privilege Conference appeared in the *Toronto Star*, I received a number of emails. The one I'm about to quote from reinforces the idea about the vaulted Canadian diversity as animating our Canadian lives. The person writes:

> I am appalled with the WHITE PRIVILEGE CONFERENCE you are promoting. Our Prime Minister tells us "diversity is our strength" and you want to cause diversity [*sic*], in Canada [but I think they meant to say "division"]. . . .
>
> The conference advertisement made me ashamed to be a Canadian, and it made me ashamed to have served my country in the Army for 39 years.
>
> You still have time to determine if Canada is inclusive, or if you believe Prime Minister Trudeau lied to you, too.

I quote this email because it embodies so much of the rhetoric and mythology not just of Canada but of the strategies of whiteness. The invoking of time in the army, the "destroying of our diversity," the accusation of "division," and, most of all, the writer's insistence on asking if PM Trudeau lied to me, to us, about diversity as a strength.

The word "lie" in the email jumped out at me for a number of reasons—in part because a letter like this one is asking that I, or we, conform to the national lie that Canada is a place where racial difference and inequality is a settled question, thus suggesting that white advantage is not an issue. The letter is a perfect expression of the mythology of "raceless" and "racism-free" Canada.

It is, in short, a lie and the lie that we are required to accept as a part of a compact in which race and, therefore, racism, disappear from our conversations even if it's still animating our lives.

"Because It's 2015": Obscuring Language to Do the Work of Whiteness

So on 4 November 2015, Justin Trudeau announced what was quickly hailed as the most diverse Canadian cabinet ever. As quickly as the claim of "most diverse" was uttered, it was also criticized. When asked about his diverse cabinet, in particular his gender parity, PM Trudeau quipped: "because it's 2015." On both social media and in the mainstream media, a debate about what constitutes diversity, and furthermore representation, emerged, pointing to the limits of gender parity as diversity when race and ethnicity enter the frame. The debate delimited the phenotypic features of PM Trudeau's cabinet, pointing to Indigenous, South Asian, and Middle Eastern MPs as a way to get beyond the limit of gender parity as diversity. Glaringly absent from the phenotypic cohort was Black MPs. It is at this point that we might find it important to note that the language of people of colour (POC) and "diversity" is what I would call an **obscuring language**. By this I mean that the logics of POC and diversity lack specificity and, therefore, can continue to do the work of whiteness. The invocation of "diversity" is meant to suggest that the work of race equity is being done and that representation is being worked for. But such assumptions can obscure exactly who's been included and represented as was so clear with Trudeau's cabinet composition at that moment. In this instance, the structure of whiteness fashioned its subordinates in hierarchical order.

Racism without Racists

At present, we have been making more robust calls for diversity and representation. The very people who have benefitted from the long and terrible history of racial advantage are now telling us that they will usher in this new remedy. But instead, the long discredited language of "unconscious bias" and its claims have been returned to us as the way forward in a range of governing institutions. In particular, at my university unconscious bias is the rage.

What the language of unconscious bias does is that it refuses to acknowledge how the structure of institutions reproduces particular practices and ways of being. And furthermore, it seeks to not place any one particular person as responsible for the perpetuation of those practices of advantage-making.

The French philosopher Étienne Balibar (2011) wrote of racism without race. Unconscious bias does not make a dissimilar move. It attempts the practices and behaviours without attending to institutional arrangements. In this instance, it is more like racism without *racists*. This slip is crucial for maintaining the white supremacist arrangement of our institutions without having to account for how they enforce, their reproduction, and how those inside of them are responsible for and benefit from that reproduction. Indeed, in an effort to not offend white people, we have gone as far as intalking about racism as structural to the extent that people are missing from how the structures actually work. So to be clear: white people are the face of white supremacy, and they benefit from it. We cannot avoid making that claim simply clear.

The Lies of Structural Self-Reform: Decolonizing and Indigenizing

One of the ways in which we are now told that the structures—which appear to be magically operating on their own—can reform themselves is if we indigenize them and if we decolonize them. These two ideas, appropriated from more radical calls for total transformations of how humans live today, are now being deployed to interrupt the radical political movements of Indigenous resurgence and the movement for Black lives. Why, or how, is it possible that the very people who have systematically benefitted from the advantages of those institutions will indigenize and decolonize them now?

If multicultural policies saved the nation-state as the potentially liberating movements of the 1960s and 1970s erupted, then we are in a similar moment now. "Indigenizing" and "decolonizing" are being harnessed and redeployed to preserve the structure of whiteness with a few adjustments and revisions. Indeed, if radical thinkers found "multiculturalism" in its logic of diversity wanting, "diversity," too, has returned as the most robust term now used to winnow out the radical politics and potentialities of indigenizing and decolonizing. Calls for "diversity" dressed up in indigenizing and decolonizing rhetoric fail to adequately account for whiteness as a structuring device of our institutional and everyday lives.

Diversity Rhetoric Obscures the Function of Whiteness

Diversity rhetoric obscures the function of whiteness that accrues to itself the terrain of change. That is: what must change, how it must change, at what speed it must change, and so on. It is the "common sense of diversity"—that is, the simple evidence of difference—that makes diversity so appealing. But such simplicity in this instance does not do justice to what radical calls for indigenizing and decolonizing actually ask of us.

The hard truth of the matter is that the governing administrative apparatus of whiteness is prepared to appropriate any discourse, any politics, any ideas, and any ideals that retain the post-Columbus compact, a compact whereby Europe and its derivative nations and their peoples, now marked as white, continue to be given privileged status across the globe.

To maintain such status, nation-states like Canada produce themselves and their appropriative ideas like indigenizing and decolonizing while keeping in place all the institutions that flow from the initial and ongoing colonial context. The claim that we can indigenize or decolonize without taking on the social, cultural, political, and economic arrangements of whiteness is to enter the terrain of lies. Such claims of indigenizing and decolonizing in that fashion are called "terminus," with the logic of putting history behind us. Such claims leave intact institutions not built for us, and never meaning to receive us, in the ongoing regiment of our society. In essence, then, such appropriations work to keep white supremacy intact even if unstated.

The Language of Race Obscures Whiteness

The language of race has often worked to make whiteness invisible. The idea of race and its biological determinism has been central to the apparatus that took shape to produce whiteness as an advantage. The advantage of whiteness, then, cannot be divorced from the logics of white supremacy and white superiority. The idea of white privilege is but one component of white superiority and white supremacist logics and their institutionalization of whiteness as the standard to be attained.

Once the biology of race has been discounted, another network of logics comes in to place the continued advantages of whiteness without race, which is Balibar's idea: Culture becomes it, crime becomes it, immigration becomes it, poverty becomes it, and so on. Though now well understood that race is a social construction, this does not mean that racism no longer exists. In fact, it is the idea that race no longer exists that often fuels the logics of white supremacy today. In this way, many used the nonexistence of that biological race to insist that those who are disadvantaged by lacking access to whiteness are creatures of their own making. This logic underpins the structure of whiteness and its resultant practices as the status quo and, thus, privileges whiteness's ongoing authority to shape our collective world by a singular benefit in favour of those who can't access the structure.

The Regime of Race Relations Management

To hold whiteness at bay to a certain degree, we have developed a network of sub-institutions like human rights offices and tribunals, diversity offices and officers, equity offices and officers, and so on. These offices and officers are accompanied by language like "colour-blindness," "equity," "diversity," "social justice," "post-racial," and so on. I see in all of this an apparatus invented to do important work and keep whiteness satisfied that its legitimacy is not under attack. The paradox that we find ourselves in is one in which to descend to whiteness and produce a different kind of world, we find ourselves working to pacify whiteness so that other potentialities might emerge. It is the totality of white hegemony that the transformative logics of decolonization are made to disrupt and break, producing something new.

The regime of race relations management, as Adolph Reed, Jr, once called it, sets in place a process of articulating a set of changes that seem to never occur (Reed, 2000). To respond to this "changing same," to use Amiri Baraka (1998) in another context, is to open up the lie at the heart of the race relations apparatus and regime that works to keep the structure of whiteness intact and in authority. Indeed, in today's culture we are told that telling the truth about the historical constitution of whiteness, and the ways it has ordered the world, is responsible for the re-emergence of white fascists, nationalists, and white liberal resentment, all at the same time. We are told that to seek social justice is to demonize white people. We are told that we must embrace our individualism and take responsibility for our own exclusion—if it can even be called exclusion. We are told that the very identities that white supremacist logics have given us should now be put behind us. In short, we are asked to perpetuate more lies in the service of sparing whiteness a serious and sustained look at itself.

The inability to fully engage whiteness and the structural violence that sustains it and that functions to maintain its existence is the central problem of our moment. So while race is a nonstarter, racism remains a central organizing feature of human life; and its principal function is to place whiteness in the position of authority and power continuously. To refuse the current arrangements of human life is to situate oneself in a position of calling for a different value to be accorded human life. If at present human life is valued in relation and proximity to whiteness, then to expose the violent structure of whiteness as a regime of value advantage is to enter into a confrontation with the deepest logics of our society. Whiteness as a structure, then, even shapes how in our attempts to overthrow it, we continue to coddle it and its creations with the kinds of languages and the offices I have already mentioned.

Radical Politics and Radical Political Imaginaries

What is worth noting here is that radical politics and radical political imaginaries are generously concerned with the preservation of collective personhood. And so in some ways the generosity of a radical politics has often created more than enough space for whiteness to come into itself as a betrayal of itself, and yet it never does. That's a really interesting paradox for radical politics.

To draw heavily on the work of Adolph Reed, Jr, Lyndon Barrett, and C.L.R. James, we can make sense of how the potential liberatory moments of the 1960s have been interrupted by a retrenchment of whiteness. Using their work, I marked the mid-1960s as a time when the potential overthrow of whiteness seemed possible. The social movements of the 1960s, in their short-sightedness, I think, failed to rethink value as foundational to post-Columbus orders of life. And so those social movements were easily incorporated into the existing logics and structures of "white supremacist, patriarchal, capitalism," to use the language of bell hooks (2004, p. 1). Significantly, when we look at such benefits, the benefits that derive out of those movements of the mid-1960s, what we see most clearly is that what the extension of those benefits did—and this is following Adolph Reed, Jr's argument—was to demobilize more radical calls for transformation. So what Adolph Reed, Jr, argues is that the interruption of a more radical politics to descend to whiteness got turned into a logic of "inclusion" and "diversity" and, therefore was demobilized (Reed, 2009).

Linking Value to Human Worth

So such gestures of inclusion, rather than structural destruction, are currently the means whereby late modern capitalism "devours its most cogent critics without an apparent lack of indigestion," as William Haver (1999, p. 26) once put it. It is precisely for this reason that the value of inclusion in the many senses and the way that value may be invoked, especially in monetary and racial logics, requires a rigorous re-engagement and not one dependent on white pacification to achieve its goals. Indeed, my argument is premised on the idea that value is always already linked to capital and its racial economy rather than ideas about human worth. That is, rather, that value is often *not* linked to ideas about human worth, which I believe has come to be the foundations of anti-racism, social justice, equity discourse, and so on. So you hear a lot of talk about diversity as an economic good rather than diversity as human worth. And so this

leaves the structure of whiteness still in place to endow what counts as value. One might suggest that where those mid-1960s movements stalled was in their inability to think and put into place in their own movements a politics of value that could matter and that could extend beyond their own incorporation into capitalist patriarchy. They could not reach an understanding of value that could reside outside of modern capitalist logics that was immune to the seductive pull of inclusion and the performative rectory of representation of bodies, identities, and communities.

The late Lyndon Barrett, writing with the contested theorizations of value, asserted: "to interpose no alternative value in the theoretically neutral moment of calling value into question remains equivalent to strengthening and reincarnating reified, dominant value" (1999, pp. 52–3). Barrett was getting at the ways in which our failure to think critically and rethink value helped to reproduce the very largess of white supremacy that we often imagined that we were working against. The social movements of the mid-1960s, in the broadest sense, did not rethink value. This means that the promise of a different order of planetary life was immediately compromised, and the conditions for incorporation made possible and therefore manageable in the already existent order of structural white authority, and the administrative apparatus was able to proceed. The existing conditions, therefore, become adaptable to inclusion without substantive change.

Who Will Self-Sacrifice?

As a pessimistic aside, let me declare that the benefits won by those movements are not meaningless, but rather we must now come to see those benefits for what they are—one of the expenses of deepening an already deadly culture. The problem of reorienting value is an important one for any future that seeks to produce a world in which value exists beyond the orbit of the current financialization of life in the service of white authority. C.L.R. James, in 1939, anticipating such a moment, articulated what he called a "Negro movement" that would participate in the larger possible anti-capitalist revolution but with its own and probably very different outcomes (James & McLemee, 1996). James made his comments in relation to the Communist Party's failure to both recruit and to adequately address Negro-American problems. James was in part offering a critique of whiteness and its structural logics. His analysis pointed to the ways in which various Black movements had embedded in them the ability to sacrifice for what he called "the promise of a new society," which the Communist Party failed to recognize (James & McLemee, 1996). Indeed, what James articulated is a different notion of justice that the Communist Party could neither hear nor tolerate in that moment. His utterances act like a cautionary tale for us today but in a reverse way. What are the ways in which our current apparatus for transformation might work to produce white self-sacrifice for the promise of a new society? At the moment, the answer to this question remains unclear. Thus enters "anti-white racism" as a response to an already compromised set of articulations that have yet to produce sustained and deeply meaningful change.

White Rage and "Anti-white Racism"

Here I present you with another email:

> I'm completely disgusted by your racism against Caucasians. . . . European descendent Canadian Caucasians were key players in the Underground Railroad that SAVED blacks from slavery. . . . Your conference is direct and unprovoked attack on Caucasian Canadians who are known for multicultural tolerance. . . . SHAME ON YOU.

White rage is not just words: it is also bodily constituted. Ideas live and emanate from the body, and articulation of white rage resides in white bodies too. The idea that race is biology might be behind us, but the language of race remains firmly with us. European Caucasians, Canadian Caucasians, and the resultant logics of "save Blacks from slavery" and "multicultural tolerance" have enfolded in them race as a *lingua franca* (or common language) of white consciousness. It is a consciousness used to stake authority, to render correction and approbation, and to dictate the terms under which conversations about the potential justice and readjustments of human life might proceed. Such utterances are not merely outbursts of fringe elements, but such utterances reveal the grammar of race thinking, raciology, and the structure of rightness as an authority and an authorizing force of human life. It's the banality of such utterances for white people and whiteness that such claims can be made. If race as biology is behind us, what is most definitely not behind us is the way in which whiteness and power structures are social relations and sociology.

The Work of Power

The two emails that I cited in this talk are examples of the work of power. Both of those emails were directed to a list of recipients or authorities with an appeal to action: in this case, that sanctions be enacted. The emails were sent—they just list everybody—to the prime minister, the president of Ryerson University, Dr Denise Green (vice-president of equity and community inclusion at Ryerson), the local MP, and on and on. The emails are an appeal to power, but emails also are an exercise in power, one in which whiteness seeks to draw to itself the power to punish and discipline those who refuse to inhabit the lie. Central to the structure of whiteness that I have been detailing here is a sense of power: the power to decide and to authorize that which it terms to be legitimate. Indeed, when whiteness's legitimacy is questioned, its most violent forms emerge. The claim of "anti-white racism" is just one moment in which the questioning of whiteness seeks to respond to the challenge of its hegemony by usurping the language of legitimate response to racism in order to shift the critique. We must refuse the idea of anti-white racism because it seeks to severely deform our conversations in a fashion as to produce a stalemate in which actual potential change becomes impossible.

The truth is that white people clinging to whiteness and its ideological apparatus is as bad for them as it is for the rest of us. Their inability to betray hegemonic whiteness—including whiteness as a structure of knowing, as a regimen of encountering the world, as a measure of what it means to be human, and as an arrangement for the terms in and on which we govern our collective selves—remains a danger for all of us.

New Ideas and New Ideals

If post-Columbus Enlightenment and post-Enlightenment ideas and ideals got us here, we are now in need of new ideas and new ideals. First, I want to stress that I, too, believe that modernity, as it has been idealized, remains an unfinished project. And by this I mean that many of us who are not white remain excess baggage of a modernist project that simply cannot contend with our humanity and repeatedly understands it as "less than" or not existent at all. But I don't think the modernist ideals are enough. So many of those ideals have been imagined, in particular, against Black life, that they need something more robust than a revision. Indeed, I'm interested in witnessing in my lifetime white people and whiteness abdicating their lofty place atop the human scale—that is, the disappearance of the scale altogether. We ignore the scale's

existence to our own collective peril. The current articulation of "anti-white racism" is a blunt refusal of the potential to transform. And yet the politics of transformation has consistently built on both the possibility and the desired reality that white people and whiteness can transform. In fact, many of our political compromises for a different world have been premised on such assumptions.

White People Will Have to Take Risks

White people will have to risk something here. They will have to risk that we won't do to them what they have done to us and continue to do to us. The measure of a possible future begins at the moment of the betrayal of whiteness, both in its bodily comportment and in its authority to know, narrate, administer, and thus command the terms of social relations and sociology. The idea of "race-traitor," long articulated by some of the earliest whiteness scholars, might be understood as an ethical incitement to experience whiteness differently, to forego its wages in service of another way of being in the world. The difficult truth is that white supremacy offers us no new vision of the world other than a continuation of the horrors we have already endured and, thus, is a setup for our continued asymmetrical antagonisms.

A "Pure Decolonial Project"

Over the last years, I have attempted to think through what I have come to call a "pure decolonial project." Because I do not think we can continue to invent new languages from marked disenfranchisement and its eventual remedy, nor is it politically desirable, I hold on to the promise of a decolonial future: a future yet to come. In this moment, we must wrestle with what that future might look like. We must risk putting flesh on its imagined bones. Radical politics has never

Call to Action

Think about some of the ways that white privilege affects Canada as a nation and how it might affect you personally in your everyday life. Watch recordings of different keynote speakers at Ryerson University's White Privilege Conference (2018) to learn the effects of white privilege that might not have occurred to you as a beneficiary or as a victim. Brainstorm ways that the structures in which you find yourself, be that at school, at work, at home, on a sports team, or an online space, can be purely decolonized. Work with whatever groups are embodying radical politics on these personal levels as well as at the various political levels (local, provincial, and federal) to help disrupt the structures of whiteness.

been conceived of as a notion that white people are incapable of transformation, as I said before. It has always understood its desires for another world as a collective endeavour. And in so doing, that has meant that the kind of radical politics I'm imagining here has a central role for people that are now marked as "white" to play. A pure decolonial project seriously requires us to consciously push collectively into the not-yet-known because the now-known is so deeply unsatisfactory, to put it that way, and anti-human. And most of all, a pure decolonial project and its potential future requires us all to give up our current project of the human, a project premise that dictated and enforced a partial and incomplete idea of what the human might be. And a pure decolonial project then begins with a collective refusal of the structure of whiteness as a mode of being human *at all* because of its fundamental insufficiency for what a life might actually be.

Tying It Together

To be able to actively work against colonialism and white supremacy, the reader must be able to name and understand these forces. In this chapter, whiteness is clearly described as a colonial structure that is constructed to be both pervasive and invisible in Canadian society. By looking at how prior attempts to deconstruct whiteness have fallen short, been co-opted, and eventually used to perpetuate whiteness, the chapter uses these movements of the past to inform the future of decolonial activism. This delineation of whiteness, and the ways in which hegemonic whiteness lies, obfuscates, and maintains power, will be useful context throughout the book. In the end, this chapter calls for a "pure decolonial project" and describes the role that white people, in conjunction with everyone who is subordinated by whiteness, will have to play in this decolonial future in order for the project to be successful.

DISCUSSION QUESTIONS

1. How has whiteness been constructed historically through colonization, and how have these practices persisted to the present day?
2. In what ways have institutions within settler societies such as Canada helped to secure whiteness and white privilege?
3. In Canada, how has whiteness come to evaluate who belongs and who does not?
4. How does the construction of "unconscious bias" prevent people from understanding how white privilege is embedded in the institutions

that policies like multiculturalism has claimed it has changed?

5. How do nation-states such as Canada maintain whiteness (and, therefore, white supremacy)?

SUGGESTIONS FOR FURTHER READING

Walcott, Rinaldo (Ed.). (2000). *Rude: Contemporary Black Canadian cultural criticism*. Toronto, ON: Insomniac Press. This book is an anthology of critical writing on Black Canadian culture, examining Black lives, cultures, and events in Canada and North America.

Walcott, Rinaldo. (2008). *Black like who? Writing Black Canada, 20th anniversary edition*. Toronto, ON: Insomniac Press. This book assesses the role of Black Canadians in defining Canada and provides insight into Black culture in North America.

Walcott, Rinaldo. (2016). *Queer returns: Essays on multiculturalism, diaspora and Black studies*. Toronto, ON: Insomnia Press. This book questions what it means to live in a multicultural society, how diaspora affects identity, and how Blackness complicates queer politics.

MULTIMEDIA SUGGESTIONS

Keynote Speaker Jane Fernandes, Ryerson White Privilege Conference, May 2018

https://ryecast.ryerson.ca/80/Watch/12582.aspx This is a recording of Jane Fernandes's address, which discusses how white privilege and hearing privilege intertwine in both her personal and professional experience and challenges the deaf community to recognize and respond to racism and white privilege that still exist in spite of other oppressions facing them.

Keynote Speaker Shirley Cheechoo, Ryerson White Privilege Conference, May 2018

https://ryecast.ryerson.ca/80/Watch/12576.aspx This recording of Cree Nation member Shirley Cheechoo's talk is about her experience in the residential school system and the effect of white privilege on her life.

REFERENCES

Balibar, Étienne. (2011). The genealogical scheme: Race or culture? *Trans-Scripts: An Interdisciplinary Journal in the Humanities and Social Sciences*, 1–9.

Baraka, Amiri. (1998). *Black music*. New York, NY: De Capo Press.

Barrett, Lyndon. (1999). *Blackness and value: Seeing double*. Cambridge, UK: Cambridge University Press.

Haver, William. (1999). Another university now: A practical proposal for a new foundation of the university. In Kay Armatage (Ed.), *Equity and how to get it: Rescuing graduate studies* (pp. 25–37). Toronto, ON: Inanna Publications and Educational.

hooks, bell. (2004). Understanding patriarchy. Retrieved from https://imaginenoborders.org/pdf/zines/ UnderstandingPatriarchy.pdf.

James, Cyril Lionel Robert., & McLemee, Scott. (1996). *C.L.R. James on the "Negro question."* Jackson, MS: University Press of Mississippi.

Reed, Adolph L. (2000). *Class notes: Posing as politics and other thoughts on the American scene*. New York, NY: New Press.

Reed, Adolph L. (2009). The limits of anti-racism. *Left Business Observer*, issue 121. Retrieved from http://www.leftbusinessobserver.com/Antiracism.html.

Wilderson, Frank. (2003). The prison slave as hegemony's (silent) scandal. *Social Justice, 30*(2), 18–27.

NOTES

1. Delivered at White Privilege Conference Global, Toronto, 9 May 2018. Read about the conference at https://www.ryerson.ca/wpc-global. Watch the speech here: https://ryecast.ryerson.ca/80/Watch/12575.aspx.

2. Please see Walcott, R. (2019). The end of diversity. *Public Culture*, 31(2), 393–408. This publication is a version of the essay delivered at White Privilege Conference Global.

PART II

Gender, Christianity, and Modernity

The modernity project and the colonial project of the Global North have long been fostered and justified as expressions of Christianity's mission to the world. The role of the Christian religion in colonization can be seen in the residential school system in Canada through which Christian-led institutions contributed to the genocide against First Nations communities, serving as agents of forced assimilation and destruction of First Nations languages and cultures (Zalcman, 2016, p. 74). Traditional Christianity has also been a major force for standardizing gender relations, as is evident in the history of religion-based discrimination against transgender people (Clark-King, 2016). Part II therefore analyzes the complex relationship between gender, Christianity, and modernity.

Laura Stokes's chapter, "A Transhistorical Perspective on Witch Hunts," offers a historical overview of early modern witch hunting and its various methods and objectives. Stokes discusses the key conclusions that scholars have drawn about the social and religious forces involved in the witch hunts. Her work provides students with tools to describe a witch hunt both typologically and historically and to understand the implications of early modern witch hunting for postcolonial persecutions. The author offers a typology, constructed and illustrated with historical examples from the European witch hunts of the 15th through the 18th century. Her typology can be used to critically examine contemporary religion-based persecutions, such as modern witch hunts in Africa, McCarthyism in the US, cyberbullying in Korea, or the satanic ritual abuse scare in North America. Stokes's model gives us a transcultural framework for critically comparing the Christian witch hunts with other, more recent moral crusades. We can apply this model in examining postcolonial campaigns for the demonization of religiously deviant people or nations around the world.

In "The Historical Role of Christianity/Theology in Colonialism and Its Continuing Influence on Racism, Gender, and Othering," Ruth A. Clowater examines the role of Christianity in the European conquest of the Americas. From a theologian's perspective, she explores the influence of biblical doctrines in driving this intercontinental crusade. Clowater investigates the symbiotic relationship between European imperialism and Christian evangelism in the great conquest of Indigenous peoples and the colonial slave economy. She explores the ways that these historical religious doctrines continue to influence Western society even today, despite being disavowed by many modern Christian leaders. Finally, Clowater encourages us to consider ways that non-imperialistic Christians and leaders of civil society might work together toward a decolonized future.

REFERENCES

Clark-King, Ellen. (2016). The divine call to be myself: Anglican transgender women and prayer. *Anglican Theological Review,* 98(2), 331–9.

Zalcman, Daniella. (2016). "Kill the Indian, save the man": On the painful legacy of Canada's residential schools. *World Policy Journal,* 33(3), 72–85.

CHAPTER 5

◇

A Transhistorical Perspective on Witch Hunts

Laura Stokes

Learning Objectives

In this chapter, you will:
- learn the history of witch hunting in early modern Europe;
- understand key conclusions scholars have drawn from those witch hunts;
- absorb a model for the analysis of witch hunts and other moral panics;
- apply the model and historical lessons to an examination of postcolonial persecutions.

Introduction

This chapter offers several discrete definitions of witch hunting, beginning with the specific example of the *Würzburgisches werk* that served in the European memory as the archetype of a witch hunt and a warning of its dangers. After the archetype of the witch hunt, I discuss historians' explanations of witch hunting, followed by a model of the witch hunt from its deep drivers to active persecution through four emotional regimes: naive, rumour-based, panicked, and skeptical. Lastly, the model and the fruits of historical analysis will be brought to bear on a set of more contemporary persecutions to ask whether and to what degree they can be considered witch hunts. In particular, I will focus on the example of witch hunting in postcolonial Africa.

The Great Witch Hunt: A Descriptive Exemplar (Würzburg and Bamberg)

The most intensive witch hunts of historical memory began after the spring of 1626 when a terrible frost struck the central German region of Franconia, destroying the vineyards and fields throughout the bishoprics of Würzburg and Bamberg in the midst of the spring bloom. The damages of the lost harvest were noted at length by a Franconian family chronicler, who also described the local response:

> There arose a great hue and cry among the common mob, asking why we continue to tolerate witches and sorcerers destroying the harvests (Behringer, 1995, p. 249).

The demands of the people were met by the authorities in both bishoprics, who established commissions to seek out and punish the witches. In Bamberg, the witch commission was given the use of the 25 small prisons in various towers and corners of the cities, and a new building was constructed in the market to serve as a witch prison. The city spared no one in seeking out every last witch. The witches were accused of the most profound rebellion against God, apostasy, and devil worship. The people of Franconia, in the grips of a **moral panic**, believed they were being assailed by a conspiracy of sorcerers who gathered with the devil for a nocturnal sabbath that was part inverted mass, part gratuitous perversion, and part briefing hall for the witches' assault on humanity.

A partial chronicle of the witches executed in Würzburg allows a sense of the progression of the witch hunt from a core stereotype of poor, old women to the city elite. Altogether, the chronicle lists 31 witch pyres over two years, covering the executions of some 161 witches that comprised just over 10 per cent of the estimated 1500 executions during the four-year Würzburg witch hunt (Behringer, 1995, pp. 251–2).

By 1630, the wisdom of the witch hunts in Bamberg and Würzburg was being openly questioned. A Jesuit chronicler in Paderborn wrote that "great pity swelled among the people" for the victims of the witch hunts and sharp doubts were raised whether the hundreds of people burned at the stake could possibly have been guilty and have deserved such a tormented death, given that the judges subjected the accused to every form of torture on the bare **denunciation** of condemned witches. People were beginning to think that the accused were being compelled to falsely confess (Behringer, 1995, p. 265).

This sense of injustice was heightened by the high social status of some of the condemned witches and triggered a **crisis of confidence** in the witch hunt. The witch hunt had reached into the highest echelons of the city government, including even magistrates and their families. In the summer of 1628, Johannes Junius, former mayor of Bamberg, was arrested as a witch and tortured despite his protestations of innocence. In a letter he had smuggled out of the witch prison to his daughter, Junius described how he was brought to confess after a long day of torture with thumbscrews and strappado:

> When at last the executioner led me back into the prison, he said to me: "Sir, I beg you, for God's sake confess something, whether it be true or not. Invent something, for you cannot endure the torture which you'll be put to; and even if you bear it all, yet you will not escape, not if you were an earl, but one torture will follow after another until even you say you are a witch" (Kors, 2001, p. 351).

Junius did confess that he was a witch and that he had been to the witches' sabbath when they gathered to adore their demon lord. Asked to remember who he had seen at the sabbath, Junius originally claimed to recall no faces or to have recognized no one, but the interrogator demanded a list of denunciations. Junius began by listing people he knew had already entered the witch prison, but his interrogator was unsatisfied, leading him on a mental walk of his neighbourhood to help bring names to his mind: "Take one street after another, begin at the market, go out on one street and back on the next." Junius's experience encapsulated the injustice that outside observers feared in the Franconian witch hunts: that the unbridled use of torture was producing false confessions.

> Here you have my confession, for which I must die. And they are sheer lies and made-up things, so help me God. For all this I

was forced to say through fear of the torture which was threatened beyond what I had already endured. For they never leave off with the torture till one confesses something; be he never so good, he must be a witch. Nobody escapes, though he were an earl (Kors & Peters, 2001, p. 352).

In his letter, Junius wrote to his daughter of his true guilt, his remorse at having given a false confession that would to help seal the fates of others. When he was given an opportunity to confess to a priest, Junius offered his guilt over the false testimony.

One Jesuit priest who claimed to have served as a confessor to the condemned witches during the witch hunt in Würzburg reported the same from his many conversations with the condemned: that they all wished to be forgiven for their false testimony against themselves and others. That priest, Friedrich Spee, wrote an influential treatise against the witch hunts, the *Cautio criminalis*, which was quickly translated from Latin and published in German in 1630. He described the trap of the witch prison for his imaginary witch exemplar, Gaia, and it was the same for her as it was for Johannes Junius.

She confesses or she does not confess, it is all the same. If she confesses, the case is clear and she is killed, for recantation means nothing here. If she does not confess, they torture her a second, third, and fourth time, for in this trial whatever the Commission desires is done. In the case of this *excepted crime*, they place no limits on how long, how severe, how often the torture may be used, and no one thinks that if anything gets broken they will have to pay compensation afterwards (Spee, 2003, p. 426).

The *Cautio criminalis* did not change the minds of witch hunters, but it did provide a very useful, detailed guide to the dangers of procedural laxity and the persecutory elements of early modern judicial practice. It became a handbook for officials and judges who wanted to prevent an accusation of witchcraft from turning into another *Würzburgischer werk*. It was the development of judicial resistance to witch hunting in practice that ultimately ended the witch hunts over the century that followed. The Franconian witch hunts were the most intensive witch hunts of the age, the apex of the great European witch hunt, and remembered as a dreadful example to avoid.

Why Did Witch Hunting Happen?

The rich and excellent historical literature on the European witch hunts offers many interpretations and explanations. When these various propositions are examined, however, we find time and again that exceptions were the rule. The concept of the witch and the process of the hunt were both highly plastic. They found material and drivers in many different aspects of the unfolding experiential reality of the early modern, rendering generalization problematic.

One of the strongest impressions of the European witch hunts in the modern imagination is that of its stereotypical victim, a poor, old woman. Across Europe as a whole, women accounted for about 75 per cent of the victims of the witch hunts. In some times and places, such as in Swiss Lucerne prior to 1519, all of the accused witches were women. In other times and places, such as in parts of France where rural residents feared the supernatural machinations of shepherds, the dominant witch concept was male, and men made up the majority of the accused. Witches were imagined as envious, but those accused of witchcraft did not tend to be the poor as often as they were established householders and other members of the community. Examinations of specific witch persecutions have been able to identify highly local elements of the victim stereotype, as in research on witch trials in the canton of Lucerne that reveals that many of the accused witches were established immigrants to their villages (Jäggi, 2002). Examinations of the **instrumentalization** of witchcraft accusations are more likely to reveal envy as motivation for accusers than for supposed witches. In most regions, the earliest witchcraft accusations and the majority of later witchcraft accusations tend to remain roughly within the social profile of the local witch stereotype. One of the signs that a trial had sparked into a panic and a panic into a witch hunt was the breakdown of that stereotype.

Historians have considered at length whether early modern witch hunting was *woman* hunting, a gender-targeted persecution of women who were too independent. Such an interpretation seems warranted for specific accusations, but it does not bear up under a more sustained, general examination. One argument that witch hunting was a gender-specific attack focuses on the special case of midwives, who were occasionally identified by early modern observers as particularly notorious or dangerous witches. The infamous witch-hunting manual the *Malleus maleficarum* (*Hammer of the witches*, 1486; see Multimedia Suggestions at the end of the chapter) argued that midwives are especially prone to witchcraft and particularly courted by the sect of the witches. In the witch hunt in Würzburg, the contemporary chronicler had indicated that a midwife was the original source of witchcraft in the region. The belief that midwives were special targets of the witch hunts has held sway in modern scholarship, linked to the historical rise of the male medical profession (Ehrenreich & English, 2010). Archival research has brought this thesis into serious question, demonstrating not only that midwives were not particularly likely to be accused as witches but that midwives enjoyed a measure of social immunity to witch hunting because of their crucial importance to the community.

Beyond the focus on midwifery, witch hunting has been widely understood as a persecutory expression of European misogyny. As many feminist scholars of the witch hunts have noted, the negative stereotype of the female witch still has power in the present day. "Witch" has been an insult flung at women as a form of gender enforcement and social control for more than 500 years, and for all of that time it has been a potentially deadly insult somewhere. This knowledge has structured women's responses to the efforts of control exerted over them, enhancing the power of those efforts. Thus, the word "witch" and the history of witch hunting are critically important to understanding the background of European misogyny against which feminist theory largely developed.

If we fail to attend to the 25 per cent of witch-hunt victims who were men, however, we miss an important truth about witch hunting. The history of the witch hunts in Europe reveals the importance of the openness of the witch concept and its capacity to expand to include men as well as women, children as well as adults, rich as well as poor. The universal applicability of the witch concept allows for the full expression of instrumentalization during a witch hunt. Not only were not all witches women, but the European misogyny that animated the witch hunters also animated the most vocal defenders of the witches. Johannes Nider, a Dutch doctor who famously defended witches in a 1573 treatise, grounded his defence in his professional medical understanding of the constitutional and intellectual weaknesses of women and their senile tendency for dementia. Nider may be the father of the insanity defence and a defender of witches, but he did both by considering women imbecilic. On the other side of the knife, the infamously misogynist demonologist Heinrich Kramer, author of the *Malleus maleficarum*, was at other moments in his career an ardent defender of a number of young female mystics in Italy about whom other clerics were alarmed in distinctly misogynistic terms (Herzig, 2013). The early modern witch hunts, despite having an unquestionably misogynistic bent, were not a straightforward application of European misogyny.

Another powerful interpretation of the witch hunts, the **acculturation** thesis, argues that the process was part of the Christianization of rural Europe. The most extreme, widely disproven version proposes that there was a surviving pagan cult in early modern Europe and that the targets of the witch hunts were night-gathering goddess-worshippers. This thesis was widely disseminated in the mid–20th century, but in the 1970s when academic historians turned to the witch hunts, they found no evidence of any coherent, non-Christian survivals in the heartland of Europe. What they did find were pagan remnants embedded within rural Christian practice. Robert Muchembled argued that the witch hunts were an elite process of acculturation oriented on eliminating the pagan elements in popular culture (Muchembled, 1985). Muchembled has since stepped back from the strong version of his thesis, which posits too great a distance between elite men and popular culture. But the acculturation thesis still survives in the literature. In part, this is because early modern advocates of witch hunting were drawing on material from the early medieval struggle with paganism. The fight against superstition was a consistent refrain within the pastoral arm of the witch hunting literature. Moreover, there is an argument to be made that the period of the witch hunts did much to destroy previously widespread European beliefs in magic and magical folk practices.

The colonization of Europe may begin as early as the encounters of Neanderthals with encroaching *Homo sapiens*, but in the written records of traditional history they open with Julius Caesar's *Gallic Wars*. In Caesar's own telling, it was a brutal campaign that employed mass slaughter to instill fear and elicit obedience. It pays to recall that the Roman term "decimation" (literally, to kill one in ten) was used as tool of internal military discipline. The Christianization of early medieval Europe was also a force of colonization because it used military force and missionizing out-migration to impose new institutional and cultural hegemony. In this sense, the concern over superstitious pagan remnants that animated the late-medieval inquisition in its formation of the diabolic witch concept could be viewed as part of a medieval postcolonial process (Cohen, 2000).

A third interpretation of the witch hunts that has particularly influenced the popular imagination is Alan MacFarlane's refusal of charity thesis (MacFarlane, 1999). In his examination of witch hunts in Essex, MacFarlane found an interesting pattern in some witchcraft accusations. The accused witch, in these cases invariably a poor, old woman, had come to a particular house to beg milk or some other small favour. The household had refused the charity and sent her away, she possibly mumbling prevarications or even cursing them outright. Shortly thereafter, when the household suffered a sudden illness or death, thoughts turned to the old woman's curses, and suspicions of witchcraft were raised. Ostensibly, the curses she muttered when turned away had been an act of witchcraft, and the harm the household had suffered was laid to her blame. MacFarlane saw a more subtle process at play in the pattern, a displacement of guilt over the refusal of charity from the household to the woman they had refused. MacFarlane's interpretation fit the dominant stereotype of the witch very well. It also fit the social and economic reality of early modern Europe, particularly during the years of crisis that saw the worst witch hunts. But when historians searched for similar dynamics elsewhere, they found refusal of charity was more of an occasional pattern rather than a consistent pattern within the witch hunts as a whole.

The economic and interpersonal tensions at the heart of the refusal of charity thesis point to another dominant factor in early modern witch hunting: the weather. The frequent coincidence of bad weather and witch hunting is notable in the historical record. The starting shot of the great witch hunt was a storm in August of 1562. After the terrible drought years and lost harvests in the 1570s and 1580s came the wave of witch hunts in the 1580s and 1590s. Following the destructive, widespread frost in the spring of 1626 came the most intensive witch hunting of the age. Bad weather was so crucial to the witch concept that both Protestant and Catholic demonologists developed convoluted arguments to explain the connection between witchcraft and storms, despite its theological incoherence with providentialism (the belief that God controls all events on earth) as well as clear proscriptions against belief in magically summoned storms in medieval canon law. Wolfgang Behringer has argued strongly for the importance of the early modern climatic minimum, the Little Ice Age, in setting crucial preconditions for the witch hunts (Behringer, 2004). But here as well exceptions prove to be the rule and in so doing work against any monolithic explanation.

What these major interpretations reveal are several heavy drivers of witch hunts: the extended and intense climatic crisis, the post-Reformation processes of confessionalization and acculturation (which first Christianized according to confession, then homogenized European cultures more generally), and the early modern transformation of economic culture that would open the world of capitalism and radical inequality. These heavy drivers increased the social stress within communities and often promoted the sense of crisis crucial to shifting the local emotional regime from rumour to panic. The decision to respond to a given person or disaster with a witchcraft accusation, however, remained with the individual, for whom a variety of culturally coherent responses (of which a witchcraft accusation was just one) existed. The concept of deep drivers thus avoids the fallacy of determinism when considering such large-scale factors in a major historical phenomenon like witch hunting.

Witch hunting was multi-causal, but what historians have found time and again is that local experience and individual choices are what determined whether or not a community descended into a witch hunt. A good example of this can be found in the southwestern German territory of the Palatinate. The larger region saw some of the most intensive witch hunting in Germany, but the Palatinate never shifted into a witch hunt, despite regular witchcraft accusations and trials. The crucial point of resistance was the development within the judicial apparatus of a system of referral. Witch trials were referred to the Tübingen theological faculty, providing a judicial review beyond the grip of any local panic (Schmidt, 2000). This system of external review, which eventually became law in many European jurisdictions, originated in specific, ad hoc procedural choices made by officials. Its efficacy was rooted in the physical distance of the consultant from the emotional regime of a community on the edge of a witch panic. Exceptions that seemed necessary in the crisis of the moment read as broken and inconsistent procedure from the emotional distance of safety. In France as well as Germany, processes of review and referral were crucial to ending the cycle of witch hunting. In France, the centralizing requirement of reviewing witch trials through the Parlement of Paris was the key mechanism used by the French state to slow and eventually stop the witch hunts (Soman, 1985).

Observing this, some have assumed that the early modern development of the state was fundamentally contrary to witch hunting, a part of early modern reason triumphing over medieval barbarism. Such a reading, which misrepresents the Middle Ages, ignores the longer history of the witch hunts and distorts the shape of the phenomenon. Throughout the 15th and 16th centuries, witch hunting appears as a tool of the territorialization process of developing states (Dillinger, 2008). Through territorialization, early modern states sought to increase the coherence of territorial boundaries with judicial, fiscal, and military control.

The relationship between the development of the early modern state and witch hunting is not linear but phase-dependent. Early in the history of the witch hunts, we often find the local state apparatus (city governments, regional lords, etc.) drawn into the persecutions for the benefit of that apparatus in its competition with other sources of justice. By acquiescing to the popular demand for witch hunting in the mid–15th century, local officials in Basel, for example, were able to bring capital justice from the rural villages to the central control of the city. Historically, imperial cities like Basel went through this territorialization process earlier than larger territories like France or Bavaria (Stokes, 2011).

When early modern centralizing forces were weak, they found advantage in supporting witch hunts. When they were strong, however, they were more likely to find advantage in ending witch hunts. The Inquisition shared with the state this relationship with witch hunts. The Inquisition has long been given a heavy share of the blame for the witch hunts because of the important role that the medieval Inquisitions played in developing persecution-ready investigative techniques and in midwifing the diabolic witch concept. In Italy and Spain, early modern Inquisitions were powerful, centralized institutions that worked against witch hunting (Henningsen, 1980).

Some of the most important aftereffects of the great witch hunt took place in the realm of politics and criminal justice. Western intellectuals in the 18th and 19th centuries made their constitutional arguments with the memory of the witch hunts in mind, taking four key collective lessons. First, they assumed that popular superstition and supernatural beliefs could be dangerous to social harmony. Second, they worried that a high degree of local autonomy could facilitate injustice. Third, they saw that lax judicial process and the lifting of usual procedures under extraordinary circumstances resulted in injustice. Fourth, they concluded that the collective state of moral panic is a crucial condition for witch hunting. All of these positions have historical validity, but each concern has been taken to a degree that has had ironic historical consequences. The promotion of Christianity in Africa, for example, undertaken to free African societies from "dangerous and backwards superstition," provided an apparatus of witchcraft persecution into a new context with deadly results. Extreme centralism, as was reached in 20th-century totalitarian states, has proven highly effective at mass persecution, even in the absence of collective support. Obsession with procedural law in the United States of America has made law into an arcane game in which money and social influence have a profound impact, rendering law highly open to instrumentalization and unconscious social biases like misogyny and racism. Lastly, in fear of stoking the darker passions of the masses, early 20th-century liberals abandoned emotional, collectivist rhetoric to the persecutory fascist wing (Beacock, 2018). Indeed, the concept of moral panic has been overused to the point that it has fallen under serious criticism (Thompson & Williams, 2014). We will return to some of these issues in considering the question of postcolonial witch hunts below, after sketching a generalized model of witch hunting.

A Model of Witch Hunting

Historians have described many different processes in the larger constellation of the European witch hunts, from the origination and development of suspicion, to different modes of resolution, through the various vicious cycles that characterized the witch hunts. The identification of vicious cycles was part of the earliest (i.e., contemporary) criticism of the witch hunts. In particular, early modern observers like Friedrich Spee were concerned with the seeming inescapability of a witchcraft accusation. "Whoever enters the witch prison must either be a witch or soon become one" under torture. Spee describes the inescapable logic of the witch prison: if the witch resists confession, it is because the Devil aids her, if she confesses, we know she is guilty. Critics of the witch hunts so emphasized this point that they have misled modern scholars sympathetic to their claims. Most thorough studies of European witchcraft trials reveal a fairly high rate of dismissal or non-finding, if not outright acquittal, of charges. Scholars are, however, quick to note that even an apparent acquittal on witchcraft charges could carry lifelong consequences and also that acquittals tended to characterize periods between witch hunts. During the intense moral panic of a witch hunt, the inescapable law of the witch prison, as Spee calls it, rises to the fore, and few if any escape accusation unscathed while the witch hunt rages (Spee, 2003).

In addition to the inescapability of the witch prison, a discursive vicious cycle appears outside the witch prison: if you deny you are a witch, it is taken as sign of being a witch. If you joke about the ridiculous suggestion, it is taken as a sign of being a witch. Any response at all to an open accusation of witchcraft, and indeed no response in particular, can be read as confirmation of the accusation (Dillinger, 2009). Like the phenomenon of inescapability, this paradox appears to be more common as the moral panic grows and comes to dominate discourse.

A different sort of vicious cycle is found in the building of the witch rumour. Moral panic grows under the influence of rumour, and a reciprocal relationship can be observed between witch beliefs and witch hunts. A feedback loop existed between one round of trials and the next round of accusations, and the local witchcraft concept became elaborated with all the baggage of the cumulative witchcraft concept. This baggage in turn contained several key elements that promoted and intensified the witch hunts. Chief among these elements was the idea of the witches' sabbath to which any given witch had presumably

been and thus could be compelled to name other attendant witches. The witches' sabbath provided a narrative mechanism for denunciations creating a snowballing effect as condemned witches gave lists of names that spawned multiple trials. This is the classic witch hunt dynamic: more and more people are accused until no one is safe.

But there is a serious flaw in the arguments about snowballing panic creating a slippery slope toward a witch hunt because they fail to account for all the witch hunts that never take place, for trials that are ended, and for communities that never join the general panic to accuse one of their own. The responses of authorities to a witch trial were crucial to whether or not a witch hunt took place. Steps taken by a single official—in sending a file for review, for example—could halt the process. Local officials, however, were subject to the same emotional regime, to borrow a term from William Reddy, as the rest of their communities (Reddy, 2001). Historians have found two crucial shifts in the emotional regime of a community that serve as turning points in the unfolding of a witch hunt. The first is the emergence of a shared moral panic, characterized by the belief that the community is under attack by witches who are hidden among them. The second is the crisis of confidence that signals the end of the witch hunt in which the community's confidence in the process of witch hunting breaks down. These are collective experiences and so can be difficult to pin down in the historical record. Not everyone individually had to share the sense of panic, but everyone would be subject to its rules. Individuals who chose openly to resist the process of witch hunting under the panic regime could be labelled witch friends and suffer heavy penalties for their resistance. Moral panic can, however, have clear indications, as when the people of Wiesensteig demanded a witch hunt from their local lord in 1563. The crisis of confidence, also a collective experience, has been easier to identify in the actions of local authorities, who frequently responded by ending the special procedural permissions of the witch hunt, by stopping the trials underway, and sometimes even by releasing the remaining accused witches from prison.

The model of witch hunting offered here is based on emotional regimes. Within this ideal type, there are four emotional regimes that characterize the relationship of a given society or community to potential witch hunting. The first regime is a naive regime, largely ignorant of the fear object (witches) or at least lacking any active rumours of malevolent witchcraft. This regime ends when a witch trial takes place within the local sphere of knowledge, often in a neighbouring territory. This first trial offers a precedent and a factual basis for rumours, initiating the rumour regime. This second regime is characterized by occasional trials, usually only by ones or twos, and by the gradual growth and proliferation of rumours about witches. The witch trials under the rumour regime tend to target only stereotypical witches. Once a rumour regime is sufficiently elaborated and widely believed, a spectacular disaster or witchcraft trial can initiate the third regime: moral panic. The panic regime is the domain of the witch hunt. It is characterized not only by individual trials and further rumours but also by chain or snowball trials, intense events that in some cases engulf whole communities in witch hunting. The usual rules of trial procedure are lifted under the panic regime. Society moves into a state of crisis that sweeps away ordinary judicial safeguards as impediments to justice against the witches. Under the panic regime, the widespread violence and injustice of the witch hunt inspires a growing skepticism. A spectacle of injustice in the process finally initiates the last regime, bringing on a crisis of confidence in the processes of witch hunting. The skeptical regime that results from this crisis is characterized by the summary dismissal of trials and release of prisoners and by the creation of rules and institutions intended to prevent similar abuses in the future.

There is a relationship between the panic regime in this model and the contemporary sociological term of analysis "moral panic," but they are not the same. Sociologists define moral panic as a state in which a particular social group is defined as a threat to society and a recognizable campaign against that group emerges (Cohen, 2002). Mass media present the group in a stylized and stereotypical fashion. The moral barricades are manned, and experts pronounce diagnoses and solutions. Moral panic makes its object into a "folk devil," elaborating the supposed sins and dangers posed by the target deviancy. The primary social expressions of moral panic are formal and spontaneous forms of social control (rules and riots) as well as the softer, if no less stigmatizing, option of treatments and cures (Goode & Ben-Yehuda, 2009). The modern sociological term "moral panic" encompasses both the rumour and panic regimes described in the model above, without providing any distinction. The concept of moral panic has received sustained criticism for its analytical weakness and political instrumentalization and may be in need of further refinement (Thompson & Williams, 2014). The articulation of the rumour and panic process into two distinct phases, as was done above, can help by providing a distinction between the ordinary injustices that characterize the negative effects of rumours and the extraordinary interjection of a state of crisis that marks a witch hunt.

Every witch hunt has identifiable heavy drivers. Early modern witch hunts were nearly overdetermined with political, social, economic, climatological, and religious stressors. It is natural that these heavy drivers, especially where their specific local importance was high enough to push through the event barrier in measurable ways, should appear as causes in scholarly analysis. The nature of heavy drivers, however, is not determinative, and counter-examples prevail. This is the nemesis of many great interpretations of the European witch hunts, which are rendered vulnerable by their identification of a locally salient heavy driver as the true cause of witch hunting.

If we construct the model as a spatial analogy, the base is an ocean with a variety of heavy drivers producing waves. In Fernand Braudel's structuralist analogy, this ocean and its waves are the *longue durée* (i.e., long time-scale historical events) and the conjunctures that structure history. Braudel gives less attention to the froth on the waves, which he describes as the ephemeral and largely inconsequential world of individuals. It is in this foam of individual experience, however, that witch accusations and trials originate. In the first phase of the model, the naive regime, the froth on the waves occasionally sends up the bubble of an accusation. The bubble may pop before it reaches a sufficient height to initiate a trial, or it might evaporate under the pressure of judicial disbelief. It is not easy for such an accusation under the naive regime to result in a confession and execution, but those that do have an important effect. They release a colour or gas that changes the regime through which our bubbles pass: the first real, local witch renders the threat immanent in the minds of the community. We can imagine the rumour regime as slightly transformed by the allegorical gas of the witch fear. Under the rumour regime, pressures from heavy drivers that might be interpreted otherwise become increasingly interpreted as the result of witchcraft. The foam on the waves produces more bubbles, and these bubbles rise more quickly through the rumour regime to produce multiple trials, confessions, and executions. The witch fear adulterates the atmosphere, increasingly transforming the expectations and perceptions of those living within its gloom. There is a critical mass dynamic in the growing witch fear because specific confessions and executions not only heighten the general atmosphere of fear but also include denunciations that draw up many new trials from the foam.

Individuals and communities often mount explicit or subtle resistance to the mounting witch fear, sending up skeptical anti-bubbles. Some communities shift directly from the rumour regime into a skeptical withdrawal from witch trials. Others bob about in the rumour regime, fear maintained by a steady stream of trials but a crucial line of resistance preventing the onset of a full-blown panic. The third regime did arrive in many communities across Europe. The titular panic of the regime can be imagined as a darkening of the gas-laden atmosphere to a blood red, drawing up accusations from the froth in a frenzy that fills the air with the bubbles of witch trials. No such visual signal exists for the historian, of course, but the panic regime is usually characterized by the lifting of key judicial safeguards and can thus be identified in the unfolding of many historical witch hunts. The dynamic of the witch hunt under the panic regime is increasingly indiscriminate, and the general relaxation of procedure increases the frequency of blatant injustice. The result is a growing skepticism that pushes against the cloud of the witch hunt until some spectacle of injustice provides the collective will to end the persecution. The skeptical regime that characterizes the end of a witch hunt provides a clear program of resistance as local memory of the negative events of the rumour and panic act to inhibit the acceptance of new accusations.

Among all these processes, drivers, and emotional regimes, what is the essence of a witch hunt? If we take the experience of witch hunting in Europe as the canonical form, we can refine the essence to a generalized definition of the two key elements, the *witch* and the *hunt*. The witch concept is a widely available, believable narrative of an evil other, and it provides a cultural framework through which to interpret the individual slings and arrows of misfortune. The hunt is a collective persecution, requiring a mechanism for persecution and a general state of moral panic.

Postcolonial Witch Hunts

If we proceed from the typological definition of witch hunting offered above, it becomes clear that some modern phenomena commonly associated with witch hunting, primarily on account of being forms of mass persecution, are typologically distinct. Excluded on the one hand must be those phenomena lacking the collusion of popular enthusiasm with elite or official programs of persecution, such as the Stalinist purges. Excluded on the other hand we find phenomena that avoid using institutional mechanisms of authority, such as the malicious rumour attacks on social media that have driven the high-profile cases of suicide in Korea. If we wish to broaden our definition to include such phenomena, we must reject the quintessential importance of collusion between the executive and the common will. It is, however, just this element of collusion and shared moral panic that allows the taking of a collective decision to loosen or remove the social and legal safeguards against mass persecution.

Other forms of mass persecution stand adjacent to witch hunts and are often analogically or even analytically bundled with them. These are mass persecutions with an ethnic or racial target: an ostensibly "real" category of social reality. One could argue that the hard social reality of Jewishness or Blackness renders such categories difficult to instrumentalize. Given the crucial nature of instrumentalization in the attacking of personal enemies through a witch hunt, this could be a serious barrier to categorizing the persecutions of minorities as witch hunts. There are two problems with assuming a hard reality to such categories, the first being their socially constructed nature and the second being the historical reality of the

Open Questions

In the discussion that follows, the author offers some answers on whether certain postcolonial persecutions should be called witch hunts. What do you think?

- In a society deeply sensitive to honour and reputation, foul rumours spawned on social media have impelled a series of Korean Internet stars to commit suicide. The persecution takes place entirely within a discursive space, and the victim executes herself. Is this a witch hunt?
- Uncounted hundreds of Black men have been shot by the police in the US. Black people are harassed in public spaces and neighbourhoods on the false assumption of criminality. A vastly disproportionate number of Black men fill the criminal justice system. Is the Black Lives Matter movement an act of resistance against a witch-hunting of African Americans?
- In the 1950s, a purge of gay and lesbian personnel from the US government was undertaken in lockstep with Joseph McCarthy's Committee on Unamerican Activities. Local police carried out raids on gay bars in Washington, DC, and thousands of homosexuals were fired from the State Department in what media labelled the Panic on the Potomac. Was it a witch hunt?
- A charismatic Pentecostal minister in Nigeria cites Exodus 22:18 to her congregants, telling parents that fussy or disobedient children may be possessed by devils. Rumours suggest exorcism by acid, and hundreds of children are attacked and some made to drink battery acid in an attempt to drive the demons out. Is it a witch hunt?

instrumentalization of personal enmity within both mass genocidal movements and the more commonplace, extended phenomena of race-based persecution in, for example, South Africa or the United States. The nature of the instrumentalization is not based in the flexibility of the despised category but in its persistent denigration and the vulnerability of anyone assigned to it to a wide variety of attacks.

When we examine the persecution of another ostensibly hard category of social reality, the attack on homosexuals during the Lavender Scare, we find Senator Joseph McCarthy activating the widespread anti-gay sentiments of mid-century America to stoke popular moral concern about communist agents (Johnson, 2004). While communism was a highly instrumentalizable accusation, it lacked sufficient capacity to stir a general sense of moral panic. Early in his campaign to find and eliminate communists, McCarthy was pushed by others to focus on "the homosexual problem." When he acceded and targeted homosexuals in particular, his persecutory program gained traction. The power of homosexuality to stir the sense of moral panic necessary for mass persecution swiftly became evident. The Panic on the Potomac, as journalists termed it, constituted a multi-layered attack on homosexuals within the public service. More than 400 state department employees were ultimately fired, gay bars and cafes in the District of Columbia were subjected to repeated raids, and the entire gay community of the city came under attack. Throughout McCarthy's persecution, charges of homosexuality, perversion, and criminality were connected to communist subornment and conspiratorial behaviour. By despising homosexuality and driving it underground, mid-century society had created a social lever that could be used to blackmail or pressure homosexuals. McCarthyism took the next step and assumed that the active communist enemy must surely have already taken advantage of such vulnerability. As it had been under the medieval inquisitions of

heresy, homosexuality became associated with a contemporary conceptual nexus of evil. The homosexual security risk was used to justify the removal of hundreds or thousands of individuals from their place in society (Johnson, 2004).

We are left with two sets of socially constructed categories along a spectrum from hard reality through highly open categories. We find the less open, more real (though still socially constructed) categories, like race or sexuality, generating emotional energy that can be effectively slaved to persecutions under the umbrella of a more open category, like witchcraft or communism. The Black person or immigrant is brought under the umbrella of the criminal type. The Jewish or queer person is brought under the umbrella of the communist. The woman becomes a witch, the Muslim person a terrorist. Analysis will be aided by the careful distinction of discriminatory social processes and the legal action of false accusation.

We have noted above that it is possible to overemphasize the reality of these categories of social identity, given the observable flexibility and socially constructed nature of such ostensibly hard categories as race or gender. The converse is also true. We risk intellectual errors if we assume too rigidly the *unreality* of the more open categories such as the witch or criminal type, which are unquestionably social constructions. The example of the terrorist label is instructive here. Following the very real attacks on the World Trade Center in New York and the Pentagon in Washington, DC, on 11 September 2001, the war on terror has displayed several hallmarks of a witch hunt, particularly in holding many of the accused under extraordinary conditions under which the usual protections of the law were not applied (United States FBI, 2007). This problem is evident also in the history of the satanic ritual abuse scare as well as in postcolonial African witch hunts, which will be discussed below. The importance of spectacular cases of real, murderous practitioners of Satanism or witchcraft should not be ignored.

The satanic ritual abuse scare, known as the "satanic panic" of the 1980s, was initiated by the Manson murders in southern California. Charles Manson and his followers claimed to be Satanists, and this claim was widely reported in the press. Although homosexuality is absent from the Manson murders, it became an important component of the satanic panic as it grew under the evangelical movement then becoming popular in American churches. Families and child care services across the United States were destroyed on the basis of highly dubious, induced, or coerced denunciations and accusations by children against their bewildered caregivers. Here the fear of supernatural evil that animated the early modern witch hunts found perhaps its fullest modern expression as frightened communities drew unconsciously on the cultural material of the early modern witch hunts. Ultimately, the judicial safeguards put in place during the Enlightenment held against the satanic panic. Although specific communities appear to have fallen into a state of moral panic, informally lifting their judicial safeguards in pursuit of the imaginary satanic sadists, the process of judicial review ended the trials and released many of those convicted. The infamous Kern County daycare case involved 36 convicted defendants, of whom two died in prison and 34 were later released (Victor, 1993).

The satanic panic was weak in part because it depended on a fear of Satan and divine punishment to motivate moral panic. While evangelical Christians were quite exercised about the reality of the devil and the work of Satanists, other Christians, non-Christians, and most particularly a-religious Americans were not moved. The accusations of child sexual abuse were by far the most alarming to the general public, but the public was still more inclined to see the cause of the evil in personal perversion rather than supernatural influence. Ultimately, the concern over child sexual abuse has been unable to play out, the reality of abuse being held in constant check by

the legal weakness of its victim-witnesses. Some critics have claimed that this embarrassing history of persecution has had a chilling effect on the testimony of children against their abusers in real cases of sexual abuse (Cheit, 2016). Given the long-standing reluctance of the courts to prosecute and convict in such cases, however, such an effect is difficult to measure at best.

African witch hunting has a complex history. Prior to European colonization, Africans had their own indigenous witchcraft concepts, practices, and fears, as well as mechanisms for persecution. There were and still are important regional differences in witchcraft practices and beliefs across Africa, just as there were in Europe (Mavhungu, 2012). Through the processes of colonization, Africa and Europe initiated a profound cultural interaction. The reception of European ideas about religion, law, and the supernatural was both destructive and fertile within the African cultural landscape, as an overview of the history of witch hunting in postcolonial Africa demonstrates. It is also important to note that European ideas were transformed through the interaction with African culture. In particular, European scholarly understandings of magic and witchcraft in the 19th and 20th centuries were heavily based on the observations of anthropologists working in colonial settings. The examination of African magic and witchcraft beliefs (especially the work of E.E. Evans-Pritchard) provided crucial elements of the definitions of these objects to historians of the European witch hunts. Given this relationship, we should perhaps take the apparent coherence of the essential nature of witchcraft in Europe and Africa with a grain of salt. But the argument has been made that this simplified definition of the witch is near-universal in human cultures (Behringer, 2004): the witch is an evil person, capable of harming others by simply wishing them ill. To the ordinary eye, the witch is indistinguishable from other people, but an expert can know witches by their signs. Such a witch concept, whatever its local elaborations, is highly open to instrumentalization. It also provides a strong social motivation to take action against witches, whether through counter-magic or direct attack. Finally, this simplified witch as evil-wisher is open to functionalization as an explanation for misfortune, and indeed the witch can be found serving as such in postcolonial African societies.

Colonial European authorities interacted with African witchcraft in three key ways. First, European missionaries generally rejected African beliefs about the supernatural and strove to replace them with normative Christian beliefs and doctrines. Second, Western anthropologists and ethnographers sought objectively to observe African cultures but still brought their biases to bear. Strong beliefs about social evolution, the "primitivity" of Africa, and the superior, "advanced" nature of European culture structured anthropologists' observations and encouraged them to see strong parallels between the superstitions of Africa and those of the European past. Finally, colonial authorities, sharing the religious and anthropological dogmas of their day and as self-conscious inheritors of the anti–witch hunting legacy of the Enlightenment, took legal and political actions against indigenous witchcraft persecutions. This meant that in Africa, witch hunting was not part of colonial acculturation, as it was in Latin America under the Catholic Inquisition (see Chapter 6). Instead, witch hunting in Africa has been a distinctly postcolonial process.

In the 18th century, the law criminalizing witchcraft in England was replaced by a law that criminalized the accusation of witchcraft, the 1735 Witchcraft and Vagrancy Act. As the titular reference to vagrancy indicates, in repealing the old witchcraft statutes Parliament was concerned with dealing with the ongoing nuisance of wandering charlatans, and so the 1735 act also set penalties for anyone offering any magical services for sale. The British carried the 1735 Witchcraft and Vagrancy Act with them into their colonial

endeavours, without much success. Although the law was replaced in the United Kingdom with the Fraudulent Mediums Act of 1951, a version of it remained in effect in Canada until 2018. In British East Africa, explicit laws against witchcraft persecution in the early 20th century failed to curtail witch fears and attacks (Behringer, 2004). In 1932, after years of frustration at its weakness in the face of witchcraft beliefs, the colonial government tried to make an example of 60 men of the Wakamba tribe in Kenya, convicting them to death "for killing an old woman they believed had cast a spell over a man's wife" (*New York Times*, 17 September 1933). The Wakamba case became entangled in appeals, and the convictions were overturned as too severe (Luongo, 2011). In 1933, a reference to that case was included in a report in the *New York Times* from the Associated Press entitled "71 Africans convicted in killing of 2 'witches.'"

> A mass "witchcraft" trial in which all of the seventy-five male inhabitants of an isolated Tanganyika village were involved resulted today in the conviction of seventy-one [of the men] as assailants of two women as witches. Sentences ranging from six months imprisonment upward were imposed. The original charge of manslaughter was reduced to one of rioting (*New York Times*, 17 September 1933).

The men were convicted of attacking and killing two women of the village, a mother and daughter who were suspected of witchcraft. The article notes colonial concern over the matter, pointing out that "The witchcraft superstition constitutes one of the most acute problems of the white administration in these sections" (*New York Times*, 17 September 1933). What is most notable to the historian, however, is the relative impotence of the colonial government. The attempt to take a hard line against witch hunts in Kenya and Tanzania was met with resistance not only from the

Indigenous people but also from the central authorities who mitigated the death sentences in the Wakamba case. The *New York Times* article quoted above makes the weakening of the charges clear. The second witch lynching was treated as a form of riot rather than as the more serious crime of homicide. Given the struggles of colonial governments in Africa to establish any semblance of the territorial control habitual for European governments, this shift in focus reflects a *real politik* adjustment on the part of colonial administrators (Luongo, 2011). Today, deadly witch trials are still conducted in Tanzania by local Sungusungu groups largely independent of state authority (see Multimedia Suggestions at the end of the chapter).

The early and consistent efforts of European colonizers in Africa to impede local witch hunts had profound unintended consequences. Some resistance movements in Africa gained political power by responding to the local demand for witch hunts. In southern Africa, both the Zimbabwe African National Union (ZANU) and the African National Congress (ANC) were deeply implicated in extrajudicial attacks on witches as anti-colonial movements became entangled with witch hunting (Behringer, 2004). In many ways, the apartheid rule in South Africa after 1948 was an extension of colonialism, and we can only speak of a postcolonial South African experience after 1994. Based on the South African experience, we can observe a late-colonial pattern of witch hunting in which a radical branch of the Liberation Party, in this case the youth arm of the ANC, began to perform the service of witch-finding as part of its grassroots community work. When the end of apartheid came in 1994, the entanglement of the ANC in rural witch hunts became something of an international embarrassment, and the overt involvement of the party was brought to an end (Behringer, 2004).

In the early post-apartheid moment, a substantial report on witchcraft beliefs, witch hunting, and witchcraft policy was commissioned by the Republic of South Africa and carried out by South African university academics, spearheaded by Victor Ralushai, professor of social anthropology at the University of Venda, one of the northern provinces particularly afflicted by witch lynchings in the 1980s and 1990s. The Ralushai report noted the significant impact of a more unified centralized response against witch lynchings in promoting a decline in the severity and frequency of incidents thereafter. It went on to argue for a novel, multi-pronged approach to the witchcraft problem. The report demonstrated at length the centrality of witchcraft beliefs to South Africans of all social stations. It argued that the belief in witchcraft was a marker of African identity and that the European laws of the colonial era should be replaced with traditional African methods of proving the guilt of suspected witches by admitting witch doctors and spirit mediums into court (Behringer, 2004).

This embrace of witchcraft prosecution has found root in a variety of postcolonial juridical settings. The Central African Republic has been widely criticized in the early 21st-century press for imprisoning witchcraft suspects. A video article on Al Jazeera's *People and Power* in 2010 (see Multimedia Suggestions) demonstrated the potential humanity and even progressive potential of that system but simultaneously confirmed the truth of Ralushai's claim about the near-ubiquity of the witchcraft belief among the African elite. The emergence of reports in 2015 that rebels in the country had conducted quasi-judicial witch trials and witch burnings is saddening but hardly surprising (Esslemont, 2015).

Postcolonial governments and scholars in Africa are clearly grappling with the complexity of the witchcraft issue. Some of the African churches, however, have taken on a terrifying new role in the persecution of witchcraft, promoting a Pentecostal witch hunt. Champions of a dark, diabolic, and distinctly Christian reading of the long-standing African witch fear have emerged, particularly within

Call to Action

Resisting persecution is a deeply individual responsibility. You can participate by thinking like a citizen; this means distrusting fearmongering and watching for signs of persecution and moral panic within your local institutions. It is important to speak up by demanding prosecutorial accountability and counteracting rhetorical prejudice by demanding tolerance. Persecution happens in myriad ways and on the microscale—act locally to fight prejudice based on any aspect of collective identity. Share good knowledge, and pass on the wise and the good. Lastly, fight for academic open access to counterbalance the free availability of early modern demonology online.

the Zionist churches in Africa (Behringer, 2004). These churches, inspired by but distinct from the Anglo-American Pentecostal movement, embrace the mystical, experiential, and supernatural within their worship and practice in a manner that breaks radically with the post-miraculous, Enlightened mainstream Protestant churches. Within the Zionist movement, charismatic ministers have forced the African belief in involuntary, inborn witchcraft into a Christian mold, arguing that fussy, disobedient, or sickly children may be carrying a devil about in the stomach. Widespread reports have emerged from Nigeria in particular of children attacked by their own parents and forced to drink acid or gasoline in an effort to drive the demons out. Ironically, those children who survive the attack and flee their families often take refuge at the churches that had (broadly) denounced them. Those churches, in turn, proclaim themselves to be rescuers of the children, saying that they rehabilitate the afflicted children through confession and gentler forms of exorcism (see *The Guardian*, "Children are targets," in Multimedia Suggestions).

To what degree can we read witchcraft persecutions in contemporary Africa as a postcolonial process? The Pentecostal witch hunts grapple with both colonial and precolonial cultural heritage in distinctly postcolonial conditions. One historian of African witchcraft has noted its modernity in its utility within the postcolonial interstitial, between and within the structural elements of modernity (Geschiere, 1997). The fear and violence against suspected witches in Africa today is a problem for African states to resolve. The intellectual grappling of the African elite with the reality of witchcraft and the importance of witchcraft beliefs to African identity is a crucial part of this. The colonial experience of European missionizing and denigration of African cultures drives a wedge between the European experience of ending their witch hunts during the Enlightenment and Africans working for justice in their societies today.

Tying It Together

A witch hunt is a social crisis of the first order riding a perfect storm of conditions: a collective persecution of people identified with a socially constructed fear object, unfolding in both institutional and popular contexts, driven by large-scale social stress, and activated by personal enmity. When the term "witch hunt" is thrown into public debate, it is useful to parse the term and identify the particular element of witch hunting at play. Is a social process of demonization taking place? Are social institutions being instrumentalized in individual or collective attacks? Is a sense of moral panic growing under the influence of a rumour regime? All of these are socially dangerous and rightfully draw the attention of public intellectuals and cultural critics. Analytically, however, each is only one part of the major conjunction of conditions that can create a full-blown witch hunt. The danger of overusing the term "witch hunt" to describe all persecutory processes is simply the danger of forgetting the true horrors of the full-blown witch hunt that can result from such processes unchecked.

DISCUSSION QUESTIONS

1. How does moral panic erode judicial safeguards? How can judicial safeguards protect against witch hunting?
2. How do stereotypes contribute to persecution? How might we fight prejudicial stereotyping?
3. What are the differences between early modern and postcolonial witch hunts? What do they have in common?
4. What is the relationship between persecution and deep drivers? How might the mitigation of deep drivers reduce prejudicial action?
5. What are the key analytical conclusions of historical scholars on the witch hunts? What light can these conclusions offer on postcolonial persecutory processes?

SUGGESTIONS FOR FURTHER READING

Behringer, Wolfgang. (2004). *Witches and witch-hunts: A global history.* Cambridge, UK: Polity Press. This book examines the history of European witchcraft and focuses on other societies where witch hunts continue to pose a major problem.

Goode, Erich, & Ben-Yehuda, Nachman. (2009). *Moral panics: The social construction of deviance.* Hoboken, NJ: Wiley-Blackwell. This book explores the genesis and dynamics of moral panics and their impacts on society.

Johnson, David K. (2004). *The Lavender Scare: The Cold War persecution of gays and lesbians in the federal government.* Chicago, IL: University of Chicago Press. This book details the repression of homosexuals in the American federal government during the McCarthy era, which ended the careers and ruined the lives of many government employees.

Geschiere, Peter. (1997). *The modernity of witchcraft: Politics and the occult in postcolonial Africa.* Charlottesville, VA: University of Virginia Press. This book explores the continued prevalence of witchcraft in African societies and its entanglement with the introduction of modern Western techniques and commodities.

MULTIMEDIA SUGGESTIONS

The Malleus Maleficarum of Heinrich Kramer & James Sprenger
http://www.malleusmaleficarum.org
This website contains a digitized version of the *Malleus maleficarium* (*The hammer of witches*), one of the most well-known medieval treatises on witchcraft.

Salem witch trials
http://salem.lib.virginia.edu/home.html
This online resource contains transcriptions of original court and personal records, as well as historical maps, from the Salem witch trials in colonial Massachusetts.

Project Gutenberg: Witchcraft (Bookshelf)
http://www.gutenberg.org/wiki/Witchcraft_
    %28Bookshelf%29
This webpage contains links to a selection of books
on the history of witchcraft as well as contemporary
accounts of witch trials. The books are digitized for
free public access.

**Al Jazeera, *People and Power*, Central African
    Republic: Witch trials**
https://youtube/3fut6NfOyZg
This investigation by *Al Jazeera English* examines
witchcraft trials in the Central African Republic.

Unreported World, Tanzania's witch hunt
https://youtube/e3RvEaUeBuk
Witches and the motivations behind witchcraft trials
in Tanzania are investigated in this short report.

***The Guardian*, Children are targets of Nigerian
    witch hunt**
https://www.theguardian.com/world/2007/dec/09/
    tracymcveigh.theobserver
Reportage on the persecution of children as witches
in Nigeria and the role of evangelical pastors in promoting the witch hunt.

REFERENCES

Beacock, Ian P. (2018). *Heartbroken: Democratic emotions,
    political subjectivity, and the unravelling of the Weimar
    Republic, 1918–1933*. PhD dissertation, Stanford
    University.

Behringer, Wolfgang (Ed.). (1995). *Hexen und hexenproz-
    esse in Deutschland*. Munich, Germany: Deutscher
    Taschenbuch Verlag.

Behringer, Wolfgang. (2004). *Witches and witch-hunts.
    A global history*. Cambridge, UK: Polity Press.

Cheit, Ross E. (2016). *The witch-hunt narrative: Politics,
    psychology, and the sexual abuse of children*. Oxford,
    UK: Oxford University Press.

Cohen, Jeffrey Jerome (Ed.). (2000). *The postcolonial Middle
    Ages*. London, UK: Palgrave.

Cohen, Stanley. (2002). *Folk devils and moral panics*.
    Abingdon-on-Thames, UK: Routledge.

Cohn, Norman. (2001). *Europe's inner demons: The demoni-
    zation of Christians in medieval Christendom*. Chicago,
    IL: University of Chicago Press.

Dillinger, Johannes. (2009). *"Evil people": A compara-
    tive study of witch hunts in Swabian Austria and the
    Electorate of Trier*, trans. Laura Stokes. Charlottesville,
    VA: University of Virginia Press.

Dillinger, Johannes, Schmidt, Jürgen Michael, & Bauer,
    Dieter (Eds.). (2008). *Hexenprozess und staatsbildung:
    Witch-trials and state-building*. Gütersloh, Germany:
    Verlag für Regionalgeschichte.

Ehrenreich, Barbara, & English, Deirdre. (2010). *Witches,
    midwives, & nurses: a history of women healers*. New
    York, NY: Feminist Press.

Esslemont, Tom. (2015). Witch burning rebels stoke Central
    African Republic violence. Reuters, 25 November.
    https://www.reuters.com/article/us-centralafrica-
    witchcraft-idUSKBN0TF03920151126.

Geschiere, Peter. (1997). *The modernity of witchcraft: Politics
    and the occult in postcolonial Africa*. Charlottesville,
    VA: University of Virginia Press.

Goode, Erich, & Ben-Yehuda, Nachman. (2009). *Moral
    panics: The social construction of deviance*. Hoboken,
    NJ: Wiley-Blackwell, 2009.

Henningsen, Gutsav. (1980). *The witches' advocate: Basque
    witchcraft and the Spanish Inquisition (1609–1614)*.
    Reno, NE: University of Nevada Press.

Herzig, Tamar. (2013) *'Christ Transformed into a Virgin
    Woman': Lucia Brocadelli, Heinrich Institoris, and
    the Defense of the Faith*. Rome: Edizioni di Storia e
    Letteratura.

Jäggi, Stefan. (2002). Luzerner Verfahren wegen Zauberei
    und Hexerei bis zur Mitte des 16. Jahrhunderts.
    Schweizerische Zeitschrift für Geschichte, 52(2), 143–50.

Johnson, David K. (2004). *The Lavender Scare: The Cold
    War persecution of gays and lesbians in the federal gov-
    ernment*. Chicago, IL: University of Chicago Press.

Kors, Alan Charles, & Peters, Edward (Eds). (2000).
    Witchcraft in Europe, 400–1700: A documentary history.
    Philadelphia, PA: University of Pennsylvania Press.

Luongo, Katherine. (2011). *Witchcraft and colonial rule
    in Kenya, 1900–1955*. Cambridge, UK: Cambridge
    University Press.

MacFarlane, Alan. (1999). *Witches in Tudor and Stuart
    England: A regional and comparative study*. Abingdon-
    on-Thames, UK: Routledge.

Mavhungu, Khaukanani. (2012). *Witchcraft in post-colonial
    Africa: Beliefs, techniques, and containment strategies*.
    Langaa RPCIG.

Muchembled, Robert. (1985). *Popular culture and elite
    culture in France, 1400–1750*, trans. Lydia Cochrane.
    Baton Rouge, LA: Louisiana State University Press.

Reddy, William M. (2001). *The navigation of feeling: A framework for the history of emotions.* Cambridge, UK: Cambridge University Press.

Schmidt, Jürgen Michael. (2000). *Glaube und skepsis: Die kurpfalz und die abendländische hexenverfolgung 1446–1685.* Gütersloh, Germany: Verlag für Regionalgeschichte.

Soman, Alfred. (1985). La décriminalisation de la sorcellerie en France. *Histoire, économie, et société, 2*(part 2), 179–203.

Spee, Friedrich von Langenfeld. (2003). *Cautio criminalis, or a book on witch trials,* trans. Marcus Hellyer. Charlottesville, VA: University of Virginia Press.

Stokes, Laura. (2011). *Demons of urban reform: Early European witch trials and criminal justice.* London, UK: Palgrave Macmillan.

Thompson, Bill, & Williams, Andy. (2014). *The myth of moral panics: Sex, snuff, and Satan.* Abingdon-on-Thames, UK: Routledge.

United States FBI. (2007). *Guantanamo Bay Inquiry.* Washington, DC: FBI.

Victor, Jeffrey S. (1993). *Satanic panic: The creation of a contemporary legend.* Chicago, IL: Open Court.

CHAPTER 6

◇

The Historical Role of Christianity/ Theology in Colonialism and Its Continuing Influence on Racism, Gender, and Othering

Ruth A. Clowater

Learning Objectives

In this chapter, you will:

- learn how European empires and the Christian church of the West formed symbiotic relationships that legitimized the conquest of Indigenous peoples and the slave trade;
- recognize ways that historical religious doctrines, even when later rejected, continue to influence Western society today;
- consider ways that Christianity and civil society might work together toward a decolonized future.

Introduction

The invasion of the American continents by European empires was fueled by greed and the desire of competing monarchs to dominate lands and peoples worldwide. This centuries-long campaign of conquest and colonization was legitimized by the Christian church. The church participated in the theft of Indigenous lands and the cultural genocide of Indigenous civilizations (King, 2013; Tinker, 1993), at times even playing a central role. Together, explorers, soldiers, settlers, and missionaries established a colonial system that even today continues to reverberate in society and in systems of civil governance.

This chapter examines some of the ways that the Western church participated in the conquest of the Americas and the religious doctrines that validated a patriarchal ordering of society modelled after European culture. Select instances of conflicts between immigrant settlers and Indigenous nations—past and present—illustrate ways that structural colonialism continues to infringe upon Indigenous rights. Until recently, church doctrine also served to perpetuate chattel slavery and segregation.

Others—any person or group of people who do not conform to the "normative" standard of Eurocentric heterosexual masculinity—have also suffered under the weight of patriarchal hegemony, both in the church and in society.

The Church of the Colonized

Ancient Israel, at various times throughout its history, had been colonized by Egyptians, Assyrians, Persians, Babylonians, Greeks, and Romans. It is from within these contexts of colonization that the ancient writings considered sacred by both Judaism and Christianity emerged. During the Roman occupation of Israel, a Jewish religious sect was founded by a rabbi named Jesus who, at least for his followers, breathed hope into what appeared to have been a hopeless situation. Jesus taught a counter-cultural alternative to oppressive political and religious regimes, frequently contrasting them to the "kingdom" (empire) of God, where those who had been marginalized would be given seats of honour at God's table (Luke 14:12–14). The message resonated among the poor and oppressed masses but threatened the Jewish leadership, so at the behest of the religious elite, the Romans executed Jesus (Mark 13:53–72).

The Jesus movement did not dissipate, and within a few centuries, Christianity had become a mainstream religious and political force. How that transpired is uncertain, but sociologist Rodney Stark presents a plausible theory that early Christians would have heeded the call to love the neighbour (Mark 12:31) and care for the sick (Luke 9:2) so that when plagues struck in ancient Rome, their works of compassion would save lives and gain converts (1997, pp. 55, 86). Additionally, as Roman subjects, early Christians could travel throughout the expansive Roman Empire, which offered opportunities for dissemination of their beliefs. Christianity was not initially perceived as a threat, but relationships with Roman authorities became strained because of the Christians'

refusal to participate in the imperial cult (emperor worship), and they were periodically subjected to waves of persecution (Jones, 1979, pp. 41–2).

When Constantine I became emperor, he legitimized Christianity and "issued an edict urging his pagan subjects to . . . adopt the Christian faith" (Jones, 1979, p. 43). Constantine was baptized before he died in 337 and was buried in the Church of the Holy Apostles in Constantinople. After his death, and despite previous refusals to worship emperors on religious grounds, Christians began to offer "sacrifice, prayer, and incense" to his statue (Jones, 1979, p. 44). Thanks to Constantine, Christianity had become the religion of the empire, so they accorded to him in death the very honour that they had refused to show his predecessors based on their **monotheistic** religious principles.

The Imperial Church

From Constantine forward, European kingdoms and the Western church formed a symbiotic relationship that worked to increase the status, power, and wealth of both. The church sought to consolidate power and expand its territories alongside the European monarchies as Roman Catholic pontiffs transformed Euro-Christian expansionism into a divine enterprise.

Christians place considerable reliance on the teachings of the Bible. Thus, for Christian empires to justify military conquest, they turned to Scripture. They found legitimization through a process of *eisegesis* (inserting meaning into texts) rather than *exegesis* (extracting meaning from texts), with the result being very flawed *hermeneutics* (interpretation). Eisegesis gave the church doctrines that, over the course of a thousand years, justified colonialism. Instead of following the biblical commandment taught by Jesus to "love your neighbour as yourself" (Matt. 22:39, New Revised Standard Version, Anglicized)—a command never limited by race, social class, religious affiliation, geography, gender, or any other condition that might have limited its scope—the church became an agent for the conquest and genocide of Indigenous peoples worldwide.

The Church's Complicity in the Conquest of the Americas

Diversity in biblical interpretation is common among Christians, but those interpretations become **heresy** when central teachings are violated: when eisegesis is substituted for exegesis in order to extract a false doctrine that conflicts with the overarching theme of the Bible.

Three heresies in particular were influential in perpetuating 500-plus years of conquest, subjugation, and Othering: the Doctrine of Discovery, the heresy that directly legitimized both the conquest of the Americas and the transatlantic slave trade; the Curse of Ham, which allowed white Christians to justify slavery and racial segregation; and Complementarianism, the doctrine that subordinates women to male authority, based upon the presumption, reinforced by centuries of Western Eurocentric Christianity, that a masculine God had ordained a patriarchal ordering of society.

The Doctrine of Discovery

What became known as the Doctrine of Discovery would set the stage for the colonizing activities that gathered steam after Columbus made his famous 1492 voyage. The origins of this doctrine lie in a series of papal pronouncements known as "bulls." In 1095, Pope Urban II issued *Terra Nullius* ("empty land"), which declared that any lands not already under the dominion of Christian empires were without legitimate owner. In 1455, Pope Nicholas V issued *Romanus Pontifex*, which authorized Portugal to buy and sell Africans while pre-emptively granting "remission of

sins to kings, all participants, and those who furnished money or troops" (Mumford, 2016, p. 32). In 1493, Pope Alexander VI declared that "barbarous nations be overthrown and brought to the faith" (*Inter Caetera*).

The popes perceived themselves as the supreme authority over both the celestial and earthly realms, with the power to "give and take kingdoms to whomsoever [they] pleased" (Mumford, 2016, pp. 32–3). Not all monarchies—England, for example—submitted to papal authority, but they all presumed European cultural superiority and embraced this same premise of discovery because it legitimized their own desires to explore and conquer the world (Mumford, 2016). Indeed, during his second voyage in 1493, Columbus landed on the Caribbean island of Borikén. Since *Terra Nullius* had established the land as "empty"—despite it already being the home of the Taíno—Columbus claimed the island for the Spanish Crown and renamed it San Juan Bautista (Saint John the Baptist). Within a short span of 50 years, the Taíno had all but disappeared, powerless as they were against the military might and deadly diseases the Europeans brought with them. By the year 1530, barely 1000 of the Taíno had survived. Gone were the culture, the language, and the people. Thus began centuries of colonial occupation of Borikén, now known as Puerto Rico, which today is a "protectorate" of the United States of America (Yale University Genocide Studies Program, 1970).

Church Participation in the Theft of Indigenous Lands

The Doctrine of Discovery established the legal basis for land ownership in the colonial era, and it continues to define ownership rights even today. In 1823, the US Supreme Court recognized Indigenous nations as "rightful occupants of the soil," but because they were no longer sovereign nations, they could not "dispose of the soil at their own will," based upon "the original fundamental principle, that discovery gave exclusive title" to the colonizer (*Johnson v. M'Intosh, 1823*). Indigenous author Thomas King summarizes the situation:

> Indians were reduced to the status of children and declared wards of the state . . . all Indian land within America now belonged to the federal government. While these rulings had legal standing only in the United States, Canada would formalize an identical relationship with Native people . . . with the passage of the Indian Act. Now it was official. Indians in all of North America were property (King, 2013, p. 81).

In South America, laws originating with colonial rule continue to trample upon Indigenous nations. The Huaorani (Waorani), a people indigenous to the Amazon rainforest, continue to fight for survival, even though they, along with other Indigenous peoples, had gained political recognition and limited autonomy in 1990. Despite this, the Ecuadoran government retains control over the subsoil and permits mining and petroleum exploration to continue (Schertow, 2007). Meanwhile, in Brazil, more than 300 Indigenous nations, including the Yanomami and Guaraní, are in their own fight for survival as Brazilian president Jair Bolsonaro walks back hard-won protections in his plan to "integrate" Indigenous people into Brazilian society, claiming as well that they control a disproportionate share of the land (BBC News, 2019).

Struggles for survival against neo-colonial oppression are also plentiful in North America. In British Columbia, for instance, "about 50 ongoing negotiations of Crown-Aboriginal treaties" have yet to be resolved, since "the vast majority of land" has never been ceded (Hall, 2013, p. 45). In New Brunswick, the Elsipogtog First Nation (Mi'kmaq) has garnered media attention for its protests against oil and gas exploration through hydraulic fracturing, or fracking. Even though the Canadian Supreme Court ruled that the "Peace and Friendship Treaties of 1760–1761" did not result in acquisition of land by the Crown and that

the Mi'kmaq "never gave up legal rights to their land" (Vowel, 2013, para. 7), the Canadian government contradicts this by claiming ownership of the natural resources underneath the surface.

Laws recognizing Indigenous rights do exist, but they often contain restrictions that give settler governments the final say by way of built-in loopholes. While the Supreme Court of Canada had ruled that the Indigenous peoples had never ceded much of the land known as British Columbia, and while it had also ruled that the Mi'kmaq had also never ceded their land in New Brunswick, this same court also determined that Parliament has "no duty to consult" before passing laws, even when those laws directly impact Indigenous peoples on their own land (*Mikisew Cree First Nation v. Canada* [2018] SCC 40).

The scenario repeats throughout the Americas. The Rama Nation, an Indigenous community in Nicaragua, risks losing a vast tropical rainforest that they have protected for centuries to *mestizo* invaders. They are also threatened by a canal project that includes a railway and an oil pipeline, violating their constitutional right to autonomy and "the mineral, forest, fishing, and other natural resources" of their communal lands (Autonomy Statute for the Regions of the Atlantic Coast of Nicaragua [Law 28, Title I, Chapter II, Art. 9, 7 Sept. 1987]). Similarly, in the US a dispute over the Dakota Access Pipeline pits Lakota Sioux against big oil, violating terms of treaties with the US government (Uenuma & Fritz, 2011). As do the struggles of the Indigenous nations in Canada, the situation with the Rama and the Sioux illustrates long-standing, present-day conflicts between settler governments and the Indigenous nations that persist in demanding the right to self-determination.

Encroachment into the Rainforest of the Rama Nation (Nicaragua)

The Rama Nation collectively owns and inhabits much of the southern Caribbean coast of Nicaragua. In 1849, Moravian missionaries arrived in Nicaragua, initially to work with the Miskitu, later extending their influence to the Rama (Board of World Mission of the Moravian Church, n.d., para. 1). Their arrival initiated:

> a large-scale decline of the Rama language, as it became replaced by Creole English. The profound cultural and psychological changes that accompanied acculturation at the hands of the missionaries are hard to imagine. Among the changes . . . were the acquisition of a negative ethnic identity. . . . In the process of conversion the Rama were made to perceive their previous state as filthy and wild (Mueller, 2002, p. 19).

The Moravian encroachment into Indigenous life mirrors the Euro-Christian evangelization in North America that began centuries earlier. In New England, between 1645 and 1675, Puritan minister John Eliot established "praying towns" that became "halfway houses for Indians" (King, 2013, p. 105). Meanwhile in Mexico, and later in California, the Spanish mission system, led by Jesuit missionary Junípero Serra, supervised "forced conversions of native peoples to Christianity and the enforcement of those conversions by imprisonment; physical violence in the form of corporal punishment; the imposition of slave labor conditions . . . [and] a living environment that was akin to a concentration camp" (Tinker, 1993, p. 42).

For the autonomous regions along the Caribbean coast of Nicaragua, the effects of colonization were minimal until President José Santos Zelaya formally "incorporated" the Caribbean territories after the British left in 1894 (Mueller, 2002, p. 21). Even then, the remoteness of the Indigenous regions helped to insulate them until civil war broke out in the 1970s. When the revolutionary Sandinistas attempted to nationalize Indigenous lands and relocate the inhabitants into settlement camps, they took up arms, since "the Indian without his land is not an Indian" (Hilario McCrea John, personal communication, 2010).

As part of a cease-fire agreement, the Indigenous nations were promised:

> The right to preserve and develop their cultural identities within the national unity, to provide themselves with their own forms of social organization, and to administer their local affairs according to their traditions . . . communal forms of land ownership . . . [and] their enjoyment, use and benefit of the waters and forests of their communal lands (Nicaragua's Constitution of 1987 with Amendments through 2005, 2018, p. 18).

Nonetheless, *mestizo* farmers steadily encroach into Rama territory, razing to the ground what had been pristine rainforest and claiming title to the land. This is more than theft; it is an affront to Rama culture: "we never go into the jungle and think, 'let's cut this all down.' Too many other people think that way, though, and they invade our lands, even today. That is why the rainforest is disappearing" (John, personal communication, 2014). The once-colonized *mestizo* seeks to become the neo-colonizer of Indigenous peoples who have inhabited the land long before Nicaragua ever became a country.

In 2014, a Hong Kong–based company broke ground on its *Gran Canal* project, an intercoastal waterway that, if completed, would be wider, deeper, and four times longer than the Panama Canal (Construction of Nicaragua canal threatens Indigenous lives and livelihoods, 2015). The canal would cut a wide swath through the entire country and destroy Rama communities, including Bankukuk Taik, the last village where the native Rama language is still spoken.

Lakota Sioux and the Black Hills (US) Land Dispute, 1876–Present

Episcopalian bishop Henry Benjamin Whipple, whom the Sioux called "Straight Tongue" (Tinker, 1993, p. 96), correctly blamed the US government for "Indian retaliations and uprisings" (Tinker, 1993, p. 103), and yet he assumed that assimilation was the only adequate solution. In 1876, Whipple represented the US government as negotiator with the Sioux and successfully "engineered the U.S. government's theft of the Black Hills from the Sioux people" (Tinker, 1993, p. viii). This treaty superseded the Fort Laramie treaty of 1868, which had guaranteed the Sioux their own "undisputed territory . . . created in perpetuity and guarded from trespass by the U.S. military" (Jewell, 2006, p. 131). Nonetheless, once gold had been discovered in the Black Hills, the government quickly forced another treaty upon them, and the Sioux lost nearly 90 per cent of their territory (Jewell, 2006, p. 133).

The Sioux Nation had been forced to sign the 1876 treaty under duress, and it was never approved by the required 75 per cent majority. The Sioux mounted a legal challenge, and more than 100 years later the US Supreme Court ruled in their favour, agreeing that "the land . . . had been taken from them wrongfully" (Uenuma & Fritz, 2011, para. 5). Instead of returning the land to its rightful owners, though, the court awarded the Sioux $102 million as compensation (Uenuma & Fritz, 2011). To date, the nation has refused to accept the settlement; the Sioux want the land back.

The 1868 Fort Laramie treaty also forms the basis of Lakota Sioux opposition to the Dakota Access Pipeline project north of the Standing Rock Sioux Reservation. The pipeline passes under the Missouri River, threatening the only source of drinking water for the reservation (Standing Rock Sioux Tribe, n.d.). The Sioux, joined by diverse Indigenous, environmental, and religious groups, have been protesting the pipeline's construction, demanding that treaty rights be honoured. Their resistance has been met with rubber bullets, water cannons, tear gas, and mass arrests (Barajas, 2016).

Protests against the Dakota Access Pipeline, including the protest camp at Standing Rock, have been a major undertaking led by Lakota Sioux in partnership with other Indigenous, environmental, and religious groups.

Church-Run Indian Schools

Religious heresy had legitimized the theft of Indigenous lands. Once in possession of the land, a fear of religious **syncretism**—a corruption of the Christian religion through assimilation of Indigenous religious practices—motivated colonizer churches to endorse the genocide of Indigenous cultures. Indigenous theologian George E. Tinker, a member of the Osage Nation, writes that the Christian missionaries who accompanied imperial soldiers "not only preached a new gospel of salvation, but also just as energetically imposed a new cultural model for existence on Indian people," having themselves confused the salvation that they preached with "the accoutrements of the missionary's cultural experience" (Tinker, 1993, p. 4).

Perhaps the most tragic attempt to impose a new cultural model, one in which churches of many denominations actively participated, was the residential school system. Indigenous children were forcibly sent to boarding schools, an environment resembling "either a military camp or a prison" (King, 2013, p. 111), where they were taught to speak, dress, and worship like the Europeans and where Indigenous languages and customs were forbidden.

In Canada, more than 150,000 children were sent to residential schools, and the last school did not close until 1996 (Madden, 2015). Even though there were warning signs early on, as evidenced by a 1907 report citing child mortality rates at the residential schools of 30 per cent in British Columbia and 50 per cent in Alberta, this did not sway Canada's Department of Indian Affairs; the deaths did not "justify a change in the policy . . . which [was] geared towards the final solution of our Indian Problem" (King, 2013, p. 114).

The trauma inflicted on Indigenous families by the residential school system continues to reverberate (the effects of historic trauma are further explored in Chapter 2). "Our young were stolen from us and sent to residential schools, day schools, and child welfare, and are now placed within an education system that . . . refuses to acknowledge our culture, our knowledge, our histories, and our Indigenous experience," laments Leanne Simpson of the Nishnaabeg Nation in Ontario (2013, pp. 51–2). This sentiment is echoed by Indigenous journalist Mary Annette Pember (Red Cliff Band Ojibwe), who had attended a residential school run by Roman Catholic nuns where the children were taught "Indian racial, cultural and spiritual inferiority" (2016, p. 6). Pember contends that the residential school experience induced a mass "intergenerational trauma" that factors into the "high rates of addiction, suicide, mental illness, sexual violence and other ills" (2016, pp. 3–4) that plague Indigenous families today.

The Curse of Ham and White Supremacy

As a principal leader of the civil rights movement in the US, Martin Luther King, Jr, once observed, "our nation was born in genocide when it embraced the doctrine that the original American, the Indian was an inferior race" (King, 1964/2010, p. 141). Conquest and genocide found legitimacy in the Doctrine of Discovery heresy, but chattel slavery and racism against all peoples of colour were justified by the Curse of Ham.

The Curse of Ham is rooted in the Old Testament story of Noah, twisted to bolster a non-biblical tradition that identifies Noah's son Ham as the ancestor of all Black people. After the great flood, Noah got drunk and "lay uncovered in his tent" (Gen. 9:21). Noah's son Ham "saw the nakedness of his father, and told his two brothers outside," so the brothers "covered the nakedness of their father" (Gen. 9:22–23). Once Noah discovered what Ham had done—which is not stated in the text—he cursed Canaan, Ham's *son*: "lowest of slaves shall he be to his brothers" (Gen. 9:25). Since Ham was the presumed

Ida B. Wells

One of the first African Americans who dared to publicly decry the lynching scourge was a woman, Ida B. Wells. Born into slavery, Wells obtained a college education and became editor of a Black newspaper called *The Free Speech*. She penned "a series of blistering editorials . . . and a stream of pamphlets and speeches [that she] delivered around the country" (Cone, 2011, Chapter 5, para. 19). In her autobiography, Wells remarked on the irony that "American Christians are too busy saving the souls of white Christians from burning in hell-fire to save the lives of Black ones from present burning in fires kindled by white Christians" (Sims, 2009, p. 82). Wells was a civil rights pioneer whose contributions were pivotal: regarding Wells's anti-lynching campaign, Frederick Douglass wrote that there was "no word equal to it in convincing power" (Douglass, 1892/2014, p. 5).

Flickr commons (identifier: storyofillinoisf00davi). E. Davis, (1922), *The story of the Illinois Federation of Colored Women's Clubs*, p. 73, Chicago: University of Illinois Press. https://www.flickr.com/photos/internetarchivebookimages/14579286127
Ida B. Wells.

ancestor of all Black people, then logically, all Blacks would be under the curse. Of course, Noah never cursed Ham (and even if he did, so what?). However, the Curse of Ham fit nicely into the narrative of white supremacy being part of God's plan. Obviously, this conclusion required a considerable amount of eisegesis, distorting Scripture almost beyond recognition, but white people allowed themselves to believe it because it reinforced their position of privilege and it justified the slave trade from which many of them benefitted economically.

Curse of Ham and the Lynching Era (1880–1940)

Slavery was eventually abolished across the Americas. In Canada, as well as in other British territories, the Act for the Abolition of Slavery took effect in 1834 by royal decree (Henry, 2014) and in the US, slavery was abolished under the Thirteenth Amendment to the US Constitution (Proclamation of the Secretary of State, 1865). Brazil brought up the rear and abolished slavery in 1888, the last country in the Americas to do so (Carvalhaes, 2017).

However, abolition did not change the minds of Christians who embraced the Curse of Ham. Slavery was followed by another dark period known as the "lynching era." Widely regarded as the founder of Black liberation theology, James H. Cone contends that between 1880 and 1940 "white Christians lynched nearly five thousand Black men and women in a manner with obvious echoes of the Roman crucifixion of Jesus" (Cone, 2011, Chapter 2, para. 1).

The Legacy of the Curse of Ham

Just as the Doctrine of Discovery had placed its seal of approval on conquest and genocide, the Curse of Ham justified the oppression of people of colour. With 21st-century hindsight, it is easy to see how the white Euro-descended colonizer, convinced of his "divine" cultural and religious superiority, would have embraced the Curse of Ham. The church has since, for the most part, admitted to the heresy of this doctrine, and settler governments have overturned laws that once discriminated based upon ethnicity, but white privilege continues, and activist groups have taken up the white supremacist banner. The 2017 "Unite the Right" rally held in Charlottesville, Virginia, a "coming-out party for an emboldened white nationalist movement" (Lind, para. 1), was just one such public display of nationalistic racism that, until recently, had mostly stayed in the shadows. The church is not responsible for these 21st-century hate groups, but it should admit to the role it has historically played in perpetuating them.

The Complementarian Movement and the Subordination of Women

In the aptly titled *Making war and minting Christians: Masculinity, religion, and colonialism in early New England*, historian R. Todd Romero (2011) writes that because belief in a masculine God was ingrained in European society and therefore

carried to the New World, "manliness remained an important measure of the success of missionary efforts and colonization. . . . It was necessary for the English to '*make* men' of the Indians before they could *make* them Christians" (Romero, 2011, p. 74). A "proper patriarchal ordering of society" would, by extension, "liberate Native women from the tyranny of . . . failed patriarchs, who embodied the antithesis of Christian manhood" (Romero, 2011, p. 83). This "could only benefit Native American women, who would then rise . . . to enjoy the status of Puritan" women (Romero, 2011, p. 75).

As with the other two heresies discussed previously, subjugation of women is rooted in a presupposition that Euro-cultural masculinity is the "divine" standard by which church and society are properly ordered. For a woman, her calling is to submit to the authority of her husband in the home and the male leadership of her church. One modern incarnation of this religious patriarchy is known as the Complementarian movement. The doctrine of Complementarianism is reactionary—its purpose is to help the church "defend against . . . evangelical feminism . . . a significant departure from what the church had practiced from its beginning [and which] reaches ultimately to the heart of the gospel" (CBMW, n.d., para. 4).

Survival of the church (and the God it represents) is contingent on perpetuating patriarchy, according to Complementarian logic. "The Bible is being undermined and the *very words of God*" corrupted when "in hundreds of places . . . the words *he, him, his, brother, father, son,* and *man*" are replaced by gender-inclusive vocabulary (CBMW, n.d., para. 9). This is eisegesis, since:

> The Greek word *anthropos* can refer to a male person. For example, "he saw a man [*anthropos*] called Matthew" (Matt. 9:9). . . . [However], it is also clear that in many contexts, and one might argue in *most* contexts, the word refers

to a *human being* . . . or, in the plural, to human beings. To continue to translate *anthropos* into masculine pronouns—at least where it is obvious that the translation is gender neutral—results in a *mistranslation* of the word *anthropos* (Throckmorton, 1985, p. 530).

Historical, Cultural, Literary, *and* Contemporary Contexts Matter

A rigid, legalistic application of the Bible leaves little room for contextualized interpretation. This completely ignores the long process of redaction of oral histories, the interpretive biases of diverse writers, the concrete historical settings in which individual books were written, the literary styles (historical narrative is not to be read as poetry and vice versa), the original languages, and the contexts in which the Bible is read today. An awareness of the complex origins of these writings ought to lead contemporary readers to be cautious with their hermeneutics. Readers also need to be mindful of their own social location. Do they read from positions of power—from a position of white privilege, for instance—or do they read from the margins? How might reading from alternate positions influence interpretation?

A cautionary tale that reflects how one's own culture can influence interpretation is found in a conflict that erupted among gentile (non-Jewish) churches of Galatia roughly 2000 years ago. Jewish-Christian missionaries felt compelled to impose religious patriarchy by insisting that converts adopt the cultural and religious norms of Judaism, including the practice of male circumcision. Paul of Tarsus wrote to the Galatian churches, urging them to reject this requirement, insisting that among them "there is no longer Jew or Greek [gentile], there is no longer slave or free, there is no longer male and female" (Gal. 3:28). Outsider Jewish missionaries had incorporated their own ethnocentric customs into their religious beliefs, based upon an unquestioned presumption of cultural superiority, and then they imposed them upon a non-Jewish people. The Bible does not reveal whether the Galatian churches ever recovered from the controversy, but the devastation that centuries of meddling by missionaries among the Indigenous nations in North America is well documented.

At times, the Israelites were the colonized and at other times the colonizer. Undeniably, in either context the ancient writings were shaped by patriarchal religion and society, and this is reflected in the language of the Bible. Even where patriarchy is not present in the original writings, it has been inserted through the translations of interpreters who also presumed patriarchy to be normative and therefore perpetuated it by inserting patriarchal language. One example is the word *diakonos* (διάκονος) or "deacon." In some Bible translations, a woman named Phoebe is correctly called a "deacon" (Rom. 16:1). The King James translates *diakonos* as "deacon" when referring to men (1 Tim. 3:12), yet *diakonos* is translated to "servant" when it refers to Phoebe.

Similarly, numerous references are made to *apostolos* (ἀπόστολος) or "apostle," a leader within the early church. Romans 16:7 mentions "Junia" (a woman's name) as an apostle. Biblical translators have resolved this perceived impossibility in assorted ways, sometimes by changing the name to a masculine form ("Junias") or by reworking the phrase so that she is not called an apostle. These matters may sound trivial, but to Christians who view the Bible as sacred literature, the impact can be significant.

European colonizers, with the active participation of the Christian church, forced themselves upon the Indigenous peoples of the Americas. Although not unanimously, the church overwhelmingly affirmed white privilege by embracing slavery and racial segregation. Many churches continue to perpetuate patriarchy by subordinating women to male authority, and they stand in judgment against LGBTQI+ individuals. Too often the church, especially when it insists on rigid dogma in defiance of evidence to the contrary, has been on the wrong side of history: Old Testament scholar Mark E. Biddle writes: "The Bible can be an instrument for evil in the hands of malevolent or even just careless interpreters" (2017, para. 11).

Looking to the Future

Corrective Hermeneutics for the Church from LGBTQI+ Theologians

Thus far in this chapter, the focus has been on the ways that colonial patriarchy in the form of Euro-masculine hegemony has marginalized Indigenous peoples, Africans and their descendants, and women. Others, particularly those who identify as non-binary or non-heterosexual, have only generally been mentioned. Rather than illustrate additional ways that Others have been excluded historically, the following are examples of alternative hermeneutics that might help the church to discover theologies of inclusion and liberate itself from its colonial-patriarchal underpinnings.

Simon Taylor, a Baptist pastor and student chaplain in the UK, challenges the notion that the "sanctity of marriage" is limited to a legal union between a heterosexual cisgender man and a heterosexual cisgender woman. Citing multiple biblical examples, Taylor observes that "marriage is one of the key ways that the Bible speaks about God's relationship to his people and creation" (Taylor, 2017, p. 44). Taylor reminds the church that God does not have a gender and that in the Bible, God "is referred to as both Mother and Father" (2017, p. 49). "Marriage points us to God and . . . is not a space for male domination of females" (p. 52).

According to theologian Phyllis Sheppard, womanist theologies apply a hermeneutical lens of "black experience and sources of knowledge, especially . . . of black women" to counteract the "destructiveness of whiteness [and] its power to render the status quo normal" (2016, pp. 153,

155). Sheppard reconciles her lesbian identity with her Christian faith by echoing the words of the apostle Paul: "Do not be conformed to the pattern of this world" (Rom. 12:2, New International Version). "God's patterns are many, varied, beautiful, and acceptable in all of their forms," she concludes (2016, pp. 163, 165).

Taylor and Sheppard provide just two examples of creative, biblically grounded hermeneutics that are inclusive and affirming to Others. Even though patriarchy was presumed by biblical writers, Others have read the biblical narrative with an interpretive lens that liberates; they see themselves as participants in the story. They present positive interpretations that restore, include, welcome, and affirm all peoples and that can help to point the church toward the kind of reciprocity that loving thy neighbour presumes.

A Call to Action for the Church

African scholar and theologian Musa Dube insists that "decolonization of inherited colonial educational systems, languages, literary canons, reading methods, and the Christian religion" are necessary to arrest the neo-colonial ideologies of both church and society (2002, p. 115). One decolonizing strategy, she asserts, is that "room . . . be made for reinterpreting the old, promoting the good, and imagining the new" (2002, p. 116). This would require a vision, commitment, and willingness to pay the price for past sins.

Decolonization of Western society demands an honest telling of Columbus's "discovery" and the centuries of devastation that followed. Public schools, funded by settler governments, continue to indoctrinate children on the Eurocentric myth of a New World, while cultural genocide, theft of land, and broken treaties remain obscure footnotes. It has never been in the self-interest of settler governments to tell their history with honesty, however, because that would contradict the heroic narrative they wish to promote, since it has been "a matter of national policy to wipe out its indigenous population" (King, 1964/2010, p. 141). Educators can still teach the truth, though, and demand that textbooks tell history from the perspectives of all participants.

Decolonization of Western Christianity also requires that the church renounce the heresy of patriarchy, rejecting the idolatry of maleness—that a masculine God has ordained a male-dominated church. Whether church denominational hierarchies will ever renounce this form of religious imperialism remains to be seen, but those who sit on the pews in those churches can demand change. The same is true with settler governments who fear the Indigenous challenge to their hegemony, failing to honour even treaties that are established law—people can change the government.

Decolonization of Western Christianity demands that the church honestly confront its participation in the conquest of the Americas. The syncretism of Euro-masculine patriarchy with religious doctrines led Christians to support the conquest and genocide of Indigenous peoples. In many respects, the church continues to perpetuate neo-colonialism through a patriarchal system that privileges male hegemony and subordinates or excludes Others. The church *can* return to its ancient roots as a church of the colonized; it

can advocate for the kind of justice, equality, and inclusion that Jesus taught.

Decolonization of both church and society calls for a decolonization of the mind. A call to decolonization can be found in Christianity's sacred book: "Do not be conformed to this world, but be transformed by the renewing of your minds, so that you may discern what is the will of God— what is good and acceptable and perfect" (Rom. 12:2). Laws already on the books, long fought for and hard won by Indigenous nations, call civil society to keep its contractual commitments. Wherever possible, stolen land should be returned to its rightful owners. For example, much of the Black Hills is public land—it could be returned.

The challenges of decolonization are daunting, but it is, for both the church and the civil societies of settler nations, "unfinished business" (Tinker, 1993, p. 5). Christian doctrine formed the basis for settler government claims to ownership of lands, so the church is "an essential component of decolonizing the myths and ideologies still undergirding the entire colonialist enterprise. Until all peoples grasp the intricate relationships binding colonialism, gender, and religion together, the dream of a genuinely new world order will remain only the shadow of an ideal" (Donaldson, 2002, p. 6).

Call to Action

Consider the calls to action for society on a broader scale listed in the chapter, and think about what you can do in your own life to embody these principles. Begin with a commitment to honour existing laws and treaties, minus the loopholes. Learn the rights and responsibilities outlined by whatever treaties that may cover the territory in which you live. Seek to undo damage wherever treaties have been violated by supporting the efforts of local Indigenous groups advocating for their own treaty rights, in whatever way they call for help. In your classes, question any history that is told through only the voice of the colonizer, and demand that the curriculum incorporate the voices and perspective of the colonized. If you attend a Christian church, organize informational sessions and invite Indigenous leaders to speak to your congregation.

Tying It Together

The aim of this chapter has been to illustrate ways that Christianity was complicit in the European conquest of the Americas. Invaders destroyed Indigenous civilizations, and the slave trade that followed was equally tragic. Since those dark days, civil laws have dismantled some aspects of racism and prejudice, but Indigenous peoples continue to be denied the right to self-determination. White supremacy continues to fester and breeds violence against ethnic minorities and Others. Women experience discrimination in the home, in the workplace, and in the church. While the Christian church is not solely responsible for all of this, it does share in the blame.

Christians, as well as adherents of other religions, would do well to embrace as fundamental doctrine a theology of inclusiveness in which all voices contribute to the global conversation regarding what it means to be human. The Taíno of Borikén were driven to the edge of extinction by Spanish conquistadores. The Rama lost their native language and much of their culture to foreign missionaries. Indigenous nations throughout the Americas continue to face threats by settler governments that refuse to comply with their own laws and respect treaties that were negotiated in good faith. All of this is antithetical to the "kingdom of God" that Jesus spoke of: a kingdom where the hidden, the forgotten, and the marginalized are welcomed (Luke 14:15–24).

DISCUSSION QUESTIONS

1. What are some ways that you might show solidarity with Indigenous nations such as the Elsipogtog of New Brunswick in their protests against fracking? For instance, you could contact legislators. What other ways might you confront your government's unwillingness to honour treaties with Indigenous nations? What do you think about the idea of returning stolen lands?

2. The struggles of the Huaorani in Ecuador, the Yanomami and Guaraní in Brazil, the Mi'kmaq in Canada, and the Lakota Sioux in the US are often characterized by mainstream media as protests against climate change, often overlooking treaty violations as the central issue. Do you think this characterization poses a danger to Indigenous demands that sovereignty of Indigenous nations be honoured? Do you see advantages to emphasizing environmental justice in this way?

3. List some of the ways that the church continues to perpetuate neo-colonialism, particularly as it intersects with civil society. What are ways this neo-colonialism is expressed in church relations with women or with LGBTQI+ communities?

4. Suggest some concrete, decolonizing steps that settler governments such as Canada and the US ought to take toward healing relations with Indigenous nations. One example would be for public schools to teach history from a perspective other than Eurocentric propaganda. What other steps might be taken? What are ways that you can be an agent for change in your own community?

5. Do you think that it is possible to depatriarchalize civil governments and society? What about religion? Why or why not? A spark can start a wildfire that can spread out of control, so what are ways *you* might spark a movement that moves society toward decolonization?

SUGGESTIONS FOR FURTHER READING

Cone, James H. (2011). *The cross and the lynching tree*. Maryknoll, NY: Orbis. This book presents a historical and theological critique of white Christianity from the perspective of the Black church in America and the role Black churches played in fighting racism and segregation in the United States.

King, Thomas. (2013). *The inconvenient Indian: A curious account of Native people in North America*. Minneapolis, MN: University of Minnesota Press. This book is a witty yet dark account of North American Indigenous history by an Indigenous scholar. King retells history in a way that highlights the cumulative effects of colonization on Native peoples, and he offers suggestions for ways to decolonization.

Tinker, George E. (1993). *Missionary conquest: The Gospel and Native American cultural genocide*. Minneapolis, MN: Fortress Press. This book provides an Indigenous perspective on the history of the Christian mission in the Americas with emphasis on how Christians attempted to impose European cultural norms on Indigenous people.

MULTIMEDIA SUGGESTIONS

"This land is for all of we" (2017: 19 minutes)
http://vimeo.com/109026969
This short film includes interviews with the Indigenous Rama people of the village of Bangkukuk about the impending construction of the Nicaragua Grand Canal. The government of Nicaragua approved the construction of a canal by a foreign company without first consulting the Indigenous peoples affected as required by national law and international conventions. The proposed canal would cut through thousands of acres of rainforest and displace many of the Indigenous Rama people.

Discovered? Or Stolen! Repudiating the Doctrine of Discovery" (2014: 6 minutes). United Church of Christ.
https://www.youtube.com/watch?time_continue=2&v=5nU9AtP9yJ8
In this video, Lakota Nation member Toni Buffalo discusses how the Doctrine of Discovery contributed to the destruction of the spirituality and culture of Native American peoples and the work of the United Church of Christ to reconcile wrongs done to Native Americans historically and today.

"Martin Luther King 'If I had sneezed'" [Excerpt from 3 April 1968 speech] (2016: 6 minutes)

https://www.youtube.com/watch?v=fgq61-owOG8
This recording is an excerpt from Martin Luther King, Jr's inspirational "mountain top" address. According to King, if he had sneezed after getting stabbed, he would have died of his injuries and would not have been around to participate in and see the results of many important events in the American civil rights movement.

"Why white evangelicals voted for Trump" (Mark Charles, 2016: 15 minutes)
https://www.youtube.com/watch?v=HKM1Fq5y7Qc
This video is an excerpt from a sermon given by Mark Charles of the Navajo Nation about why Donald Trump received 81 per cent of the white evangelical vote and 60 per cent of the white Catholic vote during the 2016 US presidential election.

Map of Indian residential schools of Canada by church denomination, Aboriginal Affairs and Northern Development Canada
http://www.aadnc-aandc.gc.ca/eng/1100100015606/1100100015611
This map displays the religious affiliation and locations of the 139 Indian residential schools in Canada recognized in the 2007 Indian Residential Schools Settlement Agreement.

REFERENCES

Autonomy statute for the regions of the Atlantic Coast of Nicaragua, Law 28. (1987) 7 September. *Centro de Asistencia Legal a Pueblos Indígenas*. Retrieved from: https://www.calpi-nicaragua.org/the-autonomy-statute-law-28.

Barajas, J. (2016). Police deploy water hoses, tear gas, against Standing Rock protestors. *PBS Newshour*, 21 November. Retrieved from: http://www.pbs.org/newshour/rundown/police-deploy-water-hoses-tear-gas-against-standing-rock-protesters.

BBC News (2019). Brazil's Indigenous people: "We fight for the right to exist." 25 April. Retrieved from: https://www.bbc.com/news/world-latin-america-48050717.

Biddle, M.E. (2017). Curse of Ham: An admonitory case-study in misreading scripture. 21 June. https://mark-biddle.com.

Board of World Mission of the Moravian Church. (n.d.). Moravian Church in Nicaragua. Retrieved from: http://moravianmission.org/partners/Nicaragua.

Carvalhaes, C. (2017). General introduction: Black religions in Brazil. *Crosscurrents*, 67(1), 6–14. doi: 10.1111/cros.12194.

Cone, J.H. (2011). *The cross and the lynching tree*. Maryknoll, NY: Orbis. Kindle Edition.

Construction of Nicaragua canal threatens Indigenous lives and livelihoods. (2015). *Cultural Survival*, 25 June. Retrieved from: https://www.culturalsurvival.org/publications/cultural-survival-quarterly/construction-nicaragua-canal-threatens-indigenous-lives.

CBMW (Council on Biblical Manhood and Womanhood). (n.d.). What's at stake? https://cbmw.org.

Donaldson, L. (2002). Introduction. In L. Donaldson & P. Kwok (Eds.), *Postcolonialism, feminism & religious discourse* (pp. 2–6). New York, NY: Routledge.

Douglass, Frederick (1892). In Wells, I.B. (2014). *Southern horrors: Lynch law in all its phases*. Union City, CA: Tembo Publishing (Original work published 1892, 1893, 1894).

Dube, M. (2002). Postcoloniality, feminist spaces and religion. In L. Donaldson & P. Kwok (Eds.), *Postcolonialism, feminism & religious discourse* (pp. 115–17). New York, NY: Routledge.

Hall, A.J. (2013). Creation, original peoples, and the colonization of a hemisphere. In S. Heinrichs (Ed.), *Buffalo shout, salmon cry* (pp. 33–46). Kitchener, ON: Herald Press.

Henry, N. L. (2014). Slavery Abolition Act, 1833. *The Canadian encyclopedia*. Retrieved from https://www.thecanadianencyclopedia.ca/en/article/slavery-abolition-act-1833.

Jewell, B. (2006). Lakota struggles for cultural survival: History, health, and reservation life. *Nebraska Anthropologist*, 21(19). Retrieved from http://digitalcommons.unl.edu/nebanthro/19.

Johnson v. M'Intosh. 21 U.S. 8 Wheat. 543 (1823).

Jones, D.L. (1979). Christianity and emperor worship from Hadrian to Constantine. *Perspectives in Religious Studies*, 6(1), 34–44.

King, M.L., Jr. (1964/2010). *Why we can't wait*. Boston, MA: Beacon Press. Kindle Edition.

King, T. (2013). *The inconvenient Indian: A curious account of Native People in North America*. Minneapolis, MN: University of Minnesota Press. Kindle Edition.

Lind, D. (2017). Unite the Right, the violent white supremacist rally in Charlottesville, explained. 14 August. Retrieved from: https://www.vox.com/2017/8/12/16138246/charlottesville-nazi-rally-right-uva.

Madden, C. (2015). Shedding light on Canada's "cultural genocide." 23 June. Retrieved from: https://www.culturalsurvival.org/news/shedding-light-canadas-cultural-genocide.

Mikisew Cree First Nation v. Canada [2018] SCC 40.

Mueller, G. (2002). *Defending Rama Indian community lands and the southeastern Nicaragua biosphere*. Four Directions Consulting. Retrieved from: http://conservation.law.ufl.edu/pdf/rama/rama_report.pdf.

Mumford, D. (2016). Slave prosperity gospel. *Homiletic*, 41(1). Retrieved from: http://www.homiletic.net/index.php/homiletic/article/view/4250.

Nicaragua's Constitution of 1987 with Amendments through 2005. (2018, 17 Jan.). Tr. Max Planck Institute. Oxford University Press. Retrieved from: https://www.constituteproject.org/constitution/Nicaragua_2005.pdf.

Pember, M.A. (2016). *Intergenerational trauma: Understanding Natives' inherited pain* (Rep.). Verona, NY: Indian Country Today Media Network. Retrieved from: https://indiancountrymedianetwork.com/free-reports/intergenerational-trauma-understanding-natives-inherited-pain.

Pope Alexander VI. (1493). The legal battle and spiritual war against Native People: The bull *Inter Caetera* (Alexander VI), 4 May. Retrieved from: www.doctrineofdiscovery.org.

Proclamation of the Secretary of State Regarding the Ratification of the Thirteenth Amendment. (1865). 18 December. US National Archives. Retrieved from: https://catalog.archives.gov/id/6247985.

Romero, R.T. (2011). *Making war and minting Christians: Masculinity, religion, and colonialism in early New England*. Boston, MA: University of Massachusetts.

Schertow, J.A. (2007). The continuing struggle of the Waorani. 11 October. Retrieved from: https://intercontinentalcry.org/the-continuing-struggle-of-the-waorani.

Sheppard, P.I. (2016). Womanist-lesbian pastoral ethics: A post-election perspective. *Journal of Pastoral Theology*, 26(3), 152–70.

Simpson, L. (2013). Liberated peoples, liberated land. In S. Heinrichs (Ed.), *Buffalo shout, salmon cry* (pp. 50–57). Kitchener, ON: Herald Press.

Sims, A.D. (2009). Nooses in public spaces: A womanist critique of lynching—a twenty-first century ethical dilemma. *Journal of the Society of Christian Ethics*, 29(2), 81–95.

Standing Rock Sioux Tribe (n.d.). History. Retrieved from: https://www.standingrock.org/content/history.

Stark, R. (1997). *The rise of Christianity: How the obscure, marginal Jesus movement became the dominant religious force in the Western world in a few centuries*. New York, NY: HarperOne.

Taylor, S. (2017). An invitation to the feast: A positive biblical approach to equal marriage. *Modern Believing,* 58(1), 41–53.

Throckmorton, B.H. (1985). Language and the Bible. *Religious Education, 80*(4), 523–38.

Tinker, G.E. (1993). *Missionary conquest: The gospel and Native American cultural genocide.* Minneapolis, MN: Fortress Press.

Uenuma, F., & Fritz, M. (2011). Why the Sioux are refusing $1.3 billion. *PBS Newshour,* 24 August. Retrieved from: http://www.pbs.org/newshour/updates/north_america-july-dec11-blackhills_08-23.

Vowel, C. (2013). The often-ignored facts about Elsipogtog. *The Star,* 14 November. Retrieved from: https://www.thestar.com/opinion/commentary/2013/11/14/the_oftenignored_facts_about_elsipogtog.html.

Yale University Genocide Studies Program (1970). Puerto Rico. 1 January. Retrieved from: https://gsp.yale.edu/case-studies/colonial-genocides-project/puerto-rico.

PART III

Gender and Development

For several decades, postcolonial feminists have examined the global economy and the gendered processes that shape the global labour market. They have explored the intersections of global and Indigenous feminist perspectives, searching for pathways to achieve environmental justice. In such works, it is important to contextualize the interactions between gender, capitalism, and globalization (Acker, 2004). The chapters of Part III combine concerns for gender equality and development, and they do so from three standpoints: Indigenous perspectives on environmental justice, postcolonial feminist perspectives on development studies, and the perspectives of migrant domestic workers seeking justice in an era of neoliberal globalization. The chapters in Part III reflect several major theoretical, empirical, and methodological contributions in the field of gender and development studies. These chapters offer an intersectional and interdisciplinary analysis of how globalization affects the process of development and its implications for social well-being and gender equality. The authors make the case for feminist economics and Indigenous feminist perspectives as useful frameworks for addressing major contemporary global challenges. They show how these perspectives indicate viable strategies for dealing with inequalities between the Global South and North, the economic polarization

within each nation, the persistence of poverty, and the world's increasing vulnerability to financial crises, food shortages, and climate change.

In "Indigenous Feminism Perspectives on Environmental Justice," Deborah McGregor explores the emergence of a distinct theoretical, methodological, and practical approach to enabling both gender and environmental justice on the basis of Indigenous feminism. This chapter examines the concept of Indigenous feminism and shows why it is important for the world. We learn about the contributions that Indigenous feminism has made to the international dialogue on environmental and water security. The chapter also indicates the value of Indigenous non-binary gender expressions. It explains the ethical principle of responsibility in relation to water justice. One of the key issues McGregor deals with is the role of the United Nations in defending the rights of Indigenous peoples. She also provides insight into the role of Indigenous legal orders in achieving justice and the importance of Indigenous knowledge systems.

In "A Postcolonial Feminist Critique of Development Studies," Fariba Solati offers a historical context on the emergence of development and post-development studies. She clarifies why postcolonial feminist critics of development differ from other critiques of the development discourse. She also explores the links between gender-related concerns and various approaches to development and considers applications of these approaches in development policies.

In "Precarious Lives, Fertile Resistance: Migrant Domestic Workers, Gender, Citizenship, and Well-Being," Denise Spitzer offers us insight into the ways that gender, racialization, and migration status are configured in the context of neoliberal globalization and the globalized labour market. The chapter examines how the precariousness of migrant lives is constructed and maintained. She investigates the rise of migrant advocacy and of collective resistance to the deleterious effects of neoliberal globalization.

REFERENCE

Acker, J. (2004). Gender, capitalism and globalization. *Critical Sociology, 30*(1), 17–41.

CHAPTER 7

◇

Indigenous Feminism Perspectives on Environmental Justice

Deborah McGregor

Learning Objectives

In this chapter, you will:

- understand the concept of Indigenous feminism and why it is an important field of study;
- learn about the contributions Indigenous feminism makes to international dialogue on environmental/water security;
- learn about Indigenous non-binary gender expressions;
- consider the ethical principle of "responsibility" in relation to water justice;
- learn about the United Nations Declaration on the Rights of Indigenous Peoples;
- examine the role of Indigenous legal orders in achieving justice;
- develop insights into Indigenous knowledge systems.

Introduction

In this chapter, you will learn about the emergence of a distinct theoretical, methodological, and practical approach for accounting for gender in relation to environmental justice called Indigenous feminism. Indigenous feminism will be defined and outlined as an important field of study to advance the contributions, insights, rights, and responsibilities of Indigenous women. While the ideology of feminism has been in existence for decades, **Indigenous feminism** has only recently emerged. Joyce Green, an Indigenous scholar, writes that Indigenous feminism seeks to "raise

issues of colonialism, racism and sexism and unpleasant synergies between these three violations of human rights" (Green, 2007, p. 20). She further remarks that if Indigenous feminists do not voice concerns and issues, such issues will not be raised at all. Indigenous feminism provides a powerful critique of colonialism, race, and gendered power relations.

You will also learn about the field of **Indigenous knowledge systems (IKS)**. Indigenous feminism emerged because academic disciplines failed to consider the unique and distinct context, history, and reality of Indigenous peoples. Indigenous feminism reveals that historical and ongoing colonial structures and processes continue to hinder the self-determination of Indigenous peoples. Indigenous feminism shows that not only is colonialism at work to dispossess Indigenous peoples, but also that racism, patriarchy, and sexism all intersect in insidious ways to discriminate, marginalize, and dehumanize women.

Indigenous knowledge systems emerged as a field of study to address the hegemony of Western knowledge. Western knowledges have contributed to the colonization and continued marginalization of Indigenous peoples, women in particular (Kermoal & Altamirano-Jiménez, 2016). The importance of Indigenous knowledges is well recognized internationally and has been for decades in the environmental realm (Kermoal & Altamirano-Jiménez, 2016). Much attention has been paid to the potential benefits of IKS in addressing local, regional, and global environmental challenges. Less attention has been paid to how knowledge is specific to "gender, age, sexuality, livelihoods, and experiences of colonization" (Kermoal & Altamirano-Jiménez, 2016, p. 9). Gender differentiation and specialization means that men and women hold different knowledges of the environment/waters and furthermore have different priorities. "Indigenous women's knowledge extends beyond the activities done by women and involves a system of inquiry that reveals Indigenous processes of observing and understanding and the protocols for being and participating in the world" (Kermoal & Altamirano-Jiménez, 2016, p. 11).

In this chapter, the concept of Indigenous feminism will be applied to environmental and water justice. This is achieved by analyzing international Indigenous environmental/water declarations generated by Indigenous women. What characteristics define a unique approach to environmental and water justice? What actions have Indigenous women taken to address their distinct experiences and concerns? What do Indigenous women envision as their future? These are some of the questions that will be addressed.

Feminism

The central characteristic of **feminism** or feminisms (socialist, radical, liberal, ecofeminist) is that it takes gender seriously as an ideological, theoretical, and methodological process intended to expose, analyze, and address the subordination of women in patriarchal societies. What is interesting about feminism, unlike other ideologies and theories, is the commitment to transformation and practice to address the subordination of women. Feminism does not just study the context, condition, and experience of women; it also seeks to address the conditions. Feminism is a highly recognizable term/concept (in Western countries, at least) because it supported and was central to a social movement. Few ideologies have managed to transcend academia and form part of the public consciousness.

Feminism remains to a certain extent "white centered, despite the active involvement of women of colour in the second and third wave feminist movement" (Huhndorf & Suzack, 2010, p. 2). Mainstream feminism remains limited in its capacity to address the unique concerns of Indigenous women relating to colonialism (both historical and ongoing). Indigenous feminism has emerged as distinct from the feminist discourse of "women of color and postcolonial feminism" (Huhndorf & Suzack, 2010, p. 1).

Indigenous/Aboriginal Feminism

Until recently, very little had been written specifically about Indigenous feminism (Huhndorf & Suzack, 2010). The relevance of Indigenous feminism in Indigenous societies has been questioned in some circles as it is argued that women enjoyed far more power, respect, and autonomy than their European counterparts (Green, 2007). The reality is that colonization has "involved their removal from positions of power, the replacement of gender roles with Western patriarchal practices and exertion of colonial control over Indigenous communities through the management of women's bodies and sexual violence" (Huhndorf & Suzack, 2010, p. 1). Further, the contemporary lived reality of Indigenous women is primarily that of racist, colonial, and patriarchal forms of oppression evidenced in both settler society and Indigenous societies. This is in part due to the forced imposition of colonial patriarchy in Indigenous societies and the subsequent internalization of such ideologies. Indigenous women are doubly subjugated because they experience oppression in dominant society and often in their own. This was evident in the public inquiry on **Missing and Murdered Indigenous Women and Girls**, which recognized that Indigenous women experience far more violence historically and currently than other women (Ambler, 2014).

Indeed, a synergy exists between feminism as an ideology and the social justice movement and Indigenous women, yet it is not uncritically embraced. Critics of Indigenous feminists and feminism balk at gendered analysis of Indigenous societies, especially of men and their role in the oppression of women. As such, Indigenous feminism does not shy away from scrutiny of Indigenous society to reveal internal oppression of women. Indigenous feminism is critical and important for revealing the intersection of gender, race, sex, colonialism, and power. Indigenous feminism embraces the theoretical as well as the practical and lived experience. Indigenous feminism has an activist orientation, with the goal of transforming society to counter "social erasure and marginalisation" of Indigenous women (Huhndorf & Suzack, 2010, p. 5). "Aboriginal feminism seeks an Aboriginal liberation that includes women and not just the conforming woman, but also the marginal and excluded, and especially the women who have been excluded from their communities by virtue of legislation and socio-historical forces" (Green, 2007, p. 25).

Indigenous feminism, applying a gendered analysis, reveals violence of all kinds, at various levels and scales, in processes of historical and contemporary colonialism. If gender was an organizing principle to colonize societies of Indigenous peoples, to undermine Indigenous women, their political, economic, social, cultural, and spiritual role, then decolonization must also include a gendered aspect (Kermoal & Altamirano-Jiménez, 2016). Indigenous feminist analysis and activism "must aim to understand the changing circumstances, the commonalities, and the specifics of Indigenous women across time and space; it must seek ultimately to attain social justice not only along gender lines but also along those of race, class and sexuality" (Huhndorf & Suzack, 2010, p. 3).

It is also critical to point out that gender is not limited to discussion about women's experience, particularly in contrast to that of men. More nuanced understanding and analysis is required to move beyond understanding gender (men/women) in strictly binary terms. **Heteropatriarchy** is an ideology of the dominant world order and has been detrimental to Indigenous peoples but particularly detrimental to women and LGBTTIQQA2s+ (Lesbian, Gay, Bisexual, Transsexual, Transgender, Intersex, Queer, Questioning, Asexual, Two-Spirited; Women's Earth Alliance [WEA] and Native Youth Sexual Health Network [NYSHN], 2014). Heteropatriarchy is defined as "[S]ystems and practices that normalize and centre male dominance; male-female gender binaries; and heterosexual identities, family units, and sexual expressions. This system is manifested in economic, material, and social disadvantages for those whose gender or sexual identity does not align with heteropatriarchy" (Williams, Fletcher, Hanson, Neapole, & Pollack, 2018, pp. 5–6).

Indigenous non-binary gender expression is the term Indigenous feminist scholar Sarah Hunt utilizes to disrupt the typically binary lens used to understand the intersection between race, colonialism, and heteropatriarchy (Hunt, 2015). "Colonial laws and ideologies have entailed the imposition of gendered and racialized categories, which have been used to ensure fewer and fewer Natives over time" (Hunt, 2015, p. 105). Colonialism acted to erase the realities of two-spirit people and non-gender-conforming people. "Gendered analyses of power in Indigenous communities had tended to focus on men and women, reinforcing the gender binary" (Hunt, 2015, p. 104). Hunt further argues that a focus on a binary-gendered analysis misses the mark in terms of understanding the impact of colonialism and patriarchy on Indigenous communities. Hunt argues that the development of an Indigenous gender-based analysis, beyond the binary, is required to account for the experience of all members of Indigenous societies (Hunt, 2015).

Anti-colonial Analysis and Indigenous Feminism

Anti-colonial scholarship addresses and critiques European colonialism's historical distortion of Indigenous peoples' political, economic, cultural, social, and spiritual lives and experiences (Johnson, Cant, Howitt, & Peters, 2007). Anti-colonial theory aims to demonstrate how Western knowledge has sought to undermine alternative ways of knowing and living in the world and the devastating consequences of such actions. As a theoretical orientation, postcolonialism deconstructs and analyzes how Eurocentric ideologies continue to marginalize Indigenous political ambitions, economic livelihoods, cultural values, and relationships with the land (Louis, 2007). Anti-colonial scholarship through such critiques generates space for other ways of being and knowing the world and shows how "colonialism is continually being enacted through status-quo approaches to sustainable development policy that are subservient to extractive modes of development" and "directly challenges the dominant 'business as usual' way of doing things" (Williams et al., 2018, p. 11). In *Women and climate change impacts and action in Canada: Feminist, Indigenous, and intersectional*

perspectives (2018), **anti-colonialism** is taken up in the following ways to analyze the current climate change agenda implications for women:

- Works with reclaiming Indigenous and local knowledge in ways that transform the economic, cultural, and political systems which are the root causes of climate change;
- Recognizes that colonial-capitalist accumulation relies on axes of exploitation that include racial, gendered, hetero-normative, other socially constructed norms and identities, and nation state lines. It applies an intersectional analysis to problematize colonial and socially constructed categories, shedding light on how these are reinforced or challenged through climate change impacts and action; and
- Recognizes the unique contributions of Indigenous and aligned Western feminisms in challenging colonial-capitalist accumulation and heteropatriarchy (Williams et al., 2018, p. 11).

Anti-colonial analysis and Indigenous feminism have their own theorists, practices, and spheres of engagement and generate space for addressing environmental/water (in)justice from a gendered lens (in this chapter, that of women). These frames of analysis are evident and asserted by Indigenous women around the world, as seen in the stated declarations of Indigenous women at various fora. Indigenous women have distinct contributions to make to the international dialogue on the global environmental crisis, in particular environmental/water justice issues including climate change. The next section examines three international declarations prepared by Indigenous women over the past two decades: the Beijing Declaration of Indigenous Women (1995); the Mandaluyong Declaration (2010); and the Lima Declaration (2013). These declarations exemplify anti-colonial and feminist articulations of how women and the people (and non-humans) they care for are affected by a continuing colonial agenda, manifested in capitalism, globalization, and trade liberalization.

Case Studies in Applying Anti-colonial and Indigenous Feminism

Indigenous women in the Global South and North are linked through coming together at various international environmental and sustainable development gatherings to collectively assert their own voices and perspectives. Indigenous women, often in opposition to the dominant environmental/sustainable development paradigm, not only offer invaluable and necessary critiques but also provide a plan of action for a more just future. Three case studies form the basis of the next section: the Beijing Declaration of Indigenous Women; the Mandaluyong Declaration of the Global Conference on Indigenous Women, Climate Change and REDD Plus; and the Lima Declaration: World Conference of Indigenous Women: Progress and Challenges Regarding the Future We Want.

The Beijing Declaration of Indigenous Women (1995)

Indigenous women involved in the development of the Beijing Declaration of Indigenous Women, convened as part of the fourth World Conference on Women, provided a powerful anti-colonial critique of what is referred to as "recolonization."

"The 'New World Order' which is engineered by those who have abused and raped Mother Earth, colonized, marginalized, and discriminated against us, is being imposed on us viciously. This is recolonization coming under the name of globalization and trade liberalization" (Beijing Declaration of Indigenous Women, 1995, 1, article 6).

We, the women of the original peoples of the world have struggled actively to defend our rights to self-determination and to our territories which have been invaded and colonized by powerful nations and interests. We have been and are continuing to suffer from multiple oppressions; as Indigenous peoples, as citizens of colonized and neo-colonial countries, as women, and as members of the poorer classes of society. In spite of this, we have been and continue to protect, transmit, and develop our Indigenous cosmovision, our science and technologies, our arts and culture, and our Indigenous socio-political economic systems, *which are in harmony with the natural laws of Mother Earth*. We still retain the *ethical and esthetic values, the knowledge and philosophy, the spirituality, which conserves and nurtures Mother Earth*. We are persisting in our struggles for self-determination and for our rights to our territories. This has been shown in our tenacity and capacity to withstand and survive the colonization happening in our lands in the last 500 years (Beijing Declaration of Indigenous Women, 1995, 1, article 5; italics mine).

The women pointed out that the broader international environmental meetings failed to critique the "new world order," stating:

This poverty is caused by the same powerful nations and interests who have colonized us and are continuing to recolonize, homogenize, and impose their economic growth development model and monocultures on us. It does not present a coherent analysis of why is it that the goals of "equality, development, and peace" becomes more elusive to women each day in spite of three UN conferences on women since 1975 (Beijing Declaration of Indigenous Women, 1995, 2, article 11).

The non-economic activities of Indigenous women have been ignored and rendered invisible, although these sustain the existence of Indigenous peoples. Our dispossession from our territorial land and water base, upon which our existence and identity depends, must be addressed as a key problem (Beijing Declaration of Indigenous Women, 1995, 2, article 7).

The Beijing Declaration offers 30 proposals and demands that signify a rejection of the new world economic order and the move to a world based on responsibility and caring for the earth to sustain all life. Indigenous feminism sentiments (although not termed in that way by the Indigenous women at the gathering) in the Beijing Declaration as distinct impacts on women are outlined throughout. Asserting Indigenous feminism as a form of critique of how women are treated in the international environmental realm also includes an assertion of Indigenous world view, legal orders, philosophies, and knowledges as part of a sustainable path forward. For example, in relation to environment/water, article 22 states that Indigenous peoples will decide what "to do with our lands and territories and to develop it an integrated, sustainable way, according to our cosmovision" (Beijing Declaration of Indigenous Women, 1995, p. 3). The first article in the declaration outlines the responsibility to care for the earth and points to the knowledge, philosophy, spirituality, and natural laws that nurture the earth. However, Indigenous lifeways are not uncritically accepted, and it is clear that those aspects that are discriminatory and disadvantage women in any way should be abolished. This is similar to the critique that Indigenous feminists make of Indigenous societies, particularly the way that colonialism has been internalized in many communities. For example, article 36 advocates that Indigenous customary laws and justice systems that are supportive of women be recognized and reinforced and those that are not be eradicated (Beijing Declaration of Indigenous Women, 1995, p. 4). The Beijing Declaration centres the concerns and calls to action of Indigenous women, pointing to human rights violations and violence against Indigenous women. It outlines a set of proposals including the right to self-determination (in all aspects: health, education, intellectual and cultural heritage, and, of critical importance here, elevating the participation of Indigenous women at every level and scale in a dialogue that affects the lives, livelihood, and sovereignty of Indigenous peoples).

The Mandaluyong Declaration (2010)

The Mandaluyong Declaration of the Global Conference on Indigenous Women, Climate Change and REDD Plus, held in Legend Villas, Philippines, in 2010, conveys similar sentiments to the Beijing Declaration of 15 years earlier. Eighty women, from 60 Indigenous Nations and 29 countries, gathered to tell their own stories of how they are differently affected by the impacts of climate change on the basis of gender. The anti-colonial critique is evident in the declaration, the women clearly critical of the world economic order.

> While we have least contributed to the problem of climate change, we have to carry the burdens of adapting to its adverse impacts. This is because of the unwillingness of rich, industrialized countries to change their unsustainable production and consumption patterns and pay their environmental debt for causing this ecological disaster. Modernity and capitalist development which is based on the use of fossil fuels and which promotes unsustainable and excessive production and consumption of unnecessary goods and services, individualism, patriarchy, and incessant profit-seeking have caused climate change (Mandaluyong Declaration, 2010, para. 1).

The delegates all point to the lived experience of Indigenous peoples and in particular how women are affected by climate change. They point to the underlying causes of climate change (modernity and capitalist development that is extractive and destructive). Climate change has contributed to the undermining of traditional livelihoods, identity, and the well-being of the people, unprecedented disasters, loss of land and communities, and food and water insecurity, all resulting in "hunger, disease and misery" (Mandaluyong Declaration, 2010, para. 3). The combined impacts of climate change point to a loss of land and lives, which has political and legal implications for the exercise of sovereignty.

Women are particularly compromised because of their caregiving role in families and communities: as "main water providers, we have to search and fight for access to the few remaining water resources" (Mandaluyong Declaration, 2010, para. 5). The declaration adds:

> Complicating these are the situations of multiple discrimination based on gender and ethnic identity. These are manifested in the lack of gender and culturally sensitive basic social services such as education and health and our lack of access to basic utility services such as water and energy. The systematic discrimination and non-recognition of our sustainable resource management and customary governance systems and their access, control and ownership over their lands, territories and resources persists (Mandaluyong Declaration, 2010).

In terms of Indigenous knowledge systems, the declaration points out that the norms, laws, knowledge, and values that guide sustainable resource governance are weakened by climate change. Yet, the women point out:

> We shared how we are addressing the issues of food, water and energy insecurity. How we are sustaining and transmitting our traditional

knowledge to the younger generations. How we are continuing our traditional land, water and forest resources management systems. How we are exerting our best to ensure the overall health and well being of our families and communities. Our efforts to recover, strengthen, use, and adapt our traditional knowledge and our ecosystems to climate change and to transmit these to our youth are bearing some good results. . . . We shared our Indigenous ways of predicting and coping with climate change–related disasters and we hope to further strengthen these knowledge and practices (Mandaluyong Declaration, 2010, p. 3).

And point out that "we continue to use and adapt our traditional knowledge and land, water, forest and natural resource management systems to climate change" (Mandaluyong Declaration, 2010, p. v3) and stress the importance of Indigenous knowledge systems as key to the future: "Our spirituality which links humans and nature, the seen and the unseen, the past, present, and future, and the living and non-living has been and remains as the foundation of our sustainable resources management and use. We believe if we continue to live by our values and still use our sustainable systems and practices for meeting our basic needs, we can adapt better to climate change" (Mandaluyong Declaration, 2010, p. 4).

The delegates who generated the Mandaluyong Declaration advocate for the recognition and implementation of the United Nations Declaration on the Rights of Indigenous Peoples (UNDRIP) as a way to help protect peoples from the risks associated with REDD Plus. Similar to the Beijing Declaration, the Mandaluyong Declaration outlines priority work areas and actions, including:

- Awareness raising, skills training workshops, information dissemination.
- Gender analysis of policies and approaches for mitigation and adaptation.

- Skills training workshops that are gender-sensitive, including the sharing of knowledge with grassroots women's organizations.

Indigenous women call for research on climate change impacts on Indigenous women and on climate change adaptation and mitigation. Ideally, such research would be conducted by Indigenous women themselves in the following areas:

- Food security and climate impacts and roles of women.
- Traditional knowledge and community forest management and the roles of Indigenous women.
- Traditional livelihoods of Indigenous women and climate change.
- Gender dimensions of adaptation and mitigation policies and measures.

Indigenous women call for enhancement of traditional practices and systems and more specifically to "reinforce Indigenous women's traditional knowledge on mitigation and adaptation and facilitate the transfer of this knowledge to the younger generations" (Mandaluyong Declaration, 2010, article 3.4).

Indigenous women call for increased political participation and policy advocacy: "Indigenous women in political and decision making bodies and processes and in the formation of the climate agenda" at all levels and scales (global, national, regional and local), essentially enabling women to speak and advocate for themselves (Mandaluyong Declaration, 2010, article 5.2).

Indigenous women advocate for a human rights–based approach to dealing with climate change, arguing in favour of "a holistic framework for a gender-sensitive, ecosystem, human rights–based and knowledge-based approach to climate adaptation and mitigation efforts (Mandaluyong Declaration, 2010, p. 7). Although the Mandaluyong Declaration was generated by Indigenous women, the space is open for going beyond

non-binary gender expressions by the inclusion of "gender-based analysis" and "sensitivity."

The Lima Declaration (2013)

The Lima Declaration: World Conference of Indigenous women: Progress and Challenges Regarding the Future We Want advocates for the principle "Nothing about us, without us" and further declares, "Everything about us, with us." The women call for "the direct, full and effective participation of Indigenous Peoples; including the vital role of Indigenous women in all matters related to our human rights, political status, and wellbeing" (Lima Declaration, 2013, para. 1). In relation to the environment:

> We, Indigenous women, affirm our responsibility to protect the Earth, our Mother. Indigenous women experience the same pain and impacts from the physical abuse and excessive exploitation of the natural world, of which we are an integral part. We will defend our lands, waters, territories and resources, which are the source of our survival, with our lives.
>
> Protection of Mother Earth is a historic, sacred and continuing responsibility of the world's Indigenous Peoples, as the ancestral guardians of the Earth's lands, waters, oceans, ice, mountains and forests. These have sustained our distinct cultures, spirituality, traditional economies, social structures, institutions, and political relations from immemorial times. Indigenous women play a primary role in safeguarding and sustaining Mother Earth and her cycles (Lima Declaration, 2013, paras. 4 & 5).

As in the Beijing and Mandaluyong declarations, the women advocate for self-determination through the UNDRIP and human rights instruments. They point out that it is Indigenous peoples who bear the burden of social and environmental harms. Women and girls bear particularly

Notable Indigenous Feminism Scholars

Here are just a few notable Indigenous feminism scholars from around the world:

- Sarah Hunt (Kwagiulth (Kwakwaka'wakw) is an excellent community-based scholar and author of *Decolonizing rape culture*. Her writing and research focuses on justice, gender, self-determination, and the spatiality of Indigenous law. Her writing and research emerge within the networks of community relations that have fostered her analysis as a community-based researcher, with a particular focus on issues facing women, girls, and two-spirit people. See her TED Talk on missing and murdered Indigenous women and girls (https://www.youtube.com/watch?v=XmJZP2liqKI).

- Zoe Todd (Métis/otipemisiw) is from Amiskwaciwâskahikan (Edmonton), Alberta, Canada. She writes about fish, art, Métis legal traditions, the Anthropocene, extinction, and decolonization in urban and prairie contexts. She is assistant professor in the Department of Sociology and Anthropology, Carleton University. See her work in 2016: An Indigenous feminist's take on the ontological turn: "Ontology" is just another word for colonialism, *Journal of Historical Sociology, 29*(1), 4–22.

- Kim Anderson (Métis) is associate professor and Canada research chair in Indigenous relations, Department of Family Relations and Applied Nutrition, University of Guelph. Her current research is focused on exploring how "all our relations" are developed and maintained in urban environments.

- Rigoberta Menchú Tum (K'iche') is a political and human rights activist from Guatemala. She is an activist and won the Nobel Peace Prize in 1992. She has since created the Indian-led political movement Winaq (Mayan: "The Wholeness of the Human Being"). See her book *I, Rigoberta Menchú* (1983) and interview on human rights (https://www.youtube.com/watch?v=ru7Hy9FDQS4).

- Aileen Moreton-Robinson (a Goenpul woman of the Quandamooka people [Moreton Bay, Queensland]) is distinguished professor of Indigenous Research at Queensland University of Technology. She is an Indigenous feminist, author, and activist for Indigenous rights. See her work *Talkin' up to the white woman: Indigenous women and feminism*, (2002), Brisbane, Australia: University of Queensland Press.

- Rauna Kuokkanen (Sápmi) is professor, Arctic Indigenous Studies, Faculty of Social Science, University of Lapland. Her research interests and writing concern Indigenous women in the north, gender and politics, self-determination, Indigenous feminist theory, Indigenous women's rights and Arctic governance, and legal and political traditions. Her newest work is titled *Restructuring relations: Indigenous self-determination, governance and gender*, published by Oxford University Press in 2018.

insidious harms, including environmental violence and human rights violations.

The anti-colonial critique is evident when the women point out that the environmental crisis faced by all is due to the rise of the "exploitive model of economic growth and development" (Lima Declaration, 2013, para. 9) and the nations' failure to uphold Indigenous and human rights.

They state that nations must: "recognize and respect our rights to land, territories and resources as enshrined in Indigenous customary law, the UNDRIP, and other international human rights instruments" (Lima Declaration, 2013, para. 10).

> Finally, we affirm that Indigenous women have knowledge, wisdom, and practical experience, which has sustained human societies over generations. We, as mothers, life givers, culture bearers, and economic providers, nurture the linkages across generations and are the active sources of continuity and positive change (Lima Declaration, 2013, para. 15).

The Indigenous feminist and Indigenous knowledge perspectives are evident in that the declaration affirms that women have knowledge and expertise that can contribute to the well-being of the earth and peoples. The women bring forward the distinct concerns, issues, and experience of Indigenous women, in addition to the unique contributions women make to addressing challenges at every scale. As in the other declarations, Indigenous sovereignty is asserted and understood as central to a sustainable future.

Conclusion

Indigenous women can offer distinct contributions to combatting the current environmental crisis based on their responsibilities and knowledge systems that have supported Indigenous societies for millennia. For decades, Indigenous women from across the globe have gathered to share their experiences, concerns, and knowledges and

---

Call to Action

Support the goals and aspirations of Indigenous women outlined in the declarations noted in the chapter. There are many ways in which this can be done in everyday practice; just some are mentioned here. Recognize that whatever happens to women happens to the earth and whatever happens to the earth happens to women. Support Indigenous women in their efforts to protect the environment whenever you can. Educate yourself: attend and participate in presentations, workshops, lectures given by Indigenous women in your community or school. Also, educate others: for example, explain to friends, family, and colleagues the importance of self-determination of Indigenous peoples through the United Nations Declaration on the Rights of Indigenous Peoples. Support non-binary people and facilitate their voices and experiences whenever possible. Support land/water-based education to reconnect with Mother Earth. If your school or community does not provide it, then demand it. You can also listen to the voices of women online. There are many resources that can be found on the Internet (videos, presentations) of women offering their own voice. When they arise, support women during times of disaster or emergencies by fundraising. Finally, follow the Lima Declaration principle: "Nothing about us, without us." This means, no decision, discussion, dialogue, or conversation about Indigenous women should occur unless Indigenous women are equal participants with a strong voice. If you do not see Indigenous women in a meeting/workshop/conference yet people are talking about issues related to and affecting Indigenous women, then call participants out and demand for the participation of Indigenous women in the discussion.

to advocate for a sustainable future. The Beijing, Mandaluyong, and Lima declarations by Indigenous women are anti-colonial in their character as they uncover the underlying reasons for ongoing environmental recolonization, dispossession, and violence. However, each declaration also lays out future priorities and plans.

It should be noted that there is a significant gap in recognizing gender beyond the man/woman binary, and work needs to be done to ensure that Indigenous non-binary gender expressions are accounted for.

Tying It Together

This chapter's main purpose was to point out that Indigenous women face unique challenges that are tied to the fate to the earth. The distinct concerns of women can be addressed by Indigenous feminism. This chapter also informs you that gender must be considered more broadly and include non-binary persons. While gender analysis has been and continues to be discussed in detail in many settings, there remain many international, national, and local fora where this is unfortunately not the case. This is especially true in regard to both Indigenous feminism and climate change policy development.

An anti-colonial analysis reveals the underlying ideologies that have resulted in the global environmental crisis. An Indigenous feminist analysis reveals that there are considerations unique to Indigenous women that UNDRIP and other human rights instruments hold as key to addressing. Indigenous women have not been silent; they have voiced their concerns and outlined calls to action and plans of action, such as those put forward in the Mandaluyong Declaration, that have not been heeded. The challenge for all of us is to listen and to act on the knowledge Indigenous women share.

DISCUSSION QUESTIONS

1. There has been Indigenous activism and resistance for countless generations, expressed in many international Indigenous declarations. Why must women assert their own voice? What is missing if women are not active or present?

2. All three declarations speak to the disproportionate violence and discrimination that Indigenous women face in every aspect of life. Why do you think this situation exists? Why has it been so easy to ignore the experience and voice of women?

3. Anti-colonial discourse reveals the destructive impacts of capitalism and colonialism on the lives of Indigenous peoples, particularly Indigenous women. What factors make women more vulnerable to the negative impacts of environmental destruction?

4. Why do you believe non-binary expressions of gender have not been adequately recognized in many international environmental fora?

5. Describe the "future" that Indigenous women have called for over the past decades.

SUGGESTIONS FOR FURTHER READING

Anderson, Kim. (2016). *A recognition of being: Reconstructing Native womanhood* (2nd edn). Toronto, ON: Canadian Women's Press. This book offers a critical approach to Indigenous feminism, examining Indigenous women's efforts at resistance to heteropatriarchy.

Kermoal, Nathalie, & Altamirano-Jimenez, Isabel. (2016). *Living on the land: Indigenous women's understanding of place*. Edmonton, AB: University of Athabasca Press. This edited volume offers insights into the nature and scope of Indigenous women's environmental knowledge. It also provides a variety of theoretical and methodological approaches to research involving Indigenous women.

Green, Joyce (Ed.). (2017). *Making space for Indigenous feminism*. Halifax, NS: Fernwood Publishing. This book is an edited volume with contributions from Indigenous feminists and allies focused on the topics of violence against women, recovery of Indigenous self-determination, racism, misogyny, and decolonization.

Suzack, Cheryl, Huhndorf, Shari, Perreault, Jeanne, & Barman, Jean (Eds). (2010). *Indigenous women and feminism: Politics, activism, culture*. Vancouver, BC: University of British Columbia Press. This book contains a collection of essays examining the historical roles of Indigenous women, their intellectual and activist work, and the relevance of contemporary literature, art, and performance for an emerging Indigenous feminism.

MULTIMEDIA SUGGESTIONS

Native Women's Association of Canada, Finding your voice, environmental toolkit for Aboriginal women (2009)

https://www.nwmo.ca/~/media/Site/Files/PDFs/2015/11/04/17/34/1705_findingyourvoice-environmentaltoolkitforaboriginalwomen.ashx?la=en

This toolkit was designed to empower, assist, and engage Aboriginal women when dealing with environmental issues affecting their communities. It is meant to provide relevant information and provide Aboriginal women with the tools they may need to ensure that their issues are being addressed and their perspectives are being heard when they are looking to effectively participate in any environmental decision-making process.

Violence on the land, violence on our bodies: Building an Indigenous response to environmental violence (2014)

http://landbodydefense.org/uploads/files/VLVBReportToolkit2016.pdf

This toolkit is the result of collaboration between the Women's Earth Alliance (WEA) and the Native Youth Sexual Health Network (NYSHN), centring on the experiences and resistance efforts of Indigenous women and young people in order to expose and curtail the impacts of extractive industries on their communities and lands. WEA invests in training and supporting grassroots women to drive solutions to our most pressing ecological concerns—water, food, land, and climate. NYSHN is a network by and for Indigenous youth that works across issues of sexual and reproductive health, rights, and justice in the United States and Canada.

Ontario Native Women's Association (ONWA), Water rights toolkit (2014)

http://www.onwa.ca/upload/documents/water-commission-toolkit-final.pdf

This toolkit was designed to empower, support, and engage Aboriginal women when dealing with water rights issues in their communities. It was created by the Ontario Indigenous Women's Water Commission (OIWWC), which strives to reassert and promote the traditional and inherent roles of Indigenous women as the caretakers of the waters by engaging in traditional practices, participating in education and planning on water issues, and forming relationships among Indigenous women.

REFERENCES

Ambler, S. (2014). *Invisible women: A call to action. A report on missing and murdered Indigenous women in Canada*. Ottawa, ON: Speaker of the House of Commons. Retrieved from: http://ywcacanada.ca/data/research_docs/00000359.pdf.

Beijing Declaration of Indigenous Women. (1995). Beijing Declaration of Indigenous Women. Fourth World Conference on Women. Retrieved from http://www.ipcb.org/resolutions/htmls/dec_beijing.html.

Green, J. (Ed.). (2007). *Making space for Indigenous feminism*. Winnipeg, MB: Fernwood Publishing.

Huhndorf, S.M., & Suzack, C. (2010). Indigenous feminism: Theorizing the issues. In Cheryl Suzack, Shari Huhndorf, Jeanne Perreault, and Jean Barman (Eds), *Indigenous women and feminism: Politics, activism, culture* (pp. 1–17), Vancouver, BC: University of British Columbia Press.

Hunt, S. (2015). The embodiment of self-determination: Beyond the gender binary. In M. Greenwood, C. Reading, & S. de Leeuw (Eds), *Determinants of Indigenous peoples' health in Canada* (pp. 104–19). Toronto, ON: Canadian Scholars' Press.

Johnson, J.T., Cant, G., Howitt, R., & Peters, E. (2007). Creating anti-colonial geographies: Embracing Indigenous peoples' knowledges and rights. *Geographical Research, 45*(2), 117–20. doi: 10.1111/j.1745-5871.2007.00441.x.

Kermoal, N., & Altamirano-Jiménez, I. (Eds). (2016). *Living on the land: Indigenous women's understanding of place*. Edmonton, AB: Athabasca University Press.

Lima Declaration. (2013). The Lima Declaration: World Conference of Indigenous Women: Progress and Challenges Regarding the Future We Want. World Conference of Indigenous Women. Retrieved from: http://www.un.org/en/ga/president/68/pdf/6132014Lima-Declaration_web.pdf.

Louis, R.P. (2007). Can you hear us now? Voices from the margin: Using Indigenous methodologies in geographic research. *Geographical Research, 45*(2), 130–9. https://doi.org/10.1111/j.1745-5871.2007.00443.x.

Mandaluyong Declaration. (2010). Mandaluyong Declaration of the Global Conference on Indigenous Women, Climate Change and REDD Plus. Manila, Philippines. Retrieved from: http://www.tebtebba.org/index.php/all-resources/file/144-indigenous-womens-declaration-on-cc-and-redd.

Native Youth Sexual Health Network. (2014). Violence on the land, violence on our bodies: Building an Indigenous response to environmental violence. Retrieved from: http://landbodydefense.org/uploads/files/ VLVBReportToolkit2016.pdf.

Williams, L., Fletcher, A., Hanson, C., Neapole, J., & Pollack, M. (2018). *Women and climate change impacts and action in Canada—Feminist, Indigenous, and intersectional perspectives*. Canadian Research Institute for the Advancement of Women and the Alliance for Intergenerational Resilience. Retrieved from: http://www.criaw-icref.ca/images/userfiles/files/Women%20and%20Climate%20Change_FINAL.pdf.

CHAPTER 8

◇

A Postcolonial Feminist Critique of Development Studies

Fariba Solati

Learning Objectives

In this chapter, you will:
- learn about the historical context in which development and post-development studies emerged;
- understand why postcolonial feminist critiques of development differ from earlier critiques of development discourse;
- learn about the historical and theoretical foundations of gender and development;
- understand the links between gender and development approaches and their applications in development policies.

Introduction

From a postcolonial feminist perspective, this chapter provides a conceptual and theoretical critique of development studies, development policies, and projects. It provides a full account of the history of the economics of development as a field of study and as a means of implementing economic policies in the countries of the Global South. It shows how and when the concept of gender was introduced to the field of development studies and how the relation between gender and development has evolved over time. It examines the different approaches to the field of women, gender, and development, underscoring the past and contemporary discussions in this field.

Any discussion about development is closely related to the history of **colonialism**. Under the idea of "improvement," many countries of the Global South had been exploited under the legitimated colonial rule from at least the 18th century by several European countries (Craggs, 2014). After World War II, colonies started to pursue self-governance and independence from their colonizers. That is when colonization was gradually replaced by development projects, which guaranteed the continuation of unequal relations of power, resulting in a continuation of exploitation of many of the ex-colonies.

According to Gustavo Esteva (1992), an influential postcolonial scholar, development projects and policies have always been based on unequal relations of power, which have resulted in unequal distribution of resources. The development policies not only exacerbate inequalities between the developed North and the developing South, they worsen the existing inequalities in the Global South, such as gender and class inequalities. To postcolonial feminists such as Sara Radcliffe (1999), Cheryl McEwan (2001), and Valeria Esquivel (2016), "development" is about power. Thus, postcolonial feminists not only challenge **patriarchal** institutions within societies, they also challenge the positions of powerful actors such as international financial institutions and transnational corporations for producing and reproducing different forms of inequalities within and across countries (Struckmann, 2018).

Development Studies and Development Projects in a Historical Context

Like other theories in the social sciences, theories of development do not emerge from a political, economic, cultural, and intellectual vacuum (Sahle, 2012). We need to examine the historical context in which these theories are developed. Development as a field of study did not exist prior to the 1940s, with its roots going back to the post–World War II period and the emergence of the postwar world order. Development discourse emerged during the **decolonization** process of most of Asia, Africa, and Latin America.

The post–World War II world was a world divided between the Soviet Union and the United States. As the postcolonial world was taking shape in the 1950s, newly independent countries found themselves, one way or another, involved in another war, the Cold War, where a clash of ideologies

was growing (Rai, 2011). Countries of the world had to identify themselves as either with the West (the US, the UK, and their allies) or with the communists (the USSR, China, and their allies).

The creation of "development" is associated with US President Harry Truman's 1949 inauguration speech (Potter, 2014b). Truman announced a "program of development" for the "underdeveloped areas" and inaugurated the "development age" (Ziai, 2017). The fundamental goal was not, however, purely humanitarian. The Western camp of the Cold War was worried that the newly independent countries would join the communist camp in their path to "development" (Ziai, 2017). Each camp offered aid packages and trade opportunities to its allied countries in the name of "development" (Rai, 2011). Trade regimes, aid packages, and funding for development projects were often tied to this alliance. The United States, representing capitalist ideology, promoted the free market and free trade while the Soviet Union promoted central planning.

The rigid binary division of the world during the Cold War gave way to another category of countries, the **Third World**. This group of countries were mainly non-aligned countries trying to find a third way between capitalist and Marxist economic systems and ideologies (Rai, 2011). The Third World, however, remained the poorest group of countries, since they shared a history of colonial exploitation. Yet different colonial histories and different processes of decolonization prevented them from having a united camp in facing the superpowers of the world (Rai, 2011).

Underdevelopment was regarded as an initial state, which rich countries had already managed to move beyond. It was assumed that poor countries could simply follow rich countries' policies in trade and governance and consequently develop. It was also believed that if the Third World were provided with the capital and the technology needed for the catching up process, they would subsequently "develop" (Potter, 2014a). Two newly established institutions, the **World Bank** and the **International Monetary Fund (IMF)** played a central role in promoting development agendas based on capitalist policies during the Cold War.

Development agendas and projects replaced the hierarchies between colonizers and colonized with the seeming equality of trading partners in a world where the "underdeveloped" lagged behind and were in need of assistance to catch up (Ziai, 2017). While the newly independent countries became the new market for Western products, the discourse of development allowed Western countries to maintain their presence in their ex-colonies (Rahnema, 1997).

The development discourse, in general, ignored the many diverse and comparable ways of living, being, and progressing. Both major approaches to development (liberal/capitalist and Marxist/communist) assumed higher rates of economic growth as the main target for development agendas. Both sides assumed that industrialization and urbanization were the key components of economic growth and in turn socio-economic development. The similarities in both approaches to development created an international consensus and understanding about the meaning of development. The postcolonial nationalist elites and states also envisioned progress as "modern," "urbanized," and "industrialized" (Rai, 2011).

Development became a top-down approach to progress. It became a meta-narrative, which ordered and explained knowledge, ignoring local and Indigenous approaches to well-being and prosperity. Since within the development discourse, the definition of progress and improvement in standards of living were limited only to higher levels of national income, those who had already achieved higher levels of national income were considered winners, and those who were lagging behind were considered losers, not only by the people in developed countries but also by the people in the Third World. According to Gustavo Esteva (1992) and

Stuart Hall (1992), this binary hierarchal division of the world created the perception of the superiority of anything Western over that of the rest of the world, so much so that millions of people perceived themselves as poor and in desperate need of following a Western model of progress. Those who were defined as underdeveloped started seeing themselves in an "inverted mirror," a mirror that belittled them (Esteva, 1992).

Consequently, the modernist ideological frameworks dictated how to "study" development. For decades, modernist definitions of development were considered the only path to progress. Nevertheless, during the 1960s many radical political perspectives emerged within social science disciplines. Political economists from the Third World, such as Raúl Prebish (1959), Paul Baran (1952), and Andre Frank (1969), questioned the modernist models of development that ignored the colonial history of these countries. During this period, theories such as Dependency Theory seriously questioned the top-down, Western-dominated pattern of development projects and development studies.

Although dependency theorists were gender-blind, they were some of the most effective critics of the liberal/neoliberal model of development (Rai, 2011). They argued that mainstream models of development were in fact "the development of underdevelopment" (Frank, 1969). For dependency theorists such as Frank, decoupling the Third World from global capitalism was the only way to progress for the less advanced countries of the South. Rooted in Marxist theory, the dependency theorists, however, focused mainly on the different levels of income (class differences) within and across countries and did not pay attention to other forms of marginalization (such as gender and racial inequalities) within societies (Rai, 2011).

In the 1980s, under Margaret Thatcher's "popular capitalism" and Ronald Reagan's neo-conservatism, neoliberalism became the dominant model for development practices and policies across the globe. With the US and UK's political leadership and economic might, the World Bank and the IMF became even more influential in implementing neoliberal development policies all over the world. The core tenets of the neoliberal approach to development are based on privatization, free trade, free capital movement, export-led economic growth, downsizing civil services and government social expenditure, eliminating subsidies, and devaluing local currencies.

At the start of the 1990s, the Soviet Union collapsed, and communism gave way to alternative ideologies. This was the end of the Cold War era, when Third World countries were no longer limited to only two sets of ideologies for their economic policies and governance. Since then, neoliberalism has been able to rule the world with almost no competition.

Mapping Development to Post-development

For decades, development continued to be linked primarily to income growth, trade, industrialization, and urbanization. Since the late 1980s, this approach to development was criticized as being extremely narrow. The wave of criticizing development discourse mainly started with scholars such as Gustavo Esteva (1985), Arturo Escobar (1985), and Majid Rahnema (1985), who questioned the modernist and Eurocentric definition of development. Influenced by Edward Said's book, *Orientalism* (1979), the postcolonial criticism of development led to criticism of many of the words used in describing the poorer nations. The struggle over the terms "underdeveloped" and "Third World" was about the way in which development was envisioned (Rai, 2011). Development was a state-led, linear, hierarchical approach to a market-led economic progress. It implied that if a country was not defined as advanced by international organizations like the World Bank and the IMF, it was backward, poor, and in need of assistance. The term "Global

South" was invented as a result, suggesting a greater interdependence between different geopolitical spaces (Escobar, 1995a).

In parallel, feminist critics of development such as Ester Boserup (1970), Marilyn Waring (1988), and Diane Elson (1995) argued that modernist approaches to development ignored gendered power relations operating within the development framework. They argued that the invisibility of women's work in the development discourse, as well as not counting women's contribution to the production and reproduction spheres, had led to severe policy imbalances, making women's dependence on men institutionalized across the Global South.

Boserup (1970) argued that modern visions of development made many women even more vulnerable as commercialization and mechanization of agriculture marginalized women's **subsistence production** in rural areas and industrialization and manufacturing created more male employment in urban areas, making women financially dependent on men. Financial dependence, it is argued, is the major factor contributing to the subordination and marginalization of women (Solati, 2017). The above criticism of development resulted in the introduction of the Gender-related Development Index (GDI) and Gender Empowerment Measures (GEM) by the United Nations. The aim of these measurements was to add a gender-sensitive dimension to the **Human Development Index**.

During the 1990s, postmodernism emerged as an alternative paradigm for the social sciences in general and development studies in particular. The postmodernist approach rejected the modernist meta-theories and meta-narratives and rigorously questioned the dominant approaches to development and Eurocentric paths to progress. It criticized the excessive generalization of Marxist and neoliberal approaches to development that all countries go through specific historical stages similar to those of European countries. All the "anti," "post," and "beyond" development stances have roots in the postmodernist approach to development (Potter, 2014a).

The Origins of Post-development and Postcolonial Perspectives

Following the writings of Ivan Illich and Michel Foucault, the first post-development publications emerged in the 1980s. Scholars such as Arturo Escobar (1985), Majid Rahnema (1985; 1992), and Ivan Illich (1973; 1997) criticized the institutions of Western modernity, arguing that capitalism teaches people to be dependent on modern products. Michel Foucault's writings (1980) were about the questions of knowledge and power and the construction of what counts as normal and true. He argued that even in science, the answer to the question of "what is true" depends on the historical, social, and political contexts. According to Foucault, the language, i.e., discourse, has real effects in practice: the description becomes "true" (Hall, 1992). His writings had significant implications on how development policy and discourse were understood and followed.

Influenced by Michel Foucault and Edward Said's writings, Arturo Escobar published *Encountering development: The making and unmaking of the Third World* in 1995, which made him one of the most influential postcolonial scholars. According to him, postcolonialism is the rejection of the entire paradigm of development, "an interest in local culture and knowledge, a critical stance towards established scientific discourses, and the defense and promotion of localized, pluralistic grassroots movements" (Escobar, 1995a, p. 215).

In addition, feminist scholars such as Irene Tinker (1990) argued that modern approaches to development were gender-blind. They argued that development discourse failed to account for power dynamics between men and women and that development had generated economic practices that had contributed to the marginalization of women, especially women who historically have been neglected and marginalized, such as peasant women in Africa (Tinker, 1990). Scholars such as Frans Schuurman (1993) believed that there was an impasse in development studies during the 1980s and 1990s that resulted in the emergence of a new tradition called the post-development school. The spread of two schools of thought, postmodernism and **post-structuralism**, helped the advancement of post-development debates (Sahle, 2012).

Post-development and Postcolonialism

Post-development shared several common features stressed by postmodernists and post-structuralists. Escobar (1995a) argued, for example, that language, words, and concepts are central in the understanding of social reality and that knowledge is socially constructed and thus not neutral. He argued that attempts to universalize knowledge led to the colonialization or subordination of other forms of knowledge and that behind the humanitarian concern of development policies, new forms of power and control were operating. The poor had become the target of more sophisticated practices called development projects (Sahle, 2012).

For postcolonial thinkers such as Escobar (1995b), development was seen as a new form of colonialism disguised under policies and projects. The argument was that development discourse has facilitated the reproduction of colonialism. Inspired by Edward Said (1979), postcolonial thinkers argue that development knowledge produced in the World Bank or the IMF is closely linked to hegemonic theories of development. A theory or idea is considered hegemonic when it is taken for granted and assumed to be articulating the truth about a social reality (Sahle, 2012). According to postcolonial perspective, development discourse therefore is hegemonic because it sets parameters for how we perceive what is right and what is good across the board without questioning the ideas influencing the discourse.

According to post-development and postcolonialist scholars such as Gustavo Esteva (1998) and Antonio Escobar (1995a), the homogenization of all societies is reductionist and simplistic because it ignores the diversities in lived histories and practised cultures of millions of people across the world. The **Structural Adjustment Programs (SAPS)** promoted by the IMF are a perfect example of the "singular prescription" Western institutions impose on all countries in need of financial assistance, ignoring the economic, political, and cultural differences across regions and countries (Sahle, 2012).

The modernist definition of progress is an economic definition, which makes "development" an economic concept. Thus, the pursuit of a good life means accumulating material wealth—i.e., a higher income—for buying more goods in the market. This has had serious gender implications, since "value" is associated with economic value and economic value is associated with tradable goods and services in the market. Thus, Western development devalues all other forms of production, skills, and activities that are not sold in the market, such as subsistence productions performed mainly by women (Esteva, 1992). Vandana Shiva called development the "new project of Western patriarchy" because it exploits women's "non-productive" work (Shiva, 1989, p. 1).

Women, Gender, and Development: Feminist Theoretical Contributions

Achieving gender equality requires involvement of diverse actors and stakeholders, such as states and international organizations, informed by critical and theoretical insights (Tiessen, Parpart, & Marchand, 2017). Modern as well as traditional discourses at national and international levels hardly ever challenged the gender relations in society in general and in development discourse in particular. Charitable development strategies (such as building schools for girls in patriarchal societies) often target women and girls without any consideration of the root causes of gender inequality.

Welfare Approach to Development

During the first phases of development practices, women came to focus only as objects of welfare concerns. The **welfare approach to development** was highly influenced by prevailing theories of modernization and economic growth (Tiessen et al., 2017). This approach to development was predominant during the 1950s to the 1970s, and it was mainly based on foreign aid. According to this approach, development issues were constructed as "problems" to be solved with policies and programs geared to addressing overpopulation and rurality (Tiessen et al., 2017). Population growth was considered the main obstacle to achieving economic growth. Based on this approach, if women bear fewer children, there will be fewer illiterate mouths to feed. Women were the main focus of this approach across the Global South, since the goal of development projects was to reduce hunger and poverty, especially in rural areas. As Martinez (2012) argues, although women's bodies were the main focus, their thoughts, experiences, and sexual and reproductive health needs were often ignored. Although targeting women for population control and defining women purely in relation to biological functions as mothers has been criticized for many decades, this approach is still dominant in contemporary policy-making (Tiessen, 2015).

Women in Development (WID): The Liberal/Neoliberal Approach to Development

Ester Boserup was the first major scholar to question the effectiveness of development projects in improving the lives of women in the Global South. In her ground-breaking book,

Women's role in economic development (1970), she argued that since development mainly has been equated to mechanization of agriculture and that development projects have generally ignored the role of women as farmers and subsistence producers, development has marginalized women. Women's access to capital and training, which is necessary for more productive production, has been very limited. Thus, women have been marginalized in the process of economic development because they gain less than men as wage workers, farmers, and traders. Since women's social status is highly associated with their economic status, by separating women's labour from waged agricultural labour, development has undermined women's social status as well.

The publication of Ester Boserup's book reinforced the importance of women's participation in development. The book was a wake-up call for development agencies and humanitarian organizations (Martinez, 2012). Based on extensive empirical evidence, Boserup showed that official statistics ignore or underestimate women's contribution to the well-being of their families, the economy, and societies. She showed that development projects had exacerbated the patriarchal division of labour and had made women's conditions worse in the agricultural sector where women performed the majority of productive activities. As Martinez (2012) argues, Boserup made women visible as a distinct analytical category, preparing the way for the Women in Development (WID) approach, which was the first major movement to consider women in development projects by major players in development such as the World Bank.

The WID framework also began to address sexual violence, discrimination, inequality in access to resources, and women's limited participation in positions of power or influence. The WID approach challenged the assumption that women would automatically gain from development policies and projects. It called for specific attention to women as "development actors," drawing on liberal

feminist demands for improving women's positions in social, economic, and political realms (Tiessen et al., 2017). WID experts also called for more accurate measures of women's access to education, training, property, credit, political power, and economic livelihood. WID was one of the significant outcomes of the liberal feminist movement. The women's movement rejected the patriarchal system that placed women under the authority of men in the private and public spheres. As a result, the General Assembly of the United Nations organized the first global conference on women, a significant step toward promoting global gender equality. It established a measure of gender inequality, recommended policies and programs to achieve gender equality, and promoted women's participation in the development process (Martinez, 2012). WID aimed to transform traditional social relations and production. It assumed that access to education, credit, and agricultural techniques would increase women's participation in the economy, improving their status and well-being. Thus, this approach was also termed the "integration approach" because its main purpose was to integrate women in production. The arguments of feminist scholars from this camp, such as Boserup, as well as international organizations such as the United Nations, were mainly about efficiency and equality—that not only should women benefit from the development process equally but also the development process itself would better achieve its goals if women were a part of the process.

Sen's "Development as Freedom" Approach

Among liberal/modernist scholars, Sen's approach to development was more sensitive to gendered relations of power. Sen's development definition went beyond meeting only the basic needs and improving capabilities (such as access to education, income, and health) (Rai, 2011). Sen (1987; 1999) defined development as freedom. He argued that legal and political freedoms as well as human rights are critical for achieving the most important kind of entitlement, the labour-based entitlement. To him, while "freedoms are instrumental to [means of] development, they are also an end of development, and therefore constitutive of it" (Rai, 2011, p. 31). Scholars following the "development as freedom" approach challenged the assumptions of modernist models of the altruistic family promoted by **neoclassical economists** (Rai, 2011). Sen argued that family is a deeply contested space where women systematically suffer from patriarchal rules and norms (Sen, 1999).

Critics of WID

While WID policies and projects improved some aspects of women's lives, gender inequality remained strong. WID policies were often criticized and described as just "add women and stir," ignoring the root causes of gender inequality and gender power dynamics within the household and the society at large (Tiessen et al., 2017).

According to the feminists from the Global South such as Gita Sen (1987), Chandra Mohanty (1988), and Naila Kabeer (1994), WID was based on an inadequate understanding of the exploitation of women. WID reflected "the individualistic concerns of women from the North, rather than the collective concerns of the poor women in the Global South" (Martinez, 2012, p. 94). The critics of WID argued that the WID approach emphasizes integrating women into the public spheres without considering the deep-rooted patriarchal institutions, such as men controlling women's movement and mobility, and gender inequalities in the private sphere, such as preferring males over females in access to food, health care, and education. Moreover, the critics argued that the WID approach complied with the capitalist structure of economic development, failing to address the differences in class and ethnicity among women (Martinez, 2012). That is why the efforts of the development agencies in training women into better integrating into economic production

did not result in meaningful improvements in women's status.

WID overlooked the social and political structures within which women were located (Rai, 2011). Scholars such as Lourdes Beneria and Gita Sen (Beneria & Sen, 1997) criticized WID, arguing that the liberal critics of development tended to ignore the history of colonization and the process of capital accumulation. To the critics such as Kabeer, WID was simply an access-based framework (Kabeer, 1994). WID's policies only improved women's access to the products of development, yet they ignored unequal gender relations of production and reproduction by overlooking patriarchal institutions operating within these societies.

Ecofeminist scholars and activists, such as Vandana Shiva (1989), also challenged the modernist paradigm of development. Ecofeminism is an ecological philosophy and a social movement that "draws on environmental studies, critiques of modernity and science, and feminist critical analyses and activism to explicate connections between women and nature, and the implications of these relationships for environmental politics" (Allison, 2010, p. 1). Ecofeminism is also an activist and academic movement that sees critical connections between both the exploitation of nature and the domination over women by men within the capitalist system. Ecofeminists advocate for intergenerational justice and sustainable development (Rai, 2011) so that future generations will be able to benefit from natural resources as well. Ecofeminists question the sustainability of development projects and their impact on the environment and, in turn, on women's well-being, especially in rural areas of the Global South.

The above criticisms are significant because they mainly come from within the liberal paradigm. As Rai (2011) indicates, these criticisms can bring about change because they use the same language as economists, NGOs, and policy-makers. However, these critics themselves have been criticized, since they have overlooked some important shortcomings of the modernist approach to development. First, they have ignored the intersectionality of class and identities, and second, they still insist on the market-led form of development, which has resulted in globalization of labour, broadening the subordinations of the disadvantaged groups across the Global South.

The Women and Development (WAD) Approach to Development

Often confused with WID, Women and Development (WAD) stemmed out of discussions in development circles in 1975. Influenced by neo-Marxist feminists such as Lourdes Beneria (1982), it focused on the relationship between women and means of production in the process of capitalist development (Tiessen et al., 2017). Contrary to Marxist-inspired theorists before them, WAD paid attention to gender-based oppression in addition to class-based oppression (Martinez, 2012). They argued that women have always been integrated into the production process but that it is the capitalist mode of production that ignores women as an integral part of production and that capitalism is the source of women's oppression. WAD called for the recognition of women's special role in the development process and acknowledged women's struggles in a patriarchal world. WAD strongly argued against women's economic exploitation within the patriarchal-capitalist economic system, which they argued was the basis of development policies.

Critiques of WAD

Typical of Marxism that considers women as a "social class" subordinated to the capitalist mode of production, WAD failed to account for the power relationships that exist at the centre of the family that are the integral part of social, economic, and political inequalities between men and women across societies (Martinez, 2012). Critics argued that WAD focused mainly on capitalism as the source of women's oppression, while unequal gender roles assigned by patriarchal traditions are as important as the unequal distribution of the means of production. Furthermore, women in non-capitalist societies, such as traditional societies and communist countries, have been exploited as well. Additionally, WAD has been criticized as being materialistic by emphasizing only women's condition in the wage-labour market at the expense of other major sources of exploitation of women such as unpaid work (Martinez, 2012).

Gender and Development (GAD): The Socialist/Feminist Approach to Development

During the 1980s, the limitations of WID and WAD were the inspiration for a new approach to development, Gender and Development (GAD). GAD was influenced by socialist feminists such as Amartya Sen (1987), Chandra Mohanty (1988), and Naila Kabeer (1994), who brought a new gendered perspective to the social, economic, and political aspects of development. Since the Structural Adjustment Programs were heavily implemented by development agencies in the 1980s, GAD mainly focused on the negative effects of debt crises across the countries of the Global South. Critical of top-down, male-biased development policies, GAD paid particular attention to how neoliberalism had contributed to the impoverishment and marginalization of women in the Global South. These scholars and activists also called for greater attention to the complexities of women's lives in the Global South (Sen & Grown, 1987). They argued that development projects that ignored the complex realities of poverty, race, ethnicity, and class were bound to fail (Tiessen et al., 2017).

One of the most influential authors associated with GAD is Chandra Mohanty. In her famous article "Under the Western eye: Feminist scholarship and colonial discourses," she argues that Western development "experts" measured gender progress with Western lenses (Mohanty, 1988). Instead of looking at people living in the Global South through Western eyes, she called for attention to the lived experiences of women and men in the Global South who are affected by race, class, and culture (Tiessen et al., 2017). Inspired by scholars such as Chandra Mohanty, GAD paid attention to placing gender within specific cultural and historical contexts, highlighting the differences in the lived experiences of women across the Global South. Mohanty's intervention set the tone for postcolonial feminist scholarship, which contributed greatly to the debates concerning representation, "Othering," and silencing women in the Global South.

Marxist/socialist feminists such as Maria Mies drastically improved the debates on gender and development. They argued that primitive accumulation is indispensable to capitalist growth and that states and international corporations exploit people of the South, particularly women, in their pursuit of capital and profit. In their influential book, *Women: The last colony* (1988), Mies, Bennholdt-Thomsen, and von Werlhof argue that women are like colonies. Within the liberal model of development, women, similar to natural resources, are treated as a means of production and are therefore appropriated and exploited. Mies argues that capitalist exploitation of wage labour was based upon the male monopoly of violence (Rai, 2011). She argues that states have institutionalized "housewifization" of women's labour within family and labour laws.

The alternative offered by feminists such as Naila Kabeer is a society based on "autonomy for women over their lives and bodies, and rejection of any state or male control over their reproductive capacity; and finally, men's participation in subsistence and nurturing work" (Kabeer, 1994, p. 66). These critics of development have been successful in initiating change. They criticized development agencies and international organizations for overlooking women's work in general and women's unpaid work in particular. They also criticized the

unequal burden of privatization of social welfare on women as the result of neoliberal policies (Rai, 2011).

GAD filled the gap left by other theoretical perspectives, since it recognized the diversity of experiences and needs of women in different parts of the world as it linked the relation of production with relations of reproduction. GAD challenged the sexual division of labour at home and in public spheres, particularly in the labour market. It stressed that "the power differences between men and women that result from this sexual division interact with other relations of dominance such as class, race, ethnicity, sexual identity, and so on" (Martinez, 2012, p. 96).

The GAD approach to development is in fact a political approach because it intends to transform unequal gendered relationships of power. It advocates for replacing capitalist market models with models that are based on cooperation and equality between sexes. Since this approach requires more radical and structural changes, it is not a popular approach among development agencies. The GAD theorists are largely concerned with the transformation of gender relations and empowering women within and beyond households. Thus, compared with the WID approach, GAD is often more confrontational and hence less influential. Yet it has been able to institutionalize gender discussions within and beyond the development discourse.

The Development Alternatives with Women for a New Era (DAWN)

At the same time that GAD was gaining influence, another approach, the Development Alternatives with Women for a New Era (DAWN), led by socialist feminists from the South such as Gita Sen (1987), launched its critiques of mainstream development. DAWN specifically criticized the neoliberal approach to women as well as development's colonial legacies (Tiessen et al., 2017).

DAWN became a transnational alternative policy group and network of feminist scholars, researchers, and activists from the Global South, who produce and disseminate analyses, proposals, and information tools oriented toward the enhancement of economic and gender justice and ecological sustainability (Rai, 2011). Since they provide policy alternatives at the international level, they have been influential in development policy-making.

Postcolonial Feminism Critics of Development

Following postcolonial scholars such as Escobar, as well as building on GAD's criticism of development discourse, many feminist scholars from the South, such as Mohanty (1988), argue that the dominant or even hegemonic Western feminist knowledges need to be decolonized and open up to other knowledges. The postcolonial and decolonial feminists assert that development discourse must include different ways of knowing produced through the everyday practices of local women, particularly Indigenous women, in order to be effective and non-colonial (Tiessen et al., 2017). Postcolonial feminists argue that development is not merely a material process. It is a social process affected by culture, politics, and economics. Economic factors are interlinked with non-economic elements and cannot be abstracted and studied in isolation. Development would not make sense without understanding of the meanings and the cultural value attributed to it by the people who are subject to it (Mannathukkaren, 2017).

According to Kirsten Holst Peterson and Anna Rutherford (1986), women in the Global South suffer from "double colonization" because they experience the oppression of colonialism and patriarchy simultaneously. A woman of the Global South has to resist the control of colonial power not only as a colonized subject but also as a woman. Following the framework laid out by Mohanty, postcolonial feminists criticized Western feminists for their tendency to assume a commonality in forms of women's oppression and activism worldwide. According to Cheryl McEwan (2001,

p. 96), "divisions among women based on nationality, race, class, religion, region, language and sexual orientation have proved more divisive within and across nations than Western theorists acknowledged." Similar arguments ensured that Western or Eurocentric political visions are no longer acceptable to women in the Global South.

Important Notes on Approaches to Women, Gender, and Development

From a postcolonial feminist perspective, it is crucial to make the following notes. First, one should be very careful not to fall into the trap of excessive generalization, which some of the above approaches often do. Not all women in the Global South experience hardship in the same way or to the same degree. Their lived experiences are vastly different. The oppressive and exploitative patriarchal traditions do not affect all women and girls equally. Moreover, the above argument does not mean that women in the North are better off compared with all women in the South. Patriarchy is global, yet women in the South, in general, experience patriarchy and face limitation much more than an average woman in the North. Furthermore, women in the Global South are not all passive, oppressed, or victims. They are courageous and creative in resisting oppression and discrimination. More important, they do not need, nor are they waiting for, women in the North to "rescue" them. They are facing a complex system of power relations, which include gender as well as class, race, age, religion, ethnicity, and sexual orientation. In each country, women are resisting male domination and oppression in different ways, challenging sexist institutions and behaviours.

Second, although the above approaches to women, gender, and development are different from each other, they all point to women's access to the means of production, i.e., paid work, as the most important factor in improving women's lives. Almost all scholars agree that, for women, the first

Gender Statistics

An overview of the living conditions experienced by millions of females in the Global South is a testament that gender inequality persists across the world. The following are a few points mentioned in the latest UN Women's Report (2018):

- Globally, women and girls are overrepresented among the poor: 330 million women and girls live on less than US$1.90 a day; that is 4.4 million more than men.
- In 18 countries, husbands can legally prevent their wives from working; in 39 countries, daughters and sons do not have equal inheritance rights; and 49 countries lack laws protecting women from domestic violence.
- Globally, 750 million women and girls were married before the age of 18, and at least 200 million women and girls in 30 countries have undergone female genital mutilation.
- Women do 2.6 times the unpaid care and domestic work that men do.
- Globally, as of September 2017, women held just 23.7 per cent of parliamentary seats.

Land and property ownership mark an end to economic vulnerability. The following are based on the World Economic Forum's latest report (Villa, 2017):

- Women own less than 20 per cent of the world's land.
- More than 400 million women in the Global South farm and produce most of the world's food supply. Yet female farmers lack equal rights to own land in more than 90 countries.
- In the Middle East and North Africa, women lack equal constitutional and statutory property rights.
- In 35 countries, widows are particularly vulnerable because they cannot inherit property from their husband.

step toward empowerment is access to and control over the means of production (Solati, 2017). Economic power is a crucial form of power and lack of it is the main source of social inequality (Blumberg, 1984). All other sources of power (such as politics and ideology) are weaker than economic power. The lower women's relative economic power, "the more likely they are to be oppressed physically, politically, and ideologically" (Blumberg, 1984, p. 75). However, one should be very careful when applying this argument to development agendas. One of the consequences of liberal/neoliberal development policies has been the feminization of global labour, which may not necessarily empower women. Many feminist scholars have criticized the feminization of the global market, arguing that women have often been exploited more than helped by being incorporated into the capitalist and patriarchal labour market. In the past three decades, transnational corporations (TNCs) and multinational companies (MNCs) have built factories offshore in countries where labour is cheaper and workers have fewer rights. The owners of capital are from rich countries, who generate enormous profits through employment of cheap, mostly female workers in the Global South. Export-led development projects

Call to Action

Run a campaign on campus called "The Faces Behind Fast Fashion" to highlight how fashion companies exploit female workers in the Global South in order to sell clothes at very low prices. This campaign entails going to your closet, examining the brands you most commonly wear, and researching the conditions of their female workers. Post pictures of the items and the women producing them on social media to call companies out about their exploitation of female workers. Demand better conditions and higher wages for these women in exchange for your loyalty to the brand. Use #WomenDeserveBetter and #FacesBehindFastFashion to spread the word.

have also used women as workers in manufacturing and agriculture on a flexible basis, not providing them with safe, secured, and fair wages and also exposing them to more male authority in the form of male management. An employment that does not lead to improvement in well-being and status is not empowering. Women's participation in the labour market should advance their ability to make decisions about their lives and improve their well-being; otherwise it becomes another source of exploitation.

Tying It Together

From a postcolonial perspective, development is the new form of colonization because it is based on unequal power relations between the countries of the North (represented by powerful states, international financial institutions, and transnational corporations) and the countries of the South. From a feminist postcolonial perspective, women in the Global South suffer from double colonization because they experience the oppression of colonialism and patriarchy simultaneously. Without paying attention to patriarchal institutions across the world, development policies and projects would not be able to improve the lives of women and girls in the Global South. Development discourse must include different ways of knowing produced through the everyday practices of local women in order to be effective and non-colonial.

DISCUSSION QUESTIONS

1. What do postcolonial feminists mean when they claim that development discourses are ahistorical?
2. Discuss the link between colonial ideas and development discourses.
3. What would be the consequence of a postcolonial feminist position for practical politics, particularly with regard to improving females' well-being?
4. What do postcolonial feminists mean by double colonization?

SUGGESTIONS FOR FURTHER READING

Elson, D. (1995). *Male bias in the development process.* New York, NY: Manchester University Press. This book examines male bias in the development process, its foundation, and evolution. Case studies cover both urban and rural settings across several different countries.

Mies, M., & Shiva, V. (2014). *Ecofeminism.* London, UK: Zed Books. This book analyzes the ecological destruction and industrial catastrophes that threaten everyday life through a North–South perspective.

Mohanty, C.T. (2003). *Feminism without borders: Decolonizing theory, practicing solidarity.* Durham, NC, and London, UK: Zed Books. This book explores important issues facing contemporary feminism, such as decolonizing and democratizing feminist practice, gender in globalization, and the evolution of interdisciplinary programs such as women's studies.

Parpart, J.L., Connelly, M.P., & Barriteau, E.V. (Eds). (2000). *Theoretical perspectives on gender and development.* Ottawa, ON: International Development Research Centre. This book focuses on the implications of theory for policy and practice, and the need to theorize gender and development to create a more egalitarian society.

MULTIMEDIA SUGGESTIONS

Development Alternatives with Women for a New Era (DAWN)

www.dawnnet.org

This is the website of the organization DAWN, a network of feminist scholars that provides a forum for feminist research, analyses, and advocacy on global issues affecting women in the Global South. Publications, events, and news related to DAWN's work can be found here.

World Bank Gender Statistics

http://databank.worldbank.org/data/reports
    .aspx?source=gender-statistics

The World Bank's gender statistics database provides customizable datasets on key gender topics.

Information about economics, demographics, health care, political participation, and the labour force are searchable by country or region.

Who's Counting? Marilyn Waring on Sex, Lies and Global Economics

https://www.youtube.com/watch?v=WS2nkr9q0VU

This documentary, featuring Marilyn Waring, discusses economics as a value system in which all goods and activities are related only to their monetary value and highlights how unpaid work often performed by women is continually unrecognized in this system.

REFERENCES

Allison, J.E. (2010). Ecofeminism and global environmental politics. In R.A. Denemark & R. Marlin-Bennet (Eds), *The international studies encyclopedia.* Hoboken, NJ: Wiley-Blackwell.

Baran, P.A. (1952). On the political economy of backwardness. *Economy and Social Studies, XX*(1), 66–84.

Beneria, L. (1982). *Women and development: The sexual division of labor in rural societies.* New York, NY: Praeger.

Beneria, L., & Sen, G. (1997). Accumulation, reproduction, and women's role in economic development: Boserup revisited. In N. Vasanathan , L. Duggan, L. Nisonoff, & N. Wiegersma (Eds.), *The women, gender and development reader.* London, UK: Zed Books.

Blumberg, R.L. (1984). A general theory of gender stratification. In R. Collins (Ed.), *Sociology theory* (pp. 23–101). San Fransisco, CA: Jossey-Bass.

Boserup, E. (1970). *Women's role in economic development.* New York, NY: St Martin's Press.

Craggs, R. (2014). Development in a global-historical context. In V. Desai & R.B. Potter (Eds), *The companion to development studies* (pp. 5–10). New York, NY: Routledge.

Elson, D. (1995). *Male bias in the development process.* Manchester, UK: Manchester University Press.

Escobar, A. (1985). Discourse and power in development: Michel Foucault and the relevance of his work to the Third World. *Alternatives X, 10*(3), 377–400.

Escobar, A. (1995a). *Encountering development: The making and unmaking of the Third World* (2nd ed.). Princeton, NJ: Princeton University Press.

Escobar, A. (1995b). Imagining a post development era. In J. Crush (Ed.), *Power of development* (pp. 211–27). London, UK: Routledge.

Esquivel, V. (2016). Power and the sustainable development goals: A feminist analysis. *Gender and Development,* (24), 9–23.

Esteva, G. (1985). Development: Metaphor, myth, threat. *Development: Seeds of Change, 3,* 78–9.

Esteva, G. (1992). Development. In W. Sachs (Ed.), *The development dictionary: A guide to knowledge as power* (pp. 6–25). London, UK; Zed Books.

Esteva, G., & Prakash, M.S. (1998). *Grassroots postmodernism: Remaking the soil of cultures.* London, UK: Zed Books.

Foucault, M. (1980). *Power/knowledge: Selected interviews and other writings, 1972–1977.* New York, NY: Pantheon Books.

Frank, A.G. (1969). *Capitalism and underdevelopment in Latin America: Historical studies of Chile and Brazil.* New York, NY: Monthly Review Press.

Hall, S. (1992). The West and the rest: Discourse and power. In S. Hall, & B. Gieben (Eds), *Formation of modernity.* London, UK: Polity Press.

Illich, I. (1973). *Tools for conviviality.* New York, NY: Harper and Row.

Illich, I. (1997). Development as planned poverty. In M. Rahnema & V. Bawtree (Eds.), *Post development reader.* London, UK: Zed Books.

Kabeer, N. (1994). *Reversed realities: Gender hierarchies in development thought.* London, UK: Verso.

McEwan, C. (2001). Postcolonialism, feminism and development: Intersections and dilemmas. *Progress in Development Studies, 1*(2), 93–111.

Mannathukkaren, N. (2017). Culture and development. In P. Haslam, J. Schafer, & P. Beaudet (Eds.), *Introduction to international development: Approaches, actors and issues,* 3rd edn (pp. 441–61). Don Mills, ON: Oxford University Press.

Martinez, A. (2012). Gender and development: The struggles of women in the Global South. In P.A. Haslam, J. Schafer, & P. Beauset (Eds.), *Introduction to international development: Approaches, actors and issues* (2nd edn, pp. 86–106). Don Mills, ON: Oxford University Press.

Mies, M., Bennholdt-Thomsen, V., & von Werlhof, C. (1988). *Women: The last colony.* London, UK: Zed Books.

Mohanty, C.T. (1988). Under Western eyes: Feminist scholarship and colonial discourse. *Feminist Review, 30,* 61–88.

Peterson, K.H., & Rutherford, A. (1986). *A double colonization: Colonial and post-colonial.* Oxford, UK: Dangaroo Press.

Potter, R.B. (2014a). The nature of development studies. In V. Desai & R.B. Potter (Eds), *The companion to development studies,* 3rd edn. London, UK, and New York, NY: Routledge Taylor and Francis Group.

Potter, R.B. (2014b). Theories, strategies and ideologies of development: An overview. In V. Desai & R.B. Potter (Eds), *The companion to development studies* (3rd edn, pp. 83–8). London, UK, and New York, NY: Routledge Taylor and Francis Group.

Prebish, R. (1959). Commercial policy in the underdeveloped countries. *American Economic Review, 49,* 251–73.

Radcliffe, S. (1999). Re-thinking development. In P. Cloke, P. Crang, & M. Goodwin (Eds), *Introducing human geography* (pp. 84–91). London, UK: Arnold.

Rahnema, M. (1985). NGO—Sifting the wheat from the chaff. *Development: Seeds of Change, 3,* 68–71.

Rahnema, M. (1992). Poverty. In W. Sachs (Ed.), *The development dictionary: A guide to knowledge as power* (pp. 6–25). London, UK; Zed Books.

Rahnema, M. (1997). Introduction. In M. Rahnema & V. Bawtree (Eds), *The post development reader* (pp. ix–xix). London, UK: Zed Books.

Rai, S.M. (2011). The history of international development: Concepts and context. In N. Visvanathan, L. Duggan, N. Wiegersma, & L. Nisonoff (Eds), *The women, gender and development reader* (2nd edn, pp. 14–21). Halifax, NS, London, ON, and New York, NY: Fernwood Publishing & Zed Books.

Sahle, E.N. (2012). Post-development and alternative to development. In P.A. Haslam, J. Schafer, & P. Beaudet (Eds), *Introduction to international development: Approaches, actors and issues* (pp. 68–85). Don Mills, ON: Oxford University Press.

Said, E. (1979). *Orientalism.* New York, NY: Vintage Books.

Schuurman, F.J. (1993). *Beyond the impasse: New directions in development theory.* Chicago, IL: University of Chcago Press.

Sen, A. (1987). *Gender and cooperative conflicts.* World Institute for Development Economics Research. Helsinki, Finland: UNU-WIDER.

Sen, A. (1999). *Development as freedom.* Oxford, UK: Oxford University Press.

Sen, G., & Grown, C. (1987). *Development crises and alternative visions: Third World women's perspectives.* London, UK: Earthscan.

Shiva, V. (1989). *Staying alive: Women, ecology and survival in India.* London, UK: Zed Books.

Solati, F. (2017). *Women, work, and patriarchy in the Middle East and North Africa.* New York, NY: Palgrave.

Struckmann, C. (2018). A postcolonial feminist critique of the 2030 Agenda for Sustainable Development: A South African application. *Agenda: Empowering Women for Gender Equity, 114*(32.1), 12–24.

Tiessen, R. (2015). Walking wombs: Making sense of the Muskoka initiative and the emphasis on motherhood in Canadian foreign policy. *Global Justice, 8,* 1–22. doi: http://dx.doi.org/10.21248/gjn.8.1.58.

Tiessen, R., Parpart, J., & Marchand, M.H. (2017). Gender and development theoretical contribution, international commitments, and global campaigns. In P.A. Haslam, J. Schafer, & P. Beaudet (Eds), *Introduction to international development: Approaches, actors and issues*, 3rd edn (pp. 84–102). Don Mills, ON: Oxford University Press.

Tinker, I. (1990). *Persistent inequalities.* New York, NY: Oxford University Press.

UN Women. (2018). *Turning promises into action: Gender equality in the 2030 Agenda for Sustainable Development.* Retrieved from http://www.unwomen. org/-/media/headquarters/attachments/sections/library/ publications/2018/sdg-report-fact-sheet-global-en. pdf?la=en&vs=3554.

Villa, M. (2017). *Women own less than 20% of the world's land. It's time to give them equal property rights.* World Economic Forum. Retrieved from https://www. weforum.org/agenda/2017/01/women-own-less-than-20-of-the-worlds-land-its-time-to-give-them-equal-property-rights.

Waring, M. (1988). *If women counted: A new feminist economics.* San Francisco, CA: Harper and Row.

Ziai, A. (2017). Post-development and alternatives to development. In P.A. Haslam, J. Schafer, & P. Beaudet (Eds), *Introduction to international development: Approaches, actors and issues* (3rd edn, pp. 65–84). Don Mills, ON: Oxford University Press.

CHAPTER 9

◇

Precarious Lives, Fertile Resistance
Migrant Domestic Workers, Gender, Citizenship, and Well-Being

Denise L. Spitzer

Learning Objectives

In this chapter, you will:
- develop a greater understanding of how the intersections of gender, racialized, and migration status are configured in the context of neoliberal globalization and the globalized labour market;
- examine how the precariousness of migrant lives is constructed and maintained;
- learn about migrant advocacy and collective resistance to the deleterious effects of neoliberal globalization.

Introduction

Our globalized world is characterized by increased movements of peoples across and within the borders of nation-states. Prominent among these flows are people, predominantly women from the **Global South**, who relocate to the **Global North** or more affluent centres in the geographic South to labour in private homes as domestic workers. Alongside the ongoing demand for domestic assistance, their movements are informed by dominant discourses and policies promoted by global economic institutions who assert that out-migration and the return of financial remittances is the answer to the legacies of colonialism, neo-colonialism, and underdevelopment experienced by countries in the Global South and by gender ideologies that herald women's sacrifice for their families.

Drawing on primary research in Canada, Hong Kong, Indonesia, and the Philippines with migrant domestic workers, this chapter highlights the ways in which global processes interacting with global gendered, racialized, and minoritized hierarchies generate **precarious working** and living conditions that inform the lives of these **migrants**. Situated in the private sphere of the household and subject to formal and informal governmental, corporate, and household policies that underscore their marginalized and often temporary status, migrant domestic workers' lives are highly circumscribed, which unsettles the possibilities of social and formal **citizenship** and can lead to deteriorating health and well-being. But as the evidence attests, migrant domestic workers are not wholly bereft. Engagement with compatriot and other migrant domestic workers not only offers social support that can mitigate the deleterious effects of their isolated living and working conditions and marginalized status but can be a site of fertile and ferocious resistance to the effects of **neoliberal globalization**.

The Context: Migration and Neoliberal Globalization

Throughout human history, populations or sub-sections thereof have been on the move, whether as part of small foraging groups in search of food, as transhumanists shifting landscapes to offer pasture to their livestock, as individual explorers, or as populations fleeing disasters—both natural and human-made. The advent of capitalism and the accompanying Western colonialist expansion-ist enterprise in the 16th century, however, laid the groundwork for the contemporary context of neoliberal globalization (Castles, 2002). More specifically, neoliberal globalization emerged out of shifts in the global economy that were sup-ported by institutions such as the International Monetary Fund (IMF), the World Bank, multina-tional corporations, and some governments begin-ning in the 1970s (Delgado Wise, Convarrubias, & Puentes, 2013). The promotion of neoliberal-ism was effected through the implementation of Structural Adjustment Programs that promoted deregulation, privatization, a greater focus on producing for export markets as opposed to local consumption, and the retreat of state expendi-tures on the public good (Desai, 2002). Multina-tional corporations benefitted from the expansion of both global commodity production chains and

outsourcing to the Global South, which helped lower costs and reduced responsibility and risk from accruing to main operations in the Global North (Castles, 2011; Delgado Wise et al., 2013). For countries in the South, neoliberal globaliza-tion has resulted in a rise in low-waged employ-ment, a massive growth in informal work, and increased environmental degradation because of privatization and the loss of local stewardship of land and resources (Delgado Wise et al., 2013). Changes in agriculture, land tenure, and environ-mental issues propelled rural-to-urban migration, contributing to the development of a large pool of surplus labour that could be deployed in low-waged jobs in the city or in another country (Del-gado Wise et al., 2013; Spitzer & Piper, 2014).

For some urban un- and underemployed and some rural residents, out-migration has become an increasingly common strategy for individual and household survival because remunerative employ-ment in their own countries is scarce and because neoliberal policies hasten the dismantling and privatization of health and social services, making living in their homelands less tenable (Delgado Wise et al., 2013; Faist, 2008). Importantly, mi-grant workers are tasked with not just sustaining their families but with enhancing the economy of their homelands through remittances shared with their networks in their countries of origin (de Haas, 2012; Faist, 2008; Spitzer, 2016a). In 2017, 258 million people—48.4 per cent of whom were women—were living outside of their country of origin; of these, 43 per cent resided in the Global South (UNDESA, 2017).

The Construction of Precarious Lives

As suggested, the precariousness that charac-terizes many migrant lives is grounded in the impact of neoliberal globalization in their home-lands, many of which contend with multiple and ongoing economic and social crises (Spitzer & Piper, 2014). Yet migrants' lives can be further destabilized by the processes by which they enter and are integrated (or not) into their host country—all of which are informed by migrants' intersectional status and by salient political and historical legacies (Spitzer, 2016b). Being inducted into precarious employment, compelled to cope with insecure migration status, and obliged to renegotiate familial and gender roles all contribute to precarious lives.

Precarious Employment

Neoliberalism has, under the guise of **labour flexibilization**, led to the removal of worker protection mechanisms (Rückert & Labonté, 2012) and fueled the expansion of precarious employment whose features include low wages, few benefits, lack of control over the work process, job insecurity, and little or no occupational health and safety oversight or protection (Lewchuk et al., 2003; Menéndez et al., 2007). Siviö et al. (2012) further characterize precarious employment as related to fears about unemployment and limited possibilities of re-employment and to a sense of powerlessness, particularly in the absence of support mechanisms such as unions. Dejardin (2008, p. 8) notes that "workers in precarious employment, without economic and social entitlements, and without long-term career prospects or equipped with few skills are more vulnerable to risks of unexpected economic downswings, job and wage losses than other workers." Concern over the prospects of unemployment further constrains workers in precarious employment from voicing complaints that might result in loss of their jobs (Siviö et al., 2012).

Notably, women workers are most likely to be allocated to precarious employment, which is "peripheral, insecure, hazardous, and low-paying" (International Labour Organization, 2003,

in Menéndez et al., 2007, p. 778). Within this context, good corporate responsibility practices heralded by multinational companies seldom extend to workers, mostly women workers, who toil at the far end of **global production chains** (Dejardin, 2008).

Migration Status

Regardless of the impetus for migration (work, permanent resettlement, fleeing persecution or disaster), countries subject individuals to state controls that determine who gains entry, for how long, and under what conditions. The categories by which migrants are classified has implications as to formal and informal policies and practices that will govern their border crossings, employment, family reunification, access to services, and settlement prospects (Goldring & Landolt, 2013). Intersectionality—referring to the mutually constituted interactions among racialized status, gender, socio-economic and migration status, country of origin, religious affiliation, sexual orientation, and educational background, among other social characteristics—situates individuals in the social hierarchy and marks individuals as potentially worthy or unworthy of entry (Spitzer, 2016a). Moreover, the legacy of colonialism underpins where individuals and communities are situated in the social landscape (Brown, Smye, & Varcoe, 2007) and therefore has implications for how migrants are able to locate themselves in their host society. As Grosfoguel (2004, p. 332) writes: "No identity in the modern world escapes the global racial/colonial formation form by coloniality on a world scale"; thus, colonial constructions of identity structure social relations in destination countries even where no previous colonial relations existed.

Citizenship, which Dobrowolsky and Tastsoglou (2006, p. 15) describe as "a legally defined but always politically significant social construction of membership and participation based on gender, age, sexuality, migrant status, class, states, ethnicity/race and other 'nodes' and forms of social division and inequality," and social and economic inclusion and exclusion are key elements of precarity. Notably, citizenship status does not always cohere with whether or how individuals take up the rights and responsibilities that the status proffers or limits, but it does affect how migrants are able to maneuver themselves in public spaces, what social goods they may access, the entitlements they may claim, and the potential certainty with which they may assert their rights to remain (Goldring & Landolt, 2013; Ong, 2006).

Importantly, migrants who may, along with their family members, be eligible for legal citizenship are subject to various demands and regulations that can enhance their sense of precariousness. For example, some countries require migrants to pass language and local knowledge tests (Wray, 2009), and in Canada applicants for permanent residency who have a family member with a criminal record may have their applications for the entire family refused (Spitzer & Torres, 2008). Unsurprisingly, those who enter a country without documentation or who become undocumented experience precarity on an ongoing basis (Goldring & Landolt, 2013).

Gender Ideology and Familial Roles

Gender ideologies embed themselves in structures, relationships, values, discourses, and the gendered social roles individuals occupy in various contexts. Changing context through migration often engenders negotiating different gender and familial roles, which for most women involves expanding their roles as breadwinners and extending their care-work responsibilities across borders. These shifting roles and the expectations associated with them further contribute to the precarity of migrant lives.

Leaving home to earn money for one's family is predicated on imagining a future that is more prosperous than what they might anticipate at home. In countries such as Indonesia and the Philippines, state-supported and popular discourses also valorize migrant workers as economic heroes reinforcing the flow of remittances (Spitzer & Piper, 2014; Yeoh, 2014). In particular, female migrants are more likely than their male counterparts to be trapped in low-income jobs where they, as dutiful wives, sisters, daughters, and mothers, may be called upon to sacrifice their own dreams of further education, of alternative work possibilities, of a different family life, or even of returning home for the good of their families who are in need of the remittances forwarded by migrant family members (Spitzer, 2011; 2012). The control that families have the potential to exert over migrant workers' (presents) and futures can further inform the uncertainty that can be woven through their lives.

Impact on Health and Well-Being

Health and well-being of migrants can be regarded as the outcomes of macro-level phenomena such as neoliberal globalization and the globalized division of labour and meso-level institutions, including gender roles and ideologies, ethnicity and racialization, migration, labour market, and social protection policies, and access to health and social services—all of which may reflect and entrench structural racism, *inter alia*, and their interactions with individual-level phenomena such as the family, household, and the body (Spitzer, 2016b). While the impact of structural racism and other macro- and meso-level phenomena may result in the expression of symptoms that do not easily fit within the confines of diagnostic labels and that may be regarded as the embodiment of marginalization (Spitzer, 2011), precarious employment in itself can be deleterious to health. The effects include high rates of musculoskeletal disorders, mental health problems (Menéndez et al., 2007), and injuries, particularly when workers experience job insecurity and uncertainty (Lewchuk et al., 2003; Siviö et al., 2012). Lack of control in the workplace as well as reduced social, organizational, and material power contribute to stress, which also has important implications for health (Brooker & Eakin, 2001).

Migrant Domestic Labour: Labouring Lives/Precarious Lives

Neoliberalism has contributed to the withdrawal of public support for health and social support programs, including day-, elder-, and home-care services, thereby shifting those responsibilities to private households—specifically to women for whom this work is deemed "natural" and inherently rewarding (Dejardin, 2008; Spitzer, 2016b). These additional responsibilities coupled with increased labour market participation have worked to increase demand for paid domestic assistance. Concomitantly, women from the Global South who are tasked with supporting their families materially and socially and who are likely to place their family's welfare above their own aspirations comprise a source of migrant domestic labour. As previously mentioned, their out-migration is further propelled by dominant discourses that herald migrant workers as heroes who, through their remittances, are contributing to the national economy (Spitzer, 2016a).

Of the more than 67 million people, approximately 83 per cent of them women, employed as domestic workers, an estimated 8.45 million women are migrants (Lim, 2016; McAuliffe & Ruhs, 2018). Because they are often left out of labour and social protection policies and legislation and operate within the private sphere of the household, domestic workers are particularly vulnerable to abuse and to violations of their labour

and human rights (Dejardin, 2008; Deshingkar & Zeitlyn, 2014). Lutz (2008) argues that the labour market for migrant domestic workers differs from that for other migrant categories because of the intimate nature of domestic labour and care-work, which is informed by gender ideologies that associate this work with women's role, and the uniquely structured relationship between employer and employee that entrenches social hierarchy and instills perceptions and sentiments of servitude (Parreñas, 2001).

State and non-state actors in both the Philippines and Indonesia, the major suppliers of migrant labour, encourage and facilitate the out-migration of their citizens. As one Philippine government official shared, "without overseas labor the Philippines would have had a social revolution. With so many entering the labor force, where could they go? Overseas work became an economic and political solution for our country" (Rodriguez, 2010, p. 76). The Philippine government has a sophisticated system of labour brokerage that has become a model for other countries, including Indonesia, and that helps to promulgate discourses that responsibilize migrants, particularly women, who are regarded as natural carers, for the economic and social development of the country (Rodriguez & Schwenken, 2013).

Migrant Domestic Workers in Hong Kong

Asia hosts the greatest concentration of migrants worldwide—the vast majority of whom are temporary workers because there are few opportunities for permanent resettlement in the region (Battisella, 2014; Gaetano & Yeoh, 2010). Moreover, the migrant work force is increasingly feminized because of the demand for domestic, care, and sex workers as well as for foreign brides (Yeoh, 2014). In 2012, 155,969 Philippine and 149,236 Indonesian migrant domestic workers were employed in Hong Kong, who along with colleagues from Thailand, Sri Lanka, and Nepal, among other countries, comprised approximately 10 per cent of the workforce such that Hong Kong had one of the highest concentrations of migrant domestic workers in the world (Kang, 2016; Lim, 2016). Migrant domestic labourers work an average of 71.4 hours per week, 20 to 30 hours more than other workers, for which they generally earn minimum wage, which for them is less than 50 per cent of what other workers earn (Kang, 2016). Employers are required to grant domestic workers a full 24-hour rest day; however, approximately one-third of workers are unable to avail themselves of the full amount of time to which they are entitled (Kang, 2016). If migrant domestic workers lose or leave their position before their contracts are completed, they must secure another post within two weeks or vacate the country—except in exceptional circumstances when the employer has died, migrated, experienced a change in financial circumstances, been abusive, or failed to meet the conditions of their employment contract.

While migrant domestic workers are subject to conditions imposed by recruitment agencies that often leave them and their families in debt in order to secure a position, country of origin figures into hiring practices. Filipino workers, who dominated the foreign domestic worker market in Hong Kong for decades, are considered better educated and more Westernized than other migrant workers but are also regarded by some as being too assertive in demanding their rights (Constable, 2007). By contrast, Indonesian workers, many of whom have low levels of education and hail from rural areas (Hugo, 2005), are deemed more traditional and docile (Constable, 2007). While these stereotypes belie the diversity of migrant domestic workers from both countries, these discourses and their impact on hiring and employer relations reflect an important aspect of their intersectional status.

Working within the confines of private households, migrant domestic workers are often vulnerable to abuse and contract violations (Spitzer & Torres, 2008; see also "A Conversation with Erwiana Sulisyaningsih and Eni Lestari" in the box on p. 150). Moreover, in Hong Kong employers often deploy home-based video surveillance to monitor the behaviour of domestic workers, further engendering a stressful work environment where, since they reside with their employers, workers have difficulty carving out a private home life outside of their employers' purview. Although migrant workers undergo medical examinations to ensure that they are in good health prior to departure from their home countries, migrant domestic workers in Hong Kong report myriad health complaints, including headaches, gastro-intestinal symptoms, insomnia, menstrual disorders, and back and neck pain (Sobritchea & de Guzman, 2006; Zulbahary & Elanvito, 2006). Employers are required to cover the costs of medical treatment (Liang, 2016), and migrant domestic workers are eligible for pregnancy and sick leave (Hong Kong Labour Dept, 2017).

Migrant Domestic Workers in Canada

With an aging populace and low population growth, Canada requires newcomers to fill jobs and contribute to the economy (Boyd, 2011). The importation of care-workers is promoted as a means of addressing the so-called care-crisis—referring to the paucity of child, elder, and disability supports that increases responsibilities for informal family caregivers, with little reference to the neoliberal agenda that contributed to the withdrawal or withholding of public assistance of these services and to the gender ideologies that assign those tasks to women, Canada has been engaged in the importation of foreign domestic workers for more than 100 years (Spitzer & Torres, 2008). Until November 2014, the iteration of the government program that facilitated the migration of foreign workers to care for children, the elderly, and persons with a disability—the Live-In Caregiver Program (LCP)—offered those who successfully completed the program a pathway to permanent residency (PR) and family reunification on Canadian soil. Prospective LCP workers had to speak, read, and write English or French, possess the equivalent of a high school education (notably, more than 60 per cent were university graduates [Kelly et al., 2011]), and have completed caregiving or related education, training, or work experience (Spitzer & Torres, 2008). Caregivers were required to reside with their employer, who was to provide them with a private lockable room. Live-in caregivers were eligible to apply for PR status and bring in immediate family members after 24 months of work within a limited time period. While acceptance was not automatic, between 2006 and 2014 an annual average of 10,740 LCP workers and their families settled permanently in Canada (Keung, 2018; Spitzer & Torres, 2008). In late 2014, the LCP was replaced by the Caregiver Program (CP), a temporary migrant worker program that, through a five-year pilot project that expires in November 2019, allows for a much more limited possibility of permanent residency status for caregivers who have cared for children or persons with high medical needs full-time in Canada for two years and in the latter case, are licensed health professionals (Government of Canada, 2018). Importantly, the

numbers of care-workers being granted PR status has dramatically declined, with a total of 1955 successful applicants in the three years since the implementation of the new regulations (Keung, 2018). In addition to narrowing the opportunity for permanent resettlement, the CP removed the co-living requirement; however, few appear to be availing themselves of this option (Keung, 2018). As the end of the CP as a five-year pilot project approaches in November 2019, the future of the CP at time of writing (January 2019) appears uncertain. As a result, the lives of migrant domestic workers awaiting a decision about their applications for PR status, and those anxious to complete CP requirements and submit a PR request before the deadline of 29 November 2019, are indeed precarious, and this insecurity has, as has been discussed, repercussions on health.

Migrant domestic care-workers in Canada report similar health complaints, including headaches, diffuse bodily pains, injuries, and mental health issues exacerbated by worries about their families and their futures (Spitzer, 2011; Spitzer & Torres, 2008). Those who reside with their employers are vulnerable not only to abuse but to demands/expectations for overtime work, and workers residing in Canada's rural areas are often isolated and at the mercy of their employers for transportation into an urban centre to access services and/or social networks (Spitzer, 2009; Spitzer & Torres, 2008). Because workers must

TABLE 9.1   Migrant care-workers in Hong Kong and Canada

Migrant care-workers	
Hong Kong	*Canada*
• Must live with employer	• Since CP implemented in 2014, not required to live with employer
• Few have private space	• Right to private, lockable room if living with employer
• Duties include housework and care labour	• Duties focus on care labour
• Work average 71 hours per week	• Maximum 48-hour work week—eligible for overtime pay after 44 hours
• No path to permanent residency	• Path to permanent residency not assured

fulfill their commitment to the CP within four years, leaving one's employ can result in periods of unemployment and anxiety about whether one can complete the program. Furthermore, with the virtual guarantee of permanent resettlement replaced by a much reduced possibility of obtaining PR status, migrant domestic workers are facing similar stress regarding the precarious nature of their migration and employment as those in Hong Kong. Those who are able to migrate are apt to encounter challenges entering the labour market as racialized workers whose credentials and work experiences are not recognized while contending with the financial demands and readjustments associated with family reunification (Torres et al., 2012).

Migrant Domestic Workers: From Precarious Work to Precarious Lives

The effects of neoliberal globalization that contribute to the economic and social insecurity further impel (predominantly) women to take up positions as foreign domestic workers. Working and primarily living in private households where they often work long hours, lack control over their work and living environment, and are isolated and surveilled contributes to deleterious effects on health and well-being that are exacerbated by the stress associated with their insecure migration and employment status, which further constrains their ability and willingness to redress the entrenched hierarchies in which they are embedded. Moreover, as they are often responsibilized for supporting their families, loss of employment is problematic. In addition, their relegation to private households often means that their interactions with others outside the family might be circumscribed for much of the workweek, reducing their exposure to the local populace and to other (potential) friends and intimates. This segregation and their limited or lack of access to social protection mechanisms contributes to social exclusion and the sense that they are only

ever partial citizens, even in the social if not legal sense. For migrant domestic workers, precarious work spills out of the confines of labour and, merging with the effects of gender, racialized, and migration status and socio-economic class, contours precarious lives.

Fertile Resistance

Migrant domestic workers are not, however, merely victims of multiple oppressions facing myriad competing demands; they are capable of demonstrating both agency—the ability to marshal social and material resources to take action on one's life—and resistance, the collective action that works to destabilize hegemonic forces and discourses (Parker, 2005; Spitzer, 2016b). Importantly, the ability to assemble the requisite resources to express agency is socially distributed such that not all persons in all circumstances are able to assert themselves, and while agency may be transformed into resistance, it does not necessarily follow. In addition, resistance, which can be both vital and potent, may be romanticized, and notably, the powerful forces that coalesce against counter-hegemonic efforts cannot be underestimated (Constable, 2007; Parker, 2005). That said, migrant domestic workers around the world are

Indonesian migrant domestic workers at International Migrants' Day protest in Hong Kong.

A Conversation with Erwiana Sulistyaningsih and Eni Lestari

Background: Indonesians Erwiana Sulistyaningsih and Eni Lestari came to Hong Kong to work as domestic labourers. Arriving in 1999, Ms Lestari's labour rights were violated by her employer, and with help from other Indonesian workers, she sought refuge in Bethune House, a shelter operated by the Asia Pacific Mission for Migrants (APMM). Since then, Eni has become a global advocate for the rights of migrant workers, and as chairperson of the International Migrants Alliance, in 2016 she became the first domestic worker to address the General Assembly of the United Nations. Ms Sulistyaningsih took up a post with a Hong Kong family and returned to Indonesia nine months later after enduring multiple forms of abuse. With the support of others, Erwiana took her employer to court where the latter was found guilty of 18 charges, fined, and sentenced to six years in prison. Ms Sulistyaningsih was named one of *Time*'s most influential people in the world in 2014 and at the time of writing was attending university in Indonesia. I spoke with both of them about their experiences and the importance of international solidarity.

Erwiana: My family are farmers. We are five people—me, my father, brother, and grandmother. We were poor, and after high school I moved to Jakarta, but the salary wasn't enough to help my family. In 2012, I entered a training centre to await a job offer as a domestic worker, and in May 2013 I was sent to Hong Kong. I returned to Indonesia in January 2014. My employer in Hong Kong treated me badly. I was given three to five slices of bread a day or one bowl of rice per day. I was allowed to sleep for four hours from 1 a.m. to 5 a.m. I was not given a rest day, not allowed out of the house, and could not access a mobile phone. I ran away and called my employment agency, but they returned me to my employer, without my passport or contract. Things with my employer got worse. She punched me in my mouth, my face, my ear, etc. After eight months, my body was so weak I couldn't work, so the employer told me to return to Indonesia. She returned my passport, gave me a ticket and 100,000 Indonesian Rupiah (~$8 USD). She took me to the airport and repeated her warning that if I said anything she would kill my family.

While waiting for my plane, some other Indonesian domestic workers approached me. At first, I was scared to talk to them because of what my employer said. One took my photo as my face was bruised and swollen; she posted it on Facebook, and she accompanied me to my home in Java. Migrant advocacy groups saw the post and began to organize around my case. They mobilized and organized a demonstration in Hong Kong that brought my situation to the attention of the media and to the authorities.

I was encouraged to take my employer to court to fight for my rights, my salary, and compensation. I didn't know anything, but the organization helped me learn about Hong Kong rules; they supported me, and I became stronger. I was not scared anymore. I want my experience to help others to learn that if you fight, you can win. People tell me that I'm brave, that I'm a "good fighter." Sometimes I feel sad, but I can handle it.

Eni: In January 2014, one organization member reported she saw a Facebook post about the abuse of a domestic worker stranded in the Hong Kong airport. We traced the person who posted the photo and asked some former Hong Kong–based domestic workers, now migrant advocates, to visit Erwiana and to gather a statement and try to organize a case. We organized demonstrations at the Indonesian consulate and at the employment agency. Soon after, we held a rally at the Hong Kong Police Department; we expected about 500 people as we had only five days to organize it, but 5000 people showed up. A second abuse victim came forward, and after Erwiana lodged a complaint with the police. The employer was arrested at the airport while she was trying to leave the country.

We learned how to help others and how to organize from Bethune House and APMM. I was picked to become a case worker. People get help but also become educated, and they are transformed into leaders. Case workers learn to be good companions, to help people without asking for something in return, and to focus on the victim. You need to help people to understand why we do what we do. We get them to participate so they can apply their new knowledge.

Solidarity is important. Erwiana won her case not because of Indonesians, and not because of her horrible abuse, but because of the solidarity across nationalities; this was key to pressuring the government. Migrant workers are international citizens, but to win we need solidarity across borders. Helping people of other sectors understand our issues requires us to educate, educate, educate and never get tired as they need to understand. Solidarity is based on unity of migrants themselves. We need political solidarity not just some money and kind words—that's not enough. We must recognize that victims are not powerless. Often victims are viewed as fragile; they need to be educated to stand alone, as you cannot be the protector. Case workers must learn this as must NGOs and faith communities. Advocacy and welfare must go hand in hand to assist victims faster to achieve their goals.

Erwiana: We want others to be in solidarity with migrants. We are human, we need your support; we cannot win if you are not supporting us. We are human and we have human rights.

Some Examples of Migrant Domestic Worker Organizations

Canada
- Association for the Rights of Household Workers (Montreal)
- Caregivers Action Centre (Toronto)
- Migrant Worker Centre (Vancouver)
- Migrante Alberta (Edmonton)
- Philippine Women's Centre of BC (Vancouver)
- Philippine Women's Centre of Ontario (Toronto)
- PINAY (Montreal)

Hong Kong
- Asia Pacific Mission for Migrants
- Association of Indonesian Migrant Workers in Hong Kong (ATKI-HK)
- Indonesian Migrant Workers Union

continued

- United Indonesians Against Overcharging (PILAR)
- United Filipinos in Hong Kong (UNIFIL-HK)

Indonesia
- INDIES
- KABAR-BUMI
- Migrant Care
- Solidaritas Perempuan

Philippines
- Center for Migrant Advocacy
- Migrant Forum in Asia
- Migrante International

engaging in collective efforts to have their rights as workers, as women, and as migrants recognized, to generate critiques against neoliberal globalization, sexism, and racism, among other issues, and to join in solidarity with other activists to work toward a more just world.

Migrant domestic workers' capacity to organize and advocate may be influenced by their ability to imagine a different life, by their opportunities to communicate freely and network with others, and by their country of residence. In the Netherlands, for example, Dutch trade unionists and foreign domestic workers formed the International Domestic Workers Network (now Federation) in 2009 (Lim, 2016), yet in countries such as Malaysia, foreigners are not allowed to lead or sometimes even join migrant advocacy organizations (Elias, 2008). In contrast, Hong Kong in its self-presentation as a transnational, global city, permits migrant workers to assemble and to express their viewpoints (Constable, 2009; Lim, 2016). Canada is also home to numerous foreign domestic care-worker organizations, such as the Association for the Rights of Household Workers, the Philippine Women's Centres, INTERCEDE, Migrant Workers Centre (formerly the West Coast Domestic Workers Association), among many others, that have been very active in lobbying for policy change (Bakan & Stasiulis, 1997; Spitzer & Torres, 2008; see box with examples of migrant domestic worker organizations).

Migrant domestic workers who participate in advocacy organizations not only learn about their human and labour rights and exchange informational, emotional, and material support, they also come to understand that the hardships they and their families face are not an individual problem but reflective of systemic issues, thereby sharpening their critique of neoliberal globalization and their understanding of gendered and racialized inequities (Torres et al., 2012). In Hong Kong, some Indonesian domestic workers credit their encounters with the more established Filipino migrant community—often through shelters operated by NGOs or migrant support organizations where they sought refuge after losing or leaving their employ—with facilitating their advocacy and organizing skills (Constable, 2009). Nation-specific organizations have proliferated, yet groups such as the Asian Migrants' Coordinating Body, which serves as an umbrella organization that facilitates coalition-building among myriad migrant worker organizations and local activists, and the Hong Kong Federation of Asian Domestic Workers—comprised of various domestic worker unions whose memberships are of foreign or local origins—are bridging constituencies (Constable, 2009; Lim, 2016). Importantly, coalitions allow for individuals to mobilize around their own cultural, national, historical, and political particularities and come together in ways that acknowledge disparate perspectives and a common agenda on specific issues. Many of these organizations in Hong Kong and elsewhere have deployed the language of human rights to forward their claims and have focused attention on the ratification of international agreements such as the International Convention on the Protection of the Rights of All Migrant Workers and Members of Their Families and the ILO's Domestic Workers' Convention (Elias, 2008; Lim, 2016). Mobilizing around these initiatives entails educating members and providing them with a local, regional, and international platform for voicing their concerns and offering alternatives (Conway, 2012). For example, organizations such as Migrante International and the International Migrants Alliance link members across borders, building a transnational movement led by migrant workers themselves (Rodriguez, 2013).

Despite the precarity of their lives, many migrant domestic workers are actively engaged in collective and fertile resistance—and/or in quotidian acts of agency that can improve individual circumstances. Engaging in active solidarity with migrant domestic workers to critique, reverse, and/or redress the deleterious effects of neoliberal globalization requires us to embrace a transversal politics grounded in a willingness to reflect on our position in the socio-political landscape, to critically unpack hegemonic discourses, and to be willing to step back and allow others, who are experts on their own lives, to lead (Conway, 2012; Mohanty, 2003).

Conclusion

Neoliberal globalization, with its focus on trade liberalization, privatization, and reductions in public spending, has helped to destabilize people's livelihoods across the globe. With fewer permanent and remunerative opportunities at home, many families in the Global South have turned to labour migration to sustain themselves. The confluence of the ongoing demand for domestic (care) labour and dominant gender ideologies that construct women as naturally inclined for this work, responsible for the well-being of their families, and willing to sacrifice themselves for others, has helped to ensure the steady out-migration of women migrant domestic workers. Often beginning their overseas assignments indebted to recruitment agencies that secure their contracts, migrant domestic workers contend with temporary migration status and isolation that leaves them vulnerable to labour and human rights violations. The desire to send remittances to their families means that workers persist in often trying circumstances where their racialized and gender status helps to entrench intra-household and societal hierarchies while their tentative migration status works to silence complaints. Although their experiences of precarity begin prior to migration, precarious migrant labour further informs and sustains the generation of precarious lives. With limited access to both legal and social citizenship, migrant domestic workers often experience an erosion of health and well-being.

These migrant workers, however, do their best to exert their own agency to mitigate their own circumstances, and, where they are able, many find ways to join with others to critique, resist, and confront neoliberal globalization by insisting: "We are workers; we are not slaves." There is an important role for transnational feminists to express solidarity with migrant domestic workers' struggles, beginning with learning more about their issues, understanding our own location within their contexts, listening more, and letting migrant workers take the lead in articulating both their concerns and their solutions for a more equitable world.

Call to Action

Research what migrant worker support and political actions exist in your area, as well as what international campaigns are currently ongoing. Volunteer with local organizations that support migrant workers in your community, and bring local attention to a current international campaign for migrant workers' rights. Want to do more? Host a film/video/arts festival featuring the stories of a diverse range of migrant workers around the world.

Tying It Together

Gendered ideologies are mobilized in the global processes of neoliberal globalization and informed by colonial and neo-colonial legacies to promulgate the out-migration of migrant domestic workers to the Global North. The precarious employment that these workers undertake—whether in Hong Kong or Canada—is a major factor in making their lives precarious. Despite the challenges, migrant domestic workers are often able to assert agency and to organize resistance to confront dominant forces of oppression and marginalization.

DISCUSSION QUESTIONS

1. How is neoliberal globalization linked to migration?
2. What drives the demand for migrant domestic workers?
3. How does precariousness affect health and well-being?
4. Why do you think the author differentiates between precarious employment and precarious lives?
5. How might you stand in solidarity with migrant domestic workers in Canada and around the world?

SUGGESTIONS FOR FURTHER READING

Flores-González, N., Guevarra, A.R., Toro-Morn, M., & Chang, G. (Eds). (2013). *Immigrant women workers in the neoliberal age*. Urbana, IL: University of Illinois Press. This edited volume highlights immigrant women working in the informal sector across the US, as well as their efforts to improve their living and working conditions.

Goldring, L., & Krishnamurti, S. (Eds). (2007). *Organizing the transnational: Labour, politics, and social change*. Vancouver, BC: University of British Columbia Press. With contributions from both academics and activists, this edited volume examines the ways in which diverse migrant communities in Canada engage with shifting domains of citizenship, identity, and collective action.

Huang, S., Yeoh, B., & Rahman, N. (Eds). (2005). *Asian women as transnational domestic workers*. Singapore: Marshall Cavendish Academic. This book offers an overview of the circumstances and experiences faced by migrant domestic workers from Asia who work in private households around the world.

Lutz, H. (Ed.). *Migration and domestic work: A European perspective on a global theme*. Aldershot, UK: Ashgate Publishing. Contributors to this

book examine the policies, discourses, and individual practices that contour the lives of migrant domestic workers in Europe.

MULTIMEDIA SUGGESTIONS

International Labour Organization, Working hours and wages for domestic workers in Asia, 30 April 2013
https://www.youtube.com/watch?v=VvF1B97YanE
This video, produced by the International Labour Organization, underscores how domestic workers are often treated as servants rather than as workers; moreover, domestic labour is not often included under work legislation. It further highlights attempts to ratify the Domestic Workers Convention, C-189.

Migrante International AVP, 8 March 2011
https://www.youtube.com/watch?v=sBZHYHzrpwc
Migrante International, a grassroots migrant advocacy organization based in the Philippines with chapters around the world, provides an overview of Overseas Filipino Workers and outlines their efforts to fight for the rights of Filipino workers across the globe.

"I was just a slave": The foreign domestic staff living a life of five-star serfdom in London. *The Guardian*, 11 January 2016
https://www.youtube.com/watch?v=V1V6QGrOFvA
Illustrating how immigration policies such as employer-tied visas are directly implicated in obstructing reports of abuse, this documentary exposes maltreatment of foreign domestic workers by wealthy employers in London, UK. Additionally, it introduces

the audience to organizations that are supporting migrant domestic workers who are trying to leave these situations.

International Migrants Alliance (IMA)
https://wearemigrants.net
The IMA is an international coalition of migrants, refugees, displaced people, and their families that analyzes and critiques neoliberal globalization, engages in solidarity campaigns, and draws attention to unjust labour practices around the world.

Migrante International
https://migranteinternational.org
Based in the Philippines but with chapters in 23 countries, Migrante International is the largest organization of Overseas Filipino Workers (OFWs) in the world. They are engaged in education, research, lobbying, and supporting OFWs and their families.

Migrant Workers Alliance for Change
http://www.migrantworkersalliance.org
The Migrant Workers Alliance for Change is an Ontario-based coalition of migrant worker advocacy and grassroots organizations, academics, faith communities, and labour groups that are engaged in campaigns to promote the rights of migrant workers in Canada.

REFERENCES

Bakan, A., & Stasiulis, D. (1997). Foreign domestic worker policy in Canada and the social boundaries of modern citizenship. In A. Bakan & D. Stasiulis (Eds), *Not one of the family: Foreign domestic workers in Canada* (pp. 29–52). Toronto, ON: University of Toronto Press.

Battisella, G. (2014). Migration in Asia: In search of a theoretical framework. In G. Battisella (Ed.), *Global and Asian perspectives on migration* (pp. 1–26). Cham, Switzerland: Springer International Publishing.

Boyd, M. (2011). Bringing care workers to Canada: Canada's migration policies. In *Women, migration and the work of care: The United States in comparative perspective* (pp. 5–10). Washington, DC: Woodrow Wilson International Center for Scholars.

Brooker, A-S., & Eakin, J. (2001). Gender, class, work-related stress and health: Toward a power-centred approach. *Journal of Community and Applied Social Psychology, 11*, 97–109.

Brown, A., Smye, V., & Varcoe, C. (2007). Postcolonial-feminist theoretical perspectives and women's health. In M. Morrow, O. Hankivsky, & C. Varcoe (Eds), *Women's health in Canada: Critical perspectives* on theory and policy (pp. 124–42). Toronto, ON: University of Toronto Press.

Castles, S. (2002). Migration and community formation under conditions of globalization. *International Migration Review, 36*(4), 1143–68.

Castles, S. (2011). Migration, crisis, and the global labour market. *Globalizations, 8*(3), 311–24.

Constable, N. (2007). *Maid to order in Hong Kong: Stories of migrant workers*. Ithaca, NY: Cornell University Press.

Constable, N. (2009). Migrant workers and the many states of protest in Hong Kong. *Critical Asian Studies, 41*(1), 143–64.

Conway, J. (2012). Transnational feminisms building anti-globalization solidarities. *Globalizations, 9*(3), 379–93.

De Haas, H. (2012). The migration and development pendulum: A critical view on research and policy. *International Migration, 50*(3), 8–25.

Dejardin, A. (2008). *Gender dimensions of globalization*. Geneva: International Labour Organization.

Delgado Wise, R., Convarrubias, H., & Puentes, R. (2013). Reframing the debate on migration, development and human rights. *Population, Space and Place, 19*, 430–43.

Desai, M. (2002). Transnational solidarity: Women's agency, structural adjustment, and globalization. In N. Naples & M. Desai (Eds), *Women's activism and globalization: Linking local struggles with transnational politics* (pp. 15–33). New York, NY: Routledge.

Deshingkar, P., & Zeitlyn, B. (2014). *Does migration for domestic work reduce poverty? A review of the literature and an agenda for research*. Working Paper 15. Falmer, Brighton, UK: University of Sussex.

Dobrowolsky, A., & Tastsoglou, E. (2006). Crossing boundaries and making connections. In E. Tastsoglou & A. Dobrowolsky (Eds), *Women, migration and citizenship: Making local, national and transnational connections* (pp. 2–35). Aldershot, UK: Ashgate Palgrave.

Elias, J. (2008). Struggles over the rights of foreign domestic workers in Malaysia: The possibilities and limitations of "rights talk." *Economy and Society, 37*(2), 282–303.

Faist, T. (2008). Migrants as transnational development agents: An inquiry into the newest round of the migration-development nexus. *Population, Space and Place, 14*, 21–42.

Gaetano, A., & Yeoh, B. (2010). Introduction to the special issue on women and migration in globalizing Asia: Gendered experiences, agency, and activism. *International Migration, 48*(6), 1–12.

Goldring, L., & Landolt, P. (2013). The conditionality of legal status and rights: Conceptualizing precarious non-citizenship in Canada. In L. Goldring & P. Landolt (Eds), *Producing and negotiating citizenship: Precarious legal status in Canada* (pp. 3–27). Toronto, ON: University of Toronto Press.

Government of Canada. (2018). Caregivers—Options for permanent residence. 27 May. Retrieved from https://www.canada.ca/en/immigration-refugees-citizenship/services/immigrate-canada/caregivers.html.

Grosfoguel, R. (2004). Race and ethnicity or racialized ethnicities? Identities within global coloniality. *Ethnicities, 4*(3), 315–36.

Hong Kong Labour Department. (2017). *Practice guide for employment of foreign domestic helpers—What domestic helpers and their employers should know*. Hong Kong: Hong Kong Labour Department. Available from: https://www.labour.gov.hk/public/wcp/FDHguide.pdf. Retrieved 28 June 2018.

Hugo, G. (2005). Indonesian international domestic workers: Contemporary developments and issues. In S. Huang, B. Yeoh, & N.A. Rahman (Eds), *Asian women as transnational workers* (pp. 54–91). Singapore: Marshall Cavendish Academic.

Kang, J. (2016). Study reveals 95% of Filipino, Indonesian helpers in Hong Kong exploited or forced labor. *Forbes*, 18 March. Retrieved from www.forbes.com/sites/johnkang/2016/03/18.

Kelly, P., Park, S., de Leon, C., & Priest, J. (2011). *Profile of live-in caregiver immigrants to Canada, 1993–2009*. TIEDI Analytical Report 18. Toronto, ON: Toronto Immigrant Employment Data Initiative.

Keung, N. (2018). Number of migrant caregivers becoming permanent residents plummets after federal changes. *Toronto Star*, 3 February. Retrieved from https://www.thestar.com/news/immigration/2018/02/03/number-of-migrant-caregivers-becoming-permanent-residents-plummets-after-federal-changes.html.

Lewchuk, W., de Wolff, A., King, A., & Polyani, M. (2003). From job strain to employment strain: Health effects of precarious employment. *Just Labour, 3*(Fall), 23–35.

Liang, C. (2016). Maid in Hong Kong: Protecting foreign domestic workers. Retrieved from https://www.migrationpolicy.org/article/maid-hong-kong-protecting-foreign-domestic-workers.

Lim, A. (2016). Transnational organising and feminist politics of difference and solidarity: The mobilisation of domestic workers in Hong Kong. *Asian Studies Review, 40*(1), 70–88.

Lutz, H. (2008). Introduction: Migrant domestic workers in Europe. In H. Lutz (Ed.), *Migration and domestic work: A European perspective on a global theme* (pp. 1–10). Aldershot, UK: Ashgate Publishing.

McAuliffe, M., & Ruhs, M. (2018). *World migration report 2018*. Geneva: International Organization for Migration.

Menéndez, M., Benach, J., Muntaner, C., Amable, M., & O'Campo, P. (2007). Is precarious employment more damaging to women's health than men's? *Social Science & Medicine, 64*, 776–81.

Mohanty, Chandra Talpade. (2003). *Feminism without borders: Decolonizing theory, practicing solidarity.* Durham, NC: Duke University Press.

Ong, A. (2006). Mutations in citizenship. *Theory, Culture & Society, 23*(2–3), 499–505.

Parker, L. (2005). Resisting resistance and finding agency: Women and medicalized birth in Bali. In L. Parker (Ed.), *The agency of women in Asia* (pp. 62–97). Singapore: Marshall Cavendish International.

Parreñas, R.S. (2001). *Servants of globalization: Women, migration and domestic work.* Stanford, CA: Stanford University Press.

Rodriguez, R.M. (2010). *Migrants for export: How the Philippines state brokers labor to the world.* Minneapolis, MN: University of Minnesota Press.

Rodriguez, R.M. (2013). Beyond citizenship: Emergent forms of political subjectivity amongst migrants. *Identities: Global Studies in Culture and Power, 20*(6), 738–54.

Rodriguez, R.M., & Schwenken, H. (2013). Becoming a migrant at home: Subjectivation processes in migrant-sending countries prior to departure. *Population, Space and Place, 19,* 375–88.

Rückert, A., & Labonté, R. (2012). The global financial crisis and health equity: Toward a conceptual framework. *Critical Public Health, 22,* 3, 267–79.

Siviö, A., Ek, E., Jorkelainen, J., Koiranen, M., Järvikoski, T., & Taanila, A. (2012). Precariousness and discontinuous work history in association with health. *Scandinavian Journal of Public Health, 40,* 360–7.

Sobritchea, C., & de Guzman, O. (2006). *Life and death on the move: The sexual and reproductive health status and needs of Filipino women migrant domestic workers.* Quezon City, Philippines: Action for Health Initiatives.

Spitzer, D.L. (2009). *Live-in caregivers in rural and small city Alberta.* (Report) Edmonton, AB: PCERII.

Spitzer, D.L. (2011). Work, worries, and weariness: Towards an embodied and engendered migrant health. In D.L. Spitzer (Ed.), *Engendering migrant health: Canadian perspectives* (pp. 23–39). Toronto, ON: University of Toronto Press.

Spitzer, D.L. (2012). Oppression and im/migrant health in Canada. In E.A. McGibbon (Ed.), *Oppression: A social determinant of health* (pp. 113–22). Halifax, NS: Fernwood Publishing.

Spitzer, D.L. (2016a). Return migrant entrepreneurship and the migration and development agenda: A focus on Filipino and Indonesian migrant workers. *Migration, Mobility, & Displacement, 2*(2), 24–39.

Spitzer, D.L. (2016b). Engendered movements: Migration, gender, and health in a globalized world. In J. Gideon (Ed.), *Handbook of gender and health* (pp. 251–67). London, UK: Elgar.

Spitzer, D.L., & Piper, N. (2014). Retrenched and returned: Filipino migrant workers in times of crisis. *Sociology, 48*(5), 1007–23.

Spitzer, D.L., & Torres, S. (2008). *Gendered-based barriers to settlement and integration for live-in caregivers: A review of the literature.* CERIS Working Paper no. 71. Toronto, ON: CERIS—The Ontario Metropolis Centre.

Torres, S., Spitzer, D.L., Hughes, K., Oxman-Martinez, J., & Hanley, J. (2012). From temporary worker to resident: The LCP and its impact through an intersectional lens. In P. Lenard & C. Straehle (Eds), *Legislated inequality: Temporary labour migration in Canada* (pp. 227–44). Montreal, QC: McGill-Queen's University Press.

UNDESA (United Nations, Department of Economic and Social Affairs), Population Division. (2017). *International migration report 2017.* New York, NY: United Nations.

Wray, H. (2009). Moulding the migrant family. *Legal Studies, 29*(4), 592–618.

Yeoh, B. (2014). Engendering international migration: Perspectives from within Asia. In G. Battisella (Ed.), *Global and Asian perspectives on migration* (pp. 139–52). Cham, Switzerland: Springer.

Zulbahary, T., & Elanvito, T. (2006). *State of health of Indonesian migrant workers: Access to health of Indonesian migrant workers.* Jakarta: Solidaritas Perempuan (Women's Solidarity for Human Rights).

PART IV

Gendering Politics: Militarism, Violence, and Security

Militarization, or the increasing role of organized aggression and armed conflict in society, continues to grotesquely shape the lives of millions of people around the world (Sutton, Morgen, & Novkov, 2008). The chapters in Part IV offer critical understanding on the causes and human costs of institutionalized violence. These chapters examine the paradigms of security, pacification, and cross-national militarization. They consider how international borders are increasingly militarized places, which are related to systems of domestic policing and imprisonment in an expanding prison-military-industrial complex. The authors critically challenge this complex by analyzing the relationships between gender, race, and militarization. Their chapters evaluate the trends of resistance in a worldwide crisis of militarization, which goes beyond examining American military engagements in the 21st century. This part of the volume offers scholarly and activist perspectives on these issues and indicates how we can move toward a more humane future. Working with a range of geographic scales and locations, the contributors examine the concrete and ideological connections among issues such as policing, border protection, and militarization. They challenge the state discourses surrounding security and order, showing how these efforts involve forms of coercive mobility that separate loved ones, disempower communities, and intensify poverty, inequality, racism, and gender or sexual oppression.

In "Globalization, Militarization, and Violence in Latin America," Jasmin Hristov explores the significance of violence as an ongoing feature in the development of capitalism in Latin America from colonial times until the present era of globalization. She applies feminist theory to indicate how the intersections of gender, class, and racial inequality have influenced the violence afflicting Latin American societies. The chapter highlights a key feature of the global economy, showing how economic policies create conditions conducive to gender inequality, violence against women, and violations of human and labour rights.

In "The Capital–State Nexus and Its War on Women," Jasmin Hristov identifies the ways in which different forms of violence interact to form vicious cycles that are reproduced across time and social space. She invites the reader to consider the essential role of women in movements of resistance and the ways that feminism and anticapitalism have been mutually supportive forces. Hristov examines how harmful ideologies regarding femininity and masculinity have sustained violence against women and how these gendered agendas intersect with other capitalist ideologies.

In "Immobilizing Bodies of Surveillance: Antioppressive Feminisms and the Decolonization of

Violence," Vanessa Lynn Lovelace and Heather M. Turcotte assess the historical context of surveillance as a colonial discourse. They explore how surveillance regulates people, land, and knowledge. They offer a detailed examination of the tactics of deconstruction and explain how such tactics expose the violence of surveillance. Lovelace and Turcotte examine how conflict zones and freedom trails become sites of surveillance. Finally, their chapter looks at how anti-oppressive feminisms can make resistance to surveillance both possible and effective.

In "Disrupting 'Security': Pacification, Accumulation, and Colonialism," Tia Dafnos problematizes "security" as a political discourse. She invites us to consider the role of academic knowledge production in generating a security discourse in the fields of criminology and security studies. Her chapter explores the ways that "pacification" has become a critical concept for analyzing security discourse. Dafnos situates international law and the current international state system in the history of European imperialism, and she examines how criminal justice systems are co-constituted with colonialism and global capitalism.

In "Gendered Omissions and Silences in Global Health Security," Colleen O'Manique offers an overview of the historical foundations of today's global health security policies. She outlines the ways in which specific political agendas shape responses to global health emergencies. Through a feminist postcolonial lens, she reveals the gendered gaps and omissions in current practices of global health governance. O'Manique proposes pathways that can start to disrupt the gendered structural violence embedded in such approaches to global health security.

REFERENCE

Sutton, B., Morgen, S., & Novkov, J. (Eds.). (2008). *Security disarmed: Critical perspectives on gender, race, and militarization.* New Brunswick, NJ: Rutgers University Press.

CHAPTER 10

◇

Globalization, Militarization, and Violence in Latin America

Jasmin Hristov

Learning Objectives

In this chapter, you will:

- learn about the origins of capitalism and colonialism;
- understand the significance of violence as an ongoing feature of the development of capitalism in Latin America from colonial times until the present era of globalization;
- apply feminist theories to understand how the intersection of gender, class, and racial inequalities has been played out across Latin American societies;
- examine key features of the global economy that create conditions conducive to gender inequality, violence against women, and human and labour rights violations.

Introduction

Latin America's history from the 1500s until the present has been characterized by two intertwining themes: 1) social relations marked by deep class, race, and gender inequalities and exploitation and 2) violence employed by those with economic and political power against the working majority and the poor for the purpose of maintaining control over resources and labour and eliminating or suppressing dissent. This chapter looks at how the relationship between capitalism, violence, and patriarchy has shaped Latin American

societies and more specifically gender relations. The chapter provides you with a historical overview of the development of capitalism in Latin America from colonial time until the era of globalization and the resulting class, gender, and racial hierarchies. We look at the key conditions necessary for capital accumulation, the mechanisms that have typically been used to secure these conditions, and the consequences of these mechanisms for human well-being. The understanding of the macro-social processes that have shaped gender relations in Latin America will serve as the foundation for the more in-depth exploration of contemporary forms of violence against women in relation to the capital–coercion nexus presented in Chapter 11. The analytical approach throughout this chapter and the next one is **dialectical**. When we say that two things are dialectically related, it means that: 1) they mutually affect each other; 2) change is ongoing—in the process of affecting each other, they are being changed; and 3) they are mutually constitutive—one cannot be completely understood without the other.

The Birth of Capitalism

Capitalism is a type of society characterized by two principal classes—those who have been dispossessed from the means of subsistence and have to sell their labour in order to survive and those who own the productive resources and hire others to work while they appropriate the value produced. It is important to remember that capitalism was not always around; it emerged as a type of society at a particular point in history. Understanding the *conditions* that made possible the birth of capitalism and the *mechanisms* that generated these conditions is crucial, since these mechanisms are still at work today, and in the process of generating the conditions they also generate poverty, inequality, militarization, and violence—the issues we tackle in this and the next chapter.

Capitalism requires three major conditions to function: *resources* (such as land, machinery, buildings, and other means of production); *labour* (workers); and *markets* of consumers. The processes that led to the development of capitalism can be traced back as far as the 1400s. The form of society that preceded capitalism was feudalism in which the two principal classes were landlords and peasants. Both had land-holding rights assigned to them by the king. Landlords or aristocrats controlled large areas of land on which peasants (serfs) had the right to live and farm on small plots in exchange for tribute to the landlord in the form of labour, in-kind, or money.

The transition to capitalism was initiated through a process referred to by Karl Marx as **primitive accumulation**—the dispossession of the direct producers from their means of subsistence. Primitive accumulation meant the expropriation of peasants' land as landlords' estates became converted into capitalist farms for commercial agriculture. Many estates became pastures for growing sheep (for wool manufacture) or lands for the mass cultivation of a single crop. This process of dispossessing serfs from their means of subsistence generated the three basic conditions necessary for capitalism: labour—peasants had no other way of surviving but to sell their labour; resources—land became a commodity; markets—because people were no longer able to produce their food and other items for everyday use, they had to buy them. In all preceding types of societies, most of the population had access to land. It was the first time in the history of humanity that such large masses of people were deprived of access to the means of their own subsistence. Primitive accumulation therefore meant a lot more than the loss of land; it also meant loss of livelihood, home, community, and culture. The evictions that began in the 1400s lasted over the next four centuries as capitalism spread throughout Europe.

Peasants resisted giving up their livelihood and becoming wage labourers. This is where the three mechanisms come into action. From its very inception until today, capitalists have always relied on these three mechanisms to deal with obstacles and dissent: *law*, *violence*, and *ideology*, all of which form part of the political realm—hence, the importance of thinking about the political (state) and economic (capital) as dialectically related. Laws were used to:

- abolish the feudal tenure of land;
- authorize the forced evictions of serfs as well as independent peasants (who used to live off the land, not belonging to any landlord). For instance, in England between 1700 and

1845, 40,000 to 50,000 small farms were swallowed up by enclosures (Mooers, 2014);

- privatize the commons (public lands) (Thomas, 2012).

Starving and homeless, dispossessed people did not automatically become wage-labourers. Many sought alternative ways of making a living such as planting gardens on public lands, begging, stealing, and forming travelling bands of peddlers or entertainers (McNally, 2011). Once again, legal mechanisms were enforced to eliminate any alternative that the dispossessed may have turned to for survival, leaving wage employment as their only option. Thus, in addition to enabling evictions, laws were also used to:

- criminalize the poor—beggars and anyone not employed; the term **vagabond** was used to label such people;
- criminalize unions;
- criminalize the act of giving alms to the poor.

Of course, to reinforce laws, violence and the threat of violence was used. Marx provides a long list of examples of this "bloody legislation" from the late 15th to the 17th century, such as ". . . whipping and imprisonment for sturdy vagabonds. They are to be tied to the cart-tail and whipped until the blood streams from their bodies . . ." and ". . . the ear-clipping and branding of those whom no one was willing to take into service" (Marx, 1867/1990, pp. 899–901).

In addition to laws and violence, the development of capitalism was characterized by an emergence of an ideology that blamed the poor for their poverty and justified severe forms of discipline for those not incorporated into the capitalist relations of production. As the state took on the role of providing care for the destitute, known as poor-relief (you can think of that as the origin of modern welfare), the poor became subject to blaming, monitoring, and stigma. Beginning in the 1500s, a body of laws known as the Poor

TABLE 10.1 Dialectical relationship between the political (state) and the economic (capital)

Political (Laws, Violence, Ideology)	Economic (Resources, Labour, Markets)
Laws were used to: • evict peasants from their land • privatize the commons • convert land into a **commodity** (something that can be bought and sold) • criminalize begging and other forms of subsistence that were outside of formal capitalist relations of production • criminalize alms-giving • criminalize workers' associations (unions) • force people to look for formal employment (Poor Laws)	*Creation of wage labourers:* • dispossession of peasants from their means of subsistence (land) • exclusion of peasants from public lands (the commons), which now become private property • elimination of other possible forms of subsistence, which generates availability of human beings with no other way to survive but to sell their labour power • competition among those looking for work → downward pressure on wages → more exploitation → more surplus value appropriated by owner of the means of production
Violence was used to: • evict peasants who resist giving up their land • punish vagabonds • repress uprisings/rebellions	*Availability of resources:* • appropriation of peasants' lands • appropriation of the commons lands
Dominant ideology: • being poor is the poor individual's fault; it is a result of laziness • receiving poor relief—a stigma • any form of subsistence other than being employed by a capitalist or by the state is bad • being employed inside the capitalist relations of production is the only acceptable way	*Creation of a market of consumers:* • people no longer produce their food, clothes, and other items used in daily living; thus, they need to purchase them as commodities

Laws was passed in England. They were based on the ideology that, in the words of one Poor Law Commissioner, "In England poverty is a crime" (Fox Piven & Cloward, 1971, p. 350). Under most of these laws, relief was given under such degrading and humiliating conditions as to "ensure that no one with any conceivable alternatives would seek public aid" and would rather "offer themselves to any employer on any terms" (Fox Piven & Cloward, 1971, p. 34).

Table 10.1 sums up the dialectical relationship between the economic and the political sphere, which is of crucial importance to comprehending not only the origins of capitalism but the mechanisms that continue to keep the capitalist system of production in place. As we can see, we cannot understand properly how the basic economic conditions required for capitalism came into place without being aware of the political mechanisms that generated and secured these conditions. At the same time, to fully understand why certain laws and ideologies became predominant, we need to look at the economic interests behind them.

Changes in Gender Relations with the Transition to Capitalism

Using the framework of the political–economic dialectic, let's now reflect on the main ways in which the emergence of capitalism affected gender relations. To examine this question, we will borrow some conceptual tools from feminist historian Silvia Federici as well as several scholars from the field of socialist feminism. To begin with, it is important to recognize that gender inequality existed prior to capitalism. According to McNally (2002), the history of human societies shows that the first gender inequalities emerged at the same time as wealth inequality. In other words, gender inequality and sexism are not tied to capitalism only but to any system based on wealth inequality.

Nonetheless, capitalism brought about new ways in which gender inequality manifests itself, and in some cases these ways have proved to be increasingly harmful.

Feminist historian Silvia Federici provides us with a compelling analysis of primitive accumulation that demonstrates the relationship between the intersection of class and gender on one hand and the political instruments that normalized **violence against women**. First, let's take a look at the economic dimension of how the transition to capitalism affected women. According to Federici (2004), the rise of capitalist relations of production led to a gendered division of labour that was much more pronounced and unequal than the one that characterized feudal society. During feudalism, in peasant households both men and women contributed to the family's subsistence, and both possessed the land in partnership with each other. Women not only worked on the farm but could dispose of the products of their labour and did not have to depend on their husbands for support. Moreover, women worked in cooperation with other women, which meant that the sexual division of labour was a source of power and protection for women as well as the basis for solidarity (Federici, 2004). However, by the 1700s with the rise of factory production, a sharper demarcation between the household sphere and the economic sphere was developed, leaving women entirely responsible for household work in addition to their work as wage-labourers (McNally, 2002) (see box on Social Reproduction Theory).

As discussed earlier, the transition to capitalism through the process of primitive accumulation relied on political instruments—violence, laws, and ideology—enacted through the state. Similarly, the consolidation of the new forms of gender inequality brought about by capitalism was also made possible by the state. Federici (2004) documents how throughout Europe between the 14th and 16th centuries, the rape of proletarian or poor women was backed by the state and brothels became legal.

Social Reproduction Theory

The **theory of social reproduction** has been developed by scholars such as Lise Vogel, Martha Gimenez, Johanna Brenner, and Susan Ferguson, who have taken Marx's theory of labour and commodity production and expanded on it in order to understand the relationship between the production of goods and services on one hand and the production of life on the other. The production of labour (i.e., the birth and raising of new workers) as well as its reproduction (the daily procedures such as cooking, cleaning, and taking care of those who are ill that enable workers to be regenerated and available for work) takes place in the home. All the work that goes into the production and reproduction of labour ensures the survival of labour power and enables capitalist exploitation to take place (Bhattacharya, 2013). Thus, Vogel (2013) explains, among working-class women, female oppression is derived from women's involvement in the process of **social reproduction** that takes place in the sphere of the home as well as exploitation at the site of production. To conclude, the central argument of **socialist feminism** is that the fundamental cause of women's oppression is neither class inequality nor "sexism" but an intricate interplay between capitalism and patriarchy (Lorber, 2012).

Gang rape of unmarried proletarian women (such as poor maids or washing women) became a common practice, and women who were raped had no other option but to earn their livelihood by prostituting themselves. Federici (2004) argues that the raping of poor women undermined class solidarity and brothels became a remedy for social protest. Both class solidarity and its logical outcome, social protest, were (and of course continue to be) the greatest threat to capitalist interests. Thus, state-sponsored violence against women and the institutionalization of prostitution proved to be a strategy for weakening the unity of the working class along lines of gender, thus lowering the threat from below, ultimately preserving class and male power.

Colonialism: The First Major Stage of Capitalist Expansion

Recall that capital requires three major conditions: land, resources, and labour. These conditions can never be secured forever within a limited geographic territory. This is why from the very beginning capitalism has been expansionary in nature. **Colonialism**, the economic, political, and military domination by one nation over another territory and its people, constituted the first major expansion of capitalism. It was a process through which capital's requirements (resources, labour, markets) could be satisfied on a global scale as various territories and their people across the Americas, and later Africa and Asia, came to be incorporated into the world capitalist economy either as labourers, as producers of raw materials or agricultural goods, or as consumers of western European goods. This economically driven expansion was made possible through enslavement, war, and genocide.

Colonies such as Brazil and those in the Caribbean, dominated by plantation-oriented agriculture, produced sugar, cacao, tobacco, and rubber and later bananas and coffee for the world economy. Others, such as Mexico, parts of Central America, and the Andean region of South America (parts of Colombia, Peru, Chile, and Bolivia) developed economies around mining. Given the richness of the land (whether its fertility or minerals deposits), securing control over it was the single most important objective of colonizers. Large landed estates, or **haciendas**, were established through concessions or land grants given by the Spanish Crown to European colonizers. These people and their descendants became the local colonial elites. It is here that the seeds of present-day social inequality and strife were sown. The history of Latin America can be visualized as a series of waves of primitive accumulation in which each wave intensified existing class inequality and poverty and each became increasingly violent:

- the initial dispossession of Indigenous people from their lands;
- the eviction of tenant farmers from *haciendas* when the latter transformed into capitalist farms;
- the evictions of squatters, or **colonos**, who engaged in subsistence agriculture on public or idle land by landlords who were expanding their landholdings;
- the encroachment of landowners onto Indigenous protected lands (such as the *resguardos* in Colombia), which were established by the Spanish Crown in an effort to prevent the Indigenous population from becoming completely extinct.

The outcome of all this has been an extremely uneven landownership structure characterized by the coexistence of large estates covering thousands of hectares (also known as **latifundios**), alongside **minifundios** (parcels of land as small as one hectare or less).

In addition to dispossessing people from the land, violence was also used to secure labour. The first institution of forced labour was the **encomienda** whereby Spanish colonizers had the legal right to forcibly extract tribute from the Indigenous population in the form of gold. With the decrease in Indigenous populations due to wars of conquest, diseases, and internal migration, African people were used as the main source of slave labour. Indigenous, peasant, and slave rebellions were violently supressed.

Class and Race

Class inequalities, of course, had racial undertones. The racialized division of labour differed according to geographic region, but generally, the most privileged class—the landowning class—was mostly of Spanish or Portuguese descent, while those working in the mines and on plantations were mostly of African descent. Domestic servants were typically Indigenous and African women. Among the tenant farmers/sharecroppers, *colonos*, landless agricultural workers, and the poor rural population in general one could find white people (of European descent), mestizos (mixed ancestry of European and Indigenous), mulattoes (mixed ancestry of European and African), and Indigenous (Oquist, 1980). Racial and class inequalities were paralleled by racially fueled violence—as Martínez (2004) puts it, white/Spaniard slave-owners in Mexico lived in a constant state of fear of a social war that gave rise to racial fantasies and helped to produce and reproduce violent behaviour. As we can see, social inequality, poverty, and violence became structural features of Latin American societies from the very beginning.

Class, Race, and Gender

The expansion of capitalism through colonialism generally degraded the status of women in non-Western societies and made them more vulnerable to violence. In societies characterized by existing gender inequality, colonial capitalism exacerbated patriarchal features through new property relations that adversely affected women as well as through systems of labour that increased women's responsibility for raising children (McNally, 2002). Sexist and racist dehumanizing ideologies depicted slave women of African descent and Indigenous women in ways that justified their brutalizing sexual exploitation—Black women were portrayed as repositories of insatiable sexual energy (McNally, 2002; Simms, 1992) and Indigenous women as "libidinous." These ideologies justified the violence that "covets the lands, the gold and the bodies of the others" (Stevenson, 1992, p. 71). "All . . . non-bourgeois others—Africans, Irish, Orientals, women, homosexuals, sex workers, and the labouring poor of Europe—were animalized, feminized and racialized" (McNally, 2002, p. 124).

In Latin America, class and race were the key variables in the subordination of women and the normalization of gender-based violence at the time. As Federici (2004) points out, capitalism must justify the contradictions built into its social relations by denigrating the nature of those it exploits. Poor women and women of colour who sought alternative forms of subsistence (as midwives, story-tellers, sex workers, or other forms of self-employment) as well as those who had special abilities such as healing or communicating with the spirits were criminalized, persecuted, and severely punished, very much like women accused of witchcraft in Europe during the emergence of capitalism (discussed in Chapter 5 of this textbook). Afro-Caribbean, Indigenous, Roma, and other poor women used to be sentenced to death or prison by the Inquisition on charges of sorcery, devil worship, and witchcraft (Few, 2002). Witch persecutions were imposed on populations with living traditions of priestesshood. Since the 1700s, there were coordinated efforts by the church and the state to suppress African religions, even those that had assimilated Catholic elements, such as Candomble and Santeria. Healing rituals were described as sorceries and African religious gatherings as diabolical (Dashu, 2000; Few, 2002). However, this cannot be understood solely as a form of cultural extermination. It was a strategy of fostering complete submissiveness

and conformity within the working classes (slaves, servants, agricultural workers, etc.) through fear. Slave-masters tortured people suspected of casting spells. Slave-master wives also engaged in the torturing of female slaves, particularly those they suspected of having sexual relations with their husbands. Common types of torture included gouging out eyes, breaking teeth, burning faces, and cutting off breasts (Dashu, 2000). These atrocities were not simply products of religious differences or the fear of unknown cultural practices. Rather, they were part of the endemic violence aimed at subjugating completely the oppressed, ensuring total submissiveness and breaking potential forms of resistance.

The sexualization of women of colour or mixed ancestry has served to justify their subjection to systematic sexual violence. As the postcolonial critique of development studies presented in Chapter 8 of this textbook argues, women's bodies are perceived as natural resources to be colonized, appropriated, and exploited. The routine rape of female slaves and servants during colonialism left a long-lasting legacy that shaped the ways in which sexuality is racialized today. For instance, Pravaz (2009) examines how colonial race and gender relations in Brazil were characterized by a fascination with the *mulata* body, which is perceived in terms of its voluptuosity and sensuality but at the same time represents a broader ideology with racist overtones that values "whitening" through "mixing." The outcome of racism, sexism, and the exoticization of African bodies has been the present-day standard of beauty whereby the most valued female bodies are those of white Brazilians who are able to embody the symbolic qualities of mulattoes (Pravaz, 2009).

The Postcolonial Period

The wars for independence were fueled by the discontent of the local economic elites with the colonial governments in Europe over terms of trade and taxes. Local elites mobilized the poor masses through a nationalist ideology that promised freedom and progress for all and pushed for unity against the European oppressors. Thus, the wars for independence were fought by the poor on behalf of the rich, who eventually became the political elite. Their vision of progress was to be achieved by adopting the neoclassical economic model based on the premise that the state should not restrict in any way the pursuit of private interests (Brockett, 1990). This, of course, led to more land dispossession, land concentration, and exploitation. The elites relied on the state army and police as well as their private armed groups to do away with subsistence agriculture and the collective ownership of land. After the abolition of slavery in the late 1800s, racial and class inequalities continued to intensify. The trend of depending on primary sector exports and importing manufactured goods continued.

The Welfare Stage and Import Substitution Industrialization (ISI)

This stage of capitalism lasted for a very short period of time—roughly from the end of the Second World War (1945) until 1980. What distinguishes this stage of capitalism from the preceding period is the approach of the state toward ensuring the long-term stability of capitalism. Whereas during the colonial and postcolonial stages (1500 to the first half of the 20th century), the state typically used legal and violent mechanisms to suppress dissent and secure the conditions necessary for capital accumulation, during this second stage states in western Europe and North America changed tactics and yielded to some of the demands of the working-class movement. It is during this period that we see the most gains for the working class, such as social safety nets, social assistance, expansion of public services, wage increases, work benefits, and other efforts

to improve the living standards of the working class and the poor. The state's intervention to mitigate the harsh impacts of capital accumulation on workers was partly a result of the fear of socialism, which had emerged in the Soviet Union, eastern Europe, China, and Cuba.

This shift in approach was reflected throughout Latin America as well. With the exception of the two countries that had socialist revolutions—Cuba and Nicaragua—various nations such as Chile, Brazil, Argentina, Colombia, Guatemala, and Mexico, for a limited time, pursued reforms aimed at partial land redistribution and workers' rights. Some of these countries also pursued what is known as **Import Substitution Industrialization (ISI)**—a development strategy aimed at reducing dependence on the importation of foreign manufactured/technology-intensive commodities and increasing the domestic production of such goods. The US had a vested interest in preventing any more socialist revolutions from emerging in the region, and so it combined military aid to right-wing governments with financial assistance for economic development through a program known as Alliance for Progress (initiated in 1961).

Counterinsurgency and the War on Communism

Large sectors of the Latin American elites were very intolerant of replacing repression with concession when it came to dealing with the threat from below. As a result, progressive governments and the worker/peasant-friendly reforms they had implemented were short-lived and abruptly interrupted by military coups that installed dictatorships throughout the hemisphere, not only reversing the few progressive laws that had been passed but also suspending civil liberties and initiating a War on Communism against the "internal enemy." The notion of the "internal enemy" is crucial because it has been at the core of all the political violence waged against left-leaning individuals and organizations, labour unions, and other social movements up until today. The **internal enemy** is part of a new form of state-building whereby the state's coercive apparatus is directed not toward an enemy outside of its territory (another country) but toward an enemy from within. This enemy is not marked by a different ethnicity, race, religion, or language. Rather, it comprises those who challenge the status quo, defend human rights, ask for social justice, or seek social transformation. The War on Communism entailed a **counter-insurgency** offensive intended to eradicate any existing revolutionary movements (guerrilla groups) and prevent the emergence of any new ones by attacking social sectors considered as fertile ground for communist indoctrination, such as peasants and labour unions. Starting in the 1950s, the US provided the ideological foundation for the counter-insurgency strategy, the training, and the military assistance that enabled Latin American states to expand their military and intelligence apparatus and create death squads and paramilitary groups to assist in combatting the "internal enemy."

Between the 1950s and the 1990s, many Latin American countries witnessed the systematic annihilation of political enemies through alarming levels of repression and the grossest acts of human rights violations. The counter-insurgency strategy led to extreme savagery such as: the killing of children by beating them against walls or throwing them alive into pits where the corpses of adults were thrown; impaling and amputating victims; opening the wombs of pregnant women; hanging fetuses by their umbilical cords from trees; and burning people alive. The overwhelming part of the most notorious human rights abusers had graduated from the **School of the Americas (SOA)**. The latter, informally known worldwide as the School of the Assassins, opened in 1963 in Fort Benning, Georgia, US, and has since trained more than 59,000 Latin American military and police personnel in counter-insurgency and low-intensity warfare. Ten of the graduates became president of their countries, and 23 became ministers of defence. One such example is General Hector Gramajo Morales, former Guatemalan defence minister, a graduate of the school and a fellow of the Edward Mason Program at the Kennedy School of Government at Harvard University, who was responsible for the rape and torture of Sister Dianna Ortiz, an American Ursuline nun. She was abducted by the Guatemalan security forces, taken to a secret prison, tortured, and raped repeatedly. Her chest and back were burned more than 111 times with cigarettes, she was lowered into an open pit packed with decapitated and tortured bodies of children, women, and men, some of whom were still alive, and swarming with rats. She was forced to cut a woman with a machete. It is important to note here that these were not isolated cases of psychopathic behaviour. Rather, US training manuals such as the *Psychological operations in guerrilla warfare* (1983) (cited in Gareau, 2004) explicitly prescribed the use of terrorism. The objective was to create fear through a phantom-like presence. The SOA closed in December 2000, but it re-opened a month later under the name Western Hemisphere Institute of Security Cooperation where essentially the same courses are being taught (Gareau, 2004). Counter-insurgency today is packaged under different names such as the War on Narco-Terrorism, but just as under the War on Communism, today's **militarization** and proliferation of paramilitary groups serves to neutralize dissent to the dominant politico-economic model.

The Rise of the Global Economy

By the 1970s, the welfare model of capitalism was already under attack by a movement of economically powerful sectors in western Europe and the US. The movement took expression in organizations and think tanks such as the Mont Pelerin

Society and argued that restrictions on the freedom of capital would lead to a socialist totalitarianism. The intellectual product of the movement is essentially the theory of neoliberalism, the main premises of which revolve around securing free mobility of capital by eliminating all kinds of barriers such as tariffs, taxation, environmental controls, and "strict/excessive" labour regulation and by privatizing state-run sectors (Harvey, 2005). When the economic crisis in the 1970s came about, characterized by inflation and economic stagnation, the movement used the crisis as a pretext to dismantle the welfare state and restore their class power by putting together a program of economic restructuring, which was adopted by governments in western Europe and North America and imposed on developing countries.

Neoliberal policies made possible the emergence of a global economy. According to a prominent sociologist of globalization, William Robinson (2004), up until the 1970s capitalism could be described as a world economy. It was only with the emergence of **global production chains** characterized by the decentralization of production that a global economy emerged. Unlike a world economy, where national economies are linked through trade but remain autonomous, in a **global economy** the production of a single commodity involves inputs of labour, resources, and technology from different countries. Thus, we see the transnational integration of national economies into a single production system. Under globalization, large sectors of the capitalist class in each country have become globally oriented—i.e., integrated into global production chains—and have become part of what is known as **global capital**. With the imposition of neoliberal policies and the implementation of free trade agreements, capital navigates in a pretty much borderless world. Companies can relocate their production to a site where they can find the lowest-cost labour force. This mobility is what gives global capital an immense advantage over workers.

Neoliberalism in Latin America

Latin American countries (except for Cuba), like many other countries in the Global South, were pressured to adopt the neoliberal agenda as part of the conditions for receiving loans from the IMF and the World Bank (WB) to service the debts they had accumulated. The Washington Consensus of the 1980s, regarded as the core message of the neoliberal recipe, was an agreement between the US Treasury, the IMF, and the WB about the right policies for developing countries. The agenda for economic restructuring that the Washington Consensus imposed on Latin America was:

- **Trade liberalization (free trade)**—the removal of any trade barriers such as tariffs and quotas
- **Foreign Direct Investment (FDI)**—physical investments and purchases by a company in a foreign country, typically by opening plants and buying buildings, factories, and land
- **Privatization**—the sale of public enterprises and assets to private owners
- **Austerity**—the drastic reduction or elimination of budget expenditures for social programs and services (Williamson & Kuczynski, 2003)

It is important to note, however, that Latin American governments implemented neoliberal policies *not* solely because of loan conditionality. Large sectors of their capitalist classes were seeking to integrate their businesses into the global economy to benefit from access to global markets. These sectors were mainly the primary resource commodity producers such as the agribusinesses, cattle-ranchers, and mining entrepreneurs. The second reason was that in exchange for implementing neoliberal policies that made it easier for foreign capital to take advantage of their labour force and resources, the US and some other states in the North provided Latin American states with military assistance that enabled them to strengthen even further their coercive apparatus and thus be able to secure in place the politico-economic model that benefitted the elite in the face of massive discontent from below.

Land and Labour: Pillars of the Global Economy

FDI in Latin America is typically found in agribusiness, mining, tourism, infrastructure, industrial/manufacturing parks, and real estate. FDI, along with other agrarian policies, has led to an agrarian restructuring marked by a shift from 1) publicly, Indigenously, and family-owned land used for subsistence food production and sale in local markets to 2) land used for large-scale industry, including agribusiness, mining, fossil fuel exploration and extraction, tourism, and infrastructure construction. The outcomes of this restructuring have been detrimental for the livelihoods of millions of small-scale farmers and their children: loss of income and home; growing landlessness; profound inequality in land ownership; food insecurity; rising poverty; declining health; disintegration of communities; and loss of culture (Bello, 2008; De Medeiros, 2007; Kay, 2001; McMichael & Schneider, 2011). In countries such as Mexico, Honduras, Colombia, Brazil, and Paraguay, small-scale farms producing food staples have been overtaken by cattle ranching and agribusiness producing cash crops such as palm oil, sugar cane, and soy. In Guatemala, Peru, and Mexico, mining is contaminating local environments, leading to serious health complications among the populations living in proximity to the mines.

The outcomes of free-trade agreements have also been detrimental for small-scale farmers and workers in the Global South. To begin with, clauses in such agreements supersede national labour or environmental laws and allow companies to sue host governments if the latter take measures that cause them a loss of profits. Second, NAFTA and other free trade agreements have forced markets in the South to absorb the surpluses of corporations in the North by destroying domestic industry and farming. In Mexico, for example, between 1991 and 2007, 4.9 million family farmers lost their livelihoods as imports of cheap US corn undercut the prices of local small-scale producers. NAFTA has also led to a decline in real wages and proliferation of coercive labour practices. Many of those dispossessed migrate to seek employment in the *maquilas* or become temporary workers in agribusinesses (Barndt, 2002) or, alternatively, migrate to the US.

Free-trade agreements, FDI initiatives, and labour deregulation have enabled the creation of **export-processing zones (EPZs)** and *maquilas*, where the assembly or partial manufacturing of products for export takes place. In 2007, some 2.5 million people worked in EPZs in Latin America, with 1.2 million in Mexico, 700,000 in Central America, and 540,000 in the Caribbean (Anner, 2015). In these zones, companies (those locally based as well as foreign) are exempt from national labour laws. The overwhelming majority of workers in *maquilas* are women, typically aged 17 to 30. Many of them are single mothers and/or primary providers for their families (Tuttle, 2012). Typically, working conditions can be described as: wages that are below the minimum wage, absence of unions, seven-day workweek, 12-hour work shifts, exposure to hazardous substances such as lead (Funari & De La Torre, 2006), temporary contracts, termination of employment without any compensation, and coercive labour practices such as forcing female employees to take contraceptives (Esbenshade, 2007) and not allowing employees to drink water so that they would not take washroom breaks. The complete disregard for occupational health regulations has generated health issues ranging from skin problems, to respiratory and kidney diseases, to leukemia (Funari & De La Torre, 2006; Sizemore, 1991). Parallel to economic exploitation, the concentration of young poor women in need of income constitutes fertile terrain for sexual exploitation. Bank Muñoz (2007) provides the example of a tortilla factory, describing the environment as racialized and sexualized despotism. Women workers are constantly pursued by managers asking for sexual favours; they are forced to flirt with managers or lose their jobs.

The Use of Violence for Dispossession and Repression

Violence on the part of the state military and police forces as well as paramilitary groups has been instrumental in the forcible removal of small-scale farmers and Indigenous groups from land of strategic economic importance for large-scale industries as well as in silencing, intimidating, and repressing labour unions and other social movements. **Paramilitary groups** comprise civilians and often former or active members of the police, military, private security companies, and criminal organizations. They are organized and funded by wealthy sectors of society, with military and logistical support provided unofficially by the state. The targets of paramilitary violence include social movements, human rights activists, and others who challenge the established political-economic model. Thanks to state and paramilitary violence, countries such as Colombia, Mexico, and Honduras have become among the most dangerous places for social activists, labour unionists, and journalists. In Colombia, paramilitary operations have made possible the transfer of 10 million hectares of land from family farmers, Indigenous groups, and Afro-descendants into the hands of the elite (Hristov, 2014). In Honduras, Guatemala, and Mexico, rural communities have been repeatedly subjected to bloody dispossession accompanied by extra-judicial executions, rape, torture, and disappearances, while activists and human rights defenders have been facing a campaign of extermination.

Tying It Together

This chapter traced the evolution of gender inequality in Latin America throughout the history of capitalist development. One of the steady features of the history of capitalism in the region has been its reliance upon violence. The persistent relationship between capital and violence has had negative implications for women's autonomy and well-being. The racist ideologies that arose during colonialism have served to justify the violence against women and people of colour and have ultimately guaranteed the dominance of capitalist male power across Latin American societies. Currently, gender inequality in Latin America is mainly expressed in the form of unequal distribution of wealth/uneven access to resources and violence against women. The processes that generate or aggravate violence against women form an integral part of the neoliberal agenda, including land dispossession, precarious working conditions in *maquilas* and EPZs, militarization, and the proliferation of non-state armed actors who violate human rights with the state's complicity. It is to this subject that we turn in the next chapter.

Call to Action

Research and then educate others on the role of US and Canadian corporate and political presence in Latin America. Volunteer with NGOs that support human rights and gender equality causes in Latin America, and join a fact-finding/human rights delegation. If you can, visit a social movement or feminist organization in Latin America (or attend a local branch meeting of one) and LISTEN.

DISCUSSION QUESTIONS

1. What are the parallels between the development of capitalism during colonialism (1500–1700s) and the spread of neoliberalism in the past 30 years with regard to the creation and/or consolidation of social inequalities based on race/ethnicity, class, and gender?

2. Why is it necessary to understand the origins and global spread of capitalism (past) as well as the mechanisms that generate the conditions for its reproduction and expansion (present) if we are to fully understand the factors that generate or aggravate violence against women?

SUGGESTIONS FOR FURTHER READING

Few, M. (2002). *Women who live evil lives: Gender, religion, and the politics in colonial Guatemala.* Austin, TX: University of Texas Press. This book looks at the experiences of Indigenous, Black, and mixed-race women who were healers, midwives, and spell-casters in Santiago de Guatemala, the capital of colonial Central America.

Mize, R.L. (2008). Interrogating race, class, gender and capitalism along the U.S.–Mexico border: Neoliberal nativism and maquila modes of production. *Race, Gender & Class, 15*(1/2), 134–55. This article considers the ways in which the intersection of *maquila* circuits of production and border militarization is a terrain that is gendered, raced, and classed.

Enloe, C.H. (2007). *Globalization and militarism: Feminists make the link.* Lanham, MD: Rowman & Littlefield. This book encourages readers to recognize the interrelatedness between the construction of dominant ideas of masculinity and femininity on one hand and militarism on the other.

Robinson, W. (2004). *A theory of global capitalism: Transnational production, transnational capitalists, and the transnational state.* Baltimore, MD: Johns Hopkins University Press. This book discusses a leading theory of global capitalism from a critical political economy approach.

MULTIMEDIA SUGGESTIONS

Maquilapolis: City of factories. (2006). Vallejo, CA: Cinemamas.
This documentary depicts the relationship between global capital and the state through a close look at the everyday realities of *maquila* workers, their working and living conditions, the destructive health and environmental impacts of the *maquilas*, and women's efforts to achieve self-empowerment.

Poto Mitan: Haitian women, pillars of the global economy. (2009). Watertown, MA: Documentary Educational Resources.
This documentary narrates the everyday reality of women working in export-processing zones in Haiti and the impacts of neoliberal policies on the majority of the population.

Paying the price: Migrant workers in the toxic fields of Sinaloa. (2009). The Chiapas Media Project
This documentary examines the impoverished lives of Mexican migrant workers employed at a foreign-owned agribusiness in Mexico producing vegetables for export to Canada. The film shows the dangerous working conditions and serious health impacts that workers, many of whom are women and children, are exposed to in the fields.

NACLA Report on the Americas
https://nacla.org/aboutus
This is the website for the magazine published by the North American Congress on Latin America (NACLA)—an independent, non-profit organization that provides information and analysis on the region and on its complex and changing relationship with the United States as tools for education and advocacy.

Latin American Perspectives
http://latinamericanperspectives.com
This website is home to an academic journal on capitalism and socialism across the Americas.

Telesurtv.net
https://www.telesurtv.net/english
This website provides critical global coverage of news with an emphasis on Latin America. It serves as an alternative to mainstream/Western media. Officially available in both English and Spanish.

UN Women Latin America and the Caribbean
http://lac.unwomen.org/en
This is the website of the United Nations organization dedicated to gender equality and the empowerment of women in the Americas and Caribbean. News, information about advocacy groups/events, and multimedia publications can be found here.

REFERENCES

Anner, M. (2015). Labor law reform and union decline in Latin America. Labour and Employment Relations Association, 60th annual proceedings.

Bank Muñoz, C. (2007). The tortilla behemoth: Sexualized despotism and women's resistance in a transnational Mexican tortilla factory. In A.L. Cabezas, E. Reese, & M. Waller (Eds), *The wages of empire: Neoliberal policies, repression, and women's poverty* (pp. 127–39). Boulder, CO: Paradigm Publishers.

Barndt, D. (2002). Picking and packing for the North: Agricultural workers at Empaque Santa Rosa. In *Tangled routes: Women, work, and globalization on the tomato trail* (pp. 165–201). Aurora, ON: Garamond Press.

Bello, W. (2008). Manufacturing a food crisis: How free-trade is destroying Third World agriculture. *The Nation.* Retrieved from https://www.thenation.com/article/manufacturing-food-crisis.

Bhattacharya, Tithi. (2013). What is social reproduction theory? 10 September. http://socialistworker.org/2013/09/10/what-is-social-reproduction-theory.

Brockett, C.D. (1990). *Land, power, and poverty: Agrarian transformation and political conflict in Central America.* Boston, MA: Unwin Hyman.

Dashu, M. (2000). Colonial hunts: South America. *Secret History of the Witches.* http://www.suppressedhistories.net/secrethistory/colhuntsouth.html.

De Medeiros, L.S. (2007). Social movements and the experience of market-led agrarian reform in Brazil. *Third World Quarterly, 28*(8), 1501–18.

Esbenshade, J. (2007). The process of exporting neoliberal development: The consequences of the growth of export processing zones in El Salvador. In A.L. Cabezas, E. Reese, & M. Waller (Eds), *The wages of empire: Neoliberal policies, repression, and women's poverty* (pp. 152–65). Boulder, CO: Paradigm Publishers.

Federici, S. (2004). *Caliban and the witch: Women, the body and primitive accumulation.* Chico, CA: AK Press.

Few, M. (2002). *Women who live evil lives: Gender, religion, and the politics in colonial Guatemala.* Austin, TX: University of Texas Press.

Fox Piven, F., & Cloward, R.A. (1971). Relief, labour, and civil disorder: An overview. In *Regulating the poor: The functions of public welfare* (pp. 3–42). New York, NY: Random House.

Funari, V., & De La Torre, S. (2006). Maquilapolis: City of factories [film]. Vallejo, CA: CineMamas.

Gareau, F.H. (2004). *State terrorism and the United States: From counterinsurgency to the War on Terrorism.* London, UK and Atlanta, GA: Clarity Press.

Harvey, D. (2005). The neoliberal state. In *A brief history of neoliberalism.* New York, NY: Oxford University Press.

Hristov, J. (2014). *Paramilitarism and neoliberalism: Violent systems of capital accumulation in Colombia and beyond.* London, UK: Pluto Press.

Kay, C. (2001). Reflections on rural violence in Latin America. *Third World Quarterly, 22*(5), 741–75.

Lorber, J. (2012). *Gender inequality: Feminist theories and politics* (5th edn). New York, NY: Oxford University Press.

McMichael, P., & Schneider, M. (2011). Food security politics and the millennium development goals. *Third World Quarterly, 32*(1), 119–39.

McNally, D. (2002). The colour of money: Race, gender, and the many oppressions of global capital. In *Another world is possible.* Winnipeg, MB: Arbeiter Ring Publishing.

McNally, D. (2011). Debt, discipline and dispossession: Race, class and the global slump. In *Global slump: The economics and politics of crisis and resistance.* Oakland, CA: PM Press.

Martínez, M.E. (2004). The black blood of New Spain: Limpieza de sangre, racial violence, and gendered power in early colonial Mexico. *The William and Mary Quarterly, 61*(3), 479–520.

Marx, K. (1867/1990). *Capital, Vol. I.* London, UK: Penguin Books.

Mize, R.L. (2008). Interrogating race, class, gender and capitalism along the U.S.–Mexico border: Neoliberal nativism and maquila modes of production. *Race, Gender & Class, 15*(1/2), 134–55.

Mooers, C. (2014). The birth of the liberal subject: Commodities, money, and citizenship. In *Imperial subjects: Citizenship in an age of crisis and empire*. New York, NY: Bloomsbury Publishing.

Oquist, P. (1980). *Violence, conflict, and politics in Colombia*. New York, NY: Academic Press.

Pravaz, N. (2009). The tan from Ipanema: Freyre, Morenidade, and the cult of the body in Rio de Janeiro. *Canadian Journal of Latin American and Caribbean Studies*, 34(67), 79–104.

Robinson, W. (2004). *A theory of global capitalism: Transnational production, transnational capitalists, and the transnational state*. Baltimore, MD: Johns Hopkins University Press.

Simms, G.P. (1992). Black women of the diaspora. In R. Bourgeault, D. Broad, L. Brown, & L. Foster (Eds), *1492–1992: Five centuries of imperialism and resistance* (*Socialist studies*, vol. 8, pp.113–34). Winnipeg, MB, and Halifax, NS: Society for Socialist Studies and Fernwood Publishing.

Sizemore, M.H. (1991). Health problems of Mexican and American workers at three maquilas in Ciudad Juárez, Mexico. *International Quarterly of Community Health Education*, 12(2), 137–48.

Stevenson, M. (1992). Columbus and the war on the Indigenous people. In R. Bourgeault, D. Broad, L. Brown, & L. Foster (Eds), *1492–1992: Five centuries of imperialism and resistance* (Socialist studies, vol. 8, p.27–45). Winnipeg, MB, and Halifax, NS: Society for Socialist Studies and Fernwood Publishing.

Thomas, M. (2012). Class, state, and power: Unpacking social relations in contemporary capitalism. In D. Brock, R. Raby, & M.P. Thomas (Eds), *Power and everyday practices* (pp. 110–27). Toronto, ON: Nelson.

Tuttle, C. (2012). *Mexican women in American factories: Free trade and exploitation on the border* (1st edn). Austin, TX: University of Texas Press.

Vogel, L. (2013). *Marxism and the oppression of women: Toward a unitary theory*. Leiden, Switzerland: Brill.

Williamson, J., & Kuczynski, P. (2003). *After the Washington Consensus—Restarting growth and reform in Latin America*. Institute for International Economics.

CHAPTER 11

◇

The Capital–State Nexus and Its War on Women

Jasmin Hristov

Learning Objectives

In this chapter, you will:
- identify the ways in which different forms of violence interact and form vicious cycles that are reproduced across time and social spaces;
- consider the indispensable role of women in movements of resistance and the ways in which feminism and anti-capitalism have been mutually nourishing;
- examine how the harmful ideologies around femininity and masculinity that sustain the violence against women intersect with other capitalist ideologies.

Introduction

In this chapter, we explore contemporary forms of violence against women as embedded in the capital–state dialectic. The latter was discussed at length in Chapter 10. The goal is to understand the political foundations of gendered violence. To this end, we consider how the violent means that facilitate capital accumulation not only generate conditions of economic deprivation and deep class inequalities but also fuel harmful ideologies of masculinity and femininity.

Gender Inequality in Latin America

The **Gender Inequality Index** is used by the United Nations to measure gender inequality in reproductive health, political participation, and economic status. It quantifies maternal mortality, adolescence birth, gender-based share of seats in parliament, enrolment in secondary education, and labour force participation rate. In 2015, Latin America and the Caribbean had a GII of 0.39, compared to a 0.28 in Europe and Central Asia, a 0.31 in East Asia and the Pacific, a 0.52 in South

Asia, and a 0.57 in sub-Saharan Africa (UNDP, 2017). The following are some of the major manifestations of gender inequality in the region outside of the domestic sphere:

- Unequal access to resources—for instance, between 1940 and 2008 women represented only 13 per cent of the beneficiaries of land reform (Seisdedos & Bonometti, 2009). According to USAID (2017), women who have access to land are eight times less likely to experience gender-based violence and 60 per cent less likely to experience domestic abuse.
- Wage gap—according to a report by the International Labour Organization (ILO) from 2013, women in Latin America continue to earn less than men across all occupational sectors (ILO, 2013).
- The feminization of poverty—higher proportion of those living in poverty are women.
- Overrepresentation of women in the informal sector.
- Under-representation of women in politics.
- The lack of reproductive rights and barriers to access to reproductive health.
- Violence against women.
- Impunity for crimes against women.

While gender inequality has been a permanent feature in Latin America's colonial and postcolonial societies, it has intensified in the era of globalization because of several mutually reinforcing processes:

1. Forced displacement, which leads to the destruction of rural livelihoods. This in turn has ripple effects that negatively affect women's economic security and well-being.
2. Precarity of employment caused by deregulation of the labour market and lack of stability due to capital's mobility.

3. Crime increase, which leads to violent environments especially in low-income neighbourhoods, placing poor women at higher risk of experiencing physical or sexual abuse (Adams, 2011).
4. The rise in illegal economies such as the transnational trafficking of illegal drugs, arms, and human beings has also led to high levels of insecurity, which, once again, place women at higher risk of being abused.
5. **Militarization**: The increase in the number of military bases and military personnel; increased presence of military and police throughout public spaces; and strengthening of the capacity of the military and police by increasing their personnel, quantity and quality of weapons, and surveillance and monitoring technology. Expanded military and police presence as part of various security projects such as Plan Colombia, the Central American Regional Security Initiative (CARSI), and the Merida Initiative (Mexico) is disproportionately affecting women in the form of sexual abuses and harassment. Militarism spreads a culture of violence and creates more access to arms, which in turn fuels domestic violence against women (Nobel Women's Initiative, 2013).
6. Conservative policies in the area of reproductive rights and health by pro-neoliberal right-wing governments—abortion laws especially disadvantage poor women by forcing them to have children despite their precarious economic situation, continue pregnancies that may have been the product of rape or incest, and risk their lives by undergoing unsafe abortion in illegal establishments. Abortion laws also criminalize young poor women who have an abortion or who are presumed to have deliberately terminated their pregnancy in cases of a miscarriage.

Violence and Human Rights Violations against Women and Children

Part of the legacy of colonialism is the evolution of violence into a means of social control, power, administration of justice, enrichment, repression, maintenance of the status quo, respect, and control over women's bodies and sexuality. Latin America suffers 33 per cent of the world's homicides despite having only 8 per cent of its population (Phillips, 2018). **Violence against women** is defined by the UN as any act of gender-based violence that results in, or is likely to result in, physical, sexual, or psychological harm or suffering, including threats of such acts, coercion, or arbitrary deprivation of liberty, whether occurring in public or in private life (Bott et al., 2012). With 12 feminicides (targeted murder of women) daily and on average 60,000 a year (CNN, 2016), Latin America has been ranked as the most violent region for women (Rodriguez, 2018). Fourteen of the 15 countries with the highest rate of **feminicide** in the world are in Latin America (CNN, 2016). The region also has the highest rate of sexual non–intimate partner violence in the world (CNN, 2016). El Salvador and Honduras display the highest rates of feminicide, with 11.2 per 100,000 and 10.2 per 100,000, respectively (NODAL, 2017). In Brazil, every day 15 women are assassinated. Nearly a third of the women over 16 years of age in this country have suffered physical or verbal abuse in the past year (BBC Mundo, 2016).

Types of Violence versus Lived Experiences: The Challenge of Categorizing Violence

While it is useful to categorize violence for analytical purposes, it is important to remember that the way people experience or perpetrate violence is a lot more complex and multifaceted.

For example, it is difficult to imagine a case-scenario in which sexual violence occurs without any elements of physical or emotional/psychological violence. Often, one form of violence such as structural violence creates conditions conducive to another, such as domestic abuse. We must also consider the fact that violence can be categorized according to many different criteria, such as the form (e.g., sexual, physical), the scale (interpersonal, collective), the objectives or conditions out of which it arises (e.g., political, domestic, structural), the type of victim according to age (e.g., women, children), the motivation (e.g., gender-based, a tool of war), and so on. These categories can intersect or overlap—for instance, sexual violence may be used as a form of political violence if the victim is a woman who is a political activist. Along the same lines, interpersonal and collective violence may feed off each other—for example, poor male youth's willingness to use violence may be harnessed for political purposes (Pearce, 2009). Therefore, looking not only at the form of violence but also at the people targeted as well as those who benefit from it can be indicative of larger power structures that are reliant on violence. Lastly, violence by men against women is inseparable from violence by men against other men. For example, it is not uncommon that the men who use rape as a weapon of war have themselves experienced gender-based violence such as forced recruitment (Carpenter, 2006) and are coerced into performing sexual violence against women.

Physical and Sexual Violence as Instrumental Violence

Instrumental violence can be defined as "violence used as means to obtain a different goal. Politically motivated and drug-related violence are classic examples of instrumental violence" (Buvinic, Morrison, & Shifter, 1999, p. 10). The following are the types of instrumental violence in the form of physical and sexual violence that women face according to the motivation of the perpetrator and/or the context within which it occurs.

Sexual Violence as a Weapon of War

Since colonial time until the present, various types of armed actors, from the state military to gangs, to paramilitary groups, have been known to use sexual violence to humiliate, demoralize, or punish the "enemy." According to Wilson (2014), rape during war is a strategy used to psychologically attack men by de-masculinizing their identities. In this sense, the bodies of women become a terrain of war (AI, 2004). In Mexico, the paramilitary group responsible for the 1997 massacre in Acteal, Chiapas, "mocked the symbols of maternity by hacking the women's breasts with machetes and extracting the fetuses from those who were pregnant" (Olivera & Furio, 2006, p. 41). Similarly, gangs of Central America such as the notorious Mara Salvatrucha are known to carve the gang's insignia on the women's dead bodies (Olivera & Furio, 2006), and one of the explanations for the notorious case of murdered women in Ciudad Juarez, Mexico, has been "the use of [women's] damaged bodies as coded languages among powerful men, businessmen, or among criminals and their gangs" (Fregoso & Bejarano, 2010, p. 14).

Sexual Violence in Sex Trafficking and Forced Recruitment

One of the major informal economies that develop under conditions of war and armed conflict or in violent environments in general is the sex industry and particularly the trafficking of women for the purpose of coerced or voluntary prostitution (Cohn, 2012; Raven-Roberts, 2012). Young women and girls are supplied as merchandise to paramilitary training camps, military bases, entertainment establishments for those employed along drug-trafficking routes, private parties of

paramilitary and drug-trafficking bosses, and other such occasions where it is not rare for the sex workers to end up mutilated or murdered (Interview, August 2017). International sex trafficking gives a transnational dimension to violence against women where it is used to force women to provide sex services and punish those who attempt to leave. For instance, in a sex-trafficking network that traffics women from Colombia to western Europe, victims were told that they had to first pay the debt incurred in the process of getting them from Colombia to Europe and threatened that if they attempted to escape, their families in Colombia would be murdered (Interview, August 2017).

Sexual Violence as Both a Means to and a Consequence of Land Dispossession

Violence against women has been used for the purpose of land dispossession. The latter is accomplished by tactics such as torturing women and men in the presence of others, leaving corpses grossly mutilated, and engaging in practices that lead the victims to experience a painful death. The following is the testimony of a person forcibly displaced by paramilitary terror who was interviewed by Amnesty International in 2003:

> A stick was pushed into the private parts of an 18-year-old pregnant girl and it appeared through [the abdomen]. She was torn apart. . . . They [army-backed paramilitaries] stripped the women and made them dance in front of their husbands. Several were raped. You could hear the screams coming from a ranch near El Salado [Department of Bolívar] (AI, 2004).

Women who have been forcibly displaced are at higher risk of sexual violence in the post-displacement period because of abductions, exacerbation of intimate-partner violence, and forced abortions (Wirtz et al., 2014). This is an important factor, given that according to the Norwegian Council for Refugees, in 2016 eight million Latin Americans were internally displaced. Moreover, under the precarious living conditions of displaced populations, female bodily processes such as "menstruation, gestation, parturition, and lactation become more burdensome, uncomfortable and dangerous," and women and girls are at risk of rape and molestation (Cockburn, 2004, p. 48).

Sexual Violence and Feminicide as an Instrument of Political Repression

Since the onset of the Cold War (1950 onwards), sexual violence and feminicide have been used in Latin America to punish, intimidate, and silence women's political participation, activism, or leadership. During the military dictatorships from the 1960s to the 1980s, rape was endemic in clandestine detention centres in Argentina, Chile, and Brazil. In El Salvador and Guatemala, soldiers received orders from their superiors to use sexual violence as a strategy of political repression against communism (Joffily, 2016).

During the neoliberal era, in countries that are otherwise categorized as democracies, sexual violence continues to be an instrument that serves the needs of capital through repression. Rape, forced disappearance, arbitrary detention, and feminicide have reached emergency proportions in Mexico, Guatemala, Honduras, and Colombia. The women targeted are members of social movements such as those for land rights or women's reproductive rights, human rights defenders, community organizers, and lawyers. In Guatemala, on average there is at least one attack on human rights defenders daily (Nobel Women's Initiative, 2013). In Colombia in 2013, every four days a female human rights defender suffered some form of a violent attack (Semana, 2013).

Honduras, consistently ranked among the most murderous countries in the world, presents another example of the multiplied risk faced by women who are involved in social movements or perform work in defence of human rights (such as journalists, lawyers, or students)—one risk for challenging the dominant politico-economic model and another for challenging patriarchy. Karla Zelaya, the communications coordinator of the peasant movement Agrarian Platform of the Aguan (*Plataforma Agraria Regional del Valle del Aguan*), recalls a time when she was forced into a vehicle while waiting for the bus. Inside the vehicle, armed men blindfolded her and began questioning her about the leaders of the movement. During the interrogation, they placed a sharp knife on her belly and began touching her in a sexual way. "I told them, 'If you are going to do anything to me, please just kill me instead,' and I begged them to allow me to speak to my mother before I die" (Interview, March 2018). Another brave woman in Honduras is Dina Mesa, a journalist, human rights defender, and a founder of the NGO Association for Democracy and Human Rights (ASOPODEHU), which supports and defends the rights of journalists, Indigenous people, women, LGBT people, and other disenfranchised groups in Honduras. Dina is the recipient of the Amnesty International Award for Journalism under Threat (2007) and Oxfam's Award for Freedom of Expression (2014). Doing this type of work in Honduras, one of the most dangerous countries in the world to be a journalist, for over 20 years, Dina has faced numerous death threats, persecution, surveillance, and a murder attempt. In addition to that, throughout her life she has encountered on numerous occasions sexual harassment and attempts at sexual abuse. The threat of sexual violence as a weapon to silence her continues to loom large in her life. When I asked her about how she manages to live with fear and if there are times when it overwhelms her, she mentioned the time when a threat she received in a text message read, "Your daughter is very hot" (Interview, April 2018).

The Assassination of Berta Cáceres: The Political–Economic Dialectic

Berta Cáceres was an Indigenous woman, environmental and human rights activist, and one of the loudest voices in defence of Indigenous communities and small-scale farmers in Honduras. She fought to defend the land and natural resources of the Lenca people (Germinando, 2018).

Background
In 2009, a military coup removed Honduras's progressive centre-left president Manuel Zelaya and installed a right-wing government that ushered in an extreme neoliberal restructuring, backed up by expansion of the military and police apparatus. The latter, along with private security forces and paramilitary groups, has been at the service of local and foreign mining companies and the agribusiness sector (Shipley, 2017). Berta co-founded the Civic Council of Indigenous and Popular Organizations of Honduras (COPINH) for the defence of Indigenous territory, natural resources, and human rights.

Her Struggle
Berta denounced the numerous human rights violations carried out by state forces and private security personnel against Indigenous communities in Honduras. Since April of 2013, COPINH engaged in opposition to the construction of the Agua Zarca Hydroelectric Project on the Gualcarque River, which is sacred for the Lenca people. As the coordinator of COPINH, Berta denounced the company, Desarrollos Energeticos S.A. (DESA), responsible for the construction of the dam, and the Honduran state, sending letters to the banks financing the projects, demanding the cancellation of the financing and denouncing the repression exercised by both the state and DESA. Berta denounced not only the Agua Zarca Hydroelectric Project but also the other 40 dams planned for Lenca territory, some financed by the CAMIF Bank, connected to the World Bank (GAIPE, 2017). Berta was a voice heard at the national and international levels because of her fierce defence of land, human rights, and nature.

Her Assassination
Thanks to COPINH's activism, DESA could not advance the construction of the hydroelectric project and thus began to threaten, repress, and harass Berta Cáceres and the other leaders of COPINH. Berta was issued an arrest warrant on charges of usurpation and damage to DESA worth more than 3 million dollars. She was detained in 2013, but because of international condemnation, the case was dismissed. Throughout 2014 and 2015, she received Facebook threats and letters. In September 2015, DESA attempted to resume the construction of the Agua Zarca Hydroelectric Dam, and COPINH responded by organizing a protest that was violently attacked. In December 2015, investigative agents of the National Civil Police arrested Olvin Mejia, who confessed that DESA had hired him to silence members of COPINH and claimed that Berta Cáceres was first on the list of people to be eliminated. Olvin was later released and began to work as a security guard at DESA. After multiple assassination attempts and threats, Berta Cáceres was murdered in March 2016 in her home at the age of 44.

continued

The five international lawyers working on Berta's case were able to identify a plot against Berta that had taken months to design and involved senior executives and employees of DESA as well as state agents (GAIPE, 2017). Nevertheless, more than two years after her death, the intellectual authors of the crime have not been charged, and COPINH members are still threatened and repressed for defending their rights as Lenca people, especially the right to free, prior, and informed consultation (Greenpeace International, 2018). Police, military, and DESA personnel have targeted those who demand an independent international commission to investigate the murder of Berta and the cancellation of the Agua Zarca Project (GAIPE, 2017). Berta's family and COPINH have asked for an independent investigation by Honduran authorities and presented the case to the Inter-American Commission of Human Rights (IACHR), the United Nations, and numerous national and international actors.

Her Legacy

Berta was awarded the Goldman Environmental Prize in 2015 after she successfully led grassroots campaigns to get the World Bank and Sinohydro, a Chinese state-owned hydropower and construction corporation and the world's largest dam builder, to stop building a hydroelectric

Berta Cáceres, in front of the river she died to protect, taken at her receipt of the Goldman Environmental Prize in 2015.

Goldman Environmental Prize

dam on the Gualcarque River (Goldman Environmental Foundation, 2018). Berta was a revolutionary who inspired many around the world to fight for the decolonization of land and bodies. In a long tradition of male leaders, the figure and leadership of Berta means a symbolic turning point for Central American social movements. Berta's feminist, horizontal leadership transformed her assassination into a symbolic crime and the pursuit for justice into a political struggle. Berta Cáceres's case is not an isolated incident but the symptom of a systemic feature—the use of violence to secure conditions for capital accumulation. According to La Via Campesina (2018), a transnational peasant movement, every three days an activist like Berta is murdered. Berta's sacrifice planted the seeds of a struggle against capitalism, racism, and patriarchy that today is embodied by hundreds of thousands of activists, minorities, and intellectuals around the world. She has become an iconic figure who has left a permanent mark on the history of social justice struggles—"Berta lives, the struggle continues." See Chapter 16 for more on Berta's legacy.

Lesbian and trans women, particularly those involved in rights advocacy, are currently one of the main targets of gender-based violence. According to one transsexual activist in Honduras, "The LGBT community is the most affected by hate crimes. We live with the fear of being assassinated at any time . . . and it's the ones who are in charge of our security—the police—that violate our rights" (Nobel Women's Initiative, 2013). Brazil is the country with the highest murder rate of LGBT (Lesbian, Gay, Bisexual, Transsexual) people in the world. The life expectancy for a trans woman of colour in Brazil is 30 years (Bowater & Moraes, 2018), and an LGBT person is murdered every 19 hours (Univision, 2018).

Domestic/Intimate-Partner Violence

The most well-known or frequently cited motivation behind gender-based violence is passion/sentimental in the context of domestic/intimate-partner violence. In Colombia in 2012, every 11 minutes a woman was a victim of intimate-partner physical abuse, and every three days a woman was killed in intimate-partner violence (Semana, 2013). In Brazil, every six hours a woman is killed by her intimate partner (BBC Mundo, 2016). More than 30 per cent of Mexican women in a recent survey said that they had been physically attacked by their former partner (Yagoub, 2017). The problem with this category of violence is that it covers up many revealing details that point in the direction of more structural causes. For instance, children who witness violence or experience violence themselves (as part of an armed conflict or criminal activity) are more likely to commit violence on others or have violence committed on them (Fregoso & Bejarano, 2010). On the other hand, cases of women who end up victimized by violence in the process of being forced into prostitution or any criminal activity, such as transporting illegal drugs, often get reported as cases of intimate-partner violence, since it is assumed that the perpetrator had a romantic relationship with the victim. Similarly, the murders of women activists are often depoliticized by being categorized as crimes of passion. All this suggests that what may appear to be a situation of domestic violence or intimate-partner violence may have much more structural and/or political undertones when it comes to its causes and consequences.

Marielle and Matheus: Two Afro-Brazilian Activists Assassinated within One-and-a-Half Months

Marielle Franco was an Afro-Brazilian queer woman, mother, sociologist, socialist, human rights defender, and councilwoman from the *favela* (poor neighbourhood) of Maré in Rio de Janeiro. She advocated against police violence and extrajudicial executions in *favelas* and for the defence of Black women and the LGBT community. In 2008, Marielle participated in a parliamentary commission that investigated para-police (paramilitary) violence in which members of the police and municipal council were implicated (Infobae, 2018). In 2016, Marielle became the fifth most voted municipal legislator (*La Vanguardia*, 2018). As part of her work, she monitored the recent wave of militarization of Rio's *favelas* that forms part of then-President Michel Temer's heavy-handed approach. On 14 March 2018, 38-year-old Marielle was shot and killed in her car along with her driver.

Matheus Passarelli was a 21-year-old Afro-Brazilian student at the Rio de Janeiro State University. Matheus/a identified as both a male and female and was a strong LGBT activist. Matheus/a was executed and burnt in the *favela* Gaúcha in Rio de Janeiro on 30 April 2018. Since 2000, the annual number of LGBT homicides in Brazil has quadrupled (Univision, 2018). The murder of Matheus/a took place in the midst of increased militarization of the city of Rio de Janeiro, which was part of right-wing President Temer's "iron-fist" approach that accompanied a wave of draconian pro-neoliberal measures.

Militarism, Machismo, and Illegal Capital in the Life of One Woman: The Micro—Macro Dialectic

Emilia lived in a small town in the Department of Quindio, Colombia. She was 16 years old when she met Edelberto, a police officer 12 years older than Emilia. She got pregnant, and the two were married. After her son was born, Edelberto was promoted to a higher-ranking position in an elite unit that came with more responsibility. Initially, she was happy because this meant an economically secure future for the family. However, Edelberto began to earn unusual amounts of money, which she realized were not his salary but came from illegal deals he made with criminals. He began to be away from home a great deal and to withhold information about his whereabouts. There was a lot more money in the household, and Emilia could now afford the clothes she always wanted, but she was not happy, since her husband would frequently arrive home drunk and she would find evidence of him having extramarital affairs. When she protested, he became abusive and aggressive. She felt undesirable and depressed. After five years of emotional and at times physical abuse and infidelity, Emilia decided to abandon the marriage. She had barely finished high school, and the only option she believed would allow her to earn sufficient money to open her own business one day was to go to Japan as a sex worker. The criminal organization that arranged to get her to Japan also paid for two cosmetic surgeries, which she had to undergo prior to her departure. She left her child with Edelberto's family. She had to stay three years in Japan to pay off the debt she owed to the trafficking organization before being allowed to return to Colombia. When she came back, she was as poor as she was when she left. In the meantime, Edelberto left the police force and began working with an army general who supplied weapons to paramilitary groups. He also locally managed the *sicarios* who service the boss of the human trafficking network that traffics women from Colombia to Spain. He began having short-term relationships with different women almost weekly. He moves around in an expensive armoured vehicle and is always armed. He says that he cannot find a woman who truly loves him, since all that women are after is his money. His nine-year-old son fears that his father may be killed at any moment and that his mother may decide to go back to Japan and leave him again (Interview, August 2017). Stories of this sort are all too common and illustrative of the ways in which the violence of capital destroys families and brutalizes women, children, and men on so many levels.

Child Marriage

Child marriage is defined as the marriage or union between two people in which one or both parties are younger than 18 years of age. Marriage requires "free and full" consent, and since consent cannot be "free and full" when one of the individuals is not sufficiently mature to make such a decision, marriage before the age of 18 can be considered forced marriage and constitutes a violation of human rights (UNICEF, 2018). Latin America's rate of child marriage of 23 per cent rivals that in high-prevalence countries in Africa and Asia. It is currently higher than that in the Middle East and North Africa. Latin America is the only region with a high rate of child marriage that is not on the decline, with one in three girls being married off before they are 18 and where births to girls under 15 are on the rise (Griffin, 2015). Brazil ranks fourth in the world for child marriage. It is estimated that the numbers may be higher if informal (common-law) unions are considered.

Of all the cases of teenagers who marry between the ages of 15 to 17, the majority are girls, and in most cases the male is considerably older.

Girls who get married before the age of 18 are at higher risk of experiencing domestic abuse as well as complication during pregnancy and birth. According to the World Health Organization (WHO), such complications are the number one cause of death among 15- to 19-year-old girls in the world (Semana, 2018). The factors driving child marriage (or marriage-like relationship with an adult) are numerous and complex. Among the key ones are:

- Poverty—some parents give their daughter in marriage hoping that she will have a better living standard and an educational opportunity provided by the husband. There have been cases, although rare, when parents "sold" their daughters. Recently, an NGO that helps women and children victims of family violence in Chiapas, Mexico, rescued a 10-year-old girl who had been sold for 30,000 pesos by her mother to a 60-year-old man (Rodriguez, 2018).
- Child abuse—girls experiencing physical and sexual abuse by a family member are more likely to start a new family early as a way of escaping the abusive domestic environment.

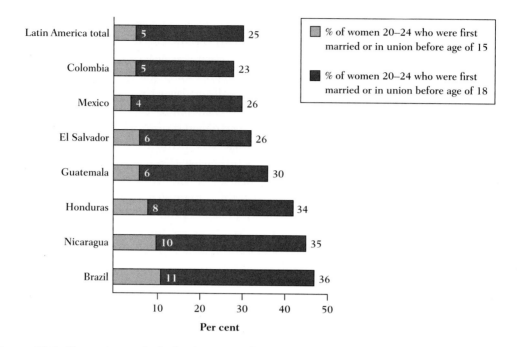

Figure 11.1 Countries with the highest prevalence of child marriage in Latin America, 2010–17

Adapted from Data and Analytics Section, Research and Policy, UNICEF Global Data Base 2018, https://data.unicef.org/topic/child-protection/child-marriage/#

- Early pregnancy—a teenage girl who has a child to raise (often the consequence of conservative abortion laws) is more likely to seek marriage as a way of securing a livelihood for herself and her child.
- Need for protection in violent environments—under circumstances of insecurity and widespread gang violence, as in the case of Central America, some girls seek to marry or move in with a gang member as a form of protection for themselves and their family (Griffin, 2015).
- War, armed conflict, and forced displacement—in Colombia, for instance, 30 per cent of adolescent internally displaced women are mothers or pregnant, compared to the national figure of 20 per cent for this age cohort (Alzate, 2007).

- Coercion—in regions with a high presence of illegal armed groups such as drug cartels or paramilitary groups, girls may be forcibly taken from their families by armed actors.

Abortion

When it comes to reproductive health and freedom, Latin America still lags behind. In El Salvador, Honduras, Nicaragua, the Dominican Republic, and Haiti, abortion is totally prohibited with no exceptions. In the rest of Latin America, it is allowed only under certain circumstances, the most common one being when the life of the woman is at risk (Clínicas de Aborto, 2018). This conservative attitude toward abortion has led to the death and criminalization of tens of thousands of women.

The Political–Economic Dialectic in Sexual Violence and Feminicide

Why Feminicide and Not Femicide?

Since the early stages of capitalism, the state has been complicit in the different forms of violence against women (Federici, 2004). The deaths of thousands of women in Latin America and the failure of states to take adequate measures has led to the birth of the term "feminicide"—a conscious effort by scholars to acknowledge the state's responsibility in femicides (Fregoso & Bejarano, 2010).

> Feminicide is a political term. It encompasses more than femicide because it holds responsible not only the male perpetrators but also the state and judicial structures that normalize misogyny. Feminicide connotes not only the murder of women by men because they are women but also indicates state responsibility for these murders whether through the commission of the actual killing, toleration of the perpetrators' acts of violence, or omission of state responsibility to ensure the safety of its female citizens.

A fact-finding mission that investigated violence against women in Mexico, Guatemala, and Honduras found that more than 95 per cent of crimes are never punished and most are never even investigated by authorities. Routine discrimination against women is an institutional feature of the justice system, and women who bring charges or petitions for justice are frequently harassed, blamed, and humiliated (Nobel Women's Initiative, 2013).

Violence against women must be understood in relation to larger structural process such as militarization, nationalism, and imperialism. Chaterjee (1996, cited in Giles & Hyndman, 2004) argues that nationalism, gender, and sexuality are mutually constitutive. Dominant definitions of what it means to be a man or a woman are interconnected with violence against civilians in the name of the nation, capital, or the family (Giles & Hyndman, 2004). Gender relations and identities encouraged by governments, the military apparatus, and other armed actors are functional to their pursuit of political and economic hegemony (Giles & Hyndman, 2004; Mohanty, Pratt, & Riley, 2009). For example, if we look at the strengthening of the state's coercive apparatus throughout Latin America (militarization) and US military intervention in the region (imperialism), we can detect the gendered, masculinized, and heterosexist practices and ideologies that further consolidate patriarchy and exacerbate women's subordination (Mohanty, Pratt, & Riley, 2009). In the highly militarized Aguan region of Honduras, peasant families live in constant fear about the safety of their daughters, since soldiers and paramilitary groups have been known to pick up girls, take them to the military installation, and force them to strip and perform sex acts (Interview, April 2018). The Honduran Center for Women's Studies reports that the rise in military expenditures has been associated with a rise in feminicides. Similarly, in Mexico the intense militarization following the launch of the War on Drugs in 2006 has led to a 40 per cent increase in feminicides. This is how Martha Ojeda, from the Coalition for Justice in the Maquiladoras, Tamaulipas, describes the Mexico–US border: "My region is a place where the population, and especially women, face shoot-outs, grenades, roadblocks. . . . Where soldiers carry out de facto raids on houses, imposing martial law, and U.S. military personnel violate national sovereignty" (Nobel Women's Initiative, 2013). In Colombia, paramilitary forces have been the most notorious and feared sexual predators. What is even more disturbing is that over the years, their victims have become increasingly younger. At present, members of such groups force peasant families living in extreme poverty to send their daughters aged 10 to 13 to the paramilitaries' property where they sexually abuse the girls and subject them to all sorts of painful and humiliating acts (Semana, 2017). Paramilitary groups not only victimize girls through direct violence but also indirectly by dictating norms and ideals of sexuality and femininity that women and young children internalize and consequently allow themselves to be molded into the objects that meet the fantasies of armed actors.

The Implications of Neoliberalism in Sexual Violence and Feminicide

As Federici (2004) explains, male-centred systems of exploitation have always relied on violence to discipline and appropriate the female body. Thus, it is important to think about how the forces that drive economic globalization create conditions that victimize women. The expansion of agribusiness and mining (two of the pillars of the global economy) has entailed present-day processes of primitive accumulation as small-scale farmers are being dispossessed and left with no other option but to sell their labour at any price in order to survive. This is the entry point to a wide range of survival options that inevitably place the dispossessed, both men and women, in conditions of increased vulnerability and risk of violence:

1. All the stressors associated with forced migration such as lack of proper nutrition, food insecurity, and inadequate housing increase the chances of domestic violence (Buvinic, Morrison, & Shifter, 1999).
2. Most forcibly displaced people migrate to the shanty towns of large urban centres where they are victimized by criminal violence. The informal nature of work in which they often engage also presents higher risks of such violence.

3. Children, especially boys, in displaced families who live in urban slums are at high risk of being recruited by gangs or criminal organizations. Even if they are not forcibly recruited, often they join "voluntarily," given the conditions of high insecurity, when belonging to a gang may be perceived as a way of having some protection.
4. Children, especially girls, in displaced families who live in urban slums are at high risk of incidents of sexual violence by gangs/criminal organizations because of the dangerous social and physical environments that they navigate. Girls are also at risk of human trafficking for the purpose of forced prostitution whereby violence and the threat of violence are the principal instruments of control.
5. Some of those displaced attempt to migrate illegally, especially people from countries such as Mexico, Honduras, Guatemala, and El Salvador, to the US and in the process are victimized by human smugglers, drug cartels, corrupt police officials, and other violent actors. Once again, sexual violence is highly prevalent under such conditions.
6. Frequently, displaced women seek employment in the *maquilas*. Here, workers are not only subjected to super-exploitation but are also sexually objectified. Bank Muñoz (2007) provides the example of a tortilla factory where she describes the environment as racialized and sexualized despotism. Women workers are constantly pursued by managers asking for sexual favours; they are forced to either flirt with managers or lose their jobs.
7. Women activists who challenge the neoliberal agenda in any way, such as those who try to start a union, who occupy land, or who rally against mining companies, are targeted by state and non-state armed actors (as discussed earlier).

Masculinities, Femininities, and Political Projects

Dominant ideologies of masculinity and femininity in Latin America serve to normalize violence and objectify women's bodies (Baird, 2012; Cockburn, 2004; Cohn, 2012; Fregoso & Bejarano, 2010; Gyles & Hyndman, 2004; Mohanty, Pratt, & Riley, 2009; Raven-Roberts, 2012; Viveros, 2001). Latin American states' history of violence is intertwined with the consolidation of violent patriarchies, the contemporary extreme expression of this being feminicide (Fregoso & Bejarano, 2010). Femininities and masculinities in Latin America vary along a continuum of subordinate and dominant. While one gender has dominated the other, domination and subordination are also determined to a large extent by class status. In this sense, those who control most of the wealth have the power to impose their definitions of femininity and masculinity on others. Within the low-income population, we find those who resist dominant definitions and challenge both class and gender inequality as well as those who subscribe to these norms.

Hegemonic Masculinity and Machismo

It is important to acknowledge here that there is no such a thing as "masculinity" in general but rather multiple masculinities. The harmful masculine identity is one that is inscribed with hegemony over other masculinities as well as over femininity, since its essence presupposes domination over other human beings (men and women). This **hegemonic masculinity** legitimates men's power vis-à-vis women and is a feature of those "men having greater power than other men, . . . with "subordinate masculinities" (Cohn, 2012). Raven-Roberts (2012) uses the term **predatory patriarchy** to refer to masculine identities infused with and constituted through violence and aggression.

In Latin America, masculinity is rooted in the hegemonic positioning over women and on competition between males (Viveros, 2001). The hegemonic masculinity takes the form of **machismo**—"the belief that women should be subordinate to the needs and desires of their male partners, taking care of them, providing them with pleasure (either as wives or partners or as approached in predatory fashion by men who would not consider marrying them) and bearing their children" (Wilson, 2014, p. 4). Viveros (2001) outlines the main elements of machismo, which include expansive sexual appetite (demonstrated by having sex with a variety of women in addition to their spouses), viewing female sexuality as an object over which the male has control, and proving manliness by displaying sexual dominance. Machismo is sustained by cultural models that assign women positions that subordinate them to the personal and institutionalized power of men. This paves the way to violence through insinuations, offensive comparisons, harassment, threats, abuse, and intimidation that eventually leads to beatings, rape, and persecution (Olivera & Furio, 2006).

Macho types of masculinity in Latin America are synonymous with social status, respect, money, sexual access to women, and violence (Baird, 2012). Boys, especially those of low socioeconomic status who have no other source of power, seek to validate their masculinity through engagement in violence as well as their domination and consumption of women, while girls' femininity can be validated through being "consumed." As Baird (2012) has found in his study on poor male youth in Medellin, Colombia, "The youths in gangs admired the gang leader . . . localised signifiers of 'doing masculinity' . . . included access to material goods such as fast motorbikes, expensive clothes and trainers, . . . and sexual access to the most coveted women in the neighbourhood" (p. 183).

Commodified Femininity

Dominant definitions of beauty and femininity in Latin America today still imply being gentle, weak, and dependent on a man and generally revolve around the principal roles women have: the reproductive and nurturing role on one hand and the sexually pleasing role on the other, leaving no space for other activities that enable the autonomous development of the woman as a human being such as education or political activism. The sexist definitions of these roles involve an inherent contradiction, since all the labour that is involved in procreation and nurturing has a physical and emotional toll that is not reconcilable with the expectations for a sexual diva with a flawless physical appearance and a sexual disposition of being eager to please. Thus, a central element of machismo culture involves an assumption that these two roles are to be performed simultaneously by different women (the wife and the lover/s). This contradiction is also one of the reasons behind the way women internalize machismo culture and put it into practice: for many women, the central goal in life is to improve their economic status by attaching themselves to a man with sufficient resources that would enable them to, after giving birth, dedicate their time and attention to taking care of their appearance (buying nice clothes, going to the gym, undergoing cosmetic surgeries, etc.) and thus pleasing the man, while delegating the nurturing and housework to the *empleada domestica* (the maid).

Subversive Femininity

Similar to the way that Indigenous, African, and poor women who challenged state authority or landowners were vilified and accused of witchcraft, today women who organize labour unions, those who demand justice for victims of state and paramilitary violence, those who struggle against land dispossession, and those who demand sexual and reproductive rights are criminalized, threatened, abused, and killed. Nevertheless, women continue to be at the forefront of social movements today. Unlike the Global North, in Latin America feminism and resistance to neoliberalism coincide almost completely in both ideas and practice. Social movements such as the Landless People's Movement in Brazil (*Movimento dos Trabalhadores sem Terra*, or MST) and the Zapatista Army of National Liberation (*Ejercito Zapatista de Liberacion Nacional*, or EZLN) have become spaces of equality, including in gender relations. In fact, women's empowerment has been one of the unintended (but wonderful) consequences in the evolution of these movements. For instance, Kampwirth (2004) has found that for women participants in the revolutionary organizations in El Salvador and Nicaragua, life within the movement "was the closest they had ever come to experiencing gender equality" (p. 14). Similarly, since the birth of the EZLN in 1994, Indigenous women have experienced profound changes in how they are viewed by others within the spheres of the family, economy, and politics. The EZLN is an Indigenous movement in Chiapas, Mexico, for land and autonomy. Initially, it began as an armed rebellion but soon afterwards transitioned into a non-armed movement. Women have served as commanders in the Zapatista army and as regional representatives, members of the autonomous government, and health and education promoters. They have formed economic collectives such as vegetable gardens and bread-making and artisan cooperatives. Women's increased presence outside the family has been accompanied by changes within the family such as a decrease in domestic violence and the right to choose when and whom to marry and how many children to have.

In the words of one Zapatista woman, "Before we didn't have any rights. Before we were not valued as women. But now we have rights as women" (Klein, 2008). Zapatista women have also played an important role in building transnational solidarity through international women's encounters hosted in Zapatista territories attended by feminists, students, teachers, peasants, Indigenous people, and other women from different countries, including the Global North. The lived experiences of people in these movements demonstrate that all forms of oppression can and should be challenged simultaneously.

Tying It Together

This chapter has provided an overview of different types of violence against women in Latin America. While there are different forms of violence according to motivation and perpetrator, political violence against women activists and human rights defenders has been the least studied one even though it has been on the rise in recent years. The issue of violence against women has been typically treated as a private/micro-level/non-political issue by academics and politicians alike. As a reaction to this, feminists across the Americas are using the term "feminicide" to signal the political roots and consequences of femicide. Political agendas at the service of capital benefit from certain definitions of masculinity and femininity and are threatened by those femininities and masculinities that subvert the dominant norms. The intersection of neoliberal restructuring with local patriarchal structures has had deadly outcomes for women, particularly poor women, women of colour, activists, and those outside heterosexual normativity. It has given rise to ideologies that normalize violence against women and treat human beings, including children, as a commodity.

Call to Action

You can establish contact with social movements and feminist organizations in Latin America and support them by disseminating material produced by them, such as urgent action calls, or by translating material into English. One example is participating in one of the international encounters organized by Zapatista women in Chiapas, Mexico. You can also participate in transnational movement events such as the World Social Forum or the Via Campesina International Conference. These are remarkable events organized outside of the capitalist consumerist logic; they are spaces of exchange based on solidarity, reciprocity, and equality. You can volunteer as an interpreter if you speak a second language. You can also collect signatures on letters that address a specific problem in a specific country (e.g., political prisoners, unlawful evictions) and send it to government officials at different levels. Write letters to the Canadian government to demand: sanctions for Canadian companies implicated in human rights abuses in Latin America, legislation on basic rules of conduct for Canadian companies abroad, and that trade and other forms of cooperation with Latin American states are conditional upon enforcement of the law against femicide on all levels and prosecution of crimes against women and girls.

DISCUSSION QUESTIONS

1. What would be one way in which the Canadian state could take a stand against gender-based violence in Latin America that would translate into a long-lasting positive impact?

2. What are some of the unintended but positive consequences of social movements for women's status and rights?

3. Reflect on some of the ways in which harmful gender ideologies in Latin America are present in North American society. What is some of the evidence of their presence?

SUGGESTIONS FOR FURTHER READING

Pailey, D. (2014). *Drug war capitalism*. Oakland, CA: AK Press. This book, written by an investigative journalist, demonstrates how terror is used to facilitate policy change and the operations of extractive industries under the cover of the War on Drugs.

Gordon, T., & Weber, J. (2016). *Blood of extraction: Canadian imperialism in Latin America*. Halifax, NS: Fernwood Publishing. This book reveals how Canadian companies operating throughout Latin America are implicated in human rights violations and contribute to further militarization and an increase in violence.

Shipley, T. (2017). *Ottawa and empire: Canada and the military coup in Honduras*. Toronto, ON: Between the Lines. This book discusses the imperialist nature of the Canadian state by examining Canada's role in the military coup in 2009 that installed a right-wing repressive regime.

Fregoso, R.L., & Bejarano, C. (Eds). (2010). *Terrorizing women: Feminicide in the Américas*. Durham, NC: Duke University Press. This book analyzes the escalation of violence against women across Latin America in the past two decades and introduces the analytical framework of feminicide.

Dominguez-Ruvalcaba, H., & Corona, I. (2012). *Gender violence at the U.S.–Mexico border: Media representation and public response*. Tucson, AZ: University of Arizona Press. This book looks at how gender-based violence is represented in media and oral narratives. In particular, it covers the most extreme manifestation of violence in the region—the feminicides in Ciudad Juarez.

Maier, E., & Lebon, N. (2010). *Women's activism in Latin America and the Caribbean: Engendering social justice, democratizing citizenship*. London, UK: Rutgers University Press. This book, particularly in parts III and IV, offers valuable insights into the struggles of present-day women's movements in different countries across the region.

MULTIMEDIA SUGGESTIONS

We women warriors: Tejiendo sabiduria. (2012). Los Angeles, CA: Todos los Pueblos Productions.
This documentary follows three Indigenous women activists from different parts of Colombia in their struggles to protect their territories in the face of warfare financed by the drug trade.

Rio Blanco Resiste
http://lab.pikaramagazine.com/guardiana-de-los-rios
This documentary film chronicles the struggle of Berta Cáceres and the Lenca people in Honduras to protect their natural environment.

Resistencia: The fight for the Aguan Valley. (2015). Naretiv Productions.
This documentary of the violent dispossession in the Aguan Valley of Honduras, a warlike region where palm-oil companies have been illegally appropriating the land of peasant cooperatives, interviews women peasant leaders and addresses foreign support for the coup in 2009.

Zapatista. (2015). San Francisco, CA: Kanopy Streaming.
This socio-political documentary details the Zapatista uprising in Mexico and its achievements

Plan Colombia: Cashing in on the drug war failure. (2003). Free Will Productions.

This documentary film demonstrates how US military funding to the Colombian state through anti-drug projects has strengthened military and paramilitary forces and led to alarming levels of repression and attacks against unionists, peasants, Indigenous groups, and other activists there.

Via Campesina

https://viacampesina.org/en

This website provides information about and publications by La Via Campesina, an international movement bringing together millions of peasants, small- and medium-size farmers, landless people, rural women and youth, Indigenous people, migrants, and agricultural workers from around the world.

Amnesty International

https://www.amnesty.org/en/latest/news

This is the website of Amnesty International, an international organization that defends human rights globally through research and campaigns. Reports on the human rights situation in each country in Latin America, as well as thematic reports according to issues, can be found here.

REFERENCES

Adams, T. (2011). Chronic violence and its reproduction: Perverse trends in social relations, citizenship and democracy in Latin America. Wilson Centre Latin American Program. Retrieved from: https://www.wilsoncenter.org/publication/chronic-violence-andits-reproduction-perverse-trends-social-relations-citizenship-and.

AI (Amnesty International). (2004). Colombia: Scarred bodies, hidden crimes—sexual violence against women in the armed conflict. 13 October. Retrieved from: http://web.amnesty.org/library/print/ENGAMR230402004?open&of=ENG-Col.

Alzate, M. (2007). The sexual and reproductive rights of internally displaced women: The embodiment of Colombia's crisis. *Disasters, 31*(1), 131–48.

Baird, A. (2012). The violent gang and the construction of masculinity amongst socially excluded young men. *Safer Communities, 11*(4), 179–90.

Bank Muñoz, C. (2007). The tortilla behemoth: Sexualized despotism and women's resistance in a transnational Mexican tortilla factory. In A.L. Cabezas, E. Reese, & M. Waller (Eds), *The wages of empire: Neoliberal policies, repression, and women's poverty* (pp. 127–39). Boulder, CO: Paradigm Publishers.

BBC Mundo. (2016). País por país: El mapa que muestra las trágicas cifras de los feminicidios en América Latina. *Redacción BBC Mundo*, 17 November. Retrieved from: http://www.bbc.com/mundo/noticias-america-latina-37828573.

Bott, S., Guedes, A., Goodwin, M., & Mendoza, J. (2012). Violence against women in Latin America and the Caribbean: A comparative analysis of population-based data from 12 countries. Pan American Health Organization. Retrieved from: https://www.paho.org/hq/index.php?option=com_content&view=article&id=8175%3A2013-violence-against-women-latin-america-caribbean-comparative-analysis&catid=1505%3Aintra-family-violence&Itemid=41342&lang=en.

Bowater, D., & Moraes, P. (2018). Brazil: Targeting trans people with impunity. Aljazeera.com. https://www.aljazeera.com/indepth/features/2015/04/brazil-targeting-trans-people-impunity-150413210248222.html.

Buvinic, M., Morrison, A., and Shifter, M. (1999). Violence in Latin America and the Caribbean: A framework for action. Sustainable Development Department, Inter-American Development Bank.

Carpenter, R. C. (2006). Recognizing gender-based violence against civilian men and boys in conflict situations. *Security Dialogue, 37*(1).

Clínicas de Aborto. (2018). Situacion legal del aborto en Latinoamerica. Retrieved from: https://www.clinicas-aborto.com.mx/legislacion/latinoamerica.

CNN. (2016). La violencia contra las mujeres en América Latina: El desolador panorama. 25 November. Retrieved from: http://cnnespanol.cnn.com/2016/11/25/la-violencia-contra-las-mujeres-en-america-latina-el-desoladorpanorama/#0.

Cockburn, C. (2004). The continuum of violence: A gender perspective on war and peace. In Wenona Giles and Jennifer Hyndman (Eds), *Sites of violence: Gender and conflict zones* (pp. 24–44). Los Angeles, CA: University of California Press.

Cohn, C. (2012). Women and wars: Contested histories, uncertain futures. In C. Cohn (Ed.), *Women and wars: Contested histories, uncertain futures* (pp. 1–24). Cambridge, UK: Polity.

Dominguez-Ruvalcaba, H., & Corona, I. (2012). *Gender violence at the U.S.–Mexico border: Media representation and public response.* Tucson, AZ: University of Arizona Press.

Federici, S. (2004). *Caliban and the witch: Women, the body and primitive accumulation.* Chico, CA: AK Press.

Fregoso, R.L., & Bejarano, C. (2010). Introduction: A cartography of feminicide in the Américas. In R. L. Fregoso & C. Bejarano (Eds), *Terrorizing women:*

Feminicide in the Américas (pp.1–41). Durham, NC: Duke University Press.

GAIPE. (2017). Represa de violencia: El plan que asesinó a Berta Cáceres. GAIPE reports.

Germinando | Espacio Agroecológico. (2018). *Feminismo, ecología y ciencia [Berta Cáceres].* Retrieved from: http://germinando.es/feminismo-ecologia-y-ciencia-2.

Giles, W., & Hyndman, J. (2004). New directions for feminist research and politics. In W. Giles & J. Hyndman (Eds), *Sites of violence: Gender and conflict zones* (pp. 301–15). Los Angeles, CA: University of California Press.

Goldman Environmental Foundation. (2018). *Fighting for their lives: Goldman Environmental Foundation.* Retrieved from: https://www.goldmanprize.org/blog/fighting-for-their-lives-goldman-prize-winners-under-threat.

Gordon, T., & Weber, J. (2016). *Blood of extraction: Canadian imperialism in Latin America.* Halifax, NS: Fernwood Publishing.

Greenpeace International. (2018). *Revealed: Investigation uncovers the plot to murder Berta Cáceres.* Retrieved from: https://www.greenpeace.org/international/story/11655/revealed-investigation-uncovers-the-plot-to-murder-berta-caceres.

Griffin, J. (2015). The "hidden" problem of child marriage in Latin America. 23 November. Retrieved from: https://theirworld.org/news/the-8216-hidden-8217-problem-of-child-marriage-in-latin-america.

ILO (International Labour Organization). (2013). Trabajo decente e igualdad de genero. http://www.ilo.org/wcmsp5/groups/public/@americas/@ro-lima/@sro- santiago/documents/publication/wcms_233161.pdf.

Infobae. (2018). *La investigación sobre el asesinato de Marielle Franco está en "la etapa final."* Retrieved from: https://www.infobae.com/america/america-latina/2018/05/11/la-investigacion-sobre-el-asesinato-marielle-franco-esta-en-la-etapa-final.

Interview. (2017, August). Ramona. Interview over Skype.

Interview. (2018, March). Karla Zelaya. Tegucigalpa, Honduras.

Interview. (2018, April). Dina Meza. Tegucigalpa, Honduras.

Joffily, M. (2016). Sexual violence in the military dictatorships of Latin America: Who wants to know. *Sur—International Journal on Human Rights, 13*(24), 165–76.

Kampwirth, K. (2004). *Feminism and the legacy of revolution: Nicaragua, El Salvador, Chiapas.* Athens, OH: Ohio University Press.

Klein, H. (2008). *We learn as we go: Zapatista women share their experiences.* 30 January. http://axisoflogic.com/artman/publish/article_25946.shtm.

La Vanguardia. (2018). *Marielle Franco, la voz guerrera de las favelas que fue silenciada por las balas.* Retrieved from: http://www.lavanguardia.com/internacional/20180315/441548890762/marielle-franco-favelas-guerrera.html.

La Via Campesina. (2018). *Las otras Berta Cáceres.* Retrieved from: https://viacampesina.org/es/las-otras-berta-caceres.

Mohanty, C., Pratt, M., & Riley, R. (2009). Introduction: Feminism and U.S wars—Mapping the ground. In R. Riley et al. (Eds), *Feminism and war: Confronting US Imperialism* (pp. 1–16). London, UK: Zed Books.

Nobel Women's Initiative. (2013). From survivors to defenders: Women confronting violence in Mexico, Honduras and Guatemala. https://nobelwomensinitiative.org/wp-content/uploads/2012/06/Report_AmericasDelgation-20121.pdf?ref=218.

NODAL. (2017). América Latina, la región más violenta para las mujeres: Hay al menos 12 femicidios diarios. 24 November. https://www.nodal.am/2017/11/america-latina-la-region-mas-violentalas-mujeres-al-menos-12-femicidios-diarios.

Olivera, M., & Furio, V. (2006). Violencia femicida: Violence against women and Mexico's structural crisis. *Latin American Perspectives, 33*(2), 104–14.

Pearce, J. (2009). Introduction: Researching democracy and social change with violence in the foreground. *IDS Bulletin, 40*(3), 1–9.

Phillips, T. (2018). Breathtaking homicidal violence: Latin America in grip of murder crisis. *The Guardian,* 26 April. Retrieved from: https://www.theguardian.com/world/2018/apr/26/latin-america-murder-crisis-violence-homicide-report?CMP=Share_iOSApp_Other.

Raven-Roberts, A. (2012). Women and the political economy of war. In C. Cohn (Ed.), *Women and wars: Contested histories, uncertain futures.* Cambridge, UK: Polity.

Rodriguez, M. (2018). Le entregó su hija de 10 años a un hombre de 60 por 30.000 pesos: El drama de los matrimonios infantiles en América Latina. *BBC Mundo,* 6 March. Retrieved from: http://www.bbc.com/mundo/noticias-america-latina-43303994.

Seisdedos, S., & Bonometti, P. (2009–10). Las mujeres en America Latina: Indicadores y datos. *Revista Ciencias Sociales,* (126/127), 75–87.

Semana. (2013). Cifras de la violencia contra la mujer. 25 November. Retrieved from: http://www.semana.com/nacion/articulo/cifras-de-la-violencia-contra-la-mujer-en-colombia/366030-3.

Semana. (2017). El depredador sexual de uraba. 15 May. Retrieved from: https://www.theguardian.com/world/2017/mar/02/colombia-paramilitaries-victims-us-court.

Semana. (2018). Le entregó su hija de 10 años a un hombre de 60 por 30.000 pesos: El drama de los matrimonios infantiles. 8 March. Retrieved from: https://www.semana.com/mundo/articulo/le-entrego-su-hija-de-10-anos-a-un-hombre-de-60-por-30000-pesos-el-drama-de-los-matrimonios-infantiles-en-america-latina/559405.

Shipley, T. (2017). *Ottawa and empire: Canada and the military coup in Honduras.* Toronto, ON: Between the Lines.

UNDP (United Nations Development Programme). (2017). Human development report. Retrieved from: http://hdr.undp.org/en/2016-report.

UNICEF. (2018). Child marriage is a violation of human rights but is all too common. Retrieved from: http://data.unicef.org/topic/child-protection/child-marriage/#.

Univision. (2018). Queman y asesinan a activista de los derechos LGBT en Brasil. Retrieved from: https://www.univision.com/noticias/america-latina/queman-y-asesinan-a-un-activista-de-los-derechos-lgbt-en-brasil.

USAID. (2017). Fact sheet: Improving women's land rights in Colombia. Retrieved from: https://land-links.org/document/fact-sheet-improving-womens-land-rights-colombia.

Viveros, M. (2001). Contemporary Latin American perspectives on masculinity. *Men & Masculinities, 3*(3), 237–60.

Wilson, T. D. (2014). Violence against women in Latin America. *Latin American Perspectives, 41*(1), 3–18.

Wirtz, A., et al. (2014). Gender-based violence in conflict and displacement: Qualitative findings from displaced women in Colombia. *Conflict and Health, 8*(10), 1–14.

Yagoub, M. (2017). Across Latin America, violence against women fuels more crime. 20 March. Retrieved from: https://www.opendemocracy.net/democraciaabierta/mimi-yagoub/across-latin-america-violence-against-women-fuels-more-crime.

CHAPTER 12

◇

Immobilizing Bodies of Surveillance
Anti-oppressive Feminisms and the Decolonization of Violence

Vanessa Lynn Lovelace and Heather M. Turcotte

Learning Objectives

In this chapter, you will:

- assess the historical context of surveillance as a colonial discourse;
- understand how surveillance regulates people, land, and knowledge;
- detail the steps of deconstruction and explain how it exposes the violence of surveillance;
- learn how conflict zones and freedom trails are sites of surveillance;
- understand how anti-oppressive feminisms make resistance to surveillance possible.

Introduction

Surveillance is a logic and practice of regulation. This chapter discusses how surveillance-as-regulation develops out of larger histories of imperial and colonial state tensions that work to produce legitimate bodies: people, geographic regions, and knowledge sets. As discussed in Chapters 2, 3, and 4 of this text, the regulation of race, gender, sexuality, and nation is central to the construction of the interstate system and our understandings of global studies. We build upon these insights to argue that Blackness is a historic site of surveillance. As Simone Browne explains, "Blackness [i]s a key site through which

surveillance is practiced, narrated, and enacted. Surveillance is nothing new to black folks. It is the fact of antiblackness" (2015, p. viii). Understanding Blackness as a historic site of surveillance refuses the normalization of surveillance that presents the United States specifically, and the **Global North** more generally, as sites of justice. Surveillance situates the people and places of the **Global South** as threats to, and problems for, individual nation-states and the international system.

To illustrate how the regulation of Blackness is central to surveillance, we construct an anti-oppressive feminist framework. **Anti-oppressive feminisms** are built through the histories of postcolonial (see Chapter 1 of this text), Third World, women of colour, transnational, Indigenous, Black, and queer feminisms (see Chapter 19 of this text). Anti-oppressive feminisms are attentive to the multiple ways "major systems of oppression are interlocking" and how "[t]he synthesis of these oppressions creates the conditions of our lives" (Combahee River Collective, 1977/2002, p. 234). Anti-oppressive feminisms draw our attention to how knowledge production enables settler-colonial, colonial, slavery, and imperial formations of nation-states. Importantly, anti-oppressive feminisms utilize the methods of deconstruction, which aim to break down unequal structures of power to resist violence and transform our relationships in more just ways. We have to make choices about the "resistance and allegiance to hegemonic Eurocentric thought and research traditions" (Brown & Strega, 2005). In other words, there are politics and power struggles in knowledge production that have a direct effect on people's lives.

We open this chapter with a question about the visibility of Blackness in surveillance. Simone Browne's quote reveals how Blackness is always on display. Browne argues that Blackness and surveillance are distinctly intertwined and "blackness is integral to developing a general theory of surveillance and, in particular, racializing surveillance" (Browne, 2015, p. 8). Race remains under-theorized in surveillance studies. We find it necessary to break down the canonical presentation of surveillance and re-centre race, particularly Blackness, to expose surveillance as a tool of **white supremacy**. This disruption shows how surveillance is violent and puts into question how people have, and continue to, develop strategies to resist this violence. In this chapter, we discuss resistance in the forms of "**conflict zones**" and "**freedom trails**" to explain how and why people, land, and knowledge are contained in the **discourse** of surveillance.

Surveillance Is a Colonial Construct

The mainstream definition of surveillance is "the act of watching a person or place, especially a person believed to be involved with a criminal activity or a place where criminals gather" (*Cambridge Dictionary*, 2018). In this definition, surveillance necessitates criminality. Leading surveillance studies scholar David Lyon argues that surveillance is "the focused, systemic and routine attention to personal details for purposes of influence, management, protection or direction" (2007, p. 14). Lyon's definition focuses not just on who is being targeted for attention but also on the surveiller's motivations. Thus, the criminal body needs focused, systemic, and routine attention so that it can be regulated and contained.

What allows for such a limited construction of surveillance to be maintained? Browne intervenes in this understanding by offering an engagement with surveillance that does not re-centre the focus on surveilling Black bodies (land, people, knowledge). Browne, instead, decentres surveillance to ask how surveillance is a project of white supremacy and what representations of surveillance we can engage with that expose the politics of what is not seen at all so that we can be accountable to our divestments. In building upon Browne's insight, we explore surveillance as a colonial construct so that we may consider ways to decolonize our relationships to surveillance, which can work toward the abolishment of surveillance and the violences it perpetuates.

Gayatri Spivak (1988) argues that epistemic violence (the violence of knowledge) affects people in both explicit and hidden ways. For instance, in the mainstream definitions of surveillance, how the criminal body is racialized is simultaneously hidden and exploited. The study of surveillance and criminality produces an illegitimate body that threatens the state and legitimate citizens (Monahan & Wood, 2018). Our geo-political histories of colonial and imperial violence ensure that the figure of the criminal to be surveilled centres on people of colour (Cacho, 2012; Schueller, 2009). The study and practice of surveillance directly targets communities of colour for regulation. These linkages illustrate how disciplinary knowledge (academic knowledge) is intimately linked to colonial and imperial histories. In what follows, we argue that the study of surveillance justifies the state-making project and makes it a necessity.

The state is made possible through direct, indirect, and settler-colonial relationships that regulate bodies of land, people, and knowledge in violent ways (Anzaldúa, 2012; Zureik, 2016). Thus, the state-making project is colonial and relies upon surveillance. State-making requires the securitization of borders, maximization of profits, regulation of population, and increasing positions of power within global affairs. Historically, processes of colonialism, slavery, and imperialism were constructed and enacted to ensure European and US control over the regions of the world it sought to extract resources from and occupy. Fundamental to colonial processes is the systematic logic and practice of racial, gender, and sexual violence that ensure Western states' dominance (Kuokkanen, 2008). In other words, the interstate system and the mechanisms of globalization are frameworks of racial, gender, and sexual violence (Agathangelou, 2004). Global affairs continue to be about the power to regulate and legitimate which bodies (land, people, knowledge) have freedom of movement.

The figure of the citizen serves as the embodied boundary of the state. **Citizenship**, then, is a state project that maintains the interstate system because it is premised on the management of power and centralizing the state, making it necessary to people's existence (Foucault, 1980; 2012; Mbembe, 2001). Citizenship status determines access to state privileges (rights and services and freedoms) while simultaneously demarcating obligations and duties. However, as M. Jacqui Alexander (1994) argues, "Not just (any) body can be a citizen" because citizenship is only available for some people. In this way, citizenship is made through systematic, structural, and interpersonal violence that denies privileges to people who have been deemed illegitimate (Browne-Marshall, 2013; Williams, 1991). More specifically, privileges are reserved for elites, historically white male elites, and those who can ascribe to the heteropatriarchal power of whiteness (Harris, 1995; Luibhéid, 2008). Communities of colour, particularly women and gender-nonconforming people of the Global South, are denied access to political and economic privileges (Reddy, 2011).

State-making relies upon global capitalist expansion that profits from the violence created by the denial of state privileges to communities of colour in the Global South. In such a system, the focal point is surveilling racial, gendered, and sexual Others because it helps differentiate which people and places are exploitable, containable, and disposable (Chang, 2000). Central to surveillance is the state's ability to regulate and manage our imaginaries, productivity, and ways of knowing and moving in the world. The parameters of citizenship establish who can and who can never be a legitimate, protected, and profitable body for the state system (Bhattacharyya, 2008; Turcotte, 2014). Thus, the state and its citizens must intensely surveille and secure all bodies that have the potential to transgress, refuse, and challenge the imagined boundaries of state legitimacy (Grewal, 2006; Lovelace & Huff, 2012; Puar & Rai, 2002).

Surveillance is an ever-shifting colonial **cartography** made possible through Western investments in imperialism, slavery, and capitalism that seek to contain, control, and rewrite ways of knowing. Military, technological, and economic capacities are often the focus for how colonialism and imperialism are able to take hold and delineate social, political, and economic relations. However, anti-oppressive feminisms remind us that it is critically important to engage with the co-constitution of research, education, and knowledge production, which includes continuous de-colonization of scholarship (Smith, 1999). In the next section, we discuss how anti-oppressive feminisms can contribute to the further decolonization of surveillance of communities who refuse to invest in the privileges of white supremacy.

Surveillance as a "Discontinuous Narrative"

White supremacy is a transnational violence that taxonomies race, gender, sexuality, class, and geography into hierarchies that privilege the logics, practices, and bodies of whiteness through the marginalization of other-than-whiteness. Anti-oppressive feminisms take into account how and why surveillance as a colonial discourse "propagate[s] violent inequalities through the knowledge claims of global power and forms of justice" (Agathangelou & Turcotte, 2010, p. 45). Throughout this section, we offer a "**discontinuous narrative**" (Pathak & Rajan, 1992) of surveillance that exposes how and why colonial violence re-spatializes people, land, and knowledge, seeking to create and confine a figure of threat through the segregation of bodies that are presented as having the potential to transgress the state. These bodies are stereotyped, learned, and managed through race, gender, and class for the protection and security of those who benefit from the inequity and hierarchies of white supremacy.

Anti-oppressive feminist insight, drawing particularly upon postcolonial, Third World, Black, and Indigenous feminisms, reveals that colonial cartographies are made through histories of conquest that misrepresent landscapes and the people who live within them (Goldstein, 2014; Mamdani, 1996; McClintock, 1995). Colonial cartographies attempt to subjugate other ways of knowing and being as a means of exerting the dominance of Eurocentric thought (Smith, 1999; Teaiwa, 2010). Geographers have participated in citizenship-making by mapping the boundaries of the state onto land masses, the body, and our minds. This process separates and excludes the world of privilege from the world of Otherness. The creation of maps (cartography) also works to institutionalize hierarchies of power (Massey, 1994; Teaiwa, 2010; Vergès, 2001). Through colonial cartographies, currently occupied and ex-colonized regions of the world are marked as sites to be surveilled (e.g., Council on Foreign Relations, 2018; Deogawanka, 2015). Without attention to how surveillance comes out of colonialism, Western discourses of "human security" obfuscate the role of state violence in the protection of whiteness.

Anti-oppressive feminisms, drawing particularly upon Black, women of colour, and transnational feminist geography, chart power–knowledge relationships on a variety of scales: from the individual to the systemic. In particular, this charting traces, makes visible, and details how geographic knowledge: 1) further regulates our understandings and social relationships and 2) creates new pathways for knowing, experiencing, and imagining freedom, conflict, and justice. It is important for us to recognize that human and physical geography has long been involved in the constructions and regulations of race, gender, sexuality, nation, and so forth (Kobayashi & Peake, 1994; Vergès, 2005). Being critical of how human and physical geography is mapped reveals how the West reinvents itself and the world through surveillance (Flusty, 2008). Colonial cartographies of surveillance, then, are the histories of how we have come to *know* which areas of the world and which people need to be watched, contained, and, at times, eradicated. Surveillance is the continued geographic investment in whiteness.

Surveillance is also a discourse. Discourses are systems of power that include beliefs, imagery, events, practices, ideas, language, and narrative exchanges (Foucault, 2012; Hall, 2009).

Discourses define and produce objects and subjects of knowledge. In other words, discourses are frameworks of regulation that produce our understandings, our world, and our position within it. We subject ourselves to, and are subjected by, discourses (Scott, 1988). Colonial discourses institutionalize "us-them narratives" (Agathangelou & Ling, 2003). Surveillance as a colonial discourse upholds a world of racial inequity that necessitates the Other be surveilled. Surveillance, then, is a discourse of racial superiority that drives the current political system, defining labouring and ruling classes based on phenotypic factors and national origins (Mudimbe, 1988); it enables conquest, enslavement, and colonization of the peoples of Asia, Africa, and the Americas (Winant, 2001).

As we have discussed thus far, the discourse of surveillance centres on unequal geographic reasoning and produces binary maps of social and physical relations (Ball, Haggerty, & Lyon, 2012). We seek to decentre the power of geographic reasoning through the method of deconstruction (Vergès, 2001). Deconstruction is a tenet of post-structuralism that aims to break down unequal structures of meaning to expose their power relationships and create new, more just meanings. It is a method concerned with radical social transformation (Derrida, 1976). Deconstruction encompasses the following methodological process:

1. Reading "texts" (words, pictures, etc.) without preconceived notions of what it presents, letting the text speak for itself;
2. Breaking down Western binary constructions that create hierarchical and confining relationships (e.g., man/woman, Black/white, West/rest) by reversing the binary, which decentres power and engages the "marginal" as central;
3. Understanding how the self constructs meaning within the text; and
4. Identifying privileged terms (those considered central to meaning) and contextualizing their history and how they became powerful.

These steps of deconstruction expose discourses as power relationships by denaturalizing the whole system of Western binary thinking (McQuillan, 2001; Scott, 1988).

Deconstruction allows the researcher to engage with their own biases and break them down. Deconstruction enables us to draw together "texts" that seemingly do not belong together, forming a discontinuous narrative and access to alternative histories. This exposure then makes us rethink what we have to do to resist the violence of surveillance. Thus, deconstruction is as much about the researcher and our ability to be open to that which we do not know as it is about the texts we are analyzing. Deconstruction focuses on how and why the narratives of surveillance can be reproduced and solidified as discourses that regulate our lives. Deconstruction accounts for multiple histories and meanings that are often consciously hidden from mainstream understandings of surveillance. As McQuillan (2001) explains, deconstruction works "to remind us that we should not assume the way we perceive the world is the same as the way the world actually is" (p. 11).

In the next section, we utilize deconstruction as a decolonial practice to challenge the staticness of surveillance and the narratives that support it. We juxtapose conflict zones and freedom trails to destabilize the understanding of Blackness as oppositional to the logic of freedom. Ultimately, conflict zones and freedom trails provide a discontinuous narrative of surveillance that exposes alternative histories, narratives, and subjectivities, along with the tensions of what/who has been presented as "in need of" surveillance.

Resisting Surveillance

Surveillance is refused and challenged in a multitude of ways by whom it targets. Yet the challenge to state violence is often met with new and additional forms of state violence. The West consistently creates "new" narratives, mechanisms, and identifying factors for containment and regulation of those who resist (Dafnos, Thompson, & French, 2016; Escobar, 1999). In the decades of decolonization (1960s–1990s) and the possibility of a postcolonial reality, the West scrambled to maintain control of the global political economy through the formation of neocolonial discourses of development, conflict zones, human security, terrorism, and often human rights (Turcotte, 2016; Williams, 2010). Colonial dominance sought to be more digestible and difficult to detect (Césaire, 1972; Escobar, 1999). These "new" surveillance discourses all work to forestall resistance and political mobilization. Importantly, they reinvigorate colonialism through more expansive frameworks of surveillance that serve Western dominance and profitability in world politics. We focus on "conflict zones" as a discourse because they illustrate how social control and state violence come together to ameliorate **white anxieties** through surveillance.

Conflict zones, we argue, are discursively and materially produced to protect Western property (land, people, knowledge) and the workings of an inequitable state system. Mainstream representations suggest that conflict zones are sites of ongoing endemic conflict that necessitate Western intervention, which serves to create a constant landscape of surveillance. Conflict zones develop through the historical reality that the nation-state comes into being because of the process of European colonization, imperialism, and African and Indigenous slavery and genocide. Conflict zones are generated within a dichotomous logic that generates an imagined geography and a material practice of where conflict and illegitimate violence happens in the world (Korf, Engeler, & Hagmann, 2010; Lipschutz & Conca, 1993; Peluso & Watts, 2001). Western knowledge production plays a key role in defining the parameters of conflict and the locations of these geographical zones. Conflict zones are presented as "outside"

the West—historically, they are located in parts of Africa, Asia, Latin America, the Middle East, and eastern Europe and disproportionately surface in the Black and brown geographies of the Third World. Conflict is often presented as the violence of multiple ethnic nationalisms that erode economic, political, and social stability (Kaldor, 1999; Klare, 2001). Conflict zones surface in times of explicit war as well as within "low intensity war" (Spira, 2012). Importantly, conflict zones are also mobilized in urban landscapes within the West, specifically by the US, to justify the War on Drugs, the War on Terror, "gang violence," and so forth (Hagerdorn, 2008).

Mainstream understandings of conflict zones present the conflict as endemic and not the result of the interstate system. However, transnational feminisms argue that the conditions of perceived endemic or "private" conflict are the direct manifestation of structural state violence (Giles & Hyndman, 2004; Sharoni, 1992; Turcotte, 2016). In other words, conflict zones are created to divert attention away from state-sponsored violence. In order for conflict zones to take hold in the Western imaginary, "Third World" populations are not properly identified with their "non-aligned" revolutionary histories as collective actors. Often located in colonized and recently decolonized states, the "Third World" exposed and refused Western occupations, war, economic plundering, and social stratifications (Prashad, 2007; Turcotte, 2011). The "Third World" was generated as a radical vision of alternative global frameworks (Okihiro, 2016; Prashad, 2007; Winant, 2001). However, these histories have been meticulously erased through the repetitive narration and international policy formation that privileges the "First World." Thus, conflict zones are a colonial retelling of the Third World that suggests it is plagued by conflict for the following reasons:

- ethnic and religious tensions
- underdevelopment

- overpopulation
- resource scarcity and extractive economies
- rebel factions
- dictatorships
- war and low-intensity wars
- since 9/11, the increase in radical Islamic terrorism and the violations of women's rights (Cutter, Richardson, & Wilbanks, 2003; Riegl, Landovsk, & Valko, 2014).

Denaturalizing this narrative of conflict zones as endemic and a natural landscape for some regions and people of the world requires a critical examination of the ongoing colonial legacies of surveillance. Importantly, the methods of deconstruction further engage with how conflict zones are connected to histories of resistance and freedom-making.

Historically, state narratives of freedom link together state-sanctioned sites of freedom to memorialize the importance of white masculinity in state-making, such as the Boston Freedom Trail. This rendering of freedom makes traceable the discourse of white supremacy (Shabazz, 2015). The Boston Freedom Trail obscures the genocidal violence of the colonists against Indigenous and enslaved peoples in order for their own (colonists') resistance and freedom to take place. For instance, if you walk the Boston Freedom Trail, you are guided along a state and privately funded historical narrative that highlights sites such as graves, speeches, and the Commons, which all convey the importance of white masculinity at the centre of how the US became a nation-state. The Boston Freedom Trail, then, is a geographic rendering of what constitutes proper freedom and thus proper citizenship.

Our understanding of freedom trails highlights the unequal power structures of global politics and the discourse of surveillance. Freedom trails are the landscapes formed by and through the process of colonized and enslaved peoples rebelling and resisting European colonization,

imperialism, slavery, and genocide. Those who challenged the colonial state engaged with alternative articulations of place-making by creating their own conditions of and for freedom—or freedom trails (Lovelace, 2017). Anti-oppressive feminisms, drawing particularly upon Black, postcolonial, and Indigenous feminisms, understand freedom as the continual process of creating a shared, communal, and livable future that is tied to land sovereignty (Agathangelou & Ling, 2009; Davis, 2012; Simpson, 2017). Our understanding of freedom trails is a challenge to conventional interpretations of freedom. However, the logic and practice of freedom takes on new meaning when one considers the state of being for those who are surveilled in a society that has consistently waged war against them. In other words, the Western narrative of freedom provides a definition, which by its very nature cannot be applied to those in places of continual surveillance (Maldonado-Torres, 2008). Freedom trails become conflict zones, and these zones work to contain and restrict movement of Black and brown geographies because of the fear of Black people in white spaces.

White anxieties are generated through people's creations of freedom trails. The threat to the state is the manifestation of white anxieties that seek to control everyone's freedom. When Others have the freedom of movement and the freedom from domination and exploitation within our white supremacist interstate system, those with state privilege invoke the discourse of surveillance and raise the stakes of citizenship. Thus, freedom generates white anxieties and the creation of conflict zones for containing Blackness. As Browne (2015) argues, "rather than seeing surveillance as something inaugurated by new technologies, such as automated facial recognition or unnamed autonomous vehicles (or drones), to see it as ongoing is to insist that we factor in how racism and antiblackness undergird and sustain the intersecting surveillances of our present order" (p. 8–9). This decentring of surveillance illustrates

Haiti on the Global Stage

On 12 January 2018, President Donald Trump stated the following to US Senators during a bipartisan meeting focused on immigration: "Why are we having all these people from shithole countries come here?" (quoted in Dawsey, 2018). His concern about "shithole countries" referred directly to Haiti, El Salvador, and African nations (Barron, 2018). Such regions and peoples of the world are produced as perpetual threats and victims—they are *criminals* who continue to both burden and necessitate inventions by the US, European nations, and the United Nations (Bigo, 2016; Buzan & Hansen, 2009). While many news media outlets (and the White House) presented Trump's statement as the result of his "growing frustration" with the proposed policy to restore protected status for immigrants already marked with protected status, the pronouncement of "shithole countries" was not a random statement of frustration. Critics described his statement as racist and immoral, calling for an immediate apology and sanctions of some kind. Trump supporters, however, applauded his statement as properly describing the so-called threat these nations pose to US nationalism and security and choosing instead to read Trump's statement as a comment on economics and not race. Importantly, Trump's perspective puts into question the concurrent history of surveillance as a discontinuous narrative.

The election of Donald Trump to the highest office in the US proves the very ideas of hate, erosion of rights, and continuous violence that Black and brown people have always continuously said existed. White supremacist violence has perpetrated against their bodies since the "founding of the Americas." The narrative of the Obama presidency was that white supremacist violence had disappeared, but it has not: it has just mutated. Trump, in all his capitalistic, heteropatriarchal, racist glory, is presented as if he were only an evil, opportunistic representative of a niche population of American society (Pérez Huber, 2016). Let us be clear: Trump and his statement are not an individualized moment. In other words, Trump is the manifestation of what we have defined as white anxieties. Trump is not exceptional; he represents the normalized systematic violence that determines citizenship and makes the surveillance of Black and brown peoples possible (Çalışkan & Preston, 2017). Such discourses are not about drawing in more citizenship possibilities; they are about recolonizing regions of the world and limiting the conditions for citizenship to those already marked with privilege.

Haiti tops the list of countries the US should not be accepting immigrants from, according to Trump. His "shithole countries" statement mobilizes fear to denigrate people from once colonized geographies and present such countries as a burdensome drain on US profitability, property, and security. This narrative subverts US colonial and imperial violence and its "racial debts" of slavery and genocide (Chakravartty & da Silva, 2012). While people of colour and immigrants' labour continue to make the US state possible and profitable, this narrative focuses on the containment and management of such bodies and their portrayal as taking away from the state (Hong, 2006). The use of the term "shithole countries" attempts to **deracialize** the politics of surveillance and citizenship construction by refusing to engage with histories of white supremacy. While Trump's question reveals a disregard for Blackness altogether, it exposes how Haiti is understood as a "shithole" country through the project of surveillance.

Continued

Anti-oppressive feminism's construction of surveillance as a discontinous narrative illustrates how conflict zones are actually freedom trails. Trump's statement about certain nations as "shitholes" and therefore not worthy of receiving immigration assistance is a statement about those nations' infrastructures, governments, economies, and, most important, populations. Trump's narrative aligns with mainstream security narratives that categorize and produce the Global South as conflict-ridden and in need of surveillance, thus necessitating further policing and securitization rather than immigration reform and assistance (Buzan & Hansen, 2009). This allows us to expose "shithole countries" as part of a longer and more complex history. Thus, Haiti tops the list of "shithole countries," not because it is the poorest nation in the Western hemisphere but because it is the only nation ever to be born out of a successful slave rebellion.

Why is Haiti so threatening? In late August of 1791, the island of Saint Domingue experienced a 13-year-long revolution. The free and enslaved Black population sought the expulsion of the French government and white slave-owning class from the island and did so through physical violence. The nation of Haiti is the result of the success of the anti-slavery, anti-colonial rebellion of Saint Domingue (Geggus, 2002; James, 1963/1989). Haiti's origins differ only slightly from that of the establishment of the US, and yet their current political and economic configurations are such that the president of one can make a statement about the other. As the only nation born of a successful slave rebellion, Haiti is both a living freedom trail and a modern-day conflict zone.

On 12 January 2010, Haiti suffered a magnitude 7.0 earthquake that devastated the nation, leaving hundreds of thousands dead and affecting millions. Haiti received billions in aid from countries, individuals, NGOs, and international organizations in the months and years following the earthquake. The earthquake also prompted changes in foreign policy in Western nations. The US extended a protected immigration status to undocumented Haitians living in the country, halting centuries-long policies aimed at controlling and minimizing Haitian contact with the US. The success of the Haitian rebellion had provoked fear that ideas of rebellion would spread in the anti-Black, slave-holding United States, and its economic, political, social, and immigration policies reflected that (Goodman, Ives, & Danticat, 2010).

Haitian people are the descendants of a group of radical revolutionary Black people who found French colonial rule antithetical to freedom. Haiti serves as the pinnacle for the fight for a space that is free from the structures, peoples, institutions, and governments that seek to enslave, enlist, and eradicate non-white peoples the world over. The Haitian people are no longer subject to direct colonial rule because they engaged in a rebellion that reverberated the world over. This history provides the context for understanding Haiti's position in the world as a conflict zone. Because of these histories, Haiti as a nation-state and as a people continues to remain threatening, in need of containment and regulation. The historical context of our current hegemonic international narratives of surveillance enmeshed with xenophobia, such as Trump's statement, can be exposed for their systemic and systematic violence. Neocolonialism and neoliberal brands of surveillance rely on the distortion of memory so that decolonial landscapes are devoid of their subjectivity and thus a voice. As in the insights of Haiti, Black rebellion and revolution and their reverberations read the interstate system as not only non-liberatory but as antithetical to the process of safety, sustainability, and freedom altogether.

whose freedom is valued, or not, which is crucial because it exposes how white supremacy hides Black resistance and acts of freedom within a landscape of conflict.

In other words, freedom trails are markedly left out of the discourse on "legitimate" sites of freedom and relegated to zones of conflict. It is because these acts were formed at the intersections of Blackness, state-making, violence, and abolition that we currently do not read these sites as freedom trails; instead, they are understood as sites for lamenting why Blackness is wrong, fearful, and in need of correction and surveillance. However, when we ask explicit questions about the political stakes of knowledge and our role within it, we begin to refuse systems of subjugation (Brown & Strega, 2005). By arguing that conflict zones and freedom trails are co-constituted, we suggest that alternative histories and subjugated knowledges have always been present. In this understanding, surveillance becomes a discontinuous narrative made visible through the relationship between conflict zones and freedom trails, which engage with the tensions and fissures of state violence. Discontinuous narratives open new pathways of, and for, decolonization and freedom-making (Tadiar, 2009).

Surveilling the Future

In approaching surveillance as a discontinuous narrative, we engage the various means of pursuing freedom by regions of the world that remain too frightening to be remembered properly in the land or social imaginary (Priest, 2010; Schlund-Vials, 2012). In juxtaposing conflict zones and freedom trails, we actively remember sites of freedom cut away from the international landscape and imagination precisely because they are Black exhibitions of freedom. In the context of anti-oppressive feminist approaches to surveillance studies, we are aware that even when we try to contribute to forms of justice, we often end up

(re)producing the very thing we are critiquing and seeking to eradicate.

When we denaturalize our relationships to geography through critical Black, postcolonial, women of colour, Indigenous, Third World, and decolonial feminist geographic methods, we are challenging submerged modes of containment and domination. Importantly, this enables new entry points and questions about our research, which produces broader and deeper **counter-cartographies** of life. In a world that privileges landscapes of domination, counter-cartographies and discontinuous narratives are needed to rework space and place and account for how human and physical geographies are interconnected, multiple, and capable of creating landscapes of justice, abolition, and freedom of movement. Thus, we can re-engage with unfinished abolitionary projects, particularly in the sites of immigration, when we denaturalize our relationships to the physical so that we can think in more complex ways about the social.

Tying It Together

Disputing the concept of surveillance through anti-oppressive feminist sensibilities reveals that the current construction of surveillance is not only limited but cannot be made to incorporate Black identity and the particular issues that are pertinent to those who exemplify and embody Blackness. Anti-oppressive feminist focus on the disruption and deconstruction of dominant, omnipotent narratives of surveillance challenges how the study and practice of gender and globalization is produced and understood. At the same time, this chapter is connected to the other chapters in this text that are concerned with the changing conditions and study of gendered race, geography, and/or social status. As a collective whole, these works expose power relations and biases about what qualifies as the postcolonial.

Call to Action

Decolonizing knowledge is a collective project that requires us to locate ourselves in the context of colonization in simultaneously oppressed and complicit ways (Walia, 2012). As Smith (1999) explains, decolonizing research is a multi-layered approach "concerned with having a more critical understanding of the underlying assumptions, motivations, and values which inform research practices" (p. 20). Research, then, is not neutral, nor objective, and thus anti-oppressive postcolonial feminist methods encourage us to examine the assumptions, motivations, and values embedded within institutionalized knowledge sets, including our own.

Identify how you participate (consciously or unconsciously) in the reproduction of knowledge inequities, and acknowledge the role of power in your reading and research. After this self-examinations, seek out more accountable modes of engagement. The role of the researcher is to ask how we can account for how knowledge contributes to inequitable social relations that subjugate other ways of knowing and being in the world.

DISCUSSION QUESTIONS

1. Who does the study of surveillance benefit the most?
2. What kind of surveillance gets studied (and which does not)?
3. How can discontinuous narratives be applied to other central tenets of gender and globalization?
4. What are the political stakes of anti-oppressive feminisms?

SUGGESTIONS FOR FURTHER READING

Alexander, M. J. (2005). *Pedagogies of crossing: Meditations on feminism, sexual politics, memory, and the sacred*. Durham, NC: Duke University Press. This book is a collection of essays by M. Jacqui Alexander, a theorist of transnational feminism. Topics discussed include the need for transnational frameworks of colonialism in queer studies and the limits and failures of liberal pluralism.

Berda, Y. (2013). Managing dangerous populations: Colonial legacies of security and surveillance. *Sociological Forum*, 28(3), 627–30. This journal article discusses historical colonial practices that served as the basis of modern palpation surveillance.

Dubois, L. (2013). *Haiti: The aftershocks of history*. New York, NY: Metropolitan Books. This book examines Haiti's colonial history as a means of understanding its current political, economic, and social conditions.

Lentin, R. (2017). Race and surveillance in the settler colony: The case of Israeli rule over Palestine. *Palgrave Communications*, 3(4 July), 1–10. https://www.nature.com/articles/palcomms201756. This article examines Israel as a state of exception and its settler-colonial control of Palestine. The article focuses on strategies of surveillance employed by the Israeli state to reinforce highly racialized practices.

McKittrick, K. (2006). *Demonic grounds: Black women and the cartographies of struggle*. Minneapolis, MN: Minnesota University Press. This book discusses how human geographies are a result of racialized connections through an exploration of the historical experiences of black women in Canada, the United States, and the Caribbean.

MULTIMEDIA SUGGESTIONS

Anne Keala Kelly. (2008). Noho hewa: The wrongful occupation of Hawai'i
ohohewa.com/about
This award-winning documentary examines the effect of US laws, economy, and militarism on the Hawaiian people, told from the perspective of Hawaiians.

Cointelpro 101, Freedom Archives
vimeo.com/15930463
This film introduces viewers to the illegal surveillance and suppression of social justice movements in the 1950s, 1960s, and 1970s by the US government through the FBI's COunter INTELligence PROgram (COINTELPRO)

The Freedom Archives
freedomarchives.org
This website contains an archive of more than 12,000 hours of audio/video recordings and print materials related to social justice movements from the 1960s to the 1990s.

The Feminist Wire
thefeministwire.com
This website provides socio-political and cultural critiques of anti-feminist, racist, and imperialist politics.

REFERENCES

Agathangelou, A.M. (2004). *The global political economy of sex: Desire, violence, and insecurity in Mediterranean nation states.* New York, NY: Palgrave Macmillan.

Agathangelou, A.M., & Ling, L.H.M. (2003). Desire industries: Sex trafficking, UN peacekeeping, and the neo-liberal world order. *Brown Journal of World Affairs,* 10(1), 133–48.

Agathangelou, A.M., & Ling, L.H.M. (2009). *Transforming world politics: From empire to multiple worlds.* New York, NY: Routledge.

Agathangelou, A.M., & Turcotte, H.M. (2010). Postcolonial theories and challenges to "First World-ism." In L. Shepard (Ed.), *Gender matters in global politics: A feminist introduction to international relations* (pp. 44–58). New York, NY: Routledge.

Alexander, M.J. (1994). Not just (any) body can be a citizen: The politics of law, sexuality and postcoloniality in Trinidad and Tobago and the Bahamas. *Feminist Review,* 48(Autumn), 5–23.

Anzaldúa, G. (2012). *Borderlands/La frontera: The new mestiza.* San Francisco, CA: Aunt Lute. (Original work published in 1987.)

Ball, K., Haggerty, K.D., & Lyon, D. (Eds). (2012). *Routledge handbook of surveillance studies.* New York, NY: Routledge.

Barron, L. (2018). A new low: The world is furious at Trump for his remark about "shithole countries." *Time,* 12 January. Retrieved from: http://time.com/5100328/shithole-countries-trump-reactions.

Bhattacharyya, G. (2008). *Dangerous brown men: Exploiting sex, violence and feminism in the war on terror.* New York, NY: Zed Books.

Bigo, D. (2016). Rethinking security at the crossroad of international relations and criminology. *The British Journal of Criminology,* 56(6), 1068–1086.

Brown, L., & Strega, S. (Eds). (2005). *Research as resistance: Critical, Indigenous, & anti-oppressive approaches.* Toronto, ON: Canadian Scholars' Press.

Browne, S. (2015). *Dark matters: On the surveillance of blackness.* Durham, NC: Duke University Press.

Browne-Marshall, G. (2013). *Race, law, and American society: 1607 to present.* New York, NY: Routledge.

Buzan, B., & Hansen, L. (2009). *The evolution of international security studies.* New York, NY: Cambridge University Press.

Cacho, L.M. (2012). *Social death: Racialized rightlessness and the criminalization of the unprotected.* New York, NY: New York University Press.

Çalışkan, G., & Preston, K. (2017). Tropes of fear and the crisis of the West: Trumpism as a discourse of post-territorial coloniality. *Postcolonial Studies,* 20(2), 199–216. doi: 10.1080/13688790.2017.1376367.

Cambridge Dictionary. (2018). Surveillance. Retrieved from: https://dictionary.cambridge.org/us/dictionary/english/surveillance#dataset-american-english.

Césaire, A. (1972). *Discourse on colonialism.* J. Pinkham, trans. New York, NY: Monthly Review Press. (Original work published in 1957.)

Chang, G. (2000). *Disposable domestics: Immigrant women workers in the global economy.* Cambridge, UK: South End Press.

Chakravartty, P., & da Silva, D.F. (2012). Accumulation, dispossession, and debt: The racial logic of global capital. *American Studies Quarterly,* 64(3), 361–85.

Combahee River Collective. (2002). A black feminist statement. In C. Moraga & G. Anzaldúa (Eds), *This bridge called my back: Writings by radical women of color* (pp. 234–44). Berkeley, CA: Third Woman Press.

Council on Foreign Relations. (2018). [Global conflict tracker, 27 June]. Retrieved from: https://www.cfr.org/interactives/global-conflict-tracker#!/global-conflict-tracker.

Cutter, S.L., Richardson, D.B., & Wilbanks, T.J. (Eds). (2003). *The geographical dimensions of terrorism.* New York, NY: Routledge.

Dafnos, T., Thompson, S., & French, M. (2016). Surveillance and the colonial dream: Canada's surveillance of Indigenous self-determination. In R. Lippert, K. Walby, I. Warren, & D. Palmer (Eds), *National security, surveillance and terror* (pp. 319–42). Cambridge, UK: Palgrave Macmillan.

Davis, A.Y. (2012). *The meaning of freedom and other difficult dialogues.* San Francisco, CA: City Lights Books.

Dawsey, J. (2018). Trump derides protection for immigrants from "shithole countries." *Washington Post.* Retrieved from: https://www.washingtonpost.com/politics/trump-attacks-protections-for-immigrants-from-shithole-countries-in-oval-office-meeting/2018/01/11/bfc0725c-f711-11e7-91af-31ac729add94_story.html?noredirect=on&utm_term=.a0f03044b0ab.

Deogawanka, S. (2015). How GIS supports the fight against terrorism. *GIS Lounge,* 29 January. Retrieved from: doi: https://www.gislounge.com/gis-supports-fight-terrorism.

Derrida, J. (1976). *Of grammatology.* G.C. Spivak, trans. Baltimore, MD: Johns Hopkin University Press.

Escobar, A. (1999). The invention of development. *Current History,* 98(631), 382–6.

Flusty, S. (2008). The banality of interdiction: Surveillance, control and the displacement of diversity. *International Journal of Urban and Regional Research,* 25(3), 658–64.

Foucault, M. (1980). Two lectures. In C. Gordon (Ed.), *Power/knowledge: Selected interviews and other writings* (pp. 78–108). New York, NY: Pantheon. (Original work published in 1976.)

Foucault, M. (2012). *Discipline and punish: The birth of the prison.* A. Sheridan, trans. New York, NY: Vintage Books. (Original work published in 1977.)

Geggus, D.P. (2002). *Haitian revolutionary studies.* Bloomington, IN: University of Indiana Press.

Giles, W., & Hyndman, J. (2004). *Sites of violence: Gender and conflict zones.* Berkeley, CA: University of California Press.

Goldstein, A. (Ed.). (2014). *Formations of United States colonialism.* Durham, NC: Duke University Press.

Goodman, A., Ives, K., & Danticat, E. (2010). Haiti devastated by largest earthquake in 200 years, thousands feared dead. *Democracy Now!* 13 January. Retrieved from: doi: http://i4.democracynow.org/2010/1/13/haiti_devastated_by_largest_earthquake_in.

Grewal, I. (2006). "Security moms" in the early twentieth century United States: The gender of security in neoliberalism. *Women's Studies Quarterly,* 34(1/2), 25–40.

Hagedorn, J. (2008). *A world of gangs: Armed young men and gangsta culture.* Minneapolis, MN: University of Minnesota Press.

Hall, S. (Ed.). (2009). *Representation: Cultural representations and signifying practices.* London, UK: Sage Publications. (Original work published in 1997.)

Harris, C.I. (1995). Whiteness as property. In K. Crenshaw, N. Gotanda, G. Peller, & K. Thomas (Eds), *Critical Race Theory: The key writing that formed the movement* (pp. 276–91). New York, NY: The New Press.

Hong, G.K. (2006). *The ruptures of American capital: Women of color, feminism and the culture of immigrant labor.* Minneapolis, MN: University of Minnesota Press.

James, C.L.R. (1963/1989). *The black Jacobins: Toussaint L'Ouverture and the San Domingo revolution.* New York, NY: Random House.

Kaldor, M. (1999). *New and old wars: Organized violence in a global era.* Stanford, CA: Stanford University Press.

Klare, M. (2001). *Resource wars: The new landscape of global conflict.* New York, NY: Metropolitan Books.

Kobayashi, A., & Peake, L. (1994). Unnatural discourse: "Race" and gender in geography. *Gender, Place and Culture,* 1(1), 225–43.

Korf, B., Engeler, M., & Hagmann, T. (2010). The geography of warscape. *Third World Quarterly,* 31(3), 385–99.

Kuokkanen, R. (2008). Globalization as racialized, sexualized violence: The case of Indigenous women. *International Feminist Journal of Politics,* 10(2), 216–33.

Lipschutz, R.D., & Conca, K. (Eds). (1993). *The state and social power in global environmental politics.* New York, NY: Columbia University Press.

Lovelace, V.L. (2017). Trailing freedom: Embodied resistance, geopolitics, and a black sense of freedom. Retrieved from University of Connecticut Dissertations, https://opencommons.uconn.edu/dissertations/1456.

Lovelace, V.L., & Huff, J. (2012). Ghost stories in the soil: Feminist notes on place and research. *International Feminist Journal of Politics,* 14(1), 154–62.

Luibhéid, E. (2008). Sexuality, migration, and the shifting line between legal and illegal status. *GLQ: A Journal of Gay and Lesbian Studies,* 14(2/3), 289–315.

Lyon, D. (2007). *Surveillance studies: An overview.* Cambridge, UK: Polity Press.

McClintock, A. (1995). *Imperial leather: Race, gender and sexuality in the colonial context.* New York, NY: Routledge.

McQuillan. M. (2001). *Deconstruction: A reader.* New York, NY: Routledge.

Maldonado-Torres, N. (2008). *Against war: View from the underside of modernity.* Durham, NC: Duke University Press.

Mamdani, M. (1996). *Citizen and subject: Contemporary Africa and the legacy of late colonialism*. Princeton, NJ: Princeton University Press.

Massey, D. (1994). *Space, place and gender*. Minneapolis, MN: Minnesota University Press.

Mbembe, A. (2001). *On the postcolony*. Berkeley, CA: University of California Press.

Monahan, T., & Wood, D.M. (Eds). (2018). *Surveillance studies: A reader*. New York, NY: Oxford University Press.

Mudimbe, V.Y. (1988). *The invention of Africa: Gnosis, philosophy, and the order of knowledge*. Bloomington, IN: Indiana University Press.

Okihiro, G. (2016). *Third World studies: Theorizing liberation*. Durham, NC: Duke University Press.

Pathak, Z., & Rajan, R.S. (1992). Shabano. In J. Butler & J. Scott (Eds), *Feminists theorize the political* (pp. 257–79). New York, NY: Routledge.

Peluso, N., & Watts, M.J. (Eds). (2001). *Violent environments*. Ithaca, NY: Cornell University Press.

Pérez Huber, L. (2016). Make America great again: Donald Trump, racist nativism and the virulent adherence to white supremacy amid U.S. demographic change. *Charleston Law Review*, 10, 215–47.

Prashad, V. (2007). *The darker nations: A people's history of the Third World*. New York, NY: The New Press.

Priest, M. (2010). "The nightmare is not cured": Emmett Till and American healing. *American Quarterly*, 62(1), 1–24.

Puar, J., & Rai, A.S. (2002). Monster, terrorist, fag: The war on terrorism and the production of docile patriots. *Social Text 72*, 20(3), 117–48.

Reddy, C. (2011). *Freedom with violence: Race, sexuality, and the US state*. Durham, NC: Duke University Press.

Riegl, M., Landovsk, J., & Valko, I. (Eds) (2014). *Strategic regions in the 21st century power politics: Zones of consensus and zones of conflict*. Newcastle, UK: Cambridge Scholars Publishing.

Schlund-Vials, C. J. (2012). *War, genocide, and justice: Cambodian American memory work*. Minneapolis, MN: University of Minnesota Press.

Schueller, M. J. (2009). *Locating race: Global sites of postcolonial citizenship*. Albany, NY: State University of New York Press.

Scott, J. (1988). Deconstruction equality-versus-difference: Or, the uses of poststructuralist theory for feminism. *Feminist Studies*, 14(1), 33–50.

Shabazz, R. (2015). *Spatializing blackness: Architectures of confinement and black masculinity in Chicago*. Champaign, IL: University of Illinois Press.

Sharoni, S. (1992). Every woman is an occupied territory: The politics of militarism and sexism and the Israeli-Palestinian conflict. *Journal of Gender Studies*, 1(4), 447–62.

Simpson, L.B. (2017). *As we have always done: Indigenous freedom through radical resistance*. Minneapolis, MN: University of Minnesota Press.

Smith, L.T. (1999). *Decolonizing methodologies: Research and Indigenous peoples*. New York, NY: Zed Books.

Spira, T.L. (2012). Neoliberal captivities: Pisagua prison and the low intensity form. *Radical History Review*, (112), 127–46.

Spivak, G.C. (1988). Can the subaltern speak? In C. Nelson & L. Grossberg (Eds), *Marxism and the Interpretation of Culture* (pp. 271–316). London, UK: Macmillan.

Tadiar, N.X.M. (2009). *Things fall away: Philippine historical experience and the makings of globalization*. Durham, NC: Duke University Press.

Teaiwa, T. (2010). Bikinis and other s/pacific n/oceans. In S. Shigematsu & K.L. Camacho (Eds), *Militarized currents: Toward a decolonized future in Asia and the Pacific* (pp. 15–31). Minneapolis, MN: University of Minnesota Press.

Turcotte, H.M. (2011). Contextualizing petro-sexual politics. *Alternatives: Global, Local, Political*, 36(3), 200–20.

Turcotte, H.M. (2014). Feminist asylums and acts of dreaming. *Feminist Theory*, 15(2), 141–60.

Turcotte, H.M. (2016). Economies of conflict: Reflecting on the (re)production of "war economies." In W. Harcourt (Ed.), *The Palgrave handbook of gender and development: Critical engagements in feminist theory and practice* (pp. 476–94). New York, NY: Palgrave Macmillan.

Vergès, F. (2001). Looking east, heading south. *African Studies Review*, 44(2), 141–9.

Vergès, F. (2005). One world, many maps. *Interventions: International Journal of Postcolonial Studies*, 7(3), 342–5.

Walia, H. (2012). Decolonizing together: Moving beyond a politics of solidarity toward a practice of decolonization. *Briarpatch*, (January/February), 27–30.

Williams, P.J. (1991). *The alchemy of race and rights*. Cambridge, MA: Harvard University Press.

Williams, R. (2010). *The divided world: Human rights and its violence*. Minneapolis, MN: University of Minnesota Press.

Winant, H. (2001). *The world is a ghetto: Race and democracy since World War II*. New York, NY: Basic Books.

Zureik, E. (2016). *Israel's colonial project in Palestine: Brutal pursuit*. New York, NY: Routledge.

CHAPTER 13

◇

Disrupting "Security"
Pacification, Accumulation, and Colonialism

Tia Dafnos

Learning Objectives

In this chapter, you will:
- problematize "security" as a political discourse;
- consider the role of academic knowledge production in producing security discourse through the fields of criminology and security studies;
- consider how "pacification" can be a critical concept for analyzing security discourse;
- situate international law and the current international state system in the history of European imperialism;
- examine how criminal justice systems are co-constituted with colonialism and global capitalism.

Introduction

From national security to food security, "security" seems to be everywhere in public discourse while being nowhere at the same time—it is perpetually elusive. Generally, security refers to a state of being safe or free from threat and danger; this is very much an **affective** condition. Experiencing fear, anxiety, unease, or uncertainty about some aspect of our lives can make us feel *insecure*, regardless of the materiality of those threats. Very few people would disagree that it is unpleasant to experience fear and anxiety and desirable to

eliminate sources of insecurity. Let's consider the implications of this. There is significant power in these feelings of security and insecurity: we can be motivated to act in certain ways or to support actions by others if we believe that they will make us feel safer and more secure, regardless of whether or not they eliminate actual sources of harm.

From a critical perspective, we might ask: what kinds of threats elicit significant responses, and what are the implications? While debates about food, income, or job security have become more common in public discourse, "security" in the Global North is predominantly associated with personal safety and national security. Historically, the sources of insecurity in this context have been and continue to be personified by dangerous Others— "criminals," "subversives," "enemies," "the uncivilized," "terrorists," "extremists," and so on. The presence of these Others produces *insecurity*, for individuals and nation-states, but has also contributed to reinforcing nation-state sovereignty and collective identities through the shared experience of threat. At the same time, security practices produce insecurity in material and affective ways for those who are construed as Other within our societies and globally. In any critical study of "security," we must ask: security for whom?

A critical understanding of security requires that we don't take "security" for granted as an objective condition with universal meaning but rather that we examine how security discourses have been used historically and in the contemporary context. In interrogating these discourses, we have to examine the role of knowledge production. The fields of criminology and security studies in particular have been complicit in producing dominant security discourses. Both fields have histories of close collaborations with state institutions such as police, corrections, government, and military. The cultivation of expert knowledge by European and Anglo-American scholars to define security, threats, and how best to achieve security has enabled imperial and colonial projects in the name of defending nation-states, the modern West, and a global order conducive to accumulation of resources and wealth.

This chapter begins with an overview of criminology and security studies, both of which take up "security" as a core problematic of study but reproduce an ideological separation between the local and global. We will consider how scholarship has contributed to **hegemonic** security discourses in the Global North. Reflecting on (post)colonial and feminist critiques, we'll consider whether it's possible to have a critical analysis of "security" that still uses the language of security. The second part of the chapter outlines a framework that adopts the concept of *pacification* to analyze how "security" is used as a political strategy to produce social, political, and economic relations locally and globally. Using this framework, we can locate the significance of security discourse to European imperialism, the creation of sovereignty doctrine, and the formation of an international state system dominated by the Global North. This historical context is important for understanding how security "threats" have been constructed as the source of personal and national *insecurities*, legitimizing coercive practices to eliminate those threats and produce order, or "peace," as the basis for security. In part three, we'll examine how this "peace-making" produces and intensifies colonial, racial, patriarchal, heteronormative, capitalist structural violence on a local scale that has global effects. In this context, people's resistance to pacification strategies and refusals to be pacified have been problematized as enduring threats to the dominant social order. Analyzed through the concept of pacification, criminalization, military operations, and humanitarian and development projects can be understood as interconnected strategies in wars of accumulation.

Studying "Security": Criminology and Security Studies

As a source of knowledge that is assumed to be objective and authoritative, academia has long played a significant role in how people understand the world. In his influential work, Michel Foucault describes knowledge as a form of power because of its capacity to shape the ways that people conduct themselves through **discourses**. In Foucault's work, discourse can be understood as "a group of statements which provide a language for talking about . . . a particular topic at a particular historical moment" (Hall, 1997, p. 72). Discourse "defines and produces the objects of our knowledge. It governs the way that a topic can meaningfully be talked about and reasoned about" (Hall, 1997, p. 72). Importantly, Foucault's conception of discourse includes both language and social practices that carry meaning. When we think or act in ways that are informed by knowledge, this is a discursive practice. At a societal level, these discursive practices may form institutions—for example, police forces and prisons—that together with representations (e.g., language, images, symbols) form "regimes of truth." Criminology and security studies have produced "regimes of truth"—ways of knowing and strategies that apply this knowledge—about "crime" and "security."

The scopes of both criminology and security studies are defined by state-derived concepts and institutions, taking for granted the state-defined categories of crime and war as objective or natural phenomena. The "classical" or conventional bodies of scholarship within these fields have therefore been oriented around "solving" the problems of crime and war to produce security by improving the effectiveness of state-based institutions: the legal and criminal justice systems (CJS) on one hand and military power and diplomacy on the other. It is not surprising that many criminologists and security scholars are also practitioners and that their fields are deeply connected with governments and state institutions through research funding and knowledge dissemination.

Criminology and security studies are academic fields that emerged and continue to be found predominately in Northern academic institutions. This does not mean that questions of justice, safety, social order, or well-being are not concerns in other places (Shilliam, 2012); what this observation does tell us is that "crime" and "security" have been defined as objects of study in ways that are particular to the Global North. As we'll see below, the way that these scholarly fields are defined reflects specificities of the societies in which they emerge. Rather than universal, the epistemological foundations and core theories of these fields are based on a Eurocentric lens.

Criminology and security studies have claimed "security" as their scholarly territory, albeit on different scales. Criminology is a field associated with sociology or psychology and is concerned with security primarily in local or domestic contexts as "crime" or "law and order" problems. Security studies, within international relations (IR), addresses security in the global or international context in terms of state or national security. This scalar separation is important because it limits our ability to think about the ways that local and global conditions are interconnected. Not only does this reify nation-state borders as "naturally" existing spaces, but it also de-politicizes and individualizes resistance and survival strategies in response to systems of oppression as "crimes." Considering the power of knowledge production, we need to examine how these fields contribute to colonialisms and global capitalism.

Criminology

Criminology involves the systematic study of criminal behaviour, patterns of crime, and social control. Like many social sciences, criminology's emergence can be traced to the influence of the Enlightenment conceptualization of people as rational, free-willed individuals driven by self-interest. This assumption about human nature lies at the heart of the liberal political philosophies that influenced the formation of political, legal, and justice systems in Europe. From these foundations to contemporary research and theories, the field of criminology exists because of the assumed role of the state as the sole legitimate provider of security through creation of law and justice institutions. Consequently, criminological research and theorizing has been largely concerned with how to improve these institutions to ensure "law and order" as a basis of security, whether by understanding "the criminal mind" or by identifying discriminatory CJS practices to be corrected.

Since the mid–20th century, Marxist, feminist, critical race, Indigenous, and anti/(post)colonial theorizing has had significant influence in the social sciences, including criminology (see, e.g., Agozino & Pfohl, 2003; Monchalin, 2016; Sudbury, 2004). Instead of taking law and "crime" categories for granted, critical perspectives study **criminalization** processes through which certain behaviours, conditions, or people become defined and treated as "criminal." Critical criminologists draw attention to the way that criminal laws and their enforcement have historically targeted marginalized groups while ignoring the harmful activities of those in dominant positions, thereby reproducing systems of oppression. These perspectives have also critiqued conventional criminology for contributing to and legitimizing these patterns of criminalization by producing a "regime of truth" about "criminality" that is infused with racist, misogynistic, heteronormative, xenophobic, bourgeois assumptions that pathologize certain people as dangerous or threatening.

Security Studies

In contrast to criminology's focus on the individual–local scale, conventional security studies revolve around the problem of state survival in a context of international conflict and thus tend to focus on military and intelligence apparatuses as means of achieving nation-state security. Security studies emerged after World War II and thus reflected global relations at the time from the perspective of the Anglo-American North. The development of security studies was most prominent in the US when "security" became a major political discourse that linked military defence to the economic security of the nation-state (Neocleous, 2008; see Chapters 8 and 12). The growth of security studies—and emergence of security discourse—has been intimately connected with political interest in producing knowledge to inform geopolitical decisions.

There is a range of critical approaches that challenge the focus on state security and warfare. Emerging in the 1980s, critical security studies (CSS) scholars aimed to expand the concept of security and the scope of the field by making the individual, rather than "the state," the referent object of security—i.e., what should be secured. "Human security" includes threats other than war, such as environmental, economic, social, or political conditions that produce insecurity in people's lives. Some CSS scholars advocate for an *emancipatory* approach that defines security as more than the absence of threats but also freedom from constraints (e.g., Booth, 1991). Another major contribution in security studies is securitization theory. Reflecting a social constructionist approach, the concept of **securitization** refers to a process through which something is discursively turned into a political issue and defined as an "existential threat" that requires a response (Buzan et al., 1998). International political sociology (IPS) scholars influenced by post-structuralism also adopt securitization as a central concept but situate it in the complexities of social relations. Bigo (2008) conceptualizes security and insecurity as inherently interdependent. He argues that security provides justification in liberal societies for *illiberal* practices that cultivate insecurity in a self-perpetuating dynamic of "(in)security."

(Post)Colonial and Feminist Critiques

Because the field of security studies has been defined by a central concern with protecting **the state**—or its inhabitants—conventional and critical approaches tend to reify the existence of nation-states and the international state system. As such, existing global conditions are taken for granted or naturalized as inevitable. An underlying assumption is that the international state system is inherently chaotic and therefore requires managing—whether through warfare, peace-making, or humanitarian intervention—to produce security. Another implication is that other conditions are ignored or subsumed to "national security." For example, poverty is understood as a human security problem because it may contribute to social instability and conflict. Security is assumed to be a desired good to be provided by states or international organizations. While CSS and emancipatory approaches focus on people rather than states, they assume that institutionalized security responses (e.g., through policing, education, political participation, poverty elimination) are desirable and that *more* security is a basis for emancipation. This thinking privileges a liberal politics, which reflects the epistemological framework of security studies based in the Global North (Agathangelou & Ling, 2009; Barkawi & Laffey, 2006; Neocleous, 2008).

One consequence of this epistemology is that security studies ignores or misrepresents the Global South. When scholars do pay attention, there is a tendency to treat resistance movements of the "weak and the powerless" "at best [as] the site of liberal good intentions or at worst a potential source of threats" (Barkawi & Laffey, 2006, p. 332). They are constructed as people and spaces that need intervention because they are incapable or because they pose threats to the North. The demand for security through military, emancipatory, or humanitarian grounds is assumed as being provided by "strong" states or international institutions. People of the Global South and Indigenous peoples in (settler) colonial states of the North are therefore erased or positioned as marginal to the making of world history (Barkawi & Laffey, 2006). The epistemology of security studies masks the violence of past and present colonialization by the Global North (Agathangelou & Ling, 2009; see Chapter 12).

Feminist scholars have critiqued the invisibilization of women and **androcentrism** in security studies and criminology. Standpoint approaches reorient the study of security from "the bottom up" based on the experiences of women

and problematize "security" as a gendered concept, which has shaped the trajectory of scholarly inquiry. The conventional domains of security—international, political, military—are traditionally male-dominated, associated with hegemonic masculine traits of strength, authority, aggression, and agency. While the field has broadened to include "human security," issues such as health and poverty are feminized as part of a non-political domestic realm that is treated as secondary to the "real" matter of national security (Khalili, 2011). Post-structural feminism deconstructs dominant discourses of gender and sex; applying this approach to "security" entails "asking what security can mean in the context of interlocking systems of hierarchy and domination and how gendered identities and ideologies (re)produce these structural insecurities" (Peterson, 1992, p. 32). Postcolonial and women of colour feminists have critiqued feminist scholarship that is limited to "adding" gender to security studies without interrogating the Eurocentric foundations of the field. The consequence is that some streams of feminist security studies have focused on gendered violence as a "foreign" problem, which casts Indigenous women, women of colour, and women in the Global South as passive victims in need of (white) First World feminism. Such narratives reproduce racist orientalist narratives in "security" discourses to justify interventions to "save" women while safeguarding the Global North (Agathangelou & Turcotte, 2010). Standpoint, post-structural, and (post)colonial feminist approaches disrupt the separation of domestic and international as separate spaces. The intersectional analyses of anti- and (post)colonial feminist approaches undo the core geopolitical categories of IR and security studies through interrogating how both states and nation(hood) are constructed through power struggles and **Othering**. Personal well-being is inherently political because experiences are shaped by systems of oppression that transcend borders while contributing to their reification. For example, the prevalence of gendered and racialized sexual violence, such as rape or emasculation, in war and in militarized societies can be understood as enactments of nationalist and imperialist hegemonic masculinities. These enactments of violence are driven by racial Othering in furthering forms of colonialism (Puar, 2007; Razack, 2008; Tickner, 2011).

Studying Security without "Security"?

Critical race, Indigenous, anti- and (post)colonial, and feminist critiques have contributed to expanding the study of "crime" and "security" by addressing the interrelated statism, racism, Eurocentrism, Orientalism, androcentrism, and heteronormativity of both academic knowledge production and security practices. While varied, these interventions raise a crucial question of whether attempting to expand or build on the concepts and theories within criminology and security studies only serves to further legitimize the global order. If both have been complicit in producing legitimation and designing strategies for colonial governance, is it possible or even desirable, for our engagement in these fields?

Considering how deeply politicized and powerful security discourse can be, some scholars have questioned whether it is possible to really critically interrogate "security" while continuing to use the terminology associated with the discourse (Neocleous & Rigakos, 2011; Peoples, 2011). How do we thoroughly unpack "security" as a discourse and analyze how it works to enact modalities of power when the discourse is so encompassing? Drawing on Foucault, how can we work from "outside" of this discourse when it shapes what's possible to think or say about "security"? From an activist-scholar perspective, is there a more effective way of refusing or subverting security discourses without reproducing similar "security-thinking" and harms?

The **binary** logic of security discourse can hinder our ability to think outside of it (Neocleous & Rigakos, 2011). A binary logic, or way of thinking and understanding the world, is structured by opposing pairs of categories that are mutually exclusive. Western thought is characterized by binary thinking; sex and gender are prime examples of this. Security discourse is based on binaries of security/insecurity, peace/war, liberal/illiberal, domestic/foreign, local/global, law enforcement/military, soft/hard power, and so on. Within dominant discourse, we can't be simultaneously secure and insecure—it must be one or the other. The other implication is that it is difficult to think outside of these pairs. Contemporary debates about the militarization of policing are a prime example (see box The Militarization Debate). The power of "security" is that it has a positive normative connotation—who wants to be unsafe, fearful, or anxious? These binaries set parameters on how we define threat and what's possible to address them.

As a way of resisting the limitations and political implications of security discourse, Neocleous (2011) proposes adopting **pacification** as a critical concept to analyze how security discourse is constructed, what it *does*, and how it has been used to do certain things. If you've heard the term "pacification," it is likely in association with colonial or war contexts. Indeed, as discussed below, pacification originated as an imperial political strategy. By using pacification as an analytical framework, we can demystify and denaturalize "security" as a universal good. As Rigakos (2011, p. 62) puts it, "do we really want to be pacified?" This offers a way of disrupting security logic binaries and the artificial disciplinary divides of criminology and security studies. This isn't just replacing one word for another; using a different concept presents another way to think about a phenomenon by disrupting assumptions and making visible relationships with other phenomena. To understand the critical analytical value of pacification, we need to situate the concept in its historical roots.

Royal Canadian Mounted Police raid on the Gidumt'en Checkpoint on unceded Wet'suwet'en territory, January 7, 2019.

Photo by Michael Toledano.

The Militarization Debate

There is significant public and scholarly debate around the militarization of police in Global North countries. The use of certain gear, weapons, technologies, and strategies such as surveillance has been critiqued as not belonging in the "normal," "domestic" realm of law enforcement. First, the underlying assumption is that police and military forces are, and have always been, separate institutions operating in separate spaces (domestic vs foreign) for distinct purposes (public order vs national defence). This obscures the historically entwined origins of police and military forces in colonial projects and the reality that for many Indigenous peoples, people of colour, poor and trans people, repressive forms of policing—harassment, detainment, death, continuous surveillance, overwhelming presence—is the norm (see Chapters 2, 10, 15, and 19). Security discourse's binary logic constrains the terms of the debate so that either a) circumstances justify "militarization" (i.e., as an exception) or b) circumstances reject it as "illiberal" and thus favour "normal" policing. In either case, the *need for security* isn't questioned, nor is the legitimacy of state institutions to respond; implicitly, this legitimizes the use of "illiberal" tactics for Others.

From Pax to Pacification

The concept of pacification has primarily been associated with military strategy, and one contemporary example is from the Vietnam War. In 1964, the US military reframed its "counter-insurgency" strategy as one of "pacification" aimed at gaining the support of the population. This pacification strategy relied on massive military presence and air bombing combined with strategies of economic and infrastructural development. The latter was part of a campaign to win "the hearts and minds" of the Vietnamese people through the promise of a "brighter, nicer new life." This "new life" would be realized by constructing liberal-capitalist political and economic institutions to suppress communism (Neocleous, 2011). Of course, this promise of reconstruction was only enabled by the military's destruction of existing infrastructures. Repressive, militaristic power works with liberal, **biopolitical** strategies to reorganize social, political, and economic relations in ideological and material ways.

The concept and practice of pacification had a much longer history as an empire-building strategy before the US operation in Vietnam. The etymological root of *pacification* is the Latin term *pax*, meaning "peace"; *pacification* therefore describes a process of making peace. One early political usage of this was the *Pax Romana*, a strategy for creating "peace" across the Roman Empire. This "peace" was produced through conquest and maintained by imposed cultural hegemony (through propaganda campaigns) along with the ever-present threat of the emperor's military power. The specific concept of "pacification" appeared in political discourses in the 16th century in the context of European imperialism and the emergence of the "modern" state system. Underlying this system was the formulation of **sovereignty doctrine**, which has become the foundation of international law and relations. This legal order evolved around the "rights" of sovereign entities (a state or ruler) in relation to other sovereigns in asserting claims to "discovered" lands. This claim includes authority to govern the territorially bounded space, including its inhabitants, without interference from external sovereigns. Violations of sovereignty would be considered legitimate grounds for war. While conventionally associated with the 1648 Peace of Westphalia, which established "equilibrium" among European nation-states, the actual groundwork for sovereignty doctrine violently emerged "through the colonial encounter" as European powers sought to justify the invasion, conquest, theft, and enslavement of Indigenous peoples, lands, and resources while protecting themselves from similar violation (Anghie, 1996, p. 332).

During early European imperialism in the Americas, a tension emerged in countries like England, France, Spain, Portugal, and Holland: If Indigenous peoples (categorized as "Indians" by colonizers) were recognized as human and thus as sovereign peoples, then invasion, resource theft, and conquest would be illegitimate violations of their sovereignty. In the mid-1500s, Charles V, King of Spain and ruler of the Holy Roman Empire, turned to theologian Francisco de Vitoria to address this quandary. While Catholic Church doctrine had legitimated European conquest on the basis that non-Christians were "heathens," Vitoria took the position that "Indians" were human and had rightful ownership of their property as Europeans did. Were Spain's activities illegitimate? Vitoria argued that "Indians" and Europeans were bound by the same "natural laws," including the principle of *reason* (*jus gentium*), which upholds the inherent right of sovereigns to travel and engage in trade. Preventing a sovereign entity from exercising this right would be "barbarism," a violation of law considered to be an "act of war" (Vitoria, 1557, in Anghie, 1996, p. 326). Through this logic, Vitoria rationalized Spanish colonization as a "just war" (*jus in bello*) in response to Indigenous resistances to invasion (Anghie, 1996).

European powers justified colonization as a legal and moral *defensive* action to protect *their* sovereignty. This rationale was further supported by racism. Although Vitoria recognized Indigenous peoples as human, he maintained that their cultural differences from the *norm* (Christianity) meant they were not sovereign peoples. By virtue of cultural and political differences, understood as inferiority, Indigenous peoples were violating Europe's *jus gentium*. This provided further legitimization for Spanish invasion to convert and transform Indigenous societies (Anghie, 1996). European legal texts at the time articulated a similar logic: Indigenous peoples were perceived as failing to use their land "productively," which was interpreted as negating any legitimate claim to ownership and, thus, to sovereignty. The assertion of racial and cultural superiority is inherent in both the eliminatory and the "civilizing" discourses of colonialism (see Chapters 2 and 6).

Since Indigenous peoples were defined by their cultural and political differences and by their *resistance* to Spanish colonizers, war was *"inevitable and endless"* (Anghie, 1996, p. 328; emphasis added). For Vitoria, the purpose of ("just") war was "to establish peace and security." Drawing on Vitoria, King Philip II declared in 1573 that all of Spain's future colonial projects would be referred to as "pacifications" rather than "conquests" to be more palatable to the Spanish people (Neocleous, 2014, p.32). The description of conquest as bringing or making "peace" was a rhetorical move masking the violence of conquest while reinforcing the superiority of Europeans colonizers and legitimating imperialism.

To summarize, pacification refers to a process of enforcing a specific kind of "peace" through military domination and repression but also through *persuasive* tactics to capture the "hearts and minds" of a population. This "civilizing" strategy aims to produce hegemonic order by cultivating cultural norms based on liberal ideology and convincing people that this order is their only option for *security* (Khalili, 2012; Neocleous, 2011). Persuasive strategies include education, cultural assimilation, building infrastructures like roads or wells, and cultivating relationships with influential community members. As a process of constituting "peace," pacification tactics destroy and repress *existing* forms of social, political, and economic relations.

Pacifying Global Order

As evident in the historical use of pacification strategies, they express sovereign power. Foucault (1995) describes **sovereign power** as embodied in the exclusive right—or prerogative—of rulers to "take life" and compel obedience of their subjects through direct and repressive means. Military force, execution, and torture are examples of sovereign exercises of power. While we might associate this kind of rule with authoritarianism, prerogative power is a defining feature of most states. In liberal democracies, sovereign power is largely delegated through policing, intelligence services, and judicial and correctional systems. All of these institutions have legal authority to use force to "keep the peace." Sovereign power is also exercised by governments to take "exceptional measures" in the name of security. This can be directed at perceived "enemies" within or outside the nation-state. This prerogative is part of sovereignty doctrine, which recognizes the authority of states to govern without interference unless threatened by others.

If the sovereign state is the only entity entitled to legitimately use force, then all other uses of force would be considered illegitimate. This is enforced through criminal law within the state and through international laws. Sovereignty doctrine is based on mutual recognition of status—while an entity might assert political and territorial authority, it might not be recognized by dominant nation-states. Consequently, any exercise of force—including forms of resistance—would be deemed illegitimate and could be construed as a security threat (see, e.g., Chapters 2, 10, and 16). This would provide justification for interventions by "legitimate" states to (re)establish order.

International law has gained hegemonic status as a neutral and objective institution that exists to ensure security. However, it is important to situate sovereignty doctrine, which underlies international law, in this history of how European powers rationalized colonialism by categorizing Indigenous nations as a) lacking sovereign status because of political or cultural "difference" and/or b) having infringed on Europeans' sovereignty by refusing invasion. The creation of legal doctrines such as **terra nullius** let European powers legitimize their imperial expansion and protect their interests from other nation-states by criminalizing colonial resistance (see Chapters 2 and 6). Contemporary military and humanitarian interventions must be read in this historical colonial context and the use of *moral* justifications based on the assumed morality of the liberal West (Pierce & Rao, 2006).

Let's reconsider the concept of *securitization*: a process of turning something into a *political* issue and defining it as an "existential threat" that requires an exceptional response. This is more likely to occur when the claim is made by people with social, political, or moral authority and if it resonates with existing associations of threat such as past conflicts or racist discourses. Considering the historical evolution of sovereignty doctrine and the international laws that govern state relations, we can situate securitization as a distinctly political strategy of asserting sovereign power. Claiming that there is a threat to existence—of the state, the life of the population, public or global order, collective identity, economy, political ideology (e.g., "our way of life")—and acting to eliminate the threat demonstrates and potentially *expands* sovereign power.

Pacification as an Analytical Concept: Disrupting Binaries

If we understand "security" as a political discourse that is used as a pacification strategy, we avoid falling into an analytical trap of reproducing hegemonic discourse by assuming security to be an intrinsically universal good. By extension, we can avoid reifying the state by placing it and its institutions in historical context. The concept of pacification makes analytical connections between local conditions and global order as co-constituted (Neocleous, 2011), which foregrounds the violence of colonialism and accumulation that underlies social, political, and economic relations. Understanding "law and order" measures "at home"—such as stop-and-frisk or "carding" practices (see Chapter 15)—as pacification leads us to ask what kind of order is being created and how does this fit within broader systems of power beyond the nation-state. What kinds of social relations or identities are being suppressed? Whose "security" is being ensured? Whose "security" is being sacrificed?

Conceptually, pacification disrupts the binaries of security/insecurity and peace/war (see Neocleous & Rigakos, 2011). Rather than oppositional conditions—in which the presence of one negates the other—they are politicized discourses that describe conditions and practices that are co-constitutive. The binary makes it seem paradoxical to think of structural violence—whether in terms of incarceration or war—as inherent to (liberal-democratic) *peace*. The binary of war and peace masks the enduring violence that constitutes "peace" as a specific social order. Analytically, we can study the way that "security" or "peace-making" produce order without being constrained by binaries of police/military, consent/coercion, or soft/hard tactics. These forms are not mutually exclusive. If we think of tactics as being either liberal or illiberal, we end up accepting "liberal" strategies as desirable and legitimate. If understood as pacification, we can acknowledge the specificities of these tactics—for example, physical force *is* different from implementing new economic policies—but also that they both contribute to (re)producing a particular social, political-economic order. We're not implicitly validating interlocking systems of colonialism, capitalism, racism, and heteropatriarchy that are part of this order and constituted by pacification tactics.

As a process of making "peace," the concept of pacification implies that there is *resistance*. This foregrounds the experiences of those who are being "sacrificed" for the security of others. If there were no resistance, pacification strategies would not be necessary. As conveyed throughout the chapters in this volume, resistance includes a spectrum of "failed consent and positive refusal" of colonial projects (Simpson, 2014, p. 128): from collective forms of political mobilization (e.g.. protest, rebellion, insurgency, social movements) to everyday ways that people challenge or refuse the ordering of their lives by oppressive systems. There is a dialectical relationship between pacification tactics and resistance strategies; they are adapted in response to others and to local and global climates. Pacification strategies therefore shift over time and in different spaces because there are *ongoing* power struggles.

Finally, another crucial binary to disrupt is that of *norm/exception*. As noted, sovereign power often operates through declaring "exceptional measures" to legitimize violence in the name of security. Exceptional measures are framed as aberrations in a normally "peaceful" society but necessitated by the existential threat. Like *peace/war*, this binary masks the interlocking gendered, racialized, class-based structures of violence that are everyday lived experiences for those who are systematically "sacrificed" to secure global colonial-capitalist processes of accumulation. Rather than exceptional, these structures of violence are the foundations of social and global order. The concept of pacification reminds us that the pursuit of

"security" constitutes the "threats" that produce anxieties.

Securing Colonial-Capitalist Order

At the core of "security" is the affective dimension. Fear, unease, and anxiety can be intensified when there is an identifiable source for those feelings. As critical race and postcolonial scholars (e.g., Aimé Césaire, Frantz Fanon, Edward Said) have shown, Othering constitutes not just a homogenous collective Other but also a collective "we" that have a common interest in being "secure" from the Other. This is why "security" is an inherently imperialistic discourse (Stoler, 2016). Through dehumanization and distancing, Othering makes the punishment and "sacrifice" of others morally tolerable or even necessary: "If you want to live, the other must die" (Foucault, 2003, p. 255). Othering is essential to sovereign power because it defines a collective (national) identity to be defended.

Security discourses draw on and contribute to the organization of social identities by constructing us-and-them and enforcing categorizations through pacification practices. While colonialism, racism, and heteropatriarchy endure through systematic Othering and being structurally embedded in institutions like law, Otherness is not static and interlocks in different ways in specific contexts. For example, Puar (2007) shows how the intensification of racist orientalist Othering following the events of 11 September 2001 mobilized a homonationalist identity of "proper" (monogamous and married) homosexuality, whiteness, and consumerism. As Puar (2007) writes, the "folding in of homosexuality into the 'us' of the 'us-versus-them' nationalist rhetoric" (p. 43) occurs by constructing Muslim and Arab Others as intensely homophobic, "improperly sexual," and misogynistic (p. 14; also see Chapter 3). Similarly, white women's safety has frequently been invoked in discourses criminalizing men of colour and migrants; passive, fragile femininity symbolizes nationhood that must be defended. At the same time, liberal feminism has been complicit in campaigns to "emancipate" Othered women, supporting and increasingly leading military and humanitarian interventions in the Global South (Puar, 2007; Razack, 2004; 2008). Women of the Global South are constructed as less "enlightened" and lacking in agency to challenge their oppression. By implication, women of the Global North are modern and liberated. The "human security" of women and LGBTQI people of colour is therefore assumed to come through their adoption of liberalism and Western gender norms (Abu-Lughod, 2002; Puar, 2007; Razack, 2008). Campaigns to liberate "oppressed women"—in domestic and foreign spaces—positions the North as saviour, entrenching an orientalist divide. White, Global North feminist activism and scholarship has been central to these discourses (Agathangelou & Turcotte, 2010). By co-constituting the self and Other as oppositional, binary logic denies or minimizes the racist homophobia and misogyny of the Global North and furthers (neo)colonialism.

Security for Whom?

Imperialism and colonization have fostered a global order in which the North has benefitted from the theft of resources (and people) over centuries. As Fanon (2004, p. 58) wrote, "Europe is literally the creation of the Third World. The riches which are choking it are those plundered from the underdeveloped peoples." At the core of global capitalism is original or "primitive" accumulation, which occurs through dispossessing people of the means of sustenance and production and then extracting wealth from those sources. The decimation of populations, plunder of resources, environmental destruction, subjugation of political and economic relations, and repression of

cultural and linguistic practices have produced precariousness. Mbembe (2003) describes these conditions as **necropolitical** as peoples' lives are regulated by continuous exposure to social and political death. In turn, these conditions fuel the affective insecurities experienced in the Global North, which underlie the expansion of policing and carceral institutions to protect "us"—from the enduring threat of Indigenous Others, whose presence disrupts the sovereign claim of colonial occupiers; racialized diasporic Others within the metropoles of empire; or visible poor and working classes in global centres of capitalism.

These insecurities are the fodder for continued pacification projects in the name of "human security." As examined in Chapters 8, 9, 12, and 14, states and international organizations of the Global North have justified their ongoing interventions as necessary to address "underdevelopment," the contemporary code-word for "inferiority" (Khalili, 2012, p. 128). According to liberal-capitalist standards, "underdevelopment" of social, political, and economic systems fosters local instability and, thus, poses potential threat to the "developed" world (Duffield, 2001). Echoing the civilizing discourses of earlier colonialisms, "human security" discourse has become the primary justification for military interventions and presence, coupled with Structural Adjustment Programs (SAPs) and humanitarian development projects. These neoliberal development projects reorganize the economic, political, and social relations of an "underdeveloped" society modelled on free market principles and "social engineering" to build "good governance" through institutions and policies related to poverty reduction, liberal human rights, and civil society participation (Hindess, 2005). One effect of social engineering is disruption of gender relations because projects "uphold and enact particular [Western] notions of both masculinity and femininity in their very enactment" (Peoples & Vaughan-Williams, 2014, p. 165). SAPs and other forms of neoliberal economic restructuring often have gendered effects that contribute to increasing women's dependency, poverty, and exposure to violence. These conditions increase women's exposure to criminalization, which is reflected in the growing rates of women's imprisonment across the Global South and North (Agozino, 2004; Sudbury, 2004).

The positive connotations of "human security" and "development" mask the coercive dimensions of these processes. In addition to gender relations, pacification strategies have historically exploited and re-formed social divisions of class, caste, and ethnicity. Social reorganization institutes neoliberal governance, which enables regulation of societies of the Global South through free market principles such as liberalization and privatization. This opens up opportunities for further economic exploitation by corporations and wealthier states by enabling "legitimate" access to natural resources. These developmental programs are made possible by conditions of duress as a result of the destructiveness of military operations and legacies of colonialism. "Underdevelopment" discourse undermines people's political capacities unless they adopt a liberal model of political engagement. Refusal to embrace restructuring as a condition of financial or humanitarian assistance has potential consequences—the denial of essential aid and/or being construed as a recalcitrant security threat. Rather than reparations or addressing the massive disparities of wealth to equalize "life chances," these pacification projects more deeply entrench the North/South divide, further justifying continued interventions (Duffield, 2001; also see Chapters 10 and 16).

"Global Lockdown"

Sudbury (2004) uses the term "global lockdown" to situate criminalization processes and the exponential growth of carceral systems around the world in the context of global capitalism. The carceral refers to repressive spaces of confinement, including jails, prisons, immigration detention centres, psychiatric hospitals, refugee camps, and Indian residential schools. While these institutions are distinct from one another, they are interdependent spaces of physical containment and surveillance "that warehouse those who are surplus or resistant to the new world order" (Sudbury, 2004, p. xii). While resistance challenges the legitimacy of this order, the "surplus" who are immaterial to capitalism—as owners, workers, or consumers—are a source of uncertainty. Both are "out of order."

Like legal systems, surveillant and carceral institutions originated in the colonial encounter, as discussed in Chapter 12. The design of slave ships (Browne, 2015; Rediker, 2008) prefigures Jeremy Bentham's panopticon, an idealized model for prisons that was "a colonial invention . . . devised on Europe's colonial frontier with the Ottoman Empire" (Mitchell, 1991, p. 35). Colonial spaces were and still are testing grounds for policing, punishment, intelligence, and surveillance techniques that "boomerang" between colonies and metropoles (Foucault, 2003, p. 103). Systems of "law and order" and colonial warfare are co-constituted. The establishing of prisons, surveillance technologies (e.g., checkpoints), and "preventative" policing strategies in colonial contexts are means of suppressing resistance and protecting colonial interests but are also part of engineering carceral and judicial infrastructures modelled on liberal ideals.

The concept of "global lockdown" lets us think about the ways that these carceral institutions are continuous with SAPs and social engineering as forms of compartmentalization, which are simultaneously repressive and constitutive (Fanon, 2004; Mbembe, 2003). Compartmentalization enforces displacement and enables surveillance through reserves, camps (internment, work, refugee), fences, checkpoints, Indian residential schools, roadblocks, walls, child apprehension, and prisons. These dispersed spaces of containment form "carceral archipelagos" of empire that open up spaces for desirable circulation for production or accumulation (Foucault, 1995; Nichols, 2014; Stoler, 2016).

Conclusion

Critiquing "security" and "peace" as political discourses doesn't mean that the conditions associated with being safe or free from threat such as the necessities of life, autonomy, love, fulfilment, coexistence, absence of violence, etc., are not desirable or possible or should not be worked for. Nor does it mean that interventions are never needed. What critique does is disrupt hegemonic discourse and foreground how these ideals have been politicized and deployed in ways that reproduce systems of domination contingent on the oppression or elimination of others on local and global scales. It moves us to think of ways to foster freedom from fear, threat, and anxiety that reject the sacrificing of others.

Counter-hegemonic scholarship and activist work have made visible how academic knowledge production is deeply entangled with practices of imperialism and global capitalism. The evolution of criminology and security studies has entrenched an ideological separation between "crime" and international security, which reinforces liberal binaries that structure the way that we think about "security" as either internal or external to the nation-state. (Post)colonial, Indigenous, critical race, and feminist analyses decentre the top-down, state-defined lenses of security studies and criminology to show how security discourses have been invoked to justify the structural violence of colonial invasion, enslavement, dispossession, displacement, criminalization, and incapacitation. These scholars have shown how the destructiveness of this violence is also constitutive of collective identities through an us-versus-them binary. Part of the political accomplishment of security discourse is in reinforcing the legitimacy of state violence to defend "us" from colonial, racialized, foreign, gender- and sex-subversive Others.

The concept of pacification is a strategy for studying "security" that disrupts the ideological lines drawn by criminology and security studies by foregrounding the violence of imperialism and colonialism underlying contemporary social, political, and economic relations. It emphasizes that "order" or "peace" is actively being done to (re)produce oppressive systems because people are also actively resisting.

Disrupting the binaries of security discourse is essential for social justice because it rejects the de-politicization and criminalization of resistances and refusals. Thinking about the way that "security" is constituted rather than accepting definitions of threat counters the divisiveness of Othering that pits us against each other. This is crucial to forge solidarities across the lines drawn by state borders, compartmentalization, and identity categories in order to challenge interlocking systems of oppression. If "security" is a politicized concept, then radical critique that disrupts by getting to the root of the "problem" is inherently political.

Tying It Together

This chapter offers "pacification" as a counter-hegemonic analytical lens to disrupt "security" discourses that underlie a wide range of oppressive processes examined throughout this book. As in the other chapters, we can trace the entanglement of Northern academic knowledge production to violence enacted in processes of nation-building and global capital. Disrupting the binds of "security" thinking, which fosters Othering, is crucial to build trans-local alliances and solidarities across struggles.

> ## Call to Action
>
> Find out what kinds of "security" initiatives have been proposed or implemented in your community within the past year (it could involve law, police, schools, public spaces, health, poverty, or economic issues). What was the issue being securitized? Whose security is primarily being addressed? Can you think of any ways that this initiative could be creating or exacerbating affective (risk, fear, anxiety, uncertainty) or material "insecurity" for some people? How might we address the underlying issue without potentially harming others? Find out whether there have been campaigns or organizing that challenge criminalization and securitization practices.

DISCUSSION QUESTIONS

1. What makes you feel secure? Think about the things that make you feel safe, and make a list of things that make you feel unsafe or fearful. If you feel comfortable doing so, share your list with a partner or group. What are the commonalities and differences? How might you explain these observations based on what you've read?

2. How do conventional criminology and security studies reproduce dominant security discourses?

3. Identify and deconstruct an example, other than those discussed in this chapter, of how gender and/or racialization have been used to construct a specific security problem, either as the referent object or as the threat.

4. Think about the words we use to describe people who encounter the criminal justice system. Compare the words "criminal" and "prisoner"—what are the assumptions that come to mind? Do they imply different relations? Reflect on your own use of these terms.

5. Select an example of a conflict discussed in one of the other chapters in this textbook. Applying the framework of pacification, explain how "security" discourse is used to delegitimize and criminalize resistance movements.

SUGGESTIONS FOR FURTHER READING

Agozino, Biko. (2003). *Counter-colonial criminology: A critique of imperialist reason*. London, UK: Pluto Press. This book is an incisive anti-colonial interrogation of the complicity of criminology in European and US imperialism.

Khalili, Laleh. (2012). *Time in the shadows: Confinement in counterinsurgencies*. Stanford, CA: Stanford University Press. This book is an engaging analysis of the continuities of confinement and detention strategies used in the US "War on Terror" and Israeli occupation of Palestine with earlier colonial warfare.

Sudbury, Julia. (2004). *Global lockdown: Race, gender, and the prison-industrial complex*. New York, NY: Routledge. This edited collection of black, Indigenous, and women of colour feminist scholars and prison activists examines the structural violence of mass incarceration as a manifestation of global colonial-capitalism.

Peoples, Columba, & Vaughan-Williams, Nick. (2014). *Critical security studies: An introduction*. London, UK: Routledge. This book provides a survey of security studies from a critical perspective.

MULTIMEDIA SUGGESTIONS

The hunted and the hated: An inside look at the NYPD's stop-and-frisk program. (2012), Dir. Ross Tuttle; 13 minutes
https://www.youtube.com/watch?v=7rWtDMPaRD8
This short documentary examines the institutionalized racism underlying the NYPD's stop-and-frisk program from the perspectives of young Black men targeted by the policy and from anonymous NYPD officers.

La battaglia di Algeri (The Battle of Algiers) (1966). Dir. Gillo Pontecorvo; 123 minutes
This film about the Algerian resistance against French colonial occupation in the 1950s serves as a commentary on urban guerrilla warfare and has been used in US military training. The Algerian anti-colonial resistance had a significant influence on the development of pacification theories by French Colonel David Galula. His writings, based on France's pacification and counter-insurgency strategies against the Algerian resistance, have informed US military counter-insurgency doctrine.

Kanehsatake: 270 years of resistance (1993). Dir. Alanis Obomsawin; 120 minutes
In 1990, Mohawks from Kanehsatake engaged in a 78-day standoff to defend Kanien'kéhaka (Mohawk) lands from being turned into a golf course. The documentary follows the Mohawks' resistance and the Canadian state's exercise of sovereign power in the context of a long history of colonial dispossession.

Critical Resistance. *What is abolition?*
http://criticalresistance.org/about/not-so-common-language
This website provides a toolkit for thinking critically about safety and well-being outside of dominant security discourse.

REFERENCES

Abu-Lughod, L. (2002). Do Muslim women really need saving? Anthropological reflections on cultural relativism and its Others. *American Anthropologist, 104*(3), 783–790. https://doi.org/10.1525/aa.2002.104.3.783.

Agathangelou, A.M., & Ling, L.H.M. (2009). *Transforming world politics: From empire to multiple worlds* (1st ed.). London, UK, and New York, NY: Routledge.

Agathangelou, A.M., & Turcotte, H.M. (2010). "Feminist" theoretical inquiries and "IR." *Oxford Research Encyclopedia of International Studies*. https://doi.org/10.1093/acrefore/9780190846626.013.374.

Agozino, B. (2004). Nigerian women in prison: Hostages in law. In J. Sudbury (Ed.), *Global lockdown: Race, gender, and the prison-industrial complex* (pp. 185–200). New York, NY: Routledge.

Agozino, B., & Pfohl, S. (2003). *Counter-colonial criminology: A critique of imperialist reason*. London, UK: Pluto Press.

Anghie, A. (1996). Francisco De Vitoria and the colonial origins of international law. *Social & Legal Studies, 5*(3), 321–36. https://doi.org/10.1177/096466399600500303.

Barkawi, T., & Laffey, M. (2006). The postcolonial moment in security studies. *Review of International Studies, 32*(2), 329–52.

Bigo, D. (2008). Globalized (in)security: The field and the ban-opticon. In D. Bigo & A. Tsoukala (Eds), *Terror, insecurity and liberty. Illiberal practices of liberal regimes after 9/11* (pp. 10–48). New York, NY: Routledge.

Booth, K. (1991). Security and emancipation. *Review of International Studies, 17*(4), 313–26.

Browne, S. (2015). *Dark matters: On the surveillance of blackness*. Durham, NC: Duke University Press.

Buzan, B., Wæver, O., & Wilde, J. de. (1998). *Security: A new framework for analysis*. Boulder, CO: Lynne Rienner Publishers.

Duffield, M. (2001). *Global governance and the new wars: The merging of development and security*. London, UK, and New York, NY: Zed Books.

Fanon, F. (2004). *The wretched of the earth*. R. Philcox, trans. New York, NY: Grove Press.

Foucault, M. (1995). *Discipline and punish: The birth of the prison*. New York, NY: Vintage Books.

Foucault, M. (2003). *"Society must be defended": Lectures at the Collège de France, 1975–1976*. D. Macey, trans. New York, NY: Picador.

Hall, S. (Ed). (1997). *Representation: Cultural representations and signifying practices*. Thousand Oaks, CA: Sage.

Hindess, B. (2005). Investigating international anti-corruption. *Third World Quarterly, 26*(8), 1389–98. https://doi.org/10.1080/01436590500336864.

Khalili, L. (2011). Gendered practices of counterinsurgency. *Review of International Studies, 37*(4), 1471–91.

Khalili, L. (2012). *Time in the shadows: Confinement in counterinsurgencies*. Stanford, CA: Stanford University Press.

Mbembe, A. (2003). Necropolitics. *Public Culture, 15*(1), 11–40.

Mitchell, T. (1991). *Colonising Egypt*. Berkeley, CA: University of California Press.

Monchalin, L. (2016). *The colonial problem: An Indigenous perspective on crime and injustice in Canada*. Toronto, ON: University of Toronto Press.

Neocleous, M. (2008). *Critique of security*. Montreal, QC: McGill-Queen's University Press.

Neocleous, M. (2011). "A brighter and nicer new life": Security as pacification. *Social & Legal Studies, 20*(2), 191–208.

Neocleous, M. (2014). *War power, police power*. Edinburgh, UK: Edinburgh University Press.

Neocleous, M., & Rigakos, G.S. (Eds). (2011). *Anti-security*. Ottawa, ON: Red Quill Books.

Nichols, R. (2014). The colonialism of incarceration. *Radical Philosophy Review, 17*(2), 435–55.

Peoples, C. (2011). Security after emancipation? Critical theory, violence and resistance. *Review of International Studies, 37*(3), 1113–35.

Peoples, C. & Vaughan-Williams, N. (2014). *Critical security studies: An introduction* (2nd edn). New York, NY: Routledge.

Peterson, V.S. (Ed.). (1992). *Gendered states: Feminist*. Boulder, CO: Lynne Rienner Publishers.

Pierce, S., & Rao, A. (Eds). (2006). Discipline and the Other body: Humanitarianism, violence and the colonial exception. In *Discipline and the Other body: Correction, corporeality, colonialism* (pp.1–35). Durham, NC: Duke University Press.

Puar, J. K. (2007). *Terrorist assemblages: Homonationalism in queer times*. Durham, NC: Duke University Press.

Razack, S. (2004). *Dark threats and white knights: The Somalia Affair, peacekeeping, and the new imperialism*. Toronto, ON: University of Toronto Press.

Razack, S. (2008). *Casting out: The eviction of Muslims from Western law and politics*. Toronto, ON: University of Toronto Press.

Rediker, M. (2008). *The slave ship: A human history*, reprinted. New York, NY: Penguin Books.

Rigakos, G. S. (2011). "To extend the scope of productive labour": Pacification as a police project. In *Anti-security* (pp. 57–84). Ottawa, ON: Red Quill Books.

Shilliam, R. (Ed.). (2012). *International relations and non-Western thought: Imperialism, colonialism and investigations of global modernity*. London, UK: Routledge.

Simpson, A. (2014). *Mohawk interruptus: Political life across the borders of settler states*. Durham, NC: Duke University Press.

Stoler, A.L. (2016). *Duress: Imperial durabilities in our times*. Durham, NC: Duke University Press.

Sudbury, J. (Ed.). (2004). *Global lockdown: Race, gender, and the prison-industrial complex*. New York, NY: Routledge.

Tickner, J.A. (2011). Feminist security studies: Celebrating an emerging field. *Politics & Gender, 7*(4), 576–81.

CHAPTER 14

◇

Gendered Omissions and Silences in Global Health Security

Colleen O'Manique

Learning Objectives

In this chapter, you will:
- learn about the historical foundations of today's global health security policy;
- consider how specific political agendas shape responses to global health emergencies;
- examine, from a feminist postcolonial lens, the gendered gaps and omissions in current practices of global health governance;
- learn about proposed pathways that could begin to disrupt the gendered structural violence embedded in approaches to global health security.

Introduction

Over the course of the past four decades, there has been a steady increase in attention paid to global health outside of the scientific fields of biomedicine and public health policy. Human health has increasingly been understood as a national and global security issue in response to the rise in lethal pandemics and humanitarian emergencies. **Global health security** focuses on the containment of disease outbreaks that can potentially spread across borders and pose threats to populations and economies. In response, a critical field of scholarship on global health security has emerged. Here, global health is understood as an issue linked to the broader analysis of the power relations shaping global health. While this

burgeoning field of research has been helpful in critically interrogating global health security policies and practices, what has been left out are critical feminist voices that address the impacts of current health security practices on different flesh-and-blood bodies.

This chapter aims to address the following question: in the current practices of global health security, whose bodies have value? It casts a postcolonial feminist lens on the responses to two recent global health emergencies: the Ebola Virus Disease (EVD) epidemic that began in 2013 in Guinea, devastating the Mano River region of West Africa; and the Zika virus epidemic that began in 2015 in Brazil and spread throughout the Americas. It argues that current discourses and practices of global health security fail to question the local conditions that shape viral outbreaks and spread. Ignored are the conditions within which people in the zones of the emergency live their lives—conditions that have been shaped by histories of colonial violence. Furthermore, it argues that today's contemporary global economic and ecological crises are, on the face of it, health emergencies. They are crises that are felt in the flesh, through disease, disability, and death. And these crises are a product of gendered, classed, and racialized power relations that maintain a hierarchy in which some bodies have value and others do not.

This chapter begins with an account of the antecedents to today's practices of global health security. It briefly outlines their foundations in the history of the European slave trade, the conquest of the "New World" and colonization, and the postwar emergence of the development industry. The next two sections present the two examples that illuminate the gendered **structural violence** emerging from recent responses to pandemic disease "threats." These accounts are based on a combination of primary sources from the UN and government organizations, feminist/civil society advocates, and academic publications. Taken together, they expose how the dominant practices of global health security differently affect classed, racialized, and gendered bodies. The concluding section suggests what might be required in order to move toward a more expansive governance of global health that addresses "threats" before they become emergencies and that strengthens the autonomy and agency of diverse communities to live healthy and meaningful lives.

The Origins of Global Health

Global health today is both a security project and a development project. We can locate its roots in the history of the European conquest of the world and the evolution of the practices and policies to control infectious disease (King, 2002, p. 64). From the beginning of the Atlantic slave trade, disease transmission was widespread among Europeans and Africans along the West African shoreline, and the overcrowded and unsanitary hollowed spaces of the slave ships further constituted highly efficient spaces of disease transmission. Between 1502 and 1870, approximately 11.4 million Africans were forced into slavery and removed from their homes to be transported to the New World as disposable labour (Birn, Pilay, & Holtz, 2009, p. 25). Here, upwards of 15 per cent of captured slaves died in middle passage (Birn et al., 2009, p. 25).

The health security strategies to counter the transmission of disease aboard the slave ships included medical examinations performed by ship surgeons, the quarantining of people and goods suspected of harbouring infectious disease, and in some cases the forcible removal of infected people by throwing them into the ocean (Muskateem, 2011, p. 312). The bodies of captive women and men represented considerable profits for distant merchants, brokers, slave traders, and mine and plantation owners. Calculations as to the maintenance of basic necessities to keep these bodies alive were made accordingly (Muskateem, 2011). For those who survived, the brutal working and living conditions translated into life expectancies averaging three years past their time of arrival in the New World (Blackburn, 1997). The Indigenous population was also brutally affected as pathogens such as smallpox and measles were brought to the Americas by the Europeans. Some estimates contend that upward of 90 per cent of Indigenous people perished, with the Spanish clergy rationalizing these deaths as God's punishment for the "Indian's bestial behaviour" (Federici, 2004, p. 86).

The medical history of much of the colonized world was shaped by the demand for labouring bodies for mines, plantations, roads, and railways, as well as to fulfill the labour of **social reproduction** for the European population. Indigenous people were also enslaved or compelled to work in in the mines, plantations, or homes of the Europeans. Silvia Federici documents the systematic destruction of Indigenous women's role in social reproduction as an essential feature of colonization (2004). Their access to land and their power and authority over seeds and the crops they cultivated were important foundations of their power and autonomy. Colonization resulted in the erosion of this power with the diversion of labour away from local care economies and subsistence farming to the plantations or to the care of settler populations.

In places in Africa where single-gender labour migration of males to urban areas became the norm and women and children stayed in rural areas, women's household labours intensified as they alone provided for their families and communities. Disease flourished in growing urban areas where proper sanitation, public health, and hygiene were lacking and where well-defined boundaries, or *cordon sanitaire*, separated Europeans from the local populations.

Health security was essential for the expansion of commercial trade and colonial networks of the 18th century. But the lack of consensus on the causes of disease made it difficult for European nations to formally agree on international standards of practice, since adopting such standards might have interfered with their individual commercial interests. This changed in the latter part of the 19th century when advances in the medical sciences led to the discovery of the germ theory of disease transmission. This in turn led to the beginnings of the international standardization of systems of medical knowledge and health practice (Arner, 2013, pp. 773–5). These developments prompted a series of international sanitary conferences, beginning in Paris in 1851, to address containment strategies for cholera, plague, and yellow fever. They eventually culminated in the International Sanitary Regulations of 1903—the precursor to today's legally binding International Health Regulations (IHR). Indeed, the public health measures adopted in 19th-century Europe helped to bring major epidemic illnesses under control through better living and working conditions, water, sanitation, and nutrition. These measures, however, were not extended to vast parts of the world under colonial occupation. Furthermore, they did little to undermine the dominance of a regime of global health that focused on disease containment and biomedical technologies to control infectious disease (Birn, 2012).

This regime of global health was disrupted with the emergence of the development industry after World War II, as was illuminated in Chapter 8. This was the time, according to Arturo Escobar, when mass poverty was "discovered," providing the anchor for state intervention within the general model of liberal-capitalist economies (Escobar, 1995). Eurocentrism was written on the slate of the colonization: the undermining of people's cultures, economies, and political systems, the possession of land, the extraction of labour and other resources (Trietler & Boatcâ, 2016, p. 161). The structural and political inequalities between the Global North and South forged through centuries of colonization have been masked by the deepening professionalization, de-politicization, and capture of "development" by private actors (Banks, Hulme, & Edwards, 2014, p. 709). Entrenched racialized and gendered systems of privilege remain intact and naturalize difference (Hawkesworth, 2016).

Since its inception in the postwar period, the development industry has evolved into a top-down, technical project to deliver "progress" to the poor that recasts the "problems" of poverty from the political realm to the more "neutral" realms of science, technology, and economics. Together the International Monetary Fund (IMF) and the World Bank (WB) have used the indebtedness of national governments in the former colonies to dictate policies to eliminate government support for the **social determinants of health** (SDH) and to keep their extractive economies friendly to **global capital**. While population and development policies have been designed to foster economic growth, they have been intricately involved in shaping the life chances of differently classed and racialized women, their intimate lives, and their gendered labour across the globe (Hawkesworth, 2016, p. 162).

Postwar Global Health

The World Health Organization (WHO) was established in 1948 as the UN specialized agency with the mandate to "'improve the health of the world's inhabitants." The WHO, in principle, embraced a broad understanding of health in its first constitution as "a state of complete physical, mental, and social well-being and not merely the absence of disease or infirmity." It did this again 30 years later with the Alma Ata Declaration of 1978 by signalling support for the WHO campaign "Health Care for All by the Year 2000." One of a number of UN "New World Order" declarations, Alma Ata had as its objective "the attainment by all citizens of the world by the year 2000 of a level of health which will permit them to lead a socially and economically productive life" (WHO, 1978). The primary means to achieving this was outlined as primary health care (PHC) (WHO, 1978). There was a clear recognition that disease and poverty were deeply intertwined and that health policies should be community-driven, support local health priorities, and the SDH (WHO, 1978).

Beginning in the early 1980s with the turn toward neoliberalism, Alma Ata was replaced by cost recovery, privatization, and "selective primary health care." This approach focused on the few diseases responsible for the greatest mortality. It was also at this time that the power of the WHO and other UN organizations to steer the global health agenda began to erode. In the 1980s, the World Bank, pharmaceutical companies, private businesses, and corporate philanthropists began to gain influence in shaping global health policy both within and outside of UN bodies. Single-disease campaigns that focused on technological quick fixes crowded out health prevention policies and health systems strengthening.

Civil society organizations and networks such as Development Alternatives with Women for a New Era (DAWN) and the People's Health Movement continue to keep health justice on the global agenda in the context of the deepening corporatization of the official actors. International NGOs such as Doctors Without Borders and the Red Cross respond to critical health disparities, filling the gaps when an acute humanitarian emergency erupts. These are overwhelmingly in places where public health systems barely exist and where health's social determinants are scarce. Examples of this can be seen in Haiti after the 2010 earthquake and in the aftermath of Hurricane Maria that devastated Puerto Rico and parts of the Caribbean in 2017.

Lakoff understands today's management of global health as consisting of two overlapping regimes: global health security and **humanitarian biomedicine** (2010). Global health security involves the social construction of, and responses to, specific diseases as "threats" to global and/or national security, known as Public Health Emergencies of International Concern (PHEIC). Recent examples are SARS, Ebola Virus Disease, and Zika. Humanitarian biomedicine focuses its attention on "threats" to human health that are less virulent and geographically contained: medical emergencies such as cholera epidemics and famines that might result from civil unrest, refugee movements, and "natural" disasters. The regime of global health security acts to maintain the continued function of the global economy for continued economic growth and profit-making, while humanitarian biomedicine exists to save individual lives. However, there are significant overlaps. For example, in the year 2000, HIV/AIDS was one of the first pathogens to be constructed explicitly as a national and global security crisis by the UN Security Council. Here, the central concern was that the spread of the virus could negatively impact good governance, economic growth, and productivity and lead to state fragility. This represented a threat to both nation-states and geopolitical interests. Once a disease outbreak is defined as a national or global security threat, justifications can be made for the enactment of extraordinary measures.

As Lakoff (2010) has suggested, both projects are "apolitical" in that they are socio-technical projects that can be seen essentially as responses to the erosion of the basic constituents of health and bare life. We can understand the technologies of global health as responses to the erosion of many people's access to the social determinants of health: to clean water and sanitation; to nutritious food; to shelter and security; to bodily autonomy and integrity; and to preventative and comprehensive health care and medicine. Health security addresses the "universal vulnerability" of the global economy to "health-related shocks," while humanitarian biomedicine addresses the individual suffering of people. In Lakoff's view, humanitarian biomedicine constitutes "a philanthropic palliative to nation-states lacking public health infrastructure in exchange for the right of international health organizations to monitor their populations for outbreaks that may threaten wealthy nations" (2010, p. 75). The common understanding now is that *we are all* under increasing threat from novel pathogens that cross national borders—that diseases do not discriminate. But this is simply not the case.

The practices constituting global health security today focus on infectious disease security, with International Health Regulations codifying the legally binding protocols to be followed by all nations (Davies, Karmadt-Scott, & Rushton, 2015). Significant investments have been made to shore up international networks for epidemic alert and response and strengthen disease surveillance, laboratory systems, and risk communication, as well as the production and stockpiling of drugs. These investments are highly uneven and influenced by vested interests; "Western" countries focus more on their own preparedness, while the beleaguered UN system copes with assisting poor countries (Weir, 2015). This is not to discount the dangers that specific "health security" risks pose to different populations. But many countries have health systems characterized by poor disease surveillance, water and sanitation, and public health care systems. Access to medicines can be highly variable and dependent on income, and the "diseases of poverty" are endemic. According to UN Habitat, approximately one billion people live in slum conditions—the ideal sites for viral spread.

The emergency discourses that dominate the institutional landscape are often described through the discourse of rights, development, and humanitarianism. This discourse serves to mask vested interests and corporate political influence (Biehl & Petryna, 2013). Humanitarian biomedicine is delivered through non-governmental actors such as Doctors Without Borders, the Bill and Melinda Gates Foundation, and the Global Fund to HIV/AIDS, Tuberculosis and Malaria as a means of avoiding "political entanglement" (Lakoff, 2010). The provision of drugs, vaccines, and bed-nets, and emergency food aid and hospitals in zones of war, famine, or natural disaster are necessary *because* of the structural violence that characterizes the current global order.

The drivers of novel disease outbreaks, such as the interrelated processes of increased human mobility and migration, rapid urbanization, and the growth and consolidation of our increasingly globalized agro-industrial food system, remain intact. The impacts of climate change and loss of biodiversity and habitat transform the life cycles of animals that can intensify zoonoses—animal diseases that can be transmitted to humans. Large industrial farms provide ideal breeding grounds for viruses to mutate into more lethal ones. We are aware that these processes exist, but they remain poorly understood (Bardosch, 2016; Bennett and McMichael, 2012; Davis, 2005). Given this reality, it is likely that our planet will experience new and more virulent viral epidemics.

People to Note in the Field

Feminist scholars whose research examines the intersections of gender, social reproduction, and health in the context of contemporary neoliberal governance are:

Emma-Louise Anderson
Sophie Harman
Belinda Bennett
Sara E. Davies
Aisha Fofana Ibrahim
Rosalind Petchesky
Emilia Rayes
Maria Tanyag

Whose Bodies Matter?

Feminist scholars have exposed the pathways between contemporary **neoliberal governance** at both international and state levels and the local conditions that underpin poverty and deepen gendered insecurities that are experienced differently by different racialized, classed, and gendered bodies. They have illuminated the essential contradiction between the "public" sphere of politics and economics and the "private" sphere of the household and its feminized labours where the activities of social reproduction—the unpaid and invisible care labours that keep bodies alive—are undertaken. Continued economic growth depends upon the intensification of this contradiction. This invisible care labour is largely the responsibility of girls and women and the existing socially constructed gendered and racialized divisions of labour (Marchand & Runyan, 2011; Peterson, 2012)

Some people are insulated from these "threats" while others are on the front lines. The labour of keeping bodies alive in the context of a PHEIC is gendered labour. Novel pathogens and their emergency responses can reinforce and intensify existing multi-layered and gendered inequalities. The global responses to Ebola and Zika clearly illustrate how they constitute forms of power that intensify the pre-existing embodied

hierarchies of difference. This chapter now turns to two case studies: Ebola Virus Disease and Zika.

Ebola Virus Disease

Ebola Virus Disease (EVD) is a severe, often fatal illness transmitted through infected fruit bats or primates to humans as well as by direct human-to-human contact through body fluids. The first outbreaks of EVD happened in the mid-1970s in villages in Central Africa and were small and localized. The most recent epidemic began in a remote village in Guinea in 2013 and went undetected for months. During this time, the virus spread across borders to Liberia and Sierra Leone, its un-detection and subsequent spread escalating into a "global health emergency" (WHO, 2014). Abdulla and Rashid note that the major international actors who could have responded early to the outbreak were hesitant to act until it had become a raging sub-regional epidemic (2017, p. 11). Intervention came only after it received international attention, with the justification couched in highly securitized language (Abdulla & Rashid, 2017, p. 11). The crisis framing of the Ebola epidemic intensified after a single case showed up in the United States (on 23 October 2014) at which point it was framed in the media as an "African" disease with potential "global" consequences (Nokov,

2015, p. 9). Media in North America focused on the potential risk to American citizens and the legitimacy of strategies of containment—of border controls, suspension of airline travel, contact tracing, and quarantine of people from the region, despite any evidence that these strategies would have a positive effect (Dionne & Seay, 2015, p. 7).

The slate upon which the outbreak in the region was written was the legacies of colonialism and the protracted violent conflicts that brutalized Sierra Leone and Liberia from the late 1980s and spread to Guinea in 2001, which ended in a fragile post-conflict peace in 2003. Conflicts in the region fostered highly militarized societies and the "absence of strong local institutions that might diagnose and stop such outbreaks and care for the afflicted" (Farmer, 2015). The vast wealth of the small political elite tied to resource extraction and the development industries was in stark contrast to the insecurity of the majority of the population (Anderson & Beresford, 2016; Bardosh, Leach, & Wilkinson, 2015; Farmer, 2015). The region shared the legacies of enslavement and colonization that shaped the developmental trajectories of their economies and polities. All three countries have endured neoliberal restructuring through World Bank Structural Adjustment Programs (SAPs). Today, they are largely export-driven economies dominated by minerals and cash crops. All three are highly gender-stratified societies characterized by labour exploitation, deep rural impoverishment, high levels of youth unemployment, and the rapid growth of slums.

The WHO declared EVD a PHEIC in August of 2014. In Liberia, it took months for medical outreach and infrastructure to reach hard-hit areas, and the epidemic had largely passed by the time Ebola treatment centres and community care centres were on the ground (Bardosch, Leach, & Wilkinson, 2016, p. 78). While a more rapid response would indeed have made a difference, as Bardosh, Leach, and Wilkinson explain, "the interlocking socio-political, economic and historical processes that have effectively perpetuated deep-seated inequalities in income, health

and political inclusion is where the source of the epidemic was located" (2016, p. 76). They characterize the response as fragmented, confusing, and top-down, with messages that bred suspicion of strangers, severely under-equipped health systems that were rapidly overwhelmed, a dramatic collapse of civil society and local economies, personal tragedy as loved ones died, and the normalization of road checkpoints, curfews, and massive quarantine (2016, pp. 77–8).

Aisha Fofana Ibrahim illuminates the ways in which gendered structural inequalities played out in the crisis in Sierra Leone. The social position of girls and women as the first line of response meant that for months they were responsible for the sick in the absence of basic knowledge and protections. The health care system was under-resourced and unable to provide essential care. This meant that women took on the care burden that the state and other actors were not providing, often becoming sole providers for children when men succumbed to disease or were unable to provide sustenance. The closure of schools presented additional care burdens for women and an increased risk for girls. Ibrahim argues that many of the disproportionate gendered social costs could have been avoided (2017, p. 167). Sophie Harman's literature survey of gender narratives in Ebola strategies and in World Bank and WHO health system strengthening plans uncovered a number of "conspicuous invisibilities" at every point in the international response (2016). While some attention was paid to the different biological impact on men and women, such as the maternal health crisis that unfolded as health systems were overwhelmed by Ebola patients, Harman noted that the gendered norms of care and social reproduction were invisible (2016, p. 524). When women were mentioned in broader reports, it was often in a few scant sentences, and there was little evidence that specific concerns were addressed in the wider response (2016, pp. 528–30). Women were reduced to the "vulnerable group" of mothers, with no acknowledgement of their role as caregivers in both formal and informal health care systems, in caring for orphaned children and as traders and income providers. Women's particular vulnerabilities to personal and economic losses, despite their critical roles in food production and cross-border trade, were also ignored (Diggins & Mills, 2015; IASC 2015).

In the context of the Ebola outbreak, the tendency was to emphasize "non-modern" or "culturalist" explanations for women's specific vulnerabilities, such as maternal mortality, as located exclusively in patriarchal practices. These types of narratives work to deflect attention from deep structures of inequality. While it was abundantly clear that patriarchal practices existed, this explanation masked the extent to which these practices were linked to broader structures of impoverishment and inequality. Diggins and Mills pointed out that:

> Given the utterly shattered state of [Sierra Leone's] post-war health system, we might question how logical it was to view poor reproductive health as evidence of gender discrimination; or how possible it could ever be to address Ebola or maternal mortality as stand-alone problems, in isolation from each other or more comprehensive structural investment, building the basic capacity of health care systems (2015, p. 2).

Although the virus was contained, the gendered consequences of the epidemic in West Africa will remain for years to come. The "emergency within the emergency" (Vetter et al., 2016) is the thousands of Ebola survivors with a range of longer-term aftereffects of the virus. Some are very serious and include neurological complications, vision problems, severe fatigue, and muscle weakness. Mental health challenges of survivors are magnified by increased food insecurity, the scarcity of access to medical services, the closing of schools and businesses, and local people's distrust of the health care system (Vetter et al., 2016,

pp. 85–9). Caring for survivors may well intensify women's unpaid care labours for years to come. Calls from the Inter-Agency Standing Committee Reference Group on Humanitarian Action highlight the most pressing issues for gender justice in the epidemic's aftermath: they call for an explicit gender-integrated response and the participation of women and girls in all communities in the recovery process across the board (IASC, 2015). This response includes calls for livelihood support and for the protection of women and girls in the context of the curtailment of security, including family planning and access to contraception, social and justice services, girls' education, and entitlements for caregivers (IASC, 2015).

Zika

The Zika virus, first discovered in 1947 in Uganda, is transmitted through the bite of the *Aedes aegypti* species of mosquito. Zika can also be transmitted through the blood, semen, and vaginal fluids of an infected person. It is a relatively mild virus; about 80 per cent of people with Zika are asymptomatic, and when symptoms do occur, they are typically mild.

According to an investigative report, *The Zika effect* (2016), reports of one confirmed case of "the deadly mosquito virus Zika" drew media attention to "a foreign pathogen threatening U.S. shores" (2016). Zika was declared a PHEIC by the director-general of the WHO in February 2016 because of a significant cluster of microcephaly in infants born to mothers with the virus in Brazil. In October 2015, the Brazil Ministry of Health reported a 20-fold increase in cases in infants that corresponded to a high prevalence of suspected Zika cases in the northeast of the country. The virus spread throughout South and Central America and into the Caribbean and the United States. However, the overwhelming number of babies born with microcephaly remained concentrated in the northeast of Brazil: 2366 of the global 2726 cases, as of 23 February 2017 (PAHO/WHO, 2017). It has been confirmed that Zika is the cause of microcephaly in newborn babies exposed to the Zika virus in utero. These babies have smaller than usual brains and can face a lifetime of mental disabilities of varying intensity, as well as seizures and sight and hearing problems.

The burden of the response to the Zika outbreak fell to women who were of childbearing age or who were pregnant. The mainstay of prevention was to minimize exposure to mosquito bites by eliminating mosquito vectors through public health campaigns, personal protective measures such as wearing long sleeves, pants, and hats, using insect repellent and bed nets, and staying indoors with screened or closed windows or air-conditioning. Women were specifically instructed to put off pregnancy through the use of **family planning** and contraception. Screening and monitoring for congenital birth defects was recommended for pregnant women. There was silence on the very different realities of girls and women with regard to the extent to which their material circumstances allowed them to follow such directives.

The great majority of women who gave birth to babies with Zika in Brazil lived in dense zones of poverty where access to such protections was not readily available. In the city of Recife, considered "ground zero" of the epidemic, volunteers and soldiers went door to door to provide information to people on how to protect themselves. But as journalist Sarah Bosley reported, many women in the *favelas* could not afford insect repellent, let alone a new set of window screens. Given the absence of piped water and sanitation, vector

Rozilene Ferreira with her three-month-old son, Arthur, waiting their turn to see a doctor at a hospital in Recife, Brazil, in 2016.

Mauricio Lima/The New York Times/Redux

control was difficult. The proliferation of the mosquito population in the poor *favelas* of Brazil is the consequence of inadequate municipal sewage management, extremely dense urban development, and the reliance on open-reservoir stagnant drinking water (Truong et al., 2016, p. 1089).

But the directive to avoid pregnancy was the most problematic. Although research on the sexual transmission of the virus is ongoing, the current science demonstrates that it can remain in semen longer than in other bodily fluids and that the majority of cases of sexual transmission have been male-to-female (CDC, 2017). The HIV/AIDS pandemic exposed the complexities of addressing "high risk" sexual behaviour, of how critical poverty, poor health care systems, gender-based violence, and racialized and gendered inequalities exposed the utility of particular policy responses (O'Manique, 2004). It became clear that sexual behaviour takes place within a broader context of power relations, including gendered power relations. For the impoverished women living in the centre of the Zika health emergency, 56 per cent of pregnancies were unintended (Roa, 2016, p. 843). According to Roa, shaping the "tragic failures of reproductive health and rights" was the poor quality of sex education, poor access to contraception, a high prevalence of gender-based violence, and gendered power relations that made the negotiation of safe sex less than straightforward (2016, p. 843).

Furthermore, laws that govern girls' and women's sexual reproductive rights in South America are among the most restrictive and punitive in the world. In Brazil, abortion is a crime punishable by up to three years in jail, with exceptions for rape or when the woman's life is at risk. Wealthy women can find discreet and safe access to abortion services, but poor women must seek out clandestine and dangerous ways to terminate pregnancies (Yamin, 2016). Donald Trump's reinstatement of the "global gag rule," which withholds USAID funding from any organization overseas that so much as offers information on reproductive health services, including abortion, has produced a chilling effect in the region while emboldening evangelical legislators to further curtail women's exercise of sexual and reproductive health rights. The impact falls on poor mothers, who face the long-term burden of caring for children throughout their lives; the effects on their education and livelihoods are ignored in policy responses (Bosley, 2016).

The epidemic has, however, mobilized feminist activists throughout the Americas against the antipathy toward women's sexual and reproductive health rights in global health governance as well as in state laws. It has also cast a light on the systemic inequality and structural violence experienced by racialized women living in critical poverty.

What Do Ebola and Zika Tell Us?

Lost from view is that unequal global disease burden and its impacts are a consequence of deep structures of inequality and structural violence, regardless of their specific biological origins. The chronic, endemic diseases of poverty and inequality do not have the potential to dramatically disrupt the states and material interests of Northern countries. Nor do they pose a direct threat to the lives of the rich. But new pathogens will likely continue to develop with increasing frequency and speed, given that the conditions of their emergence are intensifying rather than abating. Recent studies illuminate that climate change and biodiversity loss are feeding off each other and that the human destruction of nature is rapidly eroding the capacity to provide food, water, and security for billions of people (Watts et al., 2018). Capital accumulation by some depends on exploiting the resources of labour of others and, as Salleh points out, "undercuts the very materiality of environmental conditions that make it possible" (2016, p. 953). In spite of the extent to which climate change can be linked to the lifestyles of the affluent, affluence-related climate impacts are not on the global agenda.

According to the *World inequality report 2018*, the bottom half of the global population owns less

Emerging Research

Feminist political ecology is an emerging field of research that critically examines the relationships between ecological destruction, social-economic inequalities rooted in contemporary global capitalism, and gender injustices. In communities experiencing both the economic and ecological impacts of our current economic model, it is the invisible and undervalued labour of social reproduction that ensures not only bare life and human health. This labour in many instances also protects the local ecosystems that are vital to human health. This feminized labour will continue to intensify with increased inequality and the impacts of climate change. It is in this context that we can understand the limitations of both health security and humanitarian biomedicine.

than 1 per cent of global wealth, while the richest 10 per cent owns 88 per cent; the top 1 per cent alone owns half. While the Eurocentric development model exploits both nature and bodies, the institutionalization of both global health security and humanitarian biomedicine invites technocratic and market-based solutions and entrenches neoliberal systems of political and economic management. The approaches pose no threat to corporate profits and private power and in fact support its expansion into "development." This illuminates the urgency of developing a deeper understanding of the gendered and racialized structural violence that shapes both the conditions that incubate health emergencies and their responses. This is an important project not just for girls and women but for humanity as a whole.

How Do We Address These Violences and Legacies?

Competing and overlapping conceptions of health security remain. They are reflected in the tension between the conception of health as a human security issue linked to a deeper analysis of the ideological and structural forces that shape human health and the dominant view of health as a national and global security concern in which new pathogens need to be contained so as not to disrupt endless growth. The dominant narratives continue to pay little attention to the conditions that cause

humanitarian crises. Nor do they address in any meaningful way the social suffering of those who fall ill or experience most intensely the multiple impacts of epidemics. We know that we are not all "equally vulnerable," yet current responses intensify the gendered and racialized violences that are structured into the deeply troubling world that is our home. There is a need for a deeper analysis of these conditions, how they have become normalized, and why they persist in contemporary practices.

The two cases point to the need for a shift from the dominance of emergency responses that focus only on the crisis and its containment and that leave the foundations of health emergencies and the foundations of structural violence intact. Today's health emergencies leave deep scars on the bodies and lives of people who already pay the largest price for a world order that does not sustain the exercise of human rights, life, or dignity. Without denying the need for rapid responses in the face of infectious diseases, it is becoming clear that the two primary regimes of global health are not working.

A starting point in terms of emergency responses should involve paying closer attention to the impacts of health emergencies on the most vulnerable. The current regime of global health security is not accountable to those who undertake the vast bulk of care labour in the context of gendered and racialized structural violence. Nor does it begin to address the material conditions that nurture viral contagion and disease spread. Today, we are

> **Call to Action**
>
> There are many organizations and movements committed to structural change in the arenas of gender and health. Among them are Development Alternatives with Women for a New Era (DAWN), Women's Global Network for Reproductive Rights (WGNRR), and The People's Health Movement. It is also critical to understand the symbiotic relationship of all life on the planet—human, animal, and plant—and our profound interdependence. Other organizations, such as the Extinction Rebellion, support movements for ecological justice and also require a diversity of voices and actions. Join one of the organizations mentioned, or find a group based in your own community that you can support through volunteering.

witnessing the growth of political movements for climate and economic justice, anti-racism, gender and sexuality rights, and democracy. What is at the core of all these movements is the basic quest for the rights of all people to flourish within their communities—in essence, the right to genuine health security, with flesh-and-blood bodies at the centre.

Tying It Together

This chapter has cast a critical feminist lens on contemporary practices of global health security. It has argued that today's responses to global health emergencies have been shaped by legacies of conquest and colonization and are compatible with current practices of neoliberal capitalist development. The examples of recent responses to Ebola Virus Disease and Zika demonstrate some of the concrete ways in which current practices of global health security can intensify the gendered and racialized violences experienced by women in the zone of the emergency response. They also leave intact the material conditions that nurture viral contagion and disease spread in the first place. Responses make invisible those who are most vulnerable and who undertake the vast bulk of care labour in the context of gendered and racialized structural violence. There is a need to understand and address the structural conditions that nurture humanitarian crises and the social suffering of those who fall ill or experience most intensely the multiple impacts of health emergencies.

DISCUSSION QUESTIONS

1. What is health? What are the necessary conditions for all humans (regardless of nationality, class, age, race, sexuality, ability, etc.) to live a healthy life, both physically and mentally?

2. What are the structural conditions (the social determinants of health) that engender the good or bad health of various populations?

3. How are the legacies of colonialism and our contemporary neoliberal project shaping health inequalities today?

4. What understanding of health underpins the dominant discourses and practices of 1) health security and 2) humanitarian biomedicine?

5. In what ways can a feminist postcolonial framework broaden and deepen more generally our understanding of human health?

SUGGESTIONS FOR FURTHER READING

Davies, S.E., & Bennett, B. (2016). A gendered human rights analysis of Ebola and Zika: Locating gender in global health emergencies. *International Affairs, 92*(5), 1041–60. This paper expands on the gender-blindness of responses to public health emergencies and the extent to which international advisories acknowledge the impact of gender inequalities existing in health emergencies.

Forana, I.A. (2017). "I am a woman. How can I not help?" Gender performance and the spread of Ebola in Sierra Leone. In I. Abdullah & I. Rashid (Eds), *Understanding West Africa's Ebola epidemic* (pp. 163–86). London, UK: Zed Books. This book chapter is based upon findings from a study of the impact of EVD on women and girls. The author was the main researcher.

Petchesky, R. (2012). Biopolitics at the crossroads of sexuality and disaster: The case of Haiti. Sexuality Policy Watch Working Paper 8. Retrieved from: https://www.sxpolitics.org/wp-content/uploads/2012/04/spw-wp8-rpetchesky-in-schrecker-2012-biopolitics-at-the-crossroads-of-sexuality-and-disaster-the-case-of-haiti.pdf. This working paper rethinks public health crises through the perspective of Foucauldian biopolitics and feminist-intersectional theory.

MULTIMEDIA SUGGESTION

On The Media Podcast: The Zika Effect, 12 Feb. 2016

https://www.wnycstudios.org/story/on-the-media-2016-02-12

This podcast illuminates how Zika serves as a window into global questions surrounding climate change and reproductive rights.

REFERENCES

Abdullah, I., & Rashid, I. (2017). *Understanding West Africa's Ebola epidemic: Towards a political economy.* London, UK: Zed Books.

Anderson, E.-L., & Beresford, A. (2016). Infectious injustice: The political foundations of the Ebola crisis in Sierra Leone. *Third World Quarterly, 37*(3), 468–86.

Arner, K. (2013). Making global commerce into international health diplomacy: Consuls and disease control in the age of revolutions. *Journal of World History, 24*(4), 771–96.

Banks, N., Hulme, D., & Edwards, M. (2014). NGOs, states, and donors revisited: Still too close for comfort? *World Development, 66,* 707–18.

Bardosh, K. (2016). Unpacking the politics of zoonosis research and policy. In K. Bardosh (Ed.), *One health: Science, politics, and zoonotic disease in Africa.* Abingdon, UK: Routledge.

Bardosh, K., Leach, M., & Wilkinson, A. (2016). The limits of rapid response: Ebola and structural violence in West Africa. In K. Bardosh (Ed.), *One health: Science, politics, and zoonotic disease in Africa.* Abingdon, UK: Routledge.

Bennett, C., & McMichael, A. (2012). Global environmental change and human health. In T. Shrecker (Ed.), *The Ashgate research companion to the globalization of health.* Farnman, UK: Ashgate.

Biehl, J., & Petryna, A. (2013). *When people come first: Critical studies in global health.* Princeton, NJ: Princeton University Press.

Birn, A.E. (2012). From plagues to peoples: Health in the global/international agenda. In T. Schrecker (Ed.), *The Ashgate research companion to the globalization of health* (pp. 39–60). Farnham, UK: Ashgate.

Birn, A.E., Pillay, Y., and Holtz, T.H. (2009). *Textbook on international health* (3rd edn). Oxford, UK: Oxford University Press.

Blackburn, Robin. (1997). *The making of world slavery: From the baroque to the modern, 1492–1800.* New York, NY: Verso.

Bosley, S. (2016). Heartbreak and hardship for women in Brazil as Zika crisis casts deep shadow. *The Guardian International,* 5 May. Available at: https://www.theguardian.com/global-development/2016/may/05/zika-crisis brazil-women-heartbreak-hardship (accessed 24 February 2017).

CDC (Centres for Disease Control). (2017). *Centres for Disease Control: Zika and sexual transmission.* Atlanta, GA: CDC. Available at: https://www.google.ca/search?q=Zika+chances+of+spread+through+sex-&ie=utf-8&oe=utf-8&gws_rd=cr&ei=ZbCxWJeN MKu3jwTK0bHYBQ (accessed 29 January 2017).

Davies, S., Karmadt-Scott, A., & Rushton, S. (2015). *Disease diplomacy: International norms and global health security*. Baltimore, MD: John Hopkins University Press.

Davis, M. (2005). *Monster at our door: The global threat of avian influenza*. New York, NY: New Press.

Diggins, J., & Mills, E. (2015). The pathology of inequality: Ebola in West Africa. IDS Practice Paper in Brief. London, UK: Institute of Development Studies/UK Aid.

Dionne, K.Y., & Seay, L. (2015). Perceptions about Ebola in America: Othering and the role of knowledge about Africa. *Political Science and Politics, 48*(1), 6–7.

Escobar, A. (1995). *Encountering development: The making and unmaking of the Third World*. Princeton, NY: Princeton University Press.

Facundo, A., Chancel, L., Piketty, T., Saez, E., & Zucman, G., The World Inequality Report 2018. accessed at https://wir2018.wid.world/credits.html

Farmer, P. (2015). The caregivers disease. *London Review of Books*, 21 May.

Federici, S. (2004). *Caliban and the witch: Women, the body and primitive accumulation*. New York, NY: Autonomedia.

Harman, S. (2016). Ebola, gender, and the conspicuously invisible women in global health governance. *Third World Quarterly, 37*(3), 524–41.

Hawkesworth, M. (2016). *Embodied power: Demystifying disembodied politics*. New York, NY: Routledge.

IASC (Inter-Agency Standing Committee Reference Group for Humanitarian Action). (2015). *Humanitarian crisis in West Africa (Ebola) gender alert*. Geneva, Switzerland: World Health Organization. Available at: www.unwomen.org/~/media/headquarters/attachments/sections/library/publicatins/2015/iasc%20gender%20reference%20group%20-%20gender%20alert%20west%20africa%20ebola%202%20%20february%202015.pdf (accessed October 20 2016).

Ibrahim, A.F. (2017). "I am a Woman. How can I not help?" Gender performance and the spread of Ebola in Sierra Leone. In I. Abdukla & Ismail Rashid (Eds), *Understanding West Africa's Ebola epidemic*. London, UK: Zed Books.

King, N.B. (2002). Security, disease, commerce: Ideologies of post-colonial global health. *Social Studies of Science, 32*(5–6), 763–89.

Lakoff, A. (2010). Two regimes of global health. *Humanity: An International Journal of Human Rights, Humanitarianism, and Development, 1*(1), 59–79.

Marchand, M., & Runyan, A.S. (2011). Introduction: Feminist sightings of global restructuring: New and old conceptualizations. In M. Marchand & A. Runyan (Eds), *Gender and global restructuring: Sightings, sites and resistances*. New York, NY: Routledge.

Muskateem, S. (2011). "She must go overboard & shall go overboard": Diseased bodies and the spectacle of murder at sea. *Atlantic Studies, 8*(3), 301–16.

Nokov, J. (2015). Infecting the Constitution. *Political Science and Politics, 48*(1), 9–10.

O'Manique, C. (2004). *Neoliberalism and AIDS crisis in sub-Saharan Africa: Globalization's pandemic*. Basingstoke, UK: Palgrave Macmillan.

PAHO/WHO. (2017). Zika cumulative cases. 23 February. Available at www.paho.org/hq/index.php?option=com_content&view=article&id=12390&mid=42090 (accessed 24 February 2017).

Peterson, V.S. (2012). Rethinking theory. *International Feminist Journal of Politics, 14*(1), 1–31.

Roa, M. (2016). Zika virus outbreak: Reproductive health and rights in Latin America. *The Lancet, 387*, 843.

Salleh, A. (2016). Climate, water and livelihood skills: A post-development reading of the SDGs. *Globalizations, 13*(6), 952–9.

The Zika Effect. (2016). On The Media Podcast. 12 February. https://www.wnycstudios.org/story/on-the-media-2016-02-12.

Trietler, V.B., & Boatcâ, M. (2016). Dynamics of inequality in global perspective. *Current Sociology, 64*(2), 159–71.

Truong, L., Gonnerman, G., Simonich, M.T., & Tanguay, R.L. (2016). Assessment of the developmental and neurotoxicity of the mosquito control larvicide, Priproxyfen, using embryonic zebrafish. *Environmental Pollution, 218*, 1089–93.

Vetter, P., Kaiser, L., Schibler, M., Cigenecki, I., & Bauch, D.G. (2016). Sequelae of Ebola Virus Disease: The emergency within the emergency. *Lancet Infectious Diseases, 16*(6), e82–91.

Watts, N., et al. (2018). The *Lancet* countdown on health and climate change: From 25 years of inaction to a global transformation for public health. *Lancet, 391*, 581–630.

Weir, L. (2015). Inventing global health security: 1994–2005. In S. Rushton & J. Youde (Eds), *Routledge handbook of global health security*. London, UK: Routledge.

WHO (World Health Organization). (1978). *Declaration of Alma Ata*. Geneva, Switzerland: WHO. Available at: http://www.euro.who.int/__data/assets/pdf_file/0009/113877/E93944.pdf (accessed 17 June 2016).

Yamin, A.E. (2016). To fight Zika, we must fight poverty and powerlessness and ensure that women enjoy their rights. Boston, MA: FXB Center for Health and Human Rights, Harvard University. Available at: http://fxb.harvard.edu/4941-2/> (accessed 21 December 2016).

PART V

Bodies of Activism

The chapters in Part V contribute to the literature exploring types of global solidarity work that are creatively redefining what activism involves (as seen in the works of N. Naples and M. Desai [2002]). In addition, the chapters in this part of the collection examine the current presumptions of neoliberal globalization and expose the ways that these presumptions generate both constraints and possibilities for activists to engage in challenging racism and its intersections with gender. Through evaluating case studies from across the globe, we see how intersectionality and inequality are contextualized in shaping women's agencies, gender relations, identities, politics of belonging, and means of empowerment. In addition, these chapters examine how people who experience inequality and the politics of exclusion or social injustice by virtue of their gender, ethnicity, and/or class are the most vulnerable to the new adversities that appear in the process of globalization.

In "Making All Black Lives Matter: Transnational Genealogies of Resistance," Robyn Maynard explores Black feminist activist movements in both the Global North and South. She invites us to examine contemporary inequalities facing Black communities through a transnational, postcolonial, and intersectional lens. Her chapter offers a historical perspective on the global realities of anti-Black racism and the present-day Black social movements. Readers will learn about Black feminist movements worldwide and gain a greater understanding of community-led activist practices.

In "Global Mining and Decolonial Feminist Activism," Tracy Glynn examines the role of resource extraction in ongoing projects of colonialism, imperialism, and hegemonic masculinity. She investigates how global resource extraction has particular effects on women, including women from different social groupings. Glynn shows the various ways that women respond to exploitative resource extraction, and she underscores the importance of a decolonial feminist praxis for activism at resource extraction sites.

In "Forced Sterilization in Times of Sustainable Development," Ana Isla examines the contradictions of global politics in United Nations institutions. In particular, she analyzes the relationship between reproductive rights and population growth. This chapter reveals the relationships between debt, environmental crisis, and forced sterilization in Peru. Isla helps us to differentiate between reproductive rights and voluntary surgical contraceptive programs. Overall, the chapter sheds light on the impact of forced sterilization policies and the current levels of violence toward women in Peru.

In "Grannies, Rockers, and Oil Rigs: Mobilizing Age in Intersectional Climate Justice Alliances," May Chazan and Melissa Baldwin invite us to explore and define solidarity as a concept. They help us to better understand what is meant by solidarity among people who are identified by their differences. These authors look at a case of women mobilizing their own social location and specifically how the Raging Grannies have mobilized age, gender, and whiteness toward political ends. The chapter considers various practices of solidarity within and beyond frontline protest. Chazan and Baldwin ask what it means to explore our own social locations and to see what those locations might offer for participation in difference coalitional movements. The chapter invites us to consider whose needs and perspectives are ideally foregrounded in a coalitional politics that strives toward critical relationships based on solidarity.

In "The Demand: Pasts, Presents, and Futures of Black, Indigenous, and Queer of Colour Feminisms," Aleyda Marisol Cervantes Gutierrez, Tahlia Natachu, Belina Letesus Seare, Tamara Lea Spira, Mollie Jean West, and Verónica Nelly Vélez explore the histories of Black, Indigenous, and queer of colour feminisms as they intersect with contemporary student movements. These authors help us to recognize the inherent power of students to challenge institutional violence. Their chapter offers tools for mapping the legacies of radical feminist struggles in relation to racial, sexual, and gender justice culminating on university campuses today. An examination of the connections between student activism on college campuses and broader activist networks such as the Movement for Black Lives is also undertaken in this chapter. Readers will learn how student movements are formed on national and local levels and the differences between movements based on neoliberal "inclusion" and those grounded in collective liberation. The authors explain the importance of developing collective consciousness as a tool for resisting institutional tactics that are designed to isolate students and prevent their struggles from connecting. This is a chapter that helps students to situate themselves within the larger genealogy of struggle and movement organizing.

REFERENCE

Naples, N., & Desai, M. (2002). *Women's activism and globalization: Linking local struggles and transnational politics*. New York, NY: Routledge.

CHAPTER 15

◇

Making Black Lives Matter
Race, Resistance, and Global Movements for Black Liberation

Robyn Maynard

Learning Objectives

In this chapter, you will:

- discover Black feminist activist movements from the Global North and South;
- examine contemporary inequalities facing Black communities through a transnational, postcolonial, and intersectional lens;
- gain a historical perspective on the global realities of anti-Black racism as well as present-day Black social movements;
- learn about Black feminist movements worldwide;
- understand community-led activist practices.

Introduction

The principal aim of this chapter is to introduce readers to global contemporary Black liberation movements in the Black diaspora, with a particular focus on Black feminist organizing in Brazil and North America. To place these movements in their proper historical context, readers will be introduced to global histories of the transatlantic slave trade and colonization and the enduring legacies of **state (and state-sanctioned) violence** on and across the Black diaspora. Unique attention is granted, where possible, to the realities of cis and transgender women and gender non-conforming (GNC) people. While grounded in an intersectional, postcolonial understanding of oppression, this chapter provides the reader with snapshots of the **Black radical tradition** (Robinson, 1983) in the Global North and South, pointing to the need for a trans-national understanding of **anti-Black racism** and the structural conditions faced by Black women and GNC people in the diaspora as well as organized resistance to racial and gendered discrimination.

History: Slavery and Colonialism as Global Practices, with Global Legacies

In order to understand contemporary Black liberation struggles in the diaspora, it is necessary to understand histories of slavery and colonialism because these are central facets to the history of

Black life in the Caribbean and the Americas. Slavery was a global project, which, alongside colonialism and settler colonialism, reorganized much of the world and its inhabitants into hierarchies of "race," including hierarchies of proximity to who was deemed to be a human being based on traits assumed to be inborn and natural. While "race" has been debunked as a real scientific category—at least as far as it affects attributes like intelligence, motivation, and other measures—racial pseudo-science, eugenics, and culturalist forms of racism have nonetheless structured, for centuries, the distribution of power within and across the world's populations. Notions of "race" have been used to create and justify hierarchical categories of personhood. White, male, and European subjects occupy the highest position and Black subjects deemed as hardly human or entirely subhuman, less than sentient, less able to feel pain, prone to danger and crime. Black Brazilian philosopher Denise Ferreira da Silva writes that "[r]acial subjection . . . can no longer be distinguished from global subjection" (2007, p. xix). And indeed, the meanings assigned to Blackness resonate globally and do not begin or end with any particular nation. Following from the works of Caribbean philosopher and social theorist Sylvia Wynter (1995), it is clear that with the institutionalisation of global colonization and slavery, the meaning of "Blackness" became, globally, synonymous with a lesser form—or *genre*—of human life.

The social grammar of race—and the global denigration of Blackness—that was globalized in the 15th century emerged as a justification for Black enslavement—that is, it occurred with and from the massive social, political, and economic violence of chattel slavery and the centuries-long massive exploitation of the labour of enslaved Black peoples across the Americas. The profits emerging from slavery made the "civilized" world possible from an economic perspective and also created the conditions for the massive global inequalities facing "under-developed"

(re: over-exploited) nations of Africa and the Caribbean (see Rodney, 1981; Williams, 1944). Europe and its former colonial outposts, the settler colonies of the US, Canada, and Australia, have an economic base formed, broadly, from the economies of the transatlantic slave trade and the widespread institutionalization of slavery from the 15th to the 19th century.

Yet even as the modern world was built on stolen Black labour—and, in settler colonies such as the US, and Canada, on *stolen lands*—this was never without massive large-scale resistance, freedom-making, and large- and small-scale rebellions on the part of the enslaved, which continually posed massive challenges to the social, economic, and political orders violently imposed by Europeans. This is true on a global scale: as Caribbean political theorist C.L.R. James (1999), (May, 2008) and African-American thinker and activist Anna Julia Cooper have documented, the 1791 Haitian revolution—the first successful slave rebellion—challenged the political and epistemic dominance of the French empire.

From enslavement to the present, Black women have contributed in large numbers toward resistance efforts, both local and transnational in scope. Yet historians of Black radicalism are only beginning to catch up to this reality. Black women have always taken part in formal and informal organizing efforts and have been part of crafting the broader political and theoretical aspects of Black liberation work. This is a reality that Black feminist historians are only beginning to uncover. Joy James, an important Black feminist intellectual, has addressed the fact that even well-known Black radical women like Assata Shakur, while elevated as icons, continue to have their radical intellectual and political contributions absented from public memory (James, 1999).

Black women have always played central roles in both resisting and theorizing Black oppression and resistance.[1] Studies on Black feminism frequently centre, or focus entirely, on Black women in the US. Of course, Black women in the United States have played an important role in contributing to political theorizations about Black women's lives, as well as toward shaping activism and organizing for subsequent generations, as seen in the lives and legacies of Harriet Tubman and Sojourner Truth. In another example, in the late 19th century Ida B. Wells, an African-American activist and journalist, took part in transatlantic anti-lynching campaigns, drawing attention to extralegal racist violence with impacts that were definitively global in their scope (Silkey, 2015). In 1974, a Black feminist collective based in the United States, the Combahee River Collective, addressed Black women's marginalization vis-à-vis their gender, race, and class, naming this the "interlocking" nature of oppression (1986). These overlapping forms of oppression were addressed, as well, by Angela Y. Davis in *Women, race and class* (1981) and in the 1980s/1990s explicated as "intersectionality" by Kimberlé Williams Crenshaw, Black feminist legal theorist (2019). Yet more recently, Carole Boyce Davies (2008) has addressed earlier genealogies of this term, as forwarded by Caribbean-born Black communist feminist Claudia Jones (1949), who theorized the *triple oppression* of Black women in "An end to the neglect of the Negro woman" (1949).

Yet despite ongoing US cultural hegemony, Black women have been contributing to political theory and challenging racial and sexual discrimination on a global scale across centuries. Black women's involvement in slave rebellions transcends national borders. In the first successful slave rebellion, Haitian women like Cécile Fatiman, a voudou priestess, played an important role in the ceremony that preceded the launch of the Haitian revolution in 1791, along with Anacaona, Catherine Flon, also active in revolutionary struggle, even as their histories are often overlooked because of the gendered nature of popular memory (Accilien et al., 2006). Enslaved Black women in Barbados played important roles in organized

revolt, marronage, and developing community-based survival strategies (Beckles, 2000). Black women also resisted with their individual acts of bravery and courage. In Montreal, for example, Marie-Joseph Angélique, an enslaved Black woman, was hanged and burned in 1734 as punishment for her alleged involvement in a fire that destroyed the Old Port of the city (Cooper, 2006). Further, throughout the 20th century, Black women in Costa Rica, the United Kingdom, and well beyond were part of global pan-African freedom struggles (Leeds, 2013; Perry, 2015).

Global Legacies in the Present

Black Lives Matter today is arguably among the most *visible* embodiments of a resurgent Black (feminist) politic and movement, but there is a long and global history of Black feminist organizing—that is, organizing led by Black women addressing racial *and* gendered oppression (alongside a multitude of others). Racism today can be identified by what Black feminist geographer Ruth Wilson Gilmore defines as "the state-sanctioned or extralegal production and exploitation of group-differentiated vulnerability to premature death" (2007, p. 28). Yet racism is not experienced identically by all racialized groups and is also experienced differently according to factors like gender, sexuality, class, (dis)ability, and religion, among others. Across generations, Black women, often but not always identifying as feminist, have created multiple ways of identifying the multiple experiences of domination that occur simultaneously for Black women because of inseparable lived realities of their gender, race, and class, generally stemming from a global and anti-colonial perspective.

The US is frequently seen as the epicentre of racial anti-Black violence as well as global Black struggle—yet the violence of the transatlantic slave trade was global, and liberation-oriented struggles, too, have never been contained by

246 Part V Bodies of Activism

national borders or centred solely in the US. The legacy of the dehumanization of Black life evolved globally throughout slavery and continued after its abolition. For example, sociologist Vilna Bashi has documented that anti-Blackness has spanned across Canada, the United States, and the United Kingdom from the 16th century onward, under which "free" (i.e., un-enslaved) Black migration was both heavily controlled and actively discouraged through a series of formal and informal measures (Bashi, 2004).

In the empirical realm, significant efforts have been made recently by human rights organizations to draw attention to the ongoing realities facing Black communities worldwide as a legacy of the transatlantic slave trade. For instance, the United Nations declared 2015–24 the "International Decade for People of African Descent," based on the global realities of "multiple, aggravated or intersecting forms of discrimination" that render the global African diaspora—including migrants/refugees/asylum-seekers—uniquely precarious and marginalized when compared to other racial groups and thus requiring a distinct analysis (United Nations, 2018). The UN has acknowledged this to be a legacy of slavery and has decried ongoing, virulent, and widespread "[r]acism, structural discrimination, marginalization, hate speech and hate crimes" facing the African diaspora, whether as descendants of enslaved Africans or as migrants and/or refugees (United Nations Department of Public Information and the Office of the United Nations High Commissioner for Human Rights, n.d.). The world over, Black women play major roles in countering anti-Black racism in all of its incarnations. In the US, for example, under the rubric of #Sayhername, activist-scholars like Andrea Ritchie and Kimberlé Williams Crenshaw, who co-authored the report of the same name, have played an important role in bringing the realities of Black women from the margins into the mainstream (2015; see also Ritchie, 2017).

Moving outside a US-based frame, the following two case studies address the racial and gendered dimensions of anti-Black racism as well as how Black feminist organizing has responded.

Brazil

The next part of this chapter looks toward Brazil in order to illuminate anti-Blackness and Black resistance in the Global South.

Snapshot of Contemporary Realities Faced by Black Communities in Brazil

In 2005, Black persons made up nearly half (49.6 per cent) of the Brazilian population (Ciconello, 2008, p. 3). Two-thirds of prisoners are Black (including male and female prisoners). Women's incarceration has risen by 570 per cent in recent years (Geledés, 2016, p. 28). In 2013, Black women made up 51.8 per cent of the female population and 27.7 per cent of the total population of the country (IPEA, 2013, in Geledés, 2016, p. 11). Approximately 75 per cent of Black women live in poverty, frequently without access to sanitation, piped water, or garbage collection (Geledés, 2016, p. 11).

There was a 54.2 per cent increase in the murders of Black women between 2003 and 2013; in the same period, the rate of homicides of white women went down by 9.3 per cent (Geledés, 2016, p. 5). According to a report by Amnesty International, 79 per cent of the 1275 recorded killings by on-duty police officers in Rio between 2010 and 2013 were of Black persons (Amnesty International, 2015). While there is little data collected on the realities of LGBT Black populations in Brazil, available data suggests that Black LGBT populations are particularly vulnerable to sexual violence as well as to police abuse (Geledés, 2016, p. 25).

Nearly two-thirds of Black youths (64 per cent) "have dropped out of secondary education or are becoming increasingly old for the grades they are in at lower educational levels" as compared to 42 per cent of white youths (IPEA, 2007, p. 284, in Ciconello, 2008, p. 4).

Black Activism in Brazil

Black resistance in Brazil dates back nearly half a millennium. Tianna Paschel writes, "When we define the Black Lives Matter movement beyond a hashtag and a specific organizational configuration, we find that Afro–Latin Americans, just like African Americans in the U.S., have long articulated demands to be recognized as fully human" (2017). In South America and the Caribbean, maroon societies—made up of those who have escaped slavery—persisted across both regions spanning the 17th to 19th century. Enslaved peoples across the Americas resisted and fought the institution of slavery for generations in Brazil and well beyond (Ciconello, 2008, p. 7). One example in the early 20th century occurred in the between-war period when the Brazilian Black Front, an organization that included, at its largest point, 100,000 people, came together to address anti-Black racism and slavery's living legacy (Ciconello, 2008, p. 7). Later on, in the late 1970s, numerous Black organizations came together to form the Movimento Negro Unificado (MNU), or Unified Black Movement (Bairros, 2008, p. 50).

More recently, Black anthropologist Christen Smith has documented Black women's resistance to rampant police brutality, including Brazil's Black-led Reaja ou Será Mortx! (React or Die!) campaign geared toward addressing the genocidal conditions facing Black Brazilians (2017). Black women in Brazil have been highly visible in addressing ongoing realities of anti-Black racism, sexism, and classism. In 2015, more than 50,000 attended a march organized by and for Black women in Brazil entitled the "March against Racism and Violence and in Favour of Living Well (bem viver)" during which attendees were shot at and threatened by soldiers and ex-military officers (Geledés, 2016, p. 39). The organizers' manifesto read:

> We are 49 million black women—in other words, 25 per cent of the Brazilian population. We experience the most perverse racism and sexism by virtue of being black and women. We face daily white supremacy and patriarchy and sexism, which constitute a system of oppressions that prompt black women to fight for their own survival and the survival of their communities (National Black Women's March, 2016, p. 78).

Given that an estimated 4.2 million men and women who were captured from Africa were bought to Brazil—*more than one-third of those kidnapped and brought to the Americas*—(Andrews, in Ciconello, 2008), the role of Black feminist resistance here is of ongoing pertinence.

Canada

Next, you will learn about anti-Blackness, Black activism, and Black feminist struggle in Canada to help you think about race, gender, and resistance that happens in the **Global North** *outside* the United States.

Snapshot of Contemporary Realities Faced by Black Communities in Canada

Black populations (men and women) are incarcerated at a rate three times higher their proportion of the general population (Sapers, 2013). Black people are 70 per cent more likely to be shot by police than whites in encounters with the Toronto Police Services (OHRC, 2018).

In Toronto, 48 per cent of Black children live in families with incomes of less than $30,000 per year, as compared to 9 per cent of white children, representing a five-fold poverty rate disparity (Toronto District School Board, 2012, in Polyani et al., 2014); in Halifax, more than 33 per cent of

Black Nova Scotians are low-income in comparison to just over 15 per cent of non-Black Nova Scotians (African Nova Scotian Affairs, 2014). The last segregated school in Canada closed in 1983 in Nova Scotia, and Black youth remain subject to grossly disproportionate rates of suspension, expulsion, and streaming in large Canadian cities (Maynard, 2017).

Black Women's Activism in Canada

Slavery in pre-Confederation Canada was legal for more than 200 years until the British abolished slavery in its colonies in 1834. Black women were part of resisting slavery and later went on to address its long-standing legacies, fighting segregation, working to stop deportations, addressing police violence, and educating Black schoolchildren in the generations to follow (Bristow et al., 1994). This is the case even though Black women in Canada have been subject to high rates of poverty, economic exploitation, and erasure from the national psyche for centuries, which continues into the present (Brand, 1984; Maynard, 2017). In the 1920s through the 1950s, Black women in Ontario played important roles in organizing in their communities and internationally (Brand, 1991). In the 1970s, Caribbean-born domestic workers fought racist/sexist Canadian immigration laws (Lawson, 2013). Working against the erasure of Black women's day-to-day and more formal organizing from Canadian society and Black Canadian history, Black feminists living in Canada have continued to undertake important recoveries of Black women's histories, bringing their intellectual and political work into view. For example, in the 1980s the Black Women's Collective produced *Our Lives: Canada's first Black women's newspaper*, with participation from Angela Robertson, Dionne Brand, Afua Cooper, and Sylvia Hamilton. Bristow et al.'s *We're rooted here and you can't pull us up!* was released in 1994 and Afua Cooper's *The hanging of Angélique* in 2006, while Makeda Silvera's formative text, *Silenced! Talks with working class West Indian women about their lives and struggles as domestic workers in Canada* appeared in 1989. All of these texts played integral roles in bring Black women's lives and histories to the forefront.

More recent examples of Black women and GNC people fighting gender- and race-based injustice are Majiza Philip, a Black Montreal-based woman suing the Montreal police for breaking her arm in 2014, and a current class-action lawsuit undertaken by Arlene Gallone, who was held in solitary confinement for nine months, against Correction Services Canada (CSC), and Monica Forrester, a Black/Indigenous two-spirited sex worker activist who has been a leading voice to decriminalize sex work and for sex workers rights more broadly. As well, prison abolitionists like El Jones, poet, author of *Live from the Afrikan resistance*, host of *Black Power Hour*, and Nancy's Chair at Mount St Vincent University and grassroots organizing like queer and trans-led Black Lives Matter Toronto, who occupied police headquarters for more than two weeks in 2015 following the police killing of Andrew Loku, continue to play important public roles in challenging institutional anti-Black racism, sexism, and heteropatriarchy.

Tying It Together

Black freedom struggles have frequently been diasporic and transnational in nature, the result of the massive displacement that emerged from the forced transfer of nearly 15 million Africans over half a millennium. It is not merely theoretical to look at the transnational nature of Black struggle and of Black feminist struggle; if discrimination facing Black communities is global in its scope, so too is the response. After the assassination of Marielle Franco, a Black lesbian activist and city councillor in Rio de Janeiro who had been highly vocal about racist police killings, protests took place in New York, Paris, and Buenos Aires (Carvalho Carinhanha, 2018). Whether in Rio de Janeiro, Toronto, or London, Black activism across the diaspora and on the continent is of global relevance to freedom in the contemporary moment.

Freedom School

Public memory often privileges the more visible aspects of radical movements—demonstrations, uprisings, and public militancy—and underplays the important community-building traditions that also make up the history of Black activism in Canada and across the global Black diaspora. Yet teaching Black children to "love their Blackness" (Black Lives Matter Toronto, 2016) in a world that constantly questions the humanity of Black children is as radical and paradigm-shifting as an occupation of police headquarters. Black activism, both historically and contemporarily, has addressed injustice in a multiplicity of other ways, including at the level of education. Making far less headlines, in the summer of 2016 LeRoi Newbold, a trans activist and Black educator, organized a Freedom School for Black children aged 4 to 10. Schools in the greater Toronto area, like elsewhere in Canada and the United States, are a highly carceral and punitive institution for Black youth and children, who are disproportionately pathologized, disciplined, and expelled. Because many Black families in Toronto experience high rates of poverty, the Freedom School offered free and high-quality programming, culturally appropriate hot food, free transportation to and from Freedom School, and free childcare for younger children of the families who had enrolled their youth. Funded largely by community supporters, with many books donated by local Black bookstores, Freedom School gave Black youth access, sometimes for the first time in their lives, to an education that centred on Black dignity, resilience, the contributions of Black women, and queer and trans resistance. Along with expanding critical thinking skills and interactive art-based learning, the school taught youth to use technology that is frequently unavailable to Black youth from poor families. They learned about Marsha P. Johnson, Black trans icon, and her role in the Stonewall rebellion, the Bussa rebellion that helped to overthrow slavery in Barbados, the Haitian revolution, and the history of Marie-Joseph Angélique (Black Lives Matter Toronto, 2016).

Of course, Black radical education initiatives and feminist/proto-feminist Black education have their predecessors in generations past: for example, the incredible contributions of a Black woman teacher named Mary Bibb, whose story was captured by Afua P. Cooper (in Bristow et al., 1994), demonstrate that even in 19th-century Canada, Black communities had intervened within a racist education system. Black families fought to end segregated schooling in Ontario in 1965, and African Nova Scotians, too, have mobilized around education for generations (BLAC, 1994).

Call to Action

In the past several generations, students have played a major role in organizing against racial injustice. From the Student Nonviolent Coordinating Committee (SNCC) in the United States in the 1960s, through the anti–South African apartheid movements of the 1980s, up to #RhodesMustFall in 2015 in South Africa, students who have had the courage to stand on the right side of history have helped to fight injustice and challenge the politics of the status quo. Pay attention to what Black scholars and grassroots feminists are fighting for in your area, and find out how you can support them and get involved. Even small forms of support like fundraisers can make a major difference.

DISCUSSION QUESTIONS

1. Why is it important to recognize the global nature of anti-Black racism and resistance? Why do you think so much of the focus has been on the US-based Black liberation struggle?
2. Slavery has been formally abolished, yet persistent institutional racism continues to have an impact on Black communities. What are some other legacies of slavery embedded in state institutions beyond those addressed in this chapter?
3. Can you think of any pertinent local examples that exemplify the erasure of Black women's contributions to social justice movements? What could you do in your own work to challenge this erasure?
4. Drawing on the example of "Freedom School," can you think of other examples around the world when Black communities, educators, and parents have intervened in the "miseducation of Black youth"?
5. There are many similarities facing Black women across the Global North and the Global South—notably, the presence of anti-Black racism and misogyny. Yet the realities of Western imperialism (alongside class, education levels, etc.) mean that their lives are also structured by crucial differences. What are some important differences in the experiences of Black women in the Global North and the Global South, and how have Black women's movements worked to address this in the past?

SUGGESTIONS FOR FURTHER READING

Ware, Syrus Marcus, Hudson, Sandy, and Diverlus, Rodney. (Forthcoming). *Until we're free: Black Lives Matter in Canada*. Regina, SK: University of Regina Press. This book is an edited anthology by some of the team members of Black Lives Matter Toronto that provides context to addressing the legacy of their activism. The history of BLM-TO is discussed, as well as other topics related to Black feminist responses to state violence.

Perry, K.-K.Y. (2013). *Black women against the land grab: The fight for racial justice in Brazil*. Minneapolis, MN: University of Minnesota Press. This book is about contemporary Black women's activism in Brazil. It discusses Black women's leadership in community struggles against displacement, land grabs, and police violence.

Sharpe, C. (2016). *In the wake: On Blackness and being*. Durham, NC, and London, UK: Duke University Press. This book addresses the global conditions facing Black people's lives, spanning from Haiti to the Mediterranean Sea, looking to the always-present forms of Black being and Black refusal that cannot be contained/confined by anti-Blackness.

MULTIMEDIA SUGGESTIONS

Sisters in the struggle. Dirs Dionne Brand and Ginny Stikeman. National Film Board of Canada, Studio D, 1991, 49 minutes.
https://www.nfb.ca/film/sisters_in_the_struggle
This documentary features Black women in Canada who have been involved in feminist and labour organizing.

Say her name: The life and death of Sandra Bland. Dirs Kate Davis, David Heilbroner. 1 hour, 41 minutes, HBO.
This documentary investigates what happened to political activist Sandra Bland, who died while in police custody and whose death sparked a global conversation on the violence that Black women experience at the hands of the police.

Black perspectives, blog of the African American Intellectual History Society (AAIHS).
https://www.aaihs.org/about-black-perspectives
This blog, frequently updated, is based in the US and features informative and peer-reviewed short essays and book reviews that attend to intellectual and political work on Black life and Black struggle around the world.

REFERENCES

Accilien, C., et al. (2006). *Revolutionary freedoms: A history of survival, strength and imagination in Haiti*. Coconut Creek, FL: Caribbean Studies Press.

African Nova Scotian Affairs. (2014). African Nova Scotians today. Province of Nova Scotia.

Amnesty International. (2015). You killed my son: Homicides by military police in the city of Rio de Janeiro. Retrieved from: https://www.amnestyusa.org/files/youkilled_final_bx.pdf.

Bairros, L. (2008). A community of destiny: New configurations of racial politics in Brazil. *Souls, 10*(1), 50–3. doi: 10.1080/10999940801937771.

Bashi, V. (2004). Globalized anti-Blackness: Transnationalizing Western immigration law, policy, and practice. *Ethnic and Racial Studies, 27*(4), 584–606

Beckles, H.M. (2000). *Natural rebels: A social history of enslaved Black women in Barbados*. New Brunswick, NJ: Rutgers University Press.

BLAC (Black Learners Advisory Committee). (1994). BLAC report on education: Redressing inequity—Empowering Black learners. Halifax, NS: Black Learners Advisory Committee.

Black Lives Matter Toronto. (2016). Black Lives Matter—Toronto Freedom School Promotional. https://www.youtube.com/watch?v=ADEperDtKW8 (accessed 6 February 2016).

Boyce Davies, C. (2008). *Left of Karl Marx: The political life of Black communist Claudia Jones*. Durham, NC: Duke University Press.

Brand, D. (1984). A working paper on Black women in Toronto: Gender, race, and class. Fireweed, 19, re-published in Himani Bannerji (Ed.), (1993), *Returning the gaze: Essays on racism, feminism and politics* (pp. 220–42). Toronto, ON: Sister Vision Press.

Brand, D. (1991). *No burden to carry: Narratives of Black working women in Ontario, 1920s–1950s*. Toronto, ON: Women's Press.

Bristow, P., Brand, D., Carty, L., Cooper, A.P., Hamilton, S., & Shadd, A. (1994). *We're rooted here and they can't pull us up: Essays in African Canadian women's history*. Toronto, ON: University of Toronto Press.

Carvalho Carinhanha, A.M.d.S. (2018). Assassination in Brazil unmasks the deadly racism of a country that would rather ignore it. *The Conversation*, 12 April. Retrieved from: http://theconversation.com/assassination-in-brazil-unmasks-the-deadly-racism-of-a-country-that-would-rather-ignore-it-94389.

Ciconello, A. (2008). *The challenge of eliminating racism in Brazil: The new institutional framework for fighting racial inequality*. Oxfam International.

Combahee River Collective. (1986). *The Combahee River Collective statement: Black feminist organizing in the seventies and eighties*. Albany, NY: Kitchen Table.

Cooper, Afua. (2006). *The hanging of Angélique: The untold story of Canadian slavery and the burning of Old Montreal*. Toronto, ON: HarperCollins.

Crenshaw, K. (2019). *On intersectionality: Essential writings*. New York, NY: New Press.

Crenshaw, K., & Ritchie, A.J. (2015). Say her name: Resisting police brutality against Black women. Retrieved from: http://static1.squarespace.com/static/53f20d90e4b0b80451158d8c/t/560c068ee-4b0af26f72741df/1443628686535/AAPF_SMN_Brief_Full_singles-min.pdf.

da Silva, D.F. (2007). *Toward a global idea of race*. Minneapolis, MN: University of Minnesota Press.

Davis, A.Y. (1981). *Women, race, & class*. New York, NY: Random House.

Geledés. (2016). The human rights of Black women in Brazil: Violence and abuse. Report by Geledés: Instituto da Mulher Negra and Criola: Organização de Mulheres Negras. Retrieved from: https://www.geledes.org.br/wp-content/uploads/2016/11/Dossie-Mulheres-Negras-ING-WEB3.pdf.

Gilmore, R.W. (2007). *Golden gulag: Prisons, surplus, crisis, and opposition in globalizing California*. Berkeley, CA: University of California Press.

James, J. (1999). *Shadowboxing: Representations of Black feminist politics*. New York, NY: Palgrave.

Jones, C. (1949). An end to the neglect of the Negro woman. *Political Affairs*, June.

Lawson, E. (2013). The gendered working lives of seven Jamaican women in Canada: A story about "here" and "there" in a transnational economy. *Feminist Formations, 25*(1), 138–56.

Leeds, A. (2013). Toward the "higher type of womanhood": The gendered contours of Garveyism in the making of redemptive geographies in Costa Rica, 1922–1941. *Palimpsest, 2*(1), 1–27.

May, V.M. (2008). "It is Never a Question of the Slaves": Anna Julia Cooper's Challenge to History's Silences in Her 1925 Sorbonne Thesis. *Callaloo, 31*(3), 903–918.

Maynard, R. (2017). *Policing Black lives: State violence in Canada from slavery to the present*. Black Point, NS: Fernwood Publishing.

National Black Women's March, 18 November 2015. (2016). *Meridians: Feminism, Race, Transnationalism, 14*(1), 76–83.

OHRC (Ontario Human Rights Commission). (2018). *A collective impact*. Toronto, ON: OHRC.

Our Lives: Canada's first Black women's newspaper. (n.d.). Black Women's Collective. Available at: https://riseupfeministarchive.ca/publications/our-lives-canadas-first-black-womens-newspaper.

Paschel, T. (2017). From Colombia to the U.S.: Black lives have always mattered. In Larnies Bowen & Ayanna Legros (Eds), NACLA *Report on the Americas Special Report: A Hemispheric Approach to Contemporary Black Activism*.

Perry, K.H. (2015). *London is the place for me: Black Britons, citizenship and the politics of race*. New York, NY: Oxford University Press.

Polyani, Michael, Johnston, Lesley, Khanna, Anita, Dirie, Said, & Kerr, Michael. (2014). *The hidden epidemic: A report on child and family poverty in Toronto.* Social Planning Toronto. www.socialplanningtoronto.org/the_hidden_epidemic_a_report_on_child_and_family_poverty_in_toronto.

Ritchie, A.J. (2017). *Invisible no more: Police violence against black women and women of color.* Boston, MA: Beacon Press.

Robinson, Cedric J. (1983). *Black Marxism: The making of the Black radical tradition.* London, UK: Zed Press.

Rodney, W. (1981). *How Europe underdeveloped Africa.* Washington, DC: Howard University Press.

Sapers, H. (2013). Annual report of the Office of the Correctional Investigator 2012–2013.

Silkey, S.L. (2015). *Black woman reformer: Ida B. Wells, lynching, and transatlantic activism.* Athens, GA: University of Georgia Press.

Silvera, M. (1989). *Silenced: Talks with working class West Indian women about their lives and struggles as domestic workers in Canada* (2nd edn, first published in 1983). Toronto, ON: Sister Vision Press.

Smith, C.A. (2017). Battling anti-Black genocide in Brazil: For over a decade, antiracist movements in Brazil have sought justice for the killing of Black Brazilians by state forces. *NACLA Report on the Americas, 49*(1), 41–7.

United Nations. (2018). Background: 2015–2024 International Decade for People of African Descent. UN Web Services Section, Department of Public Information. http://www.un.org/en/events/african-descentdecade/background.shtml (accessed October 2018).

United Nations, UN Department of Public Information, and the Office of the United Nations High Commissioner for Human Rights. (n.d.). International decade for people of African descent. http://www.un.org/en/events/africandescentdecade/pdf/African%20Descent%20Booklet_WEB_English.pdf.

Williams, E.E. (1944). *Capitalism & slavery.* Chapel Hill, NC: University of North Carolina Press.

Wynter, S. (1995). 1492: A New World view. In V.L. Hyatt & R. Nettleford (Ed.), *Race, discourse, and the origin of the Americas: A New World view.* Washington, DC: Smithsonian Institution Press.

NOTE

1. I have addressed the globality of anti-Blackness and the diasporic nature of Black women's freedom struggle at greater length in Maynard, R. (in press), Toward a transnational Black feminist liberation, *Scholar and Feminist (S&F) Journal, 14*(4). (Invited.)

CHAPTER 16

◇

Global Mining and Decolonial Feminist Activism

Tracy Glynn

Learning Objectives

In this chapter, you will:

- examine how resource extraction is implicated in ongoing projects of colonialism, imperialism, and hegemonic masculinities;
- learn how global resource extraction uniquely affects women, including women from different social groupings, and the various ways that women respond to resource extraction;
- consider the importance of a decolonial feminist praxis in relation to the activism at resource extraction sites.

Introduction

Some women will never live to grow grey. Their hair will form roots with mountains and sacred rivers, their hands will form alliances with their people's land.
—A poem by Kailashana for Berta Cáceres
(http://algonquinstable.net/viewtopic
.php?f=27&t=30223)

Women experience resource extraction in similar but also unique ways, including disproportionately confronting the brunt of harms of an industry that continues to be dominated by men and pervaded by certain masculine ideas and practices. Women may resist the impacts of resource extraction in various ways depending on their membership in various social locations such as class, race, and sexuality. The women's similar but also varied experiences with resource extraction shape the way they respond, resist, cope, and survive. Activism rooted in a **decolonial feminist praxis** is challenging resource extraction that is implicated in the perpetuation of ideas and practices linked to colonialism, empire-building, and hegemonic masculinities. A decolonial feminist praxis involves tackling all forms of dehumanization that normalize sexism, racism, homophobia, transphobia, and a lack of connection and responsibility to one another and to the land and life.

Women at sites of resource extraction across the world, including Guatemala, Tanzania, Papua New Guinea, and elsewhere, say they want justice for being raped by men guarding the interests of a mining company. Indigenous women in northwestern British Columbian mining towns in Canada are being told to have sexual assault crisis plans in place for when hundreds of men come to their community to work in resource extraction camps. Women such as Berta Cáceres in Honduras and Dora Alicia Sorto Recinos in El Salvador have lost their lives for opposing resource development that they considered too risky and destructive.

This chapter will first provide an overview of how resource extraction is mired in colonial practices, the project of empire-building, and hegemonic masculinities. Second, this chapter will summarize the impacts of mining on women in several countries and discuss various forms of their resistance. Finally, a decolonial feminist approach to activism as a distinct and hopeful kind of activism will be explored.

Beyond 500 Years of Colonialism

The mining of gold, silver, copper, and other metals and minerals is at the heart of the story of conquest of the Americas, empire-building projects across Africa and Asia, and what some call the new **extractivism** or extractive imperialism in Latin America and other regions of the world today (Gordon & Webber, 2016; Veltmeyer & Petras, 2014). Ongoing processes of theft and destruction of Indigenous lands and culture are justified on racist notions that Indigenous peoples are in need of saving and a development model that prioritizes the exploitation of natural resources. An examination of the history of colonialism and imperialist interventions in mine-affected communities is important toward understanding and eradicating the inequality, oppression, and environmental devastation present in these communities today. Sites of resource extraction also offer a place to study how patriarchal attitudes and certain ideas and practices associated with hegemonic masculinities bolster oppressive social and economic structures.

The world continues to grapple with the harmful legacies of colonialism as seen in Indigenous communities in the Global North such as Canada and the United States as well as in countries of the Global South such as Guatemala,

the Philippines, and the Democratic Republic of Congo. The postcolonial period is marked by the continuance of coercive forms of domination, including state policies that back resource development despite Indigenous opposition (Hall, 2012). Furthermore, resource extraction continues to be linked to the erasure of women and violence against women. The disappearances and murders of Indigenous women and girls in Canada, Mexico, Guatemala, and elsewhere are linked to the violence committed against the land in the form of mining, fracking, damming rivers, and free trade agreements (Simpson, 2014; Smith, 2015; True, 2012). While more women are denied access to their traditional land and sources of their livelihoods as well as food and water to feed themselves and their families, they are also often denied access to wage labour at the mining operations and forced into sex work or other work in the informal economy that may put them in vulnerable positions with no social protections. The extractives industry, including its boom and bust nature that leaves workers and their families in stressful and precarious situations, is also linked to increases in domestic violence (True, 2012).

Mining, Men, and Masculinities

Mining has historically been and continues to be a male-dominated industry that is frequently associated with **hegemonic masculinities** that perpetuate misogynist ideas and actions that demean and subordinate femaleness and what society considers feminine. The prevailing masculine discourse and practices tend to also reinforce the gender binary, gender hierarchies, and heteronormativity. Mines as well as other industrial projects such as hydroelectric dams that are promoted by institutions such as the World Bank are sites where patriarchal norms are often naturalized and women's position and power are weakened. For example, these projects typically hire more men while compromising the land, thereby

Guatemala: Home to the Last Colonial Massacre and the New Frontier

The Maya and Xinca peoples of Guatemala were brutally forced from their land during the 300 years that Spain colonized their country. Various Indigenous peoples have continued to experience severe repression and forced displacement from their lands during numerous military regimes that worked closely with the United States government to support the interests of American corporations in Guatemala, such as the United Fruit Company (now Chiquita). The Canadian nickel mining corporation Inco Ltd also benefitted from its relations with the US government, specifically John Foster Dulles. Dulles and his brother, Allen, then the director of the Central Intelligence Agency (CIA), orchestrated a coup of Guatemala's Jacobo Árbenz government that had been redistributing the land to peasants away from large corporations such as the United Fruit Company in 1954. Carlos Castillo Armas, who received military training and funds from the US government to overthrow the Árbenz government, became the president of Guatemala following the coup. He immediately embraced free enterprise, including returning land to the United Fruit Company and supporting the exploitation of the country's nickel-rich hills in El Estor. Inco took over the nickel project from the American company Hanna Mining in 1960. Despite severe repression, the Maya Q'eqchi' protested their imminent displacement and dispossession for the mine, while lawyers, professors, and students in Guatemala City protested what they saw as a resource giveaway to a foreign corporation. Several of those who denounced the inadequate mining royalties and taxes applied to the mining operation were assassinated on the streets of the capital (Swift, 1977).

Maya Q'eqchi', grandmother, and community organizer Mama Maquín led a march to the town square of Panzós on 29 May 1978 to show community opposition to Inco's plans to mine nickel on their land. Mama Maquín was there with her daughter, grandson, and granddaughter. Only her granddaughter, Maria, survived the march in what historian Greg Grandin (2011) called Latin America's last colonial massacre. Fifty others died that day, either from bullets fired by the Guatemalan army in the square or from drowning in the Polochic River as they tried to escape. Maria told an audience in Guatemala City in 2010 at an event marking the anniversary of the massacre that the killers of her mother, brother, and grandmother live in her community today. Despite fearing for her life, she is not giving up on her quest to bring to justice those whom she calls the intellectual masterminds behind the massacre (Sanford, 2010/2011).

Guatemala in 2018 continues to be a dangerous place for opponents of resource extraction, with some saying that the 40-year civil war that began after the US interfered in their country has never ended. Different companies have taken over the Inco project in eastern Guatemala. In early 2007, about 700 armed men, including the police, private security, and the army, violently evicted five Mayan Q'eqchi' communities while the project was owned by Canadian company Skye Resources. Homes and crops were burned to the ground. The people of one of the razed communities, Lote Ocho, had nowhere to go after the eviction, so they returned to their lands to rebuild. Days later, hundreds of police, army, and private security returned and found only women and children there. The community's men were off in the fields. According to Elena Choc Quib, on 17 January 2007 she was beaten and raped by eight armed men carrying out the

continued

Photo by Larry Kaplow

María Maquín speaking out against a military post in Panzós: "I saw what the army does. I lived through what the army did. We should never agree to an army post here in Panzós" (Sanford, 2010/2011).
https://static.hwpi.harvard.edu/files/styles/os_files_xxlarge/public/revista/files/maria_maquin_speaking_against_military_base_by_larry_kaplow.jpg?m=1515712040&itok=kfyWKWX-

eviction. She says she miscarried the child she was eight months pregnant with at the time. Ten other women also say they were raped in the eviction, some gang-raped, that day (Daley, 2016).

Another Canadian mining company, HudBay Minerals, later took over the nickel project from Skye Resources. The violence continued. On 27 September 2009, Adolfo Ich, a beloved teacher and community organizer against the mine, was brutally murdered with a machete and bullets in front of his son. Eyewitnesses say that Minor Padilla, the head of security for the mine, killed Adolfo. On the same day that Adolfo was murdered, German Chub, a young man, was shot and left paralyzed. Adolfo's widow, Angelica Choc, German Chub, and the 11 women who say they were raped by Skye's security forces are taking HudBay to a provincial court in Canada and making history. For the first time, a case against a mining company is proceeding through a court in Canada for crimes committed at its subsidiary operations abroad. Unfortunately, their resistance has been met with more violence. Angelica's 18-year-old nephew, Héctor Manuel Choc Cuz, was beaten to death by a group of men on 31 March 2018. Angelica's family thinks the assassination was meant for her son, José, who witnessed his father's murder. To follow the historic court case, visit chocversushudbay.com.

harming women farmers in the Global South who rely on the land for sustenance and a livelihood (Braun, 2011; Lahiri-Dutt, 2013).

Despite the sexist nature of resource extraction, women have and continue to resist the onset of mining and its various impacts, but their resistance and self-determination are hindered by the global economic system, namely capitalism, and patriarchal ideas that serve to reinforce capitalism. One struggle that women face with a deeply rooted patriarchy is that male views dominate decision-making on resource extraction. For example, women in Chad and Cameroon were shut out of consultations about an oil pipeline that would traverse their land even though they make up 70 per cent of the agricultural workforce and depend on that land for their livelihood (True, 2012). Women are further oppressed by structural classism and racism at sites of resource extraction. As Carmen Mejía, a young Mayan activist against the Goldcorp Marlin mine in Guatemala, daughter of peasants, and the single mother of a young child, remarked in 2010, "We are not heard because we are women, we are Indigenous and we are campesinas." For her activism, Mejía, like many other activists against resource projects, has received death threats (Glynn, 2014).

Feminist theorists have noted that the bodies of politically active women and in particular working-class Black women and Indigenous women are destroyed differently from the bodies of men (Davis, 1983; Smith, 2015). To illustrate the sexism and racism that activists against resource extraction endure, in Ecuador in 2009 Lina Solano was singled out, charged with public disorder, and arrested for protesting the Canadian-owned IAMGOLD mine that she said would destroy protected Amazonian forests. Solano, a sociologist and the president of the Latin American Union of Women (ULAM), was quoted in *The Guardian* on 12 October 2009, saying, "There is a lot of verbal aggression from the police towards females protesting against the mines. They call us sluts and smelly Indians" (Hopkins, 2009).

Opposing resource extraction regularly unleashes state-backed violence that targets and harms certain bodies, both in the Global South and in Indigenous communities on Turtle Island (what is known as North America today). When Mi'kmaq warriors, grandmothers, and youth blocked the equipment used to explore for shale gas in the Canadian province of New Brunswick in 2013, the provincial government used militarized police to physically remove the land defenders. Sheila Joseph, a Mi'kmaq grandmother, said she was punched in the face by a police officer on National Aboriginal Day, 21 June 2013 (Howe, 2015). Across oceans, women in Papua New Guinea and Tanzania are working with activists in Canada and the US to get reparations for being raped and gang-raped by Barrick Gold's security guards or the police the mining company hired. The women say they are being forced to swallow the condoms that the men use in the rapes (Whittington, 2009). In some cases, the husbands of the survivors have shunned them and divorced them for having been raped. These are all examples of how Indigenous women and women in the Global South face special harm when they resist resource extraction by multinational corporations.

The kind of hegemonic masculinities on display at sites of resource extraction include sexist and misogynist acts such as the silencing of women's voices, the exclusion of women from the workforce, the rapes and gang-rapes of women, and the pillaging of the land that wipes out livelihoods and sacred sites that women use to grow crops and feed families. Countering hegemonic masculinities at sites of resource extraction involves, among other actions, interrogating the gendered nature of resource extraction, including the ways that miners are conceived by society as tough macho males. Society has shaped what it means to be a man and masculine; men are supposed to provide for their families, be tough, aggressive, and competitive, not show emotions, and take risks. Excuses have been made for the bad behaviour of men,

Courtesy Riley Sparks

Everlyn Gaupe, a rape survivor at Barrick Gold's Porgera mine in Papua New Guinea, speaks with protesters outside Barrick's annual general meeting in Toronto, Canada, on 25 April 2017.

including harassment and violence against women and homophobic acts (Johnston & McIvor, 2004).

When women enter a predominately male workforce, such as at a mining operation, they often experience discrimination, harassment in the workplace, and comments that they are stealing jobs from men who should be the natural breadwinners (Keck & Powell, 2006). Here, certain narratives about what it means to be a man and a miner are linked to the subordination of women. The different roles women assume at sites of resource extraction reveal a "fluidity of women's identities as workers, 'whores', and wives with a focus on transactional sex" (Bradshaw, Linneker, & Overton, 2017, p. 439). Meanwhile, women on the front lines of resistance to resource extraction often explain their active opposition in feminized terms. They often link their activism

to their identities of being a mother, a caretaker of families, and protector of the earth (Bell & Braun, 2010). By avoiding essentialist ideas about men and women and turning our attention to the normative-generating nature of certain kinds of masculinity that usurp subordinated masculinities, we can move toward greater gender equality (Connell & Messerschmidt, 2005). Furthermore, Connell (2014) argues that postcolonial thinking on masculinities and globalization needs to consider the creation of masculinities through history and global processes such as conquest, colonization, and integration into capitalist markets.

Women, Mining, and Resistance

Contemporary resource extraction across the world is increasingly being referred to as **extractivism**.

For Indigenous and rural communities that live off the land and depend on healthy lands, waters, and ecosystems to grow food and practise their culture, opposition to extractivism is considered a struggle for life. Mining disproportionately affects women. Some of the documented impacts of resource extraction on women include: restricted access to and loss of livelihoods; restricted access to and loss of sources of drinking water and food; increased workload; increased economic dependency on men; precarious and stigmatized forms of employment like sex work; workplace discrimination and sexual harassment and assault (Mercier & Gier, 2006).

Global campaigns and networks supporting communities affected by mining have emerged over the past decade; some of these networks are focused on highlighting and eradicating the gender impacts of mining. Women have organized in regional and international networks to address the problems of mining. For example, the Union Latinoamerica de Mujeres (Latin American Union of Women [ULAM]) is a network of grassroots women's organizations across Latin America committed to defending the environment and women's rights to challenge mining policies and practices. The International Women and Mining Network (RIMM), formed at the turn of the millennium, works at a global and regional level to expose and challenge the problems that women experience with mining in their communities. The network comprises mine resisters as well as women who work in mining operations, including women from community groups, non-governmental organizations, trade unions, and others.

Feminist scholars and activists addressing women's oppression, gender inequality, and violence at resource extraction sites demand that women be consulted in resource extraction proposals and gender analysis and planning in all phases of extraction. Others demand justice for women who have been physically and sexually attacked at their workplace or in their community by one of many security apparatuses used by the

extractives sector, while others oppose the onset or the expansion of any resource extraction on their lands.

In Canada, which is home to more than half of the world's publicly listed mining and exploration companies (Natural Resources Canada, 2018), targets of protest and calls for reform for communities harmed by extractivism include the banks, international financial institutions, ethical funds, publicly funded export credit agencies, and pension funds like the Canadian Pension Plan because of their financial support of controversial resource extraction projects. The World Bank has pressured governments to rewrite their mining laws to be more friendly to foreign investors, to privatize state-controlled mines, and to grant individual land titles over collectively owned land. Such schemes have paved the way for companies to gain easy access to land and rich mineral resources. Members of the United Church of Canada and the labour union Public Service Alliance of Canada, who support communities affected by Goldcorp, were shocked to learn that their pensions were invested in Goldcorp and, in the case of the United Church members, have organized for divestment, albeit unsuccessfully, within their institutions.

Colourful protests are an annual occurrence outside shareholders' meetings of companies such as Goldcorp and Barrick, while consumer-based campaigns like Earth Works' No Dirty Gold attempt to educate consumers about "where the gold in their products comes from, or how it is mined." Jewelry retailers like Tiffany's and university students buying class rings have been targeted for purchasing "unethical gold." Walmart's fair trade line of Love, Earth jewelry was supposed to be sourced responsibly, but a report on 6 January 2011 in the *Miami New Times* revealed that Love, Earth's gold comes from Utah and Nevada mines responsible for widespread pollution. (Friedman-Rudovsky, 2011).

Efforts toward ending violence against women and enacting better social welfare and more robust regulations that protect the environment, workers, and the health and welfare of communities are important. However, powerful forces stand opposed to reforms that hinder private accumulation. The ruling elite control not just the economy but also the state, courts, and media, making it extremely difficult for the masses to effect fundamental changes that the powerful minority opposes. Anti-capitalists caution against restricting activism to accommodate the capitalist system, an inherently exploitative system (Foster, 2003). Reforms, while necessary to alleviate the worst severities of the inequalities wrought by capitalism, remain limited and during economic crises are often rolled back in the name of austerity and balanced budgets. While working on reforms that better the lives of workers is important, those committed to radical social transformation goals seek production that is free from the profit motive and a global planned economy that wipes out all social inequalities, frees workers, and meets the needs of every human. Domitila Barrios de Chúngara, a Bolivian woman, miner, labour leader, feminist, and author who died of lung cancer in 2012, argued in 1978, "My people are not struggling for a small victory, for a small wage increase, a small answer there. No. My people are preparing themselves to get capitalism out of their country forever, and its domestic and foreign servants, too. My people are struggling to reach socialism" (Barrios de Chúngara & Viezzer, 1978, pp. 228–30).

Two kinds of activism deployed by women at resource extraction sites will be explored next in terms of what Stuart Kirsch (2014), author of *Mining capitalism*, calls a politics of space and a politics of time. The first kind of activism related to a politics of space encompasses the quest for justice for harms done by mining companies, including for acts of rape and murder but also for loss of land and livelihoods and other impacts. The second kind of activism, characterized as a politics of time, seeks to stop harm before it occurs.

"No Justice, No Peace"

One of the distinctively gendered ways that poor peasant or Indigenous women's public resistance to resource extraction is quelled is when they are raped by men in positions of authority, the police, security guards, and vigilantes. More than 200 women in Papua New Guinea say they have been raped by either Barrick Gold's security guards or hired police officers. As previously described, efforts to mine nickel in Guatemala by Canadian mining companies are linked to rapes and murder.

The activism around supporting survivors of violence at sites of resource conflicts denotes a politics of space. The networks mobilize resources, use convincing arguments, and work on building collective power to create enough leverage for the kinds of remedies and changes they seek (Kirsch, 2014). Rape survivors at sites of resource extraction by Canadian mining companies in Papua New Guinea, Guatemala, and Tanzania are supported by organizations such as MiningWatch Canada, an organization formed in 1999 to address the harms caused by Canadian corporations overseas and by mining in Canada. The women are also supported by grassroots solidarity groups such as the Mining Injustice Solidarity Network (MISN) and the Maritimes-Guatemala Breaking the Silence Network. The Canadian law firm known for its social justice work, Klippensteins, is representing the 11 Maya Q'eqchi women who are making history by taking Canadian mining company HudBay to a Canadian court for the actions of its subsidiary abroad.

Activists, including a number of prominent women such as Berta Cáceres, have lost their lives for opposing resource development that they considered too risky and destructive. Latin America is the most dangerous place in the world to be an environmental activist. Almost four environmentalists per week were murdered in 2017. According to Global Witness (2018), 197 people were killed in 2017 for defending land, wildlife, or

"Berta Cáceres Did Not Die! She Multiplied!"

Berta Cáceres (first mentioned in Chapter 11), an Indigenous Lenca activist against damming rivers to power multinational-owned mines in Honduras, was brazenly murdered in her home just before midnight on 2 March 2016. She was 44 years old. Berta was well known in the international environmental activist community, having won the 2015 Goldman Environmental Prize awarded to people who risk their lives for their environmental activism.

Berta, a retired teacher and mother of four, a fighter against illegal logging, plantations, and hydroelectric dams, grew up during the violence that swept Central America in the 1980s. Standing up for the oppressed was a value passed down to Berta by her mother, who housed refugees from El Salvador. Berta became a student activist, and in 1993 she co-founded the Civic Council of Popular and Indigenous Organizations of Honduras (COPINH) to defend the Lenca people and lands. As the director of COPINH, she often remarked that the assassinations of Indigenous people, people resisting resource extraction, journalists, and lawyers were occurring in a state of impunity.

Before her murder, Berta and her colleagues organized a popular resistance against the Agua Zarca hydroelectric dam on their Lenca territory in Rio Blanco—a dam that would displace people and destroy the sacred Gualcarque River. For months in 2013, under severe repression and criminalization, the Lenca people blocked the access road to the dam site. Berta told *Telesur* in 2015: "I have received direct death threats, threats of kidnapping, or disappearance, of lynching . . . threats of kidnapping my daughter, persecution, surveillance, sexual harassment."

More than 30,000 people attended Berta's funeral. Tributes to Berta poured in from organizations across the world. Solidarity actions at Honduran embassies were held around the world with banners that said, "Berta Cáceres Did Not Die, She Multiplied!" Four days after the assassination of Berta, mining justice activists in Toronto crashed the Prospectors and Developers Association of Canada's convention in that city, naming the people killed for resisting Canadian mining projects around the world. Days after Berta's assassination, on 15 March, her COPINH colleague, Nelson García, was shot and killed after returning home from a violent eviction. Nelson was 38, a father of five, and a farmer.

In June 2016, a former soldier who fled his unit told *The Guardian* that Berta Cáceres's name and the names of other activists were on a Honduran military hit list (Lakhani, 2016). Nine people have been arrested for Berta's murder, including members of the Honduran army and workers at the hydroelectric project company. The most recent arrest occurred on 2 March 2018 when David Castillo Mejia was arrested for his role in planning the murder while he was the CEO of Desarollos Energeticos (DESA), the company behind the hydroelectric dam that Berta and her Lenca community opposed (Lakhani, 2018).

Berta's daughters have continued their mother's activism. In 2016, one of them, Berta Zúñiga Cáceres, testified against Canadian mining companies and the Canada-Honduras Free Trade Agreement to a parliamentary subcommittee on human rights during a special session on Honduras. She told the Canadian Centre for Policy Alternatives in 2016 that

continued

Daniel Cima, Comisión Interamericana de Derechos Humanos via Flickr (CC BY 2.0)

Berta Zúñiga Cáceres continues in her mother's activist footsteps. Here she is testifying for the protection of the Aguán River Valley at a special hearing in Honduras in 2016.

The Lenca people have resisted colonialism for 500 years. . . . And now the genocide of my people started by the Spanish invaders continues through neocolonialism, with companies taking all the territories and resources, stealing the rivers, the water, the Earth. Thirty-five per cent of Honduras has been given as concessions to private companies. Our resistance is about confronting raw capitalism, the monster that is trying to dominate us through militarization and assassination.

natural resources. Berta's organization, COPINH, and solidarity groups in the United States and Canada are seeking justice for Berta's murder and demanding that American and Canadian foreign policy not contribute to more deaths of activists in the country.

"Consultas" and "Blockadia"

The struggles against resource extraction are rooted in places people wish to defend. People who never thought of themselves as activists and prefer to not be called protesters but rather protectors are taking part in blockades, writing letters, talking to their neighbours and the media, all in an effort to stop resource extraction and development that they consider too risky. The struggles are also interconnected globally and in response to unwanted development of resources. Their activism goes beyond "not in my backyard" calls, but rather their rallying cry is: "not here, not anywhere" (Klein, 2014).

Women in Guatemala, Colombia, Peru, Argentina, and elsewhere are part of local councils organizing "consultas" that allow community members a more democratic space for marginalized groups to vote on whether a large industrial project, like a mine, proceeds in their community (Walter & Urkidi, 2016). These consultas in Guatemala have resulted in people voting overwhelmingly against mining in their community (Glynn, 2014).

Mi'kmaq Women Occupy the Front Lines against Fracking

A flashpoint in the resistance to hydraulic fracturing (fracking) for shale gas occurred on Mi'kmaq territory in New Brunswick, Canada, in 2013. More than 40 people, Indigenous and settler allies, were arrested that year for their participation in road blockades against shale gas exploration. Mi'kmaq women occupied the front lines against fracking, including Amanda Polchies, who bent down with an eagle feather in front of a line of armed police in a moment that was captured by Inuk journalist Ossie Michelin. That photograph has since travelled the world and is now an iconic image of women's resistance.

One of the women arrested for resisting shale gas on Mi'kmaq territory was Suzanne Patles, a member of the Mi'kmaq Warriors Society. Suzanne argued that the arrests and conditions put on her violate her treaty rights. She pointed to the 1999 Supreme Court of Canada ruling that reaffirmed the Peace and Friendship Treaties between the Mi'kmaq and the British Crown. The treaties never ceded land or resources in New Brunswick. However, the Indigenous people in New Brunswick, like those in the rest of Canada, do not have the

Ossie Michelin/APTN National News

Ossie Michelin's photograph of Amanda Polchies kneeling in prayer, holding an eagle feather in front of a line of armed police, went viral within hours after he took it in 2013.

power to veto resource extraction on their lands. Suzanne's first arrest was on 9 June 2013 when she was praying in front of police officers attempting to make way for the movement of equipment of the shale gas company SWN Resources. She was arrested for obstruction and mischief and put under conditions to stay one kilometre away from the gas company's equipment. During her arrest, she explained to police officers that she was "sovereign" and in prayer (Glynn, 2014).

On 17 October 2013, the Royal Canadian Mounted Police (RCMP) violently, with dogs, pepper spray, pointed guns, and rubber bullets, raided a camp that was blocking the shale gas equipment on a highway in Rexton, near the Elsipogtog First Nation. Dozens of people were arrested. Amy Sock, a Mi'kmaq woman, showed bruises on her arms that she says were inflicted by RCMP officers. Amy's story did not garner the same media attention as the RCMP vehicles set ablaze that day. Many of the people arrested faced restrictive conditions. Hope Levi, a 21-year-old Mi'kmaq woman from Elsipogtog, was struck by a SWN truck on 2 December 2013. She intended to pursue a formal complaint but backed down when an RCMP investigator reminded her that she had breached conditions related to her 17 October arrest that stipulated she stay

continued

away from shale gas equipment. Three Mi'kmaq men who participated in the protests remained in jail for months without access to their traditional ceremonies (Howe, 2015).

The provincial Conservative government lost the election the following year in 2014 in what many felt was because of their support for shale gas. The Liberal party that was elected promised a moratorium on fracking for shale gas, which they implemented as an indefinite moratorium months after their election.

The phenomenon of "blockadia," as described by Naomi Klein (2014) and others as not one place but many places where local peoples around the world are putting their bodies on the land to stop destructive activities, denotes a politics of time that seeks to stop harm before it occurs (Kirsch, 2014). In the 1990s, Innu women, using civil disobedience and the courts, temporarily halted the opening of one of the world's largest nickel mines in Labrador, Canada, until agreements that benefitted the community were put into place (Lowe, 1998). There are many ingredients in a successful effort to stop resource extraction. Organizing local referenda and putting bodies on the land to stop resource extraction have proven effective in some places, but sometimes mines and oil and gas projects do go ahead, with devastating consequences for the local peoples and lands. Can a decolonial approach to activism be part of the struggles against resource extraction? A decolonial approach places Indigenous self-determination and Indigenous peoples' relationship to the land and all life at the forefront (Walia, 2012). How activists, accomplices, and allies can engage with decolonial feminist theory and practice is explored next.

100 Weaving Women Block Marble Mine

Aleta Baun and the Indigenous women in her community of Mollo on the western part of the island of Timor in Indonesia stopped marble mining that would have destroyed their sacred forests and water supplies through a weaving occupation. Approximately 150 women spent a year sitting on the marble rocks at the proposed quarry, weaving their traditional fabrics in protest. Known as "Mama Aleta," she has survived an assassination attempt. Others in her community have been beaten and arrested for their activism against the marble mine.

In the Mollo culture, women are expected to be homemakers and tend to their families. The Mollo people also believed it was important to have the women on the front lines of the protests and to act as the negotiators because they were the ones who use the forest for food, medicine, and dyes to survive. They were worried that if their men were put on the front lines, there would be violence. While the women protested at the quarry, domestic roles were reversed. Men provided domestic support at home, cooking, cleaning, and caring for the children.

In the face of sustained community opposition, in 2010 the marble mining company in Mollo left. Aleta won the 2013 Goldman Environmental Prize for her activism. She continues her work protecting the forests of Timor and developing economic options for her community that are more sustainable, such as weaving and agriculture.

What a Decolonial Feminist Praxis Has to Offer for Resource Extraction Struggles

There are many stories across the globe of women at the forefront of courageous struggle against harmful resource developments. Their activism highlights the need to stop the plundering of the natural world and the dehumanization associated with resource extraction. **Praxis** is needed in movements for social transformation. Praxis, the marrying of theory and practice, involves acting with a strategic purpose and engaging in perpetual reflection in order to inform future praxis. A historical awareness and analysis of colonialism and capitalism is key to understanding how numerous inequalities along lines of gender, race, ethnicity, class, and international hierarchies of states were created, intersect, and are maintained. Since resource extraction is bound with the worst harms of colonialism, imperialism, racism, sexism, and misogyny, a decolonial feminist praxis is relevant to solving today's problems with resource extraction. Decolonization, as a process and a goal, must confront capitalist social relations, including the complex ways that capitalism, patriarchy, white supremacy, and states interact and bolster colonial relationships (Coulthard, 2014; Walia, 2012).

In terms of decolonial feminist praxis, women are not treated as one universal category. A decolonial feminism acknowledges the differences among women (Bannerji, 2000; Lugones, 2010). Lugones argues that gender is itself "a violent and colonial introduction that is used to destroy peoples, cosmologies, and communities as the building ground of the 'civilized' West" (2007, p. 186). Eurocentred capitalist society and colonization constructed the gender binary and gender hierarchies where males and heterosexual norms dominate and subjugate. For example, colonization imposed an oppressive gender system on the Yoruba peoples in southwestern Nigeria, where females were subordinated. Before settler colonial contact, many Indigenous communities in North America were matriarchal, recognized more than two genders, and did not discriminate against homosexuality. Gender differences were understood in egalitarian terms and not in terms of subordination of one gender over another (Lugones, 2007). In order to defend, reclaim, and celebrate different ways of being and living in the world, understanding how the colonial project benefitted from gender differentials, transphobia, and homophobia is key in dismantling what appears as natural or normal.

Activism against extractivism has been informed by intersectionality, a useful lens that allows for a consideration of the interactive effects of a person's membership in various social groupings such as race, gender, class, and sexuality. For example, a woman from an Indigenous community at a mine site in the Global South will likely experience mining in a different way from that of a woman who is a multinational mining executive living in the Global North. An intersectional approach allows for the appreciation of similarities and continuities as well as the differences and discontinuities in people's experiences, histories, and strategies of survival and resistance (Alexander & Mohanty, 2013). Intersectionality, while offering an anti-oppressive approach to study and activism, must not be used to decentre Indigenous struggles.

Decolonial approaches acknowledge that Indigenous peoples bear the brunt of resource extraction. One analytical framework linked to decolonial feminism is feminist political ecology. Feminist political ecology uses an intersectional lens to examine the gender dimensions of nature and society (Elmhirst, 2011). Ecofeminism is a movement based on theories such as feminist political ecology that combine ecological concerns with feminism. In resource extraction struggles, questions such as who benefits and who loses from mining should be asked (Kojola, 2018). Leanne Simpson (2013), an Indigenous Michi Saagiig Nishnaabeg scholar from Canada, argues that "dispossession of Indigenous peoples from our homelands is the root causes of every problem we face whether it is missing or murdered Indigenous women, fracking, pipelines, deforestation, mining, environmental contamination or social issues as a result of imposed poverty."

Countering the neoliberal state's erasure of Indigenous women and their connection to the land, women through "**presencing**" call for attention to what is important about their lives. Presencing involves Indigenous women and girls telling the world that their lives matter (de Finney, 2014; Simpson, 2011). The acts of presencing and renewing relationships to the land thwart the colonial project's attempt to devalue the bodies of Indigenous women and girls so that they are not grieved or missed (Savarese, 2016, p. 148). For Simpson (2011, p. 96), "storied presencing" involves not only protest and insurrection but also remembrance and testimony (Savarese, 2016).

Women's presencing challenges several colonial discourses or myths, including the narrative that resource extraction brings development and prosperity for all and is the only option for healthy communities. Such claims of goodness are a classic strategy of legitimizing colonial domination as seen in the discourses used by Canadian mining executives whose companies operate in various African countries (Butler, 2015). For Glen Coulthard, author of *Red skins, white masks* (2014), Indigenous political-economic alternatives to capitalist-driven resource extraction and development are very much imaginable and desirable. He envisions democratic organizations of production and distribution through Indigenous co-operatives and possibly worker-run enterprises. For Coulthard (2013), decolonization will involve undoing systems of oppression and building

solidarity and networks of trade and mutual aid with those most harmed by globalized capital.

Decolonization involves learning and unlearning to radically re-imagine our lives and relationships with the land that are more respectful to all life. Settlers and non-Indigenous people can support Indigenous resistance by educating themselves about the histories of the lands where they reside and by honouring the voices of Indigenous resistance and offering concrete solidarity (Walia, 2012). Activists against resource extraction must act in respectful ways with Indigenous communities, centre Indigenous self-determination in their activism, and avoid tokenism (Walia, 2012). Decolonial activism goes beyond asking for recognition of rights imposed by settler states and instead seeks to trouble and dismantle the settler state (Coulthard, 2014; Walia, 2012).

"Deep Listening"

Settler and non-Indigenous feminists are encouraged to engage in "deep listening" when they encounter Indigenous feminist thinking. Decolonial feminist theorizing takes seriously Indigenous peoples' relations to the land and their sovereignty as well as spirituality. Feminists need to listen if they are to engage in a politics of resurgence that supports Indigenous peoples' sovereignty, laws, knowledges, philosophies, and practices (Weir, 2017). "The decolonization of feminism is mostly focused on Indigenous feminist movements and voices that challenge 'whitestream' feminism—not a question of speaking for others as it is listening to others speak for themselves" (Arvin, Tuck, & Morrill, 2013, in Oliver, 2017).

Transnationalism

Decolonial feminist praxis involves organizing for justice across colonial borders. Supporting struggles of women at resource extraction sites across

Call to Action

Every day, people stand up to oppression and fight for a more equal and just world. People protest on the streets, they block oil and gas pipelines in an effort to stop runaway climate change, they resist being dominated and oppressed in small but important gestures in their everyday lives, and they forge solidarities with groups of people who believe that their liberation will not come without the liberation of all oppressed groups of people. In Canada, networks such as No One Is Illegal, Defenders of the Land, and the Mining Injustice Solidarity Network engage in a decolonial feminist politics. Students have long been part of such alliance-building. They take what they learn in classrooms, rallies, and community meetings about colonialism and imperialism, and they join groups or they form groups. We must connect our struggles and take heart and be moved by the slogan: no one is free until we are all free. Attend an event in your community, or plan one to be held at your school's campus, that protests resource extraction and supports women affected by resource extraction in the Global South.

the globe means we must apply a transnational perspective to activism. For Chandra Talpae Mohanty (2017), engaging in transnational spaces means confronting carceral regimes, militarized borders, displacement of people through war, climate change and dispossession, and proto-fascist governments around the world. "What lies ahead is the hard work of deepening and consolidating the nascent solidarities that have emerged through these mobilizations, to imagine a decolonized public polity anchored in a horizontal feminist solidarity across borders and divides," wrote Mohanty (McLaren, 2017, p. viii). As Berta Cáceres remarked in her 2015 Goldman Environmental Prize acceptance speech:

> We must undertake the struggle in all parts of the world, wherever we may be, because we have no other spare or replacement planet. We have only this one, and we have to take action. The Honduran people, along with international solidarity, can get out of this unjust

situation, promoting hope, rebellion and organising ourselves for the protection of life.

Tying It Together

This chapter sought to shed light on the struggles that women wage in relation to the male-dominated resource extraction industry. Resource extraction tends to harm women in disproportionate ways. The way that women experience and resist resource extraction is related to their membership in various social locations. Indigenous women and women in the Global South who rely on healthy lands and waters to grow food and collect medicines are particularly harmed by the destructive nature of resource extraction. Activism informed by decolonial feminism is best equipped to redress and stop gender-related harms of resource extraction because it acknowledges and aims to dismantle colonial and capitalist structures that are behind such irresponsible and deadly exploitation of the earth and people.

DISCUSSION QUESTIONS

1. What is the relation between women and mining?

2. What kinds of masculinities are on display in mining communities?

3. Discuss how various forms of discrimination can overlap and affect people living in mining communities.

4. What kinds of resistance do women display at sites of resource extraction?

5. How do decolonial feminist approaches to activism at sites of resource extraction and development differ from other forms of resistance?

SUGGESTIONS FOR FURTHER READING

Barrios de Chúngara, D., & Viezzer, M. (1978). *Let me speak! Testimony of Domitila, A woman of the Bolivian mines.* New York, NY: Monthly Review Press. This book contains the testimony of Domitila Barrios de Chungara, a woman who organized the wives of Bolivian tin miners in the 1970s not only against exploitation from the mine but also against patriarchy and capitalism.

Federici, S. (2004). *Caliban and the witch: Women, the body and primitive accumulation.* New York, NY: Autonomedia. This book is an account of how women's bodies and lives were transformed to meet the requirements of colonialism and the transition to capitalism throughout history.

LaDuke, W. (1999). *All our relations: Native struggles for life and land.* Chicago, IL: Haymarket Books. This book, written by environmental activist Winona LaDuke, discusses the struggle for survival and the resistance to environmental and cultural degradation by Indigenous peoples in the United States.

Lugones, M. (2010). Toward a decolonial feminism. *Hypatia, 25*(4), 742–75. This article expands on Anibal Quijano's theorizing on gender oppression that is rooted in colonialism and capitalism. It argues that a decolonial feminism can overcome such gender oppression.

McLaren, M.A. (2017). *Decolonizing feminism: Transnational feminism and globalization.* London,

UK, and New York, NY: Rowman & Littlefield. This book contains a collection of essays on decolonizing epistemologies, methods, and knowledges in relation to rights, citizenship, immigration, solidarity, and freedom.

Simpson, L. (2011). *Dancing on our Turtle's back: Stories of Nishnaabeg re-creation, resurgence and a new emergence.* Winnipeg, MB: ARP. This book argues that reconciliation with Indigenous peoples must support the regeneration and resurgence of Indigenous languages, oral cultures, and traditional governance.

Swarr, A.L., & Nagar, R. (Eds). (2012). *Critical transnational feminist praxis.* New York, NY: SUNY Press. This book explores transnational feminist scholarship and activism in various fields. Transnational projects discussed in the book include the Guyanese Red Thread collective, the Ananya Dance Theatre, the Filipino-Canadian Youth Alliance, Sangtin, and VIVA!

Tuck, E. (2009). Suspending damage: A letter to communities. *Harvard Educational Review, 79*(3), 409–28. This open letter to researchers and educators calls on them to move away from "damage-centred" research on Indigenous communities to "desire-based frameworks" with Indigenous communities that do not depict Indigenous peoples as broken but as people with desires.

MULTIMEDIA SUGGESTIONS

Defensora (2013; 41 minutes)
This documentary is about Mayan Q'eqchi' resistance against nickel mining in Guatemala. Angelica Choc and other land defenders share their stories of seeking justice in Canadian courts for murder and rape.

Hija de la laguna (Daughter of the lake) (2015; 87 minutes)

This documentary is about an Andean woman who considers herself the daughter of the lakes that provide water to her village. When a large gold deposit is found beneath the lakes, the Peruvian government supports a multinational mining company mining the deposit.

Water warriors (2017; 22 minutes)

This short documentary tells the story of Mi'kmaq and settler allies in New Brunswick, Canada, coming together in 2013 to stop fracking for shale gas. Audiences are exposed to the motivations and tactics of shale gas opponents, including Indigenous mothers and grandmothers.

Leanne Betasamosake Simpson

https://www.leannesimpson.ca

This is the website of Leanne Betasamosake Simpson, a Michi Saagiig Nishnaabeg scholar, writer, and artist who writes fiction and non-fiction works about Indigenous issues.

Unión Latinoamericana de Mujeres (ULAM)

http://redulam.org.

This is the website of ULAM, a network of organizations run by women for the benefit of rural and Indigenous women affected by mining practices and policies in Latin America. ULAM promotes international activism and creates spaces for women to share their experiences and strengthen their alliances.

REFERENCES

Alexander, M.J., & Mohanty, C.T. (2013). *Feminist genealogies, colonial legacies, democratic futures*. New York, NY: Routledge.

Bannerji, H. (2000). *The dark side of the nation: Essays on multiculturalism, nationalism and gender*. Toronto, ON: Canadian Scholars' Press.

Barrios de Chúngara, D., & Viezzer, M. (1978). *Let me speak! Testimony of Domitila, a woman of the Bolivian mines*. New York, NY: Monthly Review Press.

Bell, S.E., & Braun, Y.A. (2010). Coal, identity, and the gendering of environmental justice activism in central Appalachia. *Gender & Society, 24*(6), 794–813.

Bradshaw, S., Linneker, B., & Overton, L. (2017). Extractive industries as sites of supernormal profits and supernormal patriarchy? *Gender & Development, 25*(3), 439–54.

Braun, Y.A. (2011). Left high and dry: An intersectional analysis of gender, dams, and development in Lesotho. *International Feminist Journal of Politics, 13*(2), 141–62.

Butler, P. (2015). *Colonial extractions: Race and Canadian mining in contemporary Africa*. Toronto, ON: University of Toronto Press.

Connell, R.W. (2014). Margin becoming centre: For a world-centred rethinking of masculinities. *NORMA-International Journal for Masculinity Studies, 9*(4), 217–31.

Connell, R.W., & Messerschmidt, J.W. (2005). Hegemonic masculinity: Rethinking the concept. *Gender & Society, 19*(6), 829–59.

Coulthard, G. (2013). For our nations to live, capitalism must die. *Nations Rising*, November.

Coulthard, G. (2014). *Red skin, white masks: Rejecting the colonial politics of recognition*. Minneapolis, MN: University of Minnesota Press.

Daley, S. (2016). Outcry echoes up to Canada: Guatemalans citing rapes and other abuses put focus on companies' conduct abroad. *The New York Times*, 3 April.

Davis, A. (1983). *Women, race and class*. New York, NY: Vintage.

de Finney, S. (2014). Under the shadow of empire: Indigenous girls' presencing as decolonizing force. *Girlhood Studies, 7*(1), 8–26.

Elmhirst, B. (2011). Introducing new feminist political ecologies. *Geoforum, 42*(2), 129–32.

Foster, J.B. (2003). A planetary defeat: The failure of global environmental reform. *Monthly Review, 54*(8), 1.

Friedman-Rudovsky, J. (2011). "Walmart greenwashing: Workers pay for the price." *Miami New Times*, 6 January. https://www.miaminewtimes.com/news/walmart-greenwashing-workers-pay-the-price-6379374

Global Witness. (2018). "At What Cost? Irresponsible business and the murder of land and environmental defenders in 2017." https://www.globalwitness.org/documents/19595/Defenders_report_layout_AW4_update_disclaimer.pdf

Glynn, T. (2014). Women in a mine's world: Barbaric capitalism faces opponents of mining and shale gas. *Canadian Dimension*, October.

Goldman Environmental Prize. (2015). "Berta Cáceres acceptance speech, 2015 Goldman Environmental Prize." Youtube: https://www.youtube.com/watch?v=AR1kwx8b0ms

Gordon, T., & Webber, J.R. (2016). *Blood of extraction: Canadian imperialism in Latin America*. Halifax, NS: Fernwood Publishing.

Grandin, G. (2011). *The last colonial massacre: Latin America in the Cold War*. Chicago, IL: University of Chicago Press.

Hall, R. (2012). Diamond mining in Canada's Northwest Territories: A colonial continuity. *Antipode, 45*(2), 376–93.

Hopkins, K. (2009). Women fight South American mines. *The Guardian,* 12 October. https://www.theguardian.com/business/2009/oct/12/women-fight-south-american-mines.

Howe, M. (2015). *Debriefing Elsipogtog: The anatomy of a struggle.* Halifax, NS: Fernwood Publishing.

Johnston, R., & McIvor, A. (2004). Dangerous work, hard men and broken bodies: Masculinity in the Clydeside heavy industries, c. 1930–1970s. *Labour History Review, 69*(2), 135–51.

Keck, J., & Powell, M. (2006). Women into mining jobs at Inco: Challenging the gender division of labor. In L. Mercier & J.J. Gier (Eds), *Mining women: Gender in the development of a global industry, 1670 to the present* (pp. 280–95). New York, NY: Palgrave Macmillan.

Kirsch, S. (2014). *Mining capitalism: The relationship between corporations and their critics.* Oakland, CA: University of California Press.

Klein, N. (2014). *This changes everything: Capitalism vs. the climate.* Toronto, ON: Alfred A. Knopf.

Kojola, E. (2018). Indigeneity, gender and class in decision-making about risks from resource extraction. *Environmental Sociology, 5*(2), 1–19.

Lahiri-Dutt, K. (2013). Bodies in/out of place: Hegemonic masculinity and kamins' motherhood in Indian coal mines. *South Asian History and Culture, 4*(2), 109–16.

Lakhani, N. (2016). Berta Cáceres's name was on Honduran military hit list, says former soldier. *The Guardian,* 21 June. https://www.theguardian.com/world/2016/jun/21/berta-caceres-name-honduran-military-hitlist-former-soldier.

Lakhani, N. (2018). Berta Cáceres murder: Ex-Honduran military intelligence officer arrested. *The Guardian,* 2 March. https://www.theguardian.com/world/2018/mar/02/berta-caceres-death-murder-ex-honduran-military-intelligence-officer-arrested.

Lowe, M. (1998). *Premature bonanza: Standoff at Voisey's Bay.* Toronto, ON: Between the Lines.

Lugones, M. (2007). Heterosexualism and the colonial/modern gender system. *Hypatia, 22*(1), 186–201.

Lugones, M. (2010). Toward a decolonial feminism. *Hypatia, 25*(4), 742–75.

McLaren, M.A. (2017). *Decolonizing feminism: Transnational feminism and globalization.* London, UK, and New York, NY: Rowman & Littlefield.

Mercier, L., & Gier, J.J. (Eds). (2006). *Mining women: Gender in the development of a global industry, 1670 to the present.* New York, NY: Palgrave-MacMillan.

Mohanty, C.T. (2017). Preface: Toward a decolonial feminism for the 99 percent. In M. McLaren (Ed.), *Decolonizing feminism: Transnational feminism and globalization* (pp. vii–xi). London, UK, and New York, NY: Rowman & Littlefield.

Natural Resources Canada. (2018). Canadian mining assets. *Nature Resources Canada Information Bulletin.* https://www.nrcan.gc.ca/mining-materials/publications/19323.

Oliver, K. (2017). The special plight of women refugees. In M. McLaren (Ed.), *Decolonizing feminism: Transnational feminism and globalization* (pp. 177–200). London, UK, and New York, NY: Rowman & Littlefield.

Sanford, V. (2010/2011). Reading "La masacre de Panzós" in Panzós on the 32nd anniversary. *Revista: Harvard Review of Latin America, X*(1), 17–19.

Savarese, J. (2016). Analyzing erasures and resistance involving Indigenous women in New Brunswick, Canada. In D. Memee Lavell-Harvard & J. Brant (Eds), *Forever loved: Exposing the hidden crisis of missing and murdered Indigenous women and girls in Canada.* Bradford, ON: Demeter Press.

Simpson, L. (2011). *Dancing on our Turtle's back: Stories of Nishnaabeg re-creation, resurgence and a new emergence.* Winnipeg, MB: ARP.

Simpson, L. (2013). *Elsipogtog everywhere.* https://www.leannesimpson.ca/writings/2013/10/20/elsipogtog-everywhere.

Simpson, L. (2014). Not murdered, not missing: Rebelling against colonial gender violence. Nations Rising Blog in their it ends here series, 5 March.

Smith, A. (2015). *Conquest: Sexual violence and American Indian genocide.* Durham, NC: Duke University Press.

Swift, J. (1977). *The Big Nickel: Inco at home and abroad.* Toronto, ON: Between the Lines.

True, J. (2012). *The political economy of violence against women.* Oxford, UK: Oxford University Press.

Veltmeyer, H., & Petras, J.F. (2014). *The new extractivism: A post-neoliberal development model or imperialism of the twenty-first century?* London, UK: Zed Books.

Walia, H. (2012). Decolonizing together: Moving beyond a politics of solidarity toward a practice of decolonization. *Briarpatch,* 1 January.

Walter, M., & Urkidi, L. (2016). Community consultations: Local responses to large-scale mining in Latin America. In de Castro et al. (Eds), *Environmental governance in Latin America* (pp. 287–325). New York, NY: Palgrave Macmillan.

Weir, A. (2017). Decolonizing feminist freedom: Indigenous relationalities. In M. McLaren (Ed.), *Decolonizing feminism: Transnational feminism and globalization* (pp. 257–88). London, UK, and New York, NY: Rowman & Littlefield.

Whittington, L. (2009). MPs told of gang rapes at mine. *The Toronto Star,* 24 November. https://www.thestar.com/news/investigations/2009/11/24/mps_told_of_gang_rapes_at_mine.html.

CHAPTER 17

◇

Forced Sterilization in Times of Sustainable Development

Ana Isla

Learning Objectives

In this chapter, you will:

- examine the contradiction in the global politics of United Nations institutions;
- learn about the relationship between reproductive rights and population growth;
- consider the link between the debt and the environmental crises because of forced sterilization in Peru;
- differentiate between reproductive rights and the Voluntary Surgical Contraceptive Program;
- consider the impact of forced sterilization policies and the current level of violence against women in Peru.

Introduction

Forced sterilization has occurred all over the world (in Puerto Rico for industrial plans, India for economic development, Canada to annihilate an ethnic group, and the United States to eradicate an "undesirable population"), but none have been linked to so-called sustainable development. This chapter links reproduction rights as central to the United Nations International Conference on Human Rights in Tehran (1968), as revitalized at the Conference on Population and Development in Cairo (1994), and as invigorated at the World Conference on Women in Beijing (1995).

However, at the Earth Summit (1992), **reproductive rights** shifted toward **family planning** defined as central to women's empowerment, reducing poverty, and achieving sustainable development (SD).

The internal context is the 1990s debt crisis in Peru when the Fujimori cabinet required new loans to refinance its **multilateral debt** and called on the International Monetary Fund (IMF) and the World Bank (WB) to restructure Peru's economy. This took place during the time that the environmental crisis was officially recognized by the United Nations (UN) through the Earth Summit (1992) that mistakenly identified three agents of global environmental problems—"poverty, uneven development, and population growth." How these two variables, debt and climate crises, connected forced sterilization to Peru's health reform agenda is the core of this chapter.

More specifically, the chapter focuses on Peru's population control program carried out between 1995 and 2001, which until now has not been officially recognized. My thesis is that forced sterilization was a program to reduce feminized bodies of the Indigenous and peasant population that was rebelling against the worst effects of the debt crisis. But the program was pleasing to those in the United Nations institutions advocating for population control. The background of forced sterilization was the debt crisis during the 1980s, which created conditions for political violence between the state and two guerrilla movements, Sendero Luminoso (Shining Path) and Movimiento Revolucionario Tupac Amaru (MRTA). The Truth and Reconciliation Commission (2003) denounced the fact that 60,000 Peruvians had been assassinated or disappeared in the battle for survival between 1980 and 2001. Disappearance has been especially prominent in the rural areas among poor, Quechua-speaking Indigenous people and Amazonians (Peru, The Truth and Reconciliation Commission, 2003).

The first section presents women speaking about their experiences with forced sterilization and the response of the Ministry of Justice 20 years later through the Register of Victims of Forced Sterilization (REVIESFO) program. The second section reviews an ecofeminist and postcolonial critique of the logic of domination and the Western feminist assumption that women as a group have identical interests and desires. The third section presents a historical account of the forced sterilization program in Peru, how it developed, and how it is related to global health governance and Peru's multilateral debt. The fourth section offers an account of the class, gender, and racialized nature of forced sterilization. The fifth segment presents feminism's struggle against forced sterilization. The sixth is an account of Peru's anti-women politics and of feminist activism against violence toward women.

Women Speaking on Their Experience of Forced Sterilization and REVIESFO

In Lima on 9 June 2017, a "Conversation: **Forced Sterilization**; Indigenous Women looking for Truth, Justice and Reparation" was observed by Victoria Tauli-Corpuz, UN special rapporteur on the rights of Indigenous peoples. At the introduction of the event, two women who had suffered forced sterilization made the following statements:

> My name is Luisa Pinedo Rango, a 54-year-old Shipibo woman from Ucayali. I was sterilized when I was 33, and I had 9 children. One day, a doctor arrived in the village of Masisea. On his first day, he visited my house, and on his second visit he obliged me to go with him to the hospital. Upon our arrival at the hospital, I was anaesthetized without knowing why and after waking up, he sent me home. Because my surgery became infected, I have permanent pain. Since then, I have not been able to contribute in my family's farm.

> My name is Dionisia Calderon Arellano from Cangallo, Ayacucho. In addition to being a victim of the regime's political violence because my husband was disappeared by the military, I was also a victim of state violence against the poor when I was sterilized without any information and without my consent. On the day of my sterilization, I was taken from the streets to the hospital. When I woke up, I was lying on a mattress placed on the floor. When I left the hospital, no medicine was given to me, and I developed an infection.

I saved myself because I had some little animals to sell. Even though the surgery was long ago, for many years the surgery hurt and burned. From sterilization, many women have died because they had nothing to sell to cure themselves from the infections. But that's not all what happened to us, sterilization also has stigmatized us in our communities. For example, people call me machona, capona (butch). Many of the women have been left alone because their husbands wanted to have children and they could not have any more. Children are the labour force on the farm.

These statements were followed by statements from other women participants, among them Sandra Enriquez, a lawyer from the Ministry of Justice, who reported that a Supreme Decree No. 006-2015-JUS declared priority attention to victims of forced sterilizations carried out between 1995 and 2001. The ministry had discovered national interest in the issue and therefore created the program Registro de Victimas de Esterilizacion Forzada (Register of Victims of Forced Sterilization, or REVIESFO). Its purpose is to create an administrative record and to provide victims with the right to physical health, psychological support, and legal defence (in case the victim decides to take legal action against the state). REVIESFO focuses on the recognition that violation of human rights took place because there was no prior information or consent. Ministerial Resolution 319-2015-JUS approved the procedure for registration of men and women who had undergone sterilization.

The registry, which has a national scope, began in January 2016 and has been developing with the support of several institutions. The Ministry of Justice has 30 lawyers in charge of the registry. However, it has been implemented in only 18 directorates of the 33 Public Defense Directorates of the Ministry of Justice. The Ministry of Women provides psychological support, and the Ministry of Health provides medical support to certify the surgery scar. Finally, the Ministry of Culture arranges language translation from Spanish to Quechua and from Quechua to Spanish.

After 20 years of women's struggles, the state, through the Ministry of Justice, finally listened to the victims. By July 2017, the Ministry of Justice had a record of victims that exceeded 5000 testimonies; however, only 2074 women have filed their complaints with the Public Ministry.

Several Peruvian organizations are insisting that forced sterilization be recognized as a form of sexual violence in order for victims to be registered in a single registry and be given access to prompt, fair, and remedial measures to ensure rehabilitation and satisfaction (including restoration of dignity and reputation). They also demand that the proceedings before the courts must include the medical personnel involved to guarantee non-repetition, to preserve collective memory from oblivion, and, in particular, to prevent revisionist or negationist rationalizations from arising. The reparatory measures must have a "transformative" power for their beneficiaries, since they live in marginalized situations.

In brief, Peruvian society as a whole has the inalienable right to know the truth about what happened and to see those responsible properly sanctioned. The following section reviews an ecofeminist and postcolonial critique of the logic of domination and the Western feminist assumption that women as a group have identical interests and desires.

Ecofeminism and Postcolonial Perspectives

This section draws on the work of ecofeminist Maria Mies and postcolonial feminists Chandra T. Mohanty and Christina Ewy. Then it applies these insights to analyze different aspects of the class-, gendered-, and racialized-based relationship of forced sterilization in Peru.

On Mies, Mohanty, and Ewy

Mies, author of *Patriarchy and capital accumulation on a world scale: Women in the international division of labour* (1986), is critical of the Eurocentric assumption that women's work has no value and that unpaid work has no value. She locates the origin of women's oppression in the interconnected systems of patriarchy, capitalism, and colonialism. She argues that when women, peasants, and Indigenous peoples are described as "closer to nature," they are made exploitable. Mies uses the term "**housewifization**" (1986, p. 106) to capture the process whereby hitherto life-sustaining work is captured, confined, devalued, and put to use in support of monetized production. This division of labour into reproductive labour (housewife, sustenance) and productive labour (breadwinning, salaried) is necessary for capitalism to function. Housewifization is a devaluation of women's work, but it also applies to those who are not biologically women. Similar to families and households, this division exists on a worldwide scale through colonialism. These feminized, socially marginal, and externalized economic sectors and actors are Indigenous people, peasants, and the so-called underdeveloped world in the North and the South when their land and products are taken from them through structural violence with little or no compensation.

Chandra T. Mohanty's "Under Western eyes: Feminist scholarship and colonial discourses" (1988) critiques inclusionary feminism by arguing that "assumptions of privilege and ethnocentric universality on the one hand, and inadequate self-consciousness about the effect of some Western scholarship on the 'third world' in the context of a world system dominated by the West, on the other, characterize a sizeable extent of Western feminist work on women in the third world. . . . It is in this process of discursive homogenization and systematization of the oppression of women in the third world that power is exercised in much of recent Western feminist discourse, and this power needs to be defined and named" (p. 63).

Christina Ewy's *Second-wave neoliberalism: Gender, race and health sector reform in Peru* (2010) argues that Fujimori's discourse of family planning (FP) was placed within the broader "struggle against poverty," orchestrated by development organizations and that he viewed family planning as a means to reduce poverty rather than to promote women's rights.

Several feminisms, liberal, radical, and third wave, have produced theories supposedly valid for all women. The truth is that our characteristics of class, ethnicity, national origin, geographical location, language, sexual orientation, gender identity, etc. complicate the female experience. Consequently, the women who inhabit bodies intersected by several types of simultaneous oppression are in a null space of protection.

Material ecofeminists have amplified the list of differences in a patriarchal society. More specifically, postcolonial feminism researches all forms of exploitation, oppression, and resistance developed by colonies against the political economy of global capital.

The goal of Fujimori's program of forced sterilization was part of the family planning effort to reduce the number of the poor, peasants, and Indigenous people. Their children, organized in guerrillas, rose up against the economic blackmail of the debt crisis to fight government class, gender, and racist policies that excluded them. From ecofeminist and postcolonial lenses, the acknowledgement of differences among women is crucial within an analysis of the classed, gendered, and racist impact of women's reproductive rights. Ignoring these differences was clearly exemplified when powerful Western feminists allowed Alberto Fujimori (a criminal dictator in Peru) to be one of the main speakers at the Beijing Official Fourth World Conference on Women: Action for Equality, Development and Peace in 1995.

To understand the magnitude of the human rights crisis fashioned by Fujimori's family planning, I include information on what happened in the Department of Ayacucho, where Los Cabitos, a military barrack, is located. It is here where 30 per cent of the assassinated and/ or disappeared lived. Here, among the tortured and dead were elementary, high school, and university students, professors, and artisans (APRODEH, COMISEDH, n.d.; Peru, Ministerio de Cultura, 2017).

In 2016, the struggle waged by relatives of the disappeared forced the government to enact Law No. 30470, Search for Missing Persons. As a result, the prosecutor ordered the excavation of an area of 170,000 square metres in the perimeter of the Los Cabitos barracks in Ayacucho (Ortiz, 2017). The forensic specialized team has unearthed more than 3000 bodies and delivered more than 1600 remains to families who had waited three decades to identify and bury the remains of their loved ones.

The photograph exhibition entitled "Disappeared: Between the Search and the Hope" organized by the Ministry of Culture, 2016–17, captured the delivery of the remains: Max Cabello's photos show individual and collective grieving; Nadia Cohen's photos show human solitudes, living with their discreet and isolated pain; Rodrigo Abad has chosen the Look of the Bereaved in which some of them direct their gaze toward the sky as if they were asking a superior

force to take revenge. Others question the viewer, looking at us frontally with pain, anger, or resignation; Maria Garcia Burgos presents the Chalina (Scarf) de la Esperanza that represents various actions taken by women in the most precarious contexts, collectively organized to break into public life, to plead for recognition of their demands; Giorgio Negro shows the Ashaninkas and Nomatsignengas from Amazonia, who waited with nostalgia or serenity for their missing family members (in the Amazon areas, it is difficult to search for missing persons because many of those assassinated were thrown into the rivers); Jose Atauje displays images of women's pain: mothers, widows, sisters, and daughters; and Miguel Mejia exhibits expressions that involve the processes of exhumation, identification, and burial: hands that clean, hands that recognize, bodies bent by crying, and bodies that bow before the loved one to say goodbye for the last time.

Within this ethnic battle, Fujimori's forced sterilization program only included a **Voluntary Surgical Contraceptive Program (vsc)** on the list of contraceptives. Following Beijing, Fujimori considerably increased the number of sterilizations carried out by army, navy, and national police doctors. For instance, in 1995 there were 90 daily voluntary surgical contraceptive operations each day; in 1996, the number went up to 224; and in 1997 there were 300 operations each day (Report of Ministry of Health Marino Costa Bauer to Fujimori on 6 June 1997, in Paez, 2011).

In Beijing, by accepting Fujimori as a speaker, some Western feminists contributed to depoliticize Peruvian feminist denunciations of disappearances and forced sterilizations. The next section discusses how the forced sterilization program, named the Reproductive Health and Family Planning Program (PNSRPF), was a direct result of the 1980s debt crisis and the 1992 Earth Summit.

A Historical Account of the Forced Sterilization Program in Peru and Its Relation to Global Health Governance and Multilateral Debts

The United Nations' Reproductive Health and Family Planning Program (PNSRPF) was immersed in contradictions between reproductive rights and demands for **population control** programs as requisite for development loans. In 1968, the UN Conference on Human Rights in Tehran, Iran, adopted Resolution XVIII on the Human Rights Aspects of Family Planning. The 1969 Declaration on Social Progress and Development, adopted by the General Assembly in Resolution 2542, affirmed the Tehran proclamation. The 1994 International Conference on Population and Development (ICPD) in Cairo, Egypt, maintained that "reproductive rights embrace certain human rights that are already recognized in national laws, international human rights documents and other relevant United Nations consensus documents." At this conference, the population issue was linked to human development, environmental protection, equity between sexes, and respect for human rights. After Cairo's conference, debates around reproductive rights continued, this time in the context of the climate crisis. At this point, family planning and global environmental politics had become contentious areas, particularly among indebted countries.

Regarding women's reproductive rights, a general agreement reached at the Cairo International Conference on Population and Development in 1994 was ratified at the Beijing Declaration and Platform for Action in 1995. However, at the Earth Summit in 1992, participating governments negotiated Agenda 21, which officially linked development and environment within the concept of **sustainable development** (SD) and became

TABLE 17.1   UN Conferences, 1968–95

Years	United Nations Conferences	City/Country	Declarations/Contradictions on Family Planning
1968	Human Rights	Tehran/Iran	Paragraph 3 reads that "couples have a basic human right to decide freely and responsibly on the number and spacing of their children and a right to adequate education and information in this respect."[1]
1969	Declaration on Social Progress and Development		Resolution 2542 urged governments to provide couples with not only the "education" but also the "means necessary to enable them to exercise their right to determine freely and responsibly the number and spacing of their children."[2]
1992	Earth Summit	Rio de Janeiro/Brazil	Population growth produces environmental degradation; therefore, a coordinated effort to reduce population must be taken through sustainable development.
1994	Population and Development	Cairo/Egypt	The Cairo conference includes the right of all to make decisions concerning reproduction, free of discrimination, coercion, and violence as expressed in human rights documents.[3]
1995	World Conference on Women	Beijing/China	The Beijing Declaration and Platform for Action reaffirmed women's reproductive rights and the right to development.

equated with economic growth that would rescue poor countries from poverty (Pearce & Warford, 1993). As global capital became prominent and neoliberal economists of the World Bank articulated a set of prescriptions designed to manage the ecology for global capital interest, the discourse of reproductive rights and population growth conflicted. Therefore, development agencies and big NGOs rejected calls for a new international economic order based on fair distribution. Instead, they coordinated efforts to reduce population, arguing that population growth produces environmental degradation and threatens the future of the earth.

In brief, the international political context for the implementation of the Reproductive Health and Family Planning Program in Peru was: the 1968 UN Conference on Human Rights and its follow-up in 1969; the 1994 International Conference on Population and Development; and the 1995 World Women's Conference. The reduction of population as a program was validated during the Earth Summit, 1992, when population growth was declared to be one of the causes of global warming and sustainable development was presented a justification for reducing population growth. The next section presents the implementation of the PNSRPF throughout the clash of United Nations institutions—between human rights and economic growth through the Stabilization and Structural Adjustment Programs of the IMF and the World Bank, respectively.

The Class, Gender, and Racialized Nature of Forced Sterilization

Current patriarchal-capitalist production ignores the material reality of human existence that is also expressed through the domination of women, feminized and racialized bodies, and nature. It relies on the overexploitation of paid and unpaid workers and manufactures an unequal exchange between men and women, between white and other ethnicities, and between the core and the periphery.

Since the 1970s, the so-called developing countries' integration with unregulated private global capital markets led to an increase in net foreign public and private indebtedness, with an increased portion of this debt of a short-term nature. By 1975, high interest rates had strangled the Peruvian economy. By 1980, the International Monetary Fund and the World Bank had "rescued" Peru's economy by imposing their first **Stabilization** and **Structural Adjustment Programs**. In this neoliberal context, restructuring implies setting up a new model of accumulation, new patterns of investment and saving, new income distribution, and the creation of capital in new ways. Latin American governments have been forced to assume responsibility for debt acquired by private corporations and local banks (often subsidiaries of transnational corporations based in the North). This obligation doubles the debt. By 1982, all Latin American countries were engulfed in their own debt crisis, which continues today and is an example of unsustainable development.

As a consequence of the debt, the implementation of IMF and WB programs prescribed population control programs as a prerequisite for development loans. Consequently, women from the indebted countries would have to stop having children. These ambitious plans could not be achieved without a government devoted to repressing the housewifized sectors that stood to lose the most from this financial greed—the poor women and men living on the margins of big cities as well as Indigenous and rural people (Isla, 1997).

In Peru by 1990, Fujimori's administration had been rescued by new loans from the IMF and the WB. By 1995, almost half of the population was not able to satisfy their basic needs, while a struggle for survival increased (Isla, 1997). In the context of the debt crisis, every decision of the indebted countries, including national family planning (NFP) programs, were internationally designed and sometimes directly managed. For instance, in Peru USAID, UNFPA (United Nations Population Fund), and AVSC International financed the program. In addition, from 1997 to 1999, at the heart of surgical contraception (SC) were government officials paid by the World Bank and the Inter-American Development Bank (IDB) under the command of Dr Augusto Meloni, director of external cooperation at the World Health Organization. Furthermore, each indebted country was allowed to orient its population program without public scrutiny. Consequently, between 1995 and 2001, during Alberto Fujimori's administration, the Stabilization and Structural Adjustment Programs of "poverty elimination" were accomplished through forcible sterilization made legal under the so-called Voluntary Surgical Contraceptive Program. Furthermore, the program was observed in silence by the so-called feminist NGOs that received overseas funds (Olivera, 2014).

According to Susana Chavez (2015; 2017), Fujimori eliminated informed consent from the "reproductive rights" of the International Conference on Population and Development (ICPD) and took advantage of the traditional discrimination against the poorest women in Peru. Chavez argues that in eliminating informed consent, the government organized a birth control program that did not guarantee choice, and it came with incentives and/or threats. Chavez also maintains that all the evidence indicates that sterilizations were part of a government policy, typical of the pragmatism that characterizes dictatorships such as those run by Fujimori and his closest supporters.

Remarkably, Fujimori's forced sterilization program was initiated in 1993, right after the Earth Summit in 1992, during the tenure of the minister of health, Jaime Freundt-Thurne Oyanguren (August 1993–October 1994), followed by Eduardo Yong Motta (October 1994–April 1996).

However, it was after the Beijing Conference (1995) in February 1996 that Fujimori summoned the courage to unveil the Reproductive Health and Family Planning Program of the Ministry of Health. Under the tenure of Marino Costa Bauer (April 1996–January 1999) and Alejandro Aguinaga (April 1999–November 2000), the program installed medical posts in all districts and in many rural communities that had risen up in arms against the misery imposed by international creditors and their national cronies.

To carry out a national program, the administration created a National Commission for Coordination of Family Planning and Reproductive Health Policies (COORDIPLAN). Among its declared issues was to decrease the high rate of maternal mortality that had reached 261 per 100,000 live births. It also aimed to reduce the national average of 3.4 children per woman, especially in rural areas, as well as clandestine abortions that usually ended in lesions or deaths. But the program focused on a single technique of population regulation: surgical contraception (SC).

Shortly after SC was initiated, the first alarms were raised by some churches and feminists, such as Giulia Tamayo of Flora Tristán, who uncovered the international scandal. Giulia Tamayo wrote a report "Nothing personal" (1999) for the Peruvian section of the Latin American and Caribbean Committee for the Defence of Women's Rights (CLADEM). She exposed the Peruvian government as having introduced, in 1993, surgical sterilization as a method of family planning for rural peasants and Indigenous people. She documented procedures undertaken in 1995 as numbering 21,901. Although she did not state how many of them were voluntary, the figures give an account of the absolute prioritization of the surgical method.

Years later, the ombudsman's office in its Reports No. 7 (Peru, Defensoria del Pueblo 7), No. 27 (Peru, Defensoria del Pueblo 27), and No. 69 (Peru, Defensoria del Pueblo 69) argued that among 157 documented cases of irregularities in

TABLE 17.2   Number of female sterilizations in Peru, by year

1996	1997	1998	1999	2000	2001	Total
81,762	109,689	25,995	26,788	16,640	11,154	272,028

Adapted from Peru, 2012, Defensoria del Pueblo 69.

the application of the method, 70 corresponded to lack of valid consent. Its Report No. 69 documented the number of female sterilizations as shown in Table 17.2.

Hilaria Supa Huaman (an Indigenous woman from Anta, Cuzco, and later a congresswoman) was the first person to denounce forced sterilization in the 1990s. Supa's book, *Threads of my life* (2008), describes the struggle of about 100 Indigenous women from her community. They denounced the tubal ligation program and the health complications in spite of the threats made against them. She showed how poor rural women were deceived by the government: "its Ministry of Health used the programs Feeding and Nutrition for Families in High Risk (PANFAR) and ADRA OFASA (a network of global offices working on 'development') to menace women with food donation cancellation if they refused the ligation" (p. 134). Supa also accused the government of persecuting those who fearlessly stood up against the Fujimori administration's human rights violations. She explains that "[D]uring this time, we, who performed the investigation and those who signed the complaints, suffered different forms of reprisal. Our homes were invaded and searched for evidence, we were subjected to telephone espionage and highway [road] surveillance by agents from the Intelligence Service, denial of service at Medical Post . . . , and so on" (p. 137). Also, during the so-called Festivales de Ligaduras de Trompas, in many cases health providers offered money or food to patients to be subjected to a voluntary surgical anticonception (VSA) (Supa, 2008).

Journalist Angel Paez (2011) organized statistics about the number of forced sterilizations in each Peruvian state and town and exposed the crisis as a plan deliberately directed by the government through quotas imposed on health personnel. He said that Fujimori even authorized the intervention of the armed forces and the national police to accelerate the devastating policy (Paez, 2011). The testimony of the anesthesiologist at the Maternal and Child Health Centre of Castilla in Piura, Rogelio Del Carmen, reported that by 1996, "doctors had to sterilize no longer two women a day but 62, according to the mandate of the Ministry of Health, in compliance with a state policy of Alberto Fujimori's regime" (Cronica Viva, 2015). The numerical goals at the national, regional, and local levels were compulsory, as evidenced in the testimonies of some doctors and nurses—that is, they were linked to their salaries and their job security. This pressure, exerted from the high authorities of the Ministry of Health, meant that a very high number of Quechua-speaking women in rural Andean and poor rural and urban areas were forcibly sterilized. Sterilization was performed without consent, through intimidation (constant visits by medical personnel to women's homes, generating in them a sense of "coercion," such as the loss of their identity documents), by deception (taking advantage of another surgical intervention during which the sterilization was carried out), or by blackmail (telling them that if they refused the operation, they would not receive support from the government or could be criminally reported).

This kind of plan is considered internationally a crime against humanity by Article 2 of the Convention for the Prevention and Punishment of the Crime of Genocide (Paris, 1948, ratified by

Peru on 24 February 1960) as well as by Article 6 of the Statute of the International Criminal Court (Rome, 1998, ratified by Peru on 10 November 2001). Finally, Article 8, 2, b, xxii of the statute includes forced sterilization among war crimes. However, in Peru there is no law against "forced sterilization"; nonetheless, "criminal types of serious or minor injuries could be invoked (Articles 121 and 122 penal code); torture (Art. 321 penal code); professional cooperation in the commission of torture (Article 322 penal code); abuse of authority (Article 376 criminal code), and, according to the circumstances, manslaughter (Article 111 penal code)" (Citroni, 1996).

However, in 2001 Fujimori, prosecuted as a head of a criminal organization, escaped to Japan, from where he resigned the presidency by fax; at the same time, his mandate was abolished by Congress. The transitional administration of Valentin Paniagua (2001–3) formed in the Congress a subcommittee to investigate persons and institutions involved in voluntary anti-conception surgery and to examine the practice of forced sterilization (Peru, Congreso, 2003). The subcommittee concluded that both Fujimori and his ministers of health were fully aware of the phenomenon and its magnitude and were kept regularly informed, without taking any action to sanction instances of forced sterilization. Consequently, the subcommittee filed Constitutional Complaint No. 151 against former President Alberto Fujimori and former health ministers Eduardo Yong Motta, Marino Costa Bauer (Evidence, 2014), and Alejandro Aguinaga for crimes against individual freedom, life, and the body and health, for the crime of conspiracy to commit a crime, and for the crime of genocide. The constitutional complaint was filed on 17 March 2003, and on 7 April of the same year the Permanent Commission of Congress (during the government of Alejandro Toledo, who is now a fugitive from Peruvian justice for money laundering) reversed the previous investigation and consent of Congress.

In short, Peru supposedly was going to have fewer poor people because Indigenous women would give birth to fewer poor people. VSC would contribute to lower demands for services from Indigenous and rural groups, facilitating compliance with IMF and World Bank programs. The next section reviews feminist struggles against forced sterilization after revelation of it created an enormous scandal in Peru and abroad and feminist organizations revealed that forced sterilization was part of the state's policy of Family Planning—Health for Everyone (*Programa Salud Basica para Todos*).

Feminism's Battle against Forced Sterilization

Since 1997, NGOs such as the Committee for Latin America and the Caribbean for the Defence of Women's Human Rights (CLADEM) and the Study for the Defence of Women (DEMUS) as well as journalists with *La Republica* and *El Comercio* have filed complaints against Fujimori and the forced sterilization program that the Public Ministry, appointed during Fujimori's administration, has scrapped. This prevented further investigation and determination of government criminal responsibility. However, on 15 June 1999, DEMUS, CLADEM, the Human Rights Association (APRODEH), the Legal Center for Reproductive Rights and Public Policy (CRLP), and the Center for Justice and International Law (CEJIL) filed a complaint with the Inter-American Commission on Human Rights (IACHR) against Peru for violating the human rights of María Mamérita Mestanza Chávez by subjecting her to a surgical sterilization that eventually resulted in her death (CIDH, 2003). The petition stated that the case of Mestanza Chávez should be analyzed as representing "a significant number of cases of women affected by the application of a governmental policy of a massive, compulsive and systematic nature that emphasized sterilization as a method to rapidly change the reproductive behavior of the population, especially poor, Indigenous and rural women" (CIDH, 2003).

The case documented that Mestanza Chavez was a peasant woman of 33, mother of seven. She and her husband were harassed about sterilization by La Encanada Health Centre in Cajamarca. The couple was told that they would go to jail if she did not get sterilized. Under such pressure, on 27 March 1998, she underwent sterilization, without any prior medical examination, at the Regional Hospital of Cajamarca. The next day, she was discharged despite suffering from vomiting and intense headaches. In April 1998, she died without receiving medical attention. Two days later, one of the medical doctors arrived at her house and took her husband to the hospital where he received 850 soles (250 USD) and warned him not to tell the police what had happened. In spite of the threats, the husband went to the Public Prosecutor's Office (Romero, 2011).

According to DEMUS, there are 18 documented cases of death caused by sterilization operations or the subsequent lack of medical attention. In several of the cases, surgical sterilization presented complications during or after the intervention, thus worsening the women's health, as in the cases of Leopoldina Vega Chipana and Victoria Vigo, and sometimes causing death. Among the dead is Celia Ramos Durand (DEMUS, 2016). DEMUS had shown that between 2004 and 2009, the Public Ministry scrapped other complaints because "[forced sterilizations] do not constitute a crime of genocide or torture and . . . crimes within the penal code would not have been established or would be prescribed" (DEMUS, 2016).

Giulia Tamayo argued that each of the accused should also be charged with war crimes because the coerced sterilization was carried out in the context of the 1980–2000 armed conflict (between the military and left-wing guerrillas) when the armed forces were used to threaten and terrorize the civilian population. After several other denunciations that were filed and influenced by the Inter-American Commission of Human Rights (IACHR), finally, on 24 November 2012, the Supra-Provincial Criminal Prosecutor of Lima decided to reopen the investigations in the Mestanza Chávez case under the heading of "crime against humanity." Also, in 2012 the UN Committee on Economic, Social and Cultural Rights as well as the UN Committee against Torture expressed its concern about Peru's forced sterilizations.

Because those complaints failed, another lawsuit was brought by the victims in Anta, Cuzco. Sterilization in this province was implemented door-to-door, and all the victims belonged to the same Indigenous ethnic group. Despite accusations, on 24 January 2014 the criminal investigation against Fujimori for ordering compulsory sterilization was again dropped on grounds of "insufficient evidence" (Servindi, 2016).

In 2005, after several trials as a head of a criminal organization, Fujimori was jailed for 25 years. On 24 December 2017, a political event took place, and Fujimori was released from jail. What transpired was that the president of Peru, Pedro Pablo Kuczinski (PPK), pardoned Fujimori of all his crimes committed against women and men to save himself from impeachment. This decision was fought on the streets and in the Inter-American Commission on Human Rights because this pardon was against the American Convention on Human Rights (*La Republica*, 2017). According to feminists, Fujimori and his cronies have not yet been accused of forced sterilization. On 12 and 27 January 2018, thousands of men and women from all over the country marched in indignation against the pardon. In the department of Cuzco, women marched with posters denouncing forced sterilization in each of its districts: 759 in the city of Cuzco, 218 in Chumbivilcas, 275 in Anta, 74 in Canchis, 49 in Quispicanchis, and 68 in Paucartambo (*La Republica*, 2018). Kuczinski couldn't survive a second impeachment for moral incapacity (Vilcachagua, 2018). On 23 January 2019, Alberto Fujimori's pardon was annulled, and he was forced back to prison.

Feminists are alarmed that Alberto Fujimori could be free from investigation and sanction for forced sterilization because he was never charged with this crime. The next section shows how human rights have been ignored by governments and their institutions; as a result, only a tiny percentage of the those who committed the violations during the internal conflict have been brought to trial, and most of them without positive results. Further, this judicial unresponsiveness has created a chilly climate for all Peruvian women.

An Account of Peru's Anti-woman Politics and Feminist Activism against Violence against Women

The continual human rights violations by government burdens households and fuels domestic violence. The indifference to women's rights by the courts, in particular to violence against women, has made Peruvian women in general more vulnerable. For instance, out of 4657 denunciations of systemic sexual violence by the military against girls and women peasants between 13 and 18 that occurred in the rural localities of Manta and Vilca in the department of Huancavelica, investigated by Peru's Truth and Reconciliation Commission in 2003, women's groups were able to take only 14 soldiers to court (Redaccion, 2017).

In 2017, Estudio para la Defensa de los Derechos de la Mujer (DEMUS) declared that

> The women of Manta and Vilca and their respective families have been waiting for justice for more than 13 years (since 2004) in which their cases were taken to the courts. However, at the end of this long criminal trial, the court issued an acquittal ruling leaving unpunished these aberrant and horrendous acts committed by 14 soldiers of the Peruvian army during the internal armed conflict that our country suffered (DEMUS, 2017).

After a long struggle, the case was reopened on 13 March 2019, and it is still ongoing.

The absence of justice for women makes violence against women highly socially acceptable. The National Observatory on Violence against Women and Members of the Family Group has reported that on average, 348 cases of violence against women are dealt with daily in the National Emergency Centres. Acts of physical and psychological violence were the most reported. The Judicial Branch, for its part, reported 79,186 cases of family violence in the year 2017 in the Lima region alone. That number is followed by the Arequipa region with 22,846 cases, Cuzco with 15,370 cases, and Piura with 13,672 cases, among the regions with the largest number. In addition, regarding the number of trials for feminicide during 2017, the Judicial Branch reported 58 in Arequipa and 52 in Lima Norte (Peru, Ministerio de la Mujer y Poblaciones Vulnerables, n.d.).

Femicide continues, an average of four women per day disappear, and when the complaint is filed, the police do not cooperate despite the fact that there is a Law No. 29585, which states that the police must receive and process the disappearance complaint immediately, without waiting 48 hours after the disappearance. In addition, when a woman disappears, the judiciary system takes over the investigation after six months when the evidence is difficult to gather. Further, a man is punished only when a battered woman has a serious injury or has been in hospital for more than 15 days.

Furthermore, in the neoliberal Congress, there is no political will to castigate the criminal because there has been no update to a judicial code that is 200 years old. Nor is there sex education in the schools because some religious organizations are opposed. For instance, Congress contributes to women's human rights violations through a policy whereby women and girls have the right to access abortion only in cases of rape, severe fetal impairment, or risk to their health or lives and by rejecting a bill recognizing civil unions for same-sex couples. Moreover, there is no decent budget for the National Plan against Gender Violence 2016–2021 (Plan Nacional Contra la Violencia de Genero 2016–2021).

The collective Ni Una Menos, a feminist group, has been organizing demonstrations since 2016 to make visible the problem of violence against women and to remind the state, the executive, the judiciary, and Congress that immediate, specific, and real action is needed to eradicate femicide, violence against women, and harassment. The collective is educating school children on preventing violence because it is imperative that they know their rights, their bodies, and how to identify an aggressor. Furthermore, it has created networks whereby they share testimonies about violence, generate community ties, and demand that an area in the judicial system be devoted to the issue of violence against women.

Conclusion

In this chapter, I have shown when and how global politics of reproductive health and family planning program enmeshed with the Stabilization and Structural Adjustment Programs of the IMF and the World Bank in Peru. The conflict between reproductive rights on a declining planet and the debt crisis deepened the vulnerability of Indigenous Quechua/Aimara-speaking women who were deceived, chained, and threatened by Fujimori's forced sterilization program. It demonstrated how global capital's entitlement to exploit and dominate the planet sees indebted countries' populations as feminized and disposable. Finally, what I learned from forced sterilization in Peru is that feminists need to explore and listen to many feminist and women's movements that are not represented in public discourses because they live at the margins, as once Black and Latino feminism did.

Tying It Together

This chapter has provided material knowledge of global economic, social, political, and environmental relations at the root of family planning. It was in examining this concept that we uncovered the nature of population control as forced sterilization in Peru.

Call to Action

It is important to be aware of global politics and condemn the racism and disrespect of diversity in the concept of population growth. You can work for free and informed choice on reproductive rights as universal by setting up a truth tent at your campus to speak truth to power. Look at the fatal connections between global capital and indebtedness, poverty, and environmental destruction. Criticize affluent environmentalists who call for population control in indebted countries while acknowledging your consumerism because the resources of the South and the colonies are sucked away to feed the bloated material "needs" of the First World. Denounce sustainable development as a framework for capital accumulation, and demand immediate foreign debt cancellation for the poor nations. Also reject Structural Adjustment Programs that eliminate basic social services in indebted countries.

DISCUSSION QUESTIONS

1. Do poor women have reproductive rights?
2. In what United Nations Summit were the proposed universal reproductive rights changed?
3. How have the debt and environment crises contributed to forced sterilization?
4. How have Peruvian feminists challenged global politics in their national governments?
5. How does the lack of justice contribute to femicide?

SUGGESTIONS FOR FURTHER READING

Salleh, Ariel. (2017). *Ecofeminism as politics: Nature, Marx, and the postmodern.* London, UK: Zed Books. This book argues that women's involvement in life-affirming activities has resulted in the development of gender-specific knowledge grounded in a material base and reality.

Federici, Silvia. (2009). *Caliban and the witch: Women, the body and primitive accumulation.* New York, NY: Automedia. This book considers how the privatization of the commons happened in the same historical period as the European witch trials that led to the devaluation of women and a new gendered division of labour.

Isla, Ana. (2015). *The "greening" of Costa Rica: Women, peasants, Indigenous people and the remaking of nature.* Toronto, ON: University of Toronto Press. This book evaluates sustainable development, as discussed at the 1992 Rio Earth Summit, and extends the assessment to the "green economy" in which goods and services provided by the planet depend on the stock exchange.

MULTIMEDIA SUGGESTIONS

This is what democracy looks like
https://www.youtube.com/watch?v=yBUZH2vCD_k
This documentary, narrated by Susan Sarandon and Michael Franti, follows the events of the 1999 World Trade Organization protests in Seattle.

Life and debt—Stephanie Black—Behind the lens
https://www.youtube.com/watch?v=4ZGI9bYg5ng
This film examines the problems caused by a globalized economy in the developing country of Jamaica. Filmmaker Stephanie Black discusses how some of these issues can also be found in other developing countries and how the American economy affects those other nations.

Try your ecological footprint
https://www.footprintnetwork.org/resources/footprint-calculator
This website provides a footprint calculator you can use to learn about how your personal ecological footprint affects the earth.

The shameful history haunting Peru's elections
https://www.theguardian.com/global-development/video/2016/apr/08/peru-election-forced-sterilisation-lima-protest-keiko-fujimori
This video highlights the forced sterilization of 300,000 Peruvians (mostly poor Indigenous women) in the 1990s under former president Alberto Fujimori.

Truth and Reconciliation Commission of Canada
http://www.trc.ca
This website contains the reports and findings of the Truth and Reconciliation Commission of Canada, the work of which is continued by the National Centre for Truth and Reconciliation in Winnipeg, Manitoba.

REFERENCES

APRODEH, COMISEDH, Centro de Información para la Memoria Colectiva y los Derechos Humanos— Defensoría del Pueblo y Luis Cintora (Director del documental "Te saludan Los Cabitos"). (n.d.). *La Republica*, "Tortura y Muerte en los Cabitos." http://larepublica.pe/data/tortura-y-muerte-en-los-cabitos.

CIDH (Comision Interamericana de Derechos Humanos). (2003). *María Mamerita Mestanza Chávez v. Peru* (2002) Case 12.191, Report No. 71/03, settlement 14 October 2002). Available at http://www.cidh.oas.org/women/Peru.12191sp.htm#_ftn1.

Citroni, Gabriella. (1996). *Justicia. Esterilizaciones forzadas en el Peru: La ucha por la justicia y contra el silencio*. Archivo PNSRPF. https://1996pnsrpf2000.wordpress.com/investigacion/derechos-humanos.

Chavez, Susana A. (2015). El Registro de Victimas de Anticoncepcion Quirurgica (AQ) Forzada. http://otramirada.pe/el-registro-de-víctimas-de-anticoncepción-quirúrgica-aq-forzada.

Chavez, Susana A. (2017). Esterilizaciones forzadas: Lo que no se puede poner en el olvido in Otra Mirada. http://otramirada.pe/esterilizaciones-forzadas-lo-que-no-se-puede-poner-en-el-olvido.

Cronica Viva. (2015). Esterilizaciones forzadas fueron parte de la política fujimorista. http://www.cronicaviva.com.pe/esterilizaciones-forzadas-fueron-parte-de-la-politica-fujimorista.

DEMUS (Estudios para la Defensa de los Derechos de las Mujeres). (2016). Archivan 77 denuncias de mujeres esterilizadas forzadamente. https://www.servindi.org/actualidad-noticias/08/12/2016/archivan-definitiva-mente-las-77-denuncias-de-mujeres-esterilizadas.

DEMUS (Estudios para la Defensa de los Derechos de las Mujeres). (2017). Sala Penal Nacional vulnera derechos de mujeres en el Caso Manta y Vilca. http://www.demus.org.pe/noticias/sala-penal-nacional-vulnera-derechos-de-mujeres-en-el-caso-manta-y-vilca.

Evidence. (2014). Esterilizaciones forzadas I. De los informes enviados por el Ministro de Salud Marino Costa Bauer al es president Alberto Fujimori. https://1996pnsrpf2000.files.wordpress.com/2014/09/informe.pdf.

Ewy, Christina. (2011). *Second-wave neoliberalism: Gender, race and health sector reform in Peru*. University Park, PN: Pennsylvania State University Press.

Isla, A. (1997). Coping with structural adjustment: Women's organizing in Peru. *Canadian Woman Studies, 13*(2), 78–84.

La Republica. (2017). La ONU, Wola y otras organizaciones se pronuncian. Reparos internacionales por indulto a Fujimori. 27 December. pp. 2–8. http://larepublica.pe/politica/1162919-naciones-unidas-y-organismos-de-ddhh-condenan-indulto.

La Republica. (2018). Crece el rechazo en las calles del sur al "Indulto Express" [fotos y video]. 12 January. http://larepublica.pe/politica/1169775-crece-el-rechazo-en-las-calles-del-sur-al-indulto-express.

Mies, Maria. (1986). *Patriarchy and accumulation on a world scale: Women in the international division of labour*. London, UK: Zed Books.

Mohanty, Chandra. (1988). Under Western eyes: Feminist scholarship and colonial discourses. *Feminist Review, (30),* 61–88.

Olivera, Roxana. (2014). Giulia Tamayo: Tenemos la razon! In Ideele No. 238. https://revistaideele.com/ideele/content/giulia-tamayo-¡tenemos-la-razón.

Ortiz, Beto. (2017). El genocidio secreto. https://peru21.pe/opinion/pandemonio-beto-ortiz/beto-ortiz-genocidio-secreto-372294.

Paez, Angel. (2011). Las esterilizaciones fueron mortiferas. https://larepublica.pe/politica/546047-las-esterilizaciones-fueron-mortiferas.

Pearce, W.W., & Warford, J.J. (1993). *World without end: Economics, environment, and sustainable development*. New York, NY: Oxford University Press.

Peru. Congreso. (2003). Subcomision investigadora de personas e instituciones involucradas en las acciones de anticoncepcion quirurgica voluntaria. http://www2.congreso.gob.pe/Sicr/ApoyComisiones/informes.nsf/InformesPorComision/C405450DEB310E6C05256CBE0076A35E.

Peru. Defensoría del Pueblo de Perú. (1998). Informe defensorial No. 7: Anticoncepción quirúrgica voluntaria I: casos investigados por la Defensoría del Pueblo, Lima.

Peru. Defensoría del Pueblo de Perú. (1999). Informe defensorial No. 27: La aplicación de la anticoncepción quirúrgica voluntaria y los derechos reproductivos II, Lima.

Peru. Defensoría del Pueblo de Perú. (2002). Informe defensorial No. 69: La aplicación de la anticoncepción quirúrgica voluntaria y los derechos reproductivos III, Lima.

Peru. Ministerio de Cultura. (2017). Desaparecidos. Entre la busqueda y la esperanza en Ayacucho. https://lum.cultura.pe/exposiciones/desaparecidos-entre-la-búsqueda-y-la-esperanza-en-ayacucho.

Peru. Ministerio de Justicia. (2016a). Government (1). https://www.minjus.gob.pe/wp-content/uploads/2016/05/RESOLUCION-MINISTERIAL-0111-2016-JUS.pdf.

Peru. Ministerio de Justicia. (2016b). Government (2). http://busquedas.elperuano.com.pe/normaslegales/aprueban-la-segunda-etapa-del-cronograma-de-implementacion-resolucion-ministerial-no-0161-2016-jus-1402386-1.

Peru. Ministerio de Justicia. (2017). Government (3). http://busquedas.elperuano.com.pe/normaslegales/aprueban-tercera-etapa-de-implementacion-del-registro-de-vic-resolucion-ministerial-no-0157-2017-jus-1537444-1.

Peru. Ministerio de la Mujer y Poblaciones Vulnerables. (n.d.). Observatorio nacional de la violencia contra las mujeres e integrantes del grupo familiar. https://www.mimp.gob.pe/webs/mimp/sistema-nacional-prevencion/galeria-imagenes.php.

Peru. The Truth and Reconciliation Commission. (2003). Final report. http://www.cverdad.org.pe/ingles/ifinal/index.php.

Redaccion. (2017). En juicio a militares por violencia sexual maltratan a víctimas. http://larepublica.pe/politica/1050579-en-juicio-a-militares-por-violencia-sexual-maltratan-a-victimas.

Romero, Cesar. (2011). Dossier esterilizaciones forzadas: Aun es tiempo de encontrar justicia. *La Republica*, 3 June. https://larepublica.pe/politica/545855-dossier-especial-esterilizaciones-forzadas-hablan-las-victimas.

Servindi. (2016). Esterilizaciones forzadas: Exculpan a Fujimori y sus ex ministros de salud. https://www.servindi.org/peru-actualidad-noticias/31/07/2016/esterilizaciones-forzadas-exculpan-fujimori-y-sus-ex-ministros.

Supa, Hilaria. (2008). *Threads of my life: The story of Hilaria Supa Huaman, a rural Quechua woman*. Penticton, BC: Theytus Books.

Tamayo G. (1999). Nada personal: Reporte de derechos humanos sobre la aplicación de la anticoncepción quirúrgica en el Perú 1996–1998. Lima, Peru: CLADEM.

Vilcachagua, P. (2018). PPK, el hombre que nunca encontró su norte. *Crónica*, 23 March. https://peru21.pe/politica/ppk-hombre-encontro-norte-cronica-400432.

NOTES

1. Resolution XVIII: Human Rights Aspects of Family Planning, Final Act of the International Conference on Human Rights. UN Doc. A/CONF. 32/41, p.15.

2. General Assembly Resolution 2542, UN Doc. A/7630.

3. ICPD Programme of Action 1994, para 7.3.

CHAPTER 18

◇

Grannies, Rockers, and Oil Rigs

Mobilizing Age in Intersectional Climate Justice Alliances

May Chazan and Melissa Baldwin

Learning Objectives

In this chapter, you will:

- examine the concept of solidarity and what is meant by solidarity across difference;
- learn what is meant by mobilizing social location, or in this case how age, gender, and whiteness were mobilized by the Raging Grannies toward political ends;
- consider different practices of solidarity within and beyond frontline protest;
- explore your own social locations and what they might offer to participation in difference coalitional movements;
- consider whose needs and perspectives are ideally foregrounded in coalitional politics that strive toward critical relationships based on solidarity.

Introduction

This chapter explores and extends the concept of **solidarity** by considering how the Seattle Raging Grannies mobilized their **social locations**, particularly their age, gender, and whiteness, in strategic ways to support the intergenerational, multi-movement climate justice coalition, ShellNo. Seattle's ShellNo Action Council, which in 2015 involved a series of sophisticated land and water actions, was a broad-based protest against Arctic oil extraction and the presence of the Shell drilling rigs in the Seattle port (en route to the Arctic). More generally, this particular coalition and its associated activism are part of a global climate justice movement—a movement of concerned groups and people worldwide who understand that while the impacts of climate change are and will continue to be globalized, these impacts are also uneven, racialized, colonial, and gendered. Indeed, it is well documented that, overwhelmingly, those who are and will be most affected by extreme weather, sea level rise, melting ice caps, and other related outcomes are Indigenous communities, communities in the Global South, communities of colour, women, youth, and people living in poverty (Mersha, 2017). With this in mind, this chapter examines one localized response to this global crisis and particularly the ways in which differently positioned activists formed and practised solidarities with the intention of centring the needs and perspectives of those most vulnerable and affected. Both the response discussed and the analysis offered are informed by postcolonial, critical race, and intersectional feminist approaches.

This chapter emerges from a close reading of an intergenerational panel about the ShellNo mobilizations, which took place as part of the Raging Grannies' 2016 biannual gathering, called an Unconvention. We analyze this panel, in which younger (20s through to 50s) Indigenous activists and activists of colour spoke of the ShellNo actions, reflecting on tactics and exploring the tensions of power and privilege in the coalition. We explore how and why different actors mobilize their social locations, bodies, and **privileges** in the process and practice of alliance-building. More specifically, we examine the ways in which the Raging Grannies mobilized their positions— how they drew on assumptions about older, white, middle-class women—to support the ShellNo coalition. We also consider how they practised their solidarity both on the frontlines of this activism and in longer-term organizing and relationship-building. In doing so, we introduce the complex, grounded practices of activist alliance-building across difference. We also address a gap in analyses of age/ing and intergenerationality within anti-racist, decolonial climate justice movements, bringing critical attention to how age and grandmotherhood can be mobilized toward political ends.

What becomes evident is that during the ShellNo actions, the Raging Grannies mobilized not only their white privilege but also their gender and age (arguably more marginal locations) to afford protection from the police for them and for more vulnerable coalition members—in other words, they deployed assumptions and stereotypes about themselves as "little old ladies" in strategic ways. We also discuss how the intersections of gender, age, and race inform their alliance-building processes, which extend beyond frontline actions into relationships, organizing spaces, and the panel in question.

This chapter begins with an introduction to key concepts, particularly solidarities across difference. It then offers background information on the Raging Grannies and their Unconvention, as well as context on the 2015 ShellNo mobilizations and on our 2016 research. Next, our analysis is divided into two parts: first, we consider how and why Grannies mobilized their positions as older white women on the frontlines of the ShellNo actions and how the younger activists of colour on the panel reflected on this mobilization; and second, we consider panelists' reflections on how the Grannies do and could mobilize those same positions behind the scenes of frontline protest through ongoing relationships and in the planning spaces of coalitional work. The chapter then closes by drawing together these learnings to think about solidarity as ongoing and daily practices, including on the frontlines of rallies, in sustained relationships, and through events like the ShellNo panel.

Conceptual Context

"Solidarity" is a hopeful political concept that is frequently deployed in transnational feminist scholarship and practice (and elsewhere) as a model of political engagement that holds possibilities for working across differences in power toward common goals (Gaztambide-Fernández, 2012; Mohanty, 2003). Yet, as David Featherstone suggests, solidarity has "rarely been the subject of sustained theorization, reflection or investigation" (2012, p. 5). Building on this work, Gavin Brown and Helen Yaffe (2014) also challenge how solidarity is often confined to particular protests or campaigns and instead urge scholars to consider that any theory or ideas about solidarity cannot be separated from the actions people take toward that solidarity. Thus, this chapter addresses the need to better theorize solidarity from a grounded perspective: to unpack the links between how solidarity is understood, how it is talked about, and how it is carried out in practice by different actors—both during frontline actions and in relationships surrounding those actions. Following Featherstone, then, we conceptualize solidarity as ongoing relations forged through political struggle that seek to challenge forms of oppression. This means that in this chapter we take up solidarity as a *doing*—an ongoing process of actions, intentions, discourse, and relationships. We look at how this *doing* is shaped by differences in power, privilege, and social positioning.

Notably, age and **aging** are rarely explicit in conceptualizing or analyzing solidarity. Even in organizing concerning climate justice by which youth and future generations are likely to be inequitably affected (that is, when there is an issue of intergenerational justice that arises from older generations' responsibilities as people who consumed fossil fuels at unsustainable rates and younger generations as the ones who are going to suffer most), there has been very little attention to intergenerational alliance-building or response. As such, we also specifically consider how different actors mobilized the bodily differences/barriers/assumptions of their different social locations and ages in strategic ways—this intergenerational element lends particularly salient insights to questions of how solidarity can be practised and how working across ages can be strategic. Thus, this chapter extends solidarity scholarship in three key ways: 1) it looks at links between solidarity theory and practice; 2) it extends thinking about solidarity from a focus on moments of "action" to also consider longer-term relationship-building; and 3) it pays explicit attention to age and to how age can also be mobilized in strategically political ways.

Our analysis also contributes to aging studies research on older women's roles in working for social change (e.g., Charpentier, Quéniart, & Jacques, 2008; McHugh, 2012; Meadows, Thurston, & Lagendyk, 2009). Scholars in this area

On "Solidarity"

"Solidarity" has its roots in labour movement organizing where it has long meant coalition-building across difference (see Featherstone, 2012). In transnational feminist scholarship, "solidarity" has been more contentious in its early assumptions of similarity across "women" and their struggles; more recently, much more explicit attention has been given in this literature to solidarities across differences in power and privilege (Mohanty, 2003). Notably, Indigenous scholars have offered compelling re-imaginings of solidarity across Indigenous, white settler, and settler of colour positions that centre making and keeping relationships and recognizing interdependence (Snelgrove, Dahmoon, & Corntassel, 2014). More and more, scholars are setting out to theorize solidarity, particularly by looking to examples of complex, intersectional mobilizations like the ShellNo coalition, both large-scale movements (Curnow & Helferty, 2018) and less visible relational forms (Chazan, 2016). These scholars are articulating ever more nuanced conceptualizations of solidarity through a variety of lenses, including critical reciprocity (Olwan, 2015), discomfort (Boudreau Morris, 2017), empathy (Liu & Shange, 2018), radical relationality (Carter, Recollet, & Robinson, 2017), and much more.

note how sexism and ageism (among other systems of power) intersect to shape older women's experiences of discrimination and also seek to shift the focus away from the burdens faced by older women to the contributions older women make to society. These scholars debunk dominant discourses of social movements as the domain of youth, depicting instead the numerous ways older women (in particular) are working for change (Richards, 2012; Sawchuk, 2013). They showcase older women's activism as a challenge to ageist and sexist stereotypes of older women as apolitical, frail, and disengaged—stereotypes that some note are not only rampant in society at large but are also widespread within many activist movements (Sawchuk, 2009).

Context: The Raging Grannies, ShellNo, and This Research

The Raging Grannies are a loose network of women: most are **cisgender**, **white settlers** over 65 years old, and many (but not all) are grandmothers. There are groups of Raging Grannies all over North America (Turtle Island). While localized groups mobilize around diverse social and environmental issues, as a movement they are best known for performing outrageous "granny activism," deploying flamboyant costumes and satirical songs to enter spaces not typically open to older women. Grannies play at stereotypes of the "little old lady," donning doilies and shawls while cussing out misogynist politicians (for an example, see https://www.youtube.com/watch?v=zpBO3euQQPY). As Dana Sawchuk notes, the Grannies "show up—invited or not—to city halls, shopping malls, nuclear power plants, armed forces recruiting centers, and antiwar and antiglobalization demonstrations to sing out their political messages to the tune of songs from days gone by" (2009, pp. 171–2). A number of scholars have studied the Raging Grannies, focusing on their tactical use of humour and satire in their activism

(Roy, 2004; 2007), the implications of their activism for later life learning and health (Narushima, 2004; Pedersen, 2010), and the ways they mobilize "little old lady" (or LOL) stereotypes as political strategy (Sawchuk, 2009). Yet, with the exception of Chazan (2016), there are no studies examining the Grannies' solidarity efforts across differences and none considering their intergenerational alliances. This is despite the fact that Raging Granny "gaggles" (localized groups) regularly work in complex activist coalitions across differences in gender, class, race, and generation/age.

Once every two years, Raging Grannies from across North America gather at their "Unconvention." Coming together as older[1] women working for change, they fill their days with workshops, guest speakers, networking, and political demonstrations. In 2016, we were invited to participate in the Raging Grannies' Unconvention for the second time, as part of Aging Activisms, Chazan's multi-faceted program of activist research, academic mentorship, and intergenerational communitybuilding (see www.agingactivisms.org) and as part of a larger five-year study (2013–18) into why and how older women across North America (including, but extending beyond, those involved in the Raging Grannies) are mobilizing for social change. Our experience at the 2016 Unconvention, and this resulting chapter, build from our own long-standing relationships with the Raging Grannies' network. Specifically, this chapter builds from our continued work with the Raging Grannies and questions of their coalitional work to look more in depth at solidarity as a process, looking less at the early stages of forming such alliances (Chazan, 2016) and more at a continuation of already-initiated solidarity practices.

At the 2016 Unconvention, some 200 Raging Grannies from across Turtle Island gathered in Seattle, on Coast Salish, xʷməθkʷəy̓əm (Musqueam), Skwxwú7mesh (Squamish) territories (Seattle, WA). While we participated extensively in the full three-day gathering, this article focuses on an analysis of the gathering's opening panel, which convened seven younger[2] activists, all of whom had participated and organized in different ways in the 2015 ShellNo actions. These actions aimed to halt Shell Oil's Arctic drilling by blocking rigs in the harbour and locking down on train tracks, among other tactics.[3] The panel grew out of the relationships that Seattle Raging Grannies had developed with panelists through their collaborations in these actions. The Seattle Raging Grannies invited panel participants to offer their perspectives on the roles Raging Grannies and older women more generally played and could play in these coalition actions; in extending these invitations, the Grannies centred the leadership of those most affected (or likely to be most affected) by climate change, including Indigenous women (particularly from Arctic communities), youth, women of colour, and people with their roots and families in the Global South. What intrigued us most about this panel was how, rather than open their gathering with their own reflections, the Grannies instead decided to ask the audience to listen as they passed the mic to these younger activists of colour. In this chapter, we draw on close readings and thematic analysis of our compiled field notes and the full transcript of the panel, as well as selected media coverage of the ShellNo actions.

From our observations, the Grannies in the audience for the ShellNo panel were predominantly, although not exclusively, white, non-Indigenous settlers over the age of 60, representing more than 12 granny groups, or gaggles, from across Turtle Island. Based on our participation in the 2014 and 2016 Unconventions and our previous research, some of the Grannies would have been Grannying since the first gaggle started (in Victoria in 1987), and many were relatively new to this style of activism; some were from larger, well-established gaggles and others from new groups formed in response to growing threats in nation-state politics on both sides of the colonial border. As we heard at the Unconvention and in our broader research, some Grannies present had identified as activists since their teenage years, while others only felt the confidence to take on this label in later life when calls on their time decreased and expectations of them (and of their femininity) shifted (Chazan & Baldwin, 2016). The older, white settler make-up of the audience was reflected in the ways in which panelists spoke, the knowledges they shared, and the messages they worked to get across.

Grannies on the Frontlines: Mobilizing Gender, Age, and Race

What became evident in this research was that on the frontlines of the 2015 ShellNo actions, the Seattle Grannies mobilized their privileges as older white women, as well as ageist assumptions about their bodies, in strategic ways as part of the intergenerational coalition. In these instances, rather than being perceived solely as an obstacle to their engagement, the Grannies' ages became a tool for them. Further, actors of different ages and social positions were able to leverage these positions differently throughout the coalition; as such, the intergenerational nature of this coalition added to the diversity and inventiveness of actions that were taken. In this section, we look at how the Grannies' mobilization of the "little old lady" parody demonstrates that this tactic is more than a visual subversion; rather, this practice is linked to the needs, assumptions, and privileges that accompany their bodies as older white women. First, we consider how the Grannies and others accommodated their bodily needs in ways that could also be strategically advantageous; second, we look at how the Grannies mobilized their older age not only in parody but also to materially confer protection to younger activists of colour and Indigenous activists; and third, we consider how the Grannies' mobilizations of their older white bodies were integral to this intergenerational coalition.

Spotlight on the Raging Grannies

Courtesy of Raging Grannies of Seattle

The Raging Grannies at the 2016 Unconvention

The Raging Grannies first organized in the late 1980s on the territories of the Coast and Straits Salish peoples (Victoria, Canada) as peace activists protesting the appearance of US submarines carrying nuclear warheads in the Victoria harbour through a series of imaginative and humorous actions. Their humour and passion quickly captured the imaginations of other older women, and groups, and gaggles began to mobilize in communities across North America, or what is known to many First Peoples as Turtle Island. Nearly 30 years later, a diverse network of more than 100 self-directed groups spans the continent, while some extend as far as Australia, England, Ireland, and Israel (see www.raginggrannies.org). They protest against numerous social and environmental injustices, including wars, fracking, climate injustice, poverty, childcare inaccessibility, denial of refugee rights, and inequitable conditions for Indigenous communities; each group (or "gaggle") determines their own issues and tactics. For more on the Raging Grannies, see Carole Roy (2004; 2007) and Acker and Brightwell (2004).

First, the Grannies deployed their well-known humour on the frontlines of several actions during ShellNo while also making choices of where, when, and how to resist based on their bodies. In one prominent action, several Grannies, channelling their boisterous parody of "little old ladies," locked themselves down on rocking chairs over train tracks in order to block oil trains from passing through to the port of Seattle. The Grannies dressed in feather boas, oversized bright hats, aprons, and shawls and hung photos of their grand- and great-grandchildren around their necks. They sat chained to their rocking chairs with cups of tea and knitting. One media account of this action described the Grannies' rocker-lockdown as a "visual victory," saying that the eldest Granny involved "[wore] her standard granny uniform of sunhat and flowing skirt, wielding every one of her 92 years like a weapon. Being a Raging Granny is all about making the most of an older woman's moral clout" (Kaplan, 2015). For the Grannies, this action allowed them to resist from their different bodies, needs, and abilities, while also parodying their older bodies. In other words, many Grannies would not have been able to participate in actions in kayaks, for instance, because of mobility challenges; rocking chairs, however, suited their bodily abilities. At the same time, by holding the line in their rockers for several hours, the Grannies opened up the younger activists to carry on with other organizing for the coalition. In this action, the bodily needs of the Grannies as older women—staying on land, being seated in rockers for the five-hour protest (which ended in their arrest)—coincided with effective political strategy for the broader coalition.

Second, while accommodating their bodies and mocking ageism with their granny performance, the Grannies could also manipulate ageist assumptions of their frailty and innocence in order to protect others. As Granny X explained, in the action described above the Grannies understood and anticipated that police would be relatively gentle with their old, white bodies and that in their

rocking chairs and aprons they would be deemed a very low threat. As another panelist explained, the train track lockdown began with a larger group of younger activists chained to oil drums alongside the Grannies. As the police arrived, the Grannies insisted that they would stay to the bitter end, and this freed up the younger activists to carry out the next set of actions and avoid one more direct encounter with police. The Grannies assumed that the police would treat them better than any others in the coalition, which proved more than true. As the five Grannies held their ground on rockers, the police took their time to cut them free as delicately as possible. Unlike many younger and racialized organizers who were arrested and held during the course of the ShellNo actions, the five Grannies who were arrested were released immediately after processing. One seasoned-activist panelist explained[4]:

[This] never happened before in my experience of doing anything. The Grannies were so gingerly treated that when they were arrested—I was one of the police liaisons and I was told that we could send a couple of "support" people with them in the van (they weren't going to be cuffed) to the police station! . . . It's not just about the particulars of an action, but it's about all of us acknowledging and taking into account that there are differences and that we need to leverage our privilege where it's wanted and back off where it's not.

Importantly, then, this action was more than a visual subversion: the Grannies placed themselves in precarious positions that their privileges as white women would otherwise preclude them from. They knew that the combination of ageist assumptions of their meekness and racist protection of white people would likely protect them from serious danger. They also acted knowing that this security is unequal: one panelist explained that, as an older white woman, "what happens when you

Tyler Tjomsland/The Spokesman-Review, via AP

A Raging Granny being arrested after locking down the railroad tracks at the ShellNo action.

put yourself on the line for direct action is quite different, and we need to remember that." The Granny hosting the panel continued, saying that their gentle treatment by police was in stark contrast to the police brutality inflicted upon young racialized people by the same officers:

> I think that it is one of the most important things Grannies can do, is to show up to these actions and protect our younger activists of colour. If the Seattle Grannies have learned nothing else, we have learned that. We have terrible racist police in Seattle, terrible, racist, violent police. . . . They always treat the Grannies really nicely. So if we are there, it's some protection for our friends.

Third, the ways in which the Grannies worked from and with their older white bodies offered much to the broader coalition that differently situated activists could not have offered. The action described above was just one of several times during the coalition that the Grannies placed their white bodies between the police and younger activists of colour. Knowing that the police would treat them kindly (even daintily), Grannies took to the front lines, locking themselves down in rockers on train tracks and also blockading entrances to the Tacoma Detention Centre during a person-of-colour-led demonstration. This way of conferring protection was something that panelists described as the most tangible and meaningful expression of solidarity during the coalition and something that could make a significant difference to people of colour's organizing in general: "we need the white allies and our white elders to come and stand in front, to be that shield." The Indigenous activists and activists of colour on the panel emphasized the importance of this kind of mobilization, noting that the Grannies' presence almost certainly inhibited the otherwise likely scenario of police brutality against younger, racialized activists.

So, with the confidence that they would be protected when others might be brutalized, the Grannies were able to stand (or sit) their ground in a way that others could not have. The most immediate and obvious *doing* of solidarity across difference, then, was this way in which the Grannies mobilized their old, white bodies, and anticipated perceptions of these bodies, to slow authorities down and confer some protection to more vulnerable activists. This means that the Grannies mobilized their privilege as white women, a tactic often discussed in writings about solidarity across difference, but they *also* mobilized their age-based marginalization, making use of the same limiting ageist stereotypes that they subvert through parody. At the same time, they were being practical about these bodies—not being the ones to jump into canoes or hang 50 feet in the air; their older bodies are an effective frontline *sometimes* and in certain contexts. What is interesting here is how assumptions and expectations of age, gender, and whiteness—that is, of frailty, harmlessness, passivity—were both completely upturned and strategically manipulated to confer protection, to stall police, to de-escalate (or at least keep from escalating) interactions with different authorities. What we typically would expect to be limiting about older age became an invaluable tool to the intergenerational resistance, and having actors of many ages, abilities, and social locations was key to this multi-tiered set of actions.

Solidarity as Longer-Term Relationships: Mobilizing "Granny" beyond the Protests

During the ShellNo panel in 2016, panelists (including one Granny) were clear that the actions were only one part of the ShellNo coalition, the coalition was not perfect, and differences in power and privilege created tensions in organizing that are critical to contend with and learn through. What also emerged from this research, then, was the importance of understanding solidarity as a process of relationship-building that extends well beyond the instance of an action or even a short-term coalition like ShellNo. It is critical to practise, understand, and examine solidarity as a longer-term process of relationship-building and to think about how race-gender-age dynamics play out in this ongoing work—this becomes evident in two different ways in this research.

First, the Unconvention panel provided an example of a continuation of the Grannies' solidarity practice—particularly in how it was organized to centre the knowledge of younger women of colour and Indigenous women while positioning the Grannies as learners and listeners and how it clearly reflected relationships that were cultivated through the coalition and that continued after the Unconvention was over. The panel was drawn together by some of the Seattle Raging Grannies to reflect on the ShellNo campaign. It was hosted by a member of the Seattle Raging Grannies, "Granny X," who had worked closely with the panelists throughout the organizing of ShellNo and who, as she said, was continuing those relationships. Alongside Granny X, the panel included a Tlingit, Haida, and Tsimshian woman and spiritual activist who is the director of Idle No More Washington and Native Women Rising and who works to protect the environment, assert sovereignty rights, and resurge Indigenous knowledges and spiritual practices; a women of colour activist who is the founder of Women of Colour Speak Out and who was a pivotal part of the kayaktivist actions; and the youngest member of the panel, a Black woman organizing with Got Green, a racial and climate justice organization. Though the panel also included a man of colour and three white settler women, we choose to focus on the knowledges of the Indigenous women and women of colour both because their insights offer the most depth in thinking about solidarities across (among) difference and because we agree with Granny X's opening to the panel: "I want to particularly honour the women of colour on our panel this morning. I really feel it is important because in our society women of colour often do the hardest work and get the least recognition."

This panel built on existing relationships, which was evident from the comfort panelists showed with Granny X. It was by design that the panel asked the predominantly white Grannies in the audience to step back and learn about their privilege. In fact, the panel was organized in a way that reflected an approach to solidarity that challenges dynamics of power. The hosting Granny introduced the panel as a way to extend her own learning from the coalition and to share this learning with Grannies around the continent, recognizing that that learning is an unending process. As part of this process, the Grannies encouraged each other to sit with the discomfort of having their whiteness exposed and confronted:

> First of all, we ask you, our grannies in the audience, to do a few things. You may hear some things that make you uncomfortable. So, we ask you to be willing to experience discomfort; it's not always a bad thing. It can be a good thing to challenge and stretch ourselves, so we ask you to be willing to experience that and to stay engaged. If you do experience discomfort, do your best to be present and keep listening, rather than, for example, trying to think of responses—to really listen for understanding, not for agreement or disagreement.

Even more, the Grannies prioritized BIPOC (Black, Indigenous, People of Colour) voices as part of the panel but also as a broader approach to solidarity. As Granny X continued:

We want to model some of the things that we Seattle Grannies learned through the whole ShellNo process and follow-ups to that. . . . One is "progressive stack," this means we will prioritize the voices which are usually marginalized in our society on the panel and when taking questions. Women of colour, other people of colour, and any LGBTQ people will speak first.

By drawing the panel together and explicitly privileging BIPOC voices, this process flipped age expectations and also flipped racist constructs of who holds authority and knowledge. This solidarity, then, was not confined to the specifics of an action and its organization, but rather, through the panel and the relationships underpinning it, the solidarity was carried on into a less direct process of learning, taking on humbleness, stepping back, and continuing relationships. So for the Grannies, the process of ongoing solidarity includes challenging entrenched assumptions about whose knowledge, wisdom, and expertise are valuable and legitimate—rather than assuming the positions of knowledge-holders/teachers/wise elders that expectations of age and race would typically confer to the Grannies, they instead positioned themselves as learners and lifted up the knowledges of younger activists of colour and Indigenous activists.

Second, throughout the panel, the BIPOC panelists also offered insight into the longer-term relationship-building that is so crucial to power-challenging alliances. In particular, the BIPOC panelists stated that the formal action in the harbour and on the train tracks was only a part of solidarity: many felt that the Grannies could have done more during the organizing of ShellNo to establish trust and support BIPOC organizers. They offered the Grannies some concrete ways that they could mobilize their age and whiteness in organizing (as they did during the actions) to deepen their solidarity and confront relations of power

Spotlight on International Solidarities

The ShellNo mobilizations involved intersectional solidarity work—working across difference, especially differences in age and relationship to the land. Though they were localized in scope, the ShellNo mobilizations were "international" in terms of both working across the Canada/United States colonial border and building nation-to-nation relations within the coalition among Indigenous activists, settlers of colour, and white settlers. There are many other examples of international solidarities that resonate with the complex, grounded practices of "solidarity" or alliance-building across difference we discuss in this chapter. Some compelling examples include: Indigenous and Inuit activists, artists, and musicians across Turtle Island, Greenland, and Hawai'i acting in solidarity with Inuit defending their sovereign right to hunt seal (see Rodgers & Scobie, 2015); (queer) Indigenous activists and activists of colour across Turtle Island acting in solidarity with Palestinians resisting occupation (see Atshan & Moore, 2014; Olwan, 2015); activists based in London organizing creative and varied actions in solidarity with the anti-apartheid movement in South Africa (see Brown & Yaffe, 2014). To learn more about conceptualizing *international* solidarities, read Ghabra and Calafell (2018), Landy, Darcy, and Gutierrez (2014), and Flesher Fominaya (2014). What are some examples of international solidarity that you have heard about or been involved in?

within activist networks. For instance, these panelists noted that in the behind-the-scenes of the organizing, there were a few "toxic white males" who manipulated their power and authority to try to control the actions and direct BIPOC organizers. They explained how in the *process* of planning the action, the Grannies could have mobilized their privileges and moral authority to call out and stand up to this behaviour. Unfortunately, no one confronted these "toxic white males," which meant that organizing was sometimes unsafe for BIPOC activists and that there was a missed opportunity to build trust and more relational solidarity. Panelists offered this idea of using the privilege and perception of wisdom/authority that the Grannies hold as older, white women in order to confront covertly racist behaviour while building up relationships with BIPOC activists. With these suggestions, panelists offered another way in which the Grannies might deploy both the privileges conferred by their whiteness and the tropes

associated with aging in their solidarity-building practices beyond particular protests.

Another way that panelists invited the Grannies to deepen their solidarity was to explain that they need to be engaged in the activisms led by BIPOC organizers and not just in coalitional spaces like ShellNo. The young Black woman on the panel urged the Grannies to show up for people of colour and mobilize their structural power:

Be there so that it looks like it's more than just people of colour asking for this one thing. . . . So, when *you* show up and *you* say Black Lives Matter, and you understand that's it's *true* in your heart, because you really believe it. You go to city council and tell them to not spend as much money to protect me, because the police are only there to protect white people. . . . Where do we need *you* where we don't have the power that we need? [italics denote vocal emphasis]

Following the 2016 Unconvention, several Grannies took these messages to heart and directly acted on them. One Granny in particular attended a workshop on decolonization offered by the Tlingit, Haida, and Tsimshian panelist. In an email to all Unconvention attendees in September 2016, this Granny urged others to gather together to join the resistance to the Dakota Access Pipeline at Standing Rock, listing a variety of ways that Grannies could directly support the water protectors there. This email prompted a scattered group of Grannies across Turtle Island to organize together to raise funds, educate themselves, and take action, both in Standing Rock and in their own communities. This response recalls what one panelist eloquently said: "What does winning look like? Winning looks like defeating Shell, right? Winning should *also* look like creating lasting coalitions and trust with people of colour and white people so that whenever we are in that position there's no need to rebuild."

Overall, then, the solidarity practices revealed in this research suggest that Grannies engaged in, and have been invited to engage in, alliance-building within and beyond specific protests. What becomes important here is that the specific "action" or protest is not the only site or outlet for solidarity; rather, if we think of solidarity as a "doing," a "becoming," a "process," then relationships, learning, listening, and carrying these into daily living becomes most significant. We saw this in how the Grannies organized the panel to prioritize younger BIPOC voices and to position themselves as learners. We also saw this in how panelists discussed the possibilities for the Grannies, as older, white women with credibility and perceived moral authority, to call out racism, colonialism, and white supremacy in community organizing circles and to open spaces for BIPOC organizers to take leadership roles in the longer-term resistance efforts. What seems most salient is that this solidarity process was animated through relationships: the "winning" relationships of lasting coalitions across difference, the relationships that surrounded the sharing during the panel, and the relationships that activated so many Grannies to take action during Standing Rock in the months after the Unconvention. Thus, solidarity in these discussions as a *process* or *doing* might require shifting the frame from tactical alliances toward goal-oriented formal protest to a process of relationship-building and giving up power that is entrenched in daily living. It is within this ongoing process that Grannies can continue the work of mobilizing their white privilege and subverting or deploying societal assumptions about their age in ways that challenge norms and upturn power.

Conclusion

This chapter explored the ways in which the Seattle Raging Grannies mobilized their social locations, particularly their age and whiteness, in strategic ways to support an intergenerational,

Courtesy of Raging Grannies of Seattle

Two ShellNo Coalition members

multi-movement climate justice coalition called ShellNo. Specifically, we examined the different ways the Grannies sought to build solidarities or alliances—their practices of allyship as a group of predominantly white, settler, older, middle-class women. By solidarity or alliance, we are referring to the Grannies' desires to work with a diverse coalition of activists, recognizing their own social locations and acting in ways that explicitly honour, respect, and centre the perspectives, knowledges, and needs of BIPOC and youth activists—those who are most marginalized in activist spaces and in white settler society more generally and those who are most likely to be affected by the negative effects of climate change. We examined how, in their various actions, the Grannies strategically deployed the privileges and assumptions associated with their age, gender, and skin tone.

On the front lines, this meant, for instance, chaining themselves to train tracks to block oil trains, knowing that they would be arrested but also understanding that the police were likely to be much more restrained in confrontations with them than in confrontations with younger and/or racialized activists. The Grannies boldly and satirically performed ageist-sexist stereotypes of older women as innocent and frail, sitting on their rocking chairs dressed in aprons with knitting in hand. While they subverted these stereotypes by being out on the protest lines, they also mobilized these images to confer protection on themselves and on the younger and/or racialized activists working within the coalition. This made it possible for these more vulnerable activists to participate in other actions and/or to keep their distance from police forces.

This chapter also explored the concept of solidarity as a process that includes both this kind of frontline co-operation as well as complex, longer-term relationship-building. One example of the Grannies' longer-term relationship-building was the ShellNo panel they organized at their Unconvention in 2016, which we analyzed and discussed at length. In a similar spirit of respect and redress, the Grannies invited younger BIPOC activists who had been part of the ShellNo coalition to offer their perspectives on the roles Raging Grannies and older women could play in this kind of climate justice organizing. In doing so, the Grannies centred the leadership of Indigenous women (particularly from Arctic communities), youth, women of colour, and people with their roots and families in the Global South. Here too they gave explicit thought to their own whiteness and age—to the epistemic dominance they so often hold. In other words, understanding that they are most often deemed the knowers and the teachers, they worked to challenge this dynamic by asking an audience of Grannies from across the continent to listen to and consider deeply the activist teachings of the panelists. This demonstrated not only a commitment to ongoing relationship-building but also a practice of how to go about doing such relationship-building in ways that are conducive to meaningful solidarity work.

"Solidarity" and "allyship" are widely used in social movement scholarship, just as they are on the ground in activist circles. But they are contested concepts, which are not particularly well understood as practices across different contexts. Attempts have been made to create "how to" guides on being a good ally, but they tend to be quite simplistic. In addition, while much focus on allyship has to do with redressing ongoing privilege and oppression associated with systems of white supremacy and settler colonialism, there has been very limited work to date on dynamics of age and intergenerationality. This chapter thus offers an introduction to the complex, grounded practices of activist alliance-building across multiple axes of difference, addressing a gap in analyses of age/ing and intergenerationality within anti-racist, decolonial climate justice movements.

Call to Action

What climate justice work is happening in your community? Consider joining a climate justice action campaign locally or learning from Indigenous communities in your area about what work they might already be doing and how you might support it. Begin by reading and signing the Leap Manifesto, and join or start a local group (https://leapmanifesto.org/en/the-leap-manifesto). You can also support pipeline activism and stop oil extraction all over the continent. Research pipeline and fracking resistance movements near you, and support their work! (If you live in the United States? Find pipeline resistance movements at this link: https://fossilfuelresistance.org). Support the Secwepemc Nation and their "Tiny House Warriors" who are resisting the Kinder Morgan Trans Mountain Pipeline Project in southern British Columbia (http://tinyhousewarriors.com), the Unis'tot'en Camp, who are resisting three different pipeline projects that are proposed to run through unceded Unis'tot'en territory in northern British Columbia (https://unistoten.camp), or RAVEN (Respecting Aboriginal Values and Environmental Needs), an Indigenous movement resisting the Kinder Morgan pipeline (https://raventrust.com/stop-the-kinder-morgan-pipeline-project). Learn how to divest from banks that are funding oil extraction (https://gofossilfree.org/divestment/what-is-fossil-fuel-divestment), and encourage your university or college to divest from funding companies that are pushing for oil extraction by starting a divestment campaign (https://campaigns.gofossilfree.org).

Tying It Together

Drawing on postcolonial and intersectional perspectives on analyzing activisms, this chapter introduces the complex, grounded practices of "solidarity" or alliance-building across difference, presenting one localized example of coalition activism in response to the uneven and inequitable impacts of climate change. The chapter explores the different ways the Seattle Raging Grannies mobilized their social locations, particularly their age, gender, and whiteness, in strategic ways to support the intergenerational, multi-movement climate justice coalition ShellNo. Seattle's ShellNo Action Council, which formed in 2015 as a broad-based protest against Arctic oil extraction and the presence of Shell drilling rigs in the Seattle port, offers a grounded illustration of how a global climate justice movement is playing out in a local context. The ShellNo coalition, like many such groups and actions responding to climate change around the world, was premised on an intersectional understanding that while the impacts of climate change are and will continue to be globalized, these impacts are also uneven, racialized, colonial, and gendered. Within this context, the chapter considers the ways in which a group of older, white, settler, middle-class women engaged in activism by taking direction and leadership from younger activists of colour and Indigenous leaders and how they leveraged the unearned privileges bestowed on them because of their race, age, and gender. Recognizing the intergenerational inequities associated with climate change whereby older generations have consumed unsustainable levels of fossil fuels and younger generations will bear the impacts, this chapter explicitly highlights age dynamics within this coalition response. In doing so, it addresses a gap in analyses of age/ing and intergenerationality within anti-racist, decolonial climate justice movements, bringing critical attention to how age and grandmotherhood can be mobilized toward political ends.

DISCUSSION QUESTIONS

1. In your own words, how would you explain a solidarity approach to coalition activism? How might it differ from other ways of working for change (e.g., volunteering, donating to charity)?

2. Why is it important to centre the needs, perspectives, and knowledges of youth, Indigenous peoples, people of colour, women, and communities from the Global South in climate justice organizing?

3. Discuss how the Raging Grannies mobilized their age and whiteness on the frontlines of the ShellNo actions. Explain how this subverted ageist stereotypes as well as how it offered protection to others in the coalition.

4. Discuss some of the ways the Raging Grannies were practising solidarity-building (or could have practised solidarity) through longer-term ways of building relationships and/or shifting organizing practices. Give at least two examples.

5. What social locations do you occupy, or what privileges and disadvantages do you hold in society? Can you reflect on how, if you were going to participate in a coalition like that formed around ShellNo, your own understanding of your positions and locations might shape your approach to this activism?

SUGGESTIONS FOR FURTHER READING

Waziyatawin. (2012). The paradox of Indigenous resurgence at the end of empire. *Decolonization: Indigeneity, Education & Society, 1*(1), 68–85. This article examines the links between climate change, colonial extraction, destruction, commodification of lands and waters, and colonial oppression, dispossession, and violence toward Indigenous peoples. Working from this analysis, the author also argues that the resurgence and valuing of Indigenous knowledges, pathways, and practices are critical to climate struggles but also that Indigenous lifeways are dependent on ardently protecting lands and waters.

Snelgrove, Corey, Dhamoon, Rita, & Corntassel, Jeff. (2014). Unsettling settler colonialism: The discourse and politics of settlers, and solidarity with Indigenous nations. *Decolonization: Indigeneity, Education, & Society, 3,* 1–32. This roundtable discussion explores the concept of "settler" and digs into "the politics of building solidarities between Indigenous and Non-Indigenous peoples." The authors challenge these concepts of "settler" and "solidarity," unpacking these ideas to build new understandings toward relationships, accountability, and solidarity among different peoples that can challenge power and work toward struggles for decolonization.

Walia, Harsha. (2013). *Undoing border imperialism.* Edinburgh, UK: AK Press. This book draws together the academic scholarship, activist savvy, and personal lived experience of community organizer and journalist Harsha Walia into a thorough and compelling investigation of how settler colonialism, capitalism, labour exploitation, and racist nation-building collectively create and maintain border imperialism. She offers strategies building unified struggles against these systems, drawing together insights from migrant organizing, Indigenous resistance and resurgence, and racial justice struggles. Overall, she compels organizers across movements and social locations to "overcome the barriers and borders within movements in order to cultivate fierce, loving, and sustainable communities of resistance striving toward liberation."

Chazan, May. (2016). Settler solidarities as praxis: Understanding "granny activism" beyond the highly visible. *Social Movement Studies, 15*(5), 457–70. This article is closely linked to this chapter, exploring research conducted at the previous Raging Grannies Unconvention in 2014. The chapter explores how the Raging Grannies thoughtfully modify their activisms in the context of settler-Indigenous solidarity-building; the article explores the possibilities and tensions of this kind of intergenerational, decolonial work.

Caney, Simon. (2014). Climate change, intergenerational equity and the social discount rate. *Politics, Philosophy & Economy, 13*(4), 320–42. This article explores the intergenerational disparities of the effects of ongoing climate change, particularly considering the disproportionate effects on young people and future generations, and suggests several practical ways in which contemporary actors can work toward better protection for future generations.

MULTIMEDIA SUGGESTIONS

Standing Rock syllabus

https://nycstandswithstandingrock.wordpress.com/standingrocksyllabus

This syllabus was compiled by a group of Indigenous scholar-activists based across Turtle Island in response to the lack of knowledge exposed during the Standing Rock resistance in 2016. The syllabus includes many readings but also many videos, graphics, and audio materials and serves as a resource on decolonization, climate justice, and the broader social, cultural, political, environmental, and economic context of the current environmental crisis.

Aging Activisms

www.agingactivisms.org

This is the website for Aging Activisms, an activist-research collective led by May Chazan, which is concerned with why and how activists of varied ages, abilities, backgrounds, and genders work for social and political change across diverse movements and across their lives and how they tell, curate, and circulate their stories of resistance. The website includes dozens of short storytelling videos with all kinds of change-makers, offers an online community hub for a network of academics and activists of all ages, and coalesces current popular and academic conversations about aging and activisms.

Got Green

http://gotgreenseattle.org

This is the website for Got Green, a climate justice organization based in Seattle. As their website explains, "Got Green organizes for environmental, racial, and economic justice as a South Seattle-based grassroots organization led by people of color and low income people. We cultivate multi-generational community leaders to be central voices in the Green Movement in order to ensure that the benefits of the green movement and green economy (green jobs, healthy food, energy efficient & healthy homes, public transit) reach low income communities and communities of color."

Idle No More

http://www.idlenomore.ca

This is the website for the global Idle No More movement, an Indigenous nationhood movement that is also necessarily a climate justice movement, since environmental exploitation and ongoing colonization are inseparably linked. The site offers frequently updated information as well as opportunities and suggestions for becoming engaged in decolonizing work locally and globally.

REFERENCES

Acker, Alison, & Brightwell, Betty. (2004). *Off our rockers and into trouble.* Victoria, BC: Touchwood Books.

Atshan, Sa'ed, & Moore, Darnell L. (2014). Reciprocal solidarity: Where the black and Palestinian queer struggles meet. *Biography, 37*(2), 680–705.

Boudreau Morris, Katie. (2017). Decolonizing solidarity: Cultivating relationships of discomfort. *Settler Colonial Studies,* 7 (4), 456–73.

Brown, Gavin, & Yaffe, Helen. (2014). Practices of solidarity: Opposing apartheid in the centre of London. *Antipode, 46,* 34–52.

Carter, Jill, Recollet, Karyn, & Robinson, Dylan. (2017). Interventions into the maw of old world hunger: Frog monsters, kinstellatory maps, and radical relationalities in a project of reworlding. In Heather Davis-Fische (Ed.), *Canadian performance histories and historiographies* (pp. 205–31). Toronto, ON: Playwrights Canada Press.

Charpentier, Michele, Quéniart, Anne, & Jacques, Julie. (2008). Activism among older women in Quebec, Canada: Changing the world after age 65. *Journal of Women & Aging, 20,* 343–59.

Chazan, May. (2016). Settler solidarities as praxis: Understanding "granny activism" beyond the highly visible. *Social Movement Studies, 15*(5), 457–70.

Chazan, May, & Baldwin, Melissa. (2016). Understanding the complexities of contemporary feminist activism: How the lives of older women activists contest the waves narrative. *Feminist Formations, 28*(3), 70–94.

Curnow, Joe, & Helferty, Anjali. (2018). Contradictions of solidarity: Whiteness, settler coloniality, and the mainstream environmental movement. *Environment & Society, 9*(1), 145–63.

Featherstone, David. (2012). *Solidarity: Hidden histories and geographies of internationalism.* London, UK: Zed Books.

Flesher Fominaya, Cristina. (2014). International solidarity in social movements. *Interface: A Journal for and about Social Movements, 6*(2), 16–25.

Gaztambide-Fernández, Ruben A. (2012). Decolonization and the pedagogy of solidarity. *Decolonization: Indigeneity, Education & Society, 1,* 41–67.

Ghabra, Haneen, & Calafell, Bernadette Marie. (2018). From failure and allyship to feminist solidarities: Negotiating our privileges and oppressions across borders. *Text and Performance Quarterly, 38*(1–2), 38–54.

Kaplan, Sarah. (2015). Meet the 92-year-old "raging granny" who just got arrested for protesting Arctic oil drilling. *The Washington Post,* 10 June. Retrieved from: www.washingtonpost.com/news/morning-mix/wp/2015/06/10/meet-the-92-year-old-raging-granny-who-just-got-arrested-for-protesting-arctic-oil-drilling.

Landy, David, Darcy, Hilary, & Gutiérrez, José. (2014). Exploring the problems of solidarity. *Interface: A Journal for and about Social Movements, 6*(2), 26–34.

Liu, Roseann, & Shange, Savannah. (2018). Toward thick solidarity: Theorizing empathy in social justice movements. *Radical History Review, 131,* 189–98.

McHugh, Maureen. (2012). Aging, agency, and activism: Older women as social change agents. *Women & Therapy, 35*(3), 279–95.

Meadows, Lynn M., Thurston, Stephanie E., & Lagendyk, Laura E. (2009). Aboriginal women at midlife: Grandmothers as agents of change. In P.A. Monture & P.D. McGuire (Eds), *First voices: An Aboriginal women's reader* (pp. 188–99). Toronto, ON: INANNA Publications and Education.

Mersha, Sara. (2017). Black lives and climate justice: Courage and power in defending communities and Mother Earth. *Third World Quarterly,* 1–14. https://doi.org/10.1080/01436597.2017.1368385.

Mohanty, Chandra T. (2003). *Feminism without borders: Decolonizing theory, practicing solidarity.* Durham, NC: Duke University Press.

Narushima, Maya. (2004). A gaggle of Raging Grannies: The empowerment of older Canadian women through social activism. *International Journal of Lifelong Education, 25,* 28–42.

Olwan, Dana M. (2015). On assumptive solidarities in comparative settler colonialisms. *feral feminisms, 4,* 89–102.

Pedersen, Julie. (2010). The Raging Grannies: Activist grandmothering for peace. *Journal of the Motherhood Initiative, 1,* 64–74.

Richards, Naomi. (2012). The fight to die: Older people and death activism. *International Journal of Ageing and Later Life, 7*(1), 7–32.

Rodgers, Kathleen, & Scobie, Willow. (2015). Sealfies, seals and celebs: Expressions of Inuit resilience in the Twitter era. *Interface: A journal for and about social movements, 7*(1), 70–97.

Roy, Carole. (2004). *The Raging Grannies: Wild hats, cheeky songs, and witty actions for a better world.* Montreal, QC: Black Rose Books.

Roy, Carole. (2007). When wisdom speaks, sparks fly: Raging Grannies perform humour as protest. *Women's Studies Quarterly, 35*(3/4), 150–64.

Sawchuk, Dana. (2009). The Raging Grannies: Defying stereotypes and embracing aging through activism. *Journal of Women & Aging, 21*(3), 171–85.

Sawchuk, Kim. (2013). Tactical mediatization and activist ageing: Pressures, push-backs, and the story of RECAA. *MedieKultur: Journal of Media and Communication Research, 29*(54). https://doi.org/10.7146/mediekultur.v29i54.7313.

Snelgrove, Corey, Dhamoon, Rita, & Corntassel, Jeff. (2014). Unsettling settler colonialism: The discourse and politics of settlers, and solidarity with Indigenous nations. *Decolonization: Indigeneity, Education, & Society, 3,* 1–32.

NOTES

1. We use "older" to refer to women who are older than the majority of the population; most of the Grannies are older than 60.
2. Here "younger" simply means younger than the Grannies. Panelists ranged in age from their early 20s to their late 50s.
3. For further context, ShellNo was a series of actions that took place over the course of several months in 2015. The aim was to resist Shell Oil's planned Arctic drilling. These actions were partially orchestrated by the Shell-No Action Council, a collective of representatives from more than 15 organizations, community groups, and

activist groups. The ShellNo Action Council organized a wide variety of actions in order to block the Arctic drilling rig's northern passage and raise awareness. These demonstrations took place on land, in water, and even in mid-air. The kayaktivist actions (wherein hundreds went into the harbour on canoes and kayaks to create a physical barrier to the oil rig, hoping to delay its passage, knowing that Shell Oil had a narrow window in which to carry out their drilling) received the most coverage of all of the varied ShellNo mobilizations. Yet this was just one facet of a series of creative actions designed to resist on many levels. As one panelist explained: "We were using all of these different spaces and . . . we were discussing ways to actually make [our ideas] viable and make [the actions] safe for us." So organizing around these diverse actions was grounded in the physical needs and skills of those involved. It meant working across many sites of action in ways that could work for different bodies and ways of resisting: confident swimmers took to kayaks, Tlingit and Haida singers and drummers shared music, dance, and prayer on the deck of a renewable energy barge, artists created massive banners to close off a train terminal and large elaborate lanterns to move through the water, and the Grannies locked themselves and their rocking chairs to train tracks.

4. All direct quotations come from the ShellNo panel at the 2016 Raging Grannies' Unconvention.

CHAPTER 19

◇

The Demand

Pasts, Presents, and Futures of Black, Indigenous, and Queer of Colour Feminisms[1]

*Aleyda Marisol Cervantes Gutierrez, Tahlia Natachu, Belina Letesus Seare,
Tamara Lea Spira, Mollie Jean West, and Verónica Nelly Vélez*

Learning Objectives

In this chapter, you will:

- learn about the histories of Black, Indigenous, and queer of colour feminisms as they intersect with contemporary student movements;
- recognize the inherent power of students to challenge institutional violence;
- map the legacies of radical feminist struggles in relation to racial, sexual, and gender justice culminating on university campuses today;
- examine the connections between student activism on college campuses and broader activist networks such as the Movement for Black Lives;
- learn about how student movements are formed on a national and local level;
- consider the difference between movements based on neoliberal "inclusion" versus those grounded in collective liberation;
- learn the importance of developing collective consciousness as a tool to resist institutional tactics to isolate students in connecting to struggles;
- consider your situation as a student within a larger genealogy of struggle and movement organizing.

Introduction

> *This is for us, at once before and after, seeking another kind of now.*
> —Alexis Pauline Gumbs, *We can learn to mother ourselves*, 2010

In 2013, a movement was forged out of the fires that raged across the nation, fires born out of grief and rage and love, fuelled by the affirmation that Black Lives Matter and premised on the refusal to accept the routine death of Black people throughout the world. The **Movement for Black Lives** (M4BL) emerged out of the Black community's response to George Zimmerman's acquittal after he fatally shot 17-year-old Trayvon Martin. The galvanizing chant that Black Lives Matter took hold when Michael Brown was killed on 9 August 2014 by Darren Wilson. When Wilson was acquitted by the grand jury in November of 2014, this chant exploded onto the streets of Ferguson, Missouri. The protesters, framed as "rioters" in the media, were met by militarized police in riot gear, armed with tear gas, and dogs.

M4BL was framed specifically to be intergenerational, transnational, and focused on the most marginalized of Black communities, centring the lives of Black women and people who are queer, trans, femme, disabled, poor, formerly incarcerated, undocumented, immigrant, and/or Muslim (Garza, 2017). Forged by the radical hands of Alicia Garza, Patrisse Khan-Cullors, and Opal Tometi, it expanded the work of queer and Black feminist revolutionaries of the 1970s and 1980s. Its founders framed it as "an ideological and political intervention in a world where Black lives are systematically and intentionally targeted for demise" and a movement that acknowledges the way systems of power operate across borders and recognizes the importance of connection between all oppressed peoples (Herstory, 2016). They foregrounded an "affirmation of Black folks' humanity" in a country that has denied the humanity of African-descent communities since its inception. Speaking explicitly to their contemporary moment, its participants also articulated their work as an unabashed refutation of the **neoliberal** claims of "postcolonial" and "post-racial" and as an interrogation of imperialism's support of "multiculturalism" and "inclusion."

Meanwhile, on college and university campuses, a series of radical student movements erupted along similar lines. In November of 2015, the University of Missouri's (Mizzou) president resigned in the face of an intense organizing campaign challenging the university's inadequate response to white supremacy. Like M4BL—and located only 100 miles away from Ferguson—Mizzou student activists bridged critiques of white supremacy, capitalism, and patriarchy, becoming an epicentre of student struggle nationally.

Student leader Jonathan Butler credited "three Black queer women" (Garza, Tometi, and Cullers) as an inspiration for students at Mizzou, invoking Audre Lorde and James Baldwin as foremothers of the movement (Thrasher, 2015). This framing would inform a series of demands that would break out on more than 80 university campuses recognizing the leadership of "queer Black badass women" (Marquez, 2015), including on our own campus of Western Washington University.

Examining these entwined histories, this essay brings together radical Black feminist and queer of colour histories of the late 20th century with these emergent efforts for racial, sexual, and gender justice culminating on university campuses today. We ask: *What do these intellectual and political genealogies bring to bear upon contemporary challenges to structural oppression put forward by marginalized students today? How has this current generation taken up these legacies to remold, negotiate, and articulate a radical anti-racist feminist praxis of the present?* As Tav Nyong'o (2015) asks in a recent piece on student protest: "How can any institution—a school, a corporation, an army, a police force, a prison—expect to continue along with business as usual after conceding that it is founded upon structural racism and colonial settlement?" Drawing from narratives of recent student protests, we examine how a new generation is demanding that the university grapple with precisely this question by connecting their struggles to those of past and future generations.

Before moving forward, we wish to offer a few words to frame ourselves and our methods. We are a collective of students, alumni, and faculty from Western Washington University. Specifically, we write from the vantage point of these struggles as they unfolded on our campus. In the fall of 2015, a series of death threats were issued to Black woman–identified students, including authors of this essay. Far from being isolated, these events were amplified by a context of broader ongoing assaults upon students of colour and queer,

Mexico's #todaviafaltan43

On the morning of 27 September 2014, pictures of 43 future Indigenous teachers flashed across Mexican media platforms. The night before, students of the Raul Isidro Burgos Rural Teachers' School (Escuela Normal Rural Raul Isidro Burgos) in Ayotzinapa in the state of Guerrero, Mexico, were travelling to Mexico City on buses. Along the way, they were violently attacked by heavily armed local police in the town of Iguala. According to reports, the students kept yelling that they were not carrying any weapons, although they defended themselves with rocks. Students who survived the attack have not been heard from since.

According to AJ+ (2015), the official story from Mexico's attorney general is that the police handed the students to local drug gangs that killed them and burned their bodies in a nearby town in Cocula; however, an independent investigation found serious flaws in this analysis. They found it would have been scientifically impossible for 43 bodies to have been burned in Cocula. The smoke would have been seen from miles away, and the flames would have started a forest fire.

Advocacy for Human Rights in the Americas (WOLA, 2018) has compiled a list of resources and detailed information regarding the case. Specifically, a cartography map of violence was created by Forensic Architecture to "map out and examine the different narratives of the event." In this way, the project reveals a cartography of violence spanning from the street corner level of the entire state of Guerrero. It describes an act of violence that is no longer a singular event but a prolonged act, which persists to this day in the continued absence of these 43 students (Forensic Architecture, 2017).

This was not the first time the Mexican state attacked students. Let's not forget Tlatelolco's Massacre in 1968. The 43 missing students are not only a reflection of violence against students across the nation but also the violence that Indigenous people suffer at the hands of colonial states such as Mexico. Multiple news sources have discovered evidence that it was a coordinated attack involving every level of the Mexican security forces; however, what exactly happened that night in the town of Iguana remains a mystery (Forensic Architecture, 2017; Franco, 2018; Newman, 2015).

Mexico's President Andrés Manuel López Obrador has opened a new investigation, signing an executive order to establish a Truth Access investigation in Ayotzinapa's case (Acceso a la Verdad en el Caso de Ayotzinapa) in hopes of finding out what really happened to the students that night and ensure that those involved are served justice.

Protesters across Mexico continue to commemorate and fight for these students with chants such as "You took them alive and alive we want them back" (*Porque vivos se los llevaron y vivos los queremos*). Parents and other family members have not lost hope of finding their loved ones. Every 26 September, they hold a commemorative march in Mexico City where they demand justice and assert that they will not stop until they are found.

Porque todavia nos faltan 43 (Because we are still missing 43).

trans, Indigenous, working-class, immigrant, and other marginalized students on college campuses nationwide. Of course, this struggle did not occur within a vacuum; we also write as leaders in the student campaign for a Multicultural Resource Center (MRC) and in response to the list of needs put forward by the Native American Student Association (NASU), as well as ongoing work led by queer women of colour to challenge hate crimes on our campus.

Our analysis emerges from a campus on unceded appropriated territory of the Coastal Salish Indigenous peoples where an epidemic of sexual, racial, anti-immigrant, settler colonial, and xenophobic violence—much like those surfaced and critiqued by current student demands—rages on. While we currently reside on Turtle Island, several of us also hold histories of migration, carrying familial histories of political struggle marked by displacement, war, and economic imperialism, all of which inform the ways we negotiate our sense of place and community in the local context.

This grounded context is important, we submit, as we work to honour the feminist-of-colour mandate to construct "a theory of the flesh" (Moraga & Anzaldúa, 1983). That is, rather than claiming a false pretense of objectivity, this position of struggle becomes a platform for our analysis. Transnational anti-colonial feminist Anna Agathangelou (2004) writes that "[f]eminists and cultural workers must . . . begin with ourselves and our lives as the launching point for our explanatory and analytic inquiries, especially if we are committed to revolutionary and transformative politics" (p. 169). Informed by Black, feminist of colour, decolonial, and transnational feminist frameworks and movements, we are guided by bell hooks's (1994) sage claim that to "write from a place of pain" is important because it "enables us to remember and recover ourselves, it charges and challenges us to renew our commitment to an active, inclusive feminist struggle" (pp. 59–75).

Refugees of a World on Fire: Setting the (Trans)National Stage for Student Uprisings

In her powerful words framing the necessity for and potentiality of deep solidarity across difference, Jacqui Alexander draws from Cherríe Moraga's notion of a "refugee of a world on fire" as a powerful metaphor for what it means to live in the service of everyone's liberation in times of great tumult. Alexander states:

> What if we declared ourselves *perpetual* refugees in solidarity with all refugees? Not citizen, not naturalized citizen. Not immigrant. Not resident alien. But refugees fleeing some terrible atrocity far too threatening to engage, ejected out of the familiar into some unknown, still-to-be-revealed place. Refugees forced to create out of the raw smithy of fire a shape different from our inheritance with no blueprints, no guarantees? (2005, p. 265).

Alexander herself was not present in the United States when the historic feminist of colour anthology, *This bridge called my back*, was collectively written in 1981. Notably, *This bridge* helped to create a vocabulary that generations would turn to in their efforts to organize and survive as multiply marginalized feminists. By taking up Moraga's metaphor three decades later, Alexander calls upon her readers to reject the pretense of a world we know in times when nothing less than a total reinvention of the social order is necessary for the planet's survival. Alexander models what it means to creatively and effectively listen to conversations and struggles of feminists across generations as a way to raise necessary questions and evoke a consciousness to organize in the present.

This tradition of paying homage to and repurposing critical feminist vocabularies has been amplified in recent years, particularly as the world

The Chilean Winter

From 2011 to 2013, massive student protests erupted in Chile in opposition to the ongoing inaccessibility of education for the majority of youth. Both high school and university students took to the streets to let the country know that they would not accept the ongoing corporatization of education at the expense of youth. Specifically, they called for the end of a school voucher system that diverted funds from the majority of working class and poor students attending public high school. They also called for free public education through the university level funded by the government, bus passes so that youth could get to school, a more reasonable salary for teachers, and the creation of an intercultural university that would meet the needs of Indigenous Mapuche students, among other important demands.

Dubbed "the Chilean Winter" after the "Arab Spring," this movement built from the 2006 *"pingüino"* (penguin) protests initiated by high school students, which were named as such after the students' uniforms. Expressions of student struggle challenged the elite, privatized system of education, which had been initiated by the US-backed Chilean dictator Augusto Pinochet, who ruled the country from 1973 to 1990.

Throughout the movement, students created important alliances with different marginalized sectors of society. They included striking miners from one of the largest copper mines and Mapuche communities calling for an end to colonial occupation by the Chilean state. Tactics included school occupations, walkouts, major protests, hunger strikes, and even a kiss-in.

In 2016, after ongoing protests and negotiations, the Chilean state committed to a tuition-free education program. While this appeared promising, movement leaders critiqued it for failing to address the exorbitant cost of higher education. The institutions required to abide by this rule were limited, as were slots for students within participating universities. Instead of addressing the larger context of privatized education, activists argued, this legislation simply provided funds to the lowest of income families to pay into the system. As one former student leader put it, "The education market is still there, the only thing that changes is that the family doesn't have to go into debt but can pay along with everyone else. . . . Our struggle is to eradicate the education market and strengthen public education" (O'Boyle, 2016). Therefore, while the program was one step forward, it also signified the need for further struggle.

reveals itself to be "on fire" and M4BL emerged to name the intersecting violences confronting wide-scale communities. Importantly, the intellectuals and organizers of M4BL did not claim to emerge from a vacuum; rather, part of their strategy was to credit radical thinkers of the 1970s and 1980s.

"In the last several years," writes historian Yamahtta-Taylor (2017), "Black Feminism has re-emerged as the analytical framework for the activist response to the oppression of trans women of color, the fight for reproductive rights, and, of course, the movement against police violence" (p. 13). With this (re)emergence, one core text and organizing moment at the heart of it is the historic statement, "A Black feminist statement," written by the Combahee River Collective. This statement, originally written in 1977, put forward the claim that systems of domination are interlocking and called for recognition of the "simultaneity" of experiencing those interlocking systems.

By focusing on the interlocking nature of oppressions, the Combahee River Collective defined a feminism that was built around the particular experiences of Black women specifically and women of colour more broadly. Echoing the words of feminist Anna Julia Cooper, they argued that "[i]f Black women were free, it would mean that everyone else would have to be free since our freedom would necessitate the destruction of all the systems of oppression" (Eisenstein, 1978, p. 215). Centring the freedom of the most structurally dispossessed was the only way to guarantee that the movement would work in the service of total liberation instead of reproducing violence, elitism, and new exclusions. These theorizations predated the more commonly used term "intersectionality," which was later put forward by legal scholar Kimberlé Crenshaw (1991). Combahee was the first group to use the term "identity politics," by which they meant that lived experience of oppression and intimate dreams for freedom were the touch point for any social movement.

Forty years later, on 5 October 2017, in a speech organized by the University of California Berkeley Department of Gender and Women's Studies, Alicia Garza described the Combahee River Collective statement as an "intervention" and a "love letter, to us" that was "kind enough to remind us that we are not one-dimensional beings." This challenged a white mainstream feminism that still consistently asks Black women to forget about issues of race or Black Power movements that consistently asked Black women to forget about issues of gender. Garza framed Combahee as a love letter because it reminds Black women to refuse to give up their multiplicitous identities for the sake of a "false unity" within movements—movements that could have the potential to provide actual liberation had they not been so filtered (Garza, 2017).

Garza's words underscored Combahee's contemporary relevance, reading it as a necessary critique of the same kind of unity that is often called for today with the mainstreaming of "diversity," "inclusion," "multiculturalism," and even "social justice." Indeed, as recent movements and scholars have argued, in our current times of "neoliberal multiculturalism," certain racially and sexually minoritized subjects are offered false promises of safety, citizenship, and upward mobility in exchange for cooperation with the governing structures of the state and capital (Agathangelou, Bassichis, & Spira, 2008; Hong, 2015; Melamed, 2011). Far from signalling success or the end of oppression, however, such promises have an ugly underside: the growing vortex of prisons, war zones, detention centres, and other apparatuses for the management of those deemed "surplus" to the new world order (Davis, 2004; Sudbury, 2005).

Garza's work emerges from and informs the larger organizing philosophy and political praxis of the M4BL, whose leaders recognize that their own positionalities do not necessitate the authority to speak for the needs of communities throughout the nation. This underscores a key tenet of the M4BL: liberation that is not collective is not liberation at all.

The Combahee River Collective forges the key principle that "Black, other Third World, and working women have been involved in the feminist movement from its start, but both outside reactionary forces and racism and elitism within the movement itself have served to obscure our participation" (Eisenstein, 1978, p. 211). It is not that Black women have not been involved in movements throughout history and in feminist movements in particular; rather, they have been continuously asked to flatten or forget the complexities of their politics for the sake of that false unity or blotted from the historical record altogether. As Pat Parker boldly states: "I am a feminist. I am neither white nor middle class. And the women I've worked with were like me. Yet I am told that we don't exist and that we didn't exist" (Moraga & Anzaldúa, 1983, p. 241). As Parker

Ferguson, Missouri

An excellent example of Black feminist organizing emerged in Ferguson, Missouri; in August 2014, activists and organizers from across the country gathered in protest after the murder of Michael Brown and subsequent acquittal of the shooter, Officer Darren Wilson.

As these organizers in Ferguson brilliantly framed it:

> This is a movement of and for ALL Black lives—women, men, transgender and queer. We are made up of both youth AND elders aligned through the possibilities that new tactics and fresh strategies offer our movement. Some of us are new to this work, but many of us have been organizing for years. We came together in Mike Brown's name, but our roots are also in the folded streets of New Orleans and the bolded BART stations of Oakland. We are connected online and in the streets. . . . We do not cast any one of ours to the side in order to gain proximity to perceived power. Because this is the only way we will win. We can't breathe and we won't stop until Freedom (cited in Yamahtta-Taylor, 2016, pp. 172–3).

Organizers speak explicitly to the multi-dimensionality of identity and heterogeneity of the collective, echoing Audre Lorde's dictum that it was only through the honouring of true difference that the deep spark and energy for radical change would be possible. They claim their distinct roots and paths, thus affirming that their differences only make coalition stronger.

The Black Lives Matter Freedom Ride, primarily organized by Patrisse Cullors and Darnell Moore, was one of the first national in-person actions that BLM took. This effort attracted more than 500 Black people from across the country to Ferguson that August through organized transportation and lodging (Pleasant, 2015). As highlighted in the above statement, everyone who showed up was able to bring unique experience, expertise, and skills to the table, which made their actions that much stronger.

After being met with violence and militarization, the resistance occurring in the streets of Ferguson elicited responses on Twitter from Palestinians, who offered advice specifically on how to help organizers who had been hit with tear gas. This is a prime example of transnational solidarity that BLM and M4BL organizers understand as central to their movements and struggles.

and others demonstrate, Black women have created the conditions of possibility for feminism to emerge as a political force (Randolph, 2015).

Challenging this politics of erasure, M4BL centres the leadership of Black women, many of whom are queer and trans. By building out of the experiences and needs of Black women, M4BL works toward embodying the Black feminist politics that Combahee River Collective articulated some 40 years ago. The movement returns to this very statement to posit the same: that movements led by cis white men are not enough, that inclusion is not enough, and that acceptance into mainstream society is not enough when mainstream society is literally killing anyone who threatens white supremacy.

Toward the end of her lecture, Garza weaves together radical moments of past and present, saying, "I still believe that our unity is our strength . . . the unity that calls us to examine courageously the

South Africa's #StopRacismAtPretoriaGirlsHigh

In 2016, photos of young Black leaders in South Africa flooded social media outlets under the hashtag #StopRacismAtPretoriaGirlsHigh. These were the images of students at Pretoria High School for Girls who were being punished for wearing their natural hair. School officials had created a code of conduct that determined that wearing hairstyles like Afros, dreadlocks, Bantu Knots, and Braids were only allowed if they didn't exceed 10 mm in diameter. If students did not abide by the code, they were considered "disruptive," and it would be a punishable offence. However, the underlying issue had more to do with the policing of Black youth in their expression of their own humanity, and it is clear that the code was simply an iteration of anti-Blackness under the guise of school policies.

In late August, the students at Pretoria High School began organizing disruptions during classes in response to the discriminatory treatment from their school administrators. Angie Motshekga, the minister of basic education, cited the "implementation of the code" as the source of the difficulties and believed that it would have been received differently if the issue had been raised through parent bodies initially (SABC, 2016). However, this analysis proved to be a superficial and dismissive response to many students and parents who knew the rules were inextricably connected to Apartheid and manifestations of anti-Blackness in current-day South Africa.

> What the rules are doing is using a standard of white femininity and a standard of the white mode of neatness to categorize Black learners. I think that the rules are racist and discriminatory (Wazar, 2016).

These rules created an environment that taught Black students that they would never be accepted in their fullest and most whole expression of themselves. They relate to these conditions in a way that is unrecognizable to their non-Black peers. To submit to these rules would be a sacrifice of their humanity and ultimately uphold white supremacy.

> To assert our language & hair, is to assert one's cultural belonging. Schools must embrace cultural diversity #StopRacismAtPretoriaGirlsHigh (Mahr, 2016).

As students protested, they were met by force from the administration, who threatened to arrest them. The students demanded that the code of conduct be changed and for disciplinary actions to be taken against teachers or other staff members who implemented any racist policy and/or racist actions. The resistance of students was a direct threat to the structures that the school had been operating under since its inception in 1902. Pretoria High School had been an all-white school for nearly 100 years until the mid-1990s when it accepted its first Black students after Apartheid. It is important to locate the events of 2016 in the history of Apartheid because it challenges the narrative around what liberation actually materialized into for the people, particularly Black South Africans.

"It's not about just schools," said Yvette Raphael, a human rights advocate for young women and girls who attended one of the protests. "The Rainbow Nation is not a true thing. It's not reality. . . . Behind closed doors, some of things of pre-1994 are still happening" (Mahr, 2016).

The images of the Pretoria High School students crossing their arms with fists raised in the air are reminiscent of many generations of Black people resisting submission to European violence and aggression in the journey toward self-determination through wholeness.

ways that some of us are still throwing each other under the bus for a few crumbs from the masters table . . . and I believe we can do better" (Garza, 2017). The references to pivotal statements from Black women remind us that the struggle for Black lives did not begin with the Movement for Black Lives; instead, the movement is ongoing and simply changes shape and name as each new generation takes up their own understandings of oppression. It urges us not to invisiblize or forget the work that has already been done.

Invoking the actions of Rosa Parks and the words of Audre Lorde, Garza blends temporalities of struggle to show the continuities across time; she reminds her audience to continue loving themselves enough to refuse the flattening down of the self for the sake of a false unity. She gives permission to challenge a movement that fails to demand anything less than liberation for the most marginalized, the most oppressed, the most forgotten. Patrisse Khan-Cullors, too, weaves her politics out of the struggles and dreams of past generations. In her book *When they call you a terrorist: A Black Lives Matter memoir* (Khan-Cullors & Bandele, 2018), she begins each chapter with quotes from Black women—poets, artists, educators, warriors, some of whom are queer, and many who come from previous generations. The first quote is from Assata Shakur in an essay titled "To my people" and written from prison:

It is our duty to fight for our freedom.
It is our duty to win.

We must love each other and support each other.
We have nothing to lose but our chains.

Assata Shakur's prophetic statement that "we have nothing to lose but our chains" speaks to both the legacy of slavery that came before her and the transformation of slavery that surrounds her. In the era of the New Jim Crow and the white supremacist tool of mass incarceration, chains have shifted formation but remain chains nonetheless (Hartman, 2002). So the call to fight for freedom is a call to continue the vast legacy of anti-oppressive struggle. And the call to love and support each other while fighting for that freedom is an embodiment of Black feminist theory.

In describing her memoir, Khan-Cullors states, "if we can adopt Black Feminism as a movement, both in theory and practice, I think we can live" (Khan-Cullors, 2018). Khan-Cullors's (2018) assertion that it is through Black feminism "we can live" captures the essence that lives within the name of "Black Lives Matter." Living becomes possible when Black lives matter: specifically, when Black, queer and trans, disabled, undocumented lives matter.

This understanding calls for a certain type of politics: a politics centred around abolition. **Abolition** is key because survival and freedom depend upon the destruction of any and all institutions that perpetuate oppression. But, as Khan-Cullors (2018) stresses, abolition is not just about destruction. It is also about creation and about the "imagining of something else" (Khan-Cullors, 2018) and dreaming of a better world. It's about working toward a world that *This bridge* names "El Mundo Zurdo," a place where "the colored, the queer, the poor, the female, the physically challenged" would "feel at home" (Moraga & Anzaldúa, 1983, p. 196). It is through this radical imagining that Black feminism has built its tradition of radical love. It is where validation is given for those who dare to ask for something more and where the truth of our lived realities becomes fully realized.

University Scale: Understanding the Capacity of Heat to Change the Shape of Things

It is against this broader political backdrop that nationwide student-led movements of 2015 began coalescing, with the events at the University of Missouri serving as a public focal point. This all came to a head on 10 October 2015. The catalyst for a flurry of university student demands emerged at the University of Missouri's homecoming parade.

University of Missouri: Concerned Student 1950

Eleven Black university students and members of a student group named Concerned Student 1950 interrupted the parade to publicly address the past and present climate of racism on campus. During the demonstration, the university president failed to respond appropriately; he allowed his car to hit the demonstrators and then sat complacently in the violence of the bystanders.

Following this heinous reaction, the group Concerned Student 1950 put forward a list of demands. They demanded an apology from, and subsequent removal of, the university president for his "gross negligence" and repeated failure to

acknowledge or address systematic oppression and anti-Blackness within the university. They demanded that a "comprehensive racial awareness and inclusion curriculum" be taught throughout the university and an increase in the percentage of Black faculty and staff. They demanded an increase in funding and resources for the counselling centre and the social justice centres on campus. They demanded that the university president address his failure to adequately respond to anti-Blackness or listen to the needs of Black students concerning race and racism. They demanded the university revisit the Legion of Black Collegians' demands that were presented in 1969. Together, the demands created an interjection into the daily racism and anti-Blackness experienced across campus and the university's "business as usual" attitude in the midst of it all. Student organizers' refusal to accept the routine violence at their institution reflects what Cherríe Moraga describes as a "politic born out of necessity" (Moraga & Anzaldúa, 1983, p. 23). This, to paraphrase Audre Lorde, stemmed from a politics that had nothing to do with "altruism" and everything to do with "survival" (Lorde, 2009).

Student body president Jonathan Butler began a hunger strike on 2 November 2015 when the University of Missouri failed to appropriately respond to Concerned Student 1950's second demand that the university president step down. On the sixth day of the hunger strike, Concerned Student 1950 held a strategy meeting with alumni, who explained to the students that they needed people outside of their group to validate them in order for a broader audience to listen. On the seventh day of the hunger strike, Mizzou's football team joined in support by refusing to practise or play until the university addressed the demands from Concerned Student. The football team joined the hunger strikers on the Carnahan Quadrangle and said to the media, "let this be a testament to all the other athletes across the country. That you do have power" (Dietrich, Bajaj, & Marvin, 2016).

The statement from the football team asserting the existence of the power already within reminds us of the poem Cherríe Moraga wrote in 1981 titled "The welder." Her poem uses the metaphor of a welder to explain that we already have what we need for a revolution but revolution only becomes possible when "things get hot enough" to create "fusion" (Moraga & Anzaldúa, 1983, p. 219). The "welder," she writes, "understands the capacity of heat / to change the shape of things," (p. 220) understands that our world is heating up quite literally from global climate change, politically from the fires of protest, and emotionally from the culmination of centuries of oppression. The welder understands that this heat is required to create change and is "suited to work / within the realm of sparks / out of control" (p. 220). Concerned Student 1950, already working in the realm of sparks, giving oxygen to the heat that was already there, was creating heat to change the shape of things. Concerned Student 1950 was demanding that their lives matter too.

Student organizers within Concerned Student 1950 led protests, worked tirelessly against the administration in the face of systematic oppression, and refused to let their needs be ignored or silenced. Apparent in the name, this is a group of students that "represents every Black student admitted to the University of Missouri since [the first in 1950] and their sentiments regarding race-related affairs affecting their lives at a predominantly white institution" (Concerned Student, 2015). The foundation for Concerned Student 1950 is built on the legacy of Black students that came before them. Grounding themselves in that historical legacy of anti-Blackness at Mizzou, Concerned Student 1950 begins with the acknowledgement of every Black student before them, echoing the spirit of M4BL and Combahee, recognizing the history that preceded them.

Concerned Student 1950 also called students to action across the nation. With the University of Missouri standing to lose $1 million if the football team refused to play their next game, the Athletics Department released a statement supporting the football team's solidarity with Concerned Student 1950. On 9 November 2015, university officials held an emergency meeting during which the president of Mizzou gave a statement of his official resignation as well as an apology to students and an acknowledgement of their experiences of racism. In response, Concerned Student 1950 rallied together on the lawn, making a statement with the very clear distinction that "this is a movement, not a moment" (Dietrich et al., 2016).

In the end, the actions of Concerned Student 1950 voiced a promise to future generations of students who would take up the same anti-oppressive struggle and make it their own. The list of demands, like the Combahee River Collective's statement, was also a love letter to those future generations of Black students attending Mizzou. It was framed as a love letter because their demands attempted to address the needs of those who would come after them. This was evident in the way that they demanded a strategic plan to "increase retention rates for marginalized students" (Concerned Student, 2015). It is also evident in their demand for an increase in Black faculty and staff. And it is apparent in their relentless organizing, protesting, and dreaming of a university that would not stop short for Black lives.

Following the list of demands at Mizzou, students at more than 100 other colleges and universities across the nation released demands for their own schools. Among these were demands released at our own campus of Western Washington University. In what follows, we offer a closer snapshot of the ways such dynamics unfolded locally.

WWU: Taking the Power into Our Own Hands

On 23 November 2015, a series of sexualized death threats were issued to Black women students at Western Washington University through social media. This occurred as racial and gendered tensions were on the rise, particularly as feminist students of colour and anti-racist students organized to challenge the iconography and meaning of the school mascot—a Viking. This challenge to the white hypermasculinity of the mascot was part of broader campaigns on the part of students to "claim their education," to paraphrase Adrienne Rich's call in 1977, including demands for a truly democratic multicultural centre that would respond to the needs of students of colour. Students were also working to decolonize the university, specifically through a series of needs put forward by the Native American Student Association (NASU) in May 2016. This context set the stage for a core tenet of radical Black queer and anti-racist feminist thought that became actualized under fire in our own lives—that of collective self-determination and the taking of power into our own hands.

When the death threats were issued, it had been a month and a half since the school shooting at Umpqua Community College in Oregon. It had been less than 12 days since racial death threats were made on a popular social media platform against Black students at the University of Missouri, Howard University, and Northwest Missouri State University. It had been six days since the racial death threats at Lewis and Clark College and three days since a Black student was assaulted by three white men on the Lewis and Clark College campus (Silverstein, 2015). It also coincided with the day that five Black Lives Matter protesters were shot in Minneapolis. Such events heightened the sense of fear and danger at the time that the racial death threats and threats of sexual assault were made through that same anonymous social media platform against Western Washington University's student body president, a Black woman, and one of this chapter's authors.

The threats were made by Western students who lived within a five-mile radius of the student body president and had access to the student body president's personal information, including her full name and address. The sense of urgency and fear sparked was also informed by the national landscape in which such threats were being made and carried out.

And yet, despite this broader context, university administration failed to adequately address the magnitude of seriousness that underwrote those threats. Their response, which came after Black women, other students of colour, and queer students assembled their own response team and spent 12 hours monitoring threats themselves, was to provide one individual student with police protection. This response failed to acknowledge the routine and systematic anti-Blackness within policing, thus failing to acknowledge the lived realities of Black people throughout the United States. It also failed to acknowledge or engage with the visceral fear that shook Black and Brown Western students after the threats were made.

At 5 pm on 23 November, the university president called a meeting with campus officials, the student body president, and the student vice-president of diversity, who had also been directly targeted. The students made it clear that their priority was ensuring that the message going out to campus kept Black students and students of colour at the forefront of the conversation, especially with the threats that had been made. They asked to help construct the initial message. They asked for a campus-wide alert. They asked for help in monitoring the threats online the evening of the 23rd. None of these requests was honoured. Although the university did cancel classes the following day, it only did so because Black students urged Western's president to act. The student leaders knew that students of colour wouldn't come to class, let alone leave their homes, while they were being targeted by death threats.

Later, it was confirmed that upon learning the nature of the threats, many students of colour didn't leave their dorms, even to get meals from the cafeteria. Official university communication didn't convey threats of lynching and raping against Black students but rather that "social media was being used for hate speech targeted at Western students of colour." It went on to describe the events that took place as "teachable moments"—a moment to learn from, reflect upon, and benefit from, with the central focus being the education of white male students previously unaware of these issues.

Not only did the university refuse to give adequate protection to targeted students, it proclaimed that the threats were not a threat to "general" campus safety. This made it achingly clear *whose* lives Western valued and whose were regarded as already disposable. In addition to isolating those targeted, the university responded through the logic of criminality and the ensuing pursuit of "bad" individuals. As the university president said in a general message to all students and employees:

> Yesterday, we observed social media being used for hate speech targeted at Western students of color. I need to be VERY clear here: we are not talking the merely insulting, rude, offensive commentary that trolls and various other lowlifes seem free to spew, willy nilly, although there has been plenty of that, too. No, this was hate speech.

By insisting upon the language of "hate crimes," the campus administration turned one act of institutionalized racism and sexism into an isolated event. The students who were targeted implored him to raise this as a systemic issue and to ensure that Black students and students of colour would be protected. They also asked that their calls for protection be linked to curricular demands of students of colour, as well as campaigns for adequate space for a multicultural centre, an increase in faculty of colour, and broader supports for under-represented and under-served students.

Instead, the logic of crime and punishment was set in motion, thus reproducing the hyper-masculine aggressiveness that students critiqued in the mascot itself. As the president's message continued:

> Have no doubt: this is not a capitulation to those I described as trolls and lowlifes. We are going after them. Rather, the pause is necessary so that we may learn more as we advance the law enforcement investigation and, together, plan responses that will make us stronger. In a phrase I often hear you use, it is because "Western Cares."

The language of the "lowlife" reproduces racist and classist hierarchies of value, despite its utilization to label those issuing the death threats (Cacho, 2012). This served to perpetuate the idea that the death threats and racism had been issued by one bad individual and were not part and parcel of the university structure itself. This was remarkable given the broader context of social movements unearthing the foundations of slavery, colonialism, nationalism, and sexual violence. By ending his statement with the phrase "Western Cares," the university administrator produced the university itself as a bastion of goodness to be set against the seeming aberration of one individual, who would be targeted and punished for his wrongdoings.

In response to this, campus organizers created a framework that placed the threats of 2015 in the broader context of student struggles that had been taking place at Western for the past century. Here, a brief note of context is important. In 1969, Western became the second school in the nation to establish a College of Ethnic Studies, just after San Francisco State University. This was the result of several years of organizing and strategizing led by students and faculty who believed there needed to be a space for students of colour to learn their respective histories and for all students to be able to engage with curriculum that addressed the political climate that was taking form throughout the 1960s (Vendiola, 2015) and into the 1970s.

With this history in mind—and with university demands being formed across the nation to address anti-Blackness—students at Western Washington University quickly formed the Student Assembly for Power and Liberation (SAPL). SAPL is a coalition organized by students who are Black, Indigenous, Latinx, Asian, and Pacific Islander, many of whom are women and queer. Their first act was to give a statement at the Board of Trustees meeting in Seattle on 12 February 2016 to address the lack of accountability within the university in terms of racism, and anti-Blackness in particular. They discussed the legacy of colonialism, the culture of anti-Blackness, and specific examples of "acts of violence." They ended their statement, significantly, with the same quote that Mizzou students shouted during protests and the same quote that Patrisse Khan-Cullors used to begin her memoir:

It is our duty to fight for our freedom.
It is our duty to win.
We must love each other and support each other.
We have nothing to lose but our chains.

Their call and response in Assata Shakur's words is at once an acknowledgement of the work of previous iterations of Black liberation struggles and a nod of solidarity toward Black university students across the nation, including the Black Liberation Collective and M4BL. By quoting Assata Shakur, SAPL draws connections between the specific instances of racism and sexual violence on Western's campus, the Black liberation struggles occurring across the nation, and the work being done within M4BL, locating all within a broader political genealogy of feminist political struggle. It captures the way that focusing on the local context while maintaining a national and global lens "eventually . . . spreads like wildfire," (Khan-Cullors, 2018). This embodies and reinvigorates the foundational transnational decolonial feminist principle to root our work with integrity within our local cultural context in tandem with others in different geopolitical locations (Mohanty, 2003).

Like the university student demands that spread like wildfire after University of Missouri students made theirs, SAPL wrote their own list of demands for Western. Students came forward in recognition that their abuse, their experiences of violence took place because of certain relationships of power and because of certain legacies of oppression that structured the university that housed them. Students came forward with demands because, as Erykah Badu states, "the pain to remain the same outweighed the pain to change" (Olsson et al., 2011).

In the wake of the events surrounding November 2015, Western officials made it evident how quickly the most vulnerable students are often the collateral damage of the university's failures. One of the significant ways that SAPL responded to the threats of November 2015 was by constructing a framework that addressed the structural conditions that had normalized these kinds of assaults on student bodies, minds, and spirits at Western for generations. Audre Lorde demonstrates the use of the erotic as power in reminding us that "our acts against oppression become integral with self, motivated and empowered from within" (Lorde, 1984b, p. 58). Lorde suggests that we can only understand our true source of power when we connect to this emotional and spiritual consciousness. Many students who are subjected to trauma by the institution experience these assaults at a deep psychological level that can be so foreign to our peers. "Dominance culture" doesn't allow these realities to become articulate, and so we further repress this pain. Not only is our healing dependent on us being able to have real conversations that are supported by the institutions, but these pains also become incredibly important points of information for all communities who seek to transform any experience. "The erotic is a measure between the beginnings of our sense of self and the chaos of our strongest feelings" (Lorde, 1984b, p. 54), so any praxis that does not affirm our wholeness will inevitably continue to dehumanize and disenfranchise students. If our education systems truly seek to transform, those in power must be willing to unearth what is buried deep in the foundation of its existence.

> Spirit work does not conform to the dictates of human time, but it needs our courage, revolutionary patience, and intentional shifts in consciousness so that we can anchor the struggle for social justice within the ample space of the erotic (Alexander, 2005, p. 283).

Our political practice should not be devoid of self. Any condition we may have can be used to inform a new way of relating to ourselves and our collective transformation.

Seven Generations Before and Seven Generations After: Freedom as a Constant Struggle

On 20 April 2018, the ground-breaking ceremony for the new Multicultural Center took place at Western Washington University. While the event was held to highlight the beginning of the construction of the new centre, it also brought together more than 25 years of student organizing. Each speaker at the event commemorated different individuals and communities who had helped the organizing get to this point. During the ceremony, a group of current students came together with a banner that said "we must remember hxstory." The power of the message is deeply connected to the chronic, historical, and institutional amnesia that universities create among student organizers.

In a 2018 graduation speech, student leader Alia Taqieddin offered a parallel intervention (Taqieddin, 2018, 00:27:39–00:41:02). Recalling the events of 2015 and remembering the racialized death threats as a response to the student body president, she called upon her graduating classmates to continue "listening to the voices that came before her." Taqieddin framed student activism as a process of "linking each other's histories together," noting, in particular, that current students "dare to dream so that the generations of students after us can dream a little further and push a little harder."

The work of these students underscores a central claim that we have made in this essay: In order to pick up the torch and continue our work, it is vital for current students to locate their struggles within a larger genealogy of feminist of colour struggle—one that, as Jacqui Alexander puts it, is part of "three hundred and sixty three years, spanning continents, threading dreams, holding visions" (2005, p. 257). As we have demonstrated, M4BL, Concerned Student 1950, and SAPL all address contemporary conditions through the reinvigoration of a powerful Black feminist, Indigenous, and queer of colour praxis. Part of a broader continuity, this work both draws nourishment from previous generations of struggle and reaches forward to seed more livable futures for all.

We close, then, by paying homage to the words of recently passed Native American feminist Beth Brant, who wrote the following in 1988 in the introduction to her ground-breaking first anthology of Native American women's writing:

> These hands fight back. The police, a battering husband, white men who would rape us on the land we live on. We use our fists, our pens, our paints, our cameras. . . . Our hands live and work in the present, while pulling on the past. It is impossible for us not to do both. . . . Our hands make us a future (1988, p. 12).

Brant's beautiful image of hands that "pull on the past" while also "liv[ing] in the present" and "mak[ing] a future" (p. 12) echoes the deeper knowledge of Indigenous communities who have taught us that we do not have to walk on this earth without honouring those who came before us and those who will come after. They add weight to the questions with which we close this essay: What is our duty in this movement? What is our duty to those who paved the way and to those who are coming after? Who are the seven generations before, the seven generations after?

Brant's words underscore once more our fundamental interconnection within living legacies of struggle. We are connected because, as Audre Lorde reminds us, "there is no such thing as a single-issue struggle because we do not live single-issue lives" (Lorde, 1984a, p. 138). This is the time we have been waiting for, to see each other as refugees fighting to dream up a better world. We cannot afford to ignore each other. As exemplified by the organizers who make up the collective Movement for Black Lives, it is a fundamental understanding of our interconnectedness, remembrance, and solidarity that hold movements together. By connecting to the writers of *This bridge called my back* and "A Black feminist statement," to the organizers of the Black Power movement, to Indigenous activists responding to historical trauma (Branch, 2018), to the contemporary Movement for Black Lives, and to histories of student organizing on our own college campuses,

we can begin to forge a movement that truly reckons with the radical histories that have created the conditions under which we organize today.

For student activists in particular, a new type of urgency has emerged in this contemporary moment. As we draw from past generations, we must remember that the work for liberation does not begin or end with us. We are connected to generations of people resisting; as Angela Davis reiterates, "freedom is a constant struggle" (2016) and cannot be contained. In order to honour this legacy, we must continue to imagine a new type of solidarity that allows us to see each other collectively as "refugees in a world on fire" (Alexander, 2005). The question of solidarity is vital to our movements and our transgenerational struggles; we have to be able to see each other as a bridge, connecting the past and present, connecting us across borders.

The issues and resistances reflected in the contemporary moment are intimately connected to Black and queer of colour feminisms of the past. We are still pushing against imperialism, colonialism, patriarchy, and white supremacy in a transnational context. Keeping the fire burning is necessary in order to continue our movement, building in ways that are sustainable. Remembering our stories, connecting with the genealogies of past activists, and supporting each other through it all is the work we need to do in order to continue onward and in order to survive. We won't let this fire die.

Call to Action

Take the time to learn the histories of colonial occupation, settlement, white supremacy, and labour that have shaped your university. How have students historically organized to challenge this, and what efforts are currently underway? Craft short- and long-term goals to educate yourself and your peers, and support current campaigns to create a truly anti-racist decolonial feminist institution.

Tying It Together

This essay brings together radical Black feminist and queer of colour histories of the late 20th century with emergent efforts for racial, sexual, and gender justice occurring on university campuses today. It asks what these intellectual genealogies bring to bear upon contemporary challenges to structural oppression being put forward by marginalized students. Drawing from narratives and analysis of recent student protests challenging racial, sexual, and gendered violence on college campuses, we examine how a new generation is forcing the university to grapple with precisely this question. In so doing, we offer an anti-racist feminist lens, historicizing the significance of student protest as part of a broader lineage of decolonization as a perpetual project (Quijano & Ennis, 2000) and freedom as a "constant struggle" (Davis, 2016). This chapter thus contributes to the larger aims of this textbook by putting feminist theory into practice and helping students to understand their struggles within a larger context.

DISCUSSION QUESTIONS

1. What are some changes that have been made at your university, since its inception, because of student activism?
2. How do histories of white supremacy, gender, and settler colonial occupation shape your campus? What histories of student struggle have challenged this?
3. If you are involved in student activism at your school, do you see this as connected to broader political struggles and movements? If so, how?
4. How do you see yourself in relation to lineages of resistance? Does this chapter help you to understand your life within a broader genealogy of feminist struggle? If so, how?
5. What are your dreams and visions for a just and equitable university? What would a liberatory anti-racist, anti-colonial feminist educational institution look like?

SUGGESTIONS FOR FURTHER READING

Alexander, M.J. (2005). *Pedagogies of crossing: Meditations on feminism, sexual politics, memory, and the sacred.* Durham NC: Duke University Press. This book brings together essays by Alexander, a contemporary transnational feminist theorist. Throughout the text, Alexander contextualizes many critical imperatives for feminist and queer movements to address in response to neo-imperialism and neo-colonialism.

Ferguson, R.A. (2017). *We demand: The university and student protests.* Oakland, CA: University of California Press. This book delineates the ways in which student movements influenced the intellectual landscape of the 20th century and the backlashes that are occurring because of these shifts contemporarily. It is a great read for student activists hoping to contextualize their struggles within the broader expanse of history.

Lorde, A. (2007). *Sister outsider: Essays and speeches* (2nd ed.). Berkeley, CA: Crossing Press. This is a collection of 15 essays and speeches by Audre Lorde, an exquisite poet and activist who helped to shape women of colour feminisms. The collection will help students to ground themselves in the histories of solidarity struggles that paved the way for BLM and M4BL to emerge.

Mohanty, C.T. (2003). *Feminism without borders: Decolonizing theory, practicing solidarity.* Durham,

NC, and London, UK: Duke University Press. This book brings together two decades of writing from feminist theorist Chandra Talpade Mohanty. Mohanty uses theory and pedagogy to address dominant conceptions of multiculturalism, the corporatization of the North American academy, and transnational feminist praxis.

Moraga, C., & Anzaldúa, G. (Eds). (2015). *This bridge called my back: Writings by radical women of color* (4th ed.). Albany, NY: SUNY Press. This book is referenced often throughout this chapter because it is a profound anthology capturing the vast amount of movement-building power that Black and queer of colour feminists have. It is an essential read in its own right, but it could also be a valuable way to historicize contemporary movement politics.

Randolph, S.M. (2015). *Florynce "Flo" Kennedy: The life of a Black feminist radical.* Chapel Hill, NC: University of North Carolina Press. This book focuses specifically on the life of Florynce "Flo" Kennedy (1916–2000), a Black feminist who allied herself with Black Power movements as well as with primarily white feminist organizations. It challenges mainstream feminist movement histories to reveal that Black feminism has always been a pivotal practice in US liberation movements.

Taylor, K.-Y. (Ed.). (2017). *How we get free: Black feminism and the Combahee River Collective.* Chicago, IL: Haymarket Books. In this anthology, founding members of the Combahee River Collective as well as contemporary activists reflect on the legacies of Black feminism and its impact on today's movements.

MULTIMEDIA SUGGESTIONS

Visions of abolition: From critical resistance to a new way of life. (2011). 01:27:00
https://www.imdb.com/title/tt4379078
This documentary connects the prison industrial complex and the prison abolition movement through the voices of women.

Queerness on the front lines of #BlackLivesMatter. (2015). 00:07:02
https://www.youtube.com/watch?v=0YHs-9jIH-oo
This MSNBC special features Patrisse Khan-Cullors, a founder of the #BlackLivesMatter movement, who discusses how queer and trans people of colour are integral to the movement.

Relating to race: The College of Ethnic Studies at Western Washington State College. (2015) (00:58:14)
https://cedar.wwu.edu/hrss/hrss/hrss_events/6.
This presentation, part of the Heritage Resources Speaker Series, features Michael Vendiola's examination of the College of Ethnic Studies through primary and secondary sources. Programs focused on ethnic studies were formed in the 1960s at American universities and colleges as a result of social movements at the time.

REFERENCES

Agathangelou, A. (2004). *The global political economy of sex: Desire, violence, and insecurity in Mediterranean nation states* (1st ed.). New York, NY: Palgrave Macmillan.

Agathangelou, A., Bassichis, M., & Spira, T.L. (2008). Intimate investments: Homonormativity, global lockdown and the seductions of empire. *Radical History Review, 100,* 120–43.

AJ+ (2015). What happened to the 43 Ayotzinapa students? 24 September. Retrieved from: https://www.youtube.com/watch?v=NtDfpTWpYvw.

Alexander, J.M. (2005). *Pedagogies of crossings: Meditations on feminism, sexual politics, memory and the sacred.* Durham, NC: Duke University Press.

Branch, Z. (2018). Working toward a better justice: Race and pedagogy 2018. *South Sound Magazine,* 5 October. Retrieved from: https://southsoundmag.com/working-toward-a-better-justice-race-and-pedagogy-2018.

Brant, B. (Ed.). (1988). *A gathering of spirit: A collection by North American Indian women* (2nd ed.). Ithaca, NY: Firebrand Books.

Cacho, L. (2012). *Social death: Racialized rightlessness and the criminalization of the unprotected.* New York, NY: New York University Press.

Concerned Student 1950. (2015). List of demands. Retrieved from: https://genius.com/Concerned-student-1950-list-of-demands-annotated.

Crenshaw, K. (1991). Mapping the margins: Intersectionality, identity politics, and violence against women of color. *Stanford Law Review, 43*(6), 1241–99.

Davis, A. (2004). *Are prisons obsolete?* New York, NY: Seven Stories Press.

Davis, A. (2016). *Freedom is a constant struggle: Ferguson, Palestine, and the foundations of a movement.* Chicago, IL: Haymarket Books.

Dietrich A., Bajaj V., & Marvin, Kellan. (2016). Concerned Student 1950. 21 March. [Video File]. Retrieved from: https://fieldofvision.org/concerned-student-1950.

Eisenstein, Z. (Ed.). (1978). A Black feminist statement: Combahee River Collective. In *Capitalist patriarchy and the case for socialist feminism* (pp. 210–18). New York, NY: Monthly Review Press.

Forensic Architecture. (2017). The Ayotzinapa case: A cartography of violence. Retrieved from: https://www.forensic-architecture.org/case/ayotzinapa.

Franco, Marina. (2018). El caso Ayotzinapa: Cuatro anos de dolor e incertidumbre. *The New York Times,* 26 September. Retrieved from: https://www.nytimes.com/es/2018/09/26/ayotzinapa-estudiantes-43-mexico/?rref=collection%2Fsectioncollection%2Fnyt-es&action=click&contentCollection=43-estudiantes-desaparecidos&region=stream&module=stream_unit&version=latest&contentPlacement=1&pgtype=collection.

Garza, A. (2017). GWS keynote lecture: Black Lives Matter co-founder Alicia Garza. 24 October. [Video File]. Retrieved from: https://www.youtube.com/watch?v=ZDCxFABGkPw.

Gumbs, A. (2010). We can learn to mother ourselves: The queer survival of Black feminism 1968–1996. Doctoral dissertation. Retrieved from: https://dukespace.lib.duke.edu/dspace/bitstream/handle/10161/2398/D_Gumbs_Alexis_a_201005.pdf.

Hartman, Saidiya. (2002). The time of slavery. *South Atlantic Quarterly, 101*(4), 757–77. Retrieved from: https://www.lgbt.arizona.edu/sites/lgbt.arizona.edu/files/Hartman2002.pdf.

Herstory. (2016). Black Lives Matter. Retrieved from: https://blacklivesmatter.com/about/herstory.

Hong, G. (2015). *Death beyond disavowal: The impossible politics of difference.* Minneapolis, MN: University of Minnesota.

hooks, b. (1994). Theory as liberatory practice. In *Teaching to transgress: Education as a practice of freedom* (pp. 59–75). New York, NY: Routledge.

Khan-Cullors, P. (2018). Radio Interview with C. Brooks. 20 March. Retrieved from: https://www.radioproject.org/2018/03/patrisse-khan-cullors-call-terrorist.

Khan-Cullors, P., & Bandele, A. (2018). *When they call you a terrorist: A Black Lives Matter memoir* (1st edn). New York, NY: St Martin's Press.

Lorde, A. (1984a). Learning from the 60's. In *Sister Outsider: Essays & Speeches.* Berkeley, CA: Crossing Press.

Lorde, A. (1984b). Uses of the erotic. In *Sister Outsider: Essays & Speeches.* Berkeley, CA: Crossing Press.

Lorde, A. (2009). *I am your sister: Collected and unpublished writings of Audre Lorde* (R.P. Byrd, J.B. Cole, & B. Guy-Sheftall, Eds). New York, NY: Oxford University Press.

Mahr, K. (2016). Protests over Black girls' hair rekindle debate about racism in South Africa. *The Washington Post,* 3 September. Retrieved from: https://www.washingtonpost.com/world/africa/protests-over-black-girls-hair-rekindle-debate-about-racism-in-south-africa/2016/09/02/27f-445da-6ef4-11e6-993f-73c693a89820_story.html?noredirect=on&utm_term=.8bce6f5393f4.

Marquez, Y. (2015). Badass Black queer movement paved the way for the Mizzou movement. *AUTOSTRADALE,* 10 November. Retrieved from: https://www.autostraddle.com/badass-black-queer-women-paved-the-way-for-the-mizzou-movement-315857.

Melamed, J. (2011). *Represent and destroy: Rationalizing violence in the new racial capitalism.* Minneapolis, MN: University of Minnesota Press.

Mohanty, C. (2003). *Feminism without borders: Decolonizing theory, practicing solidarity.* Durham, NC, and London, UK: Duke University Press.

Moraga, C., & Anzaldúa, G. (Eds) (1983). *This bridge called my back: Writings by radical women of color* (2nd edn). New York, NY: Kitchen Table/Women of Color Press.

Newman, Lucia. (2015). Mexico one year after the kidnapping: "I saw it all." 27 September. Retrieved from: https://www.aljazeera.com/blogs/americas/2015/09/mexico-year-kidnapping-150926054117369.html.

Nyong'o, T. (2015). The student demand. [Web log post]. Bully Bloggers, 17 September. Retrieved from: https://bullybloggers.wordpress.c7om/2015/11/17/the-student-demand.

O'Boyle, Brendan. (2016). Free college in Chile! So what are students so mad about? *America Quarterly,* 1 January. Retrieved from: https://www.americasquarterly.org/content/free-education-frustration-chiles-student-activists.

Olsson, G., Rogell, A., Barnes, J., Glover, D., Arnö, A., Questlove, . . . MPI Media Group, film distributor. (2011). The Black Power mixtape 1967–1975: A documentary in 9 chapters. Stockholm, Sweden: Sveriges Television.

Pleasant, Liz. (2015). Meet the woman behind #BlackLivesMatter—The hashtag that became a civil rights movement. *Yes Magazine,* 1 May.

Quijano, Aníbal, & Ennis, Michael. (2000). Coloniality of power, Eurocentrism, and Latin America. *Nepantla: Views from South, 1*(3), 533–80.

Randolph, Sherrie M. (2015). *Florynce "Flo" Kennedy: The life of a Black feminist radical*. Chapel Hill, NC: University of North Carolina Press.

Silverstein, J. (2015). Police investigating beating of Black Lewis & Clark College student as possible hate crime. *New York Daily News*. Retrieved from: http://www.nydailynews.com/news/national/beating-black-lewis-clark-student-hate-crime-article-1.2443751).

Sudbury, J. (2005). *Global lockdown*. New York, NY: Routledge.

Taqieddin, A. (2018). WWU spring quarter commencement 9 am. 16 June. [Vimeo Video]. Western Washington University. Retrieved from: https://vimeo.com/275433074.

Thrasher, S.W. (2015). How racial justice advocates took over Mizzou and won. *The Guardian*, 10 November. Retrieved from: https://www.theguardian.com/us-news/2015/nov/10/racial-justice-advocates-university-of-missouri-won.

Vendiola, M. (2015). Lecture on relating to race: The College of Ethnic Studies at Western Washington State College. 13 January. Washington State Archives, Goltz-Murray Archives Building, Bellingham, WA. Retrieved from: https://cedar.wwu.edu/hrss/hrss/hrss_events/6.

Wazar, M. (2016). Interview with Mishka Wazar, journalist for *The Daily Vox*. TRT World, 1 September. Retrieved from: https://www.youtube.com/watch?v=_t8Y1UHrEoU.

WOLA. (2018). Resource page: Analysis and information on Mexico's Ayotzinapa case. 28 June. Retrieved from: https://www.wola.org/analysis/analysis-and-information-on-mexicos-ayotzinapa-case.

Yamahtta-Taylor, Keeanga. (2016). *From #BlackLivesMatter to Black liberation*. Boston, MA: Haymarket Books.

Yamahtta-Taylor, Keeanga (2017). *How we get free: Black feminism and the Combahee River Collective*. Boston, MA: Haymarket Books.

NOTE

1. This chapter is dedicated to all students across all borders taking risks and resisting injustice to receive the education they deserve. We also extend our gratitude to our beautiful intergenerational community at WWU who bravely continue to challenge hateful white supremacist violence; may we always remember our hxstories and the places from which we come. We would also like to thank Madi Stapleton for her exemplary research support, particularly in the final stages of crafting this manuscript.

2. Bainter, Norm. (1975). Ethnic studies: Chronology of a concept. *Klipsun Magazine*, 5(3), 16.

3. Barnard Center for Research on Women. (2013). What is neoliberalism? 15 August. [Vimeo video]. Retrieved from: http://sfonline.barnard.edu/gender-justice-and-neoliberal-transformations/what-is-neoliberalism.

4. Black Liberation Collective. (n.d.). Retrieved from: http://www.blackliberationcollective.org.

5. Black Lives Matter toolkit. (2016). Black Lives Matter. Retrieved from; http://sayhername.blacklivesmatter.com/toolkit.

6. Conry, C. (2018). Keynote speakers at RPNC make an impact. *The Trail*, 5 October. Retrieved from: http://trail.pugetsound.edu/?p=15351.

7. Ferguson, R. (2012). *The reorder of things*. Minneapolis, MN: University of Minnesota.

8. Humphries, A., & Marbre, S.B. (n.d.). Reparations. The Movement for Black Lives. Retrieved from: https://policy.m4bl.org/reparations.

9. Kelley, R. (2002). *Freedom dreams: The Black radical imagination*. Boston, MA: Beacon Press.

10. Lindsey, T. (2018). Black Lives Matter cofounder Patrisse Cullors is writing history—on her own terms. *Popsugar*. Retrieved from: https://www.popsugar.com/news/Patrisse-Cullors-When-Call-You-Terrorist-Interview-44514195.

11. Moeti, Koketso. (n.d.). Stop racism at Pretoria Girls High. Retrieved from: https://awethu.amandla.mobi/petitions/stop-racism-at-pretoria-girls-high.

12. Platform. (n.d.). The movement for Black lives. Retrieved from: https://policy.m4bl.org/platform.

13. Rich, Adrienne. (2005). *Claiming an education*. In Chris Anderson & Lex Runciman (Eds), *Open Questions* (pp. 608–11). New York, NY: Bedford/St Martin's.

14. SABC. (2016). Nothing controversial about PGHS hair policy: Angie Motshekga. 31 August. Retrieved from: https://myzol.co.zw/articles/1495/nothing-controversial-about-pghs-hair-policy-angie-motshekga.

15. Schatz, K., & Klein Stahl, Miriam. (2018). *Rad girls can: Stories of bold, brave, and brilliant young women* (1st edn). Berkeley, CA: Ten Speed Press.

PART VI

Narrative as Activism

An extensive body of work has already explored the potential for developing social understanding through narratives. Such studies have drawn on the frameworks of postcolonial and decolonial feminisms and offered insight on the potential of narrative performance that is grounded in both personal and public experience (see Morris & Hjort, 2012). The chapters in Part VI contribute to this literature by exploring a diversity of themes regarding power, activism, and cultural, gendered, or personal identity. The authors help us to explore postcolonial feminisms through the critical intersections of race, class, sexuality, age, and ability. The narratives presented are embedded in the experiences of everyday life. They express how the social factors of "power" and "privilege" can be used in effecting social change.

Focusing on the voices of contemporary women writers, the contributors in Part VI demonstrate the important role that literature and storytelling can play in response to gendered colonial violence. These narratives analyze the socially interventionist work of Indigenous, diasporic, Black, and queer women poets, spoken word artists, and filmmakers. These chapters pair literary interventions with recent sites of activism and policy critique. They put literature in dialogue with the debates on anti-violence to illuminate new pathways toward action.

In "Women Filmmakers of the Arab Diaspora: Transnational Perspectives," May Telmissany examines the works produced by Arab female filmmakers and situates them within the global context of transnational cinema. Readers are invited to explore the tensions between national and transnational filmmaking in terms that are relevant to gender. Telmissany asks the readers to consider film history from a postcolonial perspective.

In "Untitled," Clelia O. Rodríguez exposes the challenges that the globalization of academia presents to students from the Global South. Rodríguez demonstrates how academia is a racialized structure and examines a range of issues that must be addressed if we are to achieve the decolonization of academia.

In "Migrant Slavery and Ralph Goodale-Abdoul," El Jones helps her readers to recognize the roles of colonialism and slavery in the founding of Canada. Jones examines how the colonization of the Americas, including Canada, has involved systematic destruction of Indigenous and African cultures. She invites us to consider the ways in which the criminal justice system in Canada remains biased against Indigenous people, Black people, and people of colour, despite the commonly made claims that Canada is a free and multicultural society.

In "A Killjoy Manifesto," Sara Ahmed explores what being a "killjoy" is and how this role relates to transgressing the social obligation of being happy. We are invited to consider what it means to be unseated from the table of happiness, to examine how society disregards those who unseat the contentment of others, and to notice how certain bodies are usually blamed for such disturbance. In this final chapter, Ahmed examines the intersections between race and being a feminist killjoy.

REFERENCE

Morris, M., & Hjort, M. (2012). *Creativity and academic activism: Instituting cultural studies.* Durham, NC: Duke University Press.

CHAPTER 20

◇

Women Filmmakers of the Arab Diaspora
Transnational Perspectives

May Telmissany

Learning Objectives

In this chapter, you will:
- examine the work produced by women filmmakers of the Arab diaspora and situate it within the global context of transnational cinema;
- understand the tensions between national and transnational filmmaking in terms that are gender-specific;
- consider film history from postcolonial perspectives.

Introduction

Arab women filmmakers of the Western **diaspora** hail from a wide range of ethnic, cultural, and religious backgrounds. Their work offers an invaluable opportunity to learn about the social and economic challenges faced by women in and outside the Arab World and to shed light on their cinematic contributions within the larger context of transnational cinema. General issues relating to the status of women in Arab societies and the role played by diasporic women filmmakers in emphasizing Arab struggle against colonial oppression, social patriarchy, and religious fundamentalism are discussed in this chapter in an attempt to achieve several goals: first, to highlight Arab women filmmakers' contributions to the film history; second, to participate in the debate surrounding the Arab presence in the West following

decolonization; third, to look into the representations by and about Arab women in cinema as discrepant experiences entrenched in colonial/postcolonial discourses; and, finally, to shift the focus from the central male (and oftentimes orientalist) gaze on women to the study of film production as a site of female empowerment.

Why is it important to examine films directed by Arab women filmmakers in the Western global context? Despite the quantitative and qualitative importance of their films, Arab diasporic filmmakers, especially women, remain largely unknown. The current chapter attempts to fill the gap in scholarship regarding these filmmakers and their production. First, a sizable number of films made by established directors such as the Lebanese-French Danielle Arbid (*Un homme perdu*; *Peur de rien*) and the French-Algerian Yamina Benguigui (*Inchallah dimanche*; *Aicha*) as well as by emerging ones such as the Palestinian American Cherien Dabis (*Amreeka*; *May in the summer*) or the Saudi Haifaa Al-Mansour (*Wadjda*: *Nappily ever after*) have a definite impact on how the world perceives Arab women today. Second, in addition to being at the helm of large film crews in a rather male-dominated global film industry, women filmmakers of the Arab diaspora are increasingly recognized and celebrated in film milieus. My socio-historic approach to their work is intended to contribute to the cultural history of "women worthies" (Meriwether & Tucker, 1999) by highlighting the role played by notable Arab women in the field of transnational filmmaking.

To achieve the goals set for this study, I should first acknowledge two caveats: first, the growing local and international visibility of Arab women directors should not overshadow or minimize colonial and postcolonial discourses and tensions inherent to film production and circulation on the global scale. These tensions inform and affect modes of production and ways of expression particular to the Arab communities living in Europe and North America. Second, bearing in mind that the term "Arab" constitutes a cultural hybrid, the word should not be accounted for in essentialist terms. I refrain from using "Arab" as an ethnic frame of reference and privilege a cultural reading of the Arab diaspora based on the country of origin as well as the filmmakers' linguistic and cultural belongings.

How do women filmmakers of the Arab diaspora engage with these tensions? While criticizing the homeland's cultures of repression, many diasporic filmmakers embrace the multiplicity of their national, linguistic, and cultural belongings as they dwell in the relatively unrestricted environment of their hostland. Henceforth, their transnational identities allow them 1) to rehabilitate the cultures of their homeland while criticizing social patriarchy, political paternalism, religious fundamentalism, censorship, and lack of funding opportunities; 2) to facilitate community integration

in host societies and to overcome challenges associated, for example, with colonial/neo-colonial dynamics of coercion and mitigation; and 3) to express their dissatisfaction with the paradigm of the national "as a means of understanding production, consumption and representation of cultural identity (both individual and collective) in an increasingly interconnected, multicultural and polycentric world" (Higbee & Hwee Lim, 2010, p. 8).

Many would agree, however, that beyond the East/West divide, freedom of movement and speech has an impact on Arab filmmakers living in Europe and North America. With the opportunity to move freely across geographic, cultural, and cinematic borders, filmmakers are compelled to build bridges between homeland and hostland, articulating Arab aspirations for change and liberation and deconstructing conventional representations of gendered and nationalist identities through processes of diaspora-building and acculturation. Using cinema to construct their cultural communities, diasporic filmmakers often challenge their colonial past and their neocolonial present by critically engaging with the history of (post)colonization and by subverting the power relationship between male and female, centres and peripheries, local circuits and global networks. Marked by the nomadic fluidity of their transnational condition, filmmakers recover what James Clifford identifies as "non-Western, or not-only-Western, models for cosmopolitan life, non-aligned transnationalities struggling within and against nation-states, global technologies, and markets-resources for a fraught coexistence" (1994, p. 328).

Based on these preliminary remarks, I argue in this chapter that Arab women filmmakers living in the West belong culturally and nationally to both sides of the colonial divide, which allows them to contest the social and political power discourses promulgated on both fronts. The filmmakers' viewpoints on binaries such as self and other, secular and sacred, integration and difference are therefore conceptualized and problematized in line with the fundamental critique of patriarchal and colonial arrangements of power.

Methodological Approach

Broad in scope, this chapter attempts to offer insight into diasporic filmmaking in postcolonial contexts by asking two main questions: What are the cinematic tactics adopted by women filmmakers of the Arab diaspora to challenge Western conventions in gender-specific terms? To what extent do these tactics contribute to the creation of a new aesthetics of transnational cinema made by Arab women? To answer these questions, I rely on discourse analysis to conduct a **postcolonial reading** of the ways through which women filmmakers of the Arab diaspora cope with the complex realities of their transnational condition.

The methodological tools needed to examine the subject of transnational filmmaking from a postcolonial perspective are found in interdisciplinary fields of inquiry such as area studies (Meriwether & Tucker, 1999; Shohat, 1991), film studies (Bernstein & Studlar, 1997; White, 1998), gender theories (Elsadda, 2014), and, more broadly, theories of intersectionality (Hancock, 2016). Feminist scholars (Elsadda, 2014; Shohat, 1991; 2013) contend that while essentializing the feminization of the Orient as an inferior other, the two-fold colonial gaze on Arab women (on the basis of their ethnicity and gender) promotes cultural and national hierarchies according to which white women/white feminism become superior to non-white women/non-white feminism.

Using these approaches from a comparative literature perspective, how can one disentangle the complex relationships between film, gender, colonial history, and diasporic condition? Edward Said's **contrapuntal methodology** offers an invaluable insight into ways of comparing and contrasting discrepant experiences and multi-layered representations of self and other in (post)colonial settings.

Telmissany and Schwartz claim that a "contrapuntal reading" is a reading that recognizes and engages with different voices, identities, and texts in the contexts of both colonialism and postcolonialism (2010, p. xix). Contrapuntal methodological devices include on the one hand the description of the filmmaker's political and intellectual positions and on the other hand the analysis of the relationship between texts (in our case, films).

In sum, a contrapuntal reading takes into account the filmmaker's diasporic condition, her gendered, national, and cultural identities, when comparing her films with other films. This type of reading seeks to unravel the intercultural and intertextual links between national and transnational film productions. Methodological tools and strategies (such as the ones proposed by Edward Said) allow the researcher to explain how transnational networks help women filmmakers to build solidarities, transcend national and cultural essentialism, and challenge the East/West divide from a postcolonial standpoint.

Transnational Cinema in Theory

In film theory, notions such as accented cinema (Naficy, 2001), world cinema (Chaudhuri, 2005), transnational cinema (Ezra & Rowden, 2006), and immigration cinema (Ballesteros, 2015) testify to the importance of the cross-cultural views on cinema explored and celebrated at the turn of the new millennium. Earlier, the notion of third cinema (Solanas & Getino, 1969) bore some similarities with the notion of world cinema as a means of dismantling national cinemas produced in and by the West (see box).

Today, alternative non-Western cinematic expressions, even when produced in or in collaboration with Western countries, are interpreted by film theorists as **exilic**, accented, hybrid, diasporic, transnational, or migrant forms of contestation of the colonial East/West divide from a postcolonial standpoint. Yet instead of asserting fixed national identities in the battlefield of (post)colonial discourses, concepts of hybridity (see Stam, 2013) seem to emphasize the dire need to understand the shift in power relationships between a privileged colonizer and a disadvantaged colonized. In fact, cultural crossing and in-between identities allow the diasporic transnational filmmaker to maintain a dynamic relationship with both past and present, country of origin and host country. As Higbee and Hwee Lim note: "What is required here is a critical understanding of the political imbalances as well as the unstable and shifting identifications between host/home, individual/community, global/local and, indeed, national/transnational, as well as the tensions these generate within diasporic films" (2010, p. 12).

In other words, transnational and diasporic cultures are predicated on the tensions generated by multiple belongings, processes of mobility, and a fundamental questioning of ideologies of national uniqueness. By rejecting perceptions of and beliefs in the wholesomeness of a unique ethnicity, language, religion, and/or culture, women filmmakers of the Arab diaspora unearth the intersections between gendered, colonial, and nationalist discourses.

In this perspective, transnational filmmakers play an important role in deconstructing the relationship between homeland and hostland and in shaping a new identity in today's interconnected world. Their films present three main characteristics: 1) the need to recognize cultural multiplicity and to dismantle monolithic views on cultural productions; 2) the celebration and fulfilment of mobility and networking; and 3) the adoption of anti-nationalist attitudes as a result of colonial/postcolonial downfalls. Notwithstanding this, characteristics ought to be nuanced and differentiated at all times and in all occurrences, especially when both colonial histories and the filmmakers' individual trajectory bear inevitable differences and specificities. Assuming clear-cut boundaries between East and West is in my view futile and unproductive in the context of transnational film production. The discussion of co-production that follows helps us to understand how this mode of production is often presented as an invitation to cross the cultural borders and an opportunity to bring about aesthetic innovation.

Cinematic Theories

Accented Cinema
This concept, coined by film scholar Hamid Naficy, challenges dominant and mainstream productions through films that "signify and signify upon exile and diaspora by expressing, allegorizing, commenting upon and critiquing the home and host societies and cultures . . . by means of their artisanal and collective production modes, their aesthetics and politics of smallness and imperfection, and their narrative strategies that cross generic boundaries and undermine cinematic realism" (2001, pp. 4–5).

Immigration Cinema
Drawing on the notion of migrant literature, immigration cinema theorizes cinema authored by immigrants themselves. It also refers to films made by Western filmmakers who use the means of production of dominant cinema to politically engage with the immigrants' predicaments.

Third Cinema

This concept was formulated in the 1960s in reaction to commercial cinema and to the dominant Hollywood model of filmmaking. Argentinian film directors Fernando Solanas and Octavio Getino in their manifesto "Towards a third cinema" (1969) call for an alternative revolutionary cinema to counter both first cinema (Hollywood) and second cinema (European *film d'auteur* and bourgeois cinema).

Transnational Cinema

According to Ezra and Rowden, the concept refers to "changing ways in which the contemporary world is being imagined by an increasing number of filmmakers across genres as a global system rather than as a collection of more or less autonomous nations" (2006, p. 1). It also refers to film production and circulation on a global scale to insure the availability of a wider range of films to a wider range of audiences.

World Cinema

According to film scholar Shohini Chaudhuri, "the concept of world cinema better encapsulates the dispersed and decentred model of film production and distribution that increasingly prevails, especially if it is used to emphasise the interplays between national, regional and global levels of cinema" (2005, p. 12). However, the danger of lumping together differentiated non-Western cinemas under the label of world cinema should be recognized and avoided.

Film d'auteur

Film d'auteur is an expression coined by French film critic and filmmaker François Truffaut in the 1960s to describe cinema made by filmmakers who have developed an aesthetic signature equivalent to that of an author of a novel; for example, filmmakers such as Alfred Hitchcock, Luis Bunuel, and Roberto Rossellini (or, more recently, Quentin Tarantino, Wong Kar-wai, and Xavier Dolan) are considered *auteurs*. The expression is also used to describe non-mainstream cinemas in transnational settings. In Egyptian cinematic circles, these films are referred to by the colloquial expression *aflam mahraganat*, which means "films destined for festivals."

Co-production and *Films d'auteur*

Cinematic co-production had become the global norm in the late 1990s and prevails today at the brink of the 2020s in Arab and Western contexts. Seeking out international funds, primarily from the Global North funding circuits and more recently through South–South networks, has become in the past 20 years a trademark for excellence in the Arab film industry, with a small niche available to visible women filmmakers. The notion of **glocalization** pointing to the growing interconnectedness of global and local experiences and practices might be suitable to describe tendencies in Arab cinemas toward the heterogeneity and decentralization of film production beyond Arab borders.

Chief among the programs solicited by Arab filmmakers to support film production and distribution are the government-supported French and Emirati programs. North-South funding opportunities were offered by the French Fonds Sud Cinéma as early as 1984, favouring for many decades the making of films with a strong cultural identity. Today, more than 700 long feature films from Africa, Asia, Latin America, North Africa, and the Middle East were granted subsidies by the French funds.[1] Younger in age but equally ambitious, the SANAD film fund in Abu Dhabi (United Arab Emirates)[2] seeks to develop the regional film industry along the lines of South–South co-production networks; one of their main objectives is to insure the growth of film production originating from the Arab World.

Co-production activities, however constructive they may be, mask relationships of power inherent in the new liberal age on the one hand and the everlasting tensions between culture and empire on the other. For the sake of studying strains on local and global film funding, it is seminal to differentiate between and compare two trends in cinematic co-production made by women in the Arab context: first, co-productions by Arab women filmmakers established in Europe and North America and, second, co-productions by Arab women filmmakers residing in Arab countries.

Why is the distinction between the two categories of co-production important? In today's intersected art world, the country of residence of film directors and film crews seems to have an impact on how the cinematic discourse reconfigures national and gender identities. While the very concept of "national cinema" as an expression of nationalist yearnings has become quasi-obsolete, gender inequalities in a male-dominated field such as filmmaking are still stronger than ever. An increasing number of Arab women filmmakers

have managed to negotiate a space of freedom thanks to co-production and to the rather open space available to them in their host countries. But gender inequalities, institutional constraints, and social/political censorship still represent major challenges to Arab women filmmakers residing in Arab countries.

Co-productions do not only depend on a variety of funding sources, they also target a variety of audiences. While mainstream film production remains largely locally based and addresses home-grown audiences in countries such as Egypt, Morocco, and Lebanon, the striving film industry in those countries is often reluctant to fund non-mainstream productions (traditionally considered as *films d'auteur* or, to use an Egyptian colloquial expression, *aflam mahraganat*/films destined for festivals—see box). It is not rare therefore to see that *auteur* filmmakers residing in the Arab region travel in search of external funds and larger distribution circuits. As they emerge from the margins of dominant film industries, looking for new audiences through regional and international festivals, they struggle to attract media attention and explore new markets inside and outside of their country of origin. For example, Nadine Labaki's Lebanese-French romantic comedy *Caramel* (2007), her Lebanese-French-Italian-Egyptian comedy/drama *Where do we go now* (2011), and her Lebanese-American drama *Capernaum* (2018) are considered *films d'auteur*. Labaki's feminist approach to love, sexuality, civil war, and parenthood transgresses the boundaries of national cultures by targeting national as well as international audiences.

Are there exceptions to the rule that opposes mainstream cinema and *cinema d'auteur*? Indeed! Films made by Nadine Labaki (living in Lebanon) and Ruba Nadda (living in Canada, of Syrian background) are a case in point. Both award-winning *auteur* directors also made mainstream romantic comedies: *Sabah* (2005) by Nadda and *Caramel* (2007) by Labaki. Both won local and international attention thanks to their feminist approach to sensitive matters such as the representation of Arab/Muslim female bodies, the repression of sexuality in patriarchal environments, and the subjective (as well as subversive) interpretation of religious practices such as the hijab. In both cases, the international recognition of their films problematizes the traditional opposition of mainstream film and *film d'auteur* by showing how *auteur* Arab women filmmakers use conventional mainstream cinematic genres to disentangle fact from myth associated with their Arab and Muslim cultures and to negotiate the image the Arab and/or Muslim nations have of themselves.

As a result of these processes of glocalization, peripheral film practices in national and transnational Arab cinemas bifurcate toward South–South network-building. Take the example of Yemeni-born filmmaker and producer Khadija Al-Salami: Al-Salami, who resides in Paris, directed *I am Nojoom, age 10 and divorced* (2014), an adaptation of the eponymous book by Nujood Ali, a Yemeni child bride married at the age of nine who filed for divorce from her 20-years-older husband and eventually won her freedom. The film was co-produced by Yemen, France, and the United Arab Emirates (through funding from the Dubai International Film Festival). As the United Arab Emirates move into "fresh realms like the media economy," Kay Dickinson contends that "the resulting autonomy comes as a welcome relief against a historical backdrop of transnationalised inequity of access, commercial domination, residues of military occupation and, of course, the pressures erupting from regional differences in taste" (2016, p. 137). Notwithstanding that, emerging markets in Asia and Africa have an important influence on funding processes in the Arab region; Europe remains the largest basin and host of Arab diasporic filmmaking thanks to sustainable co-production programs and the opportunity for wider distribution through the festival circuits.

Women Filmmakers of the Transnational Turn

Within the context of film production/distribution, one can identify at least three categories of transnational women filmmakers of Arab background. To determine these categories, two criteria were taken into consideration: first, the filmmakers' places of birth and dwelling, both of which have an impact on cinematic themes and styles; second, that the films meet some or all of the characteristics of transnational filmmaking mentioned earlier—namely, cultural multiplicity, mobility/networking, and anti-nationalist attitudes.

The first category is represented by first-generation Arab-born film directors residing in the West and travelling back and forth between their homeland and their hostland. The second category refers to second-generation Western-born film directors travelling sporadically to the country of origin of their parents for the sake of making films. And the third category covers Arab-born directors who live in Arab countries and who develop cultural and financial ties with the West where they occasionally dwell for educational or film production purposes.

Film historians Rebecca Hillauer (2005) and Roy Armes (2010) provide two influential accounts on diasporic filmmaking in the context of Arab cinemas. In *Encyclopedia of Arab women filmmakers*, Hillauer notes that the history of Arab women filmmakers is inextricably bound up with emigration and exile: "Exile, not only as a training and production site, but also as a place in which certain disorientation can be perceived due to the distance from one's roots" (2005, p. 12). The author cites non-mainstream filmmakers such as the Palestinian British video artist Mona Hatoum (*Measures of distance*, 1988), the Tunisian-French Nadia El Fani (*Fifty-fifty mon amour*, 1992), and the Palestinian British Azza Al Hassan (*When the exiled films home*, 2002) as examples of exilic filmmakers who oscillate between the mystical elevation of their homeland (Middle East, North Africa) and the urge to come to terms with the colonial hostland (UK, France). The filmmakers' primary goal, however, is to achieve freedom and fulfil their life dream of becoming filmmakers, according to Hillauer. One can then assume that their maladjustment and oftentimes their estrangement within national borders become the springboard for their transnational experience as diasporic filmmakers with multiple belongings, constant mobility, and rejection of nationalist impositions.

Similarly, in *Arab filmmakers of the Middle East*, Roy Armes contends that many Arab filmmakers from the Middle East and the Maghreb, when caught in colonization/decolonization developments, are either compelled to learn cinema in Western institutions or forced into displacement and exile. In the 2000s, "their filmmaking has become, to a considerable extent, a cinema of diaspora, with residence abroad and the receipt of funding from foreign sources becoming almost the norm" (Armes, 2010, p. 28). Travelling back and forth between Europe and the Arab World, the majority of Arab diasporic filmmakers (the first and second categories) live in enforced exile or live abroad for financial reasons, according to Armes. While the third category benefits from transnational modes of production/distribution, it is primarily based in Arab countries and addresses Arab audiences.

Arab-Born Migrant Filmmakers

The notion of exile as banishment, expulsion, or forced displacement is situated at the heart of films made by the Arab-born migrant filmmakers. Many, however, have been immunized against discourses of exilic suffering as their new homes become spaces of freedom and creativity, spaces that not only allow them to move back and forth between countries and cultures but give them leeway to self-representation as both Arab

and Other, woman and human. Born in 1936, pioneering Algerian-French writer and filmmaker Asia Djebar lived in Algeria, France, and the US. In 1978, she directed *The nouba of the women of Mount Chenoua* in which she celebrates the struggles of Algerian women against the colonial rulers and against their husbands. In 2005, Djebar became the first North African person to be elected to France's most prestigious cultural institution, the *Académie française*. Award-winning Lebanese filmmaker Danielle Arbid (*Un homme perdu*; *Beirut Hotel*; *Peur de rien*), born in Beirut in 1970 and based in France since 1987, puts Lebanon and Lebanese characters in the heart of her films. Despite censorship and banning of her work in Lebanon[3] and despite her films' lack of public visibility in France, Arbid continues to tackle sensitive issues of sexuality and politics from a subversive standpoint.

Documentary filmmakers are yet another example of the active (and activist) role played by women filmmakers behind the camera. Moroccan-French filmmaker Izza Genini (*Morocco, body and soul*), born to a Jewish family in Casablanca in 1942, has lived in Paris since 1960. During the 1980s and 1990s, Genini dedicated her career to producing and directing documentary films about traditional Moroccan music.[4] Lebanese documentary filmmaker Leyla Assaf-Tengroth (*The gang of freedom*, 1994; *Not like my sister*, 2008)[5] was trained in Sweden where she has lived and worked for the Swedish television network since 1966. In her compelling film *Not like my sister*, she tackles from a feminist standpoint the issue of forced marriage and honour killing by following a conservative Syrian family living in Lebanon. In this film, she addresses the confluence of poverty and patriarchy and celebrates the fight of a Muslim young woman to break free from social and religious impositions.

Born in Cairo in 1947, Egyptian-Canadian documentarist Tahani Rached (*Four women of Egypt*, 1997; *Soraida, a woman from Palestine*,

2004) moved to Canada in 1966. She worked for the National Film Board of Canada where she directed more than 20 documentaries, many of which depict women's fight for gender equality and national freedom. Although produced by Swedish and Canadian public funds, movies by Assaf-Tengroth and Rached challenge mainstream Western assumptions about passive and segregated Arab women through the celebration of female agency and empowerment: Muslim Syrian Rim in *Not like my sister* ends up marrying the Christian young man whom she loves despite parental and community opposition, while the Palestinian Soraida lives in Ramallah under Israeli occupation and fights against Israeli apartheid.

The notion of exilic/immigrant cinema encompasses a variety of experiences that go beyond immigration to the West. Few exceptions are worth mentioning. On the one hand, Arab-born migrant filmmakers experience exile and segregation within the comfort of their homeland and reflect on their exilic condition through their characters. Palestinians living in Israel under Israeli occupation, such as the veiled Muslim Palestinian-Israeli character in Maysaloun Hamoud's debut film *In-between* (2016), and LGBTQ communities who suffer from social stigmatization and gender/sexual discrimination, such as the lesbian couples in Nadine Labaki's *Caramel* and in Cherien Dabis's *May in the summer* (2013), are examples of internal exile triggered by colonial oppression or by conservative/religious rule.

On the other hand, Arab-born migrant filmmakers do not exclusively migrate toward Europe and North America. Cases of immigration from one Arab country to another as well as cases of return to the country of birth after living and filming in the West should be taken into account. Palestinian director Mai Masri (*Frontiers of dreams and fear*, 2001) was born in Jordan in 1959 and has been based in Lebanon since the 1980s. Masri made several political documentaries about the Palestinian plight before directing her first

feature film, *3000 Nights* (2015). This French-Palestinian co-production relates the story of a young Palestinian mother who fights to protect her newborn son and to survive in an Israeli prison. Born in 1974, Palestinian director Annemarie Jacir (*Salt of the sea*, 2008; *Wajib*, 2017) studied cinema and lived in the US and is now based in Jordan. Her family drama *Wajib* (literally, "Duty"), co-produced by Palestine, France, Germany, the United Arab Emirates, and Norway, relates the story of a father and his son who set on a journey across Nazareth to hand-deliver their daughter/sister's wedding invitation to each guest.

Definite or sporadic return to the homeland is another way to identify mobility as a major characteristic of transnational and diasporic filmmaking. The return of the diasporic filmmaker fulfills an important social and political need that justifies and gives meaning to border crossing. Egyptian Canadian Tahani Rached settled back in Cairo in the early 2000s. In her harrowing documentary, *These girls* (2005), Rached follows teenage street girls in the hustle and bustle of Cairo as they face the adversities of street life from drug consumption and single motherhood to physical abuse, kidnapping, and rape. Rached's feminist and anti-government views on the situation of street girls in Cairo testify to her ability to sustain a strong network in her country of origin and to support women's struggle for recognition as equal citizens in a male-privileged society and ruled by an oligarchic political regime. In recent years, Egyptian-American directors Jehane Noujaim and Mai Iskander made award-winning documentaries about the 25 January 2011 Egyptian Revolution, presenting a vivid snapshot of the weeks and months that followed the fall of 30-year-president Hosni Mubarak (see Telmissany, 2016). Noujaim (*Control room*, 2004; *The square*, 2013), born to an Egyptian father and an American mother, raised in Kuwait and Cairo, moved to Boston in her teens. Mai Iskander (*Garbage dreams*, 2009; *Words of witness*, 2012) graduated from New York

University Tisch School of the Arts and worked for A&E and PBS. In *Words of witness*, the filmmaker follows a young veiled female journalist as she makes her way in Tahrir Square to cover the events of the uprising in 2011 and 2012. *The square* does not solely focus on female characters but shows, from a feminist standpoint, the fight led by several revolutionary groups for freedom and social justice.

Western-Born Filmmakers of Arab Descent

Fewer film directors belong to the so-called second- or third-generation of immigrants born and raised in former colonial countries (France, UK) or in North America. In these cases, the parents' forced migration is often internalized by the filmmakers and voiced in their work as it informs and subverts their own transnational experience. Yamina Benguigui, born in 1955 in France to Algerian parents, Ruba Nadda, born in 1972 in Canada to Syrian parents, and Cherien Dabis, born in 1976 in the US to Palestinian parents, oftentimes give voice to older generations in their films. Forced migration of parents, siblings, and extended families are usually triggered by internal forces such as war, political repression, and economic upheaval. Memory of displacement and migration remains therefore alive and transmittable from one generation to another.

Being French-born, Canadian-born, or American-born, however, is perceived as a social and economic privilege that helps women directors of Arab descent to build stronger roots in their Western countries of birth and to negotiate their multiple identities as Other from within. The "emotional construction of a homeland, which provides a foundational narrative of departure and a validating promise of return" (Ezra & Rowden, 2006, p. 7) and which characterizes many films produced by Arab-born film directors, is problematized and subverted in films by Western-born filmmakers of the Arab diaspora.

Yamina Benguigui (*Immigrant memories*, 1997; *Inchallah Sunday*, 2001) tells stories of Maghrebi immigration to France in an attempt to free herself from her own history and that of her migrant parents. But memory of immigration becomes an essential pillar of her work as she strives "to give the children of the immigration back the dignity that their fathers sometimes missed" (Hillauer, 2005, p. 287). In her most notable movie, *Inchallah Sunday*, the main character, Zouina, moves from Algeria to France to join her husband; she is accompanied by her three children and her mother-in-law. Set in the 1960s under the family reunification program, the film illustrates different facets of exile for economic and political reasons. As the uprooted Zouina suffers from her mother-in-law's spitefulness, her husband's negligence, and her French neighbour's intolerance, she struggles to find a space of her own, to connect with other Algerians, and to cope with her new exilic condition. Benguigui's take on immigration, however, remains largely "French" because her discourse on women and religion advocates for assimilation into the French Republic's value system characterized mainly by *laïcité*, or secularism.

The perception of the West as home and the feeling of home-ness are portrayed as part of the integration process into Western societies; this perception is also the reason behind intergenerational conflicts due to differing views on values and norms. In the movie *Amreeka* (2009), the sense of belonging of the Arab-born Christian Palestinian mother as opposed to that of her Western-born second-generation son and daughter is one of the focal points of this light-hearted social drama by Cherien Dabis. Two sisters, one established in the US and the other newly emigrated from Palestine, offer two differing perceptions of home: Raghda is nostalgic for an idealized Palestine and insists that her house located in a small town in Indiana is a Palestinian territory, while Muna, a newcomer, blends into the society and adapts to her new life as she struggles to raise her son on her own.

Muna works in a fast-food restaurant; she understands and protects her nephew and niece from their mother's identity impositions and pushes the perimeters of integration by falling in love with a Jewish man.

In her second long-feature film, *May in the summer*, Dabis shows a Christian-Jordanian-American young woman (played by Dabis) who goes back to Jordan to convince her devout Christian mother to attend her wedding to a Muslim young man. Conflicts between mother and daughter arise along cultural, religious, and generational lines. The daughter's freedom to marry outside of her religion goes hand in hand with the dissociation from conservative attitudes inherent to her culture of origin and therefore the assertion of her cultural identity as rather American/Westerner.

Ruba Nadda's debut feature film *Sabah* (2005) is a romantic comedy that received support from Nadda's idol, director-producer of Armenian descent Atom Egoyan. The film chronicles Sabah's love story with a non-Muslim Canadian and her transition from being a middle-aged socially awkward veiled woman whose life is determined by cultural belongings and religious impositions to a well-integrated Canadian-Syrian-Muslim who celebrates her hyphenated identity by embracing the values of cultural and religious multiplicity. At the film release in 2005, Nadda declared to *The Globe and Mail*: "The problem is, with my culture, everything tends to be reduced to Islam and a woman's sexuality. For some reason it's the one culture that has yet to have this issue blown wide open."[6] Nadda's second feature film, *Cairo time* (2009), is a Canadian-Irish co-production shot in Cairo about the brief and unexpected love relationship between an Egyptian Muslim male and a Canadian non-Muslim female. The filmmaker's focus shifts from the social and cultural integration of an Arab in Canada (*Sabah*) to the celebration of Cairo's urban and cultural landscapes from the standpoint of a Canadian female protagonist travelling to the Middle East. *Cairo time* received

the Best Canadian Film Award at the Toronto International Film Festival in 2009 and, following its international release, was rated best-reviewed romance of the year by Rotten Tomatoes.

Arab-Born, Arab-Dwelling Filmmakers

Women filmmakers who live in the Arab World tackle more or less the same issues depicted in the first two categories—namely, the critique of social patriarchy and male domination, the intersectional relationship between gender, religion, and identity, and the rehabilitation through self-representation of Arab women on screen. With durable connections to the West (through education, intermittent sojourns in Western countries, co-production and international distribution), Arab-born, Arab-dwelling women filmmakers transgress national and cultural borders. Empowered by their ability to challenge mainstream orientalist discourses (essentializing women as inferior, oppressed, and passive), they push the limits of what and how stories about women should be told. Thanks to the aesthetic and innovative value of their work, their films (mostly co-productions) are acclaimed by Arab and international audiences worldwide.

The Tunisian director Mufida Tlatli (*The silences of the palace*, 1994) and the Lebanese director Randa Chahal Sabbag (*The kite*, 2003) condemn social patriarchy as it echoes colonial subjugation. Female resistance to patriarchy and occupation is remarkably portrayed in both films where the national liberation of southern Lebanon, occupied by the Israelis in the 1980s, and the Tunisian independence from the French protectorate in the 1950s are carried out by female protagonists who strive to break free from male and colonial dominance. Similarly, social patriarchy is condemned in co-productions directed by the Tunisian Raja Amari (*Red satin*, 2002) and the Lebanese Nadine Labaki (*Caramel*, 2007). Both filmmakers show female protagonists who are sexually liberated within the private sphere and depict unlawful love relationships between a young woman and a married man or between a mother and her future son-in-law. Female protagonists in both films cope with the conservative patriarchal system in exchange for a small margin of freedom. Reading these four films together contrapuntally allows the viewer to distinguish forms of female resistance to both male dominance and colonial hegemony. Women are empowered through singing in *Silences of the palace* and belly dancing in *Red satin* (see Telmissany, 2013); they denounce social pressure exerted by both men and women to control women's bodies in *Caramel*, as well as their present and future through arranged marriage in *The kite*.

A wide range of well-known women cineastes who dwell in Arab countries frequently travel to Europe for education or for work. Arab-born, Arab-dwelling filmmakers benefit from transnational cinema circuits to build their film careers. The list includes the Egyptian Asma El Bakry (1947–2015), director of *Beggars and nobles* (1991), the Lebanese Jocelyne Saab (born in 1948), director of *Dunia/Kiss me not* (2005), the Moroccan Farida Ben Lyazid (born in 1948), director of *Women's wiles* (1999), the Algerian Yamina Bachir (born in 1954), author of *Rachida* (2003), and the Egyptian Marianne Khoury (born in 1958), director and producer of *Women who loved cinema* (2002), to name just a few. These and many other Arab filmmakers gained visibility in recent years thanks to their tremendous talents as film directors, editors, and producers; they also gained access to internal and external funding opportunities, international film festival programming, and global TV and digital distribution.

Conclusion

My preliminary hypothesis was that cinema is a space of liminality and uncertain borders. Because cinema is a collective endeavour and because it often travels, film production inherently lends itself to the deconstruction of boundaries between the local and the global, between us and them, self and other, West and East. Ezra and Rowden contend that "cinema is borderless to varying degrees, subject to the same uneven mobility as people" (2006, p. 5). Nevertheless, as much as border permeability seems to be an ideal that many women filmmakers of the Arab diaspora seek to achieve, power relationships between cineastes and production/distribution circles remain a site of unremitting tensions and negotiations. While the inter/multi/transcultural developments and transformations undergone by cinematic modes of production worldwide embrace (and recuperate) new voices from the former "Third World" cinemas, the aesthetics of hybridity established by filmmakers of the Arab diaspora as well as the ideological and socio-cultural dimensions of their cinematic production remain heavily reliant on funding opportunities offered by Western countries.

More recently, new production and distribution configurations proposed by leading digital entertainment services such as Netflix and Amazon propose new forms of film circulation as a global commodity.[7] These new avenues along with older ones promise to open a new era for transnational film production marked by the recognition of cultural multiplicity, the critique of nationalist impositions, and the celebration of networking and mobility. The question remains: what comes next? Will women filmmakers of the Arab diaspora relinquish this opportunity to push the boundaries of cinematic storytelling? Will they continue to revisit their colonial past and postcolonial present? Will they be compelled to tell stories differently, contrapuntally? And will global audiences be willing to watch, appreciate, and ultimately continue to fund alternative cinemas?

Call to Action

Every year, an Arab Film Festival is organized by a cultural not-for-profit organization and held in a major Canadian city (see, for example, the Montreal Arab World Festival, https://festivalarabe.com/en; the Toronto Palestinian Film Festival, http://www.tpff.ca; and the Lebanese Film Festival in Ottawa, Toronto, Montreal, Vancouver, and Halifax, https://lffcanada.com). Consider joining the organization as a volunteer or learning about the films made by women filmmakers and how you might support them. Participate in discussions about these films, and consider interviewing guest filmmakers in light of your knowledge of women filmmakers of the diaspora.

Tying It Together

This chapter deconstructs through film analysis the colonialist assumptions about the voiceless and segregated women within Arab and Muslim contexts. More specifically, the chapter highlights the contributions of Arab women migrant filmmakers to transnational cinema as they embody female empowered and successful integration. The chapter explores how these women use cinema as a decolonial force, while often working within colonial funding structures and fighting colonial barriers to access.

DISCUSSION QUESTIONS

1. Is it possible to assign a fixed national identity to films made by women filmmakers of the Arab diaspora? Explain how and why transnational film production helps Arab women filmmakers to gain international visibility.

2. It seems that co-production is a major feature of Arab diasporic cinema. Why is this happening? What are the major sources of funding of Arab diasporic cinema?

3. What is the difference between mainstream cinematography and the French notion of authored cinema (*film d'auteur*)? When answering this question, consider the impact of co-production on films made by Arab women *auteurs* filmmakers.

4. Reflect on the opportunity for women filmmakers of the Arab diaspora to subvert power structures through their films. Compare structures established and imposed by the East-West/North-South divide and structures enforced by the patriarchal system.

5. Mobility is a key to understanding the new cinematic landscape in and from the Arab world: how does mobility affect Arab-born and Western-born women filmmakers? Consider comparing filmmakers who engage with the topic of home and homeland.

SUGGESTIONS FOR FURTHER READING

Ezra, Elizabeth, & Rowden, Terry (Eds). (2006). *Transnational cinema. The film reader*. London, UK, and New York, NY: Routledge. This book contains a collection of essays divided into four sections: national cinema from a transnational perspective; global cinema in the digital age; film, migration, and diaspora; and tourism and terrorism.

Dickinson, Kay. (2016). *Arab cinema travels. Transnational Syria, Palestine, Dubai and Beyond*. London, UK: Palgrave. This book offers an account of Arab cinema today, focusing on the connections between Syrian and Palestinian cinemas and Dubai's forays into film production.

Hillauer, Rebecca. (2005). *Encyclopedia of Arab women filmmakers*. Cairo, Egypt, and New York, NY: The American University in Cairo Press. This book is a comprehensive history of Arab women filmmakers from the silent era to the end of the 20th century; in addition to biographies, filmographies, and discussions of their most important works, the book offers lively and in-depth interviews with filmmakers.

MULTIMEDIA SUGGESTIONS

Arab Cinema Center

http://acc.film/about-acc.php

This website, organized by MAD Solutions film company, is a mobile platform that connects, nurtures, and promotes the Arab film industry, bridging it with local, regional, and international festivals, markets, and audiences. The site offers information about Arab films, sources of funding, and film institutes in the Arab World.

Elcinema.com

https://www.elcinema.com/en

This is the website of the largest Arab cinema database online, offering a comprehensive search index organized by names, titles, and nationality in both English and Arabic.

Raja Amari (dir.)

Through her films, Tunisian director Raja Amari opens the door to a fresh representation of women in contemporary North African cinema through the journeys of a widowed housewife who becomes a dancer at a cabaret club (*Red satin*, 2002) and an undocumented Tunisian girl in France caught in a web of sexual tension and class differences (*Foreign body*, 2016).

Leyla Assaf-Tengroth (dir.)

The film *The freedom gang* (1994) by Lebanese-Swedish director Leyla Assaf-Tengroth, based on a true story, follows the story of a young girl who runs a youth gang in war-torn Beirut. The documentary *Not like my sister* (2008) is a documentary about Dalida, the younger sister of the lead actress in *The freedom gang* (1994) and her fight against forced marriage.

Yamina Benguigui (dir.)

The films of Yamina Benguigui focus on the immigration of Arab peoples to France. The award-winning *Mémoires d'immigrés, l'héritage maghrébin* (1997) is a series of documentaries telling the story of the Maghrebi immigrants and their families. In contrast, the fictional story *Inch Allah dimanche* (2001) focuses on the difficulties of a single family's move to France and the struggle for autonomy Algerian women continue to face.

Randa Chahal Sabbag (dir.)

The kite (2003), by Lebanese director Randa Chahal Sabag, is a story of life, love, and the absurdity of the Israeli occupation from the perspective of a young Lebanese girl living in a village at the border.

Cherien Dabis (dir.)

Filmmaker Cherien Dabis draws on her own experiences as an American born to Palestinian and Jordanian parents in her films *Amreeka* (2009), about being Arab in America, and *May in the summer* (2013), about being American in the Middle East.

Mai Iskander (dir.)

Mai Iskander's two documentaries, *Garbage dreams* (2009) and *Words of witness* (2012), follow the stories of young people in Egypt as they are forced to deal with economic and political change in their country.

Annemarie Jacir (dir.)

The films of Annemarie Jacir focus on intimate experiences of Palestinian families. *Salt of this sea* (2008) tells the story of an American-born Palestinian woman who goes to Israel and Palestine on a quest to reclaim her family's home lost during the 1948 Arab-Israeli War; *Wajib* (2017) examines the dynamic between a Palestinian father and his ex-pat son as they spend the day hand-delivering wedding invitations.

Marianne Khoury (dir.)

The documentary *Women who loved cinema part I and II* (2002) examines the women filmmakers who changed the landscape of the Egyptian film industry from the 1920s to the 1960s.

Nadine Labaki (dir.)

Director and actress Nadine Labaki's two films *Caramel* (2007) and *Where do we go now?* (2011) both use humour and centre around the experiences of women. *Caramel* is about five women at a beauty salon in Beirut dealing with everyday ups and downs, and *Where do we go now?* revolves around the conflict in a village in which a church and mosque stand side by side.

Mai Masri (dir.)

The films of Mai Masri focus on the harsh experiences of young Palestinian females. In the documentary *Frontiers of dreams and fear* (2001), two teenage girls living in refugee camps miles apart become friends via email and finally meet in person at the fence separating them at the Lebanese/Israeli border. *3000 nights* (2015) tells the fictional story of a young schoolteacher who is forced to give birth to her son after being unjustly imprisoned in an Israeli women's jail.

Ruba Nadda (dir.)

Canadian director Ruba Nadda, born to Syrian and Palestinian parents, examines romantic relationships between Muslim/Arab and non-Muslim Canadian characters. In *Sabah* (2005), a traditional Muslim woman living in Toronto falls in love with a non-Muslim Canadian man, and a non-Muslim Canadian woman visiting Cairo falls for a Muslim man in *Cairo time* (2009).

Jehane Noujaim (dir.)

The documentary films of Egyptian-American filmmaker Jehane Noujaim focus on conflicts in the Middle East. *Control room* (2004) examines the relationship between Al Jazeera and the US Central Command (CENTCOM) during the 2003 invasion of Iraq; *The square* (2013) depicts the crisis in Egypt that began with the Egyptian Revolution of 2011, which called for the resignation of President Mubarak.

Tahani Rached (dir.)

Through her documentaries, Canadian-Egyptian director Tahani Rached explores daily life for women living in the Middle East by following a group of teenage girls living on the streets of Cairo (*These girls*, 2005) and a Palestinian woman living in Ramallah (*Soraida, a woman of Palestine*, 2004).

Moufida Tlatli (dir.)

Films *The silences of the palace* (1994) and *The season of men* (2000), by Tunisian director Moufida Tlatli, examine the place of women within the social structure of Tunisia. *The silences of the palace* focuses on issues of gender, class, and sexual exploitation of women, and *The season of men* critiques the place of women within the traditional patriarchal family.

REFERENCES

Armes, Roy. (2010). *Arab filmmakers of the Middle East: A dictionary*. Bloomington, IN: Indiana University Press.

Ballesteros, Isolina. (2015). *Immigration cinema in the new Europe*. Bristol, UK: Intellect Ltd.

Bernstein, Matthew, & Studlar, Gaylyn (Eds). (1997). *Visions of the East. Orientalism in film*. New Brunswick, NJ: Rutgers University Press.

Chaudhuri, Shohini. (2005). *Contemporary world cinema. Europe, Middle East, East Asia, South Asia*. Edinburgh, UK: Edinburgh University Press.

Clifford, James. (1994). Diasporas. *Cultural Anthropology*, 9(3), 302–38.

Dickinson, Kay. (2016). *Arab cinema travels. Transnational Syria, Palestine, Dubai and beyond*. London, UK: Palgrave.

Elsadda, Hoda. (2014). Gender studies in the Arab world: Reflections and questions on the challenges of discourses, locations and history. In Jean Said Makdissi & Noha Bayoumi (Eds), *Arab feminisms: Gender and equality in the Middle East*. London, UK: I.B. Tauris.

Ezra, Elizabeth, & Rowden, Terry (Eds). (2006), *Transnational cinema: The film reader*. London, UK, and New York, NY: Routledge.

Hancock, Ange-Marie. (2016). *Intersectionality: An intellectual history*. Oxford, UK: Oxford University Press.

Higbee, Will, & Hwee Lim, Song. (2010). Concepts of transnational cinema: Towards a critical transnationalism in film studies. *Transnational Cinemas*, 1(1), 7–21.

Hillauer, Rebecca. (2005). *Encyclopedia of Arab women filmmakers*. Cairo, Egypt, and New York, NY: The American University in Cairo Press.

Meriwether, Margaret, & Tucker, Judith (Eds). (1999). *A social history of women and gender in the modern Middle East*. New York, NY: Routledge. Ebook 2018.

Naficy, Hamid. (2001). *An accented cinema: Exilic and diasporic filmmaking*. Princeton, NJ: Princeton University Press.

Shohat, Ella. (1991). Gender and culture of empire: Toward a gender ethnography of the cinema. *Quarterly Review of Film and Video, 13*(1–3), 45–84.

Shohat, Ella. (2013), *Between the Middle East and the Americas: The cultural politics of diaspora* (co-edited with E. Alsultany). Ann Arbor, MI: University of Michigan Press).

Solanas, Fernando, & Getino, Octavio. (1969). Towards a third cinema. *Tricontinental,* 14 October, 107 –132. https://ufsinfronteradotcom.files.wordpress.com/2011/05/tercer-cine-getino-solanas-19691.pdf.

Stam, Robert. (2013). Beyond third cinema. The aesthetics of hybridity. In Anthony R. Guneratne & Wimal Dissanayake (Eds), *Rethinking third cinema* (pp. 31–48). New York, NY, and London: Routledge.

Telmissany, May. (2013). Arrows of desire: Dance and power in transnational cinema. *Revue des mondes musulmans et de la Méditerranée, 134*(décembre), 157–69.

Telmissany, May. (2016). Documenting defiance: Women film-makers in Tahrir Square. *Journal of African Cinema, 8*(1), 119–30.

Telmissany, May, & Schwartz, Stephanie Tara (Eds). (2010). *Counterpoints. Edward Said's legacy.* Newcastle-upon-Tyne, UK: Cambridge Scholars Publishing.

Van de Peer, Stephanie. (2017). *Negotiating dissidence: The pioneering women of Arab documentary.* Edinburgh, UK: Edinburgh University Press.

White, Patricia. (1998). Feminism and film. In John Hill & Pamela Church Gibson (Eds), *The Oxford guide to film studies* (pp. 117–34). Oxford, UK, and New York, NY: Oxford University Press.

NOTES

1. According to the 2009 report of the Fonds Sud, 543 long features were granted funds between 1984 and 2009. Within the Arab context, 78 films from the Maghreb and 70 from the Middle East were funded. In 2012, Fonds Sud was renamed World Cinema Fund, expanding French co-production activities in European and non-European countries. https://www.cnc.fr/documents/36995/156986/les+25+ans+du+Fonds-+Sud+Cin%C3%A9ma.pdf/9c735787-db0c-6519-8de1-0e41f5757431.

2. See the Abu Dhabi Film Fund for more information: http://www.sanadfilmfund.com/en.

3. https://www.lorientlejour.com/article/753199/Danielle_Arbid_vs_l%2527Etat_libanais.html.

4. See Stefanie Van de Peer, (2017), *Negotiating dissidence: The pioneering women of Arab documentary*, Edinburgh, UK: Edinburgh University Press.

5. http://www.nordicwomeninfilm.com/person/leyla-assaf-tengroth.

6. https://www.theglobeandmail.com/life/ruba-nadda/article736739.

7. After producing the American romantic comedy *Nappily ever after* by Haifaa Al-Mansour, Netflix produced *Jinn*, a teenage drama series presented by Lebanese and Jordanian filmmakers. https://media.netflix.com/en/only-on-netflix/273887.

CHAPTER 21

◇

Untitled

Clelia O. Rodríguez

Learning Objectives

In this chapter, you will:
- consider the challenges that the globalization of academia has for students from the Global South;
- recognize how academia is a racialized structure;
- examine issues that must be addressed in order to aid in the decolonization of academia.

On "Teaching" (and Learning)

My body was taught to me. I learned to work it as per the expectations I had been assigned growing up in a Catholic household in a country where women's bodies belong to laws fabricated by men (the not-so-subtle violent practices denounced by #las17 back this up). These teachings left me marks and reminders about what it is to be a being fighting to be a human. The references leading to cultural codes administered, run, controlled, and executed by society, in the name of a proper education, cornered voices to a hole inhabited by muteness. Sign language without signifiers. My body with sombre sparkles functioning with man-made batteries, corrosive and deadly.

I learned, for instance, about the (in)significance of my uterus when I bled for the first time.

This event dictated a lifelong battle to defend my body against rulings and norms. The first bleeding woke my ovaries as if they had been called to join a trip of no return. I hadn't taken classes on how the reproductive system worked, why I was in pain, or when it was going to stop. I was given a piece of cloth and was told to change it periodically. My 12-year-old body was in shock. In a never-ending tremor. I hadn't experienced anything like it, but women in the family convinced me this was an important sign, the sign of fertility, which was meant to be treasured and blessed (a lesson on sexuality should have, as an appendix, a different reading on the meaning of blood).

My body was a cultural lesson to be learned from. Every part of me was subjected to the approval of a higher power, the omnipresence of what everyone still calls an Almighty God. Under this force, my body was cleansed of sins. I lifted words in sequences known as prayers and burned candles on Sunday to ask for forgiveness for things my body had done. The holy water poured over my head when I was a baby made me worthy of entering into a path of teachings and learnings bound to a religious life I hadn't asked for. Members of the clergy witnessed, along with my family, that I was a child of God. In comparison to unbaptized children, if I were to die I would go directly to heaven and they wouldn't. Under a state of a spiritual emergency, the careless parents would categorically fall under the rubric of negligence (no parole). The bodies of others would be eternally lit up by darkness.

In the business of my body, everyone had stakes. My soul could belong either to the Devil or to God. "Even if you hide, he's always watching what you do. He even knows your thoughts," one of my aunts would constantly remind me. Getting acquainted with baptismal rites saved me from the chance of going to hell (El Salvador in English, after all, it means The Male Saviour). Do the gender math. My female saviour was found in almost every woman who paused to reprimand me for my untamed and rebellious behaviour. My grandfather was among the few who didn't second their words, rewarding me with freedom instead. He'd encourage me to climb trees because chances were I'd get up after falling down. With his power he defended me. To him I was worth defending. He otherized others because I happened to be his exception. I now had to learn the tools of otherized other women who were not "like me."

The teachings by well-behaved women consisted in always looking at the "rejects" of society. They rejected them socially considering their wear, makeup, way of walking and talking, seeing men, and sitting down as a crucial factor to be marked as unwanted. The minute I crossed the Salvadoran political-geographical border, I realized this "reject" status was part of my status. No matter where I went or what I did. Theories of "otherness" showed me a way to look back to those early teachings on gender? (Yes, "?"). The fraction of happy childhood memories rotates around my grandfather intervening on my muteness. This pattern of dependency lasted well until my adulthood. I began using, as a trampoline, thoughts on this idea of rejection. Anglophone white writers, for instance. The "?" was grasping for air because it was brought up during discussions with my broken English accent.

"You are just like them" (the rejects)
"You are nothing like us" (the accepted)
"You are acting like them" (the rejects)
"You need to act like us" (the accepted)

On "Learning" (and Teaching)

"Could you share with the committee how you visualize teaching a Gender Studies course given your interest in decolonial approaches?" I was asked once in a Skype job interview. I paused and had the urge to hang up. I heard myself engaging in a blah-blah-blah rehearsed discourse echoing what I had read in a popular book that teaches aspiring academics how to land a job. My words imitated paragraphs stretching like elastic bands pulling in all directions my Spanglish tongue. Chances drained in a synchronized pipeline of statistics categorizing my performance as "unprepared."

After sipping a cup of chamomile tea, I thought about the prospects of asking students of all backgrounds the same questions: "Could you share with me and everyone in this room how you visualize learning a Gender Studies course given your interest in decolonial approaches, as it is outlined in the syllabus?" How will this question differ from sign language speakers born in the Global North as opposed to a Black student or from a female student raised in the Global South to a white male student?

Academic visions leave out fractions of colonial layers made of everything under the sun. Some try to make attempts to anti-colonize them once or twice, at most, granting them recognition for their (extraordinary) efforts.

To me, and many   scholars/teachers/educators/instigators/agitators/warriors
                       breathing/surviving/struggling/breathing/inspiring/learning

under

A man-made steel mantel of capitalist-driven pedagogical interventions feels like

drowning/agonizing/burning/decaying/chooooooooooking

Self-care kits don't work.

When Learning Meets the Prefix "Un"

In a posthumously written note found at the back of a black and white photo, I realize why intergenerational teaching depends on unlearning what borders us because telling the patriarchy to fuck off ain't gonna do much. Radically loving the chains will not only break them but will dissolve them to grains of salt to be washed away to a sea of interrelated and suspended laughter.

A picture of my great-grandfather taught me about the affinities of blood forced on blood across time and space: the incestuous family. The emotional learning materialized in frozen tears behind pupils that run tapes and tapes of intergenerational rape. This militarized training on the bodies of female after female expose in the photograph a smile rooted in the pillars of secrecy. It is looking at a frame, on display on the family's living room, structured on carcasses built by the deafening sounds of church bells. Envisioning learning through teaching requires unveiling the denied shadows of the darkness worn daily and stretched out through horses, buses, phones, airplanes, boats, trains, llamas, canoes, satellites.

"What are your thoughts when Globalization comes to mind?" This was a question I wrote on the blackboard in a classroom of undergraduate students at the University of Ghana. Stories and reactions followed:

Spiders webbing together to knit a mantel powerful enough to drown sorrows.
Floating bottles of water caressing themselves waiting for their 1000 year anniversary to be decomposed in the density of the Mariana Trench.
Exhaust fumes inked in decaying brownish lungs.
Chinese male workers carving sweat and setting bunkbeds on bunkbeds on bunkbeds.
Gateways to developed societies with developed minds and developed fashions.
Educational opportunities granted by Embassies, rich organizations and amazing donors.
Production, consumption, production, consumption, production, consumption, etc.
"My father left over a decade ago to find work in Nigeria and we never received $$$."
"My mother left over a decade ago to find work in Nigeria and died shortly after."

Not being interrogated at airports because I possess the European passport.
Unquestionable trade at low human and animal cost.
English only. Harvard University exchange student.

Despite the disputes, grievances, and prolonged screaming silences in the room, it became somewhat clear that thoughts on globalization landed based on historical impact tied to colonialism. Shockingly not. Globalized lives measure up on a wide scale according to height, body weight, hair and eye colour, skin pigmentation, European twirls of the tongue, brand names, social capital, plated gold, tiny stickers numbering a distant Guatemala on a banana, TOEFL scores on ex-English colonies. And, and, and.

What is the significance of thoughts when emotional disobedience kicks in? Marginalization of bodies on this earthy house has left humanity without a home. Drone-living is the new aspiring dream. Caged-living is the new norm. Satellite-living is the new universal citizenship as long as WiFi charges are covered. Racists know no geographies. Classism coerces purified objectives. Sexism, death. Even genetically modified death is transferred from generation to generation. The notion of "Elsewhere" only exists in the politics of hope as advertised in globalized propaganda adorned by white doves. Disobedience, as it relates to anything remotely close to decolonial, must rise up in daily acts and not just in textbooks. Suddenly the term "reparation" is trendy, but no one wants to give up their comfort to make that happen. One watches and reads about acts of disobedience from individuals or collectives as if it was extraordinary courage. It's not. There's nothing amazing or great in emotionally confronting violence. This is a way of living. It's reality. In educational settings, emotional disobedience deploys righteous anger in order to disarm the permanence mark of colonial civility found in walls, bibliography, ways of writing and articulating theory, evaluations, grading, rubrics of knowledge, desks, assignments, curriculums, and discourses of what it means to be successful.

Securing spots in top schools? Stop!
Feeding seeds of competition among students? Stop! Think!
Strategizing how to get an A at the cost of your health? Stop! Think! Reflect!
Failing to speak up because you won't upset the authority? Stop! Think! Reflect! Act!

I encourage students to think about and reflect on disobedience because racism, classism, and sexism dress our wounds. Agency and advocacy happen outside the parameters of the written world in a harmonious rebellion I feel as radical love. Commercialized *rebeldía* is entrenched with popularized notions of what some know as guilt, and religious folks can even look at it as indirect sins to be washed with holy water from Dakota. Getting paid to talk about advocacy or receiving awards enunciates a wishy-washy version of obedience with "dis" as a *sombrero*. Advocating, without disobedience, is a better fit in a sentence with the word "ally" in it. If you come from the conceptual North, acting within the norms, the boxes, and the frameworks places you in the right track. Follow the route of a wild salmon. We ought to celebrate swimming against currents because that's where life manifests its balance with death. It is toward defying what constitutes as civil that we find the key element at the heart of disobedience: creativity.

I integrated my grandmother's teachings and lessons into my undergraduate education. She'd appear in dreams, between pages, in titles, and in the hidden dust behind librarians' desks. Her whispers were never neutral:

Her *chanclas* instructed me how to strike back.
Her mama's recipe of *marquesote* preached survival.
Her wrinkles forced water to take detours leading to *café* from Sonsonate. Google El Salvador + genocide + 1932.
Her care for *maíz* fueled my reluctance to accept borrowed truths transported across the ocean.

Conforming to static methodologies that will only subject us to passive agendas promoting racial inequality is industrialized-talk. Participating in ongoing recruitments for talent pushes away every notion of reciprocity and exchange. To fight injustice on the other side of the fence does not require usage of Air Miles or a fast-track pass at airports. Patronizing communities to practise self-care when production is the motor of your existence is noise. Exhorting a manicured lifestyle when you are pouring leftover chemicals in the sea suffocates to death disobedience's heavy breathing. Freeing up space from saturated overheated computers, when prisons prompt a trendy disconnect between liberty and Liberty, conditions notions of time to remain enslaved to capitalist needs.

Critical pedagogy should not minimize or discourage emotional disobedience by forcing those engaged with it in normative forms of writing, thinking, creating, living, sitting down, standing up, presenting, expecting death-lines, and so forth. Pedagogy, as it spreads across hallways of higher learning spaces, must be criticized because in many cases it serves capitalist-driven agendas prompting the critical to be segregated from the pedagogy. The happiness, agony, pain, sorrow, and excitement that come with defying the ongoing deteriorating conditions of humanity must be elevated to higher grounds. I often leave marks of scribble whenever I read theory on critical pedagogy, leaving me wondering where's the critical part without the action. Despite many efforts to theorize radicalness in the North and West, learning continues to be presented in homogenizing forms, and teaching is wracked by the politics of evaluations based on the pressure to perform relationships synced into niceness (and the pressure to get tenure in some cases). Masters are those who know how to play the game, as I constantly read in higher educational journals. These same experts fill hotel conference rooms, applauding a radical figure flown from the South who debunks the same lies they praise. Delivering a talk about the extraordinary lives of extraordinary circumstances of extraordinary territories of extraordinary violence of extraordinary ways to survive satisfies the hand as it inks in blank notebooks, courtesy of the association organizing the event, the extraordinary lesson to be taught in the next class where extraordinary students will praise the extraordinary teacher for the extraordinary lesson he/she/they will soon publish in an extraordinary journal to be read by a group of extraordinary experts on extraordinary topics related to the extraordinary lives of people from the extraordinary South who will get, just maybe, a copy of the extraordinary paper where their extraordinary voices are not going to even be named because the extraordinary scholar gets, well, extraordinariness.

In a conversation I had once with a student, she wanted to know how to tear down the establishment after having read an article for another class. I remember telling her that I didn't know the answer to that. What I knew was this: the act of tearing down colonized establishments, as she had detected in the text, was probably glued on phonics, and it required a bit more than just peeling off stickers located in the globe where her *tortillas* were coming from. One must be prepared to debunk foreign policies starting with 1492 so that haitch&M clothing, tinting made possible by the DNA of children and women, can have back their fingertips. Grabbing sanitized books, covered in their entirety with the best-written engaged tactical pedagogies yet avoiding the movement to eradicate what makes us unequal outside the pristine libraries, begs for a complete revision of what is understood for critical when fused with pedagogy. Radicalness in pedagogy means liberation, like the civil rights movement in the United States. It's like a bunch of seeds uprooting hate from one territory to another in order for lakes to be born out of lava. (Fragmented borders shared by one lake in particular: Lago Güija. *El Trifinio*, they call it. Three countries claiming sovereignty over Mother Nature.) This gives us tools to intervene pedagogically and become active agents within constellations of inter-resistance and co-resistance.

Webs of inter-resistance storm out critical questions based on our lived experiences. If the soles of our shoes get familiarized with living dust cornered in invented territorial political divisions, for instance, then those footprints build cartographies linked to memories of struggles rejecting lessons on maps curated in and by colonial lessons. Stories of disasters are wrongfully attributed to the fact that many humans do not know how to choose to live according to democratic standards when in fact many of our inner struggles are seeded in teachings that have nothing to do with ways of living intrinsically tied to *aguas libres*. Medical and life insurance, trust funds, privatization of education, land exploitation, and the dissemination of fear based on peoples with other sexual and religious beliefs are the stagnated disaster

itself. My inner-being knows I must evacuate and escape. Where to go?

In the past, I have accompanied students in the quest of encouraging the politics of inter-being: What does the flow of our blood tell us? Are the reddish rivers inside our own body carrying the oxygen needed to breathe? Is the left shoulder exchanging knowledge with the right kidney? Are our feet carrying us on the wisdom of the ancestors who walked freely in ancestral lands? Are we taming our feelings in linearities that lead us nowhere? Are we dictating our fingers to reject the dialogue coming from our contaminated lungs? How are we manifesting the intergenerational lessons stored in the memory of our blocked senses? Are we making sure these planted teachings coexist with other living things from Palestine to Mapuche lands? From the oceanic currents articulating awareness to the highest peaks populated by garbage by the presence of ego-seekers? Are we energizing what's articulated when sounds of birds visit our ears?

Found-nations of InnerWellness erupt like chickenpox throughout the globe, advertising notions of happiness connected to currency dressed as harmony. This monetary movement distinguishes itself by washing off stains of blood only to be repaired by fresh cotton sheets. The higher the count of Egyptian threads in clean sheets, the higher the comfort of colonizers. Interaction is blocked by ways of organizing even to the extent of how we are supposed to look after ourselves, even in academia where policing ways of learning and teaching dominate the lives of students and teachers. The latter are often disguised under the dome of engaged learning following the same patterns of colonized thinking. Statistics don't lie. People in higher learning settings are committing suicide, ending an unwell life sustained by pillars of unattainable success. If scholars are publishing at the cost of their own lives, if students are reading the same published papers testing them on how well they understood the material, if administrators are monitoring how achievements are to be met, the so-called engaged learning is yet another way to maintain the pyramid-like organization sustained by the survival of the fittest. We read this, we analyze, and it's on repeat mode without interjecting. Why?

How well are we, as educators, informing students where funding comes from when they apply for a well-known scholarship carrying the decorum of prestige? Are we actively figuring out ways to challenge how the organization of conferences continues to marginalize humans at the cost of our own "success"? Are we writing about politics of liberation yet continuing to measure students' intelligence based on As, Bs, Cs, etc.? Where do we get to perform solidarity anonymously, and when do we publicly perform it for social capital gain? Why are representations of teachable material limited to bodies from the South as if the North wasn't the origin/cause/point of departure of the politics of presentation? When are we going to stop speaking of the next generation of scholars when what's currently being accepted as scholarly worthy is not only problematic in hiring practices and who gets to be admitted to receiving an education? Isn't this yet another motion of violence that creates a lesser of two evils? How are we expected to inspire whatever the future means under capitalism if we are eradicating those who are protecting other ways of learning and teaching? How well are we listening to voices that don't make it to academic clubs based on meritocracy and nepotism?

We can articulate theories beautifully and deconstruct them in order to present what is going to be the future cutting-edge knowledge to be sold. The ties between humanity and humans are broken. This deterioration is not alive only in the imagination of writers whose ink is marked by blood, tears, and sweat. What's often forgotten, because oopsy-daisy is real, is that co-resistance between academics working against injustice, inequality, and disparity ought to be harvested in mutual exchanges. What's often included when exchanges happen requires one side to be sacrificed, leaving the other with disadvantages. A white academic, for instance, may incorporate non-canonical texts in a syllabus and speak for people of colour without considering for a fraction of time giving up a seat in the higher table where others should be eating. At the centre should not be elevating voices at the textual level but in real life. One can't debut the daily struggles of others and get paid for it. Decolonizing syllabi is not just about diversifying the rainbow spectrum. It is about getting rid of grading schemes, allowing learners to integrate their own experiences and those of their ancestors to be fused into a curriculum around the inter-being. Decolonizing the curriculum is not just about inviting women of colour as Skype speakers. It is about them teaching the material themselves. It is about dismantling preferred notions of achievements enslaving students to the chains attached to an ivory tower. We must insist on eradicating beliefs rooted in competition, lifting and singling out one voice when we should be lifting communal work. Sticking the word "decolonizing" to an agenda to showcase that one keeps up with semantics reminds me of stamps one collects at airports.

Real talk: well-written essays published in peer-reviewed journals are read by 10 people at most because access requires privilege, money, and institutional affiliation. The angles, the core, the arguments, the subjects in those papers are people of colour. The methodologies extract, without any anesthesia, raw pain. What is it going to take for academics to stop doing that in the humanities, for instance? How many times do we have to tell you there's no way around doing this? I've heard endless times from anthropologists, sociologists, psychologists, teachers, etc.: they try doing it in less aggressive ways. Ripping out memories is no different from what corporations around the globe do to extract natural resources like water, oil, gold, etc. It is just another subtle and soft way of expanding intellectual property at the cost of many that is just another face of academic imperialism. Big dams are constructed on top of running water, ignoring life. Big conferences are organized on top of community-based dialogues, ignoring orality as a way of intergenerational learning. Big workshops are organized around topics of inequality in fancy buildings where poor people are represented, ignoring precisely that, power. Big calls for papers are announced with the target language as English, ignoring that Britain colonized practically the majority of regions in the world. When papers from those ex-colonies knock on the doors of editors, the most notorious action is to reject them. The machinery in academia functions around colonized ways of who gets to do what.

Surreal talk:

If non-white students portray anger, they get punished.

If a non-white academic challenges the academic work of a white academic, then it must be because the former doesn't understand how to fool the system and is seen as a ranter.

If a committee formed by white professors writes down the criteria for students of colour to apply for an internship run by white professionals, then the student of colour must sound in writing like a white person to be considered worthy of an interview.

If a white academic is accused of utilizing colonized curriculums, teaching strategies, stolen material from non-white scholars, the vilification goes back to the non-white person because we're making a big deal out of something that can be solved diplomatically.

Unimaginable talk:

God forgives those who repent in a timely manner.

God forgives academic corruption because accused parties somehow happen to be friends.

God forgives counter-narratives, as long as they are integrated neatly in the bibliography.

God forgives those who trespass the boundaries of creativity because they also deserve rules.

God forgives those in academic parole: pipelines, they call them.

God forgives prisoners of social justice seekers because it is only available in heaven.

God forgives the radical doers whose minds are shaped by non-standardized tests.

God forgives the trespassers of academic walls.

God forgives the ones who are born outside the numbered box.

God forgives those without keys to the grading system.

God forgives those who forget to live because they're busy worrying about breathing.

God forgives the ordinary student who gives up on becoming extraordinary.

God gives peace to those who identify as different in admission forms.

God never forgets those in need of globalization.

God always attends to militarized zones because the Queen says so.

God makes sure corporations never run out of money because taxes are also paid in hell.

God rewards democracy made in China.

God gives his thumbs up to projects funded by USAID where freedom stays in five-star hotels.

God favours markets run on nuclear waste as long as daily prayers are practised.
God increases one's faith if one erases from the mind the word "rape."
God decreases one's faith if one adorns the body with fragrances of love.

Imagine your own discourse:
Write letters as if you were leaving them printed in the walls of the uterus. Downgrade commodified time. Race racism to the burning line of the black hole. Make ways for waves that narrate stories of patience. Unholy the holiness.

Live your own discourse:
What's sanctioned has to be liberated, now. Dance in intricate patterns that no one can decipher. Protect the dirt from contaminated and genetically modified seeds. Mind the gaps, see them, face them, uproot them, fuck with them, end them.

Speak your own discourse:
Guard words as if your vision depended from them. Solidarity speaks through actions. Charity speaks through failed actions. Celebrate the sounds of humans facing torture, pain, and death for defending a non-social hierarchy. The tongue is humanity's engine. Fuel it with radical love.

Learn your own discourse:
Our linguistic birth doesn't determine who we are. It doesn't help to know where we made contact after leaving the birth canal. Geographies lie. Maps lie. Following the GPS to track down our origin is depleted because oil is not eternal. If the poles of vigilance weren't working, what would that look like?

Teach your own discourse:
Make visible how you experience breathing. Is the air in your lungs more important than my oxygen? Teach me why. Why not. What makes you think that. Who taught you that. Where did you hear the word life for the first time. When did that take place. Teach me that. Why it matters. Why it doesn't matter.

Unlearn your own discourse:
The soul doesn't need training. If you think it does, teach me why.
Question marks don't need admiration signs. Teach me why or why not.
Do your eyes see colour through pristine crystals? Teach me how to read with that vision.
Coordinates of racism, sexism, classism, caste, xenophobia, and bigotry tick-tick-tick.

Experience your own discourse:
Move to the compass of butterflies. Find a niche in nesting rather than resting on power.
Relate. Count the pigmentation of grandmother moon. Scan your bones, and indulge in
the secrets they speak of your family's past. Solidarity work is not meant to gain likes.
Destroy slowly one caged spirit at a time. Constantly seek the radiance of the sun.
Commit to decolonizing living because everything we know about our own bodies has
been taught to us. And that's worth the ride to unlearning it all.

Destroy your own discourse:
I give up on hope. Nothing will change. At least I recycle. Jails imprison criminals.
Borders protect our security. Be an ally because of guilt. Capitalize social relationships.
Strategize power to oppress sheep dressed in tranquility. Demand monolinguals. Populate
the seas with coloniality. Deny, deny, deny your racism even if you have to cry. Light up
candles with the strength of kerosene. Underdevelop natural resources. Plunder clean
water while bottling up crawling creatures with plastic. Don't accept that anti-Blackness
is a thing. Use courage to weaponize toys. Accept opportunities even if it comes from
diamonds covered in blood. Travel with non-profit organizations making big bucks
erasing the footprint of violence. Work hard to cover up traces of elitism left under the
beds of those who shelter you in the South. Write up impressions on pain on those who
feed you and your family, and turn them into academic papers. Sharpen up your pencils
and use them whenever your privilege is under attack. Retain your prayers and use them
instead of acting.

Call to Action

Think about the classes in which you are currently enrolled and how they might be perpetuating the racialized structure of academia. How are globalization and colonialism discussed in
your classrooms? Are the sources utilized written by academics who are directly affected by
these issues or who only observe them? Research the sources presented to you in the classroom,
and find an opportunity to encourage diversity in the curricula of your classes. Take opportunities to join student representation in your departments, and demand better representation from
your instructors and from your departments when hiring new instructors, when promoting new
department heads, and when engaging speakers.

Tying It Together

This chapter is a spoken-word poem that embodies the issues raised throughout this book in the
context of academia and in particular the struggles
of BIPOC academics and students to work within
the system of academia—which is a mechanism
of white supremacy and colonialism—rather than
outside it. The chapter describes strategies for

changing the system from the inside while also expressing the author's own frustration and despair. This chapter vitally interrogates the very system within which this book was written and is being read as a system that perpetuates the very forces that this book attempts to disrupt.

DISCUSSION QUESTIONS

1. How are academics of colour ignored, erased, and consumed in the name of research and academia?
2. How does the author suggest that individuals resist and begin to reform the colonization of academia?
3. What are some of the ways students of colour and students from the South are at a disadvantage in academia?
4. What are the costs of "playing the game" regarding conforming to the demands of academia for Indigenous students and students of colour?
5. What are some strategies that you can employ if you (as a racialized student) are treated poorly or if you (as a white student) witness a racialized student being treated poorly for getting angry at or challenging a white professor for their colonial teaching practices?

SUGGESTIONS FOR FURTHER READING

Rodriguez, Clelia O. (2018). *Decolonizing academia: Poverty, oppression and pain*. Halifax, NS: Fernwood Books. This book discusses the need for decolonization of academia and illustrates how academia is a racialized structure through the author's personal experiences.

Bhambra, Gurminder K. (2018). *Decolonizing the university*. London, UK: Pluto Press. This book is about the different ways to decolonize the university classroom and the challenges facing students and academics dedicated to that task.

Jack, Anthony A. (2019). *The privileged poor: How elite colleges are failing disadvantaged students*. Cambridge, MA: Harvard University Press. This book examines how university policies intensify inequalities on university campuses, despite the fact that many elite schools continue to accept increasing numbers of minority and economically disadvantaged students.

MULTIMEDIA SUGGESTIONS

Healing culture podcast #49: On decolonizing academia, with Clelia Rodriguez
https://www.youtube.com/watch?v=KomNd90KTxY
This podcast recording of an interview with author Clelia Rodriguez discusses the necessity of decolonizing academia and how teaching is political work.

Decolonizing the Curriculum, TEDx talk by Melz Owusu
https://www.youtube.com/watch?v=zeKHOTDwZxU
This video recording of Melz Owusu, a graduate of the University of Leeds who became an education officer at the university, examines how colonialism affects the education system and how students of colour are at a disadvantage in the colonialized academia through both talking and rap.

#RhodesMustFall—A moment in recent history
https://www.youtube.com/watch?v=cXY702HGV9w
This video shows the removal of the statue of Cecil John Rhodes from the University of Cape Town campus from the perspective of the activists. The statue of Rhodes was seen by many as representative of the oppressive institutional racism at the University of Cape Town. The #RhodesMustFall movement received global attention and led to a wider movement to decolonize education across South Africa.

CHAPTER 22

◇

Migrant Slavery and Ralph Goodale-Abdoul

El Jones

Learning Objectives:

In this chapter, you will:

- recognize the role of colonialism and slavery in the foundation of Canada;
- examine how the colonization of the Americas, including Canada, played a major role in the destruction of Indigenous and African cultures;
- consider how the criminal justice system in Canada is biased against Indigenous people and people of colour despite claims that Canada is a free and multicultural society.

Migrant Slavery

They sailed around the world until they hit Hispaniola
The Pope and Queen and banks all said let roll the mighty dollar
Columbus and Cortez they claimed they were explorers
The borders crossed us, we never crossed the borders
Set up the Encomendia system for the ones they called the Indians
Justified it all because they said their souls weren't Christians
Forced the tribes to work, stole the land acre by acre
Took the people as a tribute, the resources and the labour
The ones they didn't murder they took out with disease
95 per cent of the Americas murdered within the century
The Arawak, Taino, and Carib they said that they were animals
Enslaved and exterminated on the claim that they were cannibals
And when no one was left to work the land because they were all dead
They turned their eyes to Africa and said enslave the Blacks instead
So they sent their ships to prey upon West African shores
Ironically guided by the maps that were taught them by the Moors
To the Company of Royal Adventurers from the Conquistadors
The borders crossed us, we never crossed the borders

They claimed they were too delicate to work out in the heat
So they said we didn't feel the pain because we were like beasts
They developed racist ideologies to say we were inferior
And so the colour of our skin became their human criteria
And with letters from the Queen they bought and then they sold
And stacked upon each other they chained us in the hold
To work the land for sugar they brought us across the sea
Brutalized and murdered us took us from our families
Saw us just like cattle so we could be exported
The average life 10 years, until we expired from the torture
And millennia of history and humanity they had to ignore
The border crossed us we never crossed the borders
And so we worked the fields for them condemned cause we were Black
And in Europe they built cathedrals and museums from the wealth got off our backs
The developed world they call it, the cradle of civilization
Funded by the labour of forced African migration
Factories and manufacturing, banks, technology, and ports
The Industrial Revolution from the goods sent back and forth
And corporations and royal charters developed of all sorts
The borders crossed us we never crossed the borders
So now 500 years later they call themselves the first world nations
And now they got the nerve to say they're controlling immigration
And them that only ran into the Americas cause they were lost
Now say they define our movement and the spaces that we cross
And now brown and Black people from the global south to north
Have to apply to enter countries where once our movement here was forced
Trade in sex and labour is the modern slavery
Taken from the same people exploited through history
1 per cent of the population own 40 per cent of the world's assets
Globalization should be called the continuation of the middle passage
From the Hudson Bay Company to mass extermination
They take the lives from people give the rights to corporations
Land, jobs, and resources the people can't afford it
So parents leave their children just so they can support them
From nannies to fruit pickers they make domestic labour laws
Forcing movement of the people just like they did before
Taking rights over their bodies just because they're poor
Lock workers into rooms, seize papers and passports
Imprisonment, killed at checkpoints, exploited and deported
The borders crossed us we never crossed the borders
And now from Jamaica, Guatemala, Philippines and Mexico
The Wretched of the Earth still make the dollars flow
When half the world's workers labour for a dollar and a quarter

The borders crossed us we never crossed the border
Babies born in prison because their mothers are detained
Workers die on highways in vans where they are chained
Women raped and abused but no one can report it
The borders crossed us we never crossed the borders
Still working in the fields still caring for the children
No citizenship, health, education, or standard of living
Come here for a season and then they are transported
The borders crossed us we never crossed the borders
And the same people who through history have colonized the rest
Continue to take the land and hoard up all the wealth
Still living off the backs of everyone they slaughtered
The borders crossed us we never crossed the borders
Still don't want to pay a living wage, workers at their beck and call
Our bodies and our freedom they want to own them all
Say we are illegal but our history records
The borders crossed us we never crossed the borders
The borders crossed us we never crossed the borders

Ralph Goodale-Abdoul

Dear Ralph Goodale,
You say that you keep Canada safe.
Safety for who in a land that was stolen by pale faces
With guns, and smallpox blankets and scalping proclamations
Undertaking to wipe out Indigenous people on the basis
That empty land was for the taking
And that's the history of your lawmaking and your borders and your immigration
And now as your government is raking through the coals of residential schools
And calling that reconciliation
As Indigenous youth in your province die in a hail of bullets aimed by a white farmer at the back of the head
And he heads back inside to finish his dinner plate
And while all punishment is escaped
You pursue the deportation of a young Black male
On the grounds that he is a danger
To the public of this strong and free nation.
And maybe you say the name of Abdoul Abdi
Or maybe I'm mistaken and you don't even bother with the identities of the Black men you're forsaking.
I'm contemplating safety for who

When Black people in Canada were 200 years for sale
Our labour backbreaking
And Black children in the coloured home were abused on an unimaginable scale
It's heartbreaking
But you don't tell that tale, Ralph Goodale.
What Canadian values are you proclaiming
When you put bodies like Abdoul's back to Somalia on a plane
And pay human traffickers to leave them on runways
It's odd how often it seems to be the people who don't pray on Sundays
Whose mosques are shot up and no terrorism charges are laid
It's funny how often your safety requires our pain
It's funny how often Black bodies are the throwaways
It's funny how you find safety if we just go away
And the charter of human rights you just blow away
For foster kids escaping abuse who were labelled runaways
And brought into contact with the police as youth
Who stop us in the streets just for being in the wrong place
Because this is a country where Black bodies must be criminalized and surveilled
To keep the public safe.
Safety for those Canadians who say they're kind enough to let us stay as long as we behave
Who say they saved Abdoul from a country where the wars we wage are called peacekeeping
And Canadian soldiers raped young boys who weren't more than Abdoul's age when he was fleeing
And of course they got away
But you don't tell that tale
When Canada brings Abdoul Abdi as a refugee
And says how generously we embrace him
Then takes him away from his family and says the state will raise him
Race in to protect him but then neglect him and forget him
His language and culture gone without a trace
Separated from his sister, 31 homes
He might have well have lived in a suitcase
And never get around to the paperwork, the forms that are misplaced
And somehow they never leave a trail
But you just shrug your shoulders and say
It's too bad that mistakes were made
But the process must prevail
It's funny how your care looks more like hate.
This is what you call a system that is fair and rules based:
The government takes kids into the care of the state
Seizes Black and Indigenous kids at disproportionate rates
Sets them up to be sentenced to jail
Punishes Black kids in the criminal justice system then calls in CBSA

And after everyone in the system gets paid
You get rid of them like they're human waste
What will it take for you to let Black people join the human race
Ralph Goodale. You're here to keep us safe
Safety for who in a place where African refugees struggle across the Manitoba border in snow up
to their waist
I wonder when your compassion got misplaced
Cause there's no haste in this country,
For Black bodies indefinitely detained on immigration holds
But you don't hear the case, they wait
Three years or five years or eight
It's funny how they tend to be African or Haitian
Or Jamaican
It doesn't even leave a bad taste in your mouth
That bodies expire in immigration jails
And still the system moves as slow as snails
Ask Abdoul Abdi what it feels like to be erased.
Have you ever felt the nails hammered into your coffin, Ralph Goodale
Have you been encased in your own grave
Sitting in a cell in solitary confinement surrounded by the names
Of decades of deportees each signed with a date
And you'll let this be Abdoul's fate
All because by the time anyone noticed they didn't fill in the citizenship papers it was too late
I don't think I can make you feel any shame
In a system you claim has no human face
Just boxes to be ticked because the process must prevail
The Prime Minister admits the province failed Abdoul
But still you move forward without delay
We even heard Ahmed Hussen say that anti-Black racism was in play
But still you strip him of his rights and that's okay
You'll follow the rules and it doesn't matter if Abdoul lives to tell the tale
After all who took responsibility for Tina Fontaine?
So let me explain
We'll daily stand in the gale for Abdoul
And we're manning the barricades for Abdoul
These Black bodies that make you so afraid
Are humane for Abdoul.
And since our hearts contain Abdoul
We'll say free Abdoul, stop the deportation
Night and day
We'll write, tweet, call, and email
To the minister of Public Safety, the so-called honourable Ralph Goodale.

Call to Action

There are many more immigrant children besides Abdoul Abdi who have slipped through the cracks or been ill-served by the Canadian immigration system. Research organizations in your community dedicated to helping refugees to Canada—especially children—settle and adapt to life here. Do your part by volunteering, as well as calling, writing, tweeting, and otherwise raising awareness when these moments of action are needed, or start such an organization at your own university if one does not exist.

DISCUSSION QUESTIONS

1. In what ways have Indigenous and Black people been similarly affected by the colonization of the Americas?

2. How did the creation of borders by European colonists affect the First Nations and Inuit of the Americas? How did it affect slaves forcibly removed from Africa?

3. How is the Canadian criminal justice system prejudiced against Indigenous people and people of colour, particularly Black people?

Explain how the settlement of Canada is connected to that prejudice.

4. How does the "Canadian experience" differ for Indigenous people, people of colour, and white people?

5. The poems note how people can hide behind the fact that they are just following the rules of the system in order to prevent blame from falling on any particular person's shoulders. Where does individual responsibility start and end within colonial power structures?

SUGGESTIONS FOR FURTHER READING

Jones, El. (2014). *Live from the Afrikan resistance!* Halifax, NS: Roseway Publishing. This book is a collection of spoken word poetry by El Jones, a poet laureate of Halifax. The poems focus on issues of racism, poverty, and violence and represent the culture of African Nova Scotia.

Hamilton, Sylvia D. (2014). *And I alone escaped to tell you.* Kentville, NS: Gaspereau Press. This book

tells the story of the settlement of African peoples in Nova Scotia through poetry, connecting people of African descent to the Canadian story.

Coates, Ta-Nehisi. (2015). *Between the world and me.* New York, NY: Spiegel & Grau. Through a letter to his son, Ta-Nehisi Coates describes his attempt to navigate the United States' race-based history and current race-based socio-political issues.

MULTIMEDIA SUGGESTIONS

"Black Power Hour" radio show on station CKDU (Dalhousie University)
https://ckdu.ca/shows/227
This live radio show, founded by El Jones, is a means for people of colour in Nova Scotia jails to share their experiences and empower each other through poetry, music, and shout-outs.

Canada Is So Polite—El Jones
https://www.youtube.com/watch?v=V7y0IkmSVTc

This is a recording of El Jones reciting a spoken word poem about historical and societal issues in Canada that are hidden behind a facade of stereotypical "Canadian politeness."

Spoken Word—El Jones, TEDxCape Breton
https://www.youtube.com/watch?v=hS9NS08Bvk0
In this TEDx event, El Jones talks about prison justice and the importance of human connections with incarcerated individuals.

CHAPTER 23

◇

A Killjoy Manifesto

Sara Ahmed[1]

Learning Objectives

In this chapter, you will:
- understand what being a "killjoy" is and how this relates to transgressing the social obligation of being happy;
- consider what it means to be unseated in the table of happiness, how society disregards those who unseat the happiness of others, and how certain bodies are usually blamed for this;
- examine the intersections of race and being a feminist killjoy.

Introduction

A manifesto: a statement of principle, a mission statement. Manifesto: a declaration of the intent of an individual or organization or group. How can one write a manifesto around a figure, the killjoy, or an activity, killing joy?

A manifesto: to make manifest. Moynan King in her discussion of Valerie Solanas's SCUM Manifesto addresses this sense of a manifesto as making manifest. She writes, "As a manifesto, SCUM's intention is to make manifest, to render perceptible, a new order of ideas" (King, 2013, n.p.). To render a new order of ideas perceptible is simultaneously a disordering of ideas; manifestos often enact what they call for in surprising and shocking ways given how they expose the violence of an order. A feminist manifesto exposes the violence of a patriarchal order, the violence of what I call "the machinery of gender."

A manifesto not only causes a disturbance, it aims to cause this disturbance. To make something manifest can be enough to cause a disturbance. This intimacy between manifestation and disturbance has implications for how we write a killjoy manifesto. A killjoy manifesto must be grounded in an account of what exists. Why is this important? It is about what we come up against. Some of the worst abuses of power I have encountered in the academy have been when individuals make use of an equality principle as if to say, boundaries and rules are about hierarchy, so we are "free to do what we want," whereby "free to do what we want" really still means "you doing what I want you to do," given that the *we* is made up of an *I* who has power and a *you* that is subordinate by virtue of their positions within an organization. Note that "doing what we want" not only can be assumed to express an equality principle but can be articulated as a rebellion against institutional norms and authority (they would prevent us from having relationships because they assume boundaries and divisions that we have given up because we are free radicals). A killjoy manifesto cannot be about the freeing of radicals to pursue their own agendas.

A killjoy manifesto thus begins by recognizing inequalities as existing. This recognition is enacted by the figure of the killjoy herself: she kills joy because of what she claims exists. She has to keep making the same claim because she keeps countering the claim that what she says exists does not exist. The killjoy is often assumed to be inventive, to bring about what she claims; or, to use my terms, she is often assumed to be a *wall* maker. If a killjoy manifesto shows how the denial of inequality under the assumption of equality is a technique of power, then the principles articulated in that manifesto cannot be abstracted from statements about what exists. A killjoy manifesto is thus about making manifest what exists. In the labour of making manifest, we make a manifesto.

To struggle for freedom is to struggle against oppression. Angela Davis in *Blues legacies and black feminism* showed how the articulation of unfulfilled longings for freedom can also represent freedom "in more immediate and accessible terms" ([1989] 1998, p. 7). It is from oppression that freedom is given expression. A manifesto is required when a struggle is necessary to give expression to something. This is why the manifesto can be understood as a killjoy genre; we have to say it because of what is not being done. A manifesto makes an appeal by not being appealing: a manifesto is not an attractive piece of writing by existing norms or standards. It cannot be: it has to strain to be said. And yet a manifesto is appealing to those who read it; a manifesto appeals

for something by appealing to someone. A killjoy manifesto appeals to killjoys.

Manifestos are often disagreeable because they show the violence necessary to sustain an agreement. It is not just that the feminist killjoy has a manifesto. The feminist killjoy is a manifesto. She is assembled around violence; how she comes to matter, to mean, is how she exposes violence. Just remember the kill in killjoy. This figure reminds us how feminism is often understood as a form of murder; calling for the end of the system that makes "men" is often understood as killing men. We could indeed compare the figure of the murderous feminist to that of the feminist killjoy. What Valerie Solanas ([1967] 2013) does in her manifesto, very controversially, is to literalize that fantasy of the murderous feminist through imagining a feminist collective, or a mind-set, that is SCUM (Society for Cutting Up Men). It should not surprise us because one of her points was to be a cut-off point that the SCUM Manifesto was read literally; it was dismissed as literal or dismissed through literalism as intending the elimination of men. The manifesto works because it enacts the literalism that would enable its own dismissal. I have noticed this use of literalism as dismissal when working on my feminist killjoy blog. For example, when I tweeted a link to a blog post "white men;" which was retweeted by a white man, another white man called it "genosuicide." Genosuicide: the self-willed killing of a people. Or another time a student at Goldsmiths, Bahar Mustafa, allegedly used the hashtag #killallwhitemen. Valerie Solanas is brought back to life on social media. Snap. But of course if this hashtag literalizes a fantasy, you literally encounter the fantasy. The hashtag is turned back into a command; heard as the planning of genocide.

The figure of the murderous feminist is useful: it allows the survival of men to be predicated on the elimination of feminism. Much feminist creativity has literalized a fantasy that does not originate with us, including the film *A question of silence*, where the man that is killed in an act of feminist revenge stands in for all men. And in a way, of course, you are being violent in exposing violence; if you are letting the violence come out of your own pen, to travel through you, you have to let the violence spill, all over the pages. And you are in a certain way calling for the end of white men because you are calling for the end of the institution that makes white men. "White men" is an institution. We do want to bring an end to him. But of course, at another level, it is harder to redeploy the figure of the murderous feminist than the figure of the feminist killjoy. Feminists are not calling for violence. We are calling for an end to the institutions that promote and naturalize violence. Much violence that is promoted by institutions is concealed by the very use of stranger danger: the assumption that violence only ever originates with outsiders. It is because we expose violence that we are heard as violent, as if the violence of which we speak originates with us.

To be a killjoy can also mean being understood as someone who kills life because there is such an intimacy between the life principle and the happiness principle. In being against happiness you are assumed to be against life. And as such there are life risks in being a killjoy. It is not that in being assigned a killjoy (and she always begins as an assignment because the feminist killjoy is announced from a position of exteriority; she already has a life of her own before we are assigned her) we are always willing or able to receive this assignment. In fact, the figure of the feminist killjoy often comes up in situations of intense pain and difficulty: when you are seated at the table, doing the work of family, that happy object, say, you threaten that object. And you threaten the object by pointing out what is already there, in the room; again, you are not being inventive. But what a feeling: when all the negative feeling that is not revealed when the family is working becomes deposited in the one who reveals the family is not working. I will never forget that feeling of wanting to eliminate myself from a situation that I had been assumed to cause.

It Is a Downer; We Are Downers

A killjoy manifesto has company: books that bring things down, books that enact a collective frown. *The dialectic of sex* could be read as a killjoy manifesto, a book that has too quickly been dismissed as assuming technology would liberate women from biology, a book that showed that when the sexual division of labour structures everything, nothing will liberate anyone. Sarah Franklin describes how the "bulk of Firestone's manifesto was based on an analysis of what has held a certain gender stratification in place for millennia" (2010, p. 46). *The dialectic of sex* is optimistic because it accounts for how liberation is difficult to achieve. No wonder she has her killjoy moments. Firestone wants to explain why this system that is not working keeps on going, a system that she has no doubt eventually will kill us all. And for explanations, she turns to love, to romance, to the family. These institutions are promises of happiness. An institution can be organized around a promise. And they become ways of organizing living by assuming that proximity to a form will get you there. So, of course, Shulamith Firestone in turning in this direction turns to happiness. She describes her "dream action" for the women's liberation movement as a smile boycott (Firestone, 1970, p. 90). Perhaps we could call this action, following Lisa Millbank (2013), a smile strike, to emphasize its collective nature. Collectively we would strike by not smiling, a collectivity built out of individual action (not smiling is an action when smiling is a requirement for women and for those understood as serving others through paid or unpaid work) but which requires more than an individual. A smile strike is necessary to announce our disagreement, our unhappiness, with a system.

We Must Stay Unhappy with This World

The figure of the feminist killjoy makes sense if we place her in the context of feminist critiques of happiness (see Ahmed, 2010). Happiness is used to justify social norms as social goods. As Simone de Beauvoir described so astutely, "It is always easy to describe as happy a situation in which one wishes to place [others]" ([1949] 1997, p. 28). Not to agree to stay in the place of this wish might be to refuse the happiness that is wished for. To be involved in political activism is thus to be involved in a struggle against happiness. The struggle over happiness provides the horizon in which political claims are made. We inherit this horizon.

A killjoy becomes a manifesto when we are willing to take up this figure, to assemble a life not as her but around her, in her company. We are willing to killjoy because the world that assigns this or that person or group of people as the killjoys is not a world we want to be part of. To be willing to killjoy is to transform a judgment into a project. A manifesto: how a judgment becomes a project.

To think of killjoys as manifestos is to say that a politics of transformation, a politics that intends to cause the end of a system, is not a program of action that can be separated from how we are in the worlds we are in. Feminism is praxis. We enact the world we are aiming for; nothing less will do. Lesbian feminism is how we organize our lives in such a way that our relations to each other as women are not mediated through our relations to men. A life becomes an archive of rebellion. This is why a killjoy manifesto will be personal. Each of us killjoys will have our own. My manifesto does not suspend my personal story. It is how that story unfolds into action.

It is from difficult experiences, of being bruised by structures that are not even revealed to others, that we gain the energy to rebel. It is from what we come up against that we gain new angles on what we are against. Our bodies become our tools; our rage becomes sickness. We vomit; we vomit out what we have been asked to take in. Our guts become our feminist friends the more we are sickened. We begin to feel the weight of histories more and more; the more we expose the weight of history, the heavier it becomes.

We snap. We snap under the weight; things break. A manifesto is written out of feminist snap. A manifesto is feminist snap.

And: we witness as feminists the trouble feminism causes. I would hazard a guess: feminist trouble is an extension of gender trouble (Butler, 1990). To be more specific: feminist trouble is the trouble with women. When we refuse to be women, in the heteropatriarchal sense as beings for men, we become trouble, we get into trouble. A killjoy is willing to get into trouble. And this I think is what is specific about a killjoy manifesto: that we bring into our statements of intent or purpose the experience of what we come up against. It is this experience that allows us to articulate a *for*, a *for* that carries with it an experience of what we come up against. A *for* can be how we turn something about. A manifesto is *about* what it aims to bring *about*.

There is no doubt in my mind that a feminist killjoy is for something; although as killjoys we are not necessarily for the same things. But you would only be willing to live with the consequences of being against what you come up against if you are for something. A life can be a manifesto. When I read some of the books in my survival kit, I hear them as manifestos, as calls to action; as calls to arms. They are books that tremble with life because they show how a life can be rewritten; how we can rewrite a life, letter by letter. A manifesto has a life, a life of its own; a manifesto is an outstretched hand. And if a manifesto is a political action, it depends on how it is received by others. And perhaps a hand can do more when it is not simply received by another hand, when a gesture exceeds the firmness of a handshake. Perhaps more than a hand needs to shake. If a killjoy manifesto is a handle, it flies out of hand. A manifesto thus repeats something that has already happened; as we know the killjoy has flown off. Perhaps a killjoy manifesto is unhandy; a feminist flight.

When we refuse to be the master's tool, we expose the violence of rods, the violences that built the master's dwelling, brick by brick. When we make violence manifest, a violence that is reproduced by not being made manifest, we will be assigned as killjoys. It is because of what she reveals that a killjoy becomes a killjoy in the first place. A manifesto is in some sense behind her. This is not to say that writing a killjoy manifesto is not also a commitment; that it is not also an idea of how to move forward. A killjoy has her principles. A killjoy manifesto shows how we create principles from an experience of what we come up against, from how we live a feminist life. When I say principles here, I do not mean rules of conduct that we must agree to in order to proceed in a common direction. I might say that a feminist life is principled but feminism often becomes an announcement at the very moment of the refusal to be bound by principle. When I think of feminist principles, I think of principles in the original sense: principle as a first step, as a commencement, a start of something.

A principle can also be what is elemental to a craft. Feminist killjoys and other willful subjects are crafty; we are becoming crafty. There are principles in what we craft. How we begin does not determine where we end up, but principles do give shape or direction. Feminist principles are articulated in unfeminist worlds. Living a life with feminist principles is thus not living smoothly; we bump into the world that does not live in accordance with the principles we try to live.

For some reason, the principles I articulate here ended up being expressed as statements of will: of what a killjoy is willing (to do or to be)

or not willing (to do or to be). I think we can understand the some of this reason. A killjoy manifesto is a willful subject; she wills wrongly by what she is willing or is not willing to do. No wonder a willful subject has principles; she can be principled. She can share them if you can bear them.

Principle 1: I Am Not Willing to Make Happiness My Cause

It is often made into a specific requirement: you are asked to do something in order to make others happy. You are more likely to be asked to do something to make others happy when they know you are not happy with what they are doing. Maybe you are asked to participate in a wedding ceremony by those who know you are against the institution of marriage celebrated by such ceremonies. They appeal to you by appealing to their own happiness. If you refuse that appeal you are judged as being selfish, as putting your own happiness before the happiness of others.

Mean: How Could You?
A Killjoy Manifesto: Meaning from the Mean

If you are willing to refuse these appeals, then happiness is not the principle you uphold. You have not found the appeal appealing. And you do not uphold this principle in general because you have come up against this principle before: you have been asked not to say things, to do things, because it would make others unhappy. It does not follow that a killjoy does not care for the happiness of others or that she might not at times decide to do something because it contributes to the happiness of others. She is just not willing to make causing happiness her political cause.

From this everyday situation of living with the consequences of not making happiness your cause, you learn the unhappiness that happiness can cause. This first principle has been the basis of much feminist knowledge and activism: the identification of how institutions are built as promises of happiness; promises that often hide the violence of these institutions. We are willing to expose this violence: the violence of the elevation of the family, the couple form, reproductivity as the basis of a good life; the violence reproduced by organizations that identify speaking about violence as disloyalty. We will expose the happiness myths of neoliberalism and global capitalism: the fantasy that the system created for a privileged few is really about the happiness of many or the most.

To expose happiness myths is to be willing to be given a killjoy assignment.

Principle 2: I Am Willing to Cause Unhappiness

Not making happiness your cause can cause unhappiness. A killjoy is willing to cause unhappiness.

A committed killjoy has a lifetime of experience of being the cause of unhappiness. And she knows this too: when you cause unhappiness, by virtue of the desires you have or the worlds you are not willing to take up as your own, unhappiness is assumed as your cause. It is not. Being willing to cause unhappiness does not make unhappiness your cause, although we live with the assumption that unhappiness is our cause. When our desires cause unhappiness, it is often assumed we desire to cause unhappiness. You might be judged as wanting the unhappiness you cause, which is another way you become an unhappiness cause.

A killjoy is willing to live with the consequences of what she is willing. She is thus willing to be the cause of someone else's unhappiness. It does

not follow that she will not be made sad by other people being sad about her life (because they think her life is sad); it does not follow, even, that she would not feel sympathy in response to those made unhappy by her life. She will not let that unhappiness redirect her. She is willing to be misdirected.

Whose unhappiness are we willing to cause? Anybody's unhappiness: that can be the only answer to this question. But there is an "if" here. We are willing to cause institutional unhappiness if the institution is unhappy because we speak about sexual harassment. We are willing to cause feminist unhappiness if feminists are unhappy because we speak about racism. This means that: we are unhappy with this if. This means that: we are unhappy with what causes unhappiness. It can cause unhappiness to reveal the causes of unhappiness.

We are willing to cause unhappiness because of what we have learned about unhappiness from what we have been assumed to have caused. An "I" turns up here; she knows what is up from what turns up. When I spoke out publicly about sexual harassment at my college, I was identified by some as a killjoy without any sense of irony (there might have been a sense of irony given I had already professed to be her). What is important for us to note is that some feminists were part of this some. A feminist colleague said that in speaking out I was compromising "the happy and stimulating" environment that "longstanding feminists" had worked to create. I assumed I was not one of the longstanding feminists because of the stand I took. Yes, even speaking out about sexual harassment can cause feminist unhappiness. If so then: I am not willing to make feminist happiness my cause.

We have learned to hear what is at stake in such accusations. Feminism by implication is a bubble within the institution. But a feminist bubble can also operate as a mode of identification. To protect the feminist bubble you might want to protect it from exposure to the violence of the institution, a violence that is happening elsewhere (another centre, another department). Protecting the feminist bubble ends up becoming a means of protecting the institution. You do not want the institutional violence exposed to others. You would prefer to resolve the violence "in house," even though the "in house" has failed to dismantle the master's house. Is this why there is such secrecy and silence about institutional violence even among some feminists?

If Feminism Is a Bubble, We Need the Bubble to Burst

When we turn away from what compromises our happiness we are withdrawing our efforts from work that needs to be done to enable a more just and equal world. But this principle of being willing to cause unhappiness cannot be upheld by being assumed to refer only to the unhappiness of others. It is possible that we do not register some situations because to register those situations would make us unhappy. Maybe that is why the killjoy appears: because we are desperate not to register what she notices. Maybe this is why the killjoy appears to those who profess to be killjoys: our happiness too might depend on what we do not notice. Perhaps we keep our happiness through a willed oblivion. We must refuse this oblivion. If something would make us unhappy, when acknowledged, we need to acknowledge it. We are willing to cause our own unhappiness, which does not make our unhappiness our cause.

Principle 3: I Am Willing To Support Others Who Are Willing To Cause Unhappiness

A killjoy might first recognize herself in that feeling of loneliness: of being cut off from others, from how they assemble around happiness. She knows, because she has been there: to be unseated by the tables of happiness can be to find yourself in that shadowy place, to find yourself alone, on your own.

It might be that many pass through the figure of the killjoy and quickly out again because they find her a hard place to be; not to be surrounded by the warmth of others, the quiet murmurs that accompany an agreement. The costs of killing joy are high; this figure is herself a cost (not to agree with someone as killing the joy of something).

How do you persist? We often persist by finding the company of other killjoys; we can take up this name when we recognize the dynamic she names; and we can recognize that dynamic when others articulate that dynamic for us. We recognize others too because they recognize that dynamic.

Those moments of recognition are precious; and they are precarious. With a moment comes a memory: we often persist by being supported by others. We might also experience the crisis of being unsupported; support matters all the more all the less we feel supported. To make a manifesto out of the killjoy means being willing to give to others the support you received or wish you received. Maybe you are in a conversation, at home or at work, and one person, one person out of many, is speaking out. Don't let her speak on her own. Back her up; speak with her. Stand by her; stand with her. From these public moments of solidarity so much is brought into existence. We are creating a support system around the killjoy; we are finding ways to allow her to do what she does, to be who she is. We do not have to assume her permanence, to turn her figure into personhood, to know that when she comes up, she might need others to hold her up.

Audre Lorde once wrote, "Your silence will not protect you" (1984, p. 41). But your silence could protect them. And by them I mean: those who are violent, or those who benefit in some way from silence about violence. The killjoy is testimony. She comes to exist as a figure, a way of containing damage, because she speaks about damage. Over time, the time of being a feminist, we might call this feminist time, I have come to understand, to know and to feel, the costs of speaking out. I have thus come to understand, to know and to feel, why many do not speak out. There is a lot to lose, a lot, a life even. So much injustice is reproduced by silence not because people do not recognize injustice but because they do recognize it. They also recognize the consequences of identifying injustice, which might not be consequences they can live with. It might be fear of losing your job and knowing you need that job to support those you care for; it might be concern about losing connections that matter; concern that what you say will be taken the wrong way; concern that by saying something you would make something worse. To suggest that the feminist killjoy is a manifesto is not to say that we have an obligation to speak out. We are not all in the same position; we cannot all afford to speak out. Killing joy thus requires a communication system: we have to find other ways for the violence to become manifest. We might need to use guerrilla tactics, and we have a feminist history to draw on here; you can write down names of harassers on books; put graffiti on walls; red ink in the water. There are so many ways to cause a feminist disturbance.

Even if speaking out is not possible, it is necessary. Silence about violence is violence. But feminist speech can take many forms. We become more inventive with forms the harder it is to get through. Speaking out and speaking with, sheltering those who speak; these acts of spreading the word, are world making. Killing joy is a world-making project. We make a world out of the shattered pieces even when we shatter the pieces or even when we are the shattered pieces.

Principle 4: I Am Not Willing to Laugh at Jokes Designed to Cause Offence

This principle might seem very specific: it might seem that it derives from my initial three principles and that it is not worthy of being one all on its own. But I think humour is such a crucial technique for reproducing inequality and injustice. I think the fantasy of the humourless feminist (as part of a more general fantasy of humourlessness of those who question a social as well as political arrangement) does such important work. The fantasy is what makes the figure of the killjoy do her work. It is assumed she says what she does (points out sexism, points out racism) because she is herself deprived of any joy, because she cannot bear the joy of others. Often, once someone has been assigned a feminist killjoy, others then will make certain jokes, in order to cause her offence, in order to witness her ill humour. Do not be tempted to laugh. If the situation is humourless, we need not to add humour to it. If the situation is unfunny, we need not to make light of it; we need not to make it fun.

It is often through humour (say, through irony or satire) that people can keep making sexist and racist utterances. Humour creates the appearance of distance; by laughing about what they repeat, they repeat what they laugh about. This about becomes the butt of the joke. It is no laughing matter. When it is no laughing matter, laughter matters.

But, of course, humour can challenge things by bringing things to the surface; I noticed this in my survival kit. But there are differences that matter in what laughter does. Feminist humour might involve the relief of being able to laugh when familiar patterns that are often obscured are revealed. We might laugh at how white men assemble themselves by reducing whatever we do as "not white men" to identity politics. We might laugh even about being poster children of diversity; and laughing does not mean we do not experience pain and frustration at being called upon by institutions to provide them with smiling colourful faces; to make our faces theirs. But this is not laughter that allows us to repeat what causes offence; it is a reorientation toward that cause. We do not repeat it; we withdraw.

The killjoy exists in close proximity to the figure of the oversensitive subject who is too easily offended. This figure is always evoked whenever social critique is successful: that something has been closed down or removed or lost (a loss that is mourned) because others are offended, where to be offended is to be too easily offended, to be weak, soft, impressionable. "Toughen up" has become a moral imperative, one that is (like most moral imperatives) articulated by those who think they have what they claim others need. Indeed this figure of the oversensitive subject might come up in advance of such a loss, or to avoid such a loss. The moral panic over trigger warnings often evokes this figure, specifically the figure of the oversensitive student who is not attuned to the difficulty and discomfort of learning, as if to say: if we let your sensitivities become law, we lose our freedom. I would argue that freedom has become reduced to the freedom to be offensive, which is also about how those with power protect their right to articulate their own views, no matter what, no matter whom.

If not wanting histories that are violent to be repeated with such violent insistence, or at least if asking questions about the terms that enable that repetition means being deemed oversensitive, we need to be oversensitive. When you are sensitive to what is not over, you are deemed oversensitive. We are sensitive to what is not over. We are sensitive because it is not over.

Principle 5: I Am Not Willing to Get Over Histories That Are Not Over

It is not over. We say that, with insistence, as we watch others declare things over. So many declarations, and they participate in the same thing. The [former] [. . .] British prime minister, David Cameron, says that one thing that made Great Britain great was that we "took slavery off the high seas." Great Britain is remembered as the liberator of the slaves, not as perpetrator of slavery; not as a country that has benefitted from the mass enslavement of others, from the colonization of others. When colonialism is referred to in the book upon which citizenship tests are based in the United Kingdom, it is described as the system that introduced democracy, law, bringing benefits to others. A violent history of conquest and theft imagined as the gift of modernity. And today, wars are still justified as gifts, as giving freedom, democracy, and equality.

When It Is Not over, It Is Not the Time to Get Over It

A killjoy is willing to bring this history up. A memory can be willful. And so we know what happens when we do this. You are accused as the one who is getting in the way of reconciliation. You are judged as the one who has yet to do what others have done: get over it; get over yourself; let it go. You become the open wound because you won't let things heal.

We are willing to be the ones who fail the project of reconciliation. We know the success of that project is the failure to address these histories of injustice that manifest not only in the unresolved trauma of those for whom this history is a bodily inheritance, a transgenerational haunting, but also in a grossly unequal distribution of wealth and resources.

How a World Is Shaped Is Memory

And they say: but look what you have been given. Equality, diversity: they all become gifts for which we are supposed to be grateful; they become compensatory. We are not grateful when a system is extended to include us when that system is predicated on inequality and violence.

Principle 6: I Am Not Willing to Be Included If Inclusion Means Being Included in a System That Is Unjust, Violent, and Unequal

It is often an invitation: come in, be part, be grateful. Sometimes we have few options: we are workers; we work; we make do. We have to survive or even progress within an institution. But even for those of us who are included, even when we do receive benefits (we might have salaries; we might have pensions), we are not willing that inclusion: we are agreeing that inclusion requires being behind the institution, identifying with it. We are willing to speak out about the violence of the system, to strike, to demonstrate. We are willing to talk about the rods, to risk being identified as the wayward arm.

But there is a difficulty here. Because surely if you are employed by an organization, if you receive the benefit of employment, it could be said that to maintain a killjoy stance is a form of political dishonesty: you get to benefit from the institutions you critique. We need to start with our own complicity[. . .]. To be complicit should not become its own reproductive logic: that all we can do is to reproduce the logics of the institutions that employ us. In fact those who benefit from an unjust system need to work even harder to expose that injustice. For those killjoys who are in regular employment—let's call ourselves professional killjoys; some of us might even be professor killjoys—when we profess we kill joy; there is no way of overcoming this difficulty, other than by starting from it. We need to use the benefits we receive to support those who do not receive these benefits, including those within our own institutions who do not have the same securities that give us the opportunity to expose the insecurities. Within higher education this means we need to enact our solidarity with students who

are fighting for education as a right, for adjunct lecturers and faculty who do not have tenure or who are on short-term contracts, with those professional staff who do the work of maintaining the very buildings and facilities in which we do our work: cleaners, security staff, porters. I have tried to show how killing joy and willfulness also relate to the politics of labour: arms matter, which is to say some end up doing the work to reproduce the conditions that enable the existence of others. When our professional existence is enabled by the work of others, we need to use our existence to recognize that work. We need to expose the injustice of how institutions give support to some by not supporting others. And we need to support those who challenge the conditions in which they work unsupported. Willfulness is striking.

And: we must keep exposing the violence within the institutions that have included us, especially when our own inclusion occurs under the sign of diversity and equality, especially when our bodies and the products of our labour are used by institutions as evidence of inclusion. We become wall breakers. So we must talk about walls; we must show how history becomes concrete. We are not willing to allow our inclusion to support a happiness fantasy. We might need to leave, at a certain point, if our inclusion requires giving up too much, though we are not all in a position to leave.

A killjoy manifesto: requires an ongoing and willful refusal to identify our hopes with inclusion within organizations predicated on violence. I am not grateful to be included in an institution that is unequal. I am not grateful to be included in an institution in which talking about sexism and racism is heard as ungrateful. We have a history of ungrateful feminists to pick up from. Ungrateful feminists; grumpy; grump.

Together: grumps are a feminist lump. A lumpen proletariat: in feminist form with a feminist consciousness.

Principle 7: I Am Willing to Live a Life That Is Deemed by Others as Unhappy, and I Am Willing to Reject or to Widen the Scripts Available for What Counts as a Good Life

I have already noted how happiness involves the narrowing down of ways of living a life. We can be disloyal by refusing to be narrowed. We live lives deemed by others to be not happy, to be not reaching the right points of ceremony. Two women living together, refusing to have a civil partnership, refusing to get married; we are enacting our rejection of heteropatriarchy. To enact a rejection is an action performed with others.

We can come to embody an alternative family line, or an alternative to the family line. I quite like being a lesbian feminist auntie. I know that as a young woman I would have liked to have had lesbian feminist aunties, though I certainly had feminist aunties to whom I owe a great deal. We need to tell our stories to children, to those who are to come; generations need to tell each other our stories, assembled around other lives, those that are faint from under-inscription. We need to tell each other stories of different ways you can live, different ways you can be; predicated not on how close you get to the life you were assumed or expected to have, but on the queer wanderings of a life you live.

I would have liked to have known there were other ways of living, of being. I would have liked to have known that women do not have to be in relation to men. Of course, I struggled for this realization: I became a feminist; I found women's studies; I met women who taught me what I did not have to do; I found women who helped me deviate from an expectation.

Queer: The Moment You Realize What You Did Not Have to Be

We can become part of a widening when we refuse to be narrowed. And each time we reject or widen the happiness script, we become part of an opening. We have to create room if we are to live a feminist life. When we create room, we create room for others.

Principle 8: I Am Willing to Put the Hap Back into Happiness

I have noted how the word "happiness" derives from the Middle English word "hap," suggesting chance. One history of happiness is the history of the removal of its hap such that happiness is defined not in terms of what happens to you but of what you work for. In my book *The promise of happiness*, I explored how happiness even ends up being redefined against hap, especially in the psychology of Bows and positive psychology: as not something that happens (or just happens). The narrow scripts of happiness are precisely about the violence of the elimination of the hap. We need to recognize the elimination of hap before we can restore hap. We cannot simply use the lighter word as if it can get us out of here. We have to recognize the weight of the world, the heaviness of happiness, how we are brought down by the expectation that we are down. We stumble. When we stumble, when we are in line, we might feel ourselves as the obstacle to our own happiness; we might feel ourselves to be getting in the way of ourselves. Can we let ourselves be in the way? Can we be willing what we seem to be undoing? I stumble; maybe by stumbling I found you, maybe by stumbling I stumbled on happiness, a hap-full happiness; a happiness that is as fragile as the bodies we love and cherish. We value such happiness because it is fragile: it comes and goes, as we do. I am willing to let happiness go; to allow anger, rage, or disappointment be how I am affected by a world. But when happiness happens, I am happy.

A fragile happiness might be attuned to the fragility of things. We can care about the things that break off, the broken things. To care about such things is not to care for their happiness. Caring for happiness can so often translate into caring for others on the condition that they reflect back an idea you have of how a life should be lived. Perhaps we can think of care in relation to hap. We are often assumed to be careless when we break something. What would it mean to care for something, whether or not it breaks? Maybe we can reorientate caring from caring for someone's happiness to caring what happens to someone or something: caring about what happens, caring whatever happens. We might call this a hap care rather than a happiness care. A hap care would not be about letting an object go but holding on to an object by letting oneself go, giving oneself over to something that is not one's own. A hap care would not seek to eliminate anxiety from care; it could even be described as care for the hap. Caring is anxious—to be full of care, to be careful, is to take care of things by becoming anxious about their future, where the future is embodied in the fragility of an object whose persistence matters. Our care would pick up the pieces of a shattered pot. Our care would not turn the thing into a memorial but value each piece; shattering as the beginning of another story.

But we would not end up with a liberal notion: everything is equally fragile; we must care for everything equally. It is not; I do not. Some things become more fragile than others in time. In time, we attend. To attend to something that has become more easily breakable is to attend to its history, with love, and with care.

Principle 9: I Am Willing to Snap Any Bonds, However Precious, When Those Bonds Are Damaging to Myself or to Others

So many times, when a bond has been snapped, I have been told it is sad. But bonds can be violent. A bond can be diminishing. Sometimes we are not ready to recognize that we have been diminished. We are not ready. It can take psychic as well as political work to be ready to snap that bond. When you do, when you snap, it can feel like an unexpected moment that breaks a line that had been unfolding over time, a deviation, a departure. But a moment can be an achievement; it can be what you have been working for.

You might be willing to snap the bond. You might need to be willful to be willing. And you might need to recognize that others too need to work to reach a point when they can let go. Share that work. We have to share the costs of what we give up. But when we give up, we do not just lose something even when we do lose something. We find things. We find out things we did not know before—about ourselves, about worlds. A feminist life is a journey, a reaching for something that might not have been possible without snap, without the snappy encouragement of others. But a feminist life is also a going back, retrieving parts of ourselves we did not even realize we had, that we did not even realize we had put on hold.

We can hold each other by not putting ourselves on hold.

Principle 10: I Am Willing to Participate in a Killjoy Movement

Whether or not you are being difficult, you are heard as making things difficult for yourself as well as others. So much difficulty, you would think feminist killjoys would give up. And yet, when I first began presenting and talking about the feminist killjoy, when I first began working with her as well as on her, picking her up, I noticed how energetic the room would be. Sometimes speaking of her, letting her into the room to do her thing, felt like an electric shock. And she finds herself quickly in a company of killjoys: transfeminist killjoys (Cowan, 2014), ethnic killjoys (Khorana, 2013), crip killjoys (Mullow, 2013), Indigenous feminist killjoys (Barker, 2015). There will be more of that I am sure.

Why? Because the figure of the killjoy comes up whenever there are difficult histories to bring up. The killjoy is appealing not despite what she brings up but because of what she brings up. She acquires vitality or energy from a scene of difficulty. To be willing to be a killjoy, to be willing to get in the way of happiness, grasps hold of a judgment and takes it on.

We even transform the judgment into a rebellious command.

Killjoy?

Just Watch Me

Bring It On

It can be quite a pickup when we pick her up. There can be joy in finding killjoys; there can be joy in killing joy. Our eyes meet when we tell each other about rolling eyes.

You Too; You Yoo

A Fragile Movement

Snappy

So many moments are abbreviated in our equation "rolling eyes = feminist pedagogy." We are willing those moments. Moments can become movement. Moments can build a movement, a movement assembled from lighter materials. This is not a secure dwelling. We are shattered, too often; but see how the walls move.

We Are Willing to Participate in a Killjoy Movement

We Are That Movement

Watch Us Roll

Call to Action

How can you ensure that you are able to continue to oppose unjust treatment, discrimination, or behaviour in an unjust world? Get involved with local anti-racist groups, BIPOC student organization communities (even as an ally), and anti-fascist groups in order to ensure that your feminism is intersectional and you are critiquing your own feminist practices to make them less racist, ableist, heteronormative, white, and cisnormative. If your community or university does not have a group like this, consider creating one with your student union.

Tying It Together

This chapter focuses on the future of global and gender studies in the nature of intersectional feminism activism. Transgressing feminist discourse that is so often built and centred on white feminism is an important move forward in the direction of deconstructing the dominant ways of knowing in a world that is dominated by ableist, cisnormative, heteronormative, racist, and sexist ideologies. This chapter helps to facilitate this discussion while teaching students how to be more comfortable in discomfort.

DISCUSSION QUESTIONS

1. In what ways have you been a killjoy in your own life? Connect your experience to at least one of the 10 principles detailed in the chapter.
2. What different kinds of killjoy movements are there? Compare differences in type and perception of killjoys.
3. Think about an unjust system from which you benefit—it might be your job, your school, or your socio-economic class. What injustices can you identify and expose from that system?
4. Brainstorm ways in which we can support one another in being killjoys. What might that look like?
5. Principle 5 states, "I AM NOT WILLING TO GET OVER HISTORIES THAT ARE NOT OVER." What piece of Canadian history can you address as a killjoy?

SUGGESTIONS FOR FURTHER READING

Ahmed, S. (2017). *Living a feminist life*. Durham, NC: Duke University Press. This book centres on the entanglement of being a feminist critiquing and being affected by the society that you critique. Ahmed explores feminist theory through an intersectional lens within this book.

Ahmed, S. (2010). *The promise of happiness*. Durham, NC: Duke University Press. This book explores the emotional labour attached to the Western culture of being happy in which people are constantly told they need to be happy or strive for happiness.

Ahmed, S. (2012). *On being included: Racism and diversity in institutional life*. Durham, NC: Duke University Press. This book is about the theme of diversity and critiques diversity initiatives that are often implemented within institutions by also bringing in discussions on whiteness that is entrenched into the very institutions that we operate within.

MULTIMEDIA SUGGESTIONS

feministkilljoys

https://feministkilljoys.com

This is the research blog of Sara Ahmed, which explores the themes of feminist theory and being a feminist killjoy in everyday life. Ahmed also shares material from a current project inspired by her experience of supporting students through inquiries into complaints of harassment and abuse within universities.

Sara Ahmed - Complaint as Diversity Work (Mar 12, 2018)

https://www.youtube.com/watch?v=JQ_1kFwkfVE

This is a recording of Sara Ahmed's talk at Cambridge University on diversity and the workplace and addresses the difficulty of making complaints and why or how complaints are blocked.

REFERENCES

Ahmed, S. (2010). *The promise of happiness*. Durham, NC: Duke University Press.

Barker, J. (2015). The Indigenous feminist killjoy. *Tequila Sovereign*, 24 July. https://tequilasovereign.com/2015/07/24/the-indigenous-feminist-killjoy.

Butler, J. (1990). *Gender trouble: Feminism and the subversion of identity*. New York, NY: Routledge.

Cowan, T.L. (2014). Transfeminist kill/joys: Rage, love, and reparative performance. *Transgender Studies Quarterly*, *1*(4), 501–16.

Davis, A.Y. ([1989] 1998). *Blues legacies and Black feminism: Gertrude Ma Rainey. Bessie Smith*. New York, NY: Vintage.

de Beauvoir, S. ([1949] 1997). *The second sex*. Harmondsworth, UK: Penguin Books.

Firestone, S. (1970). *The dialectic of sex: The case for feminist revolution*. New York, NY: Bantam.

Franklin, S. (2010). Sexism as a means of reproduction. *New Formations*, 86, 14–23.

Khorana, S. (2013). On being an "ethnic killjoy" in the Asian century. *The Conversation*, 19 November. https://theconversation.com/on-being-an-ethnic-killjoy-in-the-asian-century-19833.

King, M. (2013). Revenge as a radical feminist tactic in the SCUM Manifesto. *Nomorepotlucks*, July/August. http://nomorepotlucks.org/site/revenge-as-radical-feminist-tactic-in-the-scum-manifesto-moynan-king.

Lorde, A. (1984). *Sister outsider: Essays and speeches*. Trumansburg, NY. The Crossing Press.

Millbank, L. (2013). The scope of action, smiling, smile "strikes" and individual action. *Radtransfem*. http://radtransfem.tumblr.com/post/40249024485/the-scope-of-action-smiling-smile-strikes-and.

Mullow, A. (2013). Bellyaching. *Social Text*, 24 October. https://socialtextjournal.org/periscope_article/bellyaching.

Solanas, V. ([1967] 2013). *SCUM manifesto*. Chico, CA: AK Press.

NOTE

1. From Sara Ahmed, (2017) Conclusion 2. A killjoy manifesto, in *Living a feminist life*, pp. 251–68. Copyright, 2017, Duke University Press. All rights reserved. Republished by permission of the copyright holder. www.dukeupress.edu

Glossary

abolition historically, a political movement to end slavery and systems of exploitation. Current abolitionists argue that slavery was never fully abolished but has resurfaced over time through prison as an institution. The current political movement supports the building of community and caring for the basic needs of all through massive investments in education, housing, health care, and institutions that will care for and nurture the physical, emotional, and intellectual needs of current and future generations. With this foundation set, abolitionists call for the eradication of the neo-slave systems of prison and for the demilitarization of everyday life.

acculturation process by which a hegemonic or colonial culture seeks to shift the culture of the subaltern closer to its own, often by attacking expressions of the subaltern culture.

adaptiveness the capacity to change one's practices and life to conform to the emerging logics and new functions within the network of social relations stemming from the development of the productive forces and relations of production.

affect emotion; describing something as affective means that it is driven by an emotional response.

aging the process of change from birth to death (as opposed to the colloquial definition, which is the process of physical and psychological decline that occurs in later life).

androcentrism being male-centric; also describes a perspective that is based on a hegemonic male positionality.

anti-Black racism the specificity of racism that targets those racialized as Black (as compared to general racism, which could describe all people of colour). Its social basis is rooted in the history of slavery and its afterlives.

anti-colonialism a theoretical approach that addresses and critiques the historical and ongoing distortion by European colonial powers of the political, economic, cultural, social, and spiritual lives and experiences of Indigenous peoples. The aim is to demonstrate how "Western" knowledge has sought to undermine alternative ways of knowing and living in the world as well as to highlight the devastating consequences of such actions.

anti-oppressive feminisms theoretical approaches that attend to the intersecting systems of oppression that create the conditions of our lives. These theories, methods, and practices are formed through the intersecting histories of Black, Indigenous, postcolonial, Third World, transnational, queer, and women of colour feminisms.

austerity the drastic reduction or elimination of budget expenditures for social programs and services.

binary dual; a pair of usually dichotomous (opposite) categories.

biopolitics a concept used by Foucault to describe a mode of governing based on regulating and managing populations. Knowledge about populations is essential to this mode. The emergence of this mode of power is associated with the shift to liberal democratic forms of government in Europe and the formation of nation-states.

Black feminism a historical and contemporary movement premised on the total liberation of humanity and the abolition of white supremacy, anti-Black racism, imperialism, capitalism, colonialism, and heteropatriarchy. There are many strands of Black feminism that can be dated back to freedom-fighters under slavery and its aftermath slavery, such as Sojourner Truth, Ida B. Wells, and Anna Julia Cooper. Black feminism influenced and enabled the "second wave" of feminism in the 20th century and has been a vital motor of every historical liberation struggle.

Black radical tradition first coined by Cedric Robinson in *Black Marxism*, this was meant to describe Black forms of resistance, refusal, and rebellion that have always accompanied the racialized violence enacted on Black peoples since slavery. This tradition continues to evolve, and in Robinson's words, "the resoluteness of the black radical tradition advances as each generation assembles the data of its experience to an ideology of liberation" (1983, p. 317).

cartography The study of maps and map-making.

child marriage the marriage or union between two people in which one or both parties are younger than 18 years of age. Marriage requires "free and full" consent, and since consent cannot be "free and full" when one of the individuals is not sufficiently mature to make such a decision, marriage before the age of 18 can be considered forced marriage and constitutes a violation of human rights.

cisgender a state of being where one's gender identity aligns with the sex one was assigned at birth as well as the corresponding socially constructed gender.

citizenship a status (both legal and social) that grants all of the rights, entitlements, privileges, obligations, duties, and sense of belonging that pertain to an individual's relationship to a place, group, or nation-state. Citizenship is also, however, made and enforced through systematic, structural, and interpersonal violence that denies privileges to people who have been deemed illegitimate.

colonialism the economic, political, and military domination of one nation over another territory and its people. It was a process through which capital's requirements (resources, labour, markets) were satisfied on a global scale as various territories and their people across the Americas, and later Africa and Asia, came to be incorporated into the world capitalist economy either as labourers, as producers of raw materials or agricultural goods, or as consumers of European goods.

colonization the process of extending political, economic, and social control by a power or state over the Indigenous populations, their lands, and life worlds. It consists of the usurpation and assumption of territory and other important resources, usually with the use of force and usually by military or civil representatives of the dominant power.

colonos used in various Latin American countries to refer to people who engage in subsistence agriculture on public or idle land; "squatters."

commodity something that can be bought and sold.

compact A legal agreement among states or between nations regarding matters that they share as a common concern.

conflict zones sites of ongoing endemic violence. When occurring in the Global South, states in the Global North sometimes intervene, which serves to create a constant landscape of surveillance.

contrapuntal methodology the consideration of counterpoints, this is an approach that recognizes and engages with different voices, identities, and texts in the contexts of both colonialism and postcolonialism. This approach takes into consideration the creator's diasporic condition (if applicable) as well as their gendered, national, and cultural identities and seeks to unravel the intercultural and intertextual links between works.

counter-cartographies a mapping of an area that refuses colonial containment and surveillance as a necessary practice of human security.

counter-insurgency in the Latin American context, this was the War on Communism aimed at eradicating any existing revolutionary movements (guerrilla groups) and prevent the emergence of any new ones by attacking social sectors considered as fertile ground for communist indoctrination such as peasants and labour unions. Counter-insurgency offensives continued to be carried out after the end of the Cold War under the labels War on Drugs and War on Terror.

criminalization process through which certain behaviours, conditions, or people become defined and treated as "criminal" and problems to be addressed through the criminal justice system.

crisis of confidence the moment when the process of witch hunting ceases to make sense to local authorities, often triggered by a recognition of their own increasing vulnerability to accusation.

decolonial feminist praxis the blending of political theory, reflection, and practice that intentionally disrupts and defeats the combined and interrelated systems of power that maintain colonial state control over colonized nations as well as male dominance.

decolonial global studies the decolonization, that is, the undoing of the basic white supremacy building blocks and thought systems that have dominated the past three centuries of the world, its understanding and practice. Decolonial here refers to first, the decentring and undoing the dominance of a White supremacist world view that naturally assumes that it has propelled Europe and whiteness into supremacy thus according itself the power to rule everywhere anytime. Seeking to understand social, political, and ontological relations from the standpoint of Indigenous, enslaved, colonized populations and ecologies allows for the possibility of decolonizing as well as rupturing the theft, ongoing capture, and obliteration of global capitalism and white supremacy.

decoloniality an analysis and practice that attempts to disrupt and defeat colonial thinking and paradigms.

decolonization the process of undoing colonization, including state independence and self-governance as a means of preventing ongoing exploitation of natural and human resources.

de-enslavement the process of rupturing and transforming the systems that force people into subjection. De-enslavement entails both the end of enslaving and the end of the expropriation of land, two of the major primary categories and pillars of capitalist accumulation.

denunciation an accusation produced by a confessed and condemned criminal; the word of one witch against another.

deracialize removal of race from political approaches and analysis, which erases or ignores differing experiences and needs based on race (i.e., racism) as well as historical policies and practices based on race (i.e., colonialism).

dialectical a two-way relationship in which the two members of the relationship continuously affect and change each other. Thus, one can be properly understood only in relation to the other.

diaspora a number of people who share a connection to a homeland, history, or culture but who are located in multiple geographic locations. The word encompasses varied experiences of expatriation, displacement, and connection; the term often refers to people who have been scattered around the world as a result of involuntary dispersions but may also refer to voluntary dispersion. Diasporic populations and cultures are perceived as transnational networks that work to both accommodate and resist their host country's norms.

discontinuous narrative the methodological practice of reading disparate texts and events in conversation with one another to disrupt the naturalization of injustice.

discourse Systems of power that include beliefs, imagery, ideas, practices, events, language, and narrative exchanges.

eisegesis the process of deriving meaning of a text through the interpreter's bias or presuppositions instead of from the text itself.

encomienda institution of forced labour whereby Spanish colonizers had the legal right to forcibly extract tribute from the Indigenous population in the form of gold in the 1500s.

enslavement the violent process of forcing people into subjection.

Eurocentric perspectives the systems of thought and practice that assume the superiority of European thinkers at the expense of the rest of thought and practice.

Eurocentrism the misleading belief that European Enlightenment and post-Enlightenment understandings, interpretations, and particular ways of experiencing and living in the world are the only or best ways in which to do so.

exegesis the process of critically examining a text in order to derive its meaning.

exilic related to exile.

export-processing zones (EPZs) areas where the assembly or partial manufacturing of products for export takes place in foreign or locally owned companies. EPZs and *maquilas* employ a largely female workforce and are exempt from national labour and environmental laws (see also *maquilas*).

extractivism the process of extracting natural resources from the earth.

family planning a set of policies and services, offered usually by governments, to reduce population growth and maternal mortality by preventing unwanted pregnancy, unsafe birthing conditions, and unsafe abortions.

feminicide a term used to emphasize state responsibility in femicide through structures, laws, and cultural tolerance that normalize misogyny.

feminism an ideological, theoretical, and methodological approach intended to expose, analyze, and address the subordination of women in patriarchal societies. Unlike other ideologies and theories, feminism does not just study the context, condition, and experiences of women but is also committed to addressing these conditions.

forced sterilization the process of surgically removing or disabling an individual's reproductive organs without their full and informed consent. It is frequently conducted through deceit, threat, bribery, or legislation by a governing body.

Foreign Direct Investment (FDI) physical investments and purchases made by a company in a foreign country, typically by opening plants and buying buildings, machines, factories, and land in the foreign country.

freedom trails the landscapes formed by and through the process of colonized and enslaved peoples rebelling and resisting European colonization, imperialism, slavery, and genocide.

gendered colonial violence violence against Indigenous women resulting from the interconnections of racism, patriarchy, and settler colonialism.

Gender Inequality Index an indicator used by the UN to measure gender inequality in reproductive health, political participation, and economic status.

global capital the accumulation of money and wealth across the entire world through wealth-generating activities that are part of production chains that span multiple nation-states.

global economy transnational integration of national economies into a single production system.

global health security an approach to international health incidents that focuses on the containment of disease outbreaks that could potentially spread to other states and pose threats to their populations and economies.

Global North economically and socially privileged states that exist and persist as a result of the legacy of colonialism and global capitalism (as opposed to being a term based on geographic location, necessarily: for example, New Zealand is categorized as being in the Global North although it is located in the southern hemisphere). States of the Global North are generally depicted as industrialized, peaceful, and democratic. The term critically challenges the static-ness of geography, states, and political economy by suggesting that the location of wealth and development can in theory be located anywhere (i.e., not just in states that have a "Western" philosophy, history, and cultural heritage).

global production chain the manufacturing of goods and services across multiple borders—and often multiple sites—along a supply network. A single commodity may use raw materials, parts, and labour from different countries; also known as "the global assembly line" or the "decentralization of production."

Global South economically and socially disadvantaged states that exist and persist through the legacy of colonialism and global capitalism (as opposed to being a term based on geographic location, necessarily: for example, Nigeria is classified as belonging to the South world, even though it is located in the northern hemisphere). States in the Global South are generally depicted as in conflict and peripheral to the global political economy. The term "Global South" critically challenges the static-ness of geography, states, and political economy by suggesting that the location of wealth and development can in theory be located anywhere (i.e., not just in states that have a "Western" philosophy, history, and cultural heritage).

global studies a field of inquiry and the interdisciplinary study of political, economic, social, legal, and ecological interconnectedness. Global studies' approaches and methods articulate and allow us to understand that the whole world is an indivisible designed assemblage. This approach focuses on the generation, development of peoples and ecologies across the whole world from a multiple-scalar perspective. This multi-scalar perspective cuts through the major assumption about global studies—that is, the division of the world into global/local. Taking this division as a given, as a simple presupposition prevents us from identifying the process through which the local is continually reproduced in tandem with the reproduction of capital on a global scale. It argues that understanding the making of the world from the lens of a country or a region is too limiting. Instead, this perspective allows us to focus on the several history movements, historical events and their mutual relations and influences that play a significant role in the emergence and assemblage of the world, its processes, and people.

glocalization coined in the late 1980s, the term is a combination of the words "localization" and "globalization" and refers to the practice of simultaneously holding local and global considerations, and the universalizing and particularizing tendencies of these considerations, when dealing with contemporary social, political, and economic systems.

hacienda a large landed estate that was established through concessions or land grants given by the Spanish Crown to European colonizers.

hegemonic masculinity/ies a set of social practices that favours and legitimizes the dominance of men in society and also suppresses and delegitimizes other ways of being a man as "subordinated" masculinities.

hegemony concept associated with Antonio Gramsci that describes a power relationship based on consent. Through political and ideological struggle, hegemony is achieved when the interests of the ruling class are accepted as the common or universal interests of everyone in society.

heresy a belief or practice that is at odds with generally accepted beliefs.

hermeneutics Interpretation of sacred writings. In the case of Christianity, this would mean interpretation of the Bible.

heteropatriarchy the centring and normalizing of male dominance, heterosexuality, and male/female gender binaries, which results in social, material, and economic disadvantages for anyone who does not align with heterosexual masculine identity and all of the ways in which this is expressed.

historic trauma the accumulation of physical and emotional injuries—including threats to the physical and emotional safety or integrity of oneself or loved ones, involving fear, horror, and helplessness—over lifetimes and generations, which can result in debilitating physical and psychological conditions and symptoms.

homonationalism the favourable association between a nationalist ideology and LGBTQ2S+ rights. For example, the identification with Western states as "advanced" and "civilized" regarding LGBTQ2S+ rights and the Global South as "homophobic" and "barbaric." There are different forms, including settler forms of homonationalism and also related orientalist forms of homonationalism.

homonormativity popularized by Lisa Duggan, the term refers to how some layers of white, middle-class queer people, cis gay men in particular, come to identify with neoliberal capitalist relations by assimilating into heteronormative ideals and constructs.

housewifization labour relations outside the protection of labour laws, not covered by trade unions and collective bargaining or based on a proper contract—more or less invisible and part of the Shadow Economy. This is the case of women's labour in the household as well as the labour of peasant and Indigenous peoples.

Human Development Index (HDI) a summary measure of average achievement in key dimensions of human development: a long and healthy life, being knowledgeable, and having a decent standard of living. The HDI was created by the United Nations Development Programme to emphasize that people's capabilities should be the ultimate criteria for assessing the development of a country rather than economic growth alone.

humanitarian biomedicine an approach to international health that focuses on equal access to care globally. This approach focuses its attention on disease and illnesses that are treatable and cause the most fatalities when not treated, which tend to be geographically contained in economically or infrastructurally poor countries, whether or not they are a potential threat to the international community.

imperialism the practice of some nation(s) having a "right" to domination or being superior and warranting rule over other nations. This justifies colonialism and neo-colonialism as well as other forms of control that can be less formal. The result is unequal relations whereby "Western" and "Northern" countries benefit from relations of exploitation with countries in the Global South.

Import Substitution Industrialization (ISI) a development strategy aimed at reducing dependence on the importation of foreign manufactured/technology-intensive commodities and increasing the domestic production of such goods.

Indian Act an 1876 consolidation of the various legislations related to "Indians" within Canada. This act, although having gone through many amendments since its first passing, is still in place and affects the lives of Status Indians in Canada, from defining who is entitled to said status to controlling political structures and resources of/to those who have status. Some who are defined as Indians by the Canadian government, including non-status First Nations, Métis, and Inuit, are not governed by the act.

Indian residential schools a colonial school system forced upon Indigenous nations within Canada with the intent of assimilating Indigenous children to the colonial culture and effecting cultural genocide (and in some cases, for example when nutrition experiments were conducted, genocide) of Indigenous nations. Attendance was mandatory and in some cases enforced through child abduction.

Indigenous feminism a theoretical approach that attempts to raise awareness around the violations of human rights that occur through the interactions between colonialism, racism, and sexism by providing a powerful critique of colonialism and race and gendered power relations.

Indigenous knowledge systems (IKS) a field of study that emerged to address the hegemony of "Western" knowledge.

Indigenous non-binary gender expressions coined by Indigenous feminist scholar Sarah Hunt to disrupt the typically binary lens used to understand the intersection between race, colonialism, heteronormality, and heteropatriarchy.

instrumentalization the use or misuse of a social process—which claims or is intended to be for a collective good—for individual gain or advantage.

instrumental violence a type of violence used as a means of achieving a goal, such as silencing political opponents or the trafficking of illegal drugs.

internal enemy an enemy of the state that is found within its own territory; an integral element of the national security doctrine that emerged in Latin America after World War II. While officially the internal enemy comprised leftist guerrillas and their supporters, in reality anyone or any organization that challenged the status quo, defended human rights, demanded social justice, or sought social transformation fell into this category. The "internal enemy" continues to be part of the national security framework at present.

International Monetary Fund (IMF) an international financial institution that provides loans and policy advice to countries that seek assistance for their development projects. The IMF's main goals are financial stability, global monetary cooperation, and promoting international trade.

labour flexibilization the movement away from long-term, steady employment to "just in time" hiring of workers in global production chains as a result of neoliberal globalization. Labour flexibility enables companies to respond to changes in market needs and to keep labour costs low at the expense of worker stability and quality of life.

latifundio(s) a large landholding.

lynching the killing of African Americans. Lynching entails torture, mutilation, burning, shooting, dragging, and hanging. Those lynched are accused of an alleged crime (e.g., rape) by a white mob that ends up depriving them of their lives without due process and equal protection of the law. See Ida B. Wells's work on lynching.

machismo both an ideology and practice based on the idea that women exist to serve the needs and desires of their male partners and to bear their children. Under this ideology, a man's sexual appetite is insatiable and justifies his right to have more than one sexual partner. "Conquering" and "possessing" women are seen as signs of manliness.

maquilas areas where the assembly or partial manufacturing of products for export takes place in foreign or locally owned companies. EPZS and *maquilas* employ a largely female workforce and are exempt from national labour and environmental laws (see also **export-processing zones**).

migrants all people who have moved across an international border or within a state but away from their usual place of residence, regardless of motivation, worker status, citizenship status, or length of stay.

militarization a process of change that involves one or more of the following: increase in the number of military bases and military personnel; increased presence of military and police throughout public spaces; and strengthening of the capacity of the military and police by increasing their personnel, quantity and quality of weapons, and surveillance and monitoring technology.

minifundio(s) small parcel of farmland land, typically between one and six hectares, with little to no infrastructure.

Missing and Murdered Indigenous Women and Girls (**MMIWG**) the public inquiry that recognized that Indigenous women have, historically and currently, experienced far more violence than any other group within Canada, while as victims they have also been deprioritized by state methods of preventing, investigating, and punishing violence.

monotheism the belief that there is only one God.

moral panic a shared sense of crisis and belief that the community is under threat from a marginalized group, facilitating the lifting of ordinary judicial safeguards against persecution.

Movement for Black Lives an international social movement to campaign for justice and against systemic racism toward Black people.

multilateral debts the loans received by governments, businesses, or individual residents of a country from institutions that involve participation from multiple states, such as UN institutions, the IMF, and the World Bank.

necropolitics a concept used by Mbembe to describe the governance of populations through sovereign power to kill and expose people to death, including social and political death.

neoclassical economists an approach to the study of the production, consumption, and transfer of wealth that treats households as economic units that have rational and altruistic decision-makers. In general, neoclassical economists do not take into account the power struggles and inequalities within or between households.

neoliberal globalization the flows of people, material, wealth, and ideas, as well as the compression of time and space, that technologies afford us, driven by the promotion of the primacy of the economy, deregulation, and privatization.

neoliberal governance a theory and mode of control that proposes that human well-being is maximized by the liberation of the economic market. The implementation of this theory results in significant cuts to the public sector and public services and the reorientation of the economy to attract investment, including the slashing of corporate taxes and the removal of labour and environmental protections.

neoliberalism the political, social, and economic restructuring of global capitalist relations in accordance with free markets, the reduction or elimination of social supports, and the contradiction of removing barriers for the free flow of capital while restricting the movement of migrants across borders. It developed in response to the global wave of struggles in the 1960s and early 1970s that began to put capitalist social relations in question and strategically incorporates social program cuts and attacks on the working class, poor people, and people of colour. Feminist and cultural critics have also linked these processes to the mainstreaming of currents within social movements and marginal identities so that "dissent" is folded into the workings of the nation-state itself.

obscuring language words intentionally chosen to be unclear or non-specific in order to allow systems of power to continue unchallenged.

Othering process of excluding groups of people considered different and/or inferior while at the same time defining the superiority or centrality of those who engage in Othering.

pacification process of making or enforcing peace. This can occur through various means, such as treaties, military operations, police and intelligence actions, and social-cultural actions. As a military strategy, pacification aims to suppress a hostile population.

paramilitary groups armed groups of civilians organized and funded by wealthy sectors of society with military and logistical support provided unofficially by the state. Their targets are social movements, human rights activists, and others who challenge the established political-economic model.

patriarchy systematic gender inequality in favour of men. Men are favoured for or exclusively granted power such as political decision-making authority, control of resources, and the ability to inherit wealth.

pinkwashing the use of "favourable" treatment of queer people to undermine opposition to oppressive practices in a particular country. Most often used in opposition to Israeli state practices that try to use this supposed "good" treatment of queer people to undermine any criticism of how Palestinians are treated under apartheid policies as homophobic or supporting homophobia.

population control policies and practices with the intent of reducing the rate of births within a state or region; for example, sterilization or contraception.

postcolonial feminist thought the thought that emerged in response to nineteenth century imperial expansion, coming to the fore in the mid-twentieth century as colonies struggled for independence and self-determination. Rejecting Western hegemony and the dominance of a singular Western epistemic purportedly born of a rationalistic Enlightenment, postcolonial thought has long concerned itself with thinking otherwise—with challenging instantiated political structures, social structures, and even modes of thought. Postcolonial feminist thought, as one might expect, prioritizes concerns with gender, feminism, and women's lives within the broader framework of postcolonialism.

postcolonial reading a way of understanding texts that deliberately considers the effects that colonization have on all forms of authorship, whether they be artistic, scholarly, scientific, etc., and attempts to actively deconstruct colonial influence in works by both colonial powers and those who were colonized. This approach takes into account racism, colonialism, and gender as part of its approach.

post-structuralism an approach to studying how knowledge is produced in which both the object itself and the systems of knowledge that produced the object (i.e., the context in which the object was created) are considered.

praxis the blending of theory, practice, and ongoing reflection.

precarious work employment that is temporary or not protected from termination, is not well paid, and comes with a paucity of benefits. Those employed in the position are relatively powerless to change the conditions of their employment.

predatory patriarchy masculine identities infused with and constituted through violence and aggression.

presencing the ways that Indigenous women and girls actively present to the world that their lives matter; used by Sandra de Finney, Leanne Simpson, and others.

primitive accumulation the dispossession of the direct producers from their means of subsistence; the separation of peasants (small-scale producers) from their land. It is the process that initiated the transition from feudalism to capitalism. According to Marx, this process is ongoing because capital requires that these conditions be reproduced for it to exist.

privatization the sale of public enterprises and assets to private owners.

privilege unearned structural advantages that come from one's social location or one's position in relation to dominant systems of power (e.g., white privilege, cisgender privilege, the privilege of citizenship, able-bodied privilege). These structural advantages are maintained through laws, policies, infrastructures, social norms, and so on, which are informed by and uphold power relations that privilege some and oppress others.

queer necropolitics a term coined by Achille Mbembe and popularized by Jasbir Puar, it is an analytical tool used to describe power dynamics in which some people (those with power—in the case of queer necropolitics, cis white gay men) create and maintain political or social structures that condemn others (those without power—in particular queer and/or trans Black, Indigenous, and people [especially women] of colour) to precarious positions that could result in loss of life.

racial capitalism the emergence and ongoing sustenance of a sort of capitalism that relies upon the elaboration, reproduction, and exploitation of notions of racial difference. It is a global capitalism concomitant with the invention of what Robinson termed "the universal Negro."

racialization the social process of ascribing a race to a particular person or group of people. This involves the social construction of race categories, the racist treatment through which some are disadvantaged, and the "Othering" that occurs with this categorization. Note that while "white" is a socially constructed race category, people socially coded as "white" are not considered "racialized" because whiteness is socially constructed as the "norm" and people who are racialized are understood to be anything other than white—literally, "Othered."

reproductive rights the ability and entitlement of couples and individuals to decide freely and responsibly how many children to have and when as well as access to the information and means by which to do so safely.

School of the Americas (SOA) opened in 1963 in Fort Benning, Georgia, US. It offers training in counter-insurgency and low-intensity warfare and has since trained more than 59,000 Latin American military and police personnel. Currently, it operates under the name Western Hemisphere Institute of Security Cooperation.

securitization process through which something (a person, group, condition, phenomenon, or idea) is defined as a threat requiring immediate response, usually from state security institutions.

settler colonialism a form of political and economic exploitation of land and resources in which the colonizing nation sent citizens to stay in the colonized nation with the intended goal of population replacement of Indigenous societies with their own. In particular, this was practised by Europeans in what is now Canada, the US, Australia, and New Zealand.

social determinants of health the systems and conditions in which people live their daily lives (through birth, growth, work, and aging) that influence their health. These forces and systems include economic policies and systems, development agendas, social norms, social policies, and political systems, as well as more personal circumstances such as class, race, gender, ability, and sexuality. All of these forces and circumstances intersect to affect things such as access to clean air and water and sanitation; to nutritious food; to shelter and security; to bodily autonomy and integrity; and to preventative and comprehensive health care and medicine, which in turn all influence health.

socialist feminism a type of feminist theory, the central argument of which is that the fundamental cause of women's oppression is the interplay between capitalism and patriarchy. Socialist feminists believe that gender inequality cannot be eliminated if class inequality persists.

social location the unique interconnected positions, privileges, oppressions, world views, and knowledges that each person holds within society. This term also refers to how these positions shape an individual's view on the world and their understanding of power.

social reproduction the daily unpaid and largely feminized labour of care carried out in households and communities that keep all household members alive. This labour allows for the regeneration of workers (through the raising of children) and is made possible through the social and political structures that enable its ongoing production, including discourses that ascribe high or low value to certain labour on the basis of gender, race, class, sexuality, geography, etc. of the labourer.

solidarity historically, the feeling and practice of political unity and coalition-building to confront power. Critical activists and scholars have noted that practices of solidarity have often resulted in people with privilege taking leadership from those who are in relative positions of oppression and are most affected by the power structures that the coalition was intended to disrupt. Critical Indigenous scholars, in particular, have called for a shift in conceptualizing solidarity as a process, as an ongoing relationship, and as interdependent rather than through a charity model of "helping" those who are more oppressed.

sovereign power the exclusive or supreme authority of an entity (an individual or a different state) to govern. In Foucault's work, sovereign power refers to a mode (technology) of power that operates through public display of brutal corporeal (bodily) punishment aimed at achieving the submission and obedience of subjects.

sovereignty doctrine set of principles underlying international law that relates to the rights of states as political entities to autonomously govern their territory and population without interference. Sovereignty doctrine derives from liberal philosophies of natural law.

Stabilization Programs measures implemented by the International Monetary Fund (IMF) that dictate spending priorities to nations indebted to the IMF. These programs include requiring that nations prioritize paying interest payments over paying for health, education, housing, and other development concerns.

state ensemble of political institutions including government, police, military, judiciary, legislature, and administrative bureaucracy that claims sovereignty as basis of legitimacy to govern a territory.

state (and state-sanctioned) violence Black and woman of colour feminists like Joy James, Andrea Ritchie, and Beth Richi in the past several decades have used this term to address forms of racial and gendered harm enacted by the state or supported by the state onto marginalized populations, especially Black, Indigenous, and other women and gender non-conforming people. Examples include police violence against Indigenous communities and the targeted child welfare removal and expulsions of Black students.

Structural Adjustment Programs (SAPs) a set of neoliberal policies administered by the World Bank and the International Monetary Fund that were required to be implemented by state governments as a condition of receiving a loan or reduction of interest rate on an existing loan from these organizations. The policies include reductions in government expenditures on social programs, ending of subsidized price controls for basic foodstuffs, elimination of import restrictions and foreign exchange controls, devaluation to encourage exports, and encouragement of private foreign investment.

structural violence the effect of systems of power to shape, cause, and maintain deeply unequal life chances, including massively unequal distribution of resources, and economic, political, and discursive power. This inequality threatens the lives of its victims, but because it is embedded in the ways in which existing systems work, there is no clear single perpetrator and can often be invisible.

subaltern a term adopted by Antonio Gramsci referring to the unrepresented group of people in a society. Subaltern subjects and classes may include peasants, workers, and other groups denied access to dominant power.

subsistence production a self-sufficiency farming and food production system in which the producers and farmers focus on growing and producing enough food to feed themselves and their families. The output is mostly for local use with little or no surplus value for trade in the market.

survivance the active and intentional survival of Indigenous people in direct opposition to the efforts of colonial erasure; coined by Gerald Vizenor.

sustainable development an approach that relies on a balance of economic growth, capital accumulation, and technological innovation to cure the current ecological crisis.

syncretism the merging of different beliefs or practices into one.

terra nullius legal doctrine justifying the acquisition of land by occupation on the basis that the land is uninhabited and does not belong to anyone (that is, anyone recognized as legitimate by the acquiring state).

theory of social reproduction an approach that argues that the labour performed in the private sphere of the home enables capitalist exploitation to take place.

Third World term now primarily used by the Global North to re-narrate regions of the world as in need of development, conflict resolution, democracy, and/or containment. Originally, however, it was a radical revolutionary political term that encompassed transnational social mobilization of Black people, Indigenous people, and people of colour against white supremacy. Generated during processes of global decolonization, it served as the radical call for Third World non-alignment to the increasing Cold War political economies of the First and Second World at the end of World War II.

trade liberalization the removal of any trade barriers or measures that are meant to protect local producers from foreign competition, such as tariffs and quotas.

vagabonds a term used during the early stages of capitalism in Britain to refer to those who were unemployed—i.e., not inside the capitalist relations of production. This included people who sought alternative forms of livelihood instead of being a wage-worker.

violence against women any act of gender-based violence that results in, or is likely to result in, physical, sexual, or psychological harm or suffering, including threats of such acts, coercion, or arbitrary deprivation of liberty, whether occurring in public or in private life.

Voluntary Surgical Contraceptive Program (VSC) a surgical procedure that blocks the ducts that carry reproductive gametes to prevent conception. The procedure is intended to be permanent and irreversible, and consent is mandatory.

welfare approach to development the implementation of policies to influence the way human infrastructure is built and expanded in order to establish a minimum quality of living expectation for residents, such as having access to food, housing, and wage work for survival.

white anxieties fear felt by white people in response to the movements and freedom-making of Black people, Indigenous people, and people of colour.

whiteness a state of being perceived as "white" by society at large based on phenotype. Also, a set of logics, ideas, and practices that work to maintain and reproduce the sense of superiority that those who are perceived as "white" are socialized to feel. As part of this maintenance of perceived superiority, benefits are conferred through conditions that produce advantages for people who are coded by the larger social structure as "white." Additionally, as part of the maintenance of superiority, anyone not seen as white is assumed to be aspiring to whiteness.

white settler non-Indigenous individuals whose ancestors migrated and stayed as part of a system of settler colonialism and who have light-coloured skin (i.e., are visually coded as "white" by others).

white supremacy a global practice of violence that uses race, gender, sexuality, class, and geography as means of establishing hierarchies that privilege the logics, practices, experiences, and bodies of whiteness through the marginalization of other-than-whiteness.

World Bank (WB) an international financial institution that provides loans and policy advice to countries that seek assistance for their development projects. The World Bank's main concerns are long-term economic growth and poverty reduction.

Index